THE CULTURES AND GLOBALIZATION SERIES, 5

The Cultures and Globalization Series brings together essays examining the reciprocal relationships between cultural change and globalization. Too often the emphasis is placed on the impact of the latter on the former – this Series aims to readdress the balance. Over the course of 5 volumes, the key contemporary topics in the cultural field are covered: from identity politics and the creative industries to cultural expression, heritage, memory and city cultural governance and policy. Written by leading experts as well as emerging scholars from all the geocultural regions of the world and various distinct disciplines, the essays offer a range of different conceptual views of contemporary cultural change, thereby providing a platform for students and academics to engage in open debate. Furthermore, they are complemented by a variety of empirical 'indicator suites' rich in colour and graphics, which present quantitative data in a highly innovative, accessible and engaging way. As a result, *The Cultures and Globalization Series* is an indispensible reference tool for students of contemporary culture.

Series Editors: Helmut K. Anheier and Yudhishthir Raj Isar

Current Volumes
Vol. 5: Cities, Cultural Policy and Governance (2012)
Vol. 4: Heritage, Memory and Identity (2011)
Vol. 3: Cultural Expression, Creativity and Innovation (2010)
Vol. 2: The Cultural Economy (2008)
Vol. 1: Conflicts and Tensions (2007)

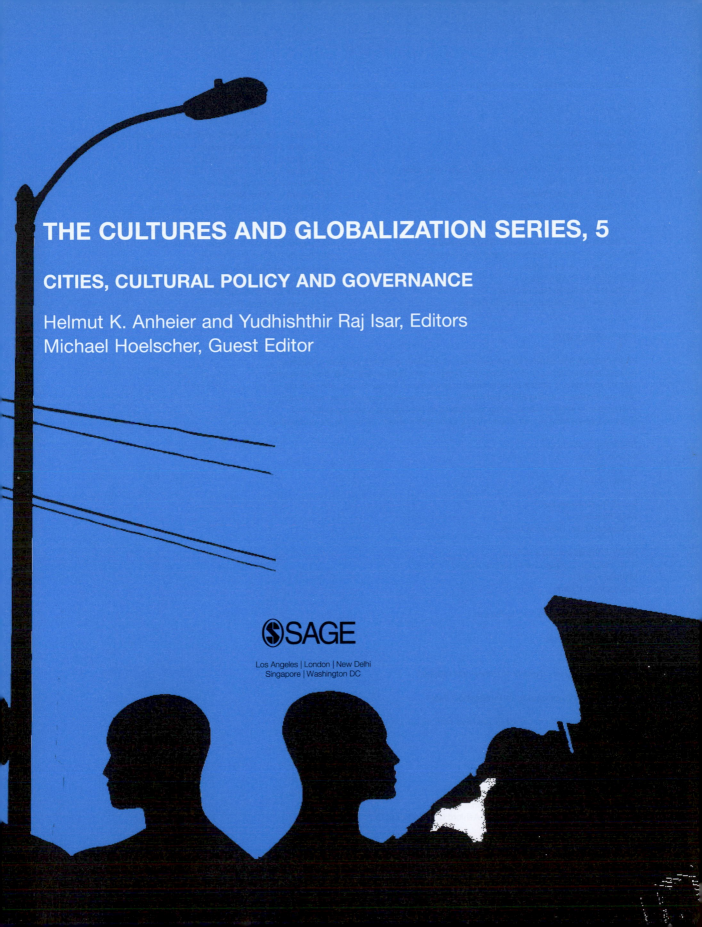

THE CULTURES AND GLOBALIZATION SERIES, 5

CITIES, CULTURAL POLICY AND GOVERNANCE

Helmut K. Anheier and Yudhishthir Raj Isar, Editors
Michael Hoelscher, Guest Editor

$SAGE

Los Angeles | London | New Delhi
Singapore | Washington DC

First published 2012

SAGE Publications Ltd
1 Oliver's Yard
55 City Road
London EC1Y 1SP

SAGE Publications Inc.
2455 Teller Road
Thousand Oaks, California 91320

SAGE Publications India Pvt Ltd
B 1/I 1 Mohan Cooperative Industrial Area
Mathura Road
New Delhi 110 044

SAGE Publications Asia-Pacific Pte Ltd
3 Church Street
#10-04 Samsung Hub
Singapore 049483

Library of Congress Control Number: 2011932692

British Library Cataloguing in Publication data

A catalogue record for this book is available from the British Library

ISBN 978-1-4462-0122-0
ISBN 978-1-4462-0123-7 (pbk)

Typeset by C&M Digitals (P) Ltd, Chennai, India
Printed and bound in Great Britain by Ashford Colour Press Ltd

This volume is dedicated to the memory of our friend and colleague Dragan Klaic (1950–2011), who supported, inspired and enriched the Series.

CONTENTS

LIST OF BOXES, FIGURES, TABLES, MAPS AND PHOTOS

Boxes

Figures

Tables

Maps

Photos

CONTRIBUTORS

Asu Aksoy teaches in the Cultural Management Programme at Istanbul Bilgi University and was also involved in the setting up of *Santralistanbul*, a new cultural complex at the site of Istanbul's first electricity power plant, as well as with Istanbul's successful bid to become a European Capital of Culture in 2010. She has recently completed a *Cultural Mapping of Istanbul* for the Turkish Ministry of Culture and Tourism and writes about urban and cultural policy in Turkey. Her earlier research was on the changing media consumption practices in Europe of Turkish-speaking migrants, a topic on which she has authored and co-authored many articles.

Helmut K. Anheier (PhD, Yale) is Dean of the Hertie School of Governance in Berlin, holds a chair in sociology at Heidelberg University and serves as Academic Director of the Center for Social Investment there. From 2001 to 2009, he was Professor of Public Policy and Social Welfare at UCLA's School of Public Affairs and Centennial Professor at the London School of Economics. Earlier, he founded and directed the Centre for Civil Society at LSE and the Center for Civil Society at UCLA. Before embarking on an academic career, he served as a social affairs officer to the United Nations. He is currently researching the nexus between globalization, civil society, and culture and is interested in policy analysis and methodological questions.

Octavio Arbeláez Tobón is a lawyer who specializes in cultural marketing. He has an MA in philosophy and is a doctoral candidate in design and creation at the National University of Caldas, Colombia. He has been professor at the National University of Colombia and the National University of Caldas, where he was dean of the Faculty of Arts. He has studied the relationship between culture and development in the transformation of Colombian cities as well as the cultural dimension of new technologies and their application to so-called 'knowledge cities' in Latin America.

Emilia Birlo (artwork) is a visual artist and fashion designer who divides her time between Berlin and Los Angeles. Her art designs can be viewed at www.birlos.de.

Laura Collier is completing a Master's in Global Communications at The American University of Paris. She has a background working and volunteering in communications for cultural institutions and NGOs in the United States, Colombia and France. She holds a Bachelor's degree from Georgetown University in Classics and German language.

Catherine Cullen has worked in the cultural arena for the last 30 years. After initial experience in publishing, editing and journalism, she became editor in chief of *LIBER*, the first European cultural supplement issued jointly by several major European newspapers. She is currently Vice-President of the Culture Committee of United Cities and Local Governments (UCLG). She has been Deputy Mayor in charge of Culture for the City of Lille, France, since 2001, and was responsible for Lille 2004, European Capital of Culture. In 2008, she also became councillor for Culture for *Lille Metropole Communauté Urbaine*.

Stuart Cunningham is Distinguished Professor of Media and Communications, Queensland University of Technology, and Director of the Australian Research Council (ARC) Centre of Excellence for Creative Industries and Innovation. His most recent books are *The Media and Communications in Australia* (with Graeme Turner) and *In the Vernacular: A Generation of Australian Culture and Controversy*. He has served as Commissioner, Australian Film Commission; foundation Chair, QPIX, Queensland's screen resource centre; Executive Council member, Australian Academy of the Humanities; Panel Chair, ARC College of Experts; President of the Council for Humanities, Arts and Social Sciences; and member of the Library Board of Queensland.

Luca Dal Pozzolo, an architect, is Vice-President of Fondazione Fitzcarraldo, an independent centre for planning, research, training and documentation on culture, arts and media management, economics and policy. He is also Director of the Cultural Observatory of Piedmont and professor at the Polytechnic of Torino and the University of Bologna. He has directed research on cultural policy, cultural economics and the management and sustainability of cultural organizations and their audiences and is the author of several books and articles on the design process, urban phenomena and local development.

Simin Davoudi is Professor of Environment Policy and Planning in the School of Architecture, Planning and Landscape at Newcastle University, UK. She is a past President of the Association of the European Schools of Planning; she has served as an expert adviser for several UK and European public bodies and has been a visiting professor at a number of European universities. *Conceptions of Space & Place in Strategic Spatial Planning* and *Planning for Climate Change* are among her latest books. http://www.ncl.ac.uk/apl/staff/profile/simin.davoudi.

Nancy Duxbury is a senior researcher and coordinator of the 'Cities, Cultures and Architecture' research group of the Centre for Social Studies at the University of Coimbra. She is also an adjunct professor with Simon Fraser University, Vancouver. From 2005 to 2008, she was the executive director of the Centre of Expertise on Culture and Communities and before that Director of Research of the Creative City Network of Canada, and Cultural Planning Analyst at the City of Vancouver. She was lead author of *Under Construction: The State of Cultural Infrastructure in Canada* (2008) and guest co-editor of a double issue of *Culture and Local Governance* on 'Culture and Sustainable Communities' (2011).

Yasser Elsheshtawy is Associate Professor of Architecture at the United Arab Emirates University. His recent research interests are urbanization patterns in Middle Eastern cities with a particular emphasis on informal urbanism, a topic on which he recently edited a special issue of the journal *Built Environment*. Among his publications are *Dubai: Behind an Urban Spectacle*, *The Evolving Arab City* and *Planning Middle Eastern Cities*. He has been a consultant for the United Nations Economic and Social Commission for Western Asia (UN-ESCWA), serves on many editorial boards, and is a columnist for *AlRoyya*, an Arabic daily specializing in financial affairs.

Terry Flew is Professor of Media and Communications at the Queensland University of Technology (QUT), in Brisbane, Australia. He is the author of *New Media: An Introduction*, *Understanding Global Media* (Palgrave) and *The Creative Industries, Culture and Policy* (SAGE) and is well known internationally in creative industries research. He has been President of the Australian and New Zealand Communication Association, and has provided expert advice to the Organization for Economic Co-operation and Development, the National Academies Forum, the Australian Communications and Media Authority, Brisbane City Council and the European Science Foundation. During 2011–12 he was seconded to the Australian Law Reform Commission to lead the National Classifications Scheme Review for the Australian Government.

Mark Gibson is author of *Culture and Power – A History of Cultural Studies* and Editor of *Continuum – Journal of Media and Cultural Studies*; he has published widely on everyday life, cultural geography and creative industries. He is Coordinator, at Monash University, of the Graduate Communications and Media Studies programme in the National Centre for Australian Studies and Research Coordinator in the School of Journalism, Australian and Indigenous Studies.

Xin Gu graduated in Civil Engineering from Shanghai Tonji University, obtained a Master's in European Urban Cultures from Manchester Metropolitan University, where she also completed her doctorate on creative industry networks and the city. She is currently a postdoctoral research fellow at Queensland University of Technology, where she is lead researcher on the ARC-financed project 'Designing Creative Clusters in China and Australia'.

Kim Gurney is a Research Associate in the University of Johannesburg's Research Centre on Visual Identities in Art and Design, exploring the nexus of culture and economics. She is also a visual artist, often engaging with gaps, disappearance and in/visibility, and a freelance journalist, with a special interest in business and culture. She holds an Honours degree in Fine Art from the University of Cape Town (South Africa), an MA in International Journalism from City University (UK) and an Honours degree in Journalism from Rhodes University (South Africa).

David Halle is Professor of Sociology at the University of California, Los Angeles. He divides his time between New York and Los Angeles. His publications include *Art Gallery Districts, Historic Preservation, and Mega Projects: Urban Change on Manhattan's Far West Side*, *New York & Los Angeles: The Uncertain Future* (edited with Andrew Beveridge), *New York & Los Angeles: Politics, Society and Culture* (ed.) and *Inside Culture: Art and Class in the American Home*.

Michael Hoelscher (PhD, Berlin) is senior lecturer at the Department of Sociology, University of Heidelberg, Germany, and Senior Research Fellow at the University of Oxford. His main fields of interest are globalization, especially European integration, cultural sociology, economic sociology, higher education, and quantitative comparative methods. He has published several journal articles in these fields.

Tom Hutton is Professor in the Centre for Human Settlements and School of Community & Regional Planning, University of British Columbia and an Associate of the Peter Wall Institute for Advanced Studies, and Green College, UBC. His research and teaching focus on urban and regional change in advanced and transitional societies, in particular the cultural economy of the city, creative industries and labour, the influence of space and built environment on the shaping of new industry formation, and the role of the inner city in cultural development. See thutton@interchange.ubc.ca.

Yudhishthir Raj Isar is an independent cultural adviser, writer and public speaker and is also Professor of Cultural Policy Studies at The American University of Paris and Eminent

Research Visitor at the University of Western Sydney. He serves on the boards of several cultural institutions. From 2004 to 2008 he was President of the international association Culture Action Europe. Previously, at UNESCO, he was Executive Secretary of the World Commission on Culture and Development; in 1986–1987 he was Executive Director of The Aga Khan Program for Islamic Architecture at Harvard University and the Massachusetts Institute of Technology.

Lucina Jiménez, PhD in Anthropology, is Director-General of the AC International Art Consortium and School (CONARTE) and President of the Mexican Communication, Culture and Arts Observatory; member of the International Group of Experts in Art Education, Culture and Citizens of the Organization of Latin American States, of the Latin American Group of Education and Culture of the UNESCO Chair for Cultural Policies and International Cooperation. She coordinates the ProIDEA Art Education research programme of the University of the Cloister of Sor Juana, the National Teaching University and CONARTE. Among her publications are *Teatro y Públicos, el lado oscuro de la Sala*, *Cultura y Democracia* and *Políticas Culturales en Transición*.

Dragan Klaic, who died on 25 August 2011, was a theatre scholar and cultural analyst. He served as a Permanent Fellow of Felix Meritis Foundation in Amsterdam and was a professor of the arts and cultural policy at the University of Leiden's Faculty of Creative and Performing Arts. He lectured widely at various universities, spoke at conferences and symposia and served as adviser, editor, researcher and trainer. His fields of engagement were contemporary performing arts, European cultural policies, strategies of cultural development and international cultural cooperation, interculturalism and cultural memory.

Linda Knudsen McAusland has over 30 years experience in the cultural sector in public policy, programme, organization and community development, with a recent focus on whole systems and transformational change. She has worked internationally and cross-culturally and most recently spent three-and-a-half years in Ukraine designing and implementing community outreach and needs assessment and also consulting on, coaching in support of, and co-designing organizational and community change processes.

Lily Kong is a Professor of Geography at the National University of Singapore. She is a social and cultural geographer, who has published widely in a number of areas, ranging from cultural policy and creative economies, to music, religion, place histories and national identities. Her work has focused on the Asian cities of Singapore, Shanghai, Hong Kong, Taipei and Beijing. Her recent books include: *Creative Cities, Creative Economies: Asian-European Perspectives*, *Singapore Hawker Centres*, *Landscapes: Ways of Imagining the World*, and *The Politics of Landscapes in Singapore: Constructions of 'Nation'*.

Kira Kosnick is Professor of Sociology at Goethe University Frankfurt. She gained her PhD in Cultural Anthropology from the New School for Social Research in 2003. Her research interests focus on transnational migration to Europe, migrant media practices, subaltern publics and the politics of cultural struggle in European urban centres. She is currently conducting a European Research Council Starting Grant Project on post-migrant youth and urban leisure practices in London, Berlin and Paris.

Abha Narain Lambah is a practising conservation architect working in Mumbai. She has authored *Through the Looking Glass: The Grade I Heritage of Mumbai* and co-authored *The Architecture of the Indian Sultanates, A City's Legacy: The Indian Navy's Heritage in Mumbai, A Conservation Manual for Owners & Occupiers: Heritage Buildings & Precincts, Mumbai* and *Conservation after Legislation: Issues for Mumbai*. She has been a columnist on heritage issues for several Indian newspapers and magazines and has served on various advisory bodies.

Charles Landry advises cities, working with them as a critical friend to harness their assets and potential. He develops his own projects using various cities as case studies from around the world such as the original 'creative city' concept, the 'intercultural city' with Phil Wood and more recently the 'creative bureaucracy'. He has written several books (see www.charleslandry.com).

Ramon Lobato, PhD, is a postdoctoral research fellow with the ARC Centre for Excellence in Creative Industries and Innovation at the Institute for Social Research, Swinburne University of Technology, Australia. He is the author of Shadow Economies of Cinema (forthcoming from the British Film Institute).

Justin McGuinness teaches communications history, research methods and urban studies at The American University of Paris, and works on the historic built environment of North African cities. Educated in England and Kuwait (MA Durham, Social Sciences; PhD Newcastle-Upon-Tyne, Town Planning), he has taught at the University of Tunis. His current research projects focus on gentrification and neo-liberal planning in Fès and Tunis and the politics of contemporary urban design in those cities.

Janet Merkel is a PhD student in urban sociology at Humboldt University, Berlin. Since 2008 she has been a research fellow of the research unit 'Cultural Sources of Newness' at the Social Science Research Center (WZB) in Berlin. Her PhD project focuses on the interrelatedness of creativity and urban spaces and investigates the role, effects, and forms of public–private coordination in urban development for the promotion of the creative industries.

Louise Mirrer has been President and CEO of the New York Historical Society since 2004. Earlier, she was Executive Vice Chancellor for Academic Affairs of the City University of New York and Professor at the CUNY Graduate Center and before that Vice Provost for Arts, Sciences and Engineering at the University of Minnesota-Twin Cities. She is a featured blogger on art, history and culture on *The Huffington Post* and has published widely on language, literature, history and women's studies. Her most recent book is *Women, Jews, and Muslims in the Texts of Reconquest Castile*.

Catherine Murray is Associate Director of the Centre for Policy Studies on Culture and Communities at Simon Fraser University, Chair of the Department of Gender, Sexuality, and Women's Studies and Professor of Communication. She has a special interest in the devolution of cultural governance to the urban sphere, cultural pluralism and emerging ethnic cultural enterprises, and their intersection with race, gender and class. See www.cultureandcommunities.ca/, murraye@sfu.ca.

Paul Nagle is the founding Executive Director of the newly established Institute for Culture in the Service of Community Sustainability ICSCS. From 2002 to 2010 he was Director of Cultural Policy for the New York City Council Member Alan Gerson. Originally a playwright, Paul was Founding Executive Director of *All Out Arts* and Founding Executive Producer for its first five festivals, as well as Managing Director and Interim

Executive Director of the Clemente Soto Vélez Cultural & Educational Center. He holds a BA in Arts Administration and an MA in cultural policy from New York University.

Kate Oakley is a writer, academic and policy analyst. She is a Visiting Professor at the Department of Cultural Policy and Management, City University in London, where she is Course Director of the MA in Cultural Leadership. She is also a Visiting Professor at the University of the Arts in London. Her research interests include the politics of cultural policy, work in the cultural industries, and regional development.

Justin O'Connor is a Professor in the Creative Industries faculty at the Queensland University of Technology, and Visiting Professor in the Department of Humanities, Shanghai Jiaotong University. Before that he was Director of the Manchester Institute for Popular Culture, Manchester Metropolitan University and Professor at the University of Leeds. While in Manchester he was responsible for that city's Nighttime Economy strategy, its Creative Industries Development Service and a new city museum.

Jordi Pascual has coordinated the 'Agenda 21 for culture' process of United Cities and Local Governments (UCLG) since 2004. He also teaches urban cultural policies and management at the Open University of Catalonia. He has been a researcher at the Autonomous University of Barcelona (1992–1996), at the Interarts Foundation (1996–2) and the Institut de Cultura-Barcelona City Council (2000–2003). He has written on the relations between urban policies, culture and sustainability (*Guide to Citizen Participation in Local Cultural Policy Development for European Cities*) and has served as a member of the Jury of the European Capital of Culture.

Edgar Pieterse is the holder of the Department of Science and Technology/National Research Foundation South African Research Chair in Urban Policy, directs the African Centre for Cities and is Professor in the School of Architecture, Planning and Geomatics at the University of Cape Town. His most recent books include: *City Futures: Confronting the Crisis of Urban Development, Counter-Currents: Experiments in Sustainability in the Cape Town region* (edited), and *The African Cities Reader: Pan-African Practices* (co-edited).

Davide Ponzini, PhD, is a researcher focusing on planning theory, urban and cultural policies at the Politecnico di Milano. He has been a visiting scholar at Yale University, Johns Hopkins University, Columbia University and Sciences Po Paris. Author of *Il territorio dei beni culturali* (2008), and co-author with Pier Carlo Palermo of *Spatial Planning and Urban Development* (2010) and with Michele Nastasi of the forthcoming *Starchitecture: Scenes, Actors and Spectacles in Contemporary Cities*.

Ferdinand Richard is a musician who at the age of 26 founded a platform for the development of urban music and artistic expression in Marseille called AMI, of which he is still the director. He is a co-founder of the emblematic *Friche Belle-de-Mai* that will be a pivotal location for the 2012 Marseille–Provence European Capital of Culture programme. He was President of the European Forum for the Arts and Heritage, now Culture Action Europe, 1996–99 and is currently President of the Roberto Cimetta Fund for the mobility of artists and cultural operators in the Mediterranean. He is a consultant to international organizations and a visiting lecturer at several universities.

Mieka Ritsema is a socio-cultural anthropologist with a focus on cities and urban life. She has a PhD in anthropology from Yale University and has taught at the University of

Botswana, Yale University, and the University of Massachusetts, Boston. Her dissertation research, supported by a Fulbright fellowship, examined the contradictions of twentieth-century modernist cities through the lens of Botswana's capital city, Gaborone. Her research and teaching explore issues and experiences of rapid urban transformation, intergenerational tensions, and place-making practices in post-colonial societies.

Kevin Robins has held professorships in Cultural Geography, Media and Communications, and Sociology. In recent years, he has worked extensively on issues of media and migration, particularly with respect to transnational Turkish migrants. He has also been involved with the Council of Europe's programme on Cultural Policy and Cultural Diversity, producing the report *The Challenge of Transcultural Diversities*. Until recently he worked with the Goldsmiths College Leverhulme Media Research Centre on questions of European media and cultural policy and at present his focus is on media cultures, with particular reference to wider questions of European identity.

Mathias Rouet is an urbanist who graduated in city planning from the University of the Sorbonne Paris 1 and in sociology from Dauphine University. He has worked with several architectural firms on the *Grand Paris* project and as a cartographer at The American University of Paris for a Paris Métropole call for proposals. His research in geography and urban sociology focuses on cultural scenes, the management of territorial conflict and urban governance.

Pier Luigi Sacco, PhD, is Professor of Cultural Economics at the IULM University, Milan and also teaches Creative Industries at the University of Italian Switzerland (USI), Lugano, and writes for *Il Sole 24 Ore*, *Saturno* and *Flash Art*. He is President of the scientific committee of the International Festival of Contemporary Art, Faenza, of the International Festival of Geography, Bardolino, of the Cultural Observatory of Marche Region and is Research Associate, Semeion Research Center, Rome. He has written prolifically on economic theory, game theory, cultural economics and cultural industries.

Katharine Sarikakis has a PhD in contemporary history and is Professor in Communication Science and Media Governance at the University of Vienna. She has held positions among others at the University of Leeds, Karlstad University, Sweden, McGill University and Hainan University, China. She is the founding co-editor of the *International Journal of Media and Cultural Politics*, and has written many articles and books in her field. She is the Chair of the Communications Law and Policy Section of the European Communication Research and Education Association (ECREA). Email: Katharine.Sarikakis@univie.ac.at.

Saskia Sassen is the Robert S. Lynd Professor of Sociology and co-chairs The Committee on Global Thought at Columbia University (www.saskiasassen.com). Her books have been translated into 21 languages. Her path-breaking *The Global City* came out in a new fully updated edition in 2001. Among her most recent works are *Territory, Authority, Rights: From Medieval to Global Assemblages* (Princeton University Press, 2008), *A Sociology of Globalization* (W.W. Norton, 2007), and the 4th fully updated edition of *Cities in a World Economy* (Sage, 2011). She is currently working on *When Territory Exits Existing Frameworks* (under contract with Harvard University Press). She contributes regularly to www.OpenDemocracy.net and www.HuffingtonPost.com.

Ihor Savchak is the founder and Director of the Centre for Cultural Management in L'viv, Ukraine. With the support of the European Cultural Foundation he has initiated and coordinates a pilot project entitled 'Elaboration of a participative cultural framework for the city of L'viv', the first ever bottom-up, community-driven cultural planning process since the country's independence in 1991.

Stephen W. Sawyer is an urban and political historian. He is currently the Chair of History and Urban Studies at The American University of Paris and since 2010 has co-directed the major in Global Cities. In his numerous articles, book chapters, edited volumes and current book projects he has focused on the political and cultural construction of scale in cities and states in Western Europe and the United States. In 2011, he completed a two-year grant, with an international and interdisciplinary team of researchers, for the city of Paris on mapping cultural amenities in the *Grand Paris*.

Annick Schramme, PhD, specializes in cultural policy and management, particularly with regard to Flanders. She is professor and academic coordinator of the Master of Management in Arts and Culture at the University of Antwerp and teaches the master class on creative and cultural industries at the Antwerp School of Management. She has published extensively in various aspects of arts and heritage policy, including the creative industries, and advises the Vice-Mayor for Culture and Tourism of the City of Antwerp on these matters. She is a board member of several cultural organizations in Flanders and the Netherlands.

Katia Segers is a professor in the department of Media Studies of the Free University of Brussels, where she has been Director of the Centre for Research on Media and Culture since 2002. She teaches also in the Master in Arts Management at the University of Antwerp. Her research and publications focus on the political economy of the cultural industries, cultural policy, children and the media and culture and media literacy. She is also the President of the Flemish Regulator for the Media, an independent external agency for the Flemish Community of Belgium and a member of the Expert Commission on Government Communication of the Flemish Parliament.

Shlomit Shulov Barkan is the area head of Public and Non-profit Organizations in the School of Business, College of Academic Studies, Israel, and also teaches at the Hebrew University, Jerusalem. She has a PhD in sociology from the University of Pennsylvania. Her work focuses on the management of non-profit organizations in the cultural and social arena and the development of strong civil society. She has extensive managerial and consulting experience in the non-profit field and business as well.

Maria Carolina Vasconcelos-Oliveira is a researcher on cultural issues, especially interested in the intersections among culture, development, public policies and urban space. She earned a Master's in Sociology at the University of São Paulo and is currently a PhD candidate there. Her Master's research on cultural institutions and audiences was recognized as one of the best in the cultural studies area by the Itaú Cultural Institute and won the *Rumos* award. She has been a member of the Labour and Development team at the Brazilian Centre for Analysis and Planning since 2005.

Phil Wood describes himself as an urban therapist. After a career in British local government in community development, cultural policy and urban regeneration, he has been since 2 a freelance analyst and activist for cities around the world, in association with the Comedia agency. He is the author (with Charles Landry) of *The Intercultural City: Planning for Diversity Advantage* (Earthscan, 2008) and is principal adviser to the Council of Europe on its Intercultural Cities programme.

Patrice Yengo, an anthropologist, is a professor at the Marien Ngouabi University of Brazzaville and is an organizer of music and theatre networks in that city. He also edits the series of publications called *Mutations et défis en Afrique central,* published by Karthala, Paris. He is currently a professor in residence at the Institute of Advanced Study in Nantes, France.

Wil Zonneveld, PhD, is professor of urban and regional development at the Faculty of Architecture and Urban Design and OTB Research Institute, Delft University of Technology, the Netherlands (www.otb.tudelft.nl). His expertise includes strategic territorial planning, the role of visions and concepts in planning, European territorial governance and the Europeanization of national territorial planning systems. He is co-editor-in-chief of the *European Journal of Spatial Development* (www.nordregio.se/ejsd/).

ACKNOWLEDGEMENTS

The Cultures and Globalization Series has benefited from the advice, support, and contributions of many individuals and organizations. We endeavour to acknowledge and thank all of them here. In the ultimate analysis, however, the co-editors alone are responsible for this final version of the publication.

International Advisory Board

Hugo Achugar (Uruguay)
Arjun Appadurai (India/USA)
Benjamin Barber (USA)
Hilary Beckles (Barbados)
Tony Bennett (United Kingdom)
Craig Calhoun (USA)
George Corm (Lebanon)
Masayuki Deguchi (Japan)
Mamadou Diouf (Senegal)
Yehuda Elkana (Israel/Hungary)
Yilmaz Esmer (Turkey)
Mike Featherstone (United Kingdom)
Sakiko Fukuda-Parr (Japan/USA)
Nathan Gardels (USA)
Anthony Giddens (United Kingdom)
Salvador Giner (Spain)
Xavier Greffe (France)
Stuart Hall (Jamaica/United Kingdom)
Seung-Mi Han (Korea)
David Held (United Kingdom)
Vjeran Katunaric (Croatia)
Nobuku Kawashima (Japan)
Arun Mahizhnan (Singapore)
Achille Mbembe (Cameroon/South Africa)
Candido Mendes (Brazil)
Catherine Murray (Canada)
Sven Nilsson (Sweden)
Walter Santagata (Italy)
James Allen Smith (USA)
Prince Hassan bin Talal (Jordan)
David Throsby (Australia)
Jean-Pierre Warnier (France)
Margaret Wyszomirski (USA)
Yunxiang Yan (China/USA)
George Yúdice (USA)

Additional Support

Research Coordination for Indicator Suites
Michael Hoelscher

Research Assistance
Matti Kunstek, Aysegül Argit, Linzhi Zhang
We also thank the students in the seminar *Stadt-Kultur-Globalisierung* held during the summer term 2010 at the University of Heidelberg for their input.

Design and Production
Indicator suites were designed by Donnie Luu (New York)

Cover and Divider Artwork
Emilia Birlo

Administration
Saskia Kyas, Hertie School of Governance
Jocelyn Guihama, School of Public Affairs, UCLA
Tijana Maneva, The American University of Paris

Financial Support

We gratefully acknowledge the financial support of the following institutions:

The Bank of Sweden Tercentenary Foundation
Compagnia di San Paolo
The Fritt Ord Institute
University of Heidelberg
Hertie School of Governance
UCLA School of the Arts and Architecture

CULTURE AND ITS MANY SPACES

Saskia Sassen

Culture is far more than a designation of a specialized institutional domain, as in expressions such as the arts or the entertainment sector. Whether the observer or practitioner know it or not, culture is an inevitable part of all endeavors, from craftwork to finance to how we use interactive technologies, notably the internet and electronic games. There is no exiting from culture or the cultural. Even in fields as unlikely as high finance, I have found that the cultural is omnipresent, notably the specialized cultures of trust that are essential given the vast amounts of money traded in seconds. Without such cultures of trust that type of trading would not be feasible.

And yet, far too often, as an object of study, culture has been confined to the self-evident domain of 'Culture'. This volume, however, like its four predecessors in *The Cultures and Globalization Series*, breaks away from that assumption: it seeks out *the cultural* in a vast range of domains, most of which we do not associate with one of the several established/conventional meaning of culture. In that sense it engages the cultural as a generic condition that is to be found in governance frameworks, in financial markets, in the making of built environments and the intermediations connecting what Henri Lefebvre conceived of as the far order of state and law, on the one hand, and the order of daily life, on the other. Though none of the authors argues it, the volume's framework seems to allow for constitutions and other foundational framings, to be conceived of as cultures of governance. Invoking Chakravarty's *Provincializing Europe*, I would posit that one outcome of this volume is to 'provincialize' presumptions of neutrality and *techne*: the chapters extend the cultural onto domains that have been thought of as technocratic, in the sense of an objectivity that escapes the cultural.

In that regard it is part of a new kind of urban scholarship that once again makes the city a strategic site for the exploration of the major challenges confronting society, challenges which tend to become concrete and urgent in cities. The city was a heuristic space – a space capable of producing knowledge about some of the major transformations of an epoch. This heuristic capacity of cities was a major factor in the beginnings of urban scholarship in our early western modernity. This is evident in the work of Simmel, Weber, Benjamin, Lefebvre, and most prominently the Chicago School, especially Park and Wirth, both deeply influenced by German sociology. These thinkers confronted massive processes – industrialization, urbanization, alienation, a new cultural formation they called 'urbanity.' Studying the city was not simply studying the urban. It was about studying the major social processes of an era.

But for much of the time since then, the city was rarely studied as a lens onto larger realities. Critical was the fact that the city ceased being the fulcrum for epochal transformations and thus a strategic site for research about non-urban processes. The urban was increasingly flattened into what came to be called 'social problems.'

Today, as we have entered a global era, the city is once again emerging as a strategic site for understanding some of the major new trends reconfiguring the social order. The city and the metropolitan region emerge as one of the strategic sites where major macro-social trends materialize and hence can be constituted as an object of study. Each of those trends is marked by specific contents and consequences. The urban moment is but one moment in their often complex, multi-sited trajectories.

The cultural presence in struggles around political, economic, technical, and legal issues centered in the realities of cities can become catalysts for changes in a whole range of institutional domains – markets, participatory governance, judicial recourse, cultures of engagement and deliberation, and rights for members of the urban community regardless of lineage and origin.

The resurgence of the city as a site for research on these major contemporary dynamics is evident in many different disciplines – sociology, anthropology, economic geography, cultural studies, and literary criticism. Most recently, economists are beginning to address the urban and regional economy in their analyses in ways that go beyond older forms of urban economics.

This volume is a significant contribution to this larger body of research and interpretation. In these authors' chapters, culture becomes a transversal condition that takes on multiple different shapes and contents. Further, it is embedded in an enormous diversity of institutional spaces, each with its specific cultural genealogies and trajectories. There are features and contents of urbanization and globalization that evince particularly distinctive instantiations of the cultural. Among these are the rise of the new information technologies, the intensifying of transnational and translocal dynamics, and the strengthening presence and voice of socio-cultural diversity. All of these are at a cutting edge of actual change. These trends do not encompass the majority of social conditions; on the contrary, most social reality probably corresponds to older continuing and familiar trends. Yet, although these trends may involve only parts of the urban condition and cannot be confined to the urban, they are strategic in that they mark the urban condition in novel ways and make it, in turn, a key research site for major urban and non-urban trends. This volume introduces the reader to a whole range of situations and conditions that capture key aspects of these three powerful global shapers. It opens new ground for research, interpretation and policy making in our emergent global urban era.

(Between Venice and Beijing, both old and grand, but in such different ways).

INTRODUCTION

Yudhishthir Raj Isar, Michael Hoelscher and Helmut K. Anheier

Cities as policy actors …

This fifth volume in *The Cultures and Globalization Series* is devoted to issues of cultural policy and governance. This policy and governance perspective complements those adopted for the four preceding volumes of the *Series*, which as a whole addresses the complex and changing intersections between the various facets and forces of globalization on the one hand and cultural change on the other. It was implicit in these earlier volumes: in relation to cultural conflicts and tensions (2007); or to the discourses and practices of the cultural and creative industries (2008); to contemporary cultural expression and creativity (2010) and to collective engagements with heritage, memory and identity (2011). Yet none of these volumes explored as objects of analysis in and of themselves the governance and policy issues raised by cultures in a globalizing world.[1] At this stage of our long-term endeavour, therefore, we consider it appropriate to do so.[2]

The present volume, like its predecessors, also attempts to provide a global perspective. But this perspective will differ significantly from the one that dominates in the 'cultural policy' literature. We understand governance in today's world as a multi-level phenomenon, as a system that involves trans-national, international, national and sub-national actors as well as governmental bodies, businesses and civil society institutions. The governance spaces these actors command have undergone significant changes in recent years, as has the influence of the latter on policy-making. While some, such as national governments, either as a matter of choice or of consequence, have lost either space or influence or both, others have gained. Among the latter we see corporations like Apple and Google, non-profit bodies like The Internet Corporation for Assigned Names and Numbers (ICANN) or The International Federation of Arts Councils and Related Agencies (IFACCA), civil society organizations such as the European Cultural Foundation or the J.P. Getty Trust, and both the old and the new media, including movements such as Creative Commons.

We also observe a resurgence of the metropolis, where the local, national, regional and global crystallize (Sassen, 1994). It is in this sense as well that, along with Scott (2008a, 2008b) and other students of urban geography, we suggest that we live in a new metropolitan age: the world is undergoing massive urbanization; the number of mega-cities is increasing, particularly in the Global South, and well-established cities such as London and New York have experienced a renaissance of a kind few would have expected even as recently as in the 1980s (see the respective indicator suites in part 2 of this volume). That these cities, along with others, such as Shanghai, Singapore or Sydney, have become 'global' players hardly seems surprising. What does stand out, however, is that these cities and others, such as Cairo, Lagos, Mexico City or Mumbai, have gained considerable influence and stature in cultural terms. They appear to have seized the opportunities offered by a globalized world better than the countries in which they are located. What is more, they appear better managed than their nation-states and seem to function more efficiently, even when their nation-states are unstable and have serious governance deficits. They are also becoming significant actors in terms of culture.

It is for this reason that the present volume is concerned with cities rather than nation-states or the international or supra-national policy actors created by them, such as UNESCO or the European Union. Most writers, most of the time, take nation-states as their principal units of analysis. Instead, the present volume will highlight cities as leading loci of cultural policy and governance. The shift from the international and the national to the regional and the local is warranted indirectly by a key finding of globalization research: rather than imposing a massive, seemingly stifling, layer of some standardized form of global culture of whatever provenance, globalization has, in many realms, led to diversity and a seemingly cacophonous *mélange* of cultural activities. These new patterns of cultural behaviour have led *inter alia* to new localisms, or to manifestations of the 'glocal' – hence the term 'glocalization' – that are hybrid forms, styles and patterns bringing together local and global elements and processes. There is a new 'city nationalism' abroad today that harks back to the city-states of the Italian Renaissance. Many cities

are creating their own imagined communities and aspiring to become part of a broader 'community of cities not marked or limited by state and/or national borders' (Paz Balibrea, 2004: 216). As shown in Figure I.1, the resulting dynamics no longer fit the conventional local-national-regional-international-transnational step function.

Yet this schematic representation should not hide the complexity of the relational pattern. First, cities are not directly part of transnational governance structures. They have neither seats nor votes at bodies such as the United Nations or the European Parliament; they do not necessarily have more voice than corporations or civil society actors in terms of advocacy. Second, they are unequally represented at national levels, and their *de jure* and *de facto* influence varies according to the type of legislative and administrative system in place. For example, Paris occupies a rather privileged position in this regard, while Los Angeles and even Berlin are less favoured by national policy frames and styles. Third, cities themselves have different governance structures that may either help or hinder their positioning in the local–global nexus. Many cities, among them Los Angeles, have highly fragmented administrative systems that make coordinated cultural policy action difficult even in the best of budgetary times. The Mayor of London has

Figure I.1 Dynamics of local and global relational patterns

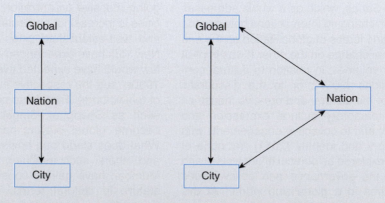

Traditional hierarchical pattern   New emerging relational pattern

far fewer policy tools and resources at his disposal than his counterparts in Berlin or Paris (see indicator suites in Part 2), not to speak of the mega-cities of the Indian sub-continent that have practically no such powers.

At the same time, there are striking similarities among cities that play a 'global' role. They are 'networked' in the sense that they form multiple intersections of movements of people, goods and services, finance, information, as well as talents and ideas. It is the density and reach of these multiplex networks that make such global cities stand out. It is also what makes their success contingent on economic, legal and social-cultural factors that emanate from both national and international sources. For this reason, they share one further characteristic: world cities often sit uncomfortably in the governance structures of nation-states and international regimes. So how do they address global governance problems, and why do some negotiate the cross-currents of globalization more successfully than others? In addressing that question, however, we must also be mindful of the diversity of the relationships between cities and globalization. As Stuart Hall wrote (2010: xi) in his Foreword to volume 3 of this *Series*:

> *Contemporary globalization in all its aspects is a process of 'combined and uneven development' – 'combined' because it draws huge differences, disparities, historical divergences and temporalities together; 'uneven' because it creates greater disparities and inequalities – in resources, wealth, income, health, welfare, material well-being and cultural power – greater even than the differences and inequalities it claims to be surpassing.*

Yet all metropolitan areas, whether they are truly 'global' in their reach – New York, Los Angeles, London, Mexico City, Mumbai, Cairo, Rio de Janeiro, Paris – or significantly large and diverse – Berlin, Cape Town, Istanbul, Lagos or Sydney – or of medium size, relatively speaking – Torino, Singapore, Stockholm – have become the 'mixing bowls' in which all the combined and uneven processes of globalization play out, particularly in the cultural field. These cities are becoming protagonists in cultural policy and politics whose importance equals and sometimes exceeds that of national governments. There are different reasons

for this. The first is the sheer size of many of these cities, which have larger populations and greater economic power than many small nation-states. A second is the strong concentration of many globalization trends within cities, regardless of their size. The Chicago School of urban sociology saw the city of the early twentieth century as a laboratory of modernity; in like manner, the globalization issues of today seem to peak in cities. Immigration, for example, is at its greatest in cities, where immigrants build up strong networks and attempt to preserve their cultures of origin, while at the same time mixing with people from many other cultural backgrounds and contributing to new forms of ongoing cultural hybridization. Multinational corporations and INGOs alike are headquartered in cities. A third reason is the greater flexibility cities enjoy in order to react to such developments and search for solutions to the policy and governance issues that they generate. In this context, then, what are the key policy and governance issues and what patterns of policy-making are emerging, where, and with what implications?

Deepening the rationale

A focus on metropolitan cultural policy and governance issues does not mean that we neglect or abandon the nation-state. However, nation-states tend to articulate and enact cultural policies primarily in terms of identity-building and protection, obeying the imperatives of what Raymond Williams once referred to as cultural policy as 'display' (Williams, 1984). While these motivations are certainly present at the local level as well – see Therborn, 2002 on the role of national capitals – cities, when compared to nation-states, appear to be interacting more dynamically, even proactively, with the challenges and opportunities of globalization. Factors of scale, accessibility and participation combine increasingly to ensure that a great deal of innovative policy-making is being made at the city level. Many of the most exciting cultural visions, projects, exchanges and networks and developments of the day are to be found in or generated by cities rather by nations.

It is at the municipal level that the patterns, processes, and outcomes associated with the 'complex connectivity' (Tomlinson, 1999) of globalization are playing out in the most challenging ways. There is increasing evidence to show that city actors – at once local governments, civil society entities and the business world – are engaging in more authentic international interactions at the policy level, in more mutual learning and exchange of experience, than are national actors (UNCHS, 2001). For example, recent debates (and many initiatives) about the economic role of the 'creative economy' and the 'creative class' have been primarily about urban policies and measures to attract and retain certain population and professional groups (see Florida, 2002; Scott, 2008a).

This city dimension was often present in the previous four volumes but was not tackled systematically. In the past few years, however, it has become abundantly clear that *the challenges and opportunities of globalization are ever more acutely perceived, felt, or actually lived at the local level*. At the same time, and in keeping with the notion of 'glocalization' referred to already, the ways in which the local interacts with the global often sidestep or contradict the so-called 'national' stances adopted by governments. Initiatives in each local community allow them to shape their own responses to cultural globalization pressures and opportunities. These responses bring up issues of governance as well. Who is in charge of cultural policy and what degree of autonomy do local actors really have in setting goals and targets?

One area of particular interest here is the *global governance* problem that affects many policy fields: the growing mismatch between the forces of globalization and the capacity of governments to steer, regulate and control. Both the 2008–09 global financial crisis and the often hapless responses to it in political capitals around the world testify to this. Unless the systemic failures of global governance are fixed through policies and institutions more adequate to the challenges of a globalized economy and global financial markets, can we do more than 'tinker' with the syndrome at best? What does this diagnosis, usually reached for financial markets or the environment, mean for cultural policy? How do metropolitan areas around the world address the global governance challenge? Could it be that the new cultural 'glocalism' is a response to governance weaknesses at national and international levels? Or is it just that, in the current 'urban turn in spatial politics', national governments are unnecessarily sacrificing regional cohesion for the 'fuelling [of] national engines of growth' (Van Winden, 2010: 103f.)?

City-level phenomena also largely confirm one of the key working hypotheses of the *Series*, which is that ever more frequently today, cultural processes play out independently of the nation-state and its policy frameworks. In some cases, of course, the nation-state has gained importance. Nevertheless, there can be little doubt that cultural processes today need to be seen through several lenses: the city or regional perspective has to be complemented by a national one, and of course both are being inflected by a transnational one as well. On the ground, however, clusterings of artists are associated with particular urban districts such as New York's Soho, museums and cultural institutions are city-created and managed, and the challenges of living together with ethnic diversity are primarily urban ones. As several chapters will show, autonomous cultural policy frameworks are being shaped increasingly by city administrations. It is therefore appropriate to focus on the cultural dimension of municipal policy and politics in order to attain the two main aims of the *Series*, namely to unpack the relationships between cultural change and globalization and to enrich the evidence base needed for informed policy-making in the cultural arena.

To be sure, national governments still articulate broad policy frameworks for culture in the arts and heritage sense. We know of course that in the USA (as in Germany) the federal government does *not* do so, but in fact this makes the argument for a local-level perspective even more compelling there. Margaret Wyszomirski observed in a previous volume (2008: 203) that in the USA key policy decisions 'are concentrated at the local level and are taking shape without the benefit of central government leadership, support, or linkage as they are in most other countries'. Everywhere, national governments put in place national administrative and institutional structures, and engage in international dialogue and cooperation. So the question is whether local actors merely imitate or emulate these visions, aims, regulatory frameworks and structures, or whether they offer alternatives to them that engage more creatively with the global. In many cases, cities *have to* interpret and apply often abstract broad national policy frameworks or, when very clearly formulated national policies exist, these provide inspiration for cultural action, but this needs to be adapted to local needs.

In other words, 'local' cultural policy-making – the tools that it employs and the relations between different kinds of public intervention in the realm of culture that obtain at the local level – cannot be analyzed in isolation from the national level. Rather, these phenomena must be explored together with and in juxtaposition to the national policy dynamics. They must also be taken up in ways that encompass the new kinds of interactions that are occurring between the two levels. Indeed, several chapters in the volume attend to such interactions. In some cases, local initiatives may be taken to palliate nation-level insufficiencies, but in the majority of instances cities set their own agendas on the basis of local conditions, needs, and expectations. Often they must also react to national trends towards decentralization. Yet even here, there is a big difference between paternalistic decentralization, which is a reckless abdication of responsibility, without regard for the local-level outcomes, and reluctant decentralization that transfers some remit to the lower level but seeks to retain control, thus burdening the local authorities with various rules and conditions. Today we are probably also seeing 'revindicated decentralization', to coin a term. There are transnational drivers of decentralization as well, for example the efforts of the European Commission, whose disbursement of EU Structural Funds for regional development has been a major factor.

Moving now from the city–nation nexus to the level of transnational flows, we see that many of the reference points or nodes of such flows and spaces are now cities rather than nations. Indeed, some of these flows have been explored in previous volumes, for example, migrations, the emergence of hybrid art-forms, or new cross-sectoral partnerships for the creation of cultural institutions. Hollywood and Bollywood are cases in point for the movie industry, as are Paris and Milan for fashion or Silicon Valley and Silicon Alley for software. The borrowing and slight modification of the places' names (Bollywood, Silicon Alley) themselves reveal the importance of the original location. Cultural forms of increasing diversity and innovativeness are emerging in transnational and transcultural space, transcending the limitations of the national imaginary in ways that suggest that 'the national logic might now actually be inhibiting more innovative cultural possibilities' (Robins, 2006: 19). Factors such as the 'nichification' attendant upon consumerist lifestyles or the demands of ethnic and linguistic pluralism are promoting frames of reference and engagement beyond as well as below nation-state

borders, such as global youth culture or diasporic communities. All these extend the horizons of collective identities and loyalties (Dahlgren, 2009), just as they also contain them within local settings as well. Cities of all sizes are now articulating visions of local culture as symbolic capital, particularly for place marketing and branding and the instrumental use of the cultural industries to boost local economic growth and employment. Even cities that do not even try to call themselves 'global' have to pay attention to global demand and information flows. Often, even if the city does not have a particularly strong cultural offer, the economic dimension of the city having become insufficient, a cultural component has to be integrated and marketed to a local audience as well as a global one. This cultural component tends increasingly to be embodied in carefully conceived events, hence the notion of 'eventful cities' (Richards and Palmer, 2010).

Hence there is a need for closer ethnographic attention to the local dynamics. For what is at stake are the size, health and diversity of the local cultural system as a whole, its very backbone. As Duxbury and Murray observed in volume 3 of the *Series* (2010: 209), 'local cultural strategies need to balance entrepreneurship with a needs-based analysis, to seek "authentic" local differentiation, and recover a dimension of playfulness in cities, not as an experience of consumption and staged commercial production but a genuine expression of creativity and a process of intercultural education and re-discovery.' It is both 'good' and 'bad' practice in relation to such issues that we shall seek to share with our readers.

While governance is not a synonym for policy, elaborating any policy in the public interest requires a strong emphasis on governance. The notion focuses on a specific aspect of policy and at the same time broadens the perspective. We understand the notion as 'the set of institutions and structures that define how public goods (or public "bads") are created and delivered to citizens and the private sector and how public policies are made' (Wei, 2001: 1).[3] On a second level, business usage in regard to the term is also relevant as the relationships between a company's management, its board, its shareholders and other stakeholders that the corporate sector seeks to nurture are equally germane to the success of cultural organizations. Corporate governance frameworks may provide 'the structure through which objectives are set and the means of attaining those objectives and monitoring performance are determined' (OECD, 2004: 11). In the cultural sector, many boards are considered to be weak governance mechanisms and this is perhaps a critical issue in the context of the current recession; similarly, there are frequent weaknesses of governance in national-level, state-run cultural organizations, which impact on their interactions with the local level. In the urban context, governance issues may also arise with regard to the numerous private–public partnerships that are taking place for developmental and infrastructural investment. Finally, as regards arts and culture practice in general, as it is supported for reasons that are at once instrinsic and instrumental, the governance of this sector needs be thought through in both instrinsic and instrumental terms.

Cultural policy, cultural politics, cultural governance

For analytical purposes we can distinguish between cultural 'policy' and 'politics', linking both notions to 'governance' in the different ways shown in the triangle diagram in Figure I.1 above. The distinction between the terms 'policy' and 'politics' is explored more fully in Chapter 32 by Isar dealing with the policy implications of the multifaceted analysis brought together in this volume. Suffice it to say here that, broadly speaking, 'policy' falls more within the purview of a problem-solving, managerial approach used by a recognized community of 'cultural policy consultants', while a focus on the 'politics' – the articulation of different values and meanings – is more characteristic of critical academic perspectives on cultural policy-making. In a sense, the distinction between the two 'torn halves' (Bennett, 2004) is comparable to that between applied and fundamental research. The common understanding of *cultural policy* refers to any 'system of ultimate aims, practical objectives and means, pursued by a group and applied by an authority [and] … combined in an explicitly coherent system' (Girard and Gentil, 1983: 13). The study of cultural policy is thus taken to be mainly what a public authority enacts in terms of cultural affairs, the latter being understood as relating to the arts and heritage. Many civil society actors – private foundations, cultural activist groups and networks and the like – also shape cultural policy in this sense; business corporations,

notably in the cultural industries, do so as well (cf. volume 2 in the *Series*, entitled *The Cultural Economy*) with impacts that rival if not exceed those of government. Cultural policy research in this universe tends to be essentially functionalist in nature, if not largely descriptive (Isar, 2009). It gathers empirical data, often but not always with the help of social science methodologies, in order to offer solutions to problems defined by a client and, consequently, its research questions rarely range beyond the delivery or non-delivery of *outputs* (in turn these are generally the outputs of institutional action). But the premises on the basis of which those outputs are defined, the values they embody, or the sometimes covert goals they pursue – in other words the *outcomes* – are rarely critiqued or called into question. There is, however, a relatively recent academic tradition also calling itself cultural policy research that does ask such questions, in a critical perspective, which leads it to focus on the subject matter rather more as cultural *politics*. Thus it targets 'the politics of culture in the most general sense: it is about the clash of ideas, institutional struggles and power relations in the production and circulation of symbolic meanings …' (McGuigan, 1996: 1). Influenced largely by cultural studies (as well as by critical sociology, e.g. Pierre Bourdieu), this perspective is inherently contested and critical.[4]

The two camps operate in parallel, but with few mutual connections. As a result, culture is a public policy domain in which there exists a bifurcation between, to put it somewhat schematically, critical and uncritical (or instrumental) analytical stances. This divide has real implications for governance in terms of regulatory oversight and overall 'system control', and our purpose for the *Series* has been to help bridge it.[5] Hence the chapters that follow in Part 1, whether in the first section on overarching themes, or in the second devoted to the experiences of individual cities, pursue this objective. With this aim in view, at the start of the project we therefore framed the issues for the benefit of our contributors on the following interconnected levels:[6]

1 the internal dynamics of cities (e.g. urban regeneration and renewal; cultural infrastructures; new modes of cultural work/employment);
2 city–city intersections (e.g., competition, branding, division of labour);
3 city–nation intersections (e.g., civil society groupings; balance between culture as economic

resource and culture as identity or difference); and

4 city–global intersections (e.g., global branding, international civil society interfaces; international organizations and transnational governments; and governance such as the EU, etc.).

Some key issues

Having set out the urban dimensions and domains of action in which *cultural policies* are being articulated and applied – or the debates around which the dynamics of *cultural politics* occur – in early 2010 we put forward a number of issues as a broad framework for the volume. As its purpose was to serve as a point of departure in soliciting contributions, our framework was not exclusive, nor was it to be a blueprint for the finished volume. It turned out to be germane and thought-provoking for our authors, however, which is why we reiterate it below:

1. Political and sociological issues

1.1. *Cultural diversity and pluralism*: as migratory flows transforming the ethnic and social heterogeneity of cities, how are city leaders devising new models of recognition, inclusion, conflict-prevention and mediation?

1.2. *Civil society entities and networks, local, regional and global*: what are the dynamics of grassroots cultural mobilization within cities as well as at the level of inter-city networks such as *United Cities and Local Governments* (UCLG)? What lessons can be learned from these diverse groupings and their interactions (or non-interactions)?

1.3. *Global organizations and city cultural policies*: how do cities interact as autonomous actors with bodies such as UNESCO, The Council of Europe or the EU?

1.4. *The tools of governance*: what hard and soft governance tools (and models underlying them) suggest themselves for policy actors in metropolitan regions? These could range from questions of budgeting and accountability to cultural audits and the use of performance measures and indicators for cultural sector organizations as well as recourse to the bridging functions of networks and platforms.

2. Socio-economic issues

2.1. *The political economy of urban cultures*: instrumental cultural and creative industries strategies were analyzed in depth in volume 2 and also to some extent in volume 3. What does today's 'state of the art' reveal that is new? What are the effects of the blurring of boundaries between for-profit and not-for-profit cultural activities, or between producers and consumers? Is there a new balance being found between city cultural development for tourists and city cultural development for (different groups of) local residents? Where are the chief investments being made: in production-centric policies or in favour of greater consumption? In institutions and infrastructure or in artistic life? What is the place of the community arts in city settings? What is their potential as a form of resistance or adaptation to globalization?

2.2. *Economic transformations and renewals (industrial decline, de-industrialization, etc.)*: how are cultural policies targeting urban regeneration and renewal in conditions of globalization. How diverse are these policies and practices? How effective are they? As regards the omnipresent trend towards gentrification as an outcome, what role do cultural organizations play? Are some of them willing accomplices? Are others merely victims, forced to move by the buzz they have created to boost the real-estate market?

2.3. *Branding*: What are the city branding formulae that are being followed and what are their impacts on the global positioning of cities, and as regards the identity, image and sense of place of their inhabitants?

2.4. *Local cultural policies and sustainable development*: how are the global dynamics of the environmental movement playing out at city level? How is the sustainability paradigm inflecting local cultural policies?

3. Urban planning issues

3.1. *City spaces and infrastructures*: how are global factors affecting policy as regards local cultural infrastructure, its nature, scale and location as well as the sustainability thereof?

3.2. *Culture in urban regeneration*: old wine in new bottles? But what exactly are these new bottles? How are heritage, the narratives of the past, and contemporary monumental cultural infrastructure, such as flagship museums, theatres and concert halls, coming together with the global discourses of the creative industries as motors of urban regeneration?

3.3. *Cities and cyberspace*: what models are emerging to create locally embedded cyber-spaces and levels of connectedness across populations and professions? How do geo-graphic space and cyberspace relate?

Responses

In keeping with the pattern established for the *Series*, Part 1 of the book is devoted to essays on issues that are overarching both conceptually and geo-politically and bring the findings of fresh research to bear. The opening chapter, by Katharine Sarikakis, looks at the cultural power of major cities in a perspective that is rather different from the usual focus on financial and trade flows. Her focus is on the political power that places certain cities at the 'commanding heights' of global cultural policy-making because they function as *centres of hege-monic political systems*. Particularly in relation to audiovisual and electronic culture policies, how do three cities – Brussels, Washington, DC, and Montevideo lead and shape both global and regional policy? The analysis focuses on the new types of concentrations of actors in these 'global cities of politics' and the processes through which they exercise control and influence on the world stage. In a similar vein, in the next chapter, Roman Lobato shifts the focus from the formal indicators of economic power to the *informal* or 'grey' and 'black' economies where we encounter a rather different map of global connectivity and cultural provision, which interacts with various 'mainstreams'. His exploration of the *circuits of media piracy* in Asia, Africa and Latin America reveals distinctive pat-terns at city level, often involving direct conflict with urban regeneration and city-branding initiatives, but also active support on the part of many cities to their informal economies for strategic reasons, which he argues will become more compelling for urban cultural policy in coming decades.

From such new ways of framing cultural govern-ance issues we move to a set of key challenges facing contemporary cities. The most obvious one is *migratory flows and cultural diversity*. Phil Wood, on

the basis of his work for the Council of Europe's 'Intercultural Cities' programme as well as broad international observation, sets out the reasons for which cities can and must take a more proactive stance to forge diverse urban societies where citizens co-create their life-worlds. A selection of examples is offered to illustrate how local government, civil society and migrants themselves are now shaping this emerging movement. Another familiar chal-lenge is that of incorporating the goals and the spirit of *sustainable development* into cultural poli-cy-making at the city level. Nancy Duxbury, Catherine Cullen and Jordi Pascual make the intel-lectual case for this and show how this new para-digm is being advanced through a wide range of local initiatives, all rooted in a pervasive and height-ened concern for grassroots public participation. Arguing that the ingredients needed to fully elaborate and impose it are all in play, the chapter describes how the United Cities and Local Government's *Agenda 21 for Culture* is playing a leadership role as an international connector in this regard and discusses the ways in which this Agenda is addressing the challenge of aligning efforts and advancing new thinking globally. While strength-ening the connections between culture and sus-tainability is a universally recognized goal already, Dragan Klaic explores another not yet recognized objective: capitalizing for the sake of cultural policy on the *'town and gown' relationships* that he finds wanting in most contemporary cities. Universities do not yet figure in the cast of cultural policy and governance players, yet there are sound reasons a more structured and structural relationship as a new frontier in this area, one that optimizes the resources of institutions of higher learning beyond the status they already confer on the cities in which they are located.

From such 'programmatic' approaches, the dis-cussion moves on to issues, tropes and practices that have dominated the discourse of culture in and for cities for several decades now. One of these is *city branding*: the strategy of identifying valuable assets that a city has to offer, developing these assets and delivering their value to attract investors, visitors and talent. Lily Kong traces the origins of city branding and explores what sorts of methods have succeeded or failed. In so doing, she stresses both positive and perverse outcomes. '*Spectacularization*' has already established itself squarely on that agenda, however, and Davide Ponzini explores how buildings or urban regeneration projects designed by star architects have become spectacles designed to contribute to 'distinction' on the global stage but may well be leading precisely to another form of homogenization. The well-known narrative of the 'Bilbao effect' accompanying the proliferation of Guggenheim Museums – and now also of antennae of the august Louvre – now enjoys great purchase everywhere, particularly in cities such as Abu Dhabi that are positioning themselves as new players on the world stage. This trend has led cities to compete in the matter of 'collecting' new buildings and cultural facilities, often with scant regard for the functions of these infrastructures and edifices both in their urban context and in the global market.

We have in this *Series* amply explored the tropes of '*creativity*' that are so dominant in cultural policy thinking today (see in particular Anheier and Isar, 2010) and indeed the notion is particularly germane at city level. It occupies a privileged place in this volume as well. Taking an analytical tack that he already deployed to good effect in volume 2 (2008), Stuart Cunningham argues here that the key tensions in discussions over what makes cities more conducive to and supportive of creativity revolve around perspectives that are either production-centric or consumption-centric. Scholars are increasingly prepared to claim priority for the city-region over the nation-state as an economic and cultural agent in the contemporary world, but are they ready to deal with major changes in the nature of cultural production and consumption themselves, he asks? Because the boundaries between the production and consumption of culture are blurring, tomorrow's citizens/consumers will expect the two to be much more interdependent. Finally, we bring our readers the most recent reflections of Charles Landry, one of the fathers of 'creativity' thinking, particular with regard to city cultural policy and governance. As Landry argues, 'everyone is in principle creative, but not equally creative, yet everyone can be more creative than they currently are'. He goes on to explore how this insight can be applied effectively to cities, where the question of creative organization takes on several layers of complexity.

The second section of Part 1 of the volume is devoted to 21 different 'City Experiences'. In each of the previous volumes, we illustrated the overarching issues from a wide range of geo-cultural perspectives as well as focus in this second section on a range of specific issues or domains with respect to

which key questions arise. In the present volume, the challenge was comparable, yet different: to illustrate the overarching issues through the very diverse experiences of a series of selected cities across the world. We started out with the idea of a set of 'City Profiles', but the notion of a profile implies that similar phenomena are being compared according to a shared analytical grid. Thus we sought initially to group cities together into clusters of shared characteristics. We thought we should have chapters on several 'global' or 'world' cities which are recognized as such in various existing classifications based on criteria such as financial and trade flows or population size. Most of these cities have also spun out cultural narratives and so we could have, say, grouped together the 'global cities' discussed in this volume – London, New York, Mexico City, Mumbai, Paris and Shanghai. But very challenging cultural issues, as well as front-edge methods of addressing them, emerge from many other cities as well, not just the 'global cities'. They emerge with equal force from cities of all shapes and sizes. We therefore sought to include analyses of the efforts and experience of metropoles already well-established in cultural terms (such as Amsterdam, Barcelona, Berlin or Istanbul), as well as of far less celebrated places whose international cultural profile is of recent origin or fabrication. We also thought it valuable to place the spotlight on the experiences of cities whose leaders and people have played the cultural card in response to dramatic urban traumas (as in Medellín, Colombia), or particular circumstances (Marseille, Torino and Venice), or through specific means of action (as in Fès or L'viv). Over and above this intrinsic diversity, however, even when urban characteristics are shared, our authors have highlighted very different sorts of achievements and challenges. This made it difficult to see the chapters as 'profiles', since each one concentrates on different facets of urban cultural policy-making and governance. For this reason, we decided to call these chapters 'City Experiences'. Also, after considering several possible ways of grouping them together, we opted in the end for a presentation in simple alphabetical order. Significantly, this ordering opens with a chapter that turns on the sustainability of a very new city – Abu Dhabi – that is creating great island cultural infrastructure practically *ex nihilo*, while it closes with a chapter that explores the severely threatened sustainability of a very old city – Venice – whose stock of cultural capital is as vast as it is ancient.

The variety of approaches is part and parcel of our editorial method, which is ecumenical in terms of both disciplines within the social sciences and the humanities and in terms of ideological preference. But the variety is above all a natural outcome of the differences between the cities themselves, whose respective cultural systems have emerged through strikingly different histories and contemporary situations. This heterogeneity is as marked in 'global cities' as it is in human settlements of less imposing proportions. In regard to cultural flourishing – or 'creativity' in cultural policy and governance – financial clout or population size are of secondary importance. Our selection represents a cross-section of germane city-based cultural issues. This is a highly plural worldscape.

Despite this plurality, however, several common threads run through all the overarching explorations and city profiles alike, and shared policy implications do emerge from them. All the chapters show that policy-making with regard to the cultural now mobilizes a broader cast of actors than ever before: not just the institutions of government, but also civil society organizations and movements, as well as the forces of the marketplace. And the dynamics of cooperation or competition between these different actors are significant in cities of all kinds. Another common thread is the powerful way in which urban development is transforming not just the urban fabric of cities, but also their cultural texture, their soul – this is evocatively presented in the photo essay of a young scholar, Mieka Ritsema, that is Chapter 33 in this volume. Part 2 of the volume, edited by Michael Hoelscher, presents quantitative data on eight of the cities and two overarching issues related to urbanization and city networks in the form of indicator suites (Anheier, 2007).

Finally, in closing, we wish to reiterate the abiding purpose of this *Series*, which is to address a range of expectations, anxieties and illusions that the encounter between cultures and globalization has generated right across the world. In the case of our cities, the expectations are tied to our current perceptions of the 'power of culture'. The anxieties arise from contradictory understandings of how cultures as resources are magnified or diminished by globalization. The illusions stem from overblown and instrumental visions of culture that simply ask it to do too much. We can only reiterate our conviction that the expectations can be justified, the anxieties allayed and the illusions dispelled by the patient and methodical marshalling of evidence in informed and conceptually sensitive ways. It is our hope that this volume too, like its four predecessors, will contribute meaningfully to that task.

Notes

1 Our understanding of 'culture' for the *Series* encompasses both the 'arts and heritage' sense of the term and a broader social science reading based on meaning-making. Hence we see 'culture' as the social construction, articulation and reception of meaning. We take it to be both the lived and creative experience for individuals as well as a body of artefacts, symbols, texts and objects, both heritage and contemporary creation, involving both enactment and representation. This allows us to embrace art and art discourse, the cultural heritage and its preservation and enhancement, the symbolic world of meanings, the commodified output of the cultural industries as well as the spontaneous or enacted, organized or unorganized cultural expressions of everyday life, including social relations. 'Globalization' we understand in the sense of today's highly accelerated movement of objects (goods, services, finance and other resources, etc.), meanings (language, symbols, knowledge, identities, etc.) and people across regions and intercontinental space (Held et al., 1999). These processes of time–space compression have accompanied the entire human story, but today their pace, depth and breadth are unprecedented.

2 Following Zürn (1998), governance in a broad sense could be defined as the sum of all collective regulations that aim at a particular problem or circumstance that needs to be solved in relation to the collective interest of certain stakeholder groups. We could also extend it to 'the traditions and institutions that determine how authority is exercised in a particular country. This includes (1) the process by which governments are selected, held accountable, monitored and replaced; (2) the capacity of governments to manage resources efficiently and to formulate, implement, and enforce sound policies and regulations; and (3) the respect of citizens and the state for the institutions that govern economic and social interactions among them' (Kaufmann, Kraay, and Zoido-Lobaton, 2000: 10).

3 In European usages there is some slippage around and between 'cultural policy' and 'cultural politics'. While *politique culturelle* in the Francophone world concerns the taken-for-granted role of the public authorities in cultural provision, and their role alone, the German notion of *Kulturpolitik* is inherently ambiguous; it could involve just that, or bring in the critical dimension we are alluding to here.

4 Some sub-disciplines, however, appear to be bridging the gap. Cultural economics, for example, engaged as it is by necessity with market forces, is now beginning to

inform policy-making for culture in, to some extent, the same way as do economists who deal with monetary policy, employment or industrial development, or like sociologists and political scientists whose findings inspire guidelines for the governance of various social and political sectors (see, for example, Throsby, 2010).

5 We are grateful to Lily Kong (see her chapter on city branding) for suggesting this choice of levels.

REFERENCES

Anheier, H. (2007) 'Introducing "Cultural Indicator" Suites'. In: Anheier, H. and Isar, Y.R. (eds.) *Conflicts and Tensions. The Cultures and Globalization Series 1*. London: SAGE Publications.

Anheier, H. and Isar, Y.R. (eds.) (2007) *Conflicts and Tensions. The Cultures and Globalization Series 1*. London: SAGE Publications.

Anheier, H. and Isar, Y.R. (eds.) (2008) *The Cultural Economy. The Cultures and Globalization Series 2*. London: SAGE Publications.

Anheier, H. and Isar, Y.R. (eds.) (2010) *Cultural Expression, Creativity and Innovation. The Cultures and Globalization Series 3*. London: SAGE Publications.

Anheier, H. and Isar, Y.R. (eds.) (2011) *Heritage, Memory and Identity. The Cultures and Globalization Series 4*. London: SAGE Publications.

Bennett, O. (2004) 'The Torn Halves of Cultural Policy Research', *International Journal of Cultural Policy*, 10(2): xxx–xx.

Dahlgren, P. (2009) *Media and Political Engagement. Citizens, Communication and Democracy*. Cambridge, UK: Cambridge University Press.

Duxbury, N. and Murray, C. (2010) 'Creative Spaces'. In: Anheier, H. and Isar, Y.R. (eds.) *Cultural Expression, Creativity and Innovation. The Cultures and Globalization Series 3*. London: SAGE Publications.

Florida, R. (2002) *The Rise of the Creative Class*. New York: Basic Books.

Girard, A. and Gentil, G. (1983) *Cultural Developments: Experiences and Policies*. Paris: UNESCO.

Hall, S. (2010) 'Foreword'. In: Anheier, H. and Isar, Y.R. (eds.) *Cultural Expression, Creativity and Innovation. The Cultures and Globalization Series 3*. London: SAGE Publications.

Held, D., McGrew, A., Goldblatt, D. and Perraton, J. (1999) *Global Transformations: Politics, Economics, and Culture*. Cambridge, UK: Polity Press.

Isar, Y.R. (2009) 'Cultural Policy: Towards a Global Survey', *Culture Unbound: Journal of Current Cultural Research* (electronic journal), 1: xxx–xx.

Kaufmann, D., Kraay, A. and Zoido-Lobaton P. (2000) 'Taking the Offensive against Corruption', *Finance and Development*. Washington, DC: IMF (June 2000).

Landry, C. (2000) *The Creative City. A Toolkit for Urban Innovators*. London: Earthscan.

Matarasso, F. and Landry, C. (1999) *Balancing Act: 21 Strategic Dilemmas in Cultural Policy*. Strasbourg: Council of Europe Publishing.

McGuigan, J. (1996) *Culture and the Public Sphere*. London: Routledge.

Organisation for Economic Co-operation and Development (OECD) (2004) *OECD Principles for Corporate Governance*. Paris: OECD.

Paz Balibrea, M. (2004) 'Urbanism, Culture and the Post-industrial City: Challenging the "Barcelona Model"'. In: Marshall, T. (ed.) *Transforming Barcelona*. London: Routledge, pp. 205–224.

Richards, G. and Palmer, R. (2010) *Eventful Cities: Cultural Management and Urban Revitalisation*. Amsterdam: Elsevir.

Robins, K. (2006) *The Challenge of Transcultural Diversities*. Final Report of the Council of Europe's transversal study on the theme of cultural policy and cultural diversity. Strasbourg: Council of Europe Publishing.

Sassen, S. (1994) *Cities in a World Economy*. Thousand Oaks, CA: Pine Forge Press.

Scott, A. (2008a) 'Cultural Economy: Retrospect and Prospect'. In: Anheier, H. and Isar, Y.R. (eds.) *The Cultural Economy. The Cultures and Globalization Series 2*. London: SAGE Publications.

Scott, A. (2008b) 'City-regions: Economic Motors and Political Actors on the World Stage'. Presentation at the School of Public Policy, UCLA. Unpublished.

Therborn, G. (2002) 'Monumental Europe: The National Years. On the Iconography of European Capital Cities', *Housing, Theory & Society*, 19(1): 26–47.

Throsby, D. (2010) *The Economics of Cultural Policy*. Cambridge: Cambridge University Press.

Tomlinson, J. (1999) *Globalization and Culture*. Chicago: University of Chicago Press.

UNCHS (United Nations Centre for Human Settlements). (2001) *Cities in a Globalizing World*. London: Earthscan.

Van Winden, W. (2010) 'Knowledge and the European City', *Tijdschrift voor economische en sociale geografie*, 101(1): 100–6.

Wei, S. (2001) *Corruption and Poor Public Governance, Project Overview*. Washington, DC: The Brookings Institution.

Williams, R. (1984) 'Reflections on the State and the Cultural Arena'. In: Appignanesi, L. (ed.) *Culture and the State*. London: Institute of Contemporary Arts.

Wyszomirski, M. (2008) 'The Local Creative Economy in the United States of America'. In: Anheier, H. and Isar, Y.R. (eds.) *The Cultural Economy. The Cultures and Globalization Series 2*. London: SAGE Publications.

Zürn, M. (1998) *Regieren jenseits des Nationalstaates. Globalisierung und Denationalisierung als Chance*. Frankfurt: Suhrkamp.

OVERARCHING ISSUES

CHAPTER 1

CITIES AS GEOPOLITICAL SPACES FOR THE GLOBAL GOVERNANCE OF CULTURE

Katharine Sarikakis

'Global cities' are generally understood to be the economic and financial centres of global capitalism, where the concentration of transnational corporations and a plethora of specialized services serve the functions of finance and trade. The author of this opening chapter explores such cities from a different angle, that of the political power that makes them central in the governance of culture internationally. These metropoles are placed at the 'commanding heights' of global policy because they function as centres of hegemonic political systems. Brussels, Washington, DC, and Montevideo are the cities whose roles in leading and shaping global and regional policy are discussed here, particularly in relation to audiovisual and electronic culture policies.

Introduction

Our everyday connection to the world takes place through familiar dots on the map that take us through cities: our physical connections and explorations, our experiencing of the cultural 'other' often begins at the international airports of city-nodes, as we travel to cities even when to reach other destinations. Our symbolic, cultural acquaintance with the world takes place through our communications media and cultural institutions with cities as the nodes of global interconnection serving as the basis from which further 'knowing' can develop. We watch the news correspondents greeting us from 'Washington' or 'London', 'Hong Kong' or 'Johannesburg', conveying to us views of the world developed about and within these urban spaces. We benefit from a plethora of cultural events in cities when they are designated as the European City of Culture or we visit cities for their cultural and leisure offers: the tourist industry has a term for it, 'city break'. We turn to cities for transnational, global human connections, for the creation of culture, to explore ideas and challenge world politics. Seattle, Genoa, Paris, Athens are 'marked' in our memory as sites of resistance to specific aspects of globalisation. London, New York, Toronto, Buenos Aires, Melbourne have become associated with the translation of human globalisation into transcultural communities.

Cities have invariably played a central role in the construction of world connections, from the ancient *polis* to the modern metropolis, across political, social, economic and cultural levels. However, in the past two decades, and as globalisation processes accelerate, cities have emerged as the main command centres of the world; not only or just confined within national geopolitical borders, but also with an expanded and complex international role to play. Scholars began paying attention to this international role by studying the ways in which cities have become geopolitical spaces and decision-making centres from where the main functions of digital capitalism are managed, namely financial markets and trade. Global cities have become the object of study in these terms, next to the study of cities as spaces rooted in the national, as distinct contexts for urban planning and urban-based cultures. Although debates rightly situate the role of the global city within international webs of connections, the connection of these two realms – the national and the global – are made largely in terms of the political economy of the 'commanding heights' of the global market. Some discussions also point to the management of culture and emergence of culture industries in global cities as part and parcel of this international political economy. Yet the connections between the governance of culture and the city as a global policy player have been insufficiently explored.

This chapter proposes the study of the global geopolitics of the city within which a range of decision-making takes place: about culture, about processes of making and consuming cultural artefacts and about processes of designing and negotiating the priorities and directions of cultural development. The chapter therefore approaches world cities as drivers and filters of cultural policy globally, rather than in terms of their own cultural projects, a range of which will be presented eloquently in other chapters in this volume. Instead, here I shall propose a different view of the city and suggest a mapping of the geopolitics of cultural governance beyond the local. I shall argue that certain cities are global *political* decision-making centres for culture. They become so because the bureaucracies headquartered there make decisions of a global impact on national and international levels and on citizens' everyday life. I argue that cultural policy-making is a process inextricably linked to the global governance of finance and trade underpinned by communication infrastructures worldwide. Three cities, Brussels, Washington and Montevideo, are taken as exemplary cases for their varying positions in global policy-making and their role in the globalisation of culture.

Culture and the city: a global affair?

The study of culture as an object of policy has been seen largely as a national affair with little attention to its international dimensions. Cities and cultural policy has been approached in relation to national parameters of power, planning and negotiation, and

the topic is understood as cultural policy *in* the city and perhaps *for* the city. Little attention has been given, however, to the role of certain cities that have become central geopolitical spaces *configured to produce global cultural policy*. Certainly, not *any* city can act as such a space, nor is culture as the object of policy a tightly prescribed unit. Rather, it is my contention here that, first, cultural governance at a national level is to a great extent subject to global policy norms, and second, that global cultural policy principles are designed among actors who are geospatially organised to interact with policy-makers. These are not only international organisations, such as the UN agencies or the International Monetary Fund, but associations of industrial coalitions, professional associations and lobbies.

The role of culture in international relations is long established. For example, initiatives to promote cultural production in the form of films or other audiovisual content in foreign markets have been a driving principle of the US State Department and the Hollywood movie industry since the beginning of the twentieth century. International markets and especially European markets were important for the economic survival of the industry but also for the cultural 'education' of Cold War era Europe in all things American (Jarvie 1990). A range of cultural exchanges among countries vary from *au pair* cultural programmes, as they exist among European and North American countries, to the 'visit' of whole museums from one country to another, such as the exhibition organised in Beijing by several German museums in 2011, and from the establishment of the European Capital of Culture programme to the flowering of national cultural diplomacy institutions, such as the Goethe Institute, the Alliance Française or the Instituto Cervantes. Culture has served as a 'public diplomacy' tool in international politics, in more outspoken efforts with the export of the American 'dream' packaged in movies or the World Service by the BBC, and in more subtle efforts by the European Commission to forge a 'European identity' (Isar 2010).

Spatially, the governance of culture involves a juxtaposition with the 'other', who exists outside the borders of the national. This takes the form of 'export/import' of cultural products, ideas, as well as forms and formats of governance. Policy philosophies are being 'exported' spatially and culturally, repeatedly. Some global, dominant examples of policy directions are the liberalisation of digital cultural content, deregulation of the media and the 'creative' industries, privatisation of digital technologies. These policy 'trends' have expanded globally, but their institutional and often ideological origins can be found in specific geographies (Chakravartty and Sarikakis 2006). For example, specific policy areas, such as European Union audiovisual policy or the promotion of its film industry, are now being adopted by Latin American and African countries. The British approach to the regulation of public funding for public media, education and other 'creative industries' is a model other countries are turning their attention to, from South Korea and Taiwan to Australia and Canada. These international spatial dimensions of cultural policy have not been studied sufficiently by either culture or media studies or policy scholars. Before I discuss in some more detail this spatiality, it is useful to contextualise it within the range of the connections between the global city and culture.

'Global cities' is a term used to describe those urban centres that become home to actors that 'produce strategic global inputs', as Sassen (2001) asserts. Sassen's investigation of the global city devotes a lot of time to the analysis of the ways in which transnational firms have created new urban centralities and peripheries through the organisation of their functions. The concentration of transnational capital in certain global urban centres derives from the functions of acquisition, cooperation and alliances, as well as the need for access to high-level experts in key industries (Sassen 2006). At the same time, these actors are in a position to provide services and goods to their clients from afar and through the facilitation of electronic communications. Hence, there co-exists, on the one hand, a dispersal of factories, offices and service outlets and, on the other hand, a concentration of economic ownership and control together with global information integration. These elements have contributed to the strategic placement of some cities as well as the reinvention of others or the reconfiguration of city centres (Sassen 2001). London and New York emerge as the major global cities (Massey [2007] 2010) because of their connections to global trade, to the seats of multinationals and to key stock markets.

Sassen notes that today's global cities are 'command points' in the organisation of the world economy, owing to the concentration of economic actors in clusters in specific global sites. They serve as key locations and marketplaces for the leading industries of the current period, whereby two elements of capital organisation are predominant, namely finance and specialised services for firms. Finally, Sassen locates core production processes as well as innovation within global major cities (Sassen 2001). Next to these, there is a network or further networks of cities that occupy vital positions in the world economy due to their specialised functions and reach within regions. Moreover, as several chapters in this volume will argue, cities present claims of global-ness in their efforts to attract global capital and often govern their external image as one associated with a 'specialisation', i.e. city of culture, 'media city' and so forth.

Deregulation and the growth of financial markets have led to an increased concentration in the operational sites of the financial industry, and subsequently in a few stock markets. Although there is some dispersal of profits and ownership through subcontracting to smaller companies worldwide, a few large firms reap the majority of profits. The way this takes place is through the specialisation of functions and sections of firms: headquarters and the producer services deliver the components of what might be called 'global control capability' (Sassen 2001). High levels of specialisation are the key to the new economy as the 'symbolic analysts' become part of a global elite that operates in a corporate, effectively borderless world. Some of the services of large companies are externalised and respond to a growing demand by companies, but also by national governments, for specialised information and analysis. Think tanks, consulting agencies and other such services are based on the ability and capacity to process complex information, which take two forms. A so-called first rank 'datum' can be accessed by anyone. A second rank 'datum' is the more complex form of information needed to execute major international deals. The capacity and capability to deal with such data is based on a combination of commanding social information material with associated interpretations and inferences that are based on cultural competencies as well as specialisations (Sassen 2001). Within this configuration, culture plays a part as a 'special' form of 'datum', the mastery of which becomes central in the nuanced processes of negotiation, analysis, evaluation and consultancy. Culture itself is also an economic activity, with market value, as the considerable focus in all current cultural policy on the 'cultural' or the 'creative industries' demonstrates (Anheier and Isar 2008).

The intersection of the global city and cultural policy can be observed on three levels, whereby culture is operationalised spatially. For one, culture becomes a significant element in the consumption and leisure practices of highly skilled workers in global cities. Due to the emergence of urban clusters in global cities dedicated geographically and infrastructurally to the operation of multinational corporations, a clustering of workers takes place whose consumption habits and needs at a cultural level shape to a great extent the 'offer' of cultural production. International publics generate international audiences in very specific localities in the urban landscape followed by international entertainment and information businesses. Culture becomes one of the 'attractions' and 'benefits' for international workforces converging into city-hubs, and so functions as an integral element of a globally divergent capitalist economy.

Under these conditions, the cultural policy landscape of the nation becomes decoupled from the monopoly of the nation state as more and more cultural activities pass on to private initiatives. This is the second level of culture; its structural configuration stretches across the axes of production and consumption. Cultural consumption has risen together with the privatisation of media and the increase of production volume through the round-the-clock business model of most communications. A series of developments in the political economy of communications has altered the cultural and communicative landscape of nations and the globe fundamentally. These changes have been studied intensively, but as a reminder, it is important to pinpoint the entry of the electronics industry into the terrain of digital communications and the digital spectrum, the convergence of technologies and mergers of companies and across industries and the interdependence of content providers and new communication technologies in communications as the core elements of the transformation of cultural governance. Also, increasingly, cultural experiencing and culture making is based on its technological realisation, from digitisation of archives and online libraries to digital audiovisual content, from interactive technologies in museum installations to non-professional online anime clips (see also Anheier and Isar 2010).

The third level of the relation of culture and the city involves the consequences of the 'technologisation'

and privatisation of culture making. Owing to the complexity of the cultural production/consumption continuum, the governance of culture takes place at a global scale at multiple levels. As a first-rank policy, the global level of governance involves policy principles. As a second-rank policy, governance is applied across core dimensions of principles in localised national, regional, urban and other geographical spaces. Both the global and the 'local' interact dialectically to a certain extent, each informing the other. However, the conditions under which the 'local' negotiates global imperatives of trade, finance and mobility are largely determined at supranational levels. This dimension is the one I shall concentrate on in the remainder of this chapter.

'New' cities of politics: Brussels, Washington, Montevideo

The governance of culture in the past 30 years parallels the geopolitical transformations of the world economy into sites of industrial production and post-industrial economies and sites of consumption. Within this process of transformation – part of which is the rise of the global city, cultural affairs, in particular cultural production, distribution and consumption – have followed the liberalisation 'exercise' of the West. Cultural institutions have succumbed to the logic of marketability and 'value for money', the popularity of cultural outputs and revenue. Moreover, technologisation has meant that a range of policies, which had little effect on everyday culture previously, attain a new centrality in the digital environment. Such are the policies of copyright and digital rights, or the retention of data on users' practices on the internet. In the process of designing policy principles, including those mentioned above, face-to-face meetings take place in various parts of the world, but the administrative dimension of the preparation and finalisation of these decisions seems concentrated in specific cities, namely Brussels and Washington. Both cities constitute central political nodes in the international policy regime of globalisation, including culture and communication. The reasons are to be found in the geospatial organisation of capitalism as a macro-level strategy that involves the designation of sites for specific purposes and functions in the system. As scholars of the French Regulation School have observed, financial capitalism requires the bureaucratic and administrative organisation of states and other organisations (Aglietta [1979] 2000). These institutions intervene to make sure that the economic system further develops and does not falter under its own internal conflicts of interests. It also generates a level of meta-governance institutions, such as think tanks, organisations, advisory boards, analysts and so forth that take this task further (Jessop 2002).

The seats of such administrations and institutional structures are located in the centre of political spaces that are identical to the geospaces of the bureaucracies of the hegemonic actors in the international policy regime. Brussels is the geopolitical manifestation of the concentration of functions of state bureaucracy that comes with its being the headquarters of the European Union. Washington, DC is the seat of the US government and the symbolic location of Western neoliberalism. I have selected these two locations precisely because of their role in initiating and pursuing wide-reaching policy agendas, including in the areas of culture

and communication, technology and civil rights. The impact of policies 'crafted' in these centres is immense and profound for the entire planet.

In the global city, corporate and service clustering evolves to facilitate the speedy and immediate exchange of information among the central players of the world economy (Sassen 2006). In Western cities cultural clustering seems to be 'mimicking' commercial tactics, whereby clusters are organised according to their portfolio of activities and functions. Moreover, clusters in the governance of culture are organised in ways enabling them to develop 'districtisation' models that depend on the existence of firms active in the cultural economy (Lazzaretti 2003; Berry et al. 2006). Clusters can also differ in terms of their positioning in the broader urban infrastructure and across their forms of market positioning, whether production or consumption oriented (Bassett 1993; Bassett et al. 2002). The geospatial clustering of Brussels and Washington, however, while entailing the principles of such networking of elites, is largely arranged around the

Map 1.1   Brussels: spatial location and clustering of actors involved in culture-related policy-making

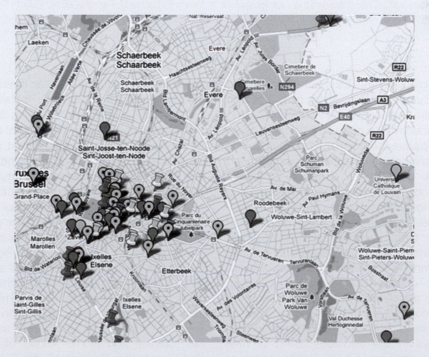

Key:

National and regional governmental institutions and associated bodies involved in policy-making processes (13): European Commission's Audiovisual Service, European Commission Headquarters, EACEA (Education, Audiovisual and Culture Executive Agency), Embassy of the USA to the EU, Embassies of Germany, Switzerland, Spain, Great Britain, France, Argentina, Paraguay, Uruguay, Brazil

Pan-European organisations (34): BITKOM e.v., Verband Privater Rundfunk und Telemedien e.v., SAA (Society of Audiovisual Authors), Digital Europe, ECTA (European Competitive Telecommunications Association), ENPA (European Newspaper Publishers' Association), FERA (European Federation of Film Directors), FAEP (European Federation of Magazines), EPC (European Policy Centre), AER (Association européenne des radios), EUROCINEMA (Association de producteurs de cinéma et de television), GESAC (European grouping of societies of authors and composers), ACE (Association des Cinémathèques Européennes), BEUC (The European Consumers' Organisation), EGBA (European Gaming and Betting Association), Pearle (Performing Arts Employers' Associations League Europe), EVA (European Visual Artists), FEP (Federation of European Book Publishers), ISFE (Interactive Software Federation of Europe), EBF (European Booksellers Federation), FES (Federation of European Screenwriters), CEPI (European Co-ordination of Independent Producers), AEPO-ARTIS (Association of European Performers' Organisations), EDIMA (European Digital Media Association), European Internet Foundation, ACT (Association of Commercial Television Europe), Eurocopya, Cable Europe, Telekom Italia, Mediaset

Belgian national organisations (4): BEA (Belgian Entertainment Association), EGMONT (Royal Institute for International Relations), Centre Culturel, Arthena – Groupement d'intérêts

Other European organisations (hosted in any European country) and with representations in other countries outside Europe (13 listed): Nokia, Siemens, Reuters Group, Eurochambers, Bertelsmann AG, Deutsche Welle, ARD, ZDF, BBC, Telefónica SA, Belgian-American Chamber of Commerce, AG for Digital Communication, Deutsche Telekom

Transnational corporations, industrial lobbies, NGOs (23 listed): MPAA (Motion Picture Association of America), IFJ (International Federation of Journalists), IETM (International network for contemporary performing arts), SIGNIS (World Catholic Association for Communications), IVF (International Video Federation), WCA (World Cinema Alliance), FIA (Fédération Internationale des Acteurs), The Internet Society, Journalists without Frontiers, IFRRO (International Federation of Reproduction Collecting Societies), International Chamber of Commerce, American Chamber of Commerce to the EU, UNESCO, Intel, Microsoft, ICMP (International Confederation of Music Publishers), Google, eBay, Yahoo, Time Warner, International Association of Audiovisual Writers and Directors, Sony Picture Entertainment

central bureaucracy of the European Union, and especially the European Commission buildings, and the White House respectively (see Map 1.1).

Brussels is effectively a city with internal invisible borders that separate the 'normal' urban Belgian life from the extraordinary global institutions cramped into a few city blocks. This spatial organisation manifests the conflict in the relation between the global and the local, whose close proximity in geographical terms is contrasted by the distance in terms of power. Other cities with clusters of global players as distinct entities are Vienna and its UNO City construction on the bank of the Danube (a natural border, opposite the rest of the city) or London City as a location symbol of reinvention of the city of London (Massey [2007] 2010). Close to 100 organisations, directly interested in and involved in various ways in the decision-making of new technologies, 'reside' around the headquarters of

the EU in Brussels. In particular, these organisations are actively involved through lobbying and direct contact in the design of Information Society policies.

For this chapter, those elements of the Information Society agenda were chosen that directly link to impacts for cultural production and consumption. The organisations shown in the map of Brussels are categorised according to whether they are governmental or not and whether they are 'domestic' (i.e. national and pan-European) or with headquarters in third countries but with transnational reach. The agenda of the Information Society suite of policies is one that involves, at an institutional level, multiple administrations of the EU. In particular, those connected to the governance of culture include the European Commission, the Committees on Culture and Education, and Civil Liberties, Justice and Home Affairs of the European Parliament, the Council of the European Union,

European Data Protection Supervisor (EDPS), European Investment Bank, European Investment Fund, European Network and Information Security Agency (ENISA), European Electronic Communications Market Authority (NRAs) and the Body of European Regulators for Electronic Communications (BEREC).

The Information Society (IS) is understood as a pillar for economic and industrial growth, cultural integration and development aid. The aim of IS policy is largely the harmonisation of laws, the opening up of national markets, turning research into marketable services and products, and overcoming regulatory fragmentation. Initiatives directly linked to cultural governance are the Digital Agenda, part of the Europe 2020 Strategy, which is focused on the interoperability of systems and economic growth and international outreach and impact, among other priorities (Europa.eu 2011); media literacy for a 'competitive audiovisual and content industry' (EC 2009/625/EC) and the creation of a single market in creative content online; data protection and copyright and related rights in the IS (Europa.eu 2008). Also, the promotion of audiovisual content in online and digital services as well as 'established' media, but within the context of digitalisation, is a core distinct area of policy in the EU. Through the Audiovisual Media Services Directive (EC 2007), the EU has extended its governance reach across many countries, through policy transfer internally and externally (Humphreys 2002, 2006), the most visible example perhaps at an international level being that of MERCOSUR (Crusafon 2010). The process of digitalisation also exemplifies a *de facto* policy transfer in terms of the choices countries are making with respect to technical standards (Garcìa Leiva and Starks 2009). This is the case of European technical standards, a core priority of the IS agenda, in the television and audiovisual services. These standards have been developed partly for historical reasons and partly as a matter of strategy to compete against major players such as Japan and the USA.

In consequence, countries need to decide (sometimes without much space for negotiation or domestic policy) as to the television systems that are to be adopted domestically. In a series of policy milestones that were developed through Brussels institutions and lobbies, the European version of the IS, a programme running from 1999 to 2005, entitled 'eEurope: An Information Society for all', focused on the development of electronic communications with a particular emphasis on technologies and the single market for cultural content. Directives on the protection of privacy, linguistic diversity and econtent led to 'eEurope 2005' and 'eContentplus', designed (2005–2008) with the aim of establishing a multinational Community programme to make digital content more 'accessible, usable and exploitable' (eContenplus website 2007; codecision COD/2004/0025). The progamme 'i2010' is the continuation of the previous programmes and is considered as part of the Lisbon Strategy to drive productivity growth and creative and competitive digital economy. Part of this agenda is the Anti-Counterfeiting Trade Agreement (ACTA) plurilateral agreement and affiliated initiatives, such as 'Creative Content in a European Digital Single Market: Challenges for the Future 2009–2010', the collective cross-border management of copyright and related rights, and the online music services Community initiative on the cross-border collective management of copyright (2010).

Washington is not the seat of a multinational polity, but it is the governance centre for one of the most hegemonic powers in international politics. As the map of the city shows (see Map 1.2), here, too, a plethora of organisations and lobbies are situated spatially in close proximity to the White House, although it does seem that some significant expansion of this clustering follows the patterns of lobby action within the District of Columbia.

At least 80 actors have been involved in the design of IS policies in the USA, mostly under the auspices of the United States Department of Commerce and its Agencies (see key to Map 1.2). Other governmental institutions involved are the National Telecommunications and Information Administration (NTIA); the National Institute of Standards and Technology (NIST); the Economic Development Administration (EDA); the International Trade Administration (ITA); the US Intellectual Property Enforcement Coordinator (IPEC); the Intellectual Property Enforcement Advisory Committees; the National Intellectual Property Rights Coordination Center; the US Copyright Office; the US Patent and Trademark Office; the Computer Crimes and Intellectual Property Section of the Department of Justice (CCIPS); the US Customs and Border Protection (CBP); the US International Trade Commission (USITC); the Trade Remedy Assistance Office (TRAO); the Office of the United States Trade Representative (USTR);

Map 1.2 Clustering of Information Society policy stakeholders in Washington, DC

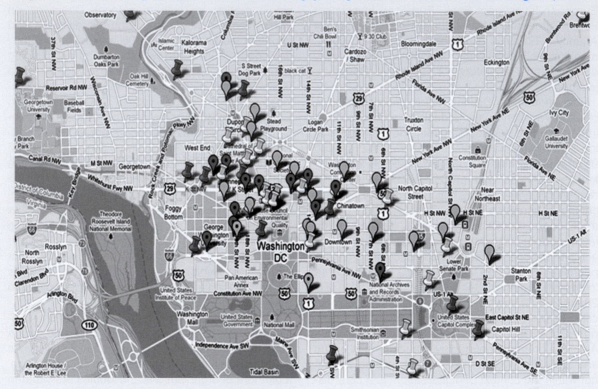

Key:

Governmental institutions and associated bodies (16): Office of the United States Trade Representative, US House of Representatives, US Copyright Office, Office of International Claims and Investment Disputes, United States Government: Washington Headquarters, FCC, Delegation of the European Union to the United States of America, Embassies of Switzerland, Germany, Spain, France, UK, Brazil, Uruguay, Paraguay, Argentina

International bodies such as representations of transnational enterprises, NGOs (13): Siemens, Nokia, OECD, World Bank, IMF, Human Rights Watch, Inter-American Development Bank, Reporters without Borders, The International Consortium of Investigative Journalists, US National Commission to UNESCO, Global Information Infrastructure Commission, ICANN (Internet Corporation for Assigned Names and Numbers)

US organisations and lobbies involved in policies relevant to the Information Society (20): IBM Institute for Electronic Government, National Public Radio, Global Trade Watch Office, Brookings Institution, National Press Club, Comcast Corporation, Heritage Foundation, Institute for Policy Studies, Association of American Publishers Inc., Hudson Institute, TIA (Telecommunications Industry Association), CATO Institute, Century Foundation, NMPA (National Music Publishers' Association), RIAA (Recording Industry Association of America), Public Broadcasting Service

Organisations involved in topics around the Information Society concept with representations in the USA and other countries on the continent (2): OAS, NAFTA Office

US corporations and lobbies with representations outside the USA (22): Disney Government Relations, Microsoft Government Affairs, Viacom Inc., IMG (The Interface Media Group Inc.), Google, News Corporation, Black Entertainment Television, Time Warner, IBM, US Chamber of Commerce, Apple Government Relations, Intel, General Electrics, Business Software Alliance, International Anti-Counterfeiting Coalition, International Intellectual Property Institute, MPAA, AP, Global Intellectual Property Center, Freedom House, VOA (Voice of America), IIPA (International Intellectual Property Alliance) the US Commercial Service; the Office of Intellectual Property Rights of the US (OIPR); and the Federal Communications Commission (FCC).

In the past 20 years, and with the launching of the 'Information Superhighway' by Al Gore, the US administration has paved the way for a series of crucial policies in the area of new communication and culture technologies. With the 1997 Framework for Global Electronic Commerce and the establishment of ICANN (the Internet Corporation for Assigned Names and Numbers) in 1998 under private law, the relation of cultural artefacts and cultural production and consumption to communication technologies has been determined as one of control over copyright. The Agreement on Trade Related Aspects of Intellectual Property and the more recent Anti-Counterfeiting Trade Agreement (ACTA) are part of a strategy that sees cultural production and the media as part of the Economic Recovery Plan, through the renewal of the 'Information Superhighway'. Policies emanating from Washington spread around the world in the form of multi- or plurilateral agreements. For example, the origins of ACTA are to be found in the American cultural and electronic industries' interest in controlling access and circulation of content and goods. At time of writing, the US administration issued 20 legislative recommendations to Congress to improve intellectual property enforcements, also in line with ACTA (The White House Blog 2011). These are continuations of a new policy agenda of digital content as prescribed in the 1998 Digital Millennium Copyright Act (DMCA) and the creation of IP enforcement obligations in bilateral and regional free trade agreements (Katz and Hinze 2009).

Montevideo is an interesting case of a city whose reach is not global, but which attracts the interest of global actors. The map of the city (Map 1.3) shows the range of clusters emerging from the location of international corporations and organisations as the capital of Mercosur. It is the seat of the Council and the Group of the Common Market and the Parlasur, the Parliament of the Mercosur, first established in 2006.

Montevideo is the seat of the Specialized Reunion of the Authorities for Cinema and Audiovisuals, which aims to create a common audiovisual market, and also to promote a common identity in the region. The city is also the place of regional initiatives following the implementation of the IS (Digital Mercosur) and the fostering of the audiovisual sector in the region. All these characteristics, as well as the emerging institutional organisation of Mercosur, manifest a similarity to the development of the European polity. Montevideo hosted the eighth round of GATT negotiations, which gave birth to the World Trade Organisation (WTO) and Agreement on

Map 1.3 Spatial clustering of actors involved in cultural policy-making in Montevideo

Key:

📍 Governmental institutions and associated bodies involved in policy (17*): Embassies of Germany, France, the USA, Great Britain, Spain, Switzerland, Paraguay, Brazil, Argentina, Mercosur Administration, RECAM, Ministry of Education and Culture, URCDP (Regulatory Unit and Control of Personal Data), Digital Mercosur Office, AGEIC (Governmental Agency for Electronic Management and for the Implementation of the Information and Knowledge Society), Delegation of the EU to Uruguay and Paraguay, ICAU (Institute for Audiovisuals and Cinema in Uruguay)

📍 International bodies such as Chambers of Commerce, representations of transnational enterprises, NGOs (13): Microsoft, Sony–Ridel SA, OLPC (One Laptop Per Child), Multicanal (Cablevisión, Grupo Clarín), US Chamber of Commerce, Spanish Chamber of Commerce, French Chamber of Commerce, Global Production Network, The Brownie Film Company, International Association of Broadcasting (AIR), German Chamber of Commerce, UNESCO

📍 Uruguayan organisations involved in policies relevant to the Information Society (63): UYTECH IT Solutions, SUDEI (Uruguayan Society of Actors), Cinemateca Uruguaya, ASOPROD (Asociación de Productores y Realizadores de Cine y Video del Uruguay), Uruguay Film Commission and Promotion, CERTuy (Centro Nacional de Respuesta a Incidentes en Seguridad Informática), Producers' Association in Montevideo, AUDEM (Uruguayan Musicians' Association), Crecoel (Co-operative for the Recycling of Electronic Devices), SUA (Uruguayan Actors' Society), Televisión Nacional Uruguay, PLAN CEIBAL, LATU (Technology Laboratory of Uruguay), Altamira Productions (Altamira Productora de Imagen), Aceituna Films, Production Company Diezcartorce, Animation Campus, Aparato Post, Control Z Films, Cinekdoque, Contenidos TV Productions, CITS (Center for Technological and Social Inclusion), FCI (Foundation of Information Technology Culture), Cordón Films Production Company, EMEU Producciones, Coral Films Production Companies, En Foco Production Company, Estudio EGG Productions, Guazú Media, FEROSA Production Company, Indias Fílmica Productions, Espectral Audio Productions, HTV-3-TAJAM Production Company, La Mayor Audio Productions, La Jolla Films, LAMA TOWN Productions, La Tribu Production Company, Efecto Cine, Locomotion Audiovisual Company, Lavorágine Films Productions, Kafka Films Productions, Medio Editores, Laroux Cine, Rain Dogs Cine Production Company, Palermo Estudio Production, Nepal Films Production Company, Paris Texas Productions, Producciones de Hacha y Tiza, Primer Plano Videoproductions, POP UP!, Fx Productions, Tarkio Film, Subtitulos TV Productions, Zur Films Production, OZ Media Productions, Transparent Films, Tokio Films, Trojan Chicken, Virginia Hinze Productions, Yema Films Production Company, Tripfilm

📍 Uruguayan organisations engaged in the implementation of the Information Society communications sector, such as the audiovisual sector, with representations in other Latin American countries (10): Megafilms, Microtime, Medio y Medio, Animalada Animations Studio, Red Cultural, Mercosur, Metropolis Production, La Productora Films Productions, El Camino Films Productions, Travelling Pro, Salado Production Company

📍 Uruguayan organisations with representations outside Latin America (8): Megafilms, Microtime, Dómino Productions, Animalada Animations Studio, Uruguayan Chamber of Commerce, Taxi Films, Librecine, Oriental Films

Trade Related Aspects of Intellectual Property Rights (TRIPS). Map 1.3 shows a vibrant national audio-visual sector. The enterprises related to the sector, the Associations and the Uruguayan Actors and Musicians' society, as well as the Uruguayan Association that represents both cinema and video producers, are located in the northwest of Montevideo. The Uruguayan Ministry of Education and Culture, the Institute for Audiovisuals and Cinema in Uruguay, the Digital Mercosur Office, the Governmental Agency for Electronic Management and for the Implementation of the Information and Knowledge Society, the Regulatory Unit and Control of Personal Data, as well as the Embassies of Argentina and Brazil (next to the office of Multicanal, belonging to the Argentinean media group *Clarín*) are in close

proximity and next to most of the media enterprises and production firms that figure in the map. Close to this dot we find the Mercosur building, where we can find the Mercosur Chamber of Audiovisual and Cinema Producers (RECAM) and, nearby, the US Embassy. Also nearby are the French, German and Spanish Embassies, the Uruguayan Chamber of Commerce, Microsoft and the International Association of Broadcasting (AIR). The majority of Uruguayan enterprises with representations outside Latin America can be found in this area as well.

As in many cities, global administrative centres operate alongside mega corporate centres and fulfil separate functions that also intersect (Sassen 2001; Massey [2007] 2010), creating networks of policy-making (Cole and John 2000). Here eight audiovisual production companies have representations outside Latin America, only one in Brussels. Only foreign organisations officially have an office or affiliates in Montevideo (Microsoft, Sony Entertainment, OLPC, The Brownie Film Co., The Global Production Network, AIR and Kodak Motion Picture). Concerning Latin American interconnectivity, nine entities of the listed have offices outside Montevideo, in Buenos Aires or Mexico City. However, it has to be underlined that associations such as Fedala (Latin American Federation of Writers and Audiovisual Directors) have no fixed organisational structure and have no regional offices, just national offices which oversee regional matters for a certain time (this year, Buenos Aires is the seat of the Fedala coordination). Regional organisations situated in Montevideo are, besides the Mercosur, the RECAM and the Digital Mercosur Office, the Media Company Cablevisión, which belongs to the Argentine media group *Clarín*, as well as the civil society organisation Red Cultural. However, today

artists, producers and cultural managers [that] integrate the network convinced that working together as a network constitutes cultural management – sharing information and exchanging of experiences. Its objective is to mobilize the geographic and cultural interaction in South America. It understands that the artistic creations and the implementations of social and cultural projects are fundamental factors of integration of the region. The network counts with more than 400 individual and institutional members from Argentina, Bolivia, Brazil, Chile, Paraguay, Uruguay, and Venezuela. (Red Cultural webpage)

This concentration represents a major regional hub and a global location for policy transfer and import into the region as a whole, through the mechanism of Mercosur. If we see Washington, DC, and Brussels as exporters of cultural and communication policies, then it is easy to understand the relation of Montevideo to them as a major 'clearing city' that adopts and adapts policy schemata. This does not mean that Montevideo is a mere 'receptor' of policy, but rather that the flow of policy models is predominantly one of 'importation'. Indicators showing the effect of EU influence reveal similar aims in media policy-making, namely to strengthen the internal market, protect cultural production and promote cultural works from within the region. The 'internationalisation' efforts of

the EU in particular have fallen on fertile ground in Latin America through incentives for networked productions and other policies that emulate the approach of European nations to their cultural industries. As Crusafon notes, 'the will of the European Union to export the European Model to other regions of the Planet has to be pointed out' (2010: 103). Figure 1.1 shows the actors involved in the design of audiovisual and Information Society policies, and particularly copyright/intellectual property policies, as they relate to cultural production and consumption, and programmes for the promotion or liberalisation of the audiovisual industries, including electronic content. This diagram also shows which constellations of actors are present in both Brussels and Washington and which other networks are present in each place. Obviously, this is neither an exclusive nor a comprehensive picture of how actors relate to the governance of cultural policies. It does demonstrate a few points clearly, however: first, that global corporations occupy a central position in the 'political' cities; second, that globally present corporations form long-lasting, inter-industrial alliances to monitor and intervene in the governance of culture across the Atlantic; and third, that other regionally dominant players are mostly third sector and professional associations. It also shows that nations with a hegemonic presence in the international policy regime are located close to the global corporations and lobbies.

Some conclusions

According to DiGaetano and Strom (2003), two distinct elements are involved in urban governance: networks of governance actors and structural arrangements of governance that determine how cities are organised around power resources. Although DiGaetano and Klemanski's study focuses on the governance of the city, it is arguable that similar conditions determine the clustering of power resources and networked actors when it comes to the political spatiality of the city in its role as a global player. The cities of Brussels, Washington and Montevideo are hegemonic in fulfilling different functions in global politics. Their bureaucracies and networks of stakeholders shape the global agendas of the governance of culture and communications. Montevideo's position in the South American region is one of emerging facilitation for the regional adoption of models of cultural governance. This role is a

Figure 1.1 Global activity of industrial lobbies in the formation of policy in Brussels, Washington, DC, and Montevideo

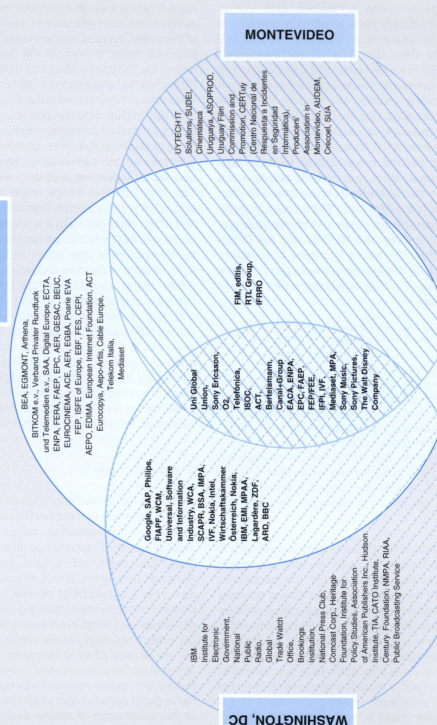

developing one and could possibly be compared to the functions of a few other places in the world, such as Addis Ababa, the seat of the African Union. Another interesting example is the role of Singapore as a city-state and its ambition to become a 'Global Media City' through the Singapore Media Fusion Plan (SMFP). The SMFP aims to encourage 'multi-agency efforts' for the development of the media sector and make Singapore the 'Trusted Global Capital for New Asia Media' (DiGaetano and Klemanski 1999: 19). The focus of the SMFP is to enhance the economic contribution of the media sector by 'engaging Singaporeans', 'boosting the industry' and 'transforming economy' (ibid.: 21–22).

The principles governing the conditions of the production and consumption of cultural goods and services are today converging upon ideas which are largely set out and negotiated within specific geospatial politics and in key cities. This process reveals an unequal relation between the core and the periphery, but it also constructs new relations of core and peripheral geographies, based on the centrality – or marginality – of decision-making about culture. It is a political process which, although largely underpinned by economic interests and conflicts among them, is not organised around economic activities *per se*, as in the global city. Hence political decision-making is vital in the construction of 'new' global cities embedded in and determining the cultural policy regime.

There are two analytically distinct but often overlapping phenomena with regard to the function of policy regimes at the international level. On the one hand, there is what we call 'policy transfer', that is, the outcome of negotiations and processes of harmonisation of laws and/or the promotion and export/import of certain policy frameworks. Such may be the promotion of the film industry package of policies or the liberalisation of telecommunications from the European Union negotiating tables to member states. This implies due process, however, within which consensus is institutionally built. In the case of the EU, for example, there is the right for 'veto' as well as unanimous voting (Humphreys 2002). On the level of international relations, the 'export' of European audiovisual policies to the Mercosur countries or other 'internationalisation' activities of the EU (Crusafon 2010, 2011) constitute such policy transfers.

The other phenomenon, policy laundering, is much more difficult to follow as there is usually little media interest in it or knowledge about it; it leaves but a scant 'paper trail' that is accessible to media and scholarship and there is little willingness to speak about it. Scholars have only recently started paying attention to this phenomenon, which means that responsibility for policies is avoided through the operation of a global system of opaque relations and/or when policies are passed that are packaged within a one-issue frame but in reality concern aims that are unpopular. Lobbying takes place outside the established processes of consultation or debate. Such is considered to be the case with ACTA, which involved the collaboration of the USA, the European Union, Japan and Switzerland in launching this particular piece of public policy in 2007 that came into force in December 2010 (ACTA 2010). The governments of Australia, Canada, the European Union (represented by the European Commission, the EU Presidency (Sweden) and EU member states), Japan, Republic of Korea, Mexico, Morocco, New Zealand, Singapore, Switzerland, and the USA were all involved. This piece of legislation was 'justified' as a necessary condition of 'harmonisation' with international standards, but its decision-making process took place under questionable conditions that do not compare favourably in terms of transparency with the internal mechanisms of nation-states and the EU. ACTA concentrates on the enforcement of control over intellectual property and throughout its negotiations has been surrounded by secrecy, although some documents were released after the end of the negotiations. It constitutes a major piece of legislation that will have profound effects on cultural consumption and culture production, by possibly criminalising the non-professional and non-commercial use of cultural artefacts by individuals (Katz and Hinze 2009). A similar 'backdoor policy' process takes place in the area of data protection and databases of personal data whereby US policies are transplanted through other policy domains – such as free trade agreements – to other countries (Yu 2009). Data protection and data monitoring have also become crucial elements in cultural production and consumption, although neither the legislative texts nor the dominant public debates refer to them as cultural policy.

International policy regimes are built by constellations of actors, such as states, corporations or international organisations. Designed over long periods of time, they involve a hegemonic power or a set of powers that drive the policy agenda and set the standards for policy transformation and normalisation in both national and regional contexts. These regimes and actors pose serious questions of legitimacy, transparency and accountability when compared to the parliamentary scrutiny or legal requirements for public consultations and debate in national politics. The gradual move from formal multilateralism to informal plurilateralism and the decline of the Bretton Woods institutions from the 1970s onwards (Katz and Hinze 2009) have meant that formally agreed processes for decision-making are now superseded by informal negotiations and the lobbying activities of a few powerful global actors. The consequences are highly problematic, as such politics robs the public of the right to scrutinise public policy and denies weaker or more vulnerable actors the opportunity and space to determine their own course of action.

Networks cooperating closely with each other for cultural governance construct new geographies in the 'global cities of politics', giving global corporations and lobbies the most international reach in terms of physical representation. The examples of Brussels and Washington demonstrate convincingly how the world is organised around global and regional players. The latter have their own pattern of attachment to institutional and power resources, as do corporations in all three cities. However, the global players are central in the development of policies in both Brussels and Washington. In these centres of governance we can see a concentration of *political* representatives of corporations, whose main function is to follow policy developments closely and intervene. Their clustering here is similar to that in all global cities, with the concentration of transnational firms and experts, but in these 'political' cities the aim is to function predominantly as political actors, that is, actors who systematically represent their own interests in the policy process. This aspect of transnational, indeed global, capital and globally active governmental institutions is one that requires more attention in our discussions of cultural governance and the city.

Acknowledgements

The author wishes to thank Sarah Ganter at the University of Vienna for extended research assistantship in the construction of the policy city maps, Jian Hui Lee at the University of Leeds as well as the editors for their constructive comments in the making of this chapter.

REFERENCES

Aglietta, Michel ([1979] 2000) *A Theory of Capitalist Regulation*. London: Verso.

Anheier, Helmut and Isar, Yudhishthir Raj (eds) (2008) *The Cultural Economy. The Cultures and Globalization Series 2*. London: SAGE.

Anheier, Helmut and Isar, Yudhishthir Raj (eds) (2010) *Cultural Expression, Creativity and Innovation. The Cultures and Globalization Series 3*. London: SAGE.

Anti-Counterfeiting Trade Agreement. Consolidated Text. Informal Predecisional/Deliberative Draft: January 18, 2010. Retrieved from: http://www.laquadrature.net/files/201001_acta.pd. Accessed 20 October, 2011.

Bassett, K. (1993) 'Urban Cultural Strategies and Urban Cultural Regeneration: A Case Study and Critique', *Environment and Planning A*, 25: 1773–1788.

Bassett, K., Griffiths, Ron and Smith, Ian (2002) 'Cultural Industries, Cultural Clusters and the City: The Example of Natural History Film-making in Bristol', *Geoforum* 33: 165–177.

Berry, Jeffrey M., Portney, Kent E., Liss, Robin, Simoncelli, and Jessica Berger, Lisa (2006) *Power and Interest Groups in City Politics*. Boston, MA: Rappaport Institute for Greater Boston. Available at: www.rappaportinstitute.org.

Chakravartty, Paula and Sarikakis, Katharine (2006) *Media Policy and Globalization*. London: Palgrave Macmillan.

Cole, Alistair and John, Peter (2000) 'Do Institutions, Policy Sectors, and Cities Matter? Comparing Networks of Local Policy Makers in Britain and France', *Comparative Political Studies*, 33 (2): 248–268.

Crusafon, Carmina (2010) 'The External Dimension of EU Audiovisual Policy: Concepts and Instruments for International Cooperation with Latin America and the Mediterranean'. Paper presented at Ecrea Conference 2010, Hamburg, October.

Crusafon, Carmina (2011) 'European Media Policy and International Relations: The Case of EU Audiovisual Policy'. In Lodge, J. and Sarikakis, K. (eds), *Culture, Mediations and the Making of Europe*. Bologna: Il Mulino.

DiGaetano, Alan and Strom, Elizabeth. (2003) 'Comparative Urban Governance, An Integrated Approach', *Urban Affairs Review*, 38 (3): 356–395.

Dominguez Moreno, J.M. and Montero, D. (2009) 'Europe as a Partner: New Spaces for Audiovisual Cooperation between Latin America and Europe', *Global Media and Communication*, 5 (1): 77–98.

Europa.eu webpage. Summaries of EU Legislation (2008). Electronic Skills for the 21st century: fostering competitiveness, growth and jobs. Online. Accessed 13.03.2011. Available from: http://europa.eu/legislation_summaries/information_society/l24152_en.htm

Europa.eu webpage. Gateway to the European Union (2011). Information Society. Overview. Online. Accessed 13.03.2011. Available from: http://europa.eu/pol/infso/index_en.htm

Garcìa Leiva, M.C. and Starks, M. (2009) 'Digital Switchover across the Globe: The Emergence of Complex Regional Patterns', *Media, Culture & Society*, 31: 787.

Humphreys, Peter (2002) 'Europeanisation, Globalisation and Policy Transfer in the European Union: The Case of Telecommunications', *Convergence*, 8: 52.

Humphreys, Peter (2006) 'Globalization, Regulatory Competition, and EU Policy Transfer in the Telecoms and Broadcasting Sectors', *International Journal of Public Administration*, 29 (4): 305–334.

Isar, Yudhishthir Raj (2010) 'Cultural Diplomacy: An Overplayed Hand?', *Public Diplomacy*, 3: 29–44.

Jarvie, Ian (1990) 'The Postwar Economic Foreign Policy of the American Film Industry: Europe 1945–1950', *Film History*, 4 (4): 277–288.

Jessop, Bob (2002) *The Future of the Capitalist State*. Cambridge: Polity Press.

Katz, E. and Hinze, G. (2009) 'The Impact of the Anti-Counterfeiting Trade Agreement on the Knowledge Economy: The Accountability of the Office of the US Trade Representative for the Creation of IP Enforcement Norms through Executive Trade Agreements', *The Yale Journal of International Law Online*, 35 (24): 24–35.

Lazzaretti, Luciana (2003) 'City of Art as a High Culture Local System and Cultural Districtualization Processes: The Cluster of Art Restoration in Florence', *International Journal of Urban and Regional Research*, 27 (3): 635–648.

Massey, Doreen ([2007] 2010) *World City*. Cambridge: Polity Press.

Red Cultural. *LA RCM en 10 puntos*. Retrieved from: http://www.redculturalmercosur.org/index.php?option=com_content&task=view&id=12&Itemid=29&lang=spanish. Accessed 22 March, 2011.

Sassen, Saskia (2001) *The Global City*. Princeton, NJ: Princeton University Press.

Sassen, Saskia (2006) *Territory, Authority, Rights: From Medieval to Global Assemblages*. Princeton, NJ: Princeton University Press.

Yu, Peter K. (2009) 'The Political Economy of Data Protection', *Chicago-Kent Law Review*, 84. Available at: http://Ssrn.Com/Abstract=1046781.

CHAPTER 2

COMMUNICATION NETWORKS, CITIES AND INFORMAL ECONOMIES

Ramon Lobato

The global city is conventionally defined as a central hub in a network of flows – of capital, people, goods and images. However, if we shift our focus away from the formal indicators of economic power and towards the grey and black economies, we encounter a rather different map of global connectivity and cultural provision. The chapter considers the relationship between informal media distribution and formal cultural policy, with reference to circuits of media piracy in Asia, Africa and Latin America.

Introduction

Long concerned with studying government support for and regulation of the arts, cultural policy analysis

is undergoing a reorientation as scholars turn their attention towards entanglements of the governmental and the cultural that take place outside the realm of policy *per se*. As the gap widens between the 'cultural sector' (museums, galleries, libraries, heritage institutions and arts organizations) and everyday sites of cultural engagement (from football fields to *Facebook*), new directions for cultural policy analysis are emerging. One indicator of this shift is the recent decision of the *International Journal of Cultural Policy* (*IJCP*) to complement its ongoing analysis of arts and culture policies with a focus on 'implicit' cultural management operating outside the realm of formal state programmes.[1] For *IJCP*, there is something to be gained from 'reaching back behind the contemporary coining of the term "cultural policy" to explore how sets of policies that could not be thematized in these terms can nevertheless be usefully understood as implicit forms of cultural policy' (Ahearne, 2009: 147). We can therefore add to the now-familiar list of objects of cultural policy analysis (arts and culture ministries, public service broadcasters, performing arts companies, heritage organizations) an array of other actors, including religious institutions, media corporations, non-governmental organizations and industry bodies.

This chapter is similarly concerned with implicit policy, by which I mean regulation, prohibition, subsidy and management that does not form part of official public policy programmes. I want to push this line of inquiry a little further, however, by considering *systems of regulation in informal rather than formal cultural economies*. What might it do to the field of cultural policy analysis to consider its constitutive 'outside', that which appears (at least at first glance) to be un-policed, un-governed and un-regulated? What can this reveal about the diversity of mechanisms for cultural management inside and outside the realm of official state policy? If one consequence of the globalization of the cultural economy has been to generate increasing difference and diversity – sometimes in tandem with cultural standardization and synchronization – then it follows that a globally-focused cultural policy study should have a corresponding attention to the diverse surfaces upon which cultural governance and control is enacted worldwide. Many of the regulatory technologies which shape how people around the world express themselves and collectively make meaning are not inscribed in policy, law or planning, yet they have very real consequences in terms of the cultural life of populations. If cultural policy analysis is to be effective as a mode of critical transnational inquiry as well as an instrumental strategy of policy evaluation, then we must take seriously the everyday forms of control that shape cultural engagement in settings where such activity occurs out of view of formal cultural institutions.

Let me illustrate this point with an anecdote. Each year for a few weeks in winter, a popular film festival takes place in Melbourne, Australia. It is a major event on the regional film calendar and attracts an array of stars, filmmakers, overseas distributors and interstate tourists to its black-tie opening night party. The festival is held across a number of cinemas in the central business district (including a public screen museum, the Australian Centre for the Moving Image), and is bankrolled by a patchwork of state, federal and local agencies and private sponsors. The official face of international film culture in Melbourne, it is the focus of much debate and gossip in cultural policy circles every year as local commentators scrutinize its programme for signs of innovation, imitation, populism or elitism. However, if you take a short stroll south of the festival precinct in the CBD, you will pass numerous DVD stores stocking imported discs of dubious legality. Among the shelves full of TV dramas and music videos, you can find subtitled copies of many of the films 'premiering' around the corner on the big screen, along with an array of other content. The discs are cheap and the subtitles unreliable, but films are often available months before they screen at the festival. Walk a little further and you pass groups of students huddled in coffee shops and walkways, chatting, smoking and playing with their phones. Some are watching short videos from *YouTube* or full-length features downloaded from file-sharing networks, and video content is swapped over coffee while tips about torrent servers and download speeds are exchanged.

Oblivious to the expensive state-funded spectacle around the corner, this sphere of cultural circulation does not show up in UNESCO statistics or urban revitalization documents. It does not attract tourists or contribute to city-branding efforts. But it does supply people with a daily diet of images and sounds, circulating diverse ideas, symbols, values and styles to equally diverse populations. In Melbourne, as in so many cities, the institutions of the cultural sector – the museum, the library, the gallery – find themselves outflanked by alternative spaces for popular cultural engagement. These spaces are not within the scope of explicit cultural policy,[2] yet they perform many of the same functions as their formal counterparts. It is important to appreciate the organizational and regulatory dynamics of these circuits if we wish to understand emerging patterns of cultural engagement and consumption.

This chapter examines some of the regulatory systems governing these informal cultural landscapes. My specific focus is on the circulation of media commodities (primarily film and books), and my frame of reference is the heated debate about intellectual property (IP) and piracy that is such a strong feature of contemporary media policy. In many cities, street vendors, informal trade associations, small-scale networks of cultural producers and sometimes even criminal organizations are the key actors in cultural regulation, rather than public servants and policymakers. Cities are hubs for informal media economies, and the relationship between urban culture, media circulation and informality is frequently co-constitutive (Sundaram, 2009).[3] This chapter surveys recent studies of informal and extra-legal media circuits across a variety of sites, drawing on literature in sociology, anthropology, media studies and policy studies.

Culture, media and informality

Thinking about cultural and media policy in the way described above requires a framework for understanding how cultural commodities circulate outside established, legal channels. The rich body of social science literature on informal economies offers such a model; it is one that is used widely in development and anthropology debates, but sparingly in cultural research. The benefit of this model is that it allows for the comparative analysis of economic and cultural systems that may otherwise appear incommensurable. Before proceeding further, it may be helpful to define informal economies and trace their roots in research and policy, for many of the early debates that formed around this idea have much to offer media and cultural policy discussions today.

The informal economies model originates in economic anthropology, sociology and development economics of the 1970s. Although definitions vary from study to study (cf. Hart, 1973; Feige, 1979; Sassen, 1994), informal economic activity is generally understood as unmeasured, unmonitored and untaxed forms of production and exchange, or as economic activity outside the regulatory gaze of the state. This idea was first popularized in studies of urban unemployment in Africa, including an International Labour Office (ILO) report (1972) on Kenya and a paper by the British anthropologist Keith Hart about urban economies in Ghana (Hart, 1973).[4] The conventional wisdom at the time was that urban unemployment in third-world cities posed a threat to stability and modernization efforts, and was best managed through large-scale development initiatives. The research by the ILO and Hart helped to make the case that the economic space understood by planners as 'unemployment' also comprised a vast number of alternative income-generating activities: hawking, small-scale commodity production, market vending, street performance, bartending, security work, begging, hustling, etc. The aim of informal economies research was to bring into the discussion these invisible income-generating activities and to take seriously their economic functions.[5]

This research was important because it cut across and reorganized the binaries that structured the theory and practice of development. In Hart's definition, the informal economy encompasses the modern (backroom electronics repairs) and the traditional (small-scale urban agriculture), the licit (cash-in-hand babysitting) and the taboo (crime, prostitution). Thus economic regulation is not limited to state policies, but also includes other forms of ground-level management and prohibition. Seeing economies through the lens of formality/ informality rather than traditional/modern, rural/ urban or legal/criminal also renders visible modes of exchange and circulation that are obscured by a focus on institutions and bureaucracies. Indeed, in the regions where this research was taking place – East Africa and West Africa – informal employment was a central rather than marginal component of national economies: it was the *norm* rather than the exception. As Hart put it, 'When half of the urban

labour force falls outside the organized labour market, how can we continue to be satisfied with indicators of economic performance which ignore their productive activities?' (1973: 88).

In the same way that the informality model was able to reorganize development and economic policy debates, so too can it contribute positively to debates in cultural policy at a time when global communication infrastructures are undergoing dramatic change. Debates around intellectual property regulation, territorial copyright, access to knowledge and digital divides could all potentially benefit from such an intervention. Since the 1970s, progressive voices in intellectual property and media policy debates have sought to rewrite international trade pacts, reform global economic institutions, and lobby powerful governments to redress persistent inequalities in global flows of information and cultural commodities.[6] The aim was to create distribution structures and regulatory frameworks which might foster a new, more democratic and equitable global communications infrastructure; the emphasis was on reform through formal policy processes. However, until recently, little attention has been paid to the *actually-existing distribution infrastructures* that carry out some of these tasks in the informal realm, or the regulatory frameworks governing them on a day-to-day basis. There is therefore a need to examine ground-level informal economies of content distribution as well as the overarching frameworks of explicit policy.

This is why any serious analysis of global media flows from a cultural policy perspective must take into account pirate networks. For much of the world's population, black and 'grey' markets provide access to a world of media – books, CDs, films, software, games – that is either not legally accessible or not accessible at an appropriate price. Yet the vast majority of the policy literature around media piracy has been about how to eradicate piracy for the benefit of copyright holders. Although a handful of policy reports have attempted to push the intellectual property debate in a different direction (Huygen et al., 2009; Karaganis, 2011), these voices are outnumbered by a much larger corpus of instrumental policy research which seeks to boost intellectual property rights, minimize violations and consolidate the evidence base linking piracy to organized crime (see IFPI, 2006; OECD, 2008; Rand Corporation, 2009).

Just as the discourse of 'unemployment' worked to obscure all the other ways in which people make a living outside salaried labour, so too is the idea of 'piracy' – defined negatively as copyright violation – working to obscure the many other policy issues arising from the informal circulation of media. There is therefore a need to rethink the conceptual categories that organize and delimit the discussion, in the same way that the informal economies model was able to productively reboot the debate about 'unemployment'. One way to do this is to reframe piracy as informal media circulation. This involves asking new questions: Who is making money from these circuits and how are they doing it? What audiences are formed here and how are they formed? How are these circuits managed and controlled? What kind of data or other information is needed for effective policy development in this area? The point is to analyze actually-existing infrastructures and assess their capacity for cultural engagement and provision, rather than to let the debate be driven solely by the imperative of top-down formal governance. Attention can then shift to the implicit forms of cultural management already at work in informal media economies.

Informal economies are rarely anarchic free markets where anything goes. Many informal circuits are subject to sophisticated forms of control, management and organization, some of which have nothing to do with explicit state-driven cultural policy. The challenge is not to see pirate or other extra-legal circuits as outside governance *in toto*, but to see them as differentially governed – largely by informal means. The next section examines some of these invisible regulatory technologies.

Informal regulation as implicit cultural policy

Informal media economies are subject to different forms of regulation, and thus different varieties of informal cultural policy. City-level, national, international and transnational forces all play a part in shaping what kinds of cultural experiences are possible in these spaces, and what commodities are made available and unavailable to populations.

Pirate markets and street vendors

Let's begin at street level, for the street is a key 'strategic site' of the informal media economy.[7] Street markets, roadside stalls, hawker stands – these are vital spaces of global media distribution and consumption. From Kuala Lumpur to Guangzhou,

Hanoi to Sao Paulo, as well as in first-world cities like New York and Rome where the urban informal economy is quite visible, streetside media is a feature of daily life. Ravi Sundaram writes of Delhi's informal street vendors and media markets as 'a vast new mediascape', which 'envelops cities like an all-pervasive skin' (2009: 5). CDs, movie soundtracks, DVDs, VCDs, books: all are ubiquitous, cheap, abundant, fixtures of the urban landscape. For much of the world's population, this is a key entry point into global media flows.

There is a longstanding tendency within public policy discussions to view street-level commerce as a zone of lawlessness and criminality. Industry groups and institutions of global media governance work to construct street-level media trade as the outside of legal media consumption, a kind of Wild West where anything goes. It is common for US trade representatives visiting East Asia to hold press conferences where they brandish fake Hollywood DVDs bought from local street stalls, presenting these as evidence of the lack of regulation which characterizes their host nations (Pang, 2006). There appears to be no cultural policy here, no intellectual property governance. The street is a kind of free-for-all, a carnival of illicit entrepreneurialism.

Yet street-level media trade is subject to many forms of regulation, even though these may be invisible from a bureaucratic and institutional perspective. The ability to participate is tightly regulated and a great deal of behind-the-scenes work goes into making these markets function effectively. Researchers in India, a nation with an estimated street vendor population of 10 million (Bhowmik, 2006), have mapped some of these regulatory dynamics. They note: 'City spaces are valuable and highly coveted. Operating on a street corner involves deals with not only civic authorities, but the local goon and the political protector' (*Seminar*, 2000: n.p.; see also Bhowmik, 2000, 2006; Singh, 2000; Rajagopal, 2004). It is rarely the case that a vendor can simply pull up a cart by the streetside and start selling their wares. Space must be rented and one's vending rights are subject to constant negotiation, regulation and interference. Informal modes of regulation to which vendors are subject include daily payments to local authorities (*tehbazari*), bribes to police and municipal officers, payment to other hawkers and community leaders, extraction of protection money by local mafias, payment of interest to money lenders, and so on. It is estimated that many vendors pay 10–20 per cent of their daily income in rent (Bhowmik, 2000). Where vending is not legally protected, vendors are subject to even higher rent extraction. Clearly, these are not common techniques in the conventional repertoires of cultural policy. Yet they perform many of the same regulatory and revenue-collecting functions, controlling who can participate in these cultural markets and under what terms. The flow-on effect is to shape – if implicitly and indirectly – the availability of cultural goods.

There are also multiple avenues for organization and activism among vendors. These constitute additional layers of informal self-governance and co-governance, foregrounding the fact that regulation is not just a top-down process. One option is for vendors to consolidate themselves into 'vote banks', mobilizing their voting power to realize local outcomes. Many seek and receive protection from political parties and lobbies. Street vendors in Mexico City, for example, have long been a power base for the PRI (Institutional Revolutionary Party). Others join local cooperatives to pool their purchasing power, or pay dues to vendor associations who negotiate on their behalf with the authorities. More formal means for organization include trade unions, which may be active at local, city, regional and national scales. Once more, India provides many examples: in Mumbai there is the Pheriwala [Street Vendor] Action Committee in Mumbai; at the national level there is the National Association for Street Vendors of India; and so on. A range of other advocates and NGOs also represent informal sector workers, including the Self-Employed Women's Association. Given the centrality of street vendors within the cultural economies of nations such as India, these organizations need to be understood as informal cultural policy actors.

The regulatory dynamics of street-level media trade vary from one part of the world to the next. Within any nation and any city, different forms of control co-exist. Yet there are common features that provide grounds for transnational comparison. As Cross and Morales (2007: 11) argue, street vendors 'around the world do recognizably similar things, but not always in the same way or for the same reasons'.[8] Crucially, there are always forms of invisible governance at work, and these function as implicit cultural policy in shaping the cultural consumption of populations and the working lives of the traders involved in these networks.

One could argue that because these layers of control and management do not directly involve the state, they do not constitute policy. But this is not entirely accurate. Municipal authorities and national governments are involved at many different levels of the street media economy. The vast majority of vendors around the world make payments to local authorities, in the form of (legal) trading and licence fees or (illegal) bribes. The police must constantly be paid off to keep them on side. Often this means that vendors must negotiate with many different layers of law enforcement: the local authorities, the traffic police, the state police, etc. In this way, the pirate media trade is actually quite heavily taxed, albeit indirectly. In effect, street pirates subsidize the state, which benefits financially from their activities.

Hybrid economies

The informal mediascape includes not only pirate networks but also 'hybrid' media circuits which combine elements of licit and illicit production and exchange. These circuits are significant from the perspective of cultural policy because they arrange the formal and the informal economies in novel combinations, revealing points of intersection and interdependency, and raising a series of questions about appropriate regulatory responses. They also foreground questions about pricing levels and business models which are of relevance to media policy debates more generally.

A striking example of a hybrid media economy is the Nigerian video industry (often referred to as Nollywood), which produces between 1,000 and 2,000 movies a year, rivalling the output of Hollywood and Bollywood. Cheaply and rapidly shot, Nigerian videos have become the quintessential popular culture form for urban Africa. They are consumed voraciously and in large numbers by audiences right across the continent, who buy VCDs (video CDs) from local street markets. Economically, Nollywood is one of few bright spots in Nigeria's moribund petro-economy, creating thousands of jobs and sustaining its own star system. Nigerian actors such as Jim Iyke and Genevieve Nnaji are now superstars throughout Africa and the diaspora.

As Brian Larkin (2004, 2008) has documented, the success of this industry can be traced back to its innovative distribution system, which *grew out of pre-existing pirate circuits* and which over time has evolved into a semi-formal network which returns revenues to producers. In the following passage, Larkin describes how the distribution system works in northern Nigeria:[9]

Nearly all of those who might be described as pirates were at the same time involved in the duplication and sale of legitimate media, and the organization that emerged made Kano the regional distribution center for electronic media in northern Nigeria and the wider Hausaphone area (which covers parts of Chad, Cameroon, Benin, Ghana, and the Sudan). The system is this: the main dealers are based at centers in Kano, like Kofar Wambai market. They then sell to distributors in other northern cities, and these in turn supply smaller urban and rural dealers who provide goods for itinerant peddlers. The system is based on a complex balance of credit and trust; and although it depends, in part, on piracy, it has evolved into a highly organized, extensive distribution system for audio- and videocassettes. (2004: 295)

As Larkin notes, distribution of Nigerian videos is characterized by intricate and informal negotiations between distributors/marketers, their local representatives, and thousands of street and market vendors. In recent years, copyright enforcement by producers and state agencies has also become a feature of the industry (Nwauche, 2003; Jedlowski, 2010). Increasingly, the Nigerian Copyright Commission and the National Film and Video Censors Board are active in monitoring street markets and video clubs for infringement – with mixed results. In this sense, Nollywood represents a hybrid pirate economy, moving from an informal mode of organization (a key factor in its rapid growth) towards a semi-formal one.

Latin American cities are home to similar hybrid media circuits. One frequently cited example is the *tecnobrega* music scene in the city of Belém in northern Brazil, where informal distribution of CDs functions as a marketing strategy for live concerts (Mizukami and Lemos, 2010). Hundreds of albums of this high-energy pop/dance music are produced annually, using samples cribbed freely from local and Western tracks. Producers give the copies for free to street vendors, who then sell them on to consumers for a nominal price (US$1–$2). In addition to showcasing the skills of the producer, the CDs also promote upcoming street parties, which is where the producers make their money back.

The popularity of *tecnobrega* events is enormous, with thousands of parties and concerts held every month (Lemos and Castro, 2008). The whole economy is informal, operating outside conventional recording and touring practices, and it relies on a dynamic mix of original and appropriated content.[10] The distribution networks, governed by tacit agreements between producers and street vendors, are efficient and extensive. The *tecnobrega* economy is attracting increasing attention from copyright reformists in Europe and the USA, who see in its flexible structure alternative futures for mainstream content industries (e.g. Bollier, 2009).[11]

These are two examples of indigenous creative industries operating outside established media business models. They rarely figure in policy discussions, precisely because they are not integrated with formal policy programmes. Yet there is much we can learn from their precedents. Both offer textbook examples of how to use culture as a driver of economic growth, and in this respect they have something to offer the voluminous cultural policy and creative industries literature on this topic (e.g. Barrowclough and Kozul-Wright, 2008). There are lessons here for other debates as well. If we define cultural policy not as the science of arts funding and urban regeneration but as the art of enriching the cultural life of communities and providing affordable access to texts and technologies of self-representation, then a different set of priorities and questions emerge. It is to these that we now turn.

Informal networks as civic infrastructures

One area that has received little sustained attention is the potential for informal media economies to function as drivers of cultural engagement, rather than as unruly forces that need to be disciplined, formalized or eradicated. To focus on these aspects is to move the debate from questions of creative industries development models to questions of cultural citizenship. With this aim in mind, I now offer some examples of how informal media networks facilitate forms of cultural provision that would not otherwise exist, due to market failures and lack of effective distribution infrastructures.

Book piracy in the developing world offers a useful point of interest here. In many Asian and Latin American nations, cheaply photocopied books provide poor communities with access to a world of ideas and information that would otherwise be off limits. Alarcón (2009) has examined the dynamics of book piracy in Peru, an organized, efficient and mature industry that is estimated to employ more people than the legal publishing industry. The Peruvian pirates are speedy (books appear on streets days after, or even before, their official release) and their reach is extensive, especially outside the capital, Lima. As Alarcón notes, 'There are vast swathes of the country with no formal bookstores' (n.p.). Pirates operate within these gaps. They have increased poor communities' access to the written word, and they have also reintroduced into circulation forgotten and out-of-print texts which have fallen through the cracks of the legal publishing industry. While there is no doubt that book piracy has eroded the economic base of the legal book trade, making it very difficult for local publishers to compete, the impact of the pirate economy on literacy levels should not be underestimated.

These pirate infrastructures[12] constitute an informal counterpart to the state-funded 'cultural sector', the reach of which is typically far more restricted. This is not to say, however, that the state is not involved in these infrastructures in other ways, nor that these networks do not create other problems. In Peru, as elsewhere, pirate economies have at times been actively supported by the state for political purposes. Alarcón notes that in the years of the Fujimori regime the government promoted piracy in order to undermine dissident publishers and local intellectual elites. This political project was aided by economic liberalization policies that opened Peru to a flood of cheap, imported technology to the detriment of local publishers. Here we see entanglements between state power and the informal economy that are characteristic of many media systems (see Box 2.1).

BOX 2.1   Formal–informal interdependence in Russia

As new research by Olga Sezneva and Joe Karaganis has established, piracy 'is not just a drain on the cultural economy in Russia – *it is one of the primary forms of that economy* and is woven into a wide range of licit practices, forms of enterprise, and patterns of consumer behavior' (2011: 154). Music, software and film piracy is the default means of media access throughout the former Soviet bloc. This reflects the prohibitively high prices of legal media goods as well as the relative novelty of intellectual property rights regimes in post-communist societies.

Copyright enforcement in Russia, as in most nations, is selective. A series of raids and crackdowns in 2006–07, conducted for the benefit of trading partners (principally the USA), has not significantly reduced pirate consumption. Rather, this enforcement effort appears to have concentrated pirate CD and DVD reproduction in the hands of a smaller number of politically protected manufacturers. Anti-piracy raids are used as a way to silence political dissent: NGOs are raided on the pretext of copyright violation, their computers confiscated and their emails pored over by the security services (Levy, 2010).

Notwithstanding these sporadic regulatory incursions, state involvement in – and support for – the pirate economy is a constitutive feature of the Russian media landscape. There is a 'web of police and security-service protection' for pirate disc factories, the largest of which are housed within military bases and nuclear power plants (Sezneva and Karaganis, 2011: 153). Guarded by government security forces, these factories are subject to political patronage. Some also produce discs for the legal market, illustrating the extent to which Russia's formal and informal media economies are integrated.

While these conditions reflect the specificities of post-Soviet Russia, with its unusual pattern of state–market relations, they are also indicative of a more general interdependence between the state and the pirate economy. In Russia, there is no clear divide between the formal and informal spheres. Intellectual property law, as a formalizing technology (Thomas, 2010), reorganizes relations between a variety of 'grey' actors, creating market opportunities and monopolies for some and driving others deeper into the black market. Cultural policy operates in the spaces between the state, legal media markets, and the informal economy.

Table 2.1 Cost of three book titles as a percentage of average income in South Africa, India and the USA

Country	The God of Small Things	Long Walk to Freedom	Oxford English Dictionary
South Africa	0.0046%	0.0069%	0.0134%
India	0.0117%	0.0273%	0.025%
USA	0.0002%	0.0003%	0.0005%

Source: Liang and Prabhala (2006)

The public-good aspects of piracy are taken up in other research. Liang and Prabhala (2006) have examined informal media economies in Africa and Asia, focusing on their relations with legal book markets. Table 2.1 compares the average retail price of selected titles in legal bookstores in India, South Africa and the USA, relative to average annual income levels in each country. Liang and Prabhala (2006: 110) come to the following conclusions:

One: absolute prices of [legal] books can be higher in the [global] south than in the north. Two: consumers in the south have to commit significantly higher proportions of their income to consume these books. Three: if consumers in the United States had to pay the same proportion of their income towards these books as their counterparts in South Africa and India, the results would be ludicrous: US$1027.50 for Mandela's Long Walk to Freedom *and US$941.20 for the* Oxford English Dictionary.

For Liang and Prabhala, the pirate economy is a solution to this pricing problem.[13] They stress that India's thriving pirate economy – fuelled by cheap imports, local IT industries, internet cafés and copy shops – means that all the books mentioned above can be bought on the streets for the equivalent of $1–$2, or photocopied for less. So the access-to-knowledge question raised by the pricing strategies of Western publishers is effectively sidestepped by moving the exchange into the informal economy.

As research like this demonstrates, informal media networks provide various kinds of civic, cultural and pedagogical goods and services which in more formalized settings would be the responsibility of the state or the market space of regulated industry. Effective public policy would benefit from attention to the public-good aspects of informal media economies – the contribution to literacy rates of pirate books and pirated DVDs (with their suspicious

but usually serviceable subtitles), the productivity benefits generated by pirated software, and so on – as well as revenue leakage for producers.

Implications for formal cultural policy

How, then, can formal institutions of cultural governance develop appropriate policy responses to informality? What are the opportunities and challenges?

One issue that makes developing policy around informal cultural economies difficult is the lack of credible data. Entertainment industry lobby groups (such as the Motion Picture Association, the International Federation of the Phonographic Industry, the Business Software Alliance) produce empirical research on pirate economies to provide ammunition for anti-piracy and IP enforcement campaigns. There is precious little alternative evidence on which to draw.[14] The point of studying pirate flows empirically would not necessarily be to establish the scale of pirate trade in different nations: from a cultural policy perspective, this is not the main question. There are other things to consider, such as the affordability of pirate goods in relation to legal media pricing, and the adequacy or inadequacy of informal infrastructures to supply a diverse range of content to audiences. The first of these issues – the global pricing problem for legal media commodities – is beginning to attract some sustained attention (Liang and Prabhala, 2006; Karaganis, 2011). However, there is less evidence available about the kinds of content that circulate and do not circulate through pirate channels.

For example, it could be quite useful to know whether Thai films or Vietnamese books or Canadian television programmes are more or less widely available in pirate economies than they are in formal legal outlets, and at what price. This would be relevant not only for analyses of the cultural preferences of national audiences (perhaps there is a bigger audience for some kinds of local content than we often assume?), but also for debates around cultural trade. To illustrate this point, let me return to the Nigerian video economy. Until 2009, when UNESCO started counting Nigeria's video releases in its global movie production surveys, there was almost no empirical data about the size of the Nigerian industry that had currency in international policy circles. As a result, Nollywood remained 'off the map' of global cultural policy. What other regional media powerhouses and emerging industries might reveal themselves if we had appropriate indicators for measuring informal flows? What else might we learn about the relative popularity of local versus imported product in various parts of the world? What implications might this have for models of cultural imperialism and cultural globalization within social and cultural theory?

It can be argued that informal street economies in developing nations are as vulnerable to cultural imperialism as formal channels. Looking at the range of DVDs in pirate stalls in Latin America, one could easily come to the conclusion that Hollywood is as dominant here as in the multiplexes. But this is not the case everywhere. For example, the pirate economy in Indonesia is building new audiences for old Indonesian films that have long been out of print, creating new niche markets for these movies through informal circulation.[15] The relationship between national cultural policy objectives and informal economies is not clear-cut. Sometimes pirate circuits work as invisible agents of cultural diversity, and sometimes not. Either way, it is worth taking seriously the proposition that in certain situations cultural policy objectives may be realized by informal circulation.

While drawing attention to possibilities of engagement between formal cultural policy and informal cultural economies, it is also necessary to be realistic about the problems of informality. Informality produces unforeseen consequences for cultural policy, which may reach beyond the specific field of media regulation and into other spheres, such as tourism and heritage. Consider the trade in touristic trinkets and postcards in Italy, sold informally near historic sites and cathedrals. Revenues from merchandise based on officially licensed images of these sites (official postcards, posters, t-shirts, and so on) contribute to maintenance and preservation efforts. With state budgets struggling to keep pace

with the costs involved, heritage sites increasingly rely on such commercial ventures. But many traders choose instead to sell cheaper, pirated merchandise, which reproduces official photographs without authorization or payment. Piracy thus damages the preservation and restoration of the sites themselves, with implications for their long-term viability.[16] This example of revenue 'leakage' involves a clear conflict between formal cultural policy initiatives and the informal media economy, presenting a rationale for intervention to stamp out unauthorized exchange. There are many other examples of informality's deleterious effects on heritage and cultural policy that we could mention here.

This raises questions about whether informal media economies should be managed through top-down policy, and the means by which this may be achieved. While the answers to such questions will always depend on the specific context, some general observations are possible. Policy intervention in informal economies typically has the effect of subjecting informal activity to greater oversight and scrutiny. The end result is to bring informality further into the realm of regulation, taxation and measurement. So policy engagement with informal economies, especially in the form of direct regulation, ends up fundamentally changing the way they operate. Sometimes this kind of policy intervention is needed. Informal media economies create problems at the same time as they offer solutions: exploitation of workers (especially women and children) is rife in the informal economy, especially in street trade. Informality facilitates the exploitation of the vulnerable and erodes the power of organized labour. Appropriate policy responses to situations such as these must be decided on a case-by-case basis.

However, it is not just about a choice of whether or not to regulate. There is also a deeper epistemological question here about what counts and does not count in policy deliberations. In the case of the Italian cathedrals, an attention to the dynamics of informality could potentially expand the category of 'heritage industry' to include the pirate postcard economies, understanding these not just as criminal activities, but also as ancillary industries which provide employment for many people within the cracks of the formal economy. While their activities are antagonistic to cultural policy objectives, the people working in these capacities still deserve an empirical presence in policy analysis. Thus the category of 'cultural sector' often needs to be expanded to render visible the diverse interdependencies between formal and informal economies.[17]

The relationship between formal cultural policy and informal cultural economies is especially interesting at city level. On the one hand, urban informal economies frequently come into direct conflict with urban regeneration and city-branding initiatives. Many cities (especially those with global city aspirations) are cracking down on informal traders with the aim of 'cleaning up the streets'. As inner urban areas gentrify and poor populations are priced out of the market, as branded stores replace street vendors, the character of cultural engagement and cultural consumption changes (Cross and Morales, 2007). These confrontations bring into focus the conflicting objectives of cultural policy, with regeneration initiatives often prioritized over the varieties of informal cultural provision that may be beneficial from the perspective of social or education policy. But this is not the only possible response. Other cities actively promote their informal economies for strategic reasons. 'Slum tours' in Brazil and India, often supported by local authorities, reveal a different kind of engagement with informality – understood here as a marketable marker of urban distinctiveness. The problems with these projects have been well documented, but if anything they gesture towards a different trajectory for urban policy engagement with the informal. It is likely that these strategies will become more common within urban cultural policy repertoires around the world in coming decades.

Conclusion

This chapter has argued that informal media circuits (including pirate circuits) are not outside policy, governance, and regulation; on the contrary, they are linked in complex ways to the state, to the cultural sector, and to mainstream media industries. Existing indexes of cultural trade (UNESCO stats, box office results, etc.) do not tell us the full story. Taking informal media flows into account provides a rather different view of where cultural production is occurring and where it is being consumed. Finally, we should not see the role of policy as being simply to formalize or discipline these circuits, because in many instances they provide cultural

materials that are not available through conventional channels. In many contexts, the key to effective cultural policy programmes and implementation will rely on strategic articulation between the state and the informal realm.

Notes

This chapter draws on my forthcoming book *Subcinema: Mapping Informal Film Distribution* (London: British Film Institute).

1 As of 2008, *IJCP* defines cultural policy as 'the promotion or prohibition of cultural practices and values by governments, corporations, other institutions and individuals', whether explicit or implicit (Ahearne and Bennett, 2009: 139).
2 They may, however, be governed indirectly through consumer protection laws or internet policy frameworks.
3 Ravi Sundaram's book *Pirate Modernity: Delhi's Media Urbanism* (2009) offers a rich and nuanced analytical framework for studying this relationship, to which the present chapter is greatly indebted.
4 See ILO (2000) and Hart (2009) for retrospective histories of the development of the informal economies model.
5 Hart's research also had a more critical epistemological ambition – to redress 'the unthinking transfer of Western categories to the economic and social structures of Africa' (Hart, 1973: 61).
6 Arguably, the first major articulation of this agenda was the NWICO (New World Information and Communication Order) campaign in UNESCO from the end of the 1970s to the mid-1980s.
7 I borrow this turn of phrase from Saskia Sassen's (1991) argument about the role of global cities in the international economy.
8 Cross and Morales (2007) argue against the use of informality as an analytical framework to understand what happens in street markets and among street vendors, although I do not share their hostility to this approach.
9 Nollywood consists of a number of different regional industries, which together make up the Nigerian video economy. The Hausa video industry in Nigeria's north differs in many ways from the Yoruba, Igbo and English-language industries, but the pattern is similar in all cases: pirate copies and originals intermingle in distribution channels.
10 The extra-legal dimensions of *tecnobrega* stem from copyright violations in sampling, not from illicit commercial distribution of original content. Liang (2009) offers an important critique of this distinction.
11 Another example of a hybrid pirate circuit can be found in Floyd's (2008) research into the pirate economy of Quichua DVDs in Ecuador, which examines the production and circulation of low-budget videos, documentary films and music videos for an indigenous community that rarely has the opportunity to hear their own language on national television. The economy is totally pirate; however,

the producers don't mind as they use the DVDs as a way to promote concerts and other events, which is where they make their money.

12 See Larkin (2008) for a sophisticated discussion of cultural infrastructures.

13 The 2011 report *Media Piracy in Emerging Economies* (Karaganis, 2011) – to which Liang contributes – develops this argument in greater depth.

14 Empirical academic studies of piracy almost always focus on online file-sharing economies, which are easier to measure via desk research. There is, however, a minor but rich tradition of ethnographic and observational studies of street-level pirate economies within the field of media anthropology (for example, Himpele, 2007; Larkin, 2008).

15 Further detail on this can be found in Lobato and Ryan (2011).

16 Thank you to Davide Ponzini for this example.

17 Of course, this would also have the effect of increasing the size and scale of many cultural industries in empirical 'mapping' studies, which may sometimes be strategically useful.

REFERENCES

Ahearne, Jeremy (2009) 'Cultural policy explicit and implicit: a distinction and some uses', *International Journal of Cultural Policy*, 15(2): 141–153.

Ahearne, Jeremy and Oliver Bennett (2009) 'Introduction', *International Journal of Cultural Policy*, 15(2): 139.

Alarcón, Daniel (2009) 'Life among the pirates', *Granta*, 109, www.granta.com/Magazine/Granta-109-Work/Life-Among-the-Pirates

Barrowclough, Diana and Zeljka Kozul-Wright (2008) *Creative Industries and Developing Countries: Voice, Choice and Economic Growth*. London: Routledge.

Bhowmik, Sharit K. (2000) 'Hawkers and the urban informal sector: a study of street vending in seven cities', National Alliance of Street Vendors of India, www.nasvinet.org/userfiles/file/A%20study%20of%20street%20vending%20in%20seven%20cities.pdf

Bhowmik, Sharit K. (2006) 'Social security for street vendors', *Seminar*, 568, www.india-seminar.com/2006/568/568_sharit_k_bhowmik.htm

Bollier, David (2009) *Viral Spiral: How the Commoners Built a Digital Republic of Their Own*. New York: New Press.

Cross, John and Alfonso Morales (2007) *Street Entrepreneurs: People, Place and Politics in Local and Global Perspective*. London: Routledge.

Feige, Edgar L. (1979) 'How big is the irregular economy?', *Challenge*, 22(5): 5–13.

Floyd, Simeon (2008) 'The pirate media economy and the emergence of Quichua language media spaces in Ecuador', *Anthropology of Work Review*, 29(2): 34–41.

Hart, Keith (1973) 'Informal income opportunities and urban employment in Ghana', *Journal of Modern African Studies*, 11(1): 61–89.

Hart, Keith (2009) 'On the informal economy: the political history of an ethnographic concept', *CEB Working Paper* No. 09/042. Brussels: Centre Emile Bernheim.

Himpele, Jeffrey (2007) *Circuits of Culture: Media, Politics, and Indigenous Identity in the Andes*. Minneapolis, MN: University of Minnesota Press.

Huygen, Annelies et al. (2009) 'Economic and cultural effects of file sharing on music, film and games'. Delft, The Netherlands: TNO Information and Communication Technology/Ministries of Education, Culture and Science, Economic Affairs and Justice.

IFPI (International Federation of the Phonographic Industry) (2006) *Piracy Report: Protecting Creativity in Music*. London: IFPI Secretariat.

International Labour Office (1972) *Employment, Incomes and Equality: A Strategy for Increasing Productive Employment in Kenya*. Geneva: ILO.

International Labour Office (2000) *The ILO and the Informal Sector: An Institutional History*. Geneva: ILO.

Jedlowski, Alessandro (2010) 'Beyond the video boom: new tendencies in the Nigerian video industry', paper presented at ASAUK writing workshop, Birmingham, 16 April.

Karaganis, Joe (ed.) (2011) *Media Piracy in Emerging Economies*. New York: Social Science Research Council.

Larkin, Brian (2004) 'Degraded images, distorted sounds: Nigerian video and the infrastructure of piracy', *Public Culture*, 16(2): 289–314.

Larkin, Brian (2008) *Signal and Noise: Media, Infrastructure, and Urban Culture in Nigeria*. Durham, NC: Duke University Press.

Lemos, Ronaldo and Oona Castro (2008) *Tecnobrega: o Pará reinventando o negócio da música*. Rio de Janeiro: Aeroplano Editora.

Levy, Clifford J. (2010) 'Russia uses Microsoft to suppress dissent', *New York Times*, 11 September, A1.

Liang, Lawrence and Achal Prabhala (2006) 'Reconsidering the pirate nation', *The Southern African Journal of Information and Communication*, 7: 108–114.

Liang, Lawrence (2009) 'Piracy, creativity and infrastructure: rethinking access to culture', SSRN eLibrary, http://ssrn.com/abstract=1436229

Lobato, Ramon (forthcoming) *Subcinema: Mapping Informal Film Distribution*. London: British Film Institute.

Lobato, Ramon and Mark Ryan (2011) 'Rethinking genre studies through distribution analysis: issues in international horror movie circuits', *New Review of Film and Television Studies*, 9(2): 188–203.

Mizukami, Pedro Nicoletti and Ronaldo Lemos (2010) 'From free software to free culture: the emergence of open business', in L. Shaver (ed.), *Access to Knowledge in Brazil: New Research on Intellectual Property, Innovation and Development*. London: Bloomsbury Academic, pp. 25–66.

Nwauche, E.S. (2003) 'Intellectual property rights, copyright and development policy in a developing country: options for sub-Saharan African countries', paper presented to the Copyright Workshop at Zimbabwe International Book Fair, www.kopinor.org/content/download/1777/13422/file/zibf.pdf

OECD (2008) *The Economic Impact of Counterfeiting and Piracy*. Paris: Organization for Economic Co-operation and Development.

Pang, Laikwan (2006) *Cultural Control and Globalization in Asia: Copyright, Piracy, and Cinema*. London: Routledge.

Rajagopal, Arvind (2004) 'The menace of hawkers: property forms and the politics of market liberalization in Mumbai', in K. Verdery and C. Humphrey (eds), *Property in Question: Value Transformation in the Global Economy*. Oxford: Berg, pp. 227–250.

Rand Corporation (2009) *Film Piracy, Organized Crime, and Terrorism*. Santa Monica, CA: Safety and Justice Program/ Global Risk and Security Center.

Sassen, Saskia (1991) *The Global City: New York, London, Tokyo*. Princeton, NJ: Princeton University Press.

Sassen, Saskia (1994) 'The informal economy: between new developments and old regulations', *The Yale Law Journal*, 103(8): 2289–2304.

Seminar (2000) Unattributed introduction to special issue on street vendors. *Seminar*, 491, www.india-seminar.com/ 2000/491/491%20problem.htm

Sezneva, Olga and Joe Karaganis (2011) 'Russia', *Media Piracy in Emerging Economies*. New York: Social Science Research Council, pp. 149–217.

Singh, Arbind (2000) 'Organizing street vendors', *Seminar*, 491 http://india-seminar.com/2000/491/491%20arbind%20 singh.htm

Sundaram, Ravi (2009) *Pirate Modernity: Delhi's Media Urbanism*. London: Routledge.

Thomas, Julian (2010) 'The law as a formalising technology: brands and the regulation of symbolic economies', paper presented at the Cultural Studies Association of Australasia annual conference, Byron Bay, 8 December.

CHAPTER 3

CHALLENGES OF GOVERNANCE IN MULTI-ETHNIC CITIES
Phil Wood

Migration and cultural diversity have become dominant metaphors for the rapid change and growing anxiety in urban communities around the world. While nation-states jealously guard their powers to police borders, dispense or deny citizenship and dabble in the shaping of national identities, it is in our cities, on a daily basis, where the business of whether we can, or cannot, find a way of living and prospering together is being performed. Powerful forces, and visceral impulses, threaten to drive us towards greater segregation, suspicion, exploitation and conflict. However, this chapter argues that cities can and must take a more proactive stance to forge diverse urban societies where citizens not only tolerate each other but co-create their world. A selection of examples is offered to illustrate how local government, civil society and migrants themselves are now shaping this emerging movement.

Introduction

Reports of the impending demise of the nation-state[1] may have been somewhat exaggerated[2] but these contortions, while trying to make sense of mesmerizing change, have been a defining factor of our age. There have been many symptoms of globalization, of which the growth in migration has been but one. However, migration seems to have become for many, including national governments, an overriding factor. And, when combined with the (not necessarily related) issue of international terrorism, it has in the minds of many been rapidly transformed into a question, a challenge and, indeed for some, an existential threat (Sassen, 1996). We now have a climate in which national politicians feel impelled to act publicly and robustly in defence of national interests and identities which, only a few years earlier, they were content to keep implicit and vague. In its most high profile cases (such as the recent Swiss referendum on the building of minarets) this has become a *kulturkampf* between Western and Muslim values. In actual fact, though, we are seeing conflicts played out across the globe between interest groups and value systems of very many hues.

Meanwhile, another symptom of systemic transformation has been the rise of the city and city-region. This has been partly through the acceleration of industrialization and rural depopulation which saw the world's urban population recently exceed 50 per cent. But we have also seen a new confidence in cities as they have realized the growing power and influence to be achieved by positioning themselves in the 'space of flows' at the nodes of global networks of financial and symbolic capital that transcend national borders (Castells, 1996). This realignment has inevitably created many paradoxes and disjunctions. In this chapter, I aim to address only one of these: cultural diversity and the governance of cities. While the nation-states jealously retain control of borders and citizenship status, the majority of migrants (and the neighbours of migrants) live, work, pray, create, procreate and die in cities. Cities appear to have little formal power to regulate or even influence who their residents will be, yet they are the places where, through the daily – and largely banal – interactions, conflicts or avoidances of people, the nature of societies will be defined (Amin, 2002). My thesis is that cities must stand up and take a more proactive role in the realms of migration, citizenship, cultural identity and (to adopt a Spanish term because no English one will do) *convivencia*. And action must move beyond the current preoccupation with legal-istic and bureaucratic entitlements and responsibili-ties to much more culturally-nuanced understanding of urban life. For a new form of local, city-based cosmopolitanism may be the best guarantee we have of achieving a world which is sustainable, equitable and beneficent rather than one gripped by fear, antagonism and atrophy. This raises some serious questions and challenges, in particular for those concerned with cultural policy in contemporary

cities in all parts of the world. In this chapter, I will try to make sense of these and offer some inspiring examples of good practice and practical ways forward.

Ways of thinking about diversity and cities

The first point to note is the scale of change, with many cities around the world now hosting substan-tial numbers of foreign-born residents, as Table 3.1 demonstrates.

While today's scale may be unprecedented in his-tory, there is no shortage of examples from the past of cities built upon constant diversity, movement and change. For better or worse, we have drawn many of our attitudes from the classic nation of migration, the United States. Take these two diametrically opposed visions of the city – as potential utopia:

Table 3.1 Top 25 world cities by percentage of foreign-born (FB) in the population

	City	Year	City Population	FB Population	% FB
1	Dubai	2002	857,233	702,931	82.00
2	Miami	2000	2,253,362	1,147,765	50.94
3	Amsterdam	2002	735,328	347,634	47.28
4	Toronto	2001	4,647,960	2,091,100	44.99
5	Muscat	2000	661,000	294,881	44.61
6	Vancouver	2001	1,967,475	767,715	39.02
7	Auckland	2001	367,737	143,417	39.00
8	Geneva	2002	427,700	164,118	38.37
9	Mecca	1996	4,467,670	1,686,595	37.75
10	The Hague	1995	441,595	161,509	36.57
11	Los Angeles	2000	9,519,338	3,449,444	36.24
12	Tel Aviv	2002	2,075,500	747,400	36.01
13	Kiev	1992	2,616,000	941,760	36.00
14	Medina	2000	5,448,773	1,893,213	34.75
15	New York	2000	9,314,235	3,139,647	33.71
16	San Francisco	2000	1,731,183	554,819	32.05
17	Riyadh	2000	4,730,330	1,477,601	31.24
18	Perth	2001	1,336,239	422,547	31.62
19	Sydney	2001	3,961,451	1,235,908	31.20
20	Jerusalem	2002	678,300	208,700	30.77
21	Melbourne	2001	3,367,169	960,145	28.51
22	Frankfurt	2000	650,705	181,184	27.84
23	Tbilisi	1999	1,339,105	370,932	27.70
24	London	2001	7,172,091	1,940,390	27.05
25	Brussels	2002	978,384	260,040	26.58

Source: Benton-Short et al. (2005: 953)

Despite cultural antagonisms ... the city [of New York] remains a model of rough-hewn cosmopolitanism and multicultural tolerance, with an astonishing mix of peoples living side by side in reasonable harmony. (Burrows and Wallace, 1999: xxiii, quoted in Grillo, 2001)

And as looming dystopia:

Most current, giddy discussions of the 'postmodern' scene in Los Angeles neglect entirely these overbearing aspects of counter-urbanization and counter-insurgency. A triumphal gloss is laid over the brutalization of inner-city neighbourhoods and the increasing South Africanization of its spatial relations. (Davis, 1992: 227, quoted in Grillo, 2000)

More prosaically, though, conventional wisdom on the relationship of cities, governance and migration has been formed from the experience of OECD countries in the post-war period. Although we might identify a variety of responses to the growth in labour migration during this time, three distinct models stand out (Bloomfield and Bianchini, 2004). First, the French approach of 'civic cultural integration', and to some extent the American 'melting pot', typify the requirement of migrants to assimilate into the majority culture in return for citizenship and civic rights. Abandoned by the US, it has been retained doggedly, but increasingly desperately, in France and may even be making a comeback in Denmark (Hedetoft, 2010). Many other countries, but classically Germany, preferred an arms-length relationship, inviting 'guest workers' to visit for labour but not to stay on for extended residence or citizenship. Largely discredited and abandoned in the 1980s, there are signs of its recent return in the guise of 'managed migration' programmes, and more explicitly and ruthlessly in the Gulf States (of which more later). Finally, the model of 'multiculturalism' adopted in Canada, Australia, the UK, the Netherlands, Sweden and latterly the US seemed to many the acme of policy formulations, but has recently come under intense scrutiny. Critics accuse it of celebrating diversity but failing to build loyalty to the nation-state and solidarity within multi-ethnic communities. Although we see the retention of many policies in many cities which are, in all but name, 'multicultural', the force of the backlash means it is now difficult to imagine a politician anywhere (with the possible

exception of Canada) being prepared to declare themselves an unqualified multiculturalist (Vertovec and Wessendorf, 2010).

A diversity of diversity

But this post-war grand narrative of migration from rural locations in the Global South to cities in the developing world is now but one of many stories to be told in the much richer and more complex environment of migration and diversity in the twenty-first century (Balbo, 2005; Stren, 2009). International migrants now represent about 190 million people and while the flow of people is still mainly South to North some 40 per cent of all movements take place *between* countries in the Global South (and if irregular migrants are added to the calculation, the balance probably tips towards the latter) (Balbo, 2009).

Very many of these movements are no longer 'one-way streets' but are made by people who move physically and culturally between two or more spaces as 'transnational' migrants. And migrants can no longer be easily pigeon-holed as young men in search of manual labour and adventure wherever they can find it. Qualified professionals, students and, increasingly, independent female workers are becoming the norm, and their destinations have become cities, and larger cities at that. These globalized 'super diverse' conurbations are magnetically attractive because they represent a nexus of employment opportunities, social connections and cultural security in an otherwise precarious world (Vertovec, 2007). But while the city might once have provided an absorptive and integrating role, it is now a far more fragmented and exclusionary place, with informality in employment, housing and citizenship appearing to be the preferred policy option of many jurisdictions (for newcomers and natives).

In a bid to face the overt negative effects of globalization, all countries in both South and North have been promoting decentralization policies ... to transfer to local government the responsibility of providing cities with the infrastructure and services required by global competition as well as the basic services required by growing numbers of the urban poor. ... consequently the attitude of many local governments is essentially of a laissez-faire type: city authorities absolve themselves from the responsibility of any pro-active supply of infrastructure and services, forcing migrant communities to rely on the private sector or self-provision to a very large extent. Lack of co-ordination among and within the many layers of government … is the norm, adding to their limited capacity to manage the issues of migration, which they often regard as only temporary and marginal. (Balbo and Marconi, 2005: 710)

And the stakes are high – very high. A sad litany of communal conflict over the last two decades, from Nigeria to India and from the Parisian *banlieues* to industrial northern England, testifies to the passions and the misery that these forces evoke. Appadurai (2006: 7) finds one explanation in the corrosive impact of the modern condition of uncertainty:

Large-scale violence is not simply the product of antagonistic identities but … itself is one of the ways in which the illusion of fixed and charged identities is produced, partly to allay the uncertainties about identity that global flows invariably produce … especially when the forces of social uncertainty are allied to other fears about growing inequality, loss of national sovereignty, or threats to local security and livelihood.

So, in the light of the critique of all recently prevailing models, the emergence of transnational migration as a reality for cities around the world, and the ever-present threat of communal conflagration, what new patterns of policy and governance can be discerned?

In the West, we at first sight see a confusing patchwork of approaches, often combining different elements of all three of the classic models. To coin a less than elegant phrase, I might describe a condition of 'neo-liberal integrationism', comprising continued openness to (highly specified) forms of migration justified purely on economic grounds; strict enforcement of tests to ascertain language, local knowledge and loyalty as the condition of citizenship; earnest public debates to determine the nature of national identity; regular sops from politicians to the 'indigenous majority' that this identity is not being compromised; pressure placed upon minorities who are seen to be 'self-segregating' themselves from the majority; while a blind eye is turned to a growing underclass of undocumented migrants performing a range of grey but useful tasks.

Elsewhere, though, we see a diversity of approaches. Japan, for example, with a growing economy but an aged population needs extra labour but cannot countenance the prospect of large alien minorities or *gaikokujin*, so has tried to restrict migration to *nikkejin* (South Americans of ethnic Japanese background) with some unexpected and perplexing consequences (Tsuda, 2000). Incredibly, there is even a growing body of thought which holds that, by investing heavily in robotics technology, Japan may one day return to a condition of complete ethnic homogeneity and fulfil all its industrial and social care labour requirements with machines rather than with potentially troublesome people (Harden, 2008; Robertson, 2010).

Cities in Latin America seem to express a far more relaxed attitude towards diversity and migration and also seem to demonstrate a great sense of municipal agency. Latin American cities, it is suggested, historically grasped autonomy from chronically weak national authorities but, in general, used their power to usher in sharply neo-liberal and entrepreneurial urban policies (Portes and Roberts, 2005), and cities became starkly segregated but on socio-economic more than ethnic grounds. However, as the last decade or so has ushered in more progressive political actors, the overriding drive has been towards achieving greater equality and openness through an urban human rights approach. Brazil introduced a City Statute in 2001, becoming the first place in the world to bring into law an explicit 'Right to the City'. Through innovations such as participatory budgeting and local master plans and the radical empowerment of neighbourhood associations, Brazilian citizens now have many of the tools with which to fashion communities with the resilience to prosper in the current climate (Fernandes, 2007). Mexico City, meanwhile, has recently brought into law a Statute for 'Hospitality, Intercultural Attention to Migrants and Human Mobility in the Federal District'. It sets policy, mechanisms and standards in the areas of hospitality, multi-ethnicity and human mobility for migrant families in the capital. It also promotes the participation of migrants as well as the public and private sectors in social planning, implementation and monitoring of policies and programmes arising from the enforcement of the law.[3]

African cities face greater pressures of migration but, in contrast to Latin America, there has been little sign of civic agency. For example, there have been many cases of xenophobia against African migrants in several South African cities (with apparent municipal insouciance) (Morris, 1998; Ostanel, 2010); and widespread evidence of segregation and conflict in West Africa (Smith, 2006; Agyei-Mensah and Owusu, 2010; Fourchard, 2011). In contrast to this, the city of Dakar has been portrayed as a haven of harmony and cross-cultural co-operation but which exists in spite, rather than because, of municipal action or policy and which may (if not consciously nurtured) be under imminent threat (Ndiaye, 2005). The general picture across Africa is thus one of city authorities which regard the integration of migrants as a low priority compared to the more pressing challenges they face.

This pattern of a 'non-policy' approach to migration is also reported in various parts of South Asia (Barbora et al., 2010; Leaf, 2010). In Bangkok, neither the municipal authorities nor civil society take migrants into account in their work, and this is portrayed as an oversight which will return to haunt the city's aspirations to become a leading regional player (Chantavanich and Vungsiriphisal, 2005). In the Indian city of Ahmedabad, city authorities are accused of progressively ignoring, and then 'air-brushing out', that city's well-documented ethnic conflicts in order to ease in their own vision of a neo-liberal 'Mega City' project (Chatterjee, 2009).

But a very different picture emerges across the Persian Gulf in Dubai and other Emirati states where a colossal property development boom has been built from the capital of foreign investors, and on the back of an army of migrant labour (mainly from the Indian sub-continent), reinforced by a very clear and deliberate policy response. The working conditions and human rights which these workers endure represents not so much a return to the 'guest worker' model, but the indentured labour system of nineteenth-century colonialism, or even a form of latter-day slavery (Hari, 2009). These workers have no right to citizenship or permanent residence and yet many have little chance of ever returning home, so exist in a legal and literal no-man's land. The state and municipality make virtually no concessions to their presence and seem content to face the challenge of global migration by attempting to hermetically seal them off from the host society. In spite of this, the migrants practise mild forms of resistance and are gradually putting down roots (Nagy, 2006; Elsheshtawy, 2008; Kanna, 2010) in these grotesque caricatures of urban community.

Challenges of governance

Having mapped out the newly evolving landscape, let us now look at the multidimensional challenges which confront cities.

Cities as international actors

Perhaps the greatest challenge to cities is the sheer pace and scale of migration which, if it continues to grow at current rates, some fear may overwhelm all but the best run and prosperous of city governance structures. There is now an emerging argument that migrant flows need to be kept to manageable levels, not only to enable receiving cities to cope, but to prevent catastrophic depopulation and destabilization in many of the countries of origin. Thus we are now seeing in some developed world cities a recognition that they share a responsibility not simply for the migration that manifests on their streets, but for that which is 'upstream' of them. In short, what can cities do to make life better in the countries of origin so that not so many people feel the desperate need to emigrate? A recent report (UNDP, 2010) charts examples of partnerships between Spanish and Moroccan and Italian and Romanian municipalities to jointly manage a previously chaotic situation which all too easily played into the hands of political extremism.[4]

A variant on this is 'city diplomacy', with cities taking on roles which might formerly have been the sole preserve of the foreign relations departments of their national governments. So, for example, we see Dutch cities making direct contact with cities in the former Yugoslavia to develop joint programmes around conflict resolution and economic development.[5]

Finally, we see an emerging trend for national and local government in countries of emigration to start thinking of their diasporic communities in terms of what they might be able to contribute in their former homelands. Of course, remittances have been and remain a powerful means of redistributing resources from the developed to the developing world, but these flows existed largely in the private world of migrant individuals and their families.

Indeed, because of often-justified suspicion of misappropriation of funds by public authorities, remittances were considered by migrants and aid organizations alike as the means most likely to ensure funds reached the people and places that most need them. However, we are now seeing examples of state and municipal agencies in countries of origin entering into formal collaboration with diasporic communities – often known as Home Town Associations (HTAs). The most developed examples of HTAs are found in Mexico's relationship with the United States, although other examples have been noted in other parts of Latin America, the Caribbean and Africa (Torres and Kuznetzov, 2006; Somerville et al., 2008; Mackay, 2010). This is for reasons of scale (there are estimated to be over 30 million people resident in the US of Mexican background, and up to 3,000 HTAs); because of the considerable degree of transnational movement and communication; and the tendency in Mexico for national government to devolve a high level of responsibility to municipalities for local governance and development. HTAs are now raising substantial funds in US migrant communities and supervising their allocation in partnership with Mexican municipalities on welfare, economic development and infrastructure projects. Another interesting aspect of these relationships is the influence on local political culture in the municipalities of origin. According to a survey carried out by the Michoacán state government migrant support agency, 37 per cent of the 113 mayors who governed in the state during 2002–2004 were returned migrants (Fox and Bada, 2008).

The city/nation interface

But many more pressing challenges may be found in a different sphere, the ever more complex relationship between cities and their national governments over the vexed issues of migration and identity.

Citizenship

While some nation-states may have devolved some of their sovereignty to supra-national bodies such as the European Union, they are less willing to surrender anything to upstart cities. But as cities come increasingly face to face with the realities of globalization, they are demanding more powers and resources to deal with them, so a tussle is under way – not least over citizenship, which national governments see as their sole preserve. However, in Spain, for example, several cities, including Madrid and Barcelona, have been experimenting with forms of local citizenship. Madrid granted local citizenship rights to migrants who had been resident in the city for six months, regardless of what status they had been given by the national government. These included rights to stand for election to neighbourhood councils and decide on the allocation of public funds to local projects. Although Madrid subsequently revoked these laws, the experiment is continuing in Barcelona and in other Catalan cities.[6]

Security policy

This is another responsibility national government has always held dearly to itself, with a very clear separation from domestic local policy, but we have seen a blurring of former rigid lines of demarcation in recent years. Following the 7 July 2005 suicide bombings in London, the British security services took a direct interest in parts of the country which they perceived as potential breeding grounds for future extremists, i.e. urban neighbourhoods of large Pakistani and Bangladeshi settlement (Thomas, 2009). The Office of Security and Counter-Terrorism introduced a scheme (the alarmingly titled Preventing Violent Extremism) in which it directed local authorities in identifying suspects vulnerable to radicalization, through the medium of youth and community workers and saturating some neighbourhoods with closed-circuit TV cameras. Many saw this as an unacceptable transgression of local democracy and there has since been a backlash in many localities, and the programme has been abolished. However, in other parts of the world local communities, migrants and civil society groups continue to suffer a heavy burden of state security surveillance and curtailment of rights in the name of anti-terrorism (Cortright, 2008).

Divergent trajectories

Although some receiving states, such as Canada, go to great lengths to settle migrant populations evenly around the country, there is an inexorable gravitation to the major and capital cities (Hyndman et al., 2006). This sets up interesting dynamics between the metropolis and the rest of the country.

In some cases (e.g. Oslo, Copenhagen and Helsinki) we are seeing the city adopting increasingly cosmopolitan policies and attitudes, while the rest of their countries seem to be moving towards less tolerant attitudes and political groupings. This is leading to the formation of transnational networks of cosmopolitan cities which may feel themselves to have more in common with each other than with their own governments and fellow countrymen.[7]

Intra-city questions

Finally, there are local governance challenges, within city hall and on the city streets. Cities are having varying degrees of success in coming to terms with the fact that in a super-diverse environment, there is always the prospect of different creeds, lifestyles and interests coming into contradiction with each other. One approach to this has been to balkanize the city into ethnic enclaves which rarely interact and therefore avoid conflict. This has been cited by critics as the downside of multiculturalism (Cantle, 2005) and, while discredited, it is still widely practised. It is certainly true that different national cultures approach conflict differently and we can see this playing out in the varying degrees of success with which different cities around the world are managing the discordance of difference.

Often city authorities seem most comfortable dealing with migration and diversity simply as an instrumental and legalistic process whereby outsiders are either rejected or moved along a conveyor belt to acceptance by the machinery of state. There is a suspicion that many cities would prefer to leave the matter at that, and avoid the messier and more ambiguous social and cultural and political-economy issues that diversity and migration throw up. My suspicion is that wilful or unintentional negligence by city authorities of these deeper questions arising from migration is merely storing up problems for the future.

I believe the real challenge that migration poses for the city governance is the need to rapidly realign its mindset, from one which delivers a 'one-size-fits-all' service to a homogeneous citizenry, to one which copes with the needs and demands of a super-diverse population. This asks serious questions of how well the city actually knows itself. Does it have the data on who is living where, how they live and who they interact with, in a world where communities of several thousand can appear or disappear in a matter of months (Van Liempt, 2010)? Does it have the intelligence and cultural competence to make sense of this data and translate it into effective policy and action? Does it have the political courage to formulate a comprehensive policy and stick to it in the face of wildfire, single-issue media storms around anything from the burka to offensive cartoons?

Cultural diversity questions will have to be asked across the full range of city functions, from education and housing to libraries and graveyard provision, and this in turn asks serious questions of the flexibility of the local political culture and bureaucratic machine to adapt to change, break out of its silos and work transversally and holistically. And while some cities may have had several decades to adapt to these conditions, others are being asked to make the transition in a matter of years, with varying degrees of success.[8]

City responses

I will now draw upon my own experiences to reflect how cities are responding to the challenges they face. As we have seen above, these are myriad and space only allows us to focus on two of these here – public space and cultural policy – which are particularly germane to this volume.

Public space

One of the most profound consequences of neo-liberal economics on cities has been the changing nature of public space. In developed countries this has been characterized by the appropriation of formerly public domains into privatized commercial and residential areas accompanied by increased security and exclusion. In the developing world the neo-liberal demand for open markets and flexibility have combined an increasing casualization of the labour market with a growing proportion of workers forced into non-contractual and informal forms of work. This affects both indigenous and migrant workers but, as can be imagined, the latter are far more susceptible, lacking the institutional structures and social networks to defend themselves. This means migrants falling back increasingly to the streets as the primary place of trade and business. Such business tends to be popular with the poorer consumers of such cities as it provides everyday and specialist goods at lower prices, but is increasingly unpopular with city authorities who perceive informal street trading as irregular, unhygienic and illegal.

In most developing world cities we now see a daily contestation between informal traders, the public, the authorities and international commercial interests to determine who will have the freedom of the streets and who will not. As the majority of such traders are either internal or foreign migrants, such interactions can have a defining influence on the quality of life of migrants in the city. South Africa, because of its high levels of migration, presents these issues in extremis, but also offers alternative scenarios dependent upon the response cities choose to make, for example in Durban (see Box 3.1). Meanwhile, with examples from Serbia (Box 3.2), Belgium and Germany (Box 3.3) below, I note other ways in which the presence of migrants has renegotiated the meaning of public space.

Box 3.1   Contesting the ecology of African public space

For many years since the fall of apartheid, the city of Durban has suggested an alternative trajectory for the South African approach to public space and diversity (Brown et al., 2010). Warwick Junction is a transport hub for the local and regional populations of the city, with some 460,000 people moving through the area each day and, not surprisingly, a wide range of trading and fringe activities proliferating nearby. One of the most prevalent of these is the medicinal herb trade for spiritual and physical ailments. Growing out of ancient Zulu traditions, this fringe activity has developed into a market of 500 informal traders, making Warwick Junction the largest Muti (herbal medicine) market in Southern Africa. But the market also features traders with long-standing or more contemporary migrant backgrounds from south and east Asia as well as the rest of Africa. There are an estimated 8,000 street traders at Warwick Junction, the majority of whom are women.

What struck me when I visited a few years ago was, first, the contrast with other South African cities: the otherworldliness of abandoned and squatted Johannesburg and the cold corporate order of Cape Town. Durban seemed messier but far more dynamic and interactive. But equally impressive was the subtle and culturally sensitive way in which the city authorities were trying to manage this bubbling cauldron of trade and ethnic exchange, which moderated its excesses while retaining it mercurial energy and distinctiveness (Dobson et al., 2009). Keith Hart (the originator of the concept of the 'informal economy') said of the Durban authorities: 'I have not come across any other example where the interests of street traders and local authorities were negotiated with mutual respect over a period as long as the Warwick project'.[9] This then appeared to be one city which was facing the challenges of globalization with a high degree of originality, competence and courage.

Or so it seemed until 2009, when Durban City Council approved plans to clear much of the site and subsidize a private developer to build a shopping mall and taxi rank (Skinner, 2009). The development was presented as something which would benefit all and make it a modern and competitive city fit to host international events such as the 2010 World Cup. This raises an important cultural policy issue. Major sporting and cultural events are presented as offering manifold benefits for cities in emerging economies, but the apparent about-face of the authorities in Durban and the obvious threat to the very special ecology which is Warwick Junction has fuelled a growing campaign of sceptical opposition.[10] One hopes that in the process of 'modernization' the city of Durban will not sacrifice its spirit of municipal inventiveness, cultural inclusiveness and street-level democracy to become just another neo-liberal clone city.

Box 3.2   Rebuilding public space in Serbia – literally

Subotica is a city in Serbia close to the border with Hungary. For most of its history its population has comprised a rich mix of Hungarians, Serbs, Croats, Macedonians, Germans, Albanians and Roma, with no group in a majority, reflecting a history of conquest, migration and accommodation. Most children grew up routinely speaking two or three languages, learning about each other's religions and living side by side. This came to an end in 1991 with the outbreak of the war that destroyed Yugoslavia. While Subotica was spared armed conflict itself, it has been profoundly changed by those tumultuous events as thousands of people left the city in a hurry. They were of all ethnic backgrounds, but generally were the best-educated and most cosmopolitan citizens who wanted no part in the nationalistic rancour; they now reside in Vienna, Berlin, New York, never to return. Their empty houses have been filled by new communities driven to Subotica from other parts of the disintegrating country. Mainly they are Serbs, nursing a deep resentment of their eviction from ancestral homes in Croatia, Bosnia and Kosovo and not especially enamoured of the cosmopolitan traditions of their new home. But another group of refugees were Muslim Roma, hounded out of Kosovo and obliged to make a new home in the meanest and most decayed parts of Subotica.

Since the war Serbia has sunk into a sullen torpor, as Europe's pariah state and, hard on the EU border, Subotica feels this exclusion most of all. It has tried to maintain its self-respect and distinctive traditions by resisting centralizing diktats from Milošević and his successors in Belgrade. However, the cosmopolis had disintegrated into a patchwork of rival tribes jealously accentuating and guarding those aspects of their identity which distinguished them, and monoglot had become the norm.

In the neighbourhood of Peščara, Serbs, Croats and Hungarians lived side by side among derelict houses and impassable roads, but such was their suspicion of each other that none were prepared to take action to rectify the situation, even though they very often could not reach the shops or schools. Also worried about this was Stevan Nikolić, leader of the outcast Roma community. One day he persuaded a friend to lend him an excavator and some tools and road materials and a small group of Roma people began repairing the road. As other (non-Roma people) passed by, Nikolić persuaded them to join in and, over the course of a week, this multi-ethnic group of neighbours who had never spoken before had created a new road for their district. So impressed was the local authority that it supported the creation of a neighbourhood council to improve the district. With the support of the city's Local Democracy Agency, many other parts of the city now also have non-sectarian neighbourhood councils.

We should never ignore the foresight of the outsider to see what is missing or to point out the absurdity of what exists.[11]

Box 3.3   Migrantas – a visual language of migration

Most global cities are now home to thousands of migrant women, but they often remain invisible and unknown to most of their fellow citizens. *Migrantas* is a collective of migrant women active in Germany and Spain who have pooled their skills into a project which aims to take the issues that arise in the daily lives of migrant women and to present them in ways which can be absorbed and understood by their fellow citizens. They quite literally reappropriate the public space with images and ideas drawn directly from migrant experience in a way that cannot be easily ignored. The process begins with *Migrantas* meeting migrant women in their own collective spaces with workshops to reflect together on the many issues of migration. Women from very different backgrounds and residency statuses exchange their experiences and express these in simple drawings, thus overcoming language shortcomings. After a careful analysis of all the drawings from different workshops, *Migrantas* culls key elements and common themes, for example the heartbreak of a family divided by distance, or the worry of one woman that other people in the street look on her as a potential terrorist. It then translates their central motifs into a visual language accessible to everyone – pictograms, the visual language of *Migrantas*. Their simple, universally understandable images stir emotions, and people from different backgrounds recognize themselves in the representations, while others gain new insights or modify their own perspectives.

All *Migrantas* projects end with an exhibition. The participants now see their drawings presented in public and experience public recognition of their voices and social participation, while visitors to the exhibitions receive an opportunity to become better acquainted with the experiences of migrant women.

One of *Migrantas*' major goals and achievements, is to make the pictograms visible in public urban spaces. They appear as posters where there is normally commercial advertising, as projected digital animations on public screens, as flyers or postcards or shopping bags. Thus migrant womens' perspectives and lived realities are taken out of the individual private space and made visible in the public space, creating an encounter which triggers reactions and self-reflection in the passer-by.[12]

Cultural policy

Rising multi-ethnicity presents a very real challenge to the cultural institutions of the city. Museums, galleries, theatres and libraries may have been created in very different times for very different audiences than the ones they now encounter, and this raises powerful questions of whether and how they should respond to change. Museums may have been created explicitly as the expression of a dominant or monolithic culture, or as part of the nation-building myth of a formerly subject people or city. Or they may simply be repositories of artefacts and symbols with meaning for an educated elite but largely illegible to others. Elena Delgado of Madrid's Museo de América is in no doubt that her profession must embrace the challenge:

The significance of a museum lies not only in its collections, but also in the reflections and insights it is able to trigger around the objects, the knowledge it provides and the multiple visions and interpretations it offers on the heritage in its care. ... As metaphorical 'free zones', museums must strive to take their place at the intersections, in those spaces where individuals and distinct cultural identities can act and interact, transform and be transformed. ... In order to become a space for negotiation, museums must disown those homogenising and discriminating values which are still very closely connected to their role in legitimising historic identity. ... One task for cultural and educational institutions should be the development of strategies to help citizens learn to live with conflict, with the other and with difference, by promoting attitudes which lead to the intersection of cultures and of knowledge. (Delgado, 2009: 8)

Box 3.4 'Me and the Other in Turin's Museums'

Italy is one country where the weight of history hangs particularly heavily, and where there has been a remarkable change in the ethnic composition of many cities. National government has taken a particularly strident stance on what it sees as the threat to Italian heritage posed by diversity, even going to the ludicrous lengths of attempting to outlaw foreign food (Owen, 2009). In response to this, a raft of Italian city museums have undertaken radical reforms of their policies and practices. Turin, which is so often the standard-bearer of cosmopolitan values in Italy, led the way and seven projects were presented in the conference 'Me and the Other in Turin's Museums'.

(Continued)

(Continued)

A common theme has been the use of artefacts to trigger reflection, reminiscence, expression and dialogue between individuals and groups who might otherwise not encounter each other, or might potentially be in conflict (Bodo et al., 2009). These include 'Tongue for Tongue', which employed story-telling as a means for cultural mediators of different backgrounds to open up and relate the collections of Turin's Museum of Anthropology and Ethnography to contemporary concerns.

Meanwhile, 'City Telling' took multi-ethnic parties of people through the city, creating personal routes that identified 'third spaces' of cultural, linguistic and aesthetic interaction. And 'There's a Garden in Every Story' in the Botanical Garden of Turin challenged locals to discover the global inter-connectedness of the city through the plants that it used; and for new migrants to make connections between old and new homelands through plants.

Museums and heritage sites occupy a special place in the multi-ethnic city, offering the opportunity of an open space in which potentially divisive and difficult issues can be approached from fresh angles which build new cultural and social capital.

Libraries too are ubiquitous city institutions whose roles and relevance have been brought into question by the speed of cultural and technological change but which, through the process of reappraisal, can offer a special contribution to the challenges of multi-ethnicity.

The first professional position that I personally ever held was to encourage unemployed people and migrants to make use of their local library as places of resource and creativity. Libraries are wonderful places but often the buildings, and even some of the librarians, were not as welcoming and accessible as they might be. Sadly, it now seems that if libraries don't make themselves more relevant to their communities they may start to disappear. This is why I was so glad to visit the Idea Stores (see Box 3.5).

Box 3.5   Idea Stores

Tower Hamlets is London's most diverse borough and is undergoing a process of gradually replacing each of its old branch libraries with Idea Stores. Designed especially by the Ghanaian architect David Adjaye to stress accessibility, transparency and flexibility, they are located next to major shops and keep the same opening hours (including Sundays) to encourage maximum usage. They have high staff numbers, including 'meeters and greeters' who are there to encourage first-time users to feel welcome and comfortable. Although still holding large book stocks, they also have space available for a wide variety of other usages to ensure they are seen by people in the neighbourhood as the centre of their community.[13]

The stated objectives of the Council are '... to bring the community together and to empower individuals to help themselves, whether it is learning to read, pursuing hobbies, expanding their knowledge or seeking a job'.

I found the physical presence of an Idea Store striking. First, it does not have a defined threshold between street and library so one is drawn inside without the feeling one is crossing any kind of boundary. This helps to create the sense of neutrality of the space which encourages users to interact. It seems significant that Adjaye was the architect chosen to bring this new concept to life. Born in Tanzania of Ghanaian parents, he grew up in several different parts of world, trained in London and now lives mainly in the Middle East and Africa. He describes his upbringing as placing him in a situation in which he had to:

Recent research suggests that the Idea Stores are managing to balance the maintenance of traditional library functions with their newer responsibilities for social inclusion and interaction (Hartley, 2005).

But urban cultures do not require an institution to give them shape and meaning – the streets will do. Festivals can be a dynamic means of expressing questions or truths about the city that have not or cannot be addressed through formal channels. Traditional carnivals, such as in Rio de Janeiro, New Orleans, Port of Spain, Venice or Cologne, are founded upon the right to public irreverence, transgression and licentiousness, and have long acted as valves to release social or political pressures. More recently, established carnivals such as London's Notting Hill or Berlin's *Karnival der Kulturen* represent a commandeering of the public space to express to the city its multi-ethnic reality (see Box 3.6).

Box 3.6   Festival Kanal: From no-go to must-go zones

Brussels is the political and administrative capital of Europe and, as such, has acquired many of the trappings of the contemporary neo-liberal city. In its patterns of ownership and land use the city centre caters increasingly for business, residential and entertainment requirements of a sophisticated and mobile professional elite. But Brussels is also a city of transnational migrants from the developing world who fashion a living at the fringes of this other city.

The schism between these two different cities is no more apparent than the two banks of the Albert Canal at Porte de Flandre. On the south side, yuppies slip out of gentrified apartments to lounge in trendy bars, while across the watery divide in Molenbeek workless or hard-pressed Moroccans and Pakistanis sip mint tea in dishevelled cafés: two worlds which barely interact or even acknowledge each other. Local activist Wim Embrechts was affronted by the complacency of this slide towards no-go areas and launched the Festival Kanal in September 2010 to shake up the city and make the canal district a 'must-go zone'. For me, the highlight was him commissioning the artist Emilio López-Menchero to make a direct and blatant intervention on the very bridge that connects the two cities. Overnight, as Brussels slept, he built an exact replica of the Checkpoint Charlie border post and then, as morning came and drivers tried to cross the bridge, he and colleagues, dressed in American and Soviet military uniforms, stopped them to remind them they were passing from one city (and ideological zone) to another. Most responded with either bemusement or amusement, but the project aroused high passion too, even resulting in an attempt at arson on the checkpoint. The artist described his work as a statement not only upon the ghettoization of Brussels, but the growing separation of the Flemish and Walloon halves of Belgium, and of the increasingly formidable barriers which 'fortress Europe' is throwing up around itself.[14]

Conclusion – a way forward

There is at present a striving to find a more sophisticated, less instrumental and more culturally-nuanced understanding of diversity in cities. We have, for example, seen 'pluricultural urbanism' (see Boudry et al., 2005), 'cosmopolitan urbanism' (Binnie et al., 2006) and 'open cities'.[15] My own preference is for the concept of interculturality because it seems best able to convey the sense of movement and dynamism which characterizes life within and between contemporary globalized cities. According to one writer, it:

> *... reminds us of interaction and encounter, i.e. what happens when a relationship of exchange is established between groups. Whereas multiculturality entails the acceptance of difference, interculturality implies that negotiation, conflict and mutual exchange exist between different groups. (García Canclini, 2006: 166)*

For me, interculturality also implies movement in the identity of individuals and groups – away from fixed and immutable positions to hybrid and multiple identities. It also accepts that conflict is not only inevitable, but a normal part of a healthy and dynamic cosmopolis (Sandercock, 2003). It advocates an agonistic approach which finds new relationships and innovations emerging from mediated conflict, rather than the antagonistic contests which currently characterize many of our diverse cities (Mouffe, 2000).

The 'Intercultural City' approach (Wood and Landry, 2008), is an attempt to equip cities with conceptual and practical toolkits for evolving distinctive governance models which respond to local conditions while riding the waves of global transformation. It maintains that integration is not a process to be undertaken by, or done to, the minorities or newcomers, but a two-way street in which all citizens must travel. In this sense it seeks to move beyond the concept of 'tolerance' (which so easily translates into indifference) to one of active engagement, negotiation and co-creation of the city. It adopts from the business world the notion of 'diversity advantage' based on the idea that, given favourable circumstances, heterogeneity will always outperform homogeneity (Page, 2007). While cities are clearly far more complex than any business, the model argues that if cities can create conditions for – and remove barriers to – inter-ethnic mixing, they are more likely to produce social and economic innovations which contribute to the common good. This notion has been taken up and refined by the Council of Europe in its Intercultural Cities programme.[16] From a pilot project of 11 European cities, the programme is now expanding to take in cities of other continents which are developing and sharing policy and practical experience on what an intercultural city might be. A comprehensive but flexible methodology has evolved which enables cities of very different sizes and context to reappraise themselves 'through an intercultural lens' and to design new alliances, policies and practices (Wood, 2009). A suite of indicators and a process of measurement have been devised, enabling cities to evaluate and compare their strengths and weaknesses (and some of the findings are provided in Part 2 of this volume), and giving them the possibility to take account of global trends but design bespoke solutions appropriate to local conditions.[17] This is important in the context of this volume because it both encourages the city to understand itself more deeply, holistically and culturally, and emboldens and empowers the city to embrace and take ownership of its diversity and shape its destiny, not from fear and exclusion of change, but through generosity of spirit and mutual enterprise.

Box 3.7   Ethnic clubbing and niche entrepreneurialism in the European metropolis

Club culture has changed the modern world. ... By now, clubs are a sector of business, an economic factor, a social authority, a cultural good, a locational advantage. Clubs are music producers. Clubs are creative pools. Clubs are the public. Clubs are niches. Club culture is a part of the modern metropolis and is, among other factors, contributing to its quality. It is indispensable. (http://www.clubcommission.de/content/blogcategory/92/44/, translated from German, visited 07/01/11.)

The above mission statement, formulated by Berlin's so-called Club Commission, an association of club and party organizers in the city, neatly sums up the new stakes that many new clubbing entrepreneurs are claiming in the context of metropolitan centres in the Global North. A recent survey published by Berlin's Tourism Marketing Agency identified clubs as the second most important cultural facilities drawing tourists to the city, just behind museums. Clubbing constitutes a central leisure activity of young adults across Europe. And while Berlin might be the official club cultural capital of contemporary Europe, other metropolitan centres have similarly understood that thriving club scenes as forms of marketable cultural entertainment constitute beneficial location factors in the globalized urban competition for a young and highly skilled labour force, economic investment and tourism. The blueprint for the post-industrial 'creative city' ranks club nightlife highly as a factor that helps to foster creative milieus. Highlighting and promoting marketable cultural events and infrastructures forms part of a tendency in contemporary urban cultural policy-making in many European cities to focus less on the socio-cultural impact that cultural policy might have on resident populations, and instead place greater emphasis on the commercial potential of culture and associated cultural industries.

In European countries, where frameworks of multiculturalism once tended to shape urban cultural policies dealing with ethnic diversity, multiculturalism has broadly been in decline. A variety of reasons can be named here: as a political paradigm, multiculturalism rested on an understanding of state government and society that has – in the UK and Germany – been superseded by neo-liberal, flexible forms of governance that position the state as facilitator rather than provider of services; a change that has also affected cultural policy-making. Politically, multiculturalism has been heavily criticized in countries such as Germany or the Netherlands as being 'too soft' on immigrants, with a political climate in the wake of September 11 and the ensuing focus on Islamist terrorism that favours 'hardline' integration policies. As a result, cultural policy-making that once sought to 'celebrate' and protect ethno-cultural diversity is now, stated in very general terms, more likely to stress its economic potential.

While immigrant populations have officially figured in this economic value-generating scenario primarily in terms of 'festivalization' (as in London's Notting Hill Carnival, Berlin's *Karneval der Kulturen* and other types of event) and ethnic cuisine, a closer look at club cultural developments in European urban centres reveals the emergence of large commercial ethnic club scenes catering almost exclusively to distinct immigrant and post-migrant audiences. Online Asian Club guides list over 20 pages of club events currently taking place in London alone, with a wide range of events from Bombay Dream nights to VIP specials on offer. Music is not necessarily a primary factor that differentiates ethnic clubbing from non-ethnic events. Thus, Kandy Nights at London's club *Piya Piya* promise R'n'B, Hip Hop and Commercial House and Garage before mentioning Indian Breaks, just as Berlin's Night of Taksim foregrounds 'hot RnB' and 'excessive House and Elektro' before adding 'Classics of 1001 Night' at Narva-Lounge. Afro-Caribbean events in Paris, however, focus heavily on particular Caribbean musical genres such as *zouk*, though these in turn are influenced by musical developments in Africa (e.g. *kizomba*) and African diasporas worldwide.

While flyposting in immigrant neighbourhoods used to be the main marketing method for ethnic clubbing ten years ago, today organizers across European cities depend heavily on online social network sites to promote their events. The latter are often held at varying locations, minimizing costs for the organizers and helping them to keep their parties 'fresh' for their demanding audiences. Thus, new types of cultural entrepreneur have emerged from and for the second and third generation of immigrants, though generations can be difficult to mark out in case of ongoing transnational migration patterns (as for the Afro-Caribbean scene in France). They share their general age group's preferences for certain types of leisure practices, such as clubbing, and make heavy use of new social technologies without simply blending into a 'mainstream' generational profile. Ethnic clubbing events in European metropolitan centres are typical instances of new forms of cultural productivity among migrants and post-migrants that rely not on ethnic community organizations or state-sponsored opportunities for socio-cultural engagement, but are market-driven and compete with other commercial leisure offerings that shape the urban fabric. They draw upon global youth cultural influences as well as transnational cultural flows between European centres, former countries of origin and diasporic locations.

These club cultural activities do not depend on funding initiatives or the goodwill of state representatives and/or old-fashioned ethnic community associations, as many migrant cultural activists used to do, but thrive instead on their ability to translate sub-cultural knowledge and social network

(Continued)

(Continued)

contacts into economically successful events. They tend not to be as publicly visible as their more established non-ethnic counterparts, such as the Berlin Club Commission that has given club entrepreneurs a voice recognized by city officials, as quite a few of them operate informally and sporadically. In cities where real estate prices are high, such as London or Paris, some organizers are forced to move to niche locations, often in urban peripheries, such as the many Afro-Caribbean events taking place in the Parisian *banlieues*. Yet they might still be taken as typical examples of a wider ethnic cultural entrepreneurialism that flourishes in European metropolitan centres. Clubbing as a cultural activity can be justified by reference to its economic benefits, above all, regardless of its ethnic inclinations, which in this particular context appear rather as a variant of taste cultures than as ethnic community affairs – despite the composition of audiences. It is the profile of taste preferences in combination with social network contacts that tends to produce mostly mono-ethnic events, not a desire for ethnic segregation. In this sense, ethnic clubbing does not differ from other types of clubbing events that target different audiences based on age, sexual preferences, musical tastes, income categories and the like.

Kira Kosnick

Notes

1 See for example Vito Tanzi (1998) *The Demise of the Nation State?* International Monetary Fund Working Paper, 98/120. Washington, DC: IMF.
2 After all, the nation-states and their central banks remained the refuge of last resort when the global financial system required a bail-out in the financial crash of 2008.
3 See *Mexico City: A Law to Embed Interculturality in the City Policies* at www.coe.int/t/dg4/cultureheritage/culture/Cities/Newsletter/newsletter12/mexico_en.ap.
4 Although this movement is not without its critics, see Raghuram (2009).
5 See www.citydiplomacy.org.
6 See http://pagines.uab.cat/translocalcat/en.
7 For example, the influential Vice-Mayor of Malmö, Sweden, Kent Andersson, has spoken widely on the topic of 'City versus State: Perspectives on urban citizenship in multicultural immigrant societies'. See http://www.international.metropolis.net/events/8th_Vienna_conf_2003/en/Metro_News_Freitag.pdf.
8 The most impressive city response I have seen to a rapid change in demographic circumstances has been in the Intercultural Plan of the city of Barcelona, www.interculturalitat.cat/.
9 See www.inclusivecities.org/Warwick_Junction.html.
10 Streetnet, the international alliance of street vendors which was originally launched in Durban in 2002, has declared a 'World Class Cities For All' Campaign, demanding a new way of dealing with such events, starting with the Commonwealth Games 2010 in Delhi and the 2014 World Cup Finals in Brazil. See www.streetnet.org.za/?page_id=250.
11 Story drawn from interviews conducted by the author. Further information on Subotica's Local Partnerships for Tolerance can be found at http://lda-subotica.org/publikacije/local-partnerships-EN.pdf.
12 More information can be found at www.migrantas.org.
13 See www.ideastore.co.uk/.
14 More information is available at http://emiliolopez-menchero.be/spip.php?article74.
15 See http://opencities.britishcouncil.org/.
16 See www.coe.int/interculturalcities.
17 See the Intercultural Cities Index at www.coe.int/t/dg4/cultureheritage/culture/cities/Index/default_en.asp.

REFERENCES

Agyei-Mensah, S. and Owusu, G. (2010) 'Segregated by neighbourhoods? A portrait of ethnic diversity in the neighbourhoods of the Accra Metropolitan Area, Ghana', *Population, Space and Place*, 16: 499–516.

Allison, P. (ed.) (2006) *David Adjaye: Making Public Buildings*. London: Whitechapel Gallery.

Amin, A. (2002) 'Ethnicity and the multicultural city: living with diversity', *Environment and Planning A*, 34(6): 959–980.

Appadurai, A. (2006) *Fear of Small Numbers: An Essay on the Geography of Anger*. Durham, NC: Duke University Press.

Balbo, M. (ed.) (2005) *International Migrants and the City*. Venice: UN-Habitat and Universita IUAV.

Balbo, M. (2009) 'Social and spatial inclusion of international migrants: local responses to a global process', SSIIM Unesco Chair Paper Series, No. 1. Venice: UNESCO.

Balbo, M. and Marconi, G. (2005) 'International migration, diversity and urban governance in cities of the South', *Habitat International*, 30(3): 706–715.

Barbora, S., Thieme, S. and Siegmann, K. (2010) 'Patterns and politics of migration in South Asia', in H. Hurni and U. Wiesmann (eds), *Global Change and Sustainable Development: A Synthesis of Research Partnerships. Perspectives of the Swiss National Centre of Competence in Research North–South*. Bern: University of Bern, 5: 313–328.

Benton-Short, L., Price, M. and Friedman, S (2005) 'Globalizing from below: the ranking of global immigrant cities', *International Journal of Urban and Regional Research*, 29(4): 945–959.

Binnie, J., Holloway, J., Millington, S. and Young, C. (eds) (2006) *Cosmopolitan Urbanism*. London: Routledge.

Bloomfield, J. and Bianchini, F. (2004) *Planning for the Intercultural City*. Bournes Green: Comedia.

Bodo, S., Gibbs, K. and Sani, M. (eds) (2009) *Museums as Places for Intercultural Dialogue: Selected Practices from Europe*. Bologna: MAP for ID Group.

Boudry, L. et al. (2005) *The Century of the City: City Republics and Grid Cities*. Brussels: Ministry of the Flemish Community.

Brown, A., Lyons, M. and Dankoco, I. (2010) 'Street traders and the emerging spaces for urban voice and citizenship in African cities', *Urban Studies*, 47(3): 666–683.

Burrows, E. and Wallace E. (1999) *Gotham: A History of New York City to 1898*. New York: Oxford University Press.

Cantle, T. (2005) *Community Cohesion: A New Framework for Race and Diversity*. Basingstoke: Palgrave Macmillan.

Castells, M. (1996) *The Rise of the Network Society*. Oxford: Blackwell.

Chantavanich, S. and Vungsiriphisal, P. (2005) 'The case of Bangkok: need for long-term national and municipal policies', in M. Balbo (ed.), *International Migrants and the City*. Vienna: UN-Habitat and Universita IUAV.

Chatterjee, I. (2009) 'Social conflict and the neo-liberal city: a case of Hindu–Muslim violence in India', *Transactions of the Institute of British Geographers*, 34: 143–160.

Cortright, D. (2008) 'Friend not foe: civil society and the struggle against violent extremism', A Report to Cordaid from the Fourth Freedom Forum and Kroc Institute for International Peace Studies at the University of Notre Dame, Notre Dame, IN.

Davis, M. (1992) *City of Quartz: Excavating the Future in Los Angeles*. London: Vintage.

Delgado, E. (2009) 'Museums as spaces of negotiation', in S. Bodo et al. (eds) *Museums as Places for Intercultural Dialogue: Selected Practices from Europe*. Bologna: MAP for ID Group.

Dobson, R., Skinner, C. and Nicholson, J. (2009) *Working in Warwick: Including Street Traders in Urban Plans*. Durban: School of Development Studies, University of Kwazulu Natal.

Elsheshtawy, Y. (2008) 'Transitory sites: mapping Dubai's "forgotten" urban spaces', *International Journal of Urban and Regional Research*, 32(4): 968–988.

Fernandes, E. (2007) 'Implementing the urban reform agenda in Brazil', *Environment and Urbanization*, 19: 177–189.

Fourchard, L. (2011) 'Lagos, Koolhaas and partisan politics in Nigeria', *International Journal of Urban and Regional Research*, 35(1): 40–56.

Fox, J. And Bada, X. (2008) 'Migrant organization and home-town impacts in rural Mexico', *Journal of Agrarian Change*, 8(2/3): 435–461.

García Canclini, N. (2006) *Diferentes, desiguales y desconectados: Mapas de la interculturalidad*. Barcelona: Gedisa.

Grillo, R. (2000) 'Plural cities in comparative perspective', *Ethnic and Racial Studies*, 23(6): 957–981.

Harden, B. (2008) 'Demographic crisis, robotic cure? Rejecting immigration, Japan turns to technology as work-force shrinks', *Washington Post*, January 7.

Hari, J. (2009) 'The dark side of Dubai', *The Independent*, April 7.

Hartley, J. (2005) 'Tower Hamlets' Idea Stores: Are They Working?', A study submitted in partial fulfilment of the requirements for the degree of Master of Arts in Librarianship, University of Sheffield.

Hedetoft, U. (2010) 'Denmark versus multiculturalism', in S. Vertovec and S. Wessendorf (eds), *The Multiculturalism Backlash: European Discourses, Policies and Practices*. London: Routledge.

Hyndman, J., Schuurman, N. and Fiedler, R. (2006) 'Size matters: attracting new immigrants to Canadian cities', *Journal of International Migration and Integration*, 6(I): 1–25.

Kanna, A. (2010) 'Flexible citizenship in Dubai: neoliberal subjectivity in the emerging "city-corporation"', *Cultural Anthropology*, 25(1): 100–129.

Leaf, M. (2010) 'Positioning the urban in Asia's international migration flows', SSIIM Unesco Chair Paper Series, No. 5. Venice: UNESCO.

Mackay, P. (2010) 'The migrating state: Mexico, migrants, and transnational governance.' A dissertation submitted to the Faculty of the Graduate School of the University of Minnesota, Minneapolis, MN.

Morris, A. (1998) '"Our fellow Africans make our lives hell": the lives of Congolese and Nigerians living in Johannesburg', *Ethnic and Racial Studies*, 22(6): 1116–1136.

Mouffe, C. (2000) *Deliberative Democracy or Agonistic Pluralism?* Vienna: Institut fur Hohere Studien.

Nagy, S. (2006) 'Making room for Migrants', *Urban Studies*, 43(1): 119–37

Ndiaye, A. (2005) 'The case of Dakar: a unique opportunity to pre-empt potential problems', in M. Balbo (ed.), *International Migrants and the City*. Venice: UN-Habitat and Universita IUAV.

Ostanel, E. (2010) 'Practice of citizenship: Mozambicans in Johannesburg, South Africa', SSIIM Unesco Chair Paper Series, No. 3. Venice: UNESCO.

Owen, R. (2009) 'Italy bans kebabs and foreign food from cities'. *The Times*, January 31.

Page, S.E. (2007) *The Difference: How the Power of Diversity Creates Better Groups, Firms, Schools and Societies*. Princeton, NJ: Princeton University Press.

Portes, A. and Roberts, B. (2005) 'The free-market city: Latin American urbanization in the years of the neoliberal experiment', *Studies in Comparative International Development*, 40(1): 43–82.

Raghuram, P. (2009) 'Which migration, what development? Unsettling the edifice of migration and development', *Population, Space and Place*, 15(2): 103–117.

Robertson, J. (2010) 'Gendering humanoid robots: robosexism in Japan', *Body and Society*, 16(1): 1–36.

Sandercock, L. (2003) *Cosmopolis 2: Mongrel Cities of the 21st Century*. New York: Continuum.

Sassen, S. (1996) *Losing Control? Sovereignty in an Age of Globalization*. New York: Columbia University Press.

Skinner, C. (2009) 'Challenging city imaginaries: street traders' struggles in Warwick Junction', *Agenda*, 81: 101–109.

Smith, D. (2006) 'Internal migration and the escalation of ethnic and religious violence in urban Nigeria', in Martin J. Murray and Garth Myers (eds), *Cities in Contemporary Africa*. Basingstoke: Palgrave Macmillan.

Somerville, W., Durana, J. and Terrazas, A. (2008) 'Hometown associations: an untapped resource for immigrant immigration?' *MPI Insight*, July, Washington, DC: Migrant Policy Institute.

Stren, R. (2009) *Diversity: A Challenge to Urban Governance*. APSA 2009 Toronto Meeting Paper. Available at SSRN: http://ssrn.com/abstract=1451015.

Thomas, P. (2009) 'Between two stools? The government's "Preventing Violent Extremism" agenda', *The Political Quarterly*, 80(2): 282–291.

Torres, F. and Kuznetsov, Y. (2006) 'Mexico: leveraging migrants' capital to develop hometown communities', in Y. Kuznetsov (ed.), *Diaspora Networks and the International Migration of Skills: How Countries Can Draw on Their Talent Abroad*. Washington, DC: The World Bank.

Tsuda, T. (2000) 'Acting Brazilian in Japan: ethnic resistance among return migrants', *Ethnology*, 39(1): 55–71.

UNDP (United Nations Development Programme) (2010) *From Migration to Development: Lessons Drawn from the Experience of Local Authorities*. Brussels: UNDP.

Van Liempt, I. (2010) '"And then one day they all moved to Leicester": the relocation of Somalis from the Netherlands to the UK explained', *Population, Space and Place*, 17(3): 254–66.

Vertovec, S. (2007) 'Super-diversity and its implications', *Ethnic and Racial Studies*, 29(6): 1024–1054.

Vertovec, S. and Wessendorf, S. (eds) (2010) *The Multiculturalism Backlash: European Discourses, Policies and Practices*. London: Routledge.

Wood, P. (ed.) (2009) *Intercultural Cities: Towards a Model for Intercultural Integration*. Strasbourg: Council of Europe.

Wood, P. and Landry, C. (2008) *The Intercultural City: Planning for Diversity Advantage*. London: Earthscan.

CHAPTER 4

CITIES AND UNIVERSITIES: A VIRTUAL CULTURAL POLICY NEXUS
Dragan Klaic

Universities are obviously important cultural players, yet they are rarely associated with cultural policy-making at the municipal level. The author of this essay explores the unexploited potential of city–university partnerships for the sake of a different kind of 'joined-up' approach to cultural policy that can benefit urban populations at large as well as the academic communities. He discusses various complementarities of interests, cites a number of exemplary cases or practices, as well as failed initiatives, and finally makes a number of practical recommendations for both university administrators and municipal authorities.

Introduction

Cities and their cultural strategies have occupied the central place in the cultural policy discourse for more than a decade, thanks to the urban revitalization agenda and its cultural component, but also because of the various creativity, creative city (Landry 2000, 2006) and creative class (Florida 2002) approaches. All these have generated powerful metaphors and kindled considerable municipal ambitions. Indeed, as Isar, Hoelscher and Anheier point out in their Introduction to this volume, under contemporary accelerated globalization, cities have become 'mixing bowls' of cultural policy, breeding grounds for new ideas and instruments, involving a 'broader mix of actors', both public and private, and a wide range of non-governmental organizations and initiatives. What curiously seem to be missing from this large cast of cultural players are universities – these institutions of higher learning are usually not associated with innovative cultural policy making on the municipal level and the broad coalitions that it successfully generates.

My intention in this essay is to explore the potentials of city–university partnerships in articulating a 'joined-up' cultural policy for the benefit of both the academic community and the urban population at large. My thesis is that municipal public authorities and universities need each other to shape an effective cultural policy, one that is capable of resisting the leveling, uniformizing impact of globalization and can produce a distinctive urban cultural constellation with clear competitive advantages. University resources complement the available municipal infrastructure of cultural provision, but an advanced level of strategic partnership would greatly enhance the appeal and standing of a university, the attractiveness of a city and the satisfaction of its inhabitants. I will explore here the complementarity of interests and resources and analyze why such partnerships are in practice quite rare and difficult to achieve and sustain. I shall cite some exemplary cases and practices, failed or abandoned initiatives and potential forms of collaboration, and will conclude with policy recommendations to the municipal authorities and university administrators.

Universities determine the identity and the appeal of many cities, especially in Europe, and are often the major employers and the biggest owners of real estate, hubs of major consumption of goods and services, economic forces bringing in public subsidies from outside, especially through grants, as well as tuition fees and private and corporate donations. The academic community – faculty, staff and students – is, because of its educational level, considered a primary cultural audience even though its actual participation in providing cultural offer might be curbed by the pressures of the academic schedule and workload. And yet, universities are often mediocre or even bad institutional citizens and town–gown relationships tend to sour and become degraded into mutual alienation and acrimony or, in the best case, mutual indifference. The impact of universities is stronger in smaller cities, but bigger cities with several universities are also beginning to appreciate the influence of their academic hubs and the value of their cultural resources for the appeal of the city itself and its quality of life.

Types of town–gown engagement

In order to develop a tentative typology of town–gown cultural policy engagement, the size of the city would figure as a primary variable. Hence a distinction could be made among:

- small European and US cities (population 50,000–150,000) whose significance has been historically determined by the long-standing operation of a university, such as Siena, Oxford, Tübingen, Coimbra, Leiden, Salamanca, Uppsala, Lund, Tartu, and also Cambridge (MA), New Haven (CT), Princeton (NJ), Palo Alto (CA) and Ann Arbor (MI), in the United States;
- large metropolitan cities that have experienced a multiplication of higher education institutions, now engaged in competition with each other, e.g., Paris, London, Berlin, Moscow, Barcelona, Istanbul, Singapore, Los Angeles, Boston, New York, Tokyo, Buenos Aires, or Rio de Janeiro; each city has a rich cultural infrastructure and its academic community is only one of its major cultural consumption constituencies;
- mid-size cities (population 150,000–750,000) that are severely affected by de-industrialization and seek to redefine their development options and priorities through a stress on knowledge generation and cultural production (Rotterdam, Lublin, Lodz, Leipzig, Goteborg ...), for which purpose they might benefit substantially from their academic resources and university cultural provisions.

Globalization has generated fierce competition for visibility, prestige and distinction among cities within each of these categories. Cities are increasingly competing with similar cities of comparative size for investment, employment opportunities, high knowledge labor force and tourists. They see their cultural resources as features that enhance the city's distinction and appeal and thus invest in their development and excellence. Hosting a university also reinforces a city's attractiveness and status, offers educational and cultural opportunities in addition to economic ones, and assures some retention of talented and ambitious young people who would otherwise pursue their education and career elsewhere. Universities are also increasingly competing for the best students and faculty, for star professors who attract outstanding graduate students and grants, for participation in externally funded research consortia, for philanthropic donations and corporate sponsorship in the form of grants, endowed chairs and stipends for students. Competition among universities for foreign students has become fierce in Europe, where the Bologna process and the Erasmus program of the EU have been major drivers of student mobility. In the USA, whose top research universities traditionally appeal to ambitious prospective graduate students from abroad, a more selective severe student visa issuance regime, imposed by the US government after 9/11, caused major concerns, voiced by Richard Florida (2005) and the presidents of the leading research universities which experienced a 30 per cent drop in foreign applications for graduate studies.

In seeking to articulate their own strategy to confront the contradictory challenges of globalization, as discussed by Hopper (2007) and many others, every city has good reason to take their university seriously since it is often the most globalized local institution – thanks to the international engagement and reputation of its faculty members and the presence of foreign students, but also in terms of the knowledge generated by different programs and departments, their research focus and output that cover a broad range of scientific fields, including distant cultures and societies, address global issues of major concern and contribute to international debates. In other words, universities often possess a concentration of knowledge pertaining to globalization that cities need to absorb in order to determine their own positions and development strategies. And in the opposite case, if the university is mediocre and utterly provincial, without international connections and reputation, disconnected from the major research on globalization issues and its foremost issues, it is very much in the interest of the city to stimulate such universities to open up and raise the level of their ambition.

With advanced de-industrialization, many cities have no other feasible future course than to focus on knowledge economy, concentrated around the university, and hope that its graduates and spin-off R&D companies will usher the city into a new economic cycle of growth, employment and a strengthened tax base. Appealing to prospective students from elsewhere and retaining 'native' university graduates are crucial city interests but feasible only if adequate jobs are available locally and if there is a vibrant cultural climate, affordable housing and other amenities. Hence some cities cooperate with the universities to create science quarters, hubs and corridors, facilitate university expansion with the help of their urban planning agencies and undertake substantial infrastructural investments in order to make construction ground available and equipped for such expansion. Inevitably, such plans raise complex issues of circulation, mass transit, parking, inhabitants and business resettlement, and could provoke confrontations with opposing civic groups and business interests. They are also sensitive to shifts in the economic climate. Before the economic recession of 2008 exploded, Yale University bought a former Bayer research campus of 135 acres in West Haven, containing 1.5 million square feet of building space. Yale is determined to concentrate its new interdisciplinary life science institutes there, although the process has been slowed down by the budget cuts that the shrinking value of the university endowment has imposed (www.yaledailynews. com). New York University's expansion plans, not only of its core campus in its Greenwich Village neighborhood, but in the uptown direction, along Sixth Avenue, by creating a 'health boulevard', have been received with enthusiasm by the construction industry, dispirited in the post-recession building slump, but guardedly by residents and local businesses.[1] Columbia University also has ambitious campus expansion plans in Upper Manhattan that will inevitably affect some residential areas. The trend to develop scientific hubs, quarters and corridors originates from the huge ground holdings of Stanford University, made partially available to various R&D spin-off enterprises and that ultimately spawned the Palo Alto–San Jose corridor, famous for an unprecedented concentration of advanced digital technology companies.

But how about cultural quarters that are jointly developed by the universities and cities? Here examples are quite rare, even though North American and European universities usually have museums, art galleries and performing arts centers that serve the academic community as well as the general public in the surrounding areas. These cultural facilities complement other cultural publicly supported facilities in the city. In some smaller towns, they provide the only cultural facility of merit. Yet interactions are not common and physical proximity does not necessarily induce cooperative attitudes between the university and municipal cultural organizations, especially as they belong to distinct administrative regimes and rely on separate funding streams. Thanks to the availability of the National Lottery money for the buildup of cultural facilities since 1994 (Bodo et al. 2004), there were in the UK several initiatives where universities, local authorities and the Arts Council collaborated to make use of this funding source and jointly create new cultural infrastructure complexes, as in Southampton, for instance. Some European cities, such as Coimbra and Vilnius, have taken advantage of the availability of the EU structural funds to revitalize their historic urban core and upgrade the context of historic university buildings and renovate them.

Municipal authorities tend to see universities on their territory as prestige enhancers and economic engines and expect that students will contribute to the vivacity of city life and spend money on leisure and culture. Local cultural organizations look at the universities as a reservoir of audience rather than as sources of relevant knowledge for their own institutional development or as sources of future qualified employees. These assumptions are often rather unrealistic, especially if students tend to remain within their sometimes remote campuses, or spend their free time in their own student cultural centers, or if many of them work hard throughout the week and then commute home for the weekend, to close-by towns and villages, thus missing the weekend attractions of the city cultural offer. With high tuition and more demanding study regimes, students in many countries have less leisure time than is often assumed, especially if they have to work several hours per week to generate extra income (Ethis et al. 2010: 50). Additionally, altered patterns of culture consumption apply to students as well: consumption of ready-made, mass-marketed, globalized cultural products prevails over locally made culture; limited involvement in cultural production – the decline of the traditional student amateur culture; the professionalization of student cultural centers; a shift to the self-made home cultural production with digital means – *YouTube* culture, as examined by Holden (2007), that enmeshes creation, production and distribution through digitization. So students spend more leisure time surfing on the internet, preoccupied with downloaded films and music or creating their own digital cultural output than attending live events or visiting museums. If they are eager to create their own cultural products, if they seek hands-on experiences, they tend to do so within university/student circles more than in the local cultural organizations that habitually offer limited participative opportunity. With increasingly diverse student populations, especially in Europe and USA, it is becoming more difficult for cultural institutions to cater to the interests of a diverse potential student audience.

Most public universities feel dependent on national ministries of education and national research funds that determine their funding, admission and study regime and faculty appointments procedures. Whether public or private, universities need the municipal authorities for the approval of their building plans, for the improvement of public transport connections, street lighting, security and parking, and for the creation of student housing, or as an interface that can help establish and nurture ties with the local business, seen as potential sponsors, donors or partners. In all these cases, universities see municipal authorities as regulators (building permits!), investors and technical facilitators. But usually not more than that. And the local cultural organizations are in the best case perceived as places where students in culture-related disciplines can perhaps do their internships. If these expectations are not fulfilled, universities become sulky and frustrated, which in turn makes it easier for the municipal authorities and cultural organizations to perceive them as self-centered and spoiled with privilege.

Cases and issues across the world

Town–gown relations have a long adversarial history in Europe since medieval times, when students at the oldest universities enjoyed the protection of the ecclesiastic authorities and thus could not be pursued by the municipalities for their unruly lifestyle and the havoc they often caused. In subsequent centuries, the urban population came to perceive students as a privileged, spoiled group that with its wealth and lifestyle provoked outrage or jealousy. Riots between students and other urban young people are a common occurrence in the history of European and North American university cities. Attitudes did change with the democratization of higher education after the Second World War, but again the political radicalization of students in the 1960s and the sexual revolution (sex, drugs and rock 'n' roll) often provoked the resentment of other city dwellers. With decentralization, universities had to deal more with the local authorities, but primarily for procedural, administrative and technical matters, not cultural policy articulation.

The limited town–gown relationships in cultural matters are best visible in the record of the European Capitals of Culture, a flagship EU cultural program, which has been running since 1985. Among some 44 cities that have carried the label so far, practically none, it seems, has made a local university or universities a strategic stakeholder in the development and the implementation of the program. This emerges from comprehensive evaluations of the program, e.g., Palmer-Rae Associates (2004) and Sassatelli (2009). Only Liverpool, European Capital of Culture in 2008, engaged two local universities to design a comprehensive monitoring and impact evaluation methodology. Among forthcoming capitals, Umea, a seventeenth-century city in the remote north of Sweden, devastated in a fire in 1888, has reached 120,000 inhabitants primarily thanks to its university, established in 1965, that with its 30,000 students and 2,000 faculty members actually determines its urban identity. Its plans for 'Cultural Capital 2014' count on several serious cooperation projects with the university in digital creation and open source software. The bid of the Dutch city of Utrecht for European Capital of Culture 2018 is being developed by the *Vreede van Utrecht*, a cultural organization, set up originally by the city and the province to develop a range of programs for the celebrations of 300 years of the Treaty of Utrecht in 2013 around the notion of a 'culture of peace'. In the meantime, *Vreede van Utrecht* has become a flexible, multifaceted cultural organization, delivering innovation, large thematic template programming and broad local and international collaborations, with a strong and steady involvement of the Utrecht University, its faculty and its international network.

The conceptual architecture of the Polish city of Lublin's bid for 2016 contains 'culture of knowledge' as one of the four main themes, and counts on the input of the local cluster of universities and colleges that account for 100,000 students in the city of 350,000 inhabitants. Without the modernization and development of the university curriculum, especially in culture-related disciplines, the city (that has tripled its culture budget in only five years and absorbs substantial cultural investments of the EU structural funds) could not count on having a critical mass of competent professionals to carry out the cultural capital program and run an expanding and revitalized cultural infrastructure.[2]

It would be one-sided to blame only cities for their inability to recognize universities as the strongholds of cultural knowledge generation – of the knowledge they need for their own cultural development and policy articulation. Universities are not easy to engage as partners. Formal commitment of university administrators and municipal leaders and formal cooperation agreements are not as a rule followed up. They rarely deliver the promised or expected impact. Universities are also difficult to engage because of their super-specialization, hierarchical authority and increased bureaucratic burden on the exercise of the core functions of teaching and research. Universities tend to operate through schools, departments, centers and institutes, while cities need combined, multifaceted, interdisciplinary know-how that can be delivered promptly only by special task forces or working teams. Faculty members, burdened with their core tasks and pressured to seek external funding for research projects and the placement of PhD students and post-docs, are also reluctant to adjust their own research interests to the needs emerging in their cultural context. Consequently, cities prefer to pay expensive outside consultants rather than to seek to package interdisciplinary academic teams that could address the complexity of urban culture from a range of interrelated disciplines: arts, cultural studies, cultural management, economy of culture, cultural policy, urban sociology and anthropology, etc.

The accreditation procedures of specific programs and degrees in North America and more recently also in Europe require some validation not only of academic peers but also from the professional field and alumni, and this is an opportunity for the cultural infrastructure to exercise some influence on the content of academic programs, curricula, the profile of the graduates and the competences they need to acquire in order to enhance their employability. Yet obviously these will involve slow and difficult processes of change and adjustment. Ambitious junior faculty members who seek to participate in the local cultural life and improve its constellation through research and knowledge generation prefer often to do so though their own private enterprises or non-profit NGOs rather than through the university infrastructure, where they expect to be blocked by senior faculty's indifference and bureaucratic impediments. Senior professors with established reputations also prefer to operate as soloist consultants and pocket extra fees rather than to involve their own colleagues and students through a university-framed arrangement. When universities or their schools and departments deliver continuous education packages and programs for culture professionals at the request of the public authorities, the commissioning party and the financier are national ministries, and their agencies are more often than not municipal authorities. An ambitious cultural program for the Polish presidency of the EU in the second half of 2011 contained a broad training program for cultural professionals: this was not assigned by the Ministry of Culture to any university but to the National Audiovisual Institute.

Universities in most parts of the world are exposed to public subsidy cuts and thus seek to diversify their funding sources. In Europe, but also in Asia, most universities are not very handy in pursuing this orientation since they neglect some obvious instruments, such as the systematic tracking of their alumni (considered in the USA to be the most precious capital and hence relentlessly pursued for voluntary contributions throughout their lifetimes!). And they fail to address their own immediate neighbors – city administrations and city cultural institutions, who could also pay them for the research and training services rendered – at much lower rates than those professional consultants charge.

Many culture departments of municipal administration do not have a set research and development budget and do not have the time and competences for a steady process of cultural policy innovation. Some of them lost specialized knowledge in a series of reorganizations and reductions of the city admin-istration staff, so that small units have became responsible for culture, sport, youth and perhaps even social welfare, a broad portfolio eliminating the chance of specialization among the staff. They are chiefly preoccupied with the subsidy allocation cycle, administration of the cultural infrastructure and its supervision, cultural investments, inter-national contacts and projects; sometimes they are directly involved in the organization of cultural manifestations or at least the coordination of such activities. Too often they act as a fire brigade, man-aging one or another urgent crisis in the city's cul-ture, an institutional deficit here or a conflict there. In many places these departments lack analytic and planning capacities, have not developed sys-tematic monitoring and evaluation procedures that would help them with the subsidy allocation among an increased number of applicants, and have only a vague notion of the cultural needs and preferences of the urban culture public and its specific constitu-encies. Thus there are enough tasks for which a city administration could engage university resources in research, consulting and policy instruments innova-tion. Every academic year, for instance, students in culture-related disciplines deliver a huge number of seminar papers, graduate and master theses on topics no one outside the university is much inter-ested in since faculty departments and programs do not orchestrate and cluster student research, even a very preliminary and pedestrian one, according to the knowledge needs in the city cultural administra-tion and cultural infrastructure.

The rare attempts to engage universities in urban cultural development sometimes fail. Some years ago Universitaet der Kuenste and Technische Uni-versitaet (TU) in Berlin staged a week-long series of seminars and workshops in order to collect ideas on how to revitalize their common neighborhood – Charlottenburg in the former West Berlin – which lost vibrancy and buzz after the reunification of the city, when much cultural action moved northeast, to Prenzlauerberg, and southeast, to Kreuzberg and Friedrichshein. No visible follow-up came from this initiative and the websites of both universities say nothing about their immediate urban context and its cultural provisions. The Center of Metropolitan Studies at the TU is more historically oriented in its research, while its recent publications, which address some current urban culture issues, do not have a specific Berlin focus. A working group that a

TU runs with the Freie Universitaet and Humboldt Universitaet, in cooperation with some Berlin muse-ums, is also focusing on the historic aspects of the urban space, not on contemporary Berlin cultural issues. The Universitaet der Kuenste has a working group researching the cultural industry dynamics in the city.

Vienna's Universitaet fuer angewandte Kunst (University of Applied Arts), a mid-nineteenth-century institution derived from the need to train museum professionals, enjoys an university status since 1970. It offers a broad range of undergraduate and graduate programs in design, art theory, practice and teaching – among which is a post-graduate program in urban strategies. Its rather assertive mission statement positions the institution as:

a determining cultural-political engine for Vienna and Austria, and a leading information and expertise centre for its subject areas. We see the 'Angewandte's' mission in the generation of a social future, for each field of study. On issues of cultural and educational policy, the 'Angewandte' shall take a clear, public stance, raise issues, and make the work of its teachers and students even more visible. We want to influence the cultural climate in Vienna and Austria. Our expertise, our future-oriented approach and our national and international networking should make us an indispensable factor in cultural politics. (www. dieangewandte.at)

And yet, there is very little discernible evidence about the implementation of this mission statement.

A remarkable initiative to turn a former power plant in Istanbul, located at the northern end of the Golden Horn, into a university and culture hub turned into a disappointment. Privately owned Bilgi University leased from the Turkish Ministry of Energy some 110,000 square meters of Santral, a former power plant that was decommissioned in the 1980s, with the intention of building its third campus, open-ing two museums, and creating a visiting artists', residence and adjacent cultural facilities. The cam-pus was indeed built, with efficient classrooms and office blocks; the envisaged artists' residence became a boutique hotel and then a high-class stu-dent dorm; the museum of energy (the former power plant installation) has a low profile and is focused on the educational market, and the modern arts museum has no collection and operates as a *Kunsthalle*, with only occasional exhibits, on loan from elsewhere. The Istanbul public comes to Santral chiefly for a few upper-class restaurants; there is also a small theater with 60 seats and a student cafeteria, but no coherent development perspective nor a synergy between the educational and cultural function. The reason is that the private owner of the Bilgi University, needing capital to develop Santral, entered into a partnership with a US commercial education company, then had a conflict with it. The US company now owns the entire university and might neglect its academic excellence and international orientation in the humanities in order to maximize profits by stressing other, more lucrative disciplines. The Turkish partner remains in charge of the Santral complex but without visible development strategy and resources (www.santralistanbul.org/main/index/). The municipal authorities of Greater Istanbul were involved only indirectly, by building a tunnel and adjacent roads that made Santral much more accessible from both sides of the Golden Horn and eliminated habitual traffic jams, but the complex remains cut off from its neighborhood, which is slowly turning from a poor into a lower middle-class one. That Istanbul was European Cultural Capital 2010 did not prompt the municipality to get involved in profiling and developing Santral.

Looking beyond Europe, one notes Singapore's transition from a harbor facility and banking center into an educational stronghold, with its ambitious buildup of university infrastructure and cultural amenities, often as a part of a university. The investment comes from the national government as Singapore is practically a city state, and cultural policies are articulated on the national level, through the Arts Council, which acts as an arts subsidy distributor, owner of several cultural venues and occasionally also as a censor. The Lasalle College of the Arts, established in 1984 as a non-profit public institution, receives financial support of the Ministry of Education. It moved to a new architecture landmark campus in 2007, broadened the range of advanced degrees, recruited an international faculty and student body and clearly aims to develop the 'creative class' that would boost Singapore as a cultural industry hub. Its public programs, including those for children, and ample venues and exhibit spaces enrich the existing cultural offer, host foreign artists and affirm the cultural diversity that marks Singapore (www.lasalle.edu.sg).

In China, it is much more difficult to discern any clear future-oriented city–university dynamics in the cultural sphere. Entire new cities are being rapidly built, existing cities are expanding exponentially, new universities are being set up, and established universities are becoming increasingly ambitious in relation to advanced research and cooperation with leading universities elsewhere. The latter in turn see the former as a recruitment pool for excellent PhD students and post-docs. Most universities have some cultural facilities and programming, rather tightly controlled, and occasionally host foreign artistic programs. International artists complain, however, that they often feel that they are being dumped by their Chinese intermediaries on a fortuitously chosen, unprepared student audience, that they are expected to cover all their expenses on a Chinese tour and earn practically nothing as a result. Municipal authorities act primarily as controlling agents, not as partners, requesting much in advance, ample pictorial and textual documentation about the programs to be featured and often delaying the authorizations that are legally required. A prevailing climate of party control and well-guarded topical taboos does little to enhance city–university cultural cooperation (Klaic 2007).

In Latin America, especially in Mexico, Argentina and Brazil, universities have nourished a tradition of critical cultural production and analysis, an activist stance of both the faculty and students, linking cultural development with socio-economic emancipation and poverty eradication through extramural engagement with deprived urban areas. A theoretical critique of the cultural dimensions of globalization, of cultural industry as a tool of imperialism, of monopolies and elitism, has been translated in continuous engagement with underprivileged groups. Cooperation with the municipal and federal state authorities is problematic because the latter tend to feed their political clients. In Mexico, where the Mexican Autonomous University has been a major hub of cultural production and programming thanks to its autonomy, a political switch of the national government after the defeat of the PRI to a neoliberal economic program weakened the involvement of the public authorities in cultural matters. In Argentina, public subsidies for culture on all levels are pitiful and even non-profit cultural production, on and off campus, relies chiefly on private patronage and sponsorship. In Brazil, under President Lula, the Ministry of Culture developed ambitious programs of cultural development as part of general social development, relying on university knowhow and cultural resources, but the reality is that several thousand municipalities have no cultural budget at all and thus cannot act as cultural players. Major corporations, however, have become major financial supporters of culture, but mainly in large cities.

Despite the enormous political and cultural shifts that took place in South Africa with the end of apartheid, universities there remain rather isolated communities and separate cultural zones, while the public authorities have radically slashed cultural budgets, now focusing on cultural industry stimulation rather than on public culture as an inclusive, emancipatory trajectory. But even these efforts have been compromised by rampant corruption and clientelism.

A new – and fascinating – question on the horizon concerns the Arab world. What will be the cultural consequences of the ongoing turmoil there, especially in Egypt, a major cultural producer for the entire region, but burdened with decades of dictatorship, huge poor and uneducated masses and unemployed university graduates who received a mediocre education? Or in Tunisia, with its high educational levels? Since the 1962 turn to 'socialism' and then in 1978 to neo-liberal market principles, the Egyptian authorities have neglected the 540 cultural centers established in the Nasser period of nationalism and Pan-Arabism, leaving them to decay physically and with scant funding for cultural activity. Moreover, the policy of guaranteed public employment for all university graduates overstaffed these centers and turned idle employees into indifferent bureaucrats (Salah Seddik 2011). The question now is to what extent an inchoate multiparty system and strengthened civil society can engage with both cultural players and universities. How can the cultural sector and civil society re-enforce each other and what synergies are imaginable between the public authorities and impoverished universities? The tensions between orthodox and/or fundamentalist Islamic and secular notions of culture and society will be certainly a major issue. Even during the Mubarak decades, government censorship and control over cultural production had its informal but influential counterpart in fundamentalist, puritan and grassroots opposition to contemporary arts, public interaction between men and women in artistic programs, public display of the human body and artistic experimentation and innovation in general. Such vigilante pressures will not fade away with the end of

dictatorship. An analysis of the cultural policies in eight Arab countries, following the methodology of the Council of Europe's *Compendium of Cultural Policies* (www.culturalpolises.net) offers valuable insights on the complexities of this cultural constellation. Some recommendations, formulated by a conference organized by the European Cultural Foundation (Hamersveld 2010), remain valid, but others need to be reviewed in the light of altered political circumstances. The municipal authorities will need to gradually rid themselves of their authoritarian attitudes while universities need to be strengthened and modernized before the two sides can engage as productive partners around some shared objectives. While these processes as well as the revitalization of public cultural centers can take many years to unfold, emerging civil society structures will have to assume the role of brokers, intermediaries and major cultural supporters, but they will inevitably reflect ideological differences and conflicting political orientations and affiliations with still to be formed political parties. So a complicated and uncertain future is to be expected.

One can perhaps clarify matters a bit by looking at Turkey, where the authoritarian and nationalist values of the Kemalist Republic clash increasingly with the re-Islamization of society, promoted in particular since 2002 by the ruling AKP party and where 87 state universities, closely supervised by a Higher Educational Council, in charge of academic appointments and curricula, have been supplemented with a growing number of private universities – some academically ambitious, such as Bilgi, some driven by various ideologies, and some by profit-making and even money laundering. These universities often have cultural functions and train future culture professionals, but they do not interact with the municipal authorities. In big cities, such as Istanbul, Ankara and Izmir, where several universities co-exist and compete, it would also be difficult to imagine how some structural city–university partnerships could be shaped. The AKP-run municipalities prefer, if at all, to communicate with universities that share its Islamic orientation, in pragmatic matters rather than in cultural policy development. A recent civil society report on cultural policy in Turkey (Ince 2011) shows that a rather vibrant civil society in Turkey, with much autonomous (NGO) cultural production, finds it difficult to engage with the universities as much as with the municipal or national authorities.

Such differences in mentality and interest are visible even in pluralist, democratic societies, such as the USA. Harvard and MIT are major cultural players in the Boston area, the University of Wisconsin in Madison, the University of Michigan in Ann Arbor, Case Western in Cleveland, the University of Indiana in Bloomington, Washington University in St Louis, and so on. Universities in many cities nurture a strong public profile, seek to enlarge and diversify their audience beyond the limits of the academic community, and reach out to poorer neighborhoods for community arts projects. However remarkable and productive these engagements are, they lack a town–gown policy basis, because most US cities have a very limited cultural policy remit and means, if at all. In addition, cities and towns run by conservative political forces often mistrust their universities as bulwarks of liberalism, progressivism and radical cultural critique and production.

There are some encouraging potentials in town–gown cultural cooperation, especially in Europe. Gothenburg University researchers in Sweden have articulated a comprehensive critique of the urban and cultural policies of the city, focused on real estate appreciation and neglecting integration and cultural participation of the underprivileged, mostly of immigrant background. They have imposed their views in public debates and have to some extent modified the attitudes and priorities of the city administration (Klaic 2009). In Malmö, also a city marked by immigration, post-industrial strategies center on research, knowhow, culture and creativity, also under the pressure of increased accessibility to Copenhagen with its rich cultural offer, now easy to reach via a new bridge. The danger is that creative people work and spend leisure time in Copenhagen and use Malmö only as a cheaper housing location, turning it into a dormitory city. The city seeks to connect Malmö institutions of higher education in joint programs and projects with the university in nearby Lund, especially in cultural and artistic disciplines resources. The candidacy of the Danish city of Arhus for the European Capital of Culture Program in 2017 seeks to involve smaller towns in north Jutland, but also relies on the cultural expertise and production of the large Arhus University. The Hague, a city that profiles itself as an international capital of peace and justice with numerous juridical institutions, specialized courts and arbitration bodies, was until 2010 rather

supportive of the initiative of the Superior School of Music and Visual Arts, *Residenzorchester* and the Nederlands Dance Theater, and supported the creation of a large integrated cultural and arts education complex in the very center of the city, in place of the Philips concert hall and Rem Kolhaas-designed Lucent Dance Theater, seeing it as a strong card in a bid to become European Capital of Culture in 2018. Harsh culture subsidy cuts, announced by the national government in 2010, and the reduction in the city's culture budget imposed by significant deficits resulting from the 2008–9 recession and construction slump, have dampened these ambitions. In the eastern part of Germany (ex-German Democratic Republic), Dresden and Leipzig, both with de-industrialization and a shrinking population, have considerable potential to engage with universities to enliven the local cultural scene and articulate a cultural development perspective around both revitalization of the rich cultural heritage and stimulation of contemporary cultural production. In London, the artistic departments of King's College seek partnership with the cultural and research facilities in the city in order to make artistic practice and research permeate other fields. However, especially in the UK, as pointed out by McGuigan (2004), but in other countries as well, university research has shifted from critical analysis and theoretical and practical elaboration of the public culture, its autonomy, inclusiveness and diversity, experimental drift and innovative temper, to a research focus on the potentially profit-making cultural industries that can more easily acquire external funding. And yet, as the cultural economist David Throsby (2010) argues consistently, the chief goal of a cultural policy is the production of cultural and not economic value. In several cities, the buildup of university campuses in the midst of urban slums and post-industrial debris (Porto Maduro in Buenos Aires, Raval in Barcelona) has had a magnetic effect and has prompted further development in quality housing, leisure facilities and general intensification of urban life. In contrast, university campuses in rural areas and very small places seem almost condemned to a self-centered existence.

The least universities can do to legitimate themselves as public cultural players is to set up their own cultural centers, clearly oriented to the urban intellectual public, with a program of lectures and discussions, in cooperation with the city cultural institutions, as the University of Amsterdam has done with its *Spui 23* platform. Or they can run their own festivals, in cooperation and with the assistance of the municipal authorities, seeking a city-wide impact and off-campus density of events, enlivening public spaces, and relying on their own international networks. The festival concepts and accents vary: international programming (in the Hungarian town of Szeged), advanced contemporary music (Huddersfield, UK), cultural diversity, interculturalism and inclusion (De Montfort University in Leicester, UK). Inevitably, these festivals also serve student recruitment or seek to boost the professional career prospects of arts and culture students.

A framework for innovation

The difficulties in shaping town–gown cultural cooperation and endorsing it with strong policy development foundations can be interpreted in a historical perspective: many universities, and not only in Europe, were established one or two centuries ago as representative institutions of national emancipation and nation and state building, with a curriculum and functions designed to buttress national identity. Globalization, the weakening of the nation-state remit through regional and even continental integration, migration, the explosive development of cultural industries and the digital revolution have altered these premises completely. Yet universities remain mostly parts of a national system and are administered, funded and supervised by national governments. They thus see ministries of education and research as their primary interlocutor.

In France, for instance, where a culture–university research and discussion platform has been in existence for quite a while, the Minister of Higher Education and Research recently appointed a commission to articulate a vision of universities as major cultural players. This commission, chaired by the sociologist Emmanuel Ethis, President of the University of Avignon, engaged in broad dialogue with academic colleagues and culture professionals and came up with no less than 128 rather inspiring recommendations (Ethis et al. 2010). Most of the proposals are applicable to all universities and most also address national government and to some extent regional and département authorities.

Few though are addressed to cities and urban agglomerations with their own cultural covenants.

Nevertheless, some recommendations are relevant to our topic, for instance: the role of universities in the digitization of cultural heritage and in fostering appreciation of the local architectural context, especially in the urban revitalization projects (recommendations 17, 82), the introduction of gastronomic cultures and local cuisine in the university cafeterias (21–22), the integration of university culture in an ecosystem of local cultural opportunities (58), universities as places of great public debates of interest to all citizens (63), attention to the culture/ecology link and absorption of sustainability objectives of the cities as formulated in the *Agenda 21 for Culture* (69), the integration of cultural figures in university governance bodies and of academics in the boards of local cultural institutions (70), the social anchoring of universities through the third life program and intergenerational and continuous learning (78), partnerships with the NGOs in the linkage of cultural and social activism (80), universities hosting programs for the European Cultural Heritage days (81) and celebrating with the city on 21 May, the World Cultural Diversity Day (85), summer terms where students engage in local cultural practices and earn credit points (93), standards for student internships in cultural institutions that will eliminate their treatment as renewable exploitable labor (96), and university-run digital TV and radio stations, in cooperation with the local media (99–101).

But to what extent will municipal politics be ready to seriously address some of these recommendations and recognize their potential benefits? The answer is quite uncertain. The economic and research potentials of the universities seem to them more important than cultural ones. To the many inspiring Ethis Commission proposals one can add some further ideas that imply not only practical cooperation between cities and universities but also innovative, joined-up cultural policy dynamics:

- The city authorities and municipal cultural institutions could engage university research resources to investigate the cultural needs, preferences, habits of the population and their satisfaction with cultural offer, the diversity and the inclusiveness of the culture audience and to design audience development and outreach strategies and actions.

- University faculty could act as advisers in the institutional development of municipal cultural organizations.
- Cities and universities could develop joint planning of urban revitalization and concentration and connectivity of cultural infrastructure.
- University scientific and arts collections and their staff could be used by city museums in a systematic manner.
- Universities could systematically pursue with city cultural organizations the placement of students as interns and ensure that their internship projects are in tune with the curriculum requirements and the host organizations needs.
- Universities, city administrations and local cultural organizations could cooperate in the launch of special events, such as festivals, museum nights, open monument days, and organize seminars, workshops, conferences and other forms of public debate, the continuing education of cultural workers and professionals and lifelong learning.
- Universities and cities could create joint platforms for cultural cooperation or temporary project organizations and teams for specific actions, or some jointly funded permanent organizations, such as observatories, research centers, or consulting firms in the field of culture.
- Cultural facilities and programs run by the university primarily for the academic community could be turned to the benefit of the city public at large and thus warrant co-financing by the city.
- Universities could be involved as partners and stakeholders in any development of a cultural strategy the city might envisage.
- Universities could develop curricular innovations and launch new culture-related specialisms, programs and degrees in accordance with the cultural development needs of the city, possibly with some form of city co-funding.
- The city could award grants to MA and PhD students who study cultural development issues of interest to the local population, thus also co-financing the generation of this needed knowledge.

These suggestions, none of which is either spectacular or revolutionary, taken together with those made by the Ethis Commission, deserve debate in international university platforms, such as the Conference of University Rectors and Presidents, but also in the numerous international networks that bring city officials together for mutual learning, such as Eurocities, the Intercultural Cities program of the Council of Europe, Creative Cities, etc. The recently established network of university research of the European Cultural Capitals planning, execution and evaluation (UnoECC) could also reinforce the university–city relationship, not in the celebratory, mega-festival spirit of these special events, but from the strategic cultural development perspective that would deliver a more lasting benefit of the ECC effort and reinforce its European and local connection.

In conclusion, it is clear that structured cultural cooperation between universities and cities, based on shared cultural policy objectives, offers a perspective of opportunities to be identified, articulated and implemented.

Notes

1 See www.nyu.edu/nyu2031/nyuinnyc/ awareness/growth-progress.php http://www.nyu.edu/nyu2031/nyuinnyc/aware ness/growth-progress.php.
2 See www.kultura.lublin.eu/wiadomosci,1,2368,Lublin_per centE2per cent80per cent93_City_of_Knowledge.html? locale=en_GB.

REFERENCES

Bodo, Carla et al. (eds) (2004) *Gambling on Culture.* Amsterdam: CIRCLE.

Ethis, Emmanuel et al. (2010) *De la culture a l'université. 128 propositions.* Paris: A. Colin. See also http://media.ensei-gnementsup-recherche.gouv.fr/file/2010/59/4/Rapport_ Commission_Culture _Universite_159594.pdf.

Florida, Richard (2002) *The Rise of the Creative Class and How It's Transforming Work, Leisure and Everyday Life.* New York: Basic Books.

—— (2005) *The Flight of the Creative Class: The New Global Competition for Talent.* New York: Harper-Collins.

Hamersveld, Ineke van (ed.) (2010) *Cultural Policies in Algeria, Egypt, Jordan, Lebanon, Morocco, Palestine, Syria and Tunisia*. Amsterdam: Boekman.

Holden, John (2007) *Logging On: Culture, Participation and the Web*. London: Demos.

Hopper, Paul (2007) *Understanding Cultural Globalization*. Cambridge: Polity Press.

Ince, Ayca (ed.) (2011) *Cultural Policy Development in Turkey: A Civic Perspective Report*. Istanbul: KPY Bilgi University.

Klaic, Dragan (2007) 'Chinese performing arts: from communist to globalized kitsch', *IIAS Newsletter* 44 (summer 2007): 18–19.

—— (2009) 'CityScape Gothenburg addresses cultural strategies of urban revival'. Black Sea/North Sea, www.intercult.se.

Landry, Charles (2000) *The Creative City*. Stroud: Earthscan.

—— (2006) *The Art of the City Making*. Stroud: Earthscan.

McGuigan, Jim (2004) *Rethinking Cultural Policy*. Maidenhead, UK: Open University Press/McGraw Hill Education.

Palmer-Rae Associates (2004) *European Cities and Capitals of Culture*. Study prepared for the European Commission. Brussels: Palmer-Rae Associates.

Salah Seddik, Rania (2011) 'Reforming cultural decentralization in Egypt'. Unpublished seminar paper, MA programme in Public Policy. Budapest: CEU.

Sassatelli, Monica (2009) *Becoming Europeans: Cultural Identity and Cultural Policies*. London: Palgrave.

Throsby, David (2010) *The Economics of Cultural Policy*. Cambridge: Cambridge University Press.

CHAPTER 5

CITIES, CULTURE AND SUSTAINABLE DEVELOPMENT
Nancy Duxbury, Catherine Cullen, and Jordi Pascual

Since the turn of the new millennium, cities have been at the heart of initiatives to include culture in sustainability planning and policy discussions, and are linked to the rise of a new, emergent model of sustainability, informed by the ideal of UNESCO's positions on the contributions of cultural diversity to sustainable development, the recovery of historical and culture-specific approaches and worldviews, and local-level community development trends. The new paradigm is being advanced through a wide range of grassroots, varied and experimental initiatives, rooted in a pervasive and heightened concern for public participation. Arguing that the ingredients needed to fully elaborate and impose it are all in play, the authors describe how the United Cities and Local Government's Agenda 21 for Culture *is playing a leadership role as an international connector in this regard.*

Introduction: the culture and sustainability paradigm

Sustainable development is the model of development that 'meets the needs of the present without compromising the ability of future generations to meet their own needs' (Brundtland Report, World Commission on Environment and Development 1987). Policy- and decision-makers are widely adopting and using this model or paradigm to plan the future of our societies. Sustainability, as defined at the UN Conference on Human Environment in Stockholm (1972), the report of the World Commission on Environment and Development, *Our Common Future* (1987), or the Agenda 21 approved in the Earth Summit of Rio de Janeiro (1992), focuses on physical ecology. In the last years of the twentieth century, environmental concerns continued to be the cornerstone of sustainable development. As the concept matures, however, increasing emphasis is being placed on interconnections between the physical ecology and the social and economic dimensions of development, leading to the three-pillar model of sustainability. In recent years, space has opened up for debate and further reflection: the role of culture in sustainability or sustainable development has emerged as a multifaceted topic of interest across a range of disciplines and contexts,[1] with parallel/complementary attention paid in many policy and urban planning contexts and the rise of a 'four-pillar' model of sustainability in a number of countries.

We argue that the 'traditional paradigm', with three dimensions or pillars of sustainable development (environmental balance, economic growth, and social inclusion) is in crisis today because it is incomplete and fails to integrate a key component: the cultural aspects of society. This traditional paradigm ignores culture or, in the best of cases, it underestimates its intrinsic importance and instrumentalizes culture for other purposes. Today, governments, civil society actors, and private companies are acknowledging that culture is a key factor to elaborate and implement local or national development strategies. The traditional paradigm also does not recognize that cultural values ultimately shape what we mean by development and determine how people see the world. In contrast, a cultural diversity approach to development paradigms brings thoughtfulness and openness, and contributes to a world with complementary, pluralized visions of development. Finally, the traditional paradigm is inadequate to address the world's challenges: can anybody neglect that today – besides an economic, a social, and an environmental crisis – the world is facing a severe cultural crisis?

Because of these points of neglect or oversight the traditional sustainability paradigm does not take into account the cultural system referred to in the Introduction to this volume, in other words the overall cultural life of a nation or city. Thus, the cultural system must continually find solid arguments to be given an opportunity to participate in debates on the future of our society with its own voice, and not as a mere instrument. We believe that the culture and sustainable development paradigm, despite the existence of both conceptual and operational challenges, contributes to a renewed platform for future discussions about sustainability. Furthermore, we believe that these discussions are an opportunity to bring together the cultural policies and cultural politics that 'are deployed by distinct communities of analytical practice',[2] including cultural policy consultants, academic researchers, and the broader cultural community itself.

The new paradigm is still in the 'phase of elaboration', following the 'pattern' of T.S. Kuhn (1962) on the evolution of paradigms in the history of science: inconsistencies and failures in the current paradigm have been detected, a growing group of actors make claims for a new paradigm, but the new one is not yet fully coherent. We believe that the new paradigm offers more solutions to major issues than the traditional sustainability paradigm. The new paradigm is useful for the cultural system because it has the potential to bring cultural issues and actors closer to general societal debates. The new paradigm is also useful for analysts and actors of sustainability and development because it better explains our world and our challenges and helps enable a diverse array of adaptations.

Conceptual origins and evolution

While much of Western thought since the Enlightenment has viewed *culture* as separate from

nature, older holistic models of society (such as the traditional medicine wheel of Aboriginal peoples or the Buddhist Dharma-Chakra) situate culture within a unified worldview and provide deep roots for the idea of culture in sustainability/sustainable development. Further groundwork for conceptual and policy development of the new paradigm was laid within a series of reports from UNESCO on culture, development, and cultural diversity, especially from the 1990s on (described below).

The contemporary impetus for culture as a fourth dimension of sustainable development emerges from cities and smaller communities, that is, from the 'grassroots' up (including locally-focused research initiatives) since the turn of the new millennium (Duxbury and Jeannotte, 2010a). More recently, it is being taken up at the national and international levels, building on the earlier results of these locally focused efforts. In these policy/planning contexts, the relation between culture and sustainable development is generally approached in two ways: first, through the development of the cultural sector itself (that is, heritage, creativity, the arts, cultural industries, crafts, etc.) and, second, through ensuring that culture has a place in 'all public policies, particularly those related to education, the economy, science, communication, environment, social cohesion, urban planning, and international cooperation' (UCLG, 2010: 2). Both aspects contribute to conceptualizing a robust role for culture in sustainable development.

In the research literature, four main conceptual threads have been brought forward to understand and position culture within sustainability:

1 *Culture as (tangible and intangible) capital* – these cultural assets with value (Throsby, 1999) are defined broadly as 'traditions and values, heritage and place, the arts, diversity and social history' (Roseland et al., 2005: 12) or more narrowly as built heritage (Gražulevičiūtė, 2006);

2 *Culture as process and way of life*, interacting with an environment and incorporating broader notions of culture as a 'whole way of life' – culture is viewed as an adaptive and iterative process 'born wherever humans had to work out a relationship with nature and themselves' (Nadarajah and Yamamoto, 2007: 22);

3 *Culture as a central binding element* providing the values underlying sustainable (or unsustainable) actions (Rana and Piracha, 2007; Brocchi, 2008) and the link between them; and

4   *Culture as creative expression* providing insights on contemporary society, environmental/sustainability issues and concerns about our future.[3]

However, as Nadarajah and Yamamoto (2007: 9) note, 'there is a dearth of studies and writing that articulate a cultural theory of a sustainable city in which (local) culture becomes a value of its own, not something merely seen as opposite to globalization and responding to it, or something of economic value, or treated as postmodern reading of a text.' In general, initiatives concerning cities, culture, and sustainability are emerging within discourses on culture and (sustainable) development, and in searches for culture-sensitive models of urbanism and city planning.

Culture and (sustainable) development

Many writers from regions such as the Pacific Islands, the Caribbean, and Africa have been adressing concerns of culture within contexts of *development*, then *sustainable development*, for some time (see, for example, Hooper, 2005; Nurse, 2006; Edozien, 2007). *Development* and *sustainable development* are typically addressed as a broad-scope concept in these writings, which emphasize the importance of cultural considerations in development strategies and techniques, reacting against (often imposed) Western development models and looking for more appropriate culturally-sensitive development models. This evolving discourse is inevitably intertwined with UNESCO's initiatives and reports, which have led international public debates on development, culture in development, and sustainable development. For example, Rana and Piracha (2007) cite the 1986 decision of UNESCO to launch the World Decade for Cultural Development (1988–97) and the 1995 report *Our Creative Diversity* as foundational developments. In 1998, the World Bank joined UNESCO in promoting culture in sustainable development (World Bank/UNESCO, 1998, 1999). Today, UNESCO continues to work on making connections between culture, sustainability, biodiversity, and sustainable development. Its *Convention on the Protection and Promotion of the Diversity of Cultural Expressions* (UNESCO, 2005) mentions the relation between culture and sustainable development in two articles:

Article 2, paragraph 6, 'Principle of sustainable development': 'The protection, promotion and maintenance of cultural diversity are an essential requirement for sustainable development for the benefit of present and future generations.'
Article 13, 'Integration of culture in sustainable development': 'Parties shall endeavour to integrate culture in their development policies at all levels for the creation of conditions conducive to sustainable development and, within this framework, foster aspects relating to the protection and promotion of the diversity of cultural expressions.'

In June 2009, the Intergovernmental Committee of the Convention approved operational guidelines for Article 13. Eight measures related to integrating a diversity of cultural expressions into sustainable development were outlined. The guidelines tend to focus on developing countries and the economic aspects of cultural industries, pointing to general facilitating conditions, optimal features for policy development processes, and values of diversity and inclusiveness. They provide conceptual advocacy for inclusion of a cultural dimension in sustainable development but are not fully explained, and remain silent on more organic, underlying cultural ecosystems (Jeannotte and Andrew, 2008).

Despite such efforts to push for the recognition of culture in sustainable development, the UN system has historically not been very supportive. As Kavaliku (2005: 24) notes, 'If we study the major global conferences of the 1990s – from Rio de Janeiro to Barbados, Cairo, Beijing, Copenhagen and Harare – their plans of action were concerned with sustainable development, but there was hardly a mention, even in dispatches, of culture'. In the Earth Summit of Rio de Janeiro (1992), culture is only mentioned in the chapter related to the sustainable development of Aboriginal communities; in the Sustainable Development Summit of Johannesburg (Rio+10) in 2002, the topic of culture as the fourth pillar of sustainability was analyzed at a Round Table convened by Mozambique and France, with very limited impact in the core of the UN system. Although there was noticeable progress during the 1992–2002 decade, the UN system tends to focus on culture as a tool for social cohesion or as an instrument for economic development (Pascual, 2009). The documents preparing the Sustainable Development Summit of Rio de Janeiro in 2012 (Rio+20) are not promising, and as yet do not reflect a full understanding of the values that culture brings to a society.

Looking more specifically at the development of cities, other researchers are investigating approaches to more culturally-sensitive models of city planning, with both conceptual and political dimensions. In general, the work comprises two sets of approaches, which are developed in the following subsections.

Culture-sensitive models of urbanism

The first set of approaches, evident among researchers located mainly in non-Western societies, searches for alternatives to Western models of city-building and urbanism, with many researchers recovering historical approaches to urban sustainability in non-Western contexts (e.g., Paliwal, 2005; Yan et al., 2008). In particular, the Kanazawa Initiative, a major research project (2000–02), examined indigenous Asian patterns of development that provided culturally-sensitive alternatives to Western models (Nadarajah and Yamamoto, 2007). The initiative was a reaction to five interrelated elements: the problematic application of Western planning models to Asian cities; the environmental unsustainability of emulating American lifestyles and development patterns in the context of rapid Asian urbanization; concern about the impact of current urbanization and economic practices on local culture and heritage; conceptual confusion as to what constitutes 'sustainable cities'; and the lack of a cultural dimension in the literature on sustainable urbanism. Rooted in detailed case studies, it put forward four alternate approaches towards 'culturally sensitive sustainable urbanism':

1 *Internal cultural transformation* – Based on 1,500 years of urban history and cultural practices in Patan, Nepal, sustainability is defined as a dialogical equilibrium maintained in three sets of relationships: between *man and economy* (economic pursuits), between *man and man* (social heterogeneity), and between *man and nature* (environment and ecology). Culture is the active process that balances these relationships to achieve sustainability. In many cases, environmental stewardship practices were embedded within cultural and religious traditions in order to sustain these practices and transmit them between generations (Tiwari, 2007).
2 *Multiculturalism and enlightened localism* – Based on examining contemporary planning and socio-cultural challenges in Penang, Malaysia, eight integrated principles are articulated to guide sustainable and culturally-informed city-building, giving prominence to multicultural diversity and 'enlightened localism' as pathways towards sustainable urbanism (Nadarajah, 2007).

3 *Urban cultural identity* – In light of cultural identity challenges in the rapidly growing city of Cheongju, Korea, the 'urban cultural system' is seen as insufficient to bring about a culturally-sensitive sustainable urbanism, and advocates for integrating culture within five sectoral/functional systems or domains of action – governance, economy, environment, spatio-physical (urban structure and development patterns), and societal systems (Choe et al., 2007).
4 *Cultural mode of production* – In the pursuit of a 'true globalization with harmony and moderation', a study of Kanazawa, Japan, focused on the operationalization of local distinctiveness through a new 'global yet varied' social and production system model (Sasaki, 2007: 174). From a sustainable city perspective, decisive factors are: (a) unique character and specialities, based on a city's traditions and culture; (b) creativity and the ability to adjust to new circumstances; and (c) cooperation between residents and the local government.

Culture as a pillar of community/urban development

Another set of approaches, based in Western societies, aims to address the neglect of culture in traditional city planning frameworks by proposing approaches to recognize and integrate cultural considerations into planning processes and strategies. These efforts reflect an emerging recognition of the 'softer' social and cultural aspects of city/community development and intercity competitiveness among urban planners, but go further to attempt to articulate the place of culture within community sustainable development and develop the scaffolding for possible cultural indicators.[4] For example, in *The Fourth Pillar of Sustainability: Culture's Essential Role in Public Planning*, Hawkes (2001) addresses the need for a cultural perspective in public planning and policy, pragmatically promoting a cultural lens in evaluating the impacts of environmental, economic, and social initiatives planned and implemented in communities. He also argues for 'an integrated framework of cultural evaluation along similar lines to those being developed for social, environmental and economic impact assessment' (Hawkes, 2006: 3). In response to the new Local Government Act of 2002, New Zealand's Ministry for Culture and Heritage promoted a *community well-being* model with four interconnected and interdependent dimensions (cultural, environmental, social, and economic) and developed a range of indicators to guide City Councils in each area (NZMCH, 2006).

The Canadian government's External Advisory Committee on Cities and Communities (2006) put forward a vision and approach to sustainable development for Canadian cities and communities that was based on a four-pillar model of sustainability, and Infrastructure Canada developed a policy that required municipalities to develop long-term Integrated Community Sustainability Plans (ICSPs) reflecting this model (Government of Canada, 2005). Since then, many local governments have developed ICSPs to guide the long-term sustainable development of their communities, although with uneven attention to the 'culture' pillar (Duxbury and Jeannotte, 2010b).

Other recent initiatives include: the *Sustainable Culture, Sustainable Communities* toolkit for Thames Gateway North Kent, England (2006); the Swedish Association of Local Authorities and Regions (SALAR) position paper on *Culture in the Sustainable Society* (2008); a sustainability action plan based on a four-pillar model, *Notre culture, au coeur du développement durable: plan d'action de développement durable*

2009–2013 (QMCCSW, 2009), developed by the Province of Quebec, Canada (see Box 5.1 and Figure 5.1); and a meeting supported by the Asia-Europe Foundation to explore the role of the arts in the context of 'sustainable creative cities' (ASEF, 2010).

These planning and policy initiatives on culture and sustainability have emerged and evolved in a context of the triad of globalization, city cultural policy, and changing governance models in which sustainability frame, long-term planning, integrated planning, community grounded processes, and alternatives to 'traditional' or 'Western development' models have played significant roles. Many of the documents encompass long-standing debates and concerns (e.g., access, participation) but grappling with these issues within a context of *sustainability* offers a qualitatively different paradigm.

The pervasive and heightened concern for grass-roots public participation in all stages of community sustainability initiatives – envisioning, planning, making decisions, and implementation – is particularly notable. Sustainable development is too vague without continuous participation of citizens in the public sphere, and culture is true participation because

Figure 5.1   Sustainability action plan developed by the Province of Quebec, Canada (QMCCSW, 2009)

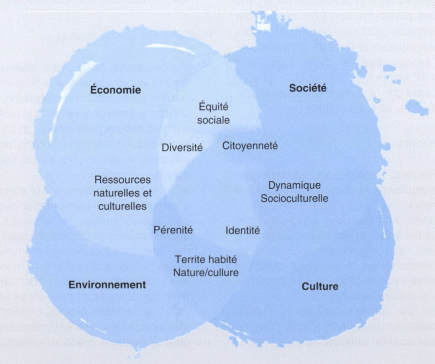

active cultural participation offers inhabitants the best opportunity to shape our societies: re-inventing the narratives on the past, shaping the expectations for today, and imagining the dreams for tomorrow. This emphasis deeply informs thinking about cultural planning within a sustainability context.

Box 5.1 Quebec's Sustainability Action Plan

In 2009, the Province of Quebec developed a sustainability action plan based on a four-pillar model. *Notre culture, au coeur du développement durable* (QMCCSW, 2009) set out in graphic form a variation of the familiar four-dimensional model and established several priorities for the Province's cultural ministry over the 2009–13 period. One priority is the development of an Agenda 21 for Culture based on the model promoted by United Cities and Local Governments (UCLG). Related to this, the Ministry intends to elaborate tools to assist municipalities to develop and implement sustainability action plans, and to develop strategic directions based on sustainability principles to guide its own regional cultural development initiatives. While the plan is comprehensive and includes priorities of relevance to local jurisdictions, such as improved conservation and restoration services for heritage properties, detailed operational guidelines for these initiatives are still being elaborated and will be ready in 2012.

The benefits of the paradigm for cultural policy

Changing a paradigm is difficult and requires a range of ingredients or prerequisites: (a) the evidence that the old paradigm is insufficient; (b) the evidence that the new 'paradigm being elaborated' is promising; (c) some bold researchers in academia voicing the virtues of the new paradigm; and (d) some 'on the field' actors implementing the new paradigm (seldom consciously, often intuitively) through concrete programmes. We believe that all these ingredients already exist. In 12 key points, this section summarizes why the paradigm of culture and sustainable development offers benefits for cultural policy.

Conceptual benefits

1 It is inclusive and it shakes an outdated concept of development. It forces the traditional players to react.
2 It offers a clear and beautiful image, easy to memorize, of the future of societies ('sustainable development'), and is inclusive of culture as part of a holistic vision of society. It does not instrumentalize culture (and, thus, it becomes acceptable to cultural actors).
3 It preserves the intrinsic values of culture (memory, creativity, diversity, dialogue, rituality) as the core of cultural policies.

4 It allows a differentiation between social and cultural stakeholders. Many social movements are genuinely interested in cultural processes, but their keyword is *equity*, which could dangerously turn to frozen identities and a paternalistic approach to freedoms. Cultural stakeholders value dynamic identities and use keywords including *risk*, *provocation*, *freedom*, *critical knowledge*, etc.

Platform for connections

5 It allows artistic and cultural stakeholders to connect to ecological stakeholders and jointly work on different aspects of sustainability. Sustainability concerns everyone, not only ecological actors.
6 It allows cultural professionals to be regarded and respected on the same footing as economists, planners, or ecologists in the field of sustainable development.
7 It leads to the involvement of civil society in the elaboration and implementation of policies. Many civil society actors (for example, in struggles against poverty or climate change) have realized that they need a cultural framework to make sense of their local actions. In many cases, they use artistic productions to illustrate their causes.
8 It recognizes arts and culture as assets for economic growth and exports of cities and nations, mainly through the creative industries, and also considers them within an integrated vision of

sustainable development. Creative industries do not escape a reassessment of how they use resources (material and immaterial).

Policy/planning

9 In a context of crisis, it provides a new tool to rethink the traditional mechanisms to support culture, rather than the traditional response to cut budgets.

10 It aligns with and supports an integrative approach to city planning which brings together and considers a multifaceted range of economic, social, cultural, and environmental costs and benefits in order to determine the most appropriate options and actions.

11 There is a growing importance of culture in international relations and diplomacy, and Agenda 21 for Culture (an initiative led by cities and local governments) plays a pioneer role in this debate.

12 All cities (small, medium-sized, and metropolises) need a cultural policy for their citizens, and not only as tourism and marketing tools. A sustainable development lens encourages wider access and participation of inhabitants.

Box 5.2   Culture and sustainable development imagined

The paradigm of culture and sustainable development entails widening the scope and width of what we currently understand by cultural policies. An attempt to visualize the new components of cultural policies was developed by the Committee on Culture of United Cities and Local Governments as a response to a consultation by UNESCO on a 'new cultural policy profile' (Pascual, 2009). The image includes the current 'inner core of cultural policies' and adds the new components that emerge when culture is related to sustainable development. This image also illustrates the potential of the new paradigm in bringing together cultural policies and politics.

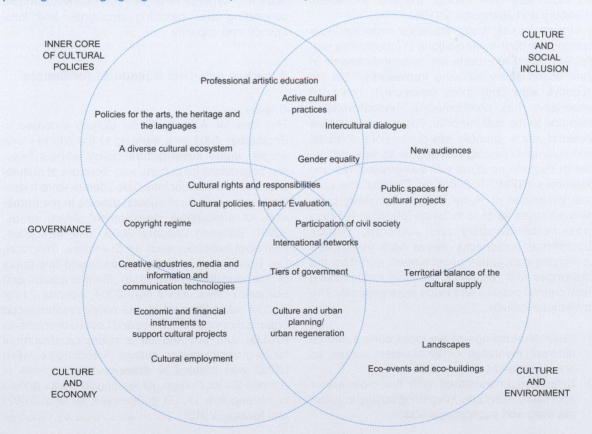

The bottlenecks: conceptual and operational

In order for the culture and sustainable development paradigm to contribute to a renewed platform for future discussions about sustainability, during its elaboration, it must address a series of conceptual and operational challenges. At present, thinking about culture in a community sustainability context is emergent and diversely conceived. In a review of scientific literature, Soini and Birkeland (2009) found that the concept of *cultural sustainability* is described in vague, diverse, and sometimes conflicting ways. In policy and planning contexts, conceptualization is generally weak. For example, in Canada, the majority of the ICSP-development guides lack a definition of culture. When provided, definitions range from the *anthropological*, focusing on community identity and values, to the *expressive*, including both heritage infrastructure and a range of arts and culture activities and resources, to a *combination* of the two, incorporating both anthropological aspects, such as language, beliefs and ways of living together, and the ways that society expresses itself through the arts and letters (Duxbury and Jeannotte, 2010b).

In some cases, 'fuzzy' guidance structures have opened the door to innovations in jurisdictions particularly eager to include the cultural dimension in their sustainability planning frameworks.[5] On the negative side (and more commonly), continued uncertainty has contributed to underdeveloped attention to the cultural pillar. For example, in New Zealand, many councils mix discussions of social and cultural well-being and appear to have difficulties in capturing cultural well-being objectives and outcomes (NZMCH, 2006). In Canada, the cultural dimension of many local sustainability planning initiatives tends to focus on (physical) heritage preservation (Duxbury and Jeannotte, 2010b). Operational bottlenecks derive both from these underlying conceptual uncertainties, and from the challenges and resistance faced in implementing local cultural policies and plans more generally. The challenges include:

1 Misunderstandings of the word *culture* and its different meanings or ambiguities: culture as way of life and culture as art.
2 Difficulties encountered with the cross-sector approach, especially integrating culture in urban planning and economic policies.
3 The complexity of the artistic world, with its great diversity of approaches and practices, from the individual to the collective, often producing a silo effect.
4 Reluctance on the part of sustainable development actors, guardians of the three-pillar system.
5 The 'culture is expensive and of no use' syndrome is a recurrent handicap for those trying to foster creativity, and it also appears when the issue of culture as the fourth pillar of sustainability is under discussion.
6 Evaluation is essential because cultural policies are, like other public policies, subject to a democratic imperative of transparency and effectiveness. However, this is a very difficult exercise, since cultural policies perhaps touch on values and the domain of the subjective more than other local policies. It is better to focus on stages of improvement rather than on quantitative criteria.

Addressing these challenges requires a combination of local and collective action. An enabling balance and synergy must be found between macro connecting and informing structures, and local agency and capacity.

A leading initiative: Agenda 21 for Culture

Origins

The idea for Agenda 21 for Culture emerged in September 2002 at a meeting in the city of Porto Alegre, where some cultural policy leaders (mayors, councillors for culture, and directors of cultural affairs of some major cities) decided to write a declaration to guide local cultural policies in the framework of sustainable development (Martí et al., 2009). Between January 2003 and May 2004, municipal networks such as Eurocities, Interlocal, Les Rencontres, and Sigma discussed five drafts of the document, mainly in Iberoamerican and European cities.[6] On 8 May 2004, Agenda 21 for Culture was approved by the newly created world organization of United Cities and Local Governments (UCLG) and adopted as a reference document for its programmes on culture. A committee within UCLG was created to advance the progress of Agenda 21 for Culture. Its leading role was ratified in consecutive UCLG congresses in Jeju (2007) and Mexico (2010).

Goals and description

Agenda 21 for Culture aims for culture to be considered the fourth pillar of sustainable development at a local level, recognizing that 'local cultural policies, based on the intrinsic values of culture (creativity, critical knowledge, diversity, memory, rituality ...) are becoming more important for democracy and citizenship'. It contains 67 articles, divided into three sections: *Principles* describe the relationship between culture and human rights, diversity, sustainability, participatory democracy, and peace; *Undertakings* concentrate on the scope of local government responsibilities, and provide a detailed description of the request for centrality of cultural policies; *Recommendations* advocate for the inclusion of cultural considerations in the programmes, budgets, and organizational charts of the various levels of government. It is now available in 19 languages, supported by training seminars and capacity-building programmes, five thematic reports, and an open-source website.

International advocacy through local adoption

Through Agenda 21 for Culture, UCLG is an active player on global cultural issues. By September 2010, 409 cities, local governments, and organizations from all over the world were linked to Agenda 21 for Culture. Its geographic coverage is growing more extensive over time, city by city: members now come from Europe, the Americas, Africa, and Australia, although Asia is still underrepresented. The formal adoption of Agenda 21 for Culture by a local government has both local and international significance: it expresses to its citizens that the local authority will strive to ensure that culture plays a key role in urban policies, and it shows a sign of solidarity and cooperation with cities and local governments around the world.

This global solidarity and cooperative advocacy was strengthened in November 2010 when the UCLG Executive Bureau officially approved a Policy Statement on 'Culture as the Fourth Pillar of Sustainable Development' at its World Summit in Mexico. With this Policy Statement, 'the members of United Cities and Local Governments share the vision that culture is the fourth pillar of sustainable development ... recognize that the trio of economic growth, social inclusion and environmental balance no longer reflect all the dimensions of our global societies [and] believe that governance at all levels – local,

national and international – should include a strong cultural dimension.'

Challenges

Agenda 21 for Culture faces several challenges. First, on an operational level, United Cities and Local Governments itself is a very young organization, with scarce resources, limited lobbying capacity, and communication limitations (among others, a difficult acronym). Second, the implementation of Agenda 21 for Culture is difficult. There is a need to link or integrate with key local planning and sustainability programmes (in some countries named 'Agenda 21'), which usually deal with three pillars. Some cities, though, have been successful in this exercise. For example, the City of Lille has integrated culture as a fully-fledged subject in the City's sustainability programme while allowing it enough flexibility and independence to continue developing its Agenda 21 for Culture. However, as discussed previously, this is still a struggle in most cities. The link – and even integration – of Agenda 21 for Culture with key local planning/sustainability programmes is often problematic but, in the long run, essential.

Third, the UCLG Committee on Culture cannot monitor what cities actually do after adopting Agenda 21 for Culture. While guidelines and support for implementation are offered, there is no definite action that results from adherence. This limits the on-the-ground impacts of adoption, and underlines why the UCLG is putting great emphasis on inter-municipal sharing of knowledge and experience about local implementation practices. Fourth, there are some internal conceptual tensions within the document. As Teixeira Coelho (2009) observes, its broad scope is difficult to synthesize (too many ideas are presented on the same plane with no hierarchy of values), some concepts are not explained in detail, and it fails to become a real 'agenda' because it does not provide specific goals and qualitative and quantitative targets. Teixeira Coelho suggests a conceptual updating of the document and claims for the involvement of civil society: 'the participation of civil society on an equal footing with local governments, sharing tasks, resources, and decision-making power, is indispensible if we truly intend to get somewhere' (Teixeira Coelho, 2009: 163).

In spite of these difficulties and issues, we believe that the Agenda 21 for Culture has advanced the debate on cultural policies and sustainable development. As a unique global structure, it brings together cities, organizations, and networks that foster relations between local cultural policies and the sustainable development of cities. It is a platform for mutual learning and exchange of experiences, for advocating on the crucial role that cities play in cultural policy and practice, and for enabling cities to contribute to global cultural governance. It has informed or influenced a wide number of local cultural strategies (e.g., Montréal, Lille, Barcelona, Lyon, Geneva, Seville, Torino, Dortmund, Toulouse, Novi Sad, Maputo, Quito, Medellin, Porto Alegre, Belo Horizonte, Buenos Aires, Diyarbakir, Çanakkale, and Redland) and a new Fund for Local Cultural Governance, launched in 2010, is expected to widen the network in yet-unrepresented countries and generate new sources of knowledge.[7]

In light of multiple challenges and informed by the knowledge gained through critical reflection (e.g., Teixeira Coelho, 2009) and implementation practices (see, e.g., Cullen, 2009), the Agenda 21 for Culture initiative continues to evolve. In 2012, the UCLG Committee on Culture will initiate a debate to write a new Agenda to be approved in 2014, in a process to involve practitioners (cities and local governments), civil society (academics, activists), and national and international institutions.

Conclusion and policy implications: international, national, local

To change a paradigm and elaborate a new one, a range of ingredients or prerequisites are required, both conceptual – evidence that the old paradigm is insufficient and that the new 'paradigm being elaborated' is promising – and operational, with active agents to carry the new paradigm forward, both researchers/scholars and 'on the field' actors implementing the new paradigm through concrete programmes. We believe that all these ingredients are in play. The current challenge is to align efforts and advance thinking while privileging the diversity of emerging approaches and contributions.

This elaboration is emergent and not yet fully coherent. It is informed by UNESCO's statements on the contributions of cultural diversity to sustainable development, the recovery of historical and culture-specific approaches and worldviews, and local-level community development trends. Further conceptual development is required. Many concepts are still 'fuzzy' and need further clarification. The overall scaffolding for the new paradigm is still being built. To facilitate this development, avenues or pathways for further thinking must be identified and enabled. Efforts must also be made to link the conceptualization efforts into policy/planning practice and on-the-ground actions. In keeping with the 'cultural diversity' approach to sustainability, this should be a highly contextualized process that must recognize specificities of places and cultures.

Operationally, it is being advanced through a wide range of grassroots experiments exploring 'new ways of living' that are being designed and implemented by non-profit organizations and community activists, and urban planners and officials innovating new ways of thinking about and organizing collective life. We have observed (and are still observing) a phase of initiatives that can be described as 'grassroots, varied, and experimental' in nature – rich with ideas and with room for original thinking and approaches, but with little consistency and difficult to synthesize in any comprehensive way. Building from this experimental phase, we are potentially entering the 'next phase' within which culture is considered in a more robust way with greater consistency and with a sense of leadership in helping to outline this next phase of cultural development for sustainable communities. Ideally, this would build on the best initial efforts, synthesis, and assessments of these efforts, and greater interconnections between theory and policy/practice. Leadership would most likely be a 'shared leadership' among leading influences in this area. UCLG's documents – *Agenda 21 for Culture*, approved in 2004, and the Policy Statement *Culture: Fourth Pillar of Sustainable Development*, approved in 2010 – are an important part of this leadership picture.

From a policy perspective, further elaboration of a culturally informed sustainability paradigm could be advanced through sound integration of culture with other domains in two ways:

• A *'culture-out' approach*: At both local and national levels, develop solid cultural policies, linked with other societal domains, so as to establish concrete objectives and actions concerning culture in areas such as education, the economy, science, communication, environment, social cohesion, urban planning, and international cooperation.

- *A cultural lens/perspective in other policy/planning domains*: At local, national, and international levels, explicitly include and integrate cultural considerations in all public policies, especially development policies and programmes on sustainable development.

In the current 'phase of elaboration' of the roles and contributions of culture to the sustainable development of cities, the idea of culture as the fourth pillar or dimension must be promoted and refined at local, national, and international levels of policy-making. Further discussion on the implications of the inclusion of culture as a pillar of sustainable development and the ways in which culturally diverse approaches can contribute to societies' necessary transitions and adaptations are very much needed.

This elaboration is contextualized at both international and local levels, informed and advanced through networked sharing of knowledge and experiences; advised by experts and 'communities of analytical practice'; and rooted in dialogue with cultural actors and the direct participation of residents/citizens. In this manner, a renewed culturally inclusive and informed paradigm of sustainable development provides a fruitful platform for collectively addressing our world's challenges, putting forth pluralized visions of urban development, and enabling a diverse array of adaptations that will be necessary as we transition into more sustainable modes of living.

Box 5.3 New Approaches to policy activism from international to local and back to global

On 1 October 2010, we opened the Institute for Cultural Strategies Institute (CSI) in New York City. Our mission is to support policy that articulates and strengthens the central role of art in civic life and enhances cultural, community and environmental sustainability. Choosing sustainability as our overarching frame, we have positioned ourselves in a global discussion, but many of our big picture inquiries are conducted in 'laboratories' at various levels of local social organization. CSI's specific aim is to support sustainability policy centred on civic participation and access in the city and then replicate this local effort in other local settings, both national and international. Our credo is that the health of an area's cultural ecology and the health of the community are absolutely interdependent.

If culture is to survive, if civil society is to survive, and if the environment is to remain conducive to our survival as a race, we need new ways of thinking and behaving. We believe that inculcating arts and culture into these discussions will make them stronger, more creative and more visionary. This will also bring arts and culture out of isolation and into contact with the other areas of the public sector around shared challenges and opportunities.

Our institute has developed some amazing cross-sector partnerships, given our brief existence so far. We are exploring gift economies, alternative currencies and taxonomies of multiple economies that occur within social organization that have no measurability by money but are nonetheless critical to social cohesion. All of these explorations of how we value what we must have in order to maintain our humanity are discussions we are having with experts and philosophers around the globe. Activists are no longer looking to the status quo in power to embrace or even seek innovative thinking. New technologies of interactivity are allowing the bypassing of ineffective traditional intermediaries. With these obstacles to progress mitigated, the acceleration of grassroots civil society organizing across sectors is breathtaking.

The cutting-edge of actualizing these behaviours and ways of being is occurring naturally in tight-knit local communities and cities. Likewise, the actual benefits that flow from our partnerships, the

(Continued)

(Continued)

'low-hanging fruit' of the work, are intended to benefit local individuals, small to mid-sized organizations and those who have traditionally been left behind due to lack of money. These communities need the scalability that comes with partnerships and collaborations, supported by policy. Major coalitions are forming quickly around open source and volunteer projects to empower the public sector and those who hold the vision of the public commons as sacred.

As lofty as the underpinning philosophies become, the ways in which these ideas are actualized through these cross-sector coalitions is in the delivery of functioning systems, tools and capabilities being made available to anyone who needs them, regardless of ability to pay: for example, the legal and financial mechanisms to allow cooperatives of small arts organizations to be able to convert to renewable energy sources together. Global challenges, global ideas, local laboratories and global solutions, not driven by money – this is indeed a major paradigm shift. The arts, no matter how small, no matter how local, are pivotal to this movement.

Paul Nagle

Notes

1 Multidisciplinary research literature reveals a wide variety of discourses within this general theme, seldom interlinking and rarely linked to policy planning. These diverse approaches offer different perspectives and insights and are important to recognize as associated, though not yet connected, elements in a broader array of knowledge – how to integrate these elements conceptually (and to operationalize their insights) is an ongoing project.

2 See Introduction to this volume.

3 For further details of these four conceptual threads, see Duxbury and Jeannotte (2010a).

4 This was also one of the main conclusions of the European URBACT I network on culture and local development led by Lille Métropole (2004–2006).

5 For example, communities in the northern Yukon Territory are described as being 'always at risk of losing capacity, cultural depth, and self-reliance' (Yukon, no date: 15). ICSP cultural sustainability goals for these communities look to a more *self-reliant community* ('one that is not losing capacity and culture') and *enhanced community identity* where development is respectful of the community's cultural identity, landmarks are preserved, cultural values are recognized as part of the planning process, and 'infrastructure development is culturally appropriate in design, placement, and approach' (p. 15).

6 The most difficult discussions focused on the length and the name of the document. Several names were considered: 'Agenda 21 for Culture', 'Declaration of Cities for Cultural Diversity', or 'An Agenda for Local Cultural Development of Cities', among others. In the end, 'Agenda 21 for Culture' was selected, offering an interesting image that connected the new cultural initiative to the successful environmental/physical ecology programme, 'Agenda 21'.

7 The Fund is promoted by the Committee on Culture and the World Secretariat of UCLG, with the support of the Spanish Development Cooperation Agency (AECID) and the City Council of Barcelona. The 2010 Call for Proposals was set at €675,000 and opened to projects led by cities and local governments, direct or indirect members of UCLG, in countries in Africa, Latin America, and the Mediterranean. The projects had to aim to locally implement Agenda 21 for Culture (involving technical assistance, training, capacity-building, etc.). The Call attracted 78 expressions of interest, 26 projects were submitted, and 11 projects received funding.

REFERENCES

Asia-Europe Foundation (ASEF) (2010) Briefing Report on Workshop 3, 'Sustainable Creative Cities: The Role of the Arts in Globalised Urban Contexts', of the 4th Connecting Civil Societies in Asia and Europe (CCS4) Conference, 1–3 October 2010, Brussels, Belgium.

Brocchi, D. (2008) The cultural dimension of sustainability, in S. Kagan and V. Kirchberg (eds), *Sustainability: A New Frontier for the Arts and Culture*. Frankfurt: Verlag für Akademische Schriften, pp. 26–58.

Choe, S.-C., Marcotullio, P.J. and Piracha, A.L. (2007) Approaches to cultural indicators, in M. Nadarajah and A.T. Yamamoto (eds), *Urban Crisis*. Tokyo: UNU Press.

Cullen, C. (2009) Lille and the Agenda 21 for Culture, in J. Pascual (ed.), *Cities, Cultures and Developments*.

Report No. 5. Barcelona: Committee on Culture of United Cities and Local Governments (UCLG).

Duxbury, N. and Jeannotte, M.S. (2010a) Culture, sustainability and communities: exploring the myths. *Oficina do CES*, No. 353. Available at: www.ces.uc.pt/publicacoes/oficina/index.php?id=2982.

Duxbury, N. and Jeannotte, M.S. (2010b) From the bottom-up: culture in community sustainability planning, paper presented at the 3rd ESA Sociology of Culture Research Network mid-term Conference, 'Culture and the Making of Worlds,' Milan, Italy, 7–9 October.

Edozien, N.N. (2007) Cultural divergence and education towards sustainable development – an African viewpoint. *Kulturelle Vielfalt*, 2 (in BNE-Journal, 2009).

External Advisory Committee on Cities and Communities (2006) *From Restless Communities to Resilient Places: Building a Stronger Future for All Canadians*. Ottawa: Infrastructure Canada.

Government of Canada (2005) *Integrated Community Sustainability Planning – A Background Paper*. Discussion paper for 'Planning for Sustainable Canadian Communities Roundtable', organized by the Prime Minister's External Advisory on Cities and Communities, 21–23 September.

Gražuleviĉiũtė, I. (2006) Cultural heritage in the context of sustainable development. *Environmental Research, Engineering and Management*, 3(37): 74–79.

Hawkes, J. (2001) *The Fourth Pillar of Sustainability: Culture's Essential Role in Public Planning*. Melbourne: Common Ground.

Hawkes, J. (2006) Creative democracy, keynote speech at 'Interacció' 2006: Community Cultural Policies', Barcelona, 25 October 2006.

Hooper, A. (ed.) (2005) *Culture and Sustainable Development in the Pacific*. Canberra: ANU ePress/Asia Pacific Press.

Jeannotte, M.S. and Andrew, C. (2008) Operational guidelines for incorporating culture into sustainable development policies: a Canadian perspective, report prepared for Department of Canadian Heritage.

Kavaliku, L. (2005) Culture and sustainable development in the Pacific, in A. Hooper (ed.), *Culture and Sustainable Development in the Pacific*. Canberra: ANU ePress/Asia Pacific Press, pp. 22–31.

Khun, T.S. (1962) *The Structure of Scientific Revolutions*. Chicago: University of Chicago Press.

Martí, J., Cullen, C., Lombardi, H., Sjöstedt, M. and Pascual, J. (2009) Agenda 21 for Culture: state of affairs and perspectives, in J. Pascual (ed.), *Cities, Cultures and Developments*. Report No. 5. Barcelona: Committee on Culture of UCLG.

Nadarajah, M. (2000) City, culture and sustainable development: towards a cultural framework for sustainable urbanization, in *Report of the International Conference on Culture in Sustainability of Cities I*. Kanazawa: IICRC, pp. 48–61.

Nadarajah, M. (2007) Culture of sustainability: multicultural reality and sustainable localism – a case study of Penang (George Town), Malaysia, in M. Nadarajah and A.T. Yamamoto (eds), *Urban Crisis*. Tokyo: UNU Press.

Nadarajah, M. and Yamamoto, A.T. (eds) (2007) *Urban Crisis: Culture and the Sustainability of Cities*. Tokyo: UNU Press.

New Zealand Ministry for Culture and Heritage (NZMCH) (2006) *Cultural Well-being and Local Government. Report 1: Definition and Context of Cultural Well-being*. Wellington: NZMCH.

Nurse, K. (2006) Culture as the Fourth Pillar of Sustainable Development, report prepared for Commonwealth Secretariat, UK.

Paliwal, P. (2005) Sustainable development and systems thinking: a case study of a heritage city. *International Journal of Sustainable Development and World Ecology*, 12(2): 213–220.

Pascual, J. (2009) *Culture and Sustainable Development: Examples of Institutional Innovation and Proposal of a New Cultural Policy Profile*. Barcelona: Committee on Culture of United Cities and Local Governments.

Quebec Ministry of Culture, Communications and the Status of Women (QMCCSW) (2009) *Notre culture, au coeur du développement durable: plan d'action de développement durable 2009–2013*. Quebec: QMCCSW.

Rana, R.S.J.B. and Piracha, A.L. (2007) Cultural frameworks, in M. Nadarajah and A.T. Yamamoto (eds), *Urban Crisis*. Tokyo: UNU Press, pp. 13–50.

Roseland, M. et al. (2005) *Towards Sustainable Communities: Resources for Citizens and their Governments*. Gabriola Island: New Society.

Sasaki, M. (2007) Towards an urban cultural mode of production: a case study of Kanazawa, Japan, I, in M. Nadarajah and A.T. Yamamoto (eds), *Urban Crisis*. Tokyo: UNU Press.

Soini, K. and Birkeland, I. (2009) From policy to practices: the discourse on cultural sustainability, paper presented at the Nordic Conference on Cultural Policy, Jyväskylä, August.

Swedish Association of Local Authorities and Regions (SALAR) (2008) *Culture in the Sustainable Society*. Stockholm: SALAR.

Teixeira Coelho, J. (2009) For an effective and contemporary Agenda 21 for Culture, in J. Pascual (ed.), *Cities, Cultures and Developments*. Report No. 5. Barcelona: Committee on Culture of United Cities and Local Governments.

Thames Gateway North Kent (2006) *Sustainable Culture, Sustainable Communities: The Cultural Framework and Toolkit for Thames Gateway North Kent*. Guilford, UK: Southeast Cultural Observatory.

Throsby, D. (1999) Cultural capital. *Journal of Cultural Economics*, 23: 3–12.

Tiwari, S.R. (2007) Transforming cultural heritage into sustainable future: a case study of Patan, Nepal in M. Nadarajah and A.T. Yamamoto (eds), *Urban Crisis*. Tokyo: UNU Press, pp. 62–106.

United Cities and Local Governments (UCLG) (2004) *Agenda for Culture*. Barcelona: UCLG.

UCLG Committee on Culture and World Secretariat (2010) *Culture: Fourth Pillar of Sustainable Development*. Policy Statement approved by the UCLG Executive Bureau in Mexico City. United Cities and Local Governments.

UNESCO (1995) *Our Creative Diversity*. Paris: UNESCO.

UNESCO (2005) *Convention on the Protection and Promotion of the Diversity of Cultural Expressions*. Paris: UNESCO.

World Bank/UNESCO (1998) 'Culture in Sustainable Development: Investing in Cultural and Natural Endowments' conference, Washington, DC.

World Bank/UNESCO (1999) *Understanding Culture in Sustainable Development: Investing in Cultural and Natural Endowments* (Conference proceedings and discussion paper). Washington, DC.

World Commission on Environment and Development (Brundtland Report) (1987) *Our Common Future.* New York: Oxford University Press.

Yan, Y. et al. (2008) Analysis of the role of the Mosuo culture in local environmental protection in Lugu Lake region. *International Journal of Sustainable Development and World Ecology,* 15: 48–55.

Yukon (Department of Community Services, Government of Yukon) (no date) *Integrated Community Sustainability Plan Template (Part 1).* Whitehorse: Government of Yukon.

CHAPTER 6

CITY BRANDING
Lily Kong

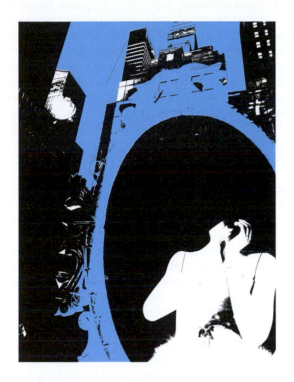

This chapter discusses the concept of city branding as a strategy of identifying valuable assets that a city has to offer, developing these assets and delivering their value to attract investors, visitors and talent. Whether a city brand is successful or not depends on whether there is good partnership, leadership, cooperation and organization. Where there is a lack of consensus on the city brand, a top-down approach in brand development and an image–reality gap, the branding is likely to fail. Specific cases of branding efforts (Bilbao, Dubai and Beijing) and the issues they encountered are briefly discussed. Finally, the chapter suggests areas for further research.

Introduction

In recent years, city branding has emerged as a fast-growing practice in various parts of the world, with governments using it as a strategy to raise the international profile of selected cities. Competition among cities for tourists, investments and other resources has intensified, and city branding is believed to be an effective strategy for cities in this competition. With such stiff competition, champions of city branding argue that neglecting such branding could cause a city to fade into obscurity. On the other hand, those that are successful can achieve or maintain economic well-being.

This chapter will begin by introducing the origins of city branding, tracing its evolution from marketing practices such as product branding and corporate branding. Second, it will present several frameworks on the conceptual thinking underpinning the development of a city brand. Third, different methods of measuring a city brand will be presented. Fourth, the key success factors for creating a strong city brand will be discussed. Fifth, the challenges encountered in each stage of city branding – from development to implementation to monitoring of the brand – will be examined. Sixth, the chapter will highlight three empirical cases of cities and their branding efforts, highlighting the challenges of sustaining a city brand. Seventh, the chapter will identify emerging trends in city branding. Finally, the chapter will discuss further areas for research that could contribute to a better understanding of city branding and its impacts.

Origins of city branding

City branding, as defined by marketing experts, is a strategy of identifying valuable assets that a city has to offer, developing these assets and delivering their value to attract investors, visitors and talent (van Gelder and Allan 2006). Creating favourable images of a city is a powerful factor in being able to appeal to and draw target groups. However, merely cultivating and conveying positive images of a city is not enough in city branding. A brand also implies 'a promise which must be kept if customers are to be satisfied…' (Henderson 2007: 263), thus emphasizing that a city brand must also deliver the value it promises and fulfil the expectations of its target audience. City branding is often carried out to raise the city's profile as a tourist destination or favoured place for business or residence, ultimately resulting in economic gains for the city (Mommaas 2002). It has also been used as a tool for regeneration and countering negative images in cities that have suffered a crisis, such as New Orleans after Hurricane Katrina (Gotham 2007), or New York after September 11 (Greenberg 2008).

The concept of branding a city extends the branding of products to the branding of places. Marketing practitioners commonly employed branding as a way to increase the value of their products and it was thought that this technique could also be used to brand places, such as cities, regions and nations. Doubts were initially raised regarding the feasibility and validity of doing so. The concern was that simply importing the technique of product branding, and applying it to a place, overlooked significant differences between a place and product (Kavaratzis and Ashworth 2006). It failed to recognize that a place is a multifaceted entity which needs to serve diverse consumers with a variety of needs, versus a product. For instance, consumers of a city could be residents seeking a good standard of living, investors desiring a stable economic environment, or tourists looking for leisure activities. In the case of a product, there is mainly one need to fulfil – to serve its functional utility. Another difference, as noted by other marketing consultants, is the complexity of branding a place due to other forces such as politics (Pike 2008), which is far less likely to be a complicating factor for products.

Corporate branding, which also stemmed from product branding, seemed to narrow the gap and provide a more reliable transferable technique for branding cities. Corporate branding represents not only the product offered, but the people, values and culture of the organization (Parkerson and Saunders 2005). It thus acknowledges the multiple dimensions of the organization as an entity, and thus those of any city's. In addition, corporate branding addresses the complexity of dealing with multiple stakeholders (Kavaratzis 2005), similar to managing the diverse user groups of a city. However, differences nevertheless exist in that corporations have clear organizational structures, whereas many cities do not, theirs often being based on networks. City branding is thus more complex, because decision-making and cooperation tends to be harder across networks (Parkerson and Saunders 2005). Applying product or corporate branding techniques to a city is thus clearly inadequate.

City branding is a form of place branding, a category which also includes nation branding and destination branding. Although nations, cities and tourist destinations are similar in that they are places, there are differences in the ways they are branded and marketed. These differences generally lie in the number of stakeholders and strategic objectives involved, according to place branding specialists Moilanen and Rainisto (2009). For example, branding larger entities, like countries and cities, usually involves more target audiences and strategic objectives than branding tourist destinations, like a resort. Other differences between nation branding and city branding, for example, will be elaborated in a later section.

Developing and measuring a city brand

Several conceptual frameworks and models have been developed in recent years to provide guidance on how to develop a strong place/city brand. Some of these frameworks highlight key areas to address in the process of brand development while others are step-by-step guides to brand development. Table 6.1 summarizes five of these conceptual frameworks and models, originating from the discipline of marketing and business.

Similarities can be observed among the different frameworks. City branding can generally be categorized into four main stages. The first stage entails preliminary and preparatory steps in planning a city brand. Its main focus is research to identify how people feel and relate towards a city or place, and what it means to them. Comparing this against how they feel about other cities provides a starting point from which to develop a stronger city brand (Morgan et al. 2004; van Gelder and Allan 2006). This stage may also include developing a shared vision of the city in years to come, a vision that unifies stakeholders and which they can aspire towards (van Gelder and Allan 2006).

The second stage involves brand identity development. Brand identity development is identified in almost all the five frameworks, indicating how important it is in the overall process of building a city brand. Brand identity is based on the core values of a city, and represents how a city wants to position itself and be perceived (Moilanen and Rainisto 2009). The ingredients for constructing a brand identity need to be drawn from various aspects of a city, such as its culture, history and people. It should help create an image reflective of the city and express the

Table 6.1 Approaches to developing a place/city brand

Authors	Approach to developing a place/city brand
Morgan et al. (2004)	1 Marketing investigation, analysis and strategic recommendations 2 Brand identity development 3 Brand launch and introduction: communicating the vision 4 Brand implementation 5 Monitoring, evaluation and review
van Gelder and Allan (2006)	1 Assessment of status quo 2 Decide a vision of the city 3 Determine the city brand strategy 4 Engage in activities that will help realize the brand 5 Monitoring progress
Trueman and Cornelius (2006)	Uses a 'Place Brand Identity Toolkit' to point out elements essential in creating a city brand identity (e.g. a multi-layered identity, brand ownership, partnership and clear communication)
Pike (2008)	Focuses on three key components to develop a destination brand: 1 Destination brand identity development 2 Destination image 3 Destination positioning
Moilanen and Rainisto (2009)	1 Start-up and organization 2 Research stage 3 Forming brand identity 4 Making, executing and enforcing the plan 5 Implementation and follow-up

values of its people (Zhang and Zhao 2009). A unique brand identity is critical in establishing a city brand that is distinct and differentiated from other cities, providing a longer-lasting competitive advantage. This is becoming increasingly crucial today as inter-city competition gets tougher, and more cities offer similar assets. For example, a city or destination may portray itself as offering cultural attractions and friendly locals, but this claim can also be echoed by many other destinations (Morgan et al. 2004).

The third stage of city branding involves implementation of the brand through actions and activities, like launching campaigns, marketing activities and related policies. This requires good organization, communication and overall management (Moilanen and Rainisto 2009). Communication of the city brand can be carried out through three types of communication – primary, secondary and tertiary. Primary communication relates to the 'communicative effects of a city's actions, when communication is not the main goal of these actions' (Kavaratzis 2005: 337). A city's actions refer, for example, to the

physical landscaping of the city, the building of infrastructure projects, the organization of the governance structure, as well as the city's behaviour such as type of events hosted – all of which communicate the brand even though it was not their main intention. In contrast, secondary communication is the 'formal, intentional communication' that occurs through marketing practices such as advertising. Finally, tertiary communication refers to word-of-mouth which occurs, for example, when a visitor to the city recommends it to other people. Tertiary communication is beyond the direct control of marketing professionals, but effective primary and secondary communication can help strengthen positive tertiary communication (Kavaratzis 2004). During this third stage of city branding, the timing in rolling out activities should be done in a way to achieve maximum impact, and checks performed to ensure activities are in line with the branding strategy (van Gelder and Allan 2006).

The final stage is the subsequent monitoring of the city brand, which is addressed in three of the five frameworks identified in Table 6.1 (Morgan et al.

2004; van Gelder and Allan 2006; Moilanen and Rainisto 2009). Monitoring ensures the city brand is being implemented as intended, for example, that it is communicated accurately. In addition, the city brand has to be regularly evaluated and adjusted to accommodate any changes in environment. Gotham's (2007) study of New Orleans demonstrates this, with the devastation of Hurricane Katrina prompting adjustment of the city's branding to counter negative publicity and reinforce its appeal as a vibrant multicultural destination.

Measuring a city brand

After developing a city brand, how have the outcomes been measured, and how might the relative successes of city brands be measured? Perhaps the most well-known method of measurement is the Anholt–GFK Roper City Brands Index (CBI), by place brand specialist Simon Anholt. This model uses six dimensions, as displayed in the hexagon in Figure 6.1, to measure the perceptions that people from other countries hold of a particular city.

A survey made up of questions based on six dimensions (Anholt 2006) is administered to people from other countries, both developed and undeveloped. The results provide the city with a score that enables it to be ranked against other cities. The six dimensions are:

1 Presence – The perception of the city's international standing on the world stage, for example, its contributions to culture and science.
2 Place – How attractive respondents find physical aspects of the city and its environment.
3 People – The perception of how friendly and welcoming the city's community is towards foreigners.
4 Prerequisites – Perception of the standard of living in a city, such as ease of finding suitable accommodation and the quality of basic amenities like healthcare.
5 Pulse – The vibrancy of the city, and availability of fun and engaging activities.
6 Potential – The educational and economic opportunities available, in terms of quality of schools and jobs available, and the business environment.

Figure 6.1   Anholt City Brand Hexagon

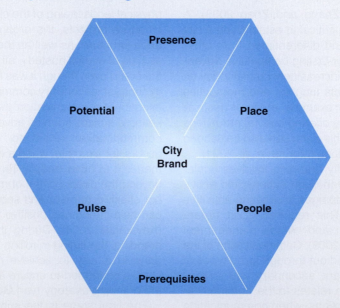

Source: Anholt, Simon. The Anholt–GFK Roper City Brands Index, www.gfkamerica.com/practice_areas/roper_pam/ placebranding/cbi/ (accessed June 2010)

The usefulness of the CBI is its specificity in measuring a city brand, and not just a general place brand that can include nations and regions. The CBI is to be distinguished from Anholt's Nation Brand Index (NBI). The CBI is premised on the belief that because cities are smaller and more homogeneous in terms of culture, climate and people than a nation, cities are usually assessed by people in more specific, and often, more functional, terms (Anholt 2006). This is also recognized by branding researchers Caldwell and Freire (2004: 59) who found that cities are perceived more from a 'functional point of view'. For example, when people consider a city, they often look at details like transport facilities and the safety of its streets. In contrast, a nation is often thought of in broader terms, such as cultural heritage and government policies.

A key quality of the CBI is that it is based on people's perceptions of the city, which may not necessarily reflect reality accurately. Some respondents would not even have visited the city in question before. For instance, a respondent may perceive a city to have a dull arts scene, but in reality, the city could have a burgeoning arts scene that is little known due to inadequate marketing. However, the CBI is premised on the belief that 'perception is reality'. Care must also be taken when drawing conclusions from a city's CBI ranking across the years. The rank assigned to a city is relative to other cities, and the rise and fall in one city's rank over consecutive years depends on the performance of other cities. For instance, if a city is ranked number five in 2009, but falls to number ten in 2010, it may not mean its absolute score has dropped. Its score could actually have increased as compared to the previous year's score, but newly-included cities in the survey could have stronger brands, resulting in the city's drop in rank (Anholt 2006).

Another model to assess branding success is the customer-based brand equity (CBBE) model. The earliest CBBE model seems to have been developed by Aaker (1991), with a similar later version by Keller (2003). The CBBE model is made up of four dimensions:

1 Brand awareness – Customers' knowledge of the destination's existence.
2 Brand associations – Degree to which the brand is linked to that product category.

3 Brand resonance – Enthusiasm in engaging with the destination.
4 Brand loyalty – Repeat visits and positive word-of-mouth (Pike 2008: 181).

Despite providing a useful framework through these four dimensions, no quantitative measures were devised initially for the customer-based brand equity model. In 2009, Boo et al. addressed this gap by devising scale items to measure quantitatively the effectiveness of destination brands. While useful, this extended model developed by a team with backgrounds in tourism studies aims to evaluate the strength of tourist destination brands in attracting tourists only, and does not specifically measure city brands. As a result, questions in the survey are limited to gathering respondents' views about the attractiveness of a place for vacation (Boo et al. 2009). Hence, the extended customer-based brand equity model does not address characteristics which are valued by users other than tourists. For example, it does not measure the stability of a city's business environment which would interest investors, nor the standard of living which would interest potential long-term residents. As a relatively new model, the customer-based brand equity model has thus far been used to study only two tourist destinations, Atlantic City and Las Vegas. On the other hand, the Anholt–GFK Roper CBI has been used yearly since 2005 to rank cities worldwide, the number of cities involved usually being around 50.

Success factors in city branding

Several factors are fundamental to the success of city branding. Hankinson, a researcher in marketing and business, examined the role of branding in 12 British cities and identified four factors as being particularly important – partnerships, organizational complexity and control, product complexity, and measurement of success (Hankinson 2001: 140). Several of these overlap with van Gelder and Allen's (2006: 9) key success factors: partnership, leadership, cooperation and organization.

Partnership refers to how diverse stakeholders of a city must cooperate to develop and implement the city brand. Stakeholders could include residents, government, urban planners and tourism organizations. Whether from the public or private sector, or the local community, all stakeholders have to be committed and agree on the vision of the city and development of the city brand (Hankinson 2001; van Gelder and Allan 2006). Moreover, these partnerships should be equal, with each stakeholder's opinion bearing equal weight and authority. Too often, the direction of the city brand is swayed to serve the interests of stakeholders who possess more power and influence (van Gelder and Allan 2006). This pitfall could result in a failed attempt at city branding. One example of how such a challenge emerged is Hong Kong's West Kowloon Cultural District where the government's attempt to develop the mega-project as a strategy for branding itself as a city with cultural assets ran into many difficulties. The government's top-down approach in its earliest phases meant that it failed to engage the public and solicit its views. It invited leading world architects to design the landmark without consulting its own cultural sector. This top-down approach, which failed to seek consensus from the bottom, led to a subsequent lack of support from the community and was one of the reasons for the many starts and stops to the West Kowloon project (Lui 2008).

Another success factor is leadership. Because the partnership is made up of diverse stakeholders, each with its own agenda and interests, it is vital to have strong leadership to reconcile and unite these stakeholders towards achieving the desired city brand. As decision-making processes and working styles differ among stakeholders, leadership is needed to establish new ways of working together effectively (van Gelder and Allan 2006). This mirrors Hankinson's (2001) identification of the importance of clear organizational roles and structures in city branding. Others have identified the importance of having leaders in city branding, sometimes using the idea of 'brand champions'. Brand champions can be government representatives, business managers or anyone in charge of managing the brand development process. They are crucial in spearheading and organizing the development of the city brand (Morgan et al. 2004; Pike 2008; Moilanen and Rainisto 2009).

Cooperation is also an essential factor for successful city branding. The willingness of partners to negotiate and discuss differing opinions is a basic but key ingredient. With multiple partners involved in city branding, the challenge of cultivating harmony and managing conflict among these different partners increases. To motivate partners to work

together, it is important for them to keep in mind the common purpose of achieving a strong city brand (van Gelder and Allan 2006).

A final success factor is organization, specifically, a brand management organization. A brand management organization is responsible for implementing the brand strategy towards the intermediate or final stages of city branding. For instance, it decides which marketing activities and events are most appropriate for conveying the city brand (van Gelder and Allan 2006). It also regularly monitors the brand strategy to ensure it is in line with the original intentions. If misalignment occurs, the city branding strategy will need to be adjusted (van Gelder and Allan 2006). The brand management organization should also leverage the local community to help communicate and convey its brand. Residents and locals of the city can serve as ambassadors of the brand.

Another attempt at identifying the key success factors in city branding and measuring a city brand is the ISE Conceptual Model where ISE stands for Index, Support and Execution. 'Index' refers to the Anholt City Brands Index which measures a city brand. 'Support' and 'Execution' are areas in which success factors are identified, whereby 'Support' refers to the management support required for effective city branding, and 'Execution' refers to strategies that must be executed to attain a successful city brand (Qian 2009). The success factors cited in the ISE Conceptual Model mostly overlap with those of other models, such as those by Hankinson (2001) and van Gelder and Allan (2006). For example, the ISE Conceptual Model again highlights the importance of a clear organizational structure in city branding, what it terms 'City branding organization', and a working environment that fosters cooperation among partners, referred to as 'City Branding Culture' (Qian 2009: 316). However, the ISE Conceptual Model also includes a success factor that is not explicitly outlined in other models, which is the importance of a unique city brand identity. It states that a distinctive brand identity is essential for successful city branding (Qian 2009). The ISE model has not been tested in practice.

Failure of city branding

City branding usually fails because of various factors: lack of consensus on the city brand, a top-down approach, and an image–reality gap. One of the requirements in the early stages of city branding is to define the city brand. This is about building the brand identity, which should express the core values of the people as drawn from their culture, heritage and identity, and represent how a city desires to be perceived. The difficulty lies in defining a city brand that is mutually agreeable to the many diverse stakeholders of a city. Cities have a multitude of people from a variety of backgrounds who are pursuing different interests in the city, whether for residence, business, employment or educational opportunities. Each of these groups may view the city in a different way, and value certain aspects of a city differently from another person. Creating a city brand acceptable to all stakeholders is an issue, and possibly the most contentious part of city branding (Zhang and Zhao 2009).

Another issue in city branding is a top-down approach that neglects the opinions of the community and other stakeholders. If opinions from the local community are not sought in conceiving the city brand, and instead, one stakeholder dominates the city branding exercise, tensions will inevitably arise. In most cases, city councils or governments play a key role in city branding, but for city branding to be successful, they should ensure that they do not monopolize the branding process or disregard input from the public. The case of the West Kowloon Cultural District in Hong Kong, as briefly described above, illustrates this issue clearly.

A third reason for the failure of city branding is that there is too much of a gap between the images projected of a city and the reality. The images created by a city to influence how it is perceived need to be realistic. If the images do not genuinely portray the city, the result is disparity between a visitor's experiences and the brand promise (Henderson 2007). Managing this gap is relevant not only to tourism, but to the locals as well. The case of Beijing and its city branding efforts illustrate this. In preparation for hosting the 2008 Olympics, Beijing officials tried to sell the image of a 'new Beijing' and spruced up parts of the city around the Olympic venues. Slogans like 'New Beijing, Great Olympics' further supported its efforts. However, neighbourhoods distant from the Olympic venues remained in their dilapidated states, and poor housing amenities remained a problem (Zhang and Zhao 2009). There was thus a gap between the images cultivated and the reality of the situation experienced by the locals. A gap can create tension and increase the risk that a city brand is rejected by locals or other stakeholders.

City branding: three empirical cases

City branding is practised by cities in many different parts of the world, from Europe to the Middle East to Asia. This section discusses briefly an example each of these regions by looking at the branding efforts of Bilbao, Dubai and Beijing, and the issues they encountered.

The city of Bilbao in Spain started out as an industrial city and was Spain's capital of steel and shipping. However, in the 1970s, it suffered the effects of the recession and experienced urban decline (Plaza 2006). Job loss was severe, unemployment rose and the population began shrinking as people left the city (Plöger 2007). A strategy for urban regeneration and recovery was developed by the authorities in the 1980s, which focused on tourism, regeneration projects and improvement in infrastructure. Efforts also involved culture-led regeneration, urban renewal, environment clean-up and formation of a high-technology sector (Plöger 2007). Possibly the most significant regeneration project in establishing the city brand was the installation of the Guggenheim Museum in Bilbao. It can be said that the Guggenheim Museum was instrumental in transforming the entire image of Bilbao (Evans 2003).

The Guggenheim Museum was viewed as a cultural and international icon that would, as the local government hoped, strengthen the city brand and boost tourism. Designed by American architect Frank Gehry, the Guggenheim Museum in Bilbao opened in 1997, drawing over one million visitors in its first year and becoming a major tourist attraction (Plöger 2007). However, controversy has surrounded the building of the Guggenheim Museum Bilbao (GMB) since the beginning, from the time plans were unveiled to build it, till today, with critics doubting its effectiveness in achieving a sustainable city brand. First, the government's decision to build GMB lacked the support of local communities (Evans 2003). The idea of importing this cultural icon, which some viewed as a 'subtle form of American hegemonic imperialism' (Plaza 2006: 453) was resisted by activists and artists in Bilbao. A bomb went off on the opening of GMB (Evans

2003). Second, there was concern that the expenses involved in building and maintaining the GMB would divert financial support from local initiatives (Garcia 2004). The cost of building the museum was €144 million and was covered totally by public sector funding (Plöger 2007). People criticized the use of such a large sum of money towards building the museum and the public subsidies that were required to cover the museum's liabilities (Plöger 2007). Third, there are opposing views regarding the effectiveness of GMB in sustaining Bilbao's city brand. Guggenheim Museums are becoming increasingly ubiquitous, having opened in Berlin, Las Vegas and potentially in other locations such as Shanghai and Rio de Janeiro (Evans 2003). As this 'Guggenheim franchise' expands worldwide, the Guggenheim Museum Bilbao risks losing its novelty. When a city depends too heavily on a single icon, it risks the weakening of its own city brand as the icon grows more commonplace (Evans 2003). Hannigan (2003) also points out that using a globalized 'product' that has no connection to the local culture and heritage of the community into which it is imported is unlikely to sustain urban regeneration in the long term.

Dubai is another city taking efforts to brand itself. From its origins as a small trading port and subsequent development into a trading centre, its vision is to further become a 'hub of global commerce, a top tourist destination and a shopping Mecca' (Bagaeen 2007: 173). To fulfil this vision, Dubai has poured money into real estate projects and the construction of signature landmarks to attract tourists and investors. Luxury residences, commercial buildings and hotels were built at an astonishing rate, as Bagaeen (2007) observed. From these have sprung the iconic Burj Al-Arab hotel, one of the world's tallest hotels, which resembles a billowing sail. Another is the Palm Jumeirah, an artificial island created in the shape of one of Dubai's symbols, the palm tree, which will accommodate hotels, villas and retail developments. The purpose of all this construction is for Dubai to project an image of progress and energy, with landmark structures to attract wealthy visitors and talent (Bagaeen 2007).

Dubai's efforts to build a brand for itself has fuelled the phenomenal pace of development in the city but also caused issues to surface which have cast doubts on the sustainability of its progress. Environmental problems have resulted from the huge pace of construction in the city. The erection of numerous glass towers means a rise in energy consumption to keep these buildings cool. Dredging and other construction processes at the Palm islands have reportedly damaged the marine environment and eroded beaches (Bagaeen 2007). Traffic is also badly congested. If development is to be sustained, the impact on the environment needs to be carefully considered and managed. Another issue is the soaring cost of living in Dubai. The real estate boom in Dubai has raised the cost of living, causing residential and commercial rent to go up. Although one of the chief objectives of Dubai's city branding efforts is to make the place attractive to foreign entrepreneurs and expatriates, the high cost of living could deter these target groups. The challenge is to make Dubai a cost-effective location that will be perceived as a suitable place for work and residence (Bagaeen 2007). Finally, there is a general feeling that Dubai is rather artificial and commercialized. Some view it simply as an aggregation of malls, theme parks and entertainment centres (Bagaeen 2007). The city's lack of soul may deter some people and undermine Dubai's efforts in city branding.

Beijing's ambition and vision was to position itself as 'an international megalopolis, a famous cultural entity and a city truly suitable for human habitation', as outlined in its City Master Plan (Zhang and Zhao 2009: 248). The process of city branding involved physical changes in the urban landscape, hosting of the 2008 Olympic Games and promotion of Beijing as both a cultural and cosmopolitan place. Huge investments were made to improve tourism infrastructure, such as high-end hotels, amusement centres and theme parks, and to develop existing historical attractions (Zhang and Zhao 2009). In the run-up to the Olympics, iconic buildings were constructed not only to serve a functional purpose, but also to symbolize Beijing's modernity. Two of the more prominent landmarks were the National Stadium, known as the 'Bird's Nest', and the National Aquatics centre with its distinct bubble-clad design. Both of these were designed by internationally renowned architects and cost millions to construct (Zhang and Zhao 2009). The entire Olympic Park, which included the athletes' Village, occupied a large area of land exceeding 1000 hectares.

However, Beijing's construction of these architectural spectacles and infrastructure did raise issues, especially among the locals. To accommodate these structures, selected housing areas in the city were demolished. People were concerned that areas like the old *hutong* would be sacrificed to make way for the Olympic Park, thus displacing residents who were less well-off (Gold and Gold 2008). The human rights group Centre on Human Rights and Evictions estimated that a total of 1.5 million Beijing residents would have been evicted by the start of the Olympic ceremony (Engel 2007). This seemed contradictory to Beijing's efforts to brand itself as a 'city truly suitable for human habitation'. Another issue was the government's treatment of the locals who had contributed to building the landmarks. Many local workers had been employed to build the Olympic landmarks, but were ordered to return to their hometowns during the Games in order to ease security and environmental pressures on the city (Zhang and Zhao 2009: 252). The government seems to have disregarded the contributions of these workers, who were often poor and disadvantaged, and failed to award them due recognition. Lastly, there are doubts as to how aligned the Olympic venues are with the brand identity of Beijing. They are indeed architectural marvels and symbols of modernity, but do not quite reflect the culture and heritage of Beijing. Locals and foreigners alike felt that the main attraction of Beijing is its rich historical heritage (Zhang and Zhao 2009: 251). Certainly, the locals identified more with this heritage than with modernity. In a survey carried out by Zhang and Zhao (2009), respondents believed that Beijing's brand identity could in fact be enhanced if it were known as an ancient capital.

Emerging trends in city branding

A key challenge emerging is the risk of homogeneity among city brands. Although one of the key principles of city branding is to create a unique brand identity, the paradox is that city brands seem to be increasing in homogeneity because cities employ similar formulas in branding (Lui 2008). For instance, many cities use mega-events as a platform to raise the profile of the city, such as the hosting of the Olympics in Turin and Beijing. Another commonly used tool is the construction of iconic landmarks to boost the visibility of a city, like the Guggenheim Museum in Bilbao. Such mega-events and spectacular architecture may not be exclusive

to that particular city and can be reproduced elsewhere. When reproduced in other cities, it can dilute the distinctiveness of a city and reduce differentiation among cities. A case in point, as discussed fully by Elsheshtawy in Chapter 10 of this volume, is that of Abu Dhabi, which aims to establish a Guggenheim museum, even though Guggenheim museums are already found or being planned for many other cities (Evans 2003).

Perhaps in response to this challenge of increasing uniformity, a developing trend is the increasing focus on creativity and local culture as valuable assets that cities can offer (Vanolo 2008), which directs attention to a city's unique characteristics and can thus be used in city branding as sources of differentiation. Creativity can be defined as the ability to create something new through innovation and originality of thought. Creativity exists not only in the realm of art, but also in other areas, such as science, politics and business (Trueman et al. 2008). To illustrate how creativity can be harnessed in building a city brand, we can look at how *haute couture* fashion in Milan contributes to the strength of its city brand (Trueman et al. 2008) and its well-established association with being a fashion capital – a position not easily copied by other cities. Trueman et al. also draw attention to how urban planners are exploring ways to harness the creative talent of its communities, multicultural population and youth as a possible tool for urban regeneration, and examine how 'creative aspects of diversity, ethnicity and demographics' can increase the value of the brand (Trueman et al. 2008: 29).

Related to creative cities and city branding is Okano and Samson's (2010) theoretical framework for promoting creativity in cities and other public spaces. The authors advocate forming an urban strategic management system when developing creative cities that will 'expand the city's capabilities and tolerance, incorporating a city's social sustainability, embracing social inclusion, dynamic learning ability and smartness, and a vision that balances points of dispute' (Okano and Samson 2010: S15). A key guideline highlighted in this framework is the recognition and utilization of arts and design in creating value for a city. For example, high-quality design of products can positively influence people's perception of the city connected to the production of those goods. City managers are advised to select themes, for instance, a vibrant arts scene, which would attract stakeholders and position the city as an interesting and lively place to reside and visit. Another guideline is tolerance in choosing themes that adequately accommodate the desires of a range of people, since a theme that is too narrow may exclude and alienate certain groups. In addition, the framework points out the importance of 'smartness' in developing effective solutions towards practical problems linked to city layout and operation. These must be addressed to satisfy basic needs and expectations of people (Okano and Samson 2010).

A phenomenon similar to the expanding role of creativity in city branding is the rise in prominence of cultural industries, such as arts and heritage, in city branding. One example is the popularity of cultural quarters as a solution to rebrand and revitalize a city (Roodhouse 2009). A cultural quarter is 'a geographical area of a city that acts as a focus for cultural and artistic activities through the presence of a group of buildings devoted to housing a range of such activities' and allows urban planners to 'preserve and encourage cultural production and consumption as well as to physically regenerate a location' (Roodhouse 2009: 82). The rich mix of art, architecture, heritage and creatives in the quarter can help create a unique identity for the city. Nurturing cultural industries in an effort to develop a city brand was also evident in Turin, which, among other initiatives, strove to support local art foundations and celebrate its local culture (Vanolo 2008).

Closing reflections

Much of the literature on city branding comes from the fields of business and marketing, and tends to focus on city branding as a tool to achieve economic benefits for the city. Emphasis is placed on attracting external visitors such as tourists, investors and business people. Less extensive is research that explores the functions of city branding other than as an economic tool, and the effects of city branding on its *internal* population – its residents. The attention Mommaas (2002) pays to the socio-cultural effects of city branding and its possible use as a source of identification for the local community is fairly singular, and there is much room for further research in this direction.

One area that deserves research attention is the socio-cultural effect of city branding on the attitude of residents towards the city; specifically, whether city branding can influence residents' loyalty to the city and their willingness to stay in the long term. Research in this area could prove crucial in the context of the modern-day challenge of retaining local talent. With barriers to migration perhaps comparatively lower than in the past, authorities and policy-makers are trying to keep talented individuals within their society and stem 'brain-drain'. Research into city branding and residents' loyalty could provide findings helpful to the management of human capital. Although a study was previously conducted on city brand attitudes, its focus was different in that it tested the relationship between city attributes and a favourable attitude towards the city brand (Merrilees et al. 2009), but did not explore how city branding itself could be used as a possible tool to influence the locals' loyalty to the city as long-term residents.

Another area of research could be the impact of growing cultural diversity on city branding. The complexity of city branding has already been linked, among other factors, to the challenge of involving multiple stakeholders with diverse interests and backgrounds. In today's increasingly global society, urban communities are made of a growing mix of different ethnicities and cultural backgrounds. Existing literature has not actually delved into how, in particular, rising multiculturalism influences the process of city branding, and the challenges and advantages it possibly brings. The findings could benefit organizations in charge of city branding by providing insight into managing growing multiculturalism in the building of a strong and unified city brand.

City branding has spawned a fast-growing literature. While evolving essentially from marketing theories of product and corporate branding, there is a realization that simply applying product/corporate branding techniques to a city is inadequate. In acknowledgement of the multifaceted dimensions of a city and its difference from a product or corporate entity, models specific to the development of city brands have been developed. These models suggest varying approaches to city branding, but generally highlight key stages, which involve researching current perceptions of the city, developing the brand identity, implementation, and monitoring of the city brand. Measuring a city brand can also be conducted using different models, but the most widely used is the Anholt City Brands Index.

Success factors of city branding are: equal partnership between stakeholders, leadership, cooperation, and a brand management organization that not only implements the brand strategy, but also monitors the brand. Issues encountered in city branding are identified, which most commonly include lack of consensus on the city brand, a top-down approach, and an image–reality gap.

An emerging challenge in city branding today is the risk of homogeneity across cities, as cities follow the same formula in city branding. To find greater sources of differentiation, a developing trend is to focus on a city's creativity and creative industries as a valuable asset in developing a unique city brand. Whether this will be successful remains to be seen, though the evidence to date suggests that the same 'creative city' strategy is being implemented in different cities (Kong et al.

2006). Finally, existing literature tends to direct city branding efforts towards attracting external visitors, and is relatively lacking in the analysis of the relationship between city branding and internal stakeholders, such as residents. More research is needed to study the influence of city branding on attitudes of residents towards the city, such as their loyalty and willingness to live there in the long term. Similarly, as cities become more multicultural, with the greater flows of people across boundaries, the impact on city branding needs to be examined.

City branding is a complex, multifaceted exercise that seems set to stay. A city's success in branding itself can position it well in the global competition, but it would only be part of any urban strategy – albeit an increasingly common, perhaps necessary if insufficient, part of a city's agenda of ambition.

REFERENCES

Aaker, D. A. (1991) *Managing brand equity*. New York: The Free Press.

Anholt, S. (2006) 'The Anholt City Brands Index: How the world views its cities', Retrieved 23 August 2011.

Bagaeen, S. (2007) 'Brand Dubai: the instant city; or the instantly recognizable city', *International Planning Studies* 12 (2), 173–197.

Boo, S., Busser, J., Baloglu, S. (2009) 'A model of customer-based brand equity and its application to multiple destinations', *Tourism Management* 30 (2), 219–231.

Caldwell, N., Freire, J. R. (2004) 'The differences between branding a country, a region and a city: applying the Brand Box Model', *The Journal of Brand Management* 12 (1), 50–61.

Engel, M. (2007) 'Olympic losers', *Financial Times Magazine* 14–15 July, p. 8.

Evans, G. (2003) 'Hard-branding the cultural city – from Prado to Prada', *International Journal of Urban and Regional Research* 27 (2), 417–440.

Garcia, B. (2004) 'Cultural policy and urban regeneration in Western European cities: lessons from experience, prospects for the future', *Local Economy* 19 (4), 312–326.

van Gelder, S., Allan, M. (2006) *City Branding: How Cities Compete in the 21st Century*. London and Amsterdam: Placebrands.

Gold, J. R., Gold, M. M. (2008) 'Olympic cities: regeneration, city rebranding and changing urban agendas', *Geography Compass* 2 (1), 300–318.

Gotham, K. F. (2007) '(Re)branding the big easy – tourism rebuilding in post-Katrina New Orleans', *Urban Affairs Review* 42 (6), 823–850.

Greenberg, M. (2008) *Branding New York: how a city in crisis was sold to the world*. New York: Routledge.

Hankinson, G. (2001) 'Location branding: a study of the branding practices of 12 English cities', *The Journal of Brand Management* 9 (2), 127–142.

Hannigan, J. (2003) 'Symposium on branding, the entertainment economy and urban place building: introduction', *International Journal of Urban and Regional Research* 27 (2), 352–360.

Henderson, J. C. (2007) 'Uniquely Singapore? A case study in destination branding', *Journal of Vacation Marketing* 13 (3), 261–274.

Kavaratzis, M. (2004) 'From city marketing to city branding: towards a theoretical framework for developing city brands', *Place Branding* 1 (1), 58–73.

Kavaratzis, M. (2005) 'Place branding: a review of trends and conceptual models', *The Marketing Review* 5 (4), 329–342.

Kavaratzis, M., Ashworth, G. J. (2006) 'City branding: an effective assertion of identity or a transitory marketing trick?', *Place Branding* 2 (3), 183–194.

Keller, K. L. (2003) *Strategic brand management*. Upper Saddle River, NJ: Prentice-Hall.

Kong, L., Gibson, C., Khoo, L.-M., Semple, A.-L. (2006) 'Knowledges of the creative economy: towards a relational geography of diffusion and adaptation in Asia', *Asia Pacific Viewpoint* 47 (2), 173–194.

Lui, T. L. (2008) 'City-branding without content: Hong Kong's aborted West Kowloon mega-project', *International Development Planning Review* 30 (3), 215–226.

Merrilees, M., Miller, D., Herington, C. (2009) 'Antecedents of residents' city brand attitudes', *Journal of Business Research* 62 (3), 362–367.

Moilanen, T., Rainisto, S. (2009) *How to brand nations, cities and destinations: a planning book for place branding.* New York: Palgrave Macmillan.

Mommaas, J. T. (2002) 'City branding: the necessity of socio-cultural goals' in *Urban Affairs* (ed.) *City branding: image building & building images.* Rotterdam: NAi Uitgevers, 32–48.

Morgan, M., Pritchard, A., Pride, R. (2004) *Destination branding: creating the unique destination proposition.* Oxford: Butterworth-Heinemann.

Okano, H., Samson, D. (2010) 'Cultural urban branding and creative cities: a theoretical framework for promoting creativity in the public spaces', *Cities* 27 (1), S10–S15.

Parkerson, B., Saunders, J. (2005) 'City branding: can goods and services branding models be used to brand cities?', *Place Branding* 1 (3), 242–264.

Pike, S. (2008) *Destination marketing: an integrated marketing communications approach.* Burlington, MA: Butteworth-Heinemann.

Plaza, B. (2006) 'The return on investment of the Guggenheim Museum Bilbao', *International Journal of Urban and Regional Research* 30 (2), 452–467.

Plöger, J. (2007) 'Bilbao city report', *Open Access publications from London School of Economics and Political Science* 43, 1–39.

Qian, M. H. (2009) 'A study of success factors in city branding: the ISE conceptual model', *Marketing Science Innovations and Economic Development*, 313–321.

Roodhouse, S. (2009) 'Understanding cultural quarters in branded cities', in Donald, S. H., Kofman, E. and Kevin, C (eds), *Branding cities: cosmopolitanism, parochialism, and social change.* New York: Routledge, 75–88.

Trueman, M., Cook, D., Cornelius, N. (2008) 'Creative dimensions for branding and regeneration: overcoming negative perceptions of a city', *Place Branding and Public Diplomacy* 4, 29–44.

Trueman, M., Cornelius N. (2006) 'Hanging baskets or basket cases? managing the complexity of city brands and regeneration', Bradford University School of Management *Working Paper Series* 6 (13).

Vanolo, A. (2008) 'The image of the creative city: some reflections on urban branding in Turin', *Cities* 25 (6), 370–382.

Zhang, L., Zhao, S. X. (2009) 'City branding and the Olympic effect: a case study of Beijing', *Cities* 26 (5), 245–254.

CHAPTER 7

COMPETING CITIES AND SPECTACULARIZING URBAN LANDSCAPES[1]

Davide Ponzini

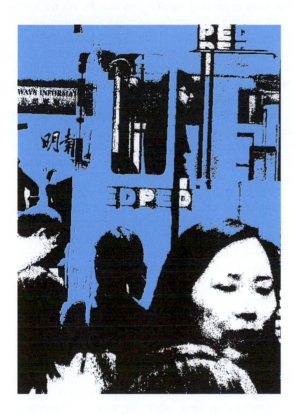

It seems that 'spectacle-ization' is necessary in order for places [...] to somehow be 'recognized' as places to enter the 'global stage'. Such cities can only be taken seriously in the new world dis/order if they are partly at least places of distinct spectacle, through events, museums, ancient remains, festivals, galleries, meetings, sport events and iconic [...] shops, universities, and especially new and refurbished iconic buildings. (Urry, 2007: 134)

Introduction

The quoted passage above suggests that a number of different elements in a city can be turned into spectacle and made to contribute to its 'distinction' on the global stage. This chapter discusses a limited set of urban spectacles, namely those designed by star architects. Over the last decade, increasing attention has been given to the role of architectural celebrities, not only in designing buildings and complexes or in regenerating urban areas, but also in relation to city branding and marketing. The narrative of the 'Bilbao effect' has spread widely in both postindustrial and 'emerging' economies, leading cities apparently to compete in the matter of 'collecting' new buildings and cultural facilities, sometimes with little regard for the functions of these infrastructures and edifices both in their urban context and in the global market.

I shall discuss this global phenomenon in the context of current urban scholarly and policy-making debates and draw on examples of spectacular architecture and international cultural projects such as the ongoing urban transformation in Bilbao and the proposal for Guggenheim museums in Europe, Asia and America. The chapter also takes up decision-making processes related to these and other branded development projects and discusses their urban implications, arguing that, although moderate success in regeneration and tourist attraction may be achieved, the high expectations of policy-makers in terms of urban regeneration and development are often not met. In addition, unbalanced and paradoxical urban effects may sometimes occur. In today's multi-sector city governance networks (typically including local government, public and non-profit cultural institutions, private real estate actors and mixed public-private agencies) culture facilities and activities are generally expected to trigger urban regeneration and economic development, but the latter evidently depends also on complex contextual factors, e.g. accessibility, availability of financial, social and cultural capital for the intervention and for economic and social complementary activities. Yet representing architectural aesthetics as a determinant factor in regeneration and economic revitalization has been the means for diffusing beliefs and behaviours among decision-makers and has provided certain actors with apparently favourable conditions. The support of a limited number of global architectural firms and of similar cultural services and institutions tends to homogenize the urban and cultural landscapes of cities while, paradoxically, these very cities seek to distinguish themselves by hiring star architects or hosting distinct cultural activities.

A better understanding of this phenomenon, and of how cultural politics might mediate various interests or induce the redistribution of positive effects in a larger set of social actors and groups, is crucial both to urban planning in general and to urban cultural policy-making in particular. In my view, the interpretation of outstanding and meaningful architectural interventions should be discussed not as the definition of isolated aesthetic spaces or as the accomplishment of a given spatial or functional order, but as the exploration of possible transformations in the urban landscape and of its different material and immaterial uses. This perspective implies a cultural conception of the urban landscape, of its material and symbolic construction through time, and not only as the accumulation of icons and spectacles to be consumed by the media, private investors or by politics.

Archistarship landings

In the beginning of 2008 three global cities welcomed a piece of architecture designed by Zaha Hadid. In a tour conceived by the fashion designer Karl Lagerfeld, Hong Kong, Tokyo and New York City hosted the colourful media and commercial circus of Chanel. Not everybody agrees whether the Chanel Mobile Art Pavilion is an actual building (with its shape inspired by the 2.55 purse by Gabrielle Chanel and exhibiting several art works), an urban scale piece of design, or a habitable public art piece. After Hong Kong, Tokyo and New York City, the world tour of the Pavilion was programmed to include London, Moscow and Paris, and it would have done so had adverse economic and financial conditions not forced Chanel to shut it down.

This example seems germane to describe the current drift towards the spectacularization of architecture and it highlights some of its aspects. The striking aesthetics are only one feature (and are not dissimilar to past phases of architecture, to tell the truth). What may be more characteristic of today are the deliberate trespassing of genre and style

boundaries, together with the importance of the public performance of the star architect, the limited interest accorded to the surrounding forms of urban living, the leveraging of locations, the intersection of private interests and the deployment of old or new symbols of contemporary cities. Chanel is not the only company seeking to link its name to the work of famous architects: de Portzamparc for Louis Vuitton in New York City, Hadid for BMW, Sanaa for Dior, and many others. Architects today have a stable place in the rich market of production of images and meanings to be sold in the form of the brand (Klingman, 2007).

In the past, many architects blurred the boundaries between different art forms. They now more and more consciously design, forge identities and perform for private companies and public administrations as well. Both Betsky (1997) and Jencks (2005) have argued that the aesthetics of enigmatic architectural icons can shape social and media visibility and be a communicative vehicle. In contemporary times, the aesthetic shock only can induce individuals to consider the artistic and communicative value of one building or a place. Bernard Tschumi (1994) conceptualized some strategies of contemporary architecture, e.g. to de-familiarize architectural views and spaces, to fragment and diversify architectural codes and languages, also by putting new design and building technologies to work. The contestation of formal and functional hierarchies is a typical means of reaching unusual and eye-catching results, requiring the user to interpret these new urban signifiers.[2] Interestingly for investors, urban promoters and others, spectacularization can result in a formal and meaningful distinction of buildings in the urban environment that turns them into images for celebrating the past, hosting cultural, entertainment or sport events, or promoting tourism. The contents of the play may vary, but a significant increase of attention to its packaging and media exposure can be witnessed (Foster, 2002). However, highlighting the importance of social and media interpretation rather than actual building and functional features seems crucial for deeper analysis of spectacularization.

Besides inducing us to rethink aesthetic categories, the example of the Chanel Mobile Art Pavilion requires us to pay further attention to the relationships between this structure and the place where this 'archistarship' lands and operates. The landing and taking-off attitude of architectural objects that are similar to the Chanel Pavilion is not totally new, as well as the disjunction between urban forms and social material and symbolic uses, but generally architecture is supposed to be a stable part of the city. Some authors, alluding to the pervasive lack of efficacy in solving contemporary urban problems, maintain that architectural discussion can occur atopically and consider individual artifacts, even if they produce surrounding urban spaces that are generic and of little value. Since this juxtaposition between the stability of urban forms and the insta-bility of hosted functions has been accepted – probably in rhetorical and instrumental ways – as unavoid-able features of contemporary cities, architecture has been theoretically legitimized to induce any potential mutation with respect to the urban context (Koolhaas, 1978). It is not possible to dismiss the relationship between architectural interventions and their urban contexts so easily without encoun-tering some potential contradictions, such as induc-ing spectacular but dysfunctional and meaningless urban places.

Hadid's Chanel Mobile Art Pavilion has been interpreted by many as an object that can be moved to any place. In fact, it demonstrates the opposite: the Pavilion moved between particular global cities that offered specialized activities and fluxes related to fashion, high accessibility and visibility, and was positioned in specific areas. For example, in New York City it was located in the Rumsey Playfield in Central Park, on Fifth Avenue and a few blocks away from Museum Mile, which includes the Guggenheim Museum and the Met-ropolitan Museum of Art. Similarly, most spec-tacular architecture that is located in ways that contrast it abruptly with the urban fabric and its multiple layering become the site of special functions, such as museums, galleries, libraries, or other private or public functions. These depend sys-tematically on the urban environment and its stability in order to survive (also financially) and to display their putative communicative, social and economic impact.

The name of the star architect has become a key factor not only in the design of projects for develop-ing and regenerating urban areas, but also in defin-ing a positive and communicative image, since visibility of interventions has been considered to be immaterial competitive factors. As Jencks has noted: 'Cities are competing against each other for icons and are using architects to drum up the

"something different"' (Jencks, 2005: 19). Currently, one can see 'emerging' countries apparently bet-ting on this rationale, leveraging the aura and visi-bility of name architects, even if this means hiring performers who do not necessarily dialogue with local culture while consolidating his/her status. As Saunders (2007: 3) has put it:

in places where big money intersects with big new urbanization, high-rise both mundane and spectacular have become aggressive assertions of a city or country's unignorability, rapid progress, and membership in modernization's big league. Dubai and now Abu Dhabi present the most mind-boggling instances of a sudden and extensive use of architecture to buy a way both into the 21st century and into the cultural traditions of (largely Western) civilization ('We'd like three Picassos, two Matisses...').

The use of cultural attractors for triggering urban development has often been coupled with the spec-tacular artifacts and flamboyant architectural per-formance (Benedikt, 1999; Gospodini, 2002; Sorkin, 2003; Saunders, 2005; Grima, 2008). Sudjic (1993: 76) is one analyst who anticipated and mocked this tendency:

There is now an international flying circus which travels the world leaving signature buildings in its wake. The major cities of the world share a need to collect them, in the same way that art galleries from Osaka to Liège need Henry Moore, David Hockney and Julian Schnabel. So Richard Meier builds essentially the same building in Frankfurt and The Hague, and Michael Graves builds apartment towers in Yokohama and offices in Atlanta.

The number of such examples is almost unlim-ited, but stories are not as simple and happily-ending as the dominant 'Bilbao effect' rhetoric tends to suggest. For example, a typical culture-led city branding mega-project for the West Kowloon Cultural District was envisioned and granted with HK$21.6 billion budget by the Government of the Hong Kong Special Administrative Region and finally designed by the archistar Norman Foster. The project was intended to promote tourism and the media visibility of a world city through interna-tional museums such as the Guggenheim and through spectacular architecture (e.g. the world's largest outdoor roof, Foster-designed museum facility) but it was heavily contested. In 2006 the city-state had to initiate a new and lengthy process of public consultation (Lui, 2008) and new project selection. In 2010 three proposals (respectively by Foster and Partners, Rem Koolhaas-OMA and Rocco Yin) were at stake, while some smaller-scale cultural and leisure activities are being promoted onsite. In this case, despite massive economic resources, the amendment to urban regulation and the star architect's aura could not bypass political confrontation and local community positions. In another instance, Renzo Piano outlined a development project in the 1,400,000 square metres of abandoned brownfields of a steel factory on the outskirts of Milan, including a new museum, a new train station, a marketplace, research and education facilities, office space and housing towers (Goldstein Bolocan and Bonfantini, 2007). Partly because of fluctuations in the real estate market and legal problems, the developer gave up long before opening the construction site. In this case, economic instability stymied the implementation of a project designed by an architect who was appreciated by both the developer and the local authorities.

Of course, many spectacular mega-projects, whether in North America, Asia or Europe, do not face such shortcomings. Emerging capitals of consumerism can count on massive economic resources, such as Doha's flamboyant sport stadia and facilities, iconic office towers and hotels, various projects signed by Pei, Isozaki, Correa, Arup, KEO and other international firms, and the subsequent accumulation of urban spectacles (Adhan, 2008). Doha may be following the archetype of the Baltimore Inner Harbor development, or most likely just competing with the closer and contemporary Dubai (Acuto, 2010). But what about other cases, such as the branded Olympics or World Expo developments, which have mushroomed in cities on all five continents? All these tend to be developed in a state of exception, and are subject to fewer limitations than most. Economic resources, *ad hoc* planning powers derogating from ordinary planning logic and procedure are legitimized by actors and urban development interests through discursive constructions such as the 'Bilbao effect'. In this sense, spectacular architecture is increasingly interpreted as an immaterial competitive factor by local coalitions, but it does not necessarily mean better projects or final urban effects.

Competing cities and the 'Bilbao effect' narrative

Influenced by trends in the global economy (e.g. the growing role of services and immaterial production, knowledge-based economy) and in Western society in particular (e.g. more leisure time, increasing expenditures on culture, entertainment and tourism, open and cosmopolitan societies), policymakers have developed a rationale for branding and marketing cities through attractive pictures, cultural amenities and spectacular artifacts, regardless of the lack of supporting evidence – in this the process is similar to other globalization rhetoric.[3] The metaphors of the entrepreneurial city, of the city as a growth and entertainment machine, are useful in describing competition among cities in such urban developments. In our current mature capitalism, cities and regions have assumed a fundamental role in wealth circulation and accumulation. David Harvey (1985, 1989a and 1989b) elaborated a conceptual framework that anticipated many empirical studies regarding contemporary social and economic organization, where cities compete in space for attracting production and workers, for specializing in consumption and entertainment, economic control and wealth redistribution. By analyzing Baltimore's urban affairs in the broader frame of late capitalist urban trends, he noted that entrepreneurial tendencies in city management were often connected with the presence of post-modern architecture, conference and retail centres, cultural and entertainment facilities, and attempts to host Olympics, Expos or sport in potentially decontextualized buildings and complexes. These phenomena can be motivated by the fact that higher financial mobility and availability limited the rise of other monopolies and consequently the economic appreciation of such places and facilities has become increasingly important for capital accumulation and circulation (Harvey, 2002). A sociologically refined interpretation of competitive trends describes contemporary cities as entertainment machines (Lloyd and Clark 2002; Clark, 2004). In order to attract specialized workers and a high-income population (people who tend to be more inclined to spend and less in need of social services), cities tend to target higher quality-of-life expectations, in terms of cultural services and entertainment. These dynamics impact local systems in terms of urban revitalization and gentrification well beyond traditional touristic flows.

The flagship project of the new Guggenheim Museum by Frank Gehry in Bilbao, opened in 1997, was interpreted as the trigger for a broader process of branding and revitalizing the city. The description of this urban transformation process by experts in the field of architecture and urban design is sometimes very simplistic. For example, in the words of an architectural critic:

> *The rust belt city [...] needed a postcard image comparable to the Eiffel Tower and the Sydney Opera House to symbolize its emergence as a player on the chessboard of a united Europe and globalized economy. It needed a monument. One building and $110 million later, Bilbao is now a contender as a world-class city, and many of the world's second- and third-tier cities have called Mr. Gehry's office, hoping for a comparable Cinderella transformation. (Giovannini, 2001: 1)*

Often, this museum has been interpreted as a piece of design on the urban scale, an artwork or a monument, probably also because it is located in a very visible site surrounded by the Nervion river, whose waters reflect the building with postcard-like effects. Furthermore, the name of the architect was important. The vice-mayor of the city stated: 'good architecture is not enough anymore: to seduce we need names' (cited in Gonzales, 2006: 847). These are among the reasons why the Guggenheim became more of an icon for the city and for its renaissance – a brand, rather than just a museum (Klingman, 2007). Furthermore, a number of urban and infrastructural projects appeared in subsequent years designed by stars such as Foster, Isozaki, Pelli and Calatrava (Gospodini, 2002).

Regarding this specific case, the insights of urban scholars are probably more accurate, less simplistic and more cautious (McNeill, 2000; Plaza, 2000 and 2006; Evans, 2003; Plaza and Haarich, 2009). If one contextualizes the construction of the museum in the broader process of transformation of the city, and analyzes different public and private

Photo 7.1 Bilbao, 2010. Frank Gehry, Guggenheim Museum; Jeff Koons, Puppy (Photographer: Michele Nastasi)

investments, the functioning of real estate mechanisms and the perverse impacts of some development projects, one notes the inconsistencies between the narration and the actual processes of urban regeneration and local development (Moulaert et al., 2002; Plöger, 2007; Ponzini, 2010). Even if the powerful narrative representing architectural aesthetics as a determinant factor in regeneration does not seem to respond to actual urban processes, the use of branded large-scale projects as a 'quick fix' for contemporary cities is widespread in Western and recently in rising Asian cities as well (Kong, 2007), sometimes covering simple economic interests, sometimes more complex political and symbolic dynamics. However, spectacular architecture and the use of star architects seem to have a more articulated set of rationalities and reasons than the urge for spectacular global competition. It would be wrong to describe this phenomenon as competition in the architectural market, let alone in the real estate market, on the basis of the assumption that each city intervenes as a collective actor, rationally collecting development projects and fine works of architecture. In the case of spectacular architecture, the collector is not a unitary decision-maker but a complex social organization which adopts rationales that are not only economic but political, and are sometimes based on cultural and social constructs. On the other hand, the architectural debate sometimes confines itself to the discussion of the aesthetics and may either fuel or alternatively pay little attention to the social and cultural constructs that are functional in creating and spreading the current starchitecture phenomenon. The numerous problems and failures of the Guggenheim Foundation in trying to start Bilbao-like processes in Taiwan, Mexico, Brazil and the United Arab Emirates tend to confirm the scepticism towards this idea of architectural collecting.

McGuggenheim: global museums and franchise urban development projects?

The dominant narrative of the 'Bilbao effect' and the expectations attached to iconic buildings and star architects' interventions are exemplified by the Guggenheim Foundation's projects around the world. The question here is not how this sort of global process is culturally indifferent to the locale, but that these projects show how the 'Bilbao effect' narrative does not always correspond to the reality of locating cultural facilities in actual urban contexts (Ockman, 2004).[4] The director of the Guggenheim Foundation claimed that, after the Bilbao experience, he received about 60 proposals for participation in urban development projects in the world (Guggenheim Foundation, 2000). A number of hypotheses and experimentations in this delocalization season faced failures that led to a further reconsideration of the Bilbao story. Rem Koolhaas designed the Las Vegas Guggenheim for the Venetian Casino. A few months after the inauguration the museum closed. To be sure, intense competition in the entertainment industry and the pace of attraction substitution in Las Vegas both exerted an influence, but there is no doubt that it was a failed experiment. In New York City, a $950 million intervention was planned for a new Gehry-designed Guggenheim Museum on the East River, including a library and educational facilities, a theatre and other public spaces. The plan slowed down, probably affected by post-9/11 adverse conditions, and it was finally cancelled. In Rio de Janeiro, Thomas Krens developed a preliminary scheme for the Brazilian Guggenheim Museum to be located in a partially underwater facility designed by Jean Nouvel. The project was halted after harsh criticism mentioning the already existing local Museum of Modern Art, designed by Afonso Eduardo Reidy, and dramatic and unsolved economic and social problems. The city of Taichung, Taiwan, envisioned a new Guggenheim designed by Zaha Hadid in order to attract cultural tourism. Local conditions, among which the absence of a nearby international airport, pushed the local government to cancel the project (Sudjic, 2005; Martinez, 2006). In Guadalajara, Mexico, after a feasibility study for a new museum, the Mexican studio Enrique Norten/ Ten Arquitectos was preferred to international teams of Jean Nouvel or Asymptote to develop the concept. This project was cancelled as well. More recently, a Guggenheim Hermitage Museum designed by Zaha Hadid was planned to open in Vilnius. At the time of writing significant doubts are being expressed about the feasibility of the project and apparently the Guggenheim Foundation alone will locate a new facility in Helsinki instead.

Only recently has Thomas Krens publicly recognized the fact that 'the new Guggenheim became a cultural symbol, but it was based on the foundation

Photo 7.2   Dubai, 2010. Skidmore Owings Merrill, Burj Khalifa (Photographer: Michele Nastasi)

of a larger system' (Koolhaas, 2007: 334). After the many years of worldwide expansion he promoted (notably the opening of smaller museums in Soho in 1992 and in Berlin, and enhancing Peggy Guggenheim's activities in Venice) – a kind of global franchising (McNeill, 2000) – the Guggenheim today is facing far less favourable conditions and has appointed a new director, Richard Armstrong, with a brief to focus more on the management of existing museums than to promote further delocalization projects.[5] Yet one of the Guggenheim ventures launched earlier still has promise. This is the Gehry-designed museum based on an aesthetic similar to the Bilbao masterpiece that was ordered by Abu Dhabi, in the United Arab Emirates, as part of a package deal including an outpost of the Louvre Museum designed by Jean Nouvel, Zaha Hadid's Performing Arts Centre, Tadao Ando's Maritime Museum, and Norman Foster's Sheikh Zayed National Museum. Together these will constitute the Cultural District of Saadiyat Island (literally, the 'Island of Happiness'; cf. Elsheshtawy, 2008, and his chapter in this volume; Ponzini, 2011).

Abu Dhabi's spectacularized Cultural District

Abu Dhabi has peculiar economic and institutional conditions, amplifying several features that are common in contemporary large-scale and culture-led development projects and in the use of star architecture (cf. Elsheshtawy's chapter in this volume). Suffice it to say here that from the political point of view the number of actors taking part in urban planning and development decision-making is very limited, in most cases concentrating all the material resources, land and financial means that are needed for large-scale cultural and urban development projects. Political consensus and legitimization seem symbolically important but are irrelevant in actual terms: laws and rules can be adapted both in the markets and in the urban planning field, where the competent office has little or non-existing power in regulating the growth engine. The marketing of projects and their link to Western culture and architecture is dominant. Urban design decisions are almost entirely made by developers proposing simplified master plans for complex development processes. In this sense, one can see the extreme urban effects of removing part of the local governments' political preoccupation in the global competition era. Abu Dhabi's economic diversification goals now need to immobilize huge capitals in the real estate market and in future urban development. The higher the value of localized capital, also due to some star architect's signature, the more credit the government can obtain from the international financial system for future investments in urban development. The only evident limit is the overall credibility of the development operations, guaranteed by the presence of international actors and cultural institutions. Nonetheless, the role of important international cultural and economic institutions is curtailed, with reference to cultural management, but not to other aspects – e.g. spatial organization, the modes and conditions of urban growth or the localization of other complementary functions – which the future management will potentially depend on (Ponzini, 2009).

The symbolic dimension of Abu Dhabi's Cultural District and many other franchise cultural projects is linked to the image of the nation and strengthened by the artistic aura of iconic architecture in a contradictory way and it shows the enormous difficulty of matching global objectives with local identities, environments and functions, which is typical of Western flagship projects (McNeill and Tewdwr-Jones, 2003). The conditions in Abu Dhabi may not be common elsewhere, but they can help us think through the general critique and the paradoxes of this contemporary trend of spectacularizing urban environments.

Critiques and paradoxes

Several issues emerge from these cases. They have to do with the cumulative effects on decision-making and investment strategy, the homogenization of the urban environment induced by spectacularization, and the role of different actors involved. If cities bet entirely on a Bilbao-like strategy, collateral effects can be expected at the level both of individual cities and in aggregated terms. Excessive attention and resources devoted to immaterial economic and political goals can affect distributive and material outcome in the medium and long term (Harvey, 1989b). The representation of cities already has its hierarchies and rankings deriving from long-term accumulation of cultural

and reputational capitals and it might be difficult to alter these despite massive investments in cultural and specialized services or in spectacularizing the urban environment.

The paradoxical effects of this entrepreneurial strategy need to be highlighted, for the multiplication of places trying to catalyze consumers' attention, to boost consumption and real estate values (Sklair, 2010), tends to reduce their uniqueness, making rather indeterminate the connections to contextual cultural meanings and symbols. The striving to put in place specialized tertiary activities tends to push real estate values towards the higher levels of geographically distant spaces. The benefits of this growth machine in term of potential wealth redistribution to actors that are not involved in real estate speculation, especially lower-income groups, can be seriously doubted (Molotch, 1976; Logan and Molotch, 1987). Besides the socially uneven effects, this strategy tends to locate cultural amenities and attractors in homogeneous and inefficient ways and create niches (Clark et al., 2002), potentially inducing irrational intra-urban competition for development and appreciation among different areas, especially in contexts that are weakly planned and that have limited public debate.

Even if one believes that tourism flows depend on the localization of one spectacular cultural facility, it is crucial to stress that the creation of more or less homologous pieces of design in different cities will reduce flows in any given place (Plaza, 2000). It is evident, however, that global flows depend on a wider set of local conditions. Furthermore, and more generally, the multiplication of similar aesthetically striking artifacts all over the world has the paradoxical effect of internationally homogenizing the urban landscape (Muñoz, 2008). Even leaving aside the fact that investing in expensive facilities may distract funding or increase the future costs of cultural management and cultural offer, any consideration of using exceptional architecture in the context of urban transformation should, at least, pay more attention to the material, political and symbolic interests promoting such use, their vested interests, their stated and unstated goals and their modes of action (Jansen, 2007). Also to be considered is the incremental composition of the specific urban landscape, including notable artifacts and different urban fabrics, as well as infrastructures and open spaces and their social meaning in the many forms of contemporary living.

Photo 7.3 Paris, 2010. La Défense (Photographer: Michele Nastasi)

In contemporary urban contexts, where architecture appears to have less and less influence over decision-making, evidently the highest concern of the key actors is not the aesthetic and functional quality of the built environment. If anything, architectural aesthetics are interpreted as instrumental for economic, political, or symbolic objectives of public and private decision-makers. The spectacularizing architect has possibly become more and more an artist who is supposedly capable of triggering positive urban development processes. For his ability to catalyze political consensus and media attention, higher fees are generally paid to him by real estate developers and politicians alike (Julier, 2005). Along similar lines, art curators and cultural institutions are able to increase their scope, reputation and turnover, sometimes interpreting their cultural mission in ways that not only instrumentalize other actors, but also are risky for the entire cultural system.

The 'Bilbao effect' narrative has been rejected in various contexts, as discussed already. In several cases, on the basis of sheer common sense or for a shrewd assessment of the political or social costs, city managers and policy-makers have been unwilling to replicate a ready-made competitiveness-boosting recipe. In many others, however, the paradoxical and perverse impacts have not been considered holistically by many decision-makers who have fostered signature cultural facilities and urban development projects. In this regard it seems important to add some final considerations.

From architectural collecting to planning urban landscapes

One perverse result of spectacularization is the homogeneity of architectural outcomes in radically different cultural, aesthetic, urban, political, economic, social and institutional contexts. This homogeneity is not due merely to a generic process of globalization but to the production and circulation of specific metaphors and narratives regarding the urban impact of spectacular architecture and their connections to financial and political mechanisms. While the narrative of competitiveness promotes urban projects that resemble one another, the territories concerned do not. The example cited at the outset of the Mobile Art Pavilion showing a piece of architecture landing and transforming the urban environment, and its obvious link with the 'Bilbao effect' narrative, reveals on the contrary that place and context are determinant. The idea of promoting the image and ultimately governing the development of a city by collecting signature architecture is still widespread today in the media, and more surprisingly among decision-makers, planners and architects. But their aspirations are deeply flawed.

At a time when the financial crisis induces cuts in spectacularization costs, it might be wise to critically contest this tendency, without falling into the easy condemnation of this or that type of architect, urban planner, developer, policy-maker or others. Aesthetically striking interventions were part of the built environment well before the post-modern age and they will continue well beyond it. In my view, therefore, the interpretation of outstanding architectural interventions ought to be discussed not in terms of isolated aesthetic spaces or as the accomplishment of a given order, but as the exploration of possible transformations in the urban landscape and of its different material and immaterial uses (Palermo, 2008; Palermo and Ponzini, 2010). Such a perspective implies a *cultural* conception of the urban landscape, of its material and symbolic construction through time, and not only as the accumulation of icons to be consumed by the media, private investors or politics.

Notes

1 This chapter presents some of the results of a broader research project carried out with the financial support of the International Research Scholarship in Memory of Giovanni Agnelli, funded by UniCredit Private Banking and the Agnelli Foundation. Part of this research has been published in Ponzini 2010, 2011; also in Ponzini and Nastasi, 2011. I offer heartfelt thanks to Michele Nastasi for selecting and allowing me to use his photos and would like to acknowledge Jill Diane Friedman's linguistic advice.

2 In the past, extreme conditions were considered in order to analyze and discuss how the attention of observers and consumers was attracted by promiscuous architectural, spectacular and communicative elements (Venturi et al., 1977). More elaborate and general theories have been recently proposed, among others, by Vidler (1992, 2000).

3 On entrepreneurial cities or regions, see Jessop (1998); on urban competitiveness strategies see Beauregard and Pierre (2000); regarding the creative city, Ponzini and Rossi (2010).

4 As correctly noted by McNeill (2000).

5 For a comment on the choice and interviews, see 'Guggenheim Chooses a Curator, Not a Showman', *New York Times* online, September 23, 2008.

REFERENCES

Acuto, M. (2010) 'High-rise Dubai urban entrepreneurialism and the technology of symbolic power', *Cities*, 27(4): 272–284.

Adhan, K. (2008) 'Rediscovering the Island: Doha's urbanity from pearls to spectacle', in Y. Elsheshtawy (ed.), *The Evolving Arab City: Tradition, Modernity and Urban Development*. London and New York: Routledge, pp. 218–257.

Beauregard, R. A. and Pierre, J. (2000) 'Disputing the global: A sceptical view of locality-based international initiatives', *Policy & Politics*, 28(4): 465–478.

Benedikt, M. (1999) 'Less for less yet: on architecture's value(s) in the marketplace', *Harvard Design Magazine*, 7: 10–14.

Betsky, A. (1997) *Icons: Magnets of Meaning*. San Francisco: Chronicle Books.

Clark, T. N. (ed.) (2004) *The City as an Entertainment Machine*. Amsterdam: Elsevier.

Clark, T. N., Lloyd, R., Wong, K. K. and Jain, P. (2002) 'Amenities drive urban growth', *Journal of Urban Affairs*, 24(5): 493–515.

Elsheshtawy, Y. (2008) 'Cities of sand and fog: Abu Dhabi's global ambition', in Y. Elsheshtawy (ed.), *The Evolving Arab City: Tradition, Modernity and Urban Development*. London and New York: Routledge, pp. 258–304.

Evans, G. (2003) 'Hard branding the cultural city: from Prado to Prada', *International Journal of Urban and Regional Research*, 27(2): 417–440.

Foster, H. (2002) *Design and Crime*. London: Verso.

Giovannini, J. (2001) 'The Bilbao effect: moving beyond national borders, city-states are emerging on the global map, powered by world-class architecture', *Red Herring Magazine*, 12 February. Available at: www.acturban.org/biennial/doc_net_cities/the_bilbao_effect.htm

Goldstein Bolocan, M. and Bonfantini, B. (eds) (2007) *Milano Incompiuta. Interpretazioni urbanistiche del mutamento*. Milan: Franco Angeli.

Gonzales, S. (2006) 'Scalar narratives in Bilbao: a cultural politics of scales approach to the study of urban policy', *International Journal of Urban and Regional Research*, 30(4): 836–857.

Gospodini, A. (2002) 'European cities in competition and the new "uses" of urban design', *Journal of Urban Design*, 7(1): 59–73.

Grima, J. (ed.) (2008) *A Critical Situation: What to Make of Starchitecture, and Who to Blame for It*. New York: Forum for Urban Design.

Guggenheim Foundation (2000) 'Press Office release #912,27 September 2000. Guggenheim Foundation Announces Planning Alliance with Frank O. Gehry & Associates and Rem Koolhaas/AMO', retrieved from www.guggenheim.org/press_releases/release_51.html on May 18, 2009.

Harvey, D. (1985) *The Urbanization of Capital: Studies in the History and Theory of Capitalist Urbanization.* Oxford: Basil Blackwell.

Harvey, D. (1989a) *The Condition of Postmodernity. An Enquiry into the Origins of Cultural Change.* Oxford: Blackwell.

Harvey, D. (1989b) 'From managerialism to entrepreneurialism: the transformation in urban governance in late capitalism', *Geografiska Annaler B*, 71(1): 3–17.

Harvey, D. (2002) 'The art of rent: globalization, monopoly, and the commodification of culture', in L. Panitch and C. Leys (eds), *Socialist Register 2002: A World of Contradictions.* Chicago: Haymarket Books, pp. 93–110.

Jansen, O. B. (2007) 'Culture stories: understanding cultural urban branding', *Planning Theory,* 6(3): 211–236.

Jencks, C. (2005) *The Iconic Building: The Power of Enigma.* London: Frances Lincoln.

Jessop, B. (1998) 'The enterprise of narrative and the narrative of enterprise: place marketing and the entrepreneurial city', in T. Hall and P. Hubbard (eds), *The Entrepreneurial City.* Chichester: Wiley, pp. 77–99.

Julier, G. (2005) 'Urban designscapes and the production of aesthetic consent', *Urban Studies*, 42(5/6): 869–887.

Klingman, A. (2007) *Brandscapes: Architecture in the Experience Economy.* Cambridge, MA: MIT Press.

Kong, L. (2007) 'Cultural icons and urban development in asia: economic imperative, national identity and global city status', *Political Geography,* 26(4): 383–404.

Koolhaas, R. (1978) *Delirious New York: A Retroactive Manifesto for Manhattan.* London: Thames & Hudson.

Koolhaas, R. (2007) 'After Bilbao: Thomas Krens' vision for Abu Dhabi as a "cultural destination"', *Volume-Al Manakh*, 12: 334–336.

Lloyd, R. and Clark, T. N. (2002) 'The city as an entertainment machine', in K. Fox Gotham (ed.), *Critical Perspectives in Urban Redevelopment.* New York: Elsevier, pp. 357–378.

Logan, J. R. and Molotch, H. L. (1987) *Uraban Fortunes: The Political Economy of Place.* Berkeley, CA: University of California Press.

Lui, T. (2008) 'City-branding without content: Hong Kong's aborted West Kowloon megaproject, 1998–2006', *International Development Planning Review*, 30(3): 215–226.

Martinez, J. (2006) 'Financing a global Guggenheim museum', Master's thesis, Louisiana State University, Baton Rouge, LA, accessibile at: http://etd.lsu.edu/docs/available/etd-04032006-174214/unrestricted/Martinez_thesis.pdf.

McNeill, D. (2000) 'McGuggenisation? National identity and globalisation in the Basque country', *Political Geography* 19(4): 473–494.

McNeill, D. and Tewdwr-Jones, M. (2003) 'Architecture, banal nationalism and re-territorialization', *International Journal of Urban and Regional Research*, 27(3): 738–743.

Molotch, H. (1976) 'The city as a growth machine: toward a political economy of place', *American Journal of Sociology*, 82(2): 309–332.

Moulaert, F., Swyngedouw, E. and Rodriguez, A. (2002) 'Neoliberal urbanization in Europe: large-scale urban development projects and the new urban policy', *Antipode*, 34(3): 547–582.

Muñoz, F. (2008) *UrBANALizaction: paisajes communes, lugares globales.* Barcelona: Gustavo Gili.

Ockman, J. (2004) 'New politics of the spectacle: "Bilbao" and the global imagination', in D. M. Lasansky and B. McLaren (eds), *Architecture and Tourism: Perception, Performance and Place.* New York: Berg, pp. 227–240.

Palermo, P. C. (2008) 'Thinking over urban landscapes: interpretations and courses of action', in G. Maciocco (ed.), *Urban Landscape Perspectives.* Heidelberg, Berlin, London, New York: Springer.

Palermo, P. C. and Ponzini, D. (2010) *Spatial Planning and Urban Development: Critical Perspectives.* Heidelberg, Berlin, London, New York: Springer.

Plaza, B. (2000) 'Evaluating the influence of a large cultural artifact in the attraction of tourism: the Guggenheim Museum of Bilbao case', *Urban Affairs Review*, 36(2): 264–274.

Plaza, B. (2006) 'The return on investment of the Guggenheim Museum in Bilbao', *International Journal of Urban and Regional Research*, 30(2): 452–467.

Plaza, B. and Haarich, S. N. (2009) 'Museums for urban regeneration? Exploring conditions for their effectiveness', *Journal of Urban Regeneration and Renewal*, 2(3): 259–271.

Plöger, J. (2007) 'Bilbao: City Report'. LSE Case Report 43. London: London School of Economics. Available online at: http://sticerd.lse.ac.uk/dps/case/cr/CASEreport43.pdf.

Ponzini, D. (2009) 'Urban implications of cultural policy networks: the case of the Mount Vernon Cultural District in Baltimore', *Environment and Planning C: Government and Policy*, 27(3): 433–450.

Ponzini, D. (2010) 'Bilbao effects and narrative defects: a critical re-appraisal of an urban narrative', *Cahiers de recherche du Programme Villes & Territoires*. Paris: Sciences Po, pp. 1–15.

Ponzini, D. (2011) 'Large-scale development projects and star architecture in the absence of democratic politics: the case of Abu Dhabi, UAE', *Cities*, 28(3): 251–259.

Ponzini, D. and Rossi, U. (2010) 'Becoming a creative city: the entrepreneurial mayor, network politics, and the promises of an urban renaissance', *Urban Studies*, 47(5): 1037–1057.

Ponzini, D. and Nastasi, M. (2011) *Starchitecture: Scenes, Actors and Spectacles in Contemporary Cities.* Turin and London: Allemandi.

Saunders, W. S. (2005) 'Preface', in W. S. Saunders (ed.), *Commodification and Spectacle in Architecture: A Harvard Design Magazine Reader.* Minneapolis, MN: University of Minnesota Press.

Saunders, W. S. (2007) 'High-rise fever, architects gone wild, instant cities', *Harvard Design Magazine*, 26(3).

Sklair, L. (2010) 'Iconic architecture and the culture-ideology of consumerism', *Theory, Culture & Society*, 27(5): 135–159.

Sorkin, M. (2003) 'Brand Aid; or, The Lexus and the Guggenheim (Further Tales of the Notorious B.I.G.ness)', *Harvard Design Magazine*, 17: 1–5.

Sudjic, D. (1993) *The 100 Mile City.* London: Flamingo.

Sudjic, D. (2005) *The Edifice Complex: How the Rich and Powerful Shape the World.* London and New York: Allen Lane.

Tschumi, B. (1994) *Architecture and Disjunction.* Cambridge, MA: MIT Press.

Urry, J. (2007) 'The power of spectacle', in *Visionary Power, Producing the Contemporary City. International Architecture Biennale Rotterdam.* Rotterdam: Nai Publishers, pp. 131–141.

Venturi, R., Scott Brown, D. and Izenour, S. (1977) *Learning from Las Vegas.* Cambridge, MA: MIT Press.

Vidler, A. (1992) *The Architectural Uncanny: Essays in the Modern Unhomely.* Cambridge, MA: MIT Press.

Vidler, A. (2000) *Warped Space: Art, Architecture and Anxiety in Modern Culture.* Cambridge, MA: MIT Press.

CHAPTER 8

THE CREATIVE CITIES DISCOURSE: PRODUCTION AND/OR CONSUMPTION?

Stuart Cunningham

The already considerable debate about what constitutes a 'creative' city becomes ever more critical as the world urbanizes at a rapid pace. In this chapter the author argues that the key tensions in discussions over what makes cities more conducive to and supportive of creativity revolve around perspectives that are either production-centric or consumption-centric. Scholars are increasingly prepared to claim priority for the city-region over the nation-state as an economic and cultural agent in the contemporary world, but are they ready to deal with major changes in the nature of cultural production and consumption themselves? A number of examples of new challenges for the creative cities 'discourse' rounds out the chapter.

Introduction

I live in a place called Brisbane. The city, along with the entire city-region of southeast Queensland

(reaching south to the Gold Coast, north to the Sunshine Coast, and westward to Toowoomba), has undergone rapid population growth over the last decade or two, fuelled mostly by internal migration from Australia's southern states. Indeed, for a period of time in the 2000s, it was the second fastest-growing city-region in the western world, second only to Phoenix, with growth rates exhibiting classic signs of sun-belt migrations during that period. Like Phoenix, southeast Queensland attracted retirees, together with those escaping higher housing costs in the larger Australian metropolises. In the most recent wave of such migration, however, professionals have, for the first time, become a significant part of the cohort moving into the region, attracted by challenging career opportunities along with the well-established lifestyle, family rearing and housing affordability factors. Although internal migration slowed down when the global financial crisis impacted on Queensland's economy, the demographics of this most recent wave would count among Richard Florida's (2002) creative professionals.

That said, Brisbane is no real contender for the upper tiers of creative cities. Indeed, in creative cities place-competition, it would stand a long way back – in the third or fourth tier – and is still emerging from a long history of political and cultural backwardness. The well-known Australian satirist Barry Humphries was at his coruscating best when he proposed that Australia is the Brisbane of the world! Nevertheless, the data show clear growth in the professional class, and this has had beneficial impacts on cultural participation and consumption. Between 2001 and 2006, the percentage of tertiary-qualified workers rose from 19.2 per cent to 23.3 per cent, while conversely the percentage of the lowest qualified workers decreased from 50.8 per cent to 43.0 per cent (Australian census data in ID 2010: 27). Accompanying this trend has been a corresponding growth of the specifically creative workforce, by which I mean the creative and support jobs related to arts, design, media and communications, not the generalised white- and no-collar workforce as defined by

Florida (see Cunningham 2011). Indeed, between the censuses of 2001 and 2006 more of these creative workforce jobs were created in Queensland than in any other state, accounting for almost a third of national growth (10,359 new creative workforce jobs appear in Queensland, which is 30 per cent of all new such jobs in Australia).

Yet, one of the defining features of Brisbane's creative workforce employment is its continuing lack of producers – the people who assemble resources, do deals and create wealth for the whole of the creative workforce. At the time of the most recent (2006) national census, Brisbane's total workforce was about 43 per cent the size of Sydney's, and its creative workforce was 29 per cent compared to Sydney. However, Brisbane had only 15 per cent of the number of producers that Sydney had, and only 18 per cent the number of directors, across screen, theatre, radio, and events. The proportion of these key creative professionals has grown a little since 1996 (when the number of Brisbane producers and directors were respectively only 12 per cent and 14 per cent of those found in Sydney). But the key point remains: the producer/director pool has always been low in Brisbane and has remained so.

Likewise, the key producer services 'soft' infrastructure in Australia is mostly found elsewhere. All the large employers and firms in the creative sector, and the bureaucratic support infrastructure, are headquartered in Sydney and Melbourne. This includes the major broadcasters, pay-TV and telecommunications companies, federal government funding agencies, regulatory bodies, internet service providers, the professional associations representing the interests of the creative sector in games, film, TV, radio, multimedia, internet, and even the consumer bodies which agitate on the consumption side.

Thus, while there has been record growth in internal migration, and a corresponding growth in the professional and creative workforces and also (following what we might expect from Florida's thesis) cultural consumption, there has not been a commensurate increase in the capacity for Brisbane to be a significant producer and wealth-creator of culture. However, the great variety of indexes available for ranking cities always provides the chance for a good news story: in *The Economist* Intelligence Unit's survey of 140 cities worldwide, Brisbane is currently 16th, while the Globalization and World Cities (GaWC) research network slots Brisbane in as a third-tier Gamma+ (see Infrastructure Australia 2010: chapter 2 and Taylor et al. 2010). Its 'liveability' has allowed Brisbane to score well in some indexes, which has been a source of civic pride and a new branding strategy, in which it is recently touted as 'Australia's new world city' (www.brisbanemarketing.com.au).

However, faced with cultural infrastructural deficit within the nation-state, Brisbane and southeast Queensland increasingly look to cultural export markets in the Asian region to align with Queensland's massive focus on commodities exports into, and tourism from, this region. Brisbane has seven sister city relationships; all are cities in east Asia or the Asia-Pacific, none is North American, South American, African or European. Major cultural initiatives such as the Asia Pacific Triennial (an art exhibition), the Asia Pacific Screen Awards (a screen competition) and the World Theatre Festival (a contemporary performance season) further turn the city-region's strategic focus outside the nation-state.

This consideration of Brisbane serves to illustrate several key points I wish to argue. Relationships between cultural consumption and cultural production are complex and may not necessarily align; indeed, the tension between production-centric and consumption-centric accounts of what makes for a creative city or city-region is, I argue, its central motive force. Brisbane exemplifies this tension. It also partakes in what is a global shift of attention from the nation-state, as the locus of economic and cultural agency, to the city-region – a central feature of the creative cities literature.

Creative cities discourse and production–consumption tensions

To engage, as this volume does, with cultural policy and politics in its urban setting, must be to engage with the creative cities discourse (CCD). Speaking to the book's themes of political economy of culture at the city level, the attraction of creative talent, city branding and urban planning, CCD is a rapidly-growing literature across many discipline fields: urban studies, urban planning, architecture, design, media communication, and cultural and economic geography. (To think of creative cities discourse is, in an instrumentalisation of Foucault, to propose that such bodies of knowledge-practice are always ordered in ways that produce as well as inhibit understanding; they are structured by tensions that need to be made explicit.) It is hybrid; the corpus consists of historical and analytical work (Hall 1998; Sassen 1994; Saxenian 1996; Scott 2000, 2005), work which is more focused on urban planning (Montgomery 2007) and work which is concerned with place-competitiveness (Florida 2002, 2005, 2006; Florida and Tinagli 2004; Landry 2000, 2006). It is a broad and deep academic discourse, often strongly policy-oriented, and thus also highly technical, when it engages with urban zoning regulations, architectural design, and the vagaries of statistics. Equally, it can be highly rhetorical, with place-competitiveness provoking what many academics might regard as egregious and tendentious displays by civic officials as they jostle to put their city on the map. Tensions, and confusions, between the descriptive and the normative abound.

Increasingly ubiquitous place-competition often draws on rigorous research and analysis but also, in the hands of many of its practitioners, is driven by the need for both hard economic and symbolic capital. Yet this strong element of ranking and tiering contrasts with approaches where every city can have its day and be creative. In the battle for city profile, there is a fundamental tension between the established pantheon of truly world-leading cities (as extolled by Sassen 1994 or Hall 1998) and the approach that offers, with appropriate strategy, policy and programmes, virtually any city the opportunity to bootstrap itself into contention (as developed by Richard Florida, Charles Landry, John Montgomery and others).

Tensions in CCD are structured by what I would call its master polarity – the tension between production-centricity and consumption-centricity. A sense of this polarity can be gleaned from the recent and quite neutral definition of the creative city by cultural economist David Throsby:

The concept of the creative city describes an urban complex where cultural activities of various sorts are an integral component of the city's economic and social functioning. Such cities tend to be built upon a strong social and cultural infrastructure; to have relatively high concentrations of creative employment; and to be attractive to inward investment because of their well-established arts and cultural facilities.
(Throsby 2010: 139)

Beneath Throsby's appealingly Arcadian vision of the creative city lies a seething, dynamic debate structured by this tension. In his important and influential *The Rise of the Creative Class*, urbanist Richard Florida (2002) neatly reversed the usual economic booster strategies employed by governments and councils throughout the developed world. Instead of inward investment to build industrial-scale production infrastructure and capacity, he famously promoted the idea that city growth strategy can be based on 'building a community that is attractive to creative people' (Florida 2002: 283). The 'creative class' (by which he meant everyone from bohemian artists to young urban professionals), by virtue of their lifestyle-based locational choices, drive city renewal and growth. The argument is that 'places with a flourishing artistic and cultural environment are the ones that generate economic outcomes and overall economic growth' (Florida 2002: 261) not because of the economic muscle of the cultural/creative industries but because of their high-tech workers' pulling power.

While Florida's work has attracted strong and sustained criticism, it is undeniable that his focus on creative occupation counterbalances the usual dependence simply on industry statistics in industry development debates. His insistence on 'creative' capital rather than the more generic 'human' capital has focused attention on the creative worker in mainstream policy debate in ways no other contribution has. The generic argument is made by Charles Landry (2000) that cities have one crucial resource – people – and that human creativity 'is replacing location, natural resources and market access as the principal key to urban dynamics' (quoted in Throsby 2010: 139). But Florida insisted that generic human capital was too imprecise a category to capture his understanding of 'urban dynamics' and instead has put the creative class centre stage (Florida 2005: 6). While the great scholars of the city (Lewis Mumford 1961, Jane Jacobs 1961, Peter Hall 1998) have observed and analysed *ex post facto*, Florida and his ilk champion policy interventions that give municipal authorities reason to consider a hitherto hidden or neglected resource.

Having said this, it is the case that the bulk of academic commentary runs against Florida. It is often argued that the definition of the creative workforce is too broad at one-third of the US workforce and there are significant problems with the implied causal relationship between the creative class and economic growth (Peck 2005). While there may be no real sense of class identity or agency in Florida's notion of the creative class, it has driven an easily stereotyped vision of inner urban, modish, bike-riding connoisseurs of nightclubs and restaurants that is weakly correlated to economic growth and social opportunity (McRobbie 2005; Oakley 2004). It has tended to create confusion and displace policies aimed at the specifically defined creative workforce and its sustainability (Cunningham 2011) as the consumption-oriented focus on discretionary expenditure by the creative class favours white-collar professionals rather than bohemians. The focus on tolerance being the key to the three Ts (talent, technology, tolerance) (Florida 2005: 7) – the centrepiece of Florida's claims to embedding a progressive politics in his research – has proven difficult to sustain. The lack of causal or even a strong correlative relationship between cultural diversity and openness and economic growth has led Florida and his team to step away from a strong adherence to tolerance as a driver (Storper and Scott 2009: 165). Essentially, the fatal flaw, for our purposes here, is that Florida tells us something about what creatives do at *leisure*, but not what they do at *work*.

This branch of the CCD contrasts with the resolutely production-centric accounts of the classic and recently-minted creative cities accounts of AnneLee Saxenian (1996), Saskia Sassen (1994), Allen Scott (2000, 2005), Michael Storper (Storper and Scott 2009), Ann Markusen (2006), Michael Curtin (2003 and forthcoming) and other key writers in the field. These writers are driven by the need to account for global economic dynamics, the effects of postfordism and flexible accumulation on contemporary creative production practice at the level of particular, and especially globally leading or emerging, cities and city-regions. Scott asserts that:

The origins of urban development and growth in modern society reside, above all, in the dynamics of economic production and work. ... To be sure, actual cities are always something vastly more than just bare accumulations of capital and labor, for they are also arenas in which many other kinds of phenomena – social, cultural, and political – flourish. We might say, to be more accurate, that localized production complexes and their associated labor markets constitute proto-urban forms around which their other phenomena crystallize in various concrete ways. (Scott 2006: 2)

Refuting the claims of consumption-centricity, Scott and Michael Storper warn that:

Recourse to amenities-based theories as a guiding principle for urban growth policy is ill-advised because their theories manifestly fail to address the basic issues of building, sustaining and transforming regional ensembles of production activities and their attendant local labor markets. (Storper and Scott 2009: 164)

The production-centric school of thought has made profound contributions to our understanding of the dynamics of global cultural dynamics and flows, and indeed dominates the commanding heights of the academic literature. But it cannot be the last word on the matter, as consumption-centric accounts play a key role for that swathe of cities (like Brisbane) which will never sit in the pantheon of first-tier cities, and to which the ministrations of those like Florida, Landry and Montgomery are directed. Again instrumentalising Foucault, the master tension in CCD between production- and consumption-centricity is a *productive* one. Policies to support production and for consumption don't necessarily align and are often in direct competition. The tension between production and consumption will remain and heighten, as we will now see, as urbanisation reaches epochal proportions, and what counts as production and consumption blur into each other under conditions of globalisation, digitisation and convergence.

The increasing centrality of CCD

2009 was the tipping point in the global history of human demographics. From this year, a majority of the world's population are living in urban areas. Doug Saunders' (2010) *Arrival City: How the Largest Migration in History is Reshaping Our World* presents the following data: advanced western urbanisation is complete. For many decades, rural dwellers have made up between 5 and 25 per cent of the population of western countries. Fewer than 5 per cent of western populations are employed in agriculture; in some cases it is as low as 2 per cent. In Asia, 41 per cent of people live in cities, and in Africa the figure is 38 per cent, but each month 5 million city dwellers are created through migration or birth in Africa, Asia and the Middle East. By 2025, it is estimated that 60 per cent of total population will live in cities, by 2050, 70 per cent or more, and by the end of the century some equilibrium will be reached at 75 per cent. This kind of urbanisation is often represented as a holocaust in waiting, by writers such as Mike Davis in *Planet of Slums* (2006), yet there are contra-accounts of slums as places where questions of sustainability, recycling and practical, low-tech innovation can be models for other parts of the world (e.g., Hamdi 2004; Hermanson 2010). This massive global urbanisation means that creative cities discourse will become, inexorably and inevitably, an increasingly important global issue.

Besides this epic demographic shift, two other megatrends are driving the rise of CCD that challenge enduring disciplinary methods, objects of study and policy frameworks. The first trend is the increasing preparedness of scholars to claim priority for the city-region over the nation-state as an economic and cultural agent in the contemporary world, as this volume's co-editors put it in their Introduction.

It's certainly the case that, under conditions of globalisation, the city-region and its relations to other city-regions are becoming major foci. But the trend can be overstated. It is a conceit of the transnational cosmopolitan left that the decline of the 'interstate system' (Lee 2010) represents an advance over the old Europe of imperial and colonising nation-states. But the new governance paradigm of the postwar world that saw a supranational entity like the European Union perform some kind of controlling function over old imperial nations also saw the post-colonising establishment of more new nation-states than ever before in history. I have myself been a strong critic of the 'decline of the nation-state' proposition (Cunningham 1992; Cunningham and Jacka 1998), arguing instead that nation-states, particularly those outside the western hegemony, exist as balances to the power of transnational economic and cultural forces and also interact interdependently with local, regional and provincial agents. Nevertheless, two decades on, cities, city-regions and city-cultures have undoubtedly become increasingly prominent actors under conditions of globalisation – I canvas momentarily cases where the nation-state is both critical, and contrary, to the creative city.

The second megatrend relates to the changing nature of cultural activity. The creative cities discourse will increase in importance into the future because the shape of culture is changing under conditions of globalisation, digitisation and convergence. Cultural production will continue to become even more digitally created and delivered on multi-platforms as barriers to entry and transaction costs on digital platforms are lowered. Cultural production will be engaged with globally while also being narrowcast within and to increasingly targeted niches. Such 'global narrowcasting' is the emergent form in which culture will be produced and consumed into the future. Cities will become ever more a balancing, anchorage point for an increasingly global and digital mobility of culture, with locative activities, events and dynamics that secure culture's real-time, real-life embodiment. Digital culture always develops alongside rearrangements and often intensifications of such embodiment: evidence for this can been seen in urbanistic congregations of user-consumers/producers, mixtures of virtual and geographically situated communities (Choi 2010). The question of 'quality of life' in burgeoning cities will bring the consumption and production polarities of the agenda closer together around the phenomenon of the 'produser' or producer-user (Bruns 2008).

As urbanisation continues apace, globally but especially in Asia, Africa and the Middle East, burgeoning city-regions will need to address their versions of CCD out of a quite different set of circumstances from those which have preoccupied the canonical writers of CCD, who have sat within the western tradition. Major city-regions will not necessarily be cultural production centres on a core–periphery model, with a small number of world-cities exporting to the rest of the world. They will consolidate along polycentric models such as the geo-linguistic regional model (Sinclair et al. 1996). Peter Hall (1998: 23) apologised for his almost exclusively western focus (with the singular exception of Tokyo–Kanagawa) in his magisterial account of *Cities in Civilisation*. Yet, given that all the largest cities in the world, with the exception of New York – as long as we count Mexico City as the global south – are now or will be non-western in the near future, it is hard to imagine a successor to Peter Hall excluding, in a twenty-first-century survey of 'cities in civilisation', cities such as Shanghai, Mexico City, Beijing ... or even Lagos.

Identifying new challenges for CCD

The structural tensions which subtend CCD are not likely to abate, but changes in modes of urbanistic congregation, and production and consumption, just outlined, mean that CCD will evolve rapidly. In this concluding section, I explore some variations on the themes of pantheons of creative cities (production-centric) or great lifestyle urbs (consumption-centric), noting where new avenues of inquiry are being generated. Each suggests intriguing extensions of what is already a very robust research agenda.

Against the assumption of waning nation-state agency, I consider the creative city as a product of direct nation-state policy prescription (Beijing) and then obverse examples – creative city initiatives where the nation-state's policy parameters are definitively worked around (film festivals; 'runaway' production hotspots such the Gold Coast). Then follow cities which lead the way as digital hotspots, where production-consumption is blurred (Seoul); and cities outside the west, and which have risen from inauspicious and informal economies (Lagos-Nollywood). The counter-discourse to that which assumes that only inner urban milieu can be significantly creative must be addressed – the creative congregation as non-metropolitan (creative suburbia, Northern Rivers, New Zealand). We conclude where we started – with the problematic of production capability in the context of predominantly lifestyle-consumption drivers (Brisbane). The examples I use come mainly from the 'eastern hemisphere' and, unashamedly so, for this helps move the discussion well away from CCD's traditional North Atlantic nexus.

The creative city as policy prescription: Beijing

The classic studies that constitute the core of CCD are clear about the complex, organic growth and multivariate causality of success factors for a creative city, and also how evanescent some success was – Hall's exemplar is Berlin in the 1920s. Despite this, and despite the dangers of template-driven, or 'cookie-cutter', approaches (Gibson 2010; Gibson and Kong 2005; Oakley 2004), cities the world over go on promoting place-competitiveness through strategies, policies and programmes. And one of, if not *the*, biggest strategy must be that for Beijing. This is no municipal council boosterism. This is nation-state *dirigisme* at its most tendentious. The intent of the Chinese authorities is for Beijing to become nothing less than a media 'capital' as well as the political capital of an emerging superpower.

For Michael Curtin (2003, 2008, and forthcoming), there are three essential elements for a media capital: industrial infrastructure driven by the logic of accumulation, human capital driven by trajectories of creative migration and a successful management of the forces of socio-cultural variation. China has systematically adopted creative clustering strategies to rapidly build capacity in, for example, lower-end animation, but the Chaoyang district in central Beijing is a monster creative cluster charged with bringing together 'mother ships' (critical ideological infrastructure in the media sector) with foreign investor-friendly new media and large entertainment developments, meanwhile reasserting Beijing's priority over Shanghai's creative industries and the lowered flag of Hong Kong.

According to Angela Huang's (2010) research, the difficulty of enacting the third of Curtin's drivers – successful management of the forces of socio-cultural variation – is hampering the development of Beijing as a media capital, even as industrial infrastructure and creative migration are proceeding apace. Foreign companies can exhaust their patience struggling to access China's domestic market through regulatory and bureaucratic intransigence. The Chinese government acts both as a regulator and market designer as well as a player in supporting national media conglomerates ('mother ships') in ways that restrict competition and entrench market power. Content and technology innovation is hampered by intra-government departmental interests. Governmental promotion of socialistic cultural homogeneity compromises the maturity of a competitive market; Chinese audiences are hungry for different cultural products and experience and turn to pirated content if such 'socio-cultural variation' is not available on mandated media outlets. While there is overwhelming nation-state investment in the development of Beijing as a creative capital, there are also considerable obstacles to be overcome if it is to be successful.

The creative city as a product of city-region rather than nation-state agency: film festivals and 'runaway' screen production

Most of the acknowledged world cities of the modern era have achieved that status through a relatively benign interdependency with the nation-state, and have been the pre-eminent urban force in that country over decades if not centuries (London, Paris, Tokyo, New York). But there is also a clear obverse of the creative city as a creature of nation-state agency; these are examples where national identity is irrelevant or the nation-state is actively opposed.

Even though nation-state governance concerns itself with 'identity building and identity protection', as the co-editors put it, this remains at the rather abstract level of Benedict Anderson's 'imagined community' (1991). More concrete, local identity building is usually left to the municipal (or state/province if there is federal governance) level. The contrast between mainstream film industry policies at the national level (production and distribution assistance based typically on national expression and identity, attempting to balance the might of Hollywood) and those of city place-marking through film festivals is instructive.

Film festivals, like festivals generally, are place-marking activities, invested in by burgeoning numbers of cities and towns, all of which are increasingly interested in announcing their status as culturally savvy and prepared to invest and to trigger further investment. It seems as though a festival is as necessary in any given town council's repertoire as roads, rates and rubbish! Indeed, a substantial part of film consumption now takes place outside the domain of mainstream film distribution and outside the purview of national film policies. A central fact of the film festival phenomenon is that its political economy is not driven by powerful distribution muscle, as the film industry itself is, but by myriad and growing numbers of civic councils, arts and tourism government agencies, states, provinces, regional authorities, private philanthropy, commercial businesses at a local more than a multinational level, and of course box office – all of whom invest in the film festival for local identity, prestige, and turnover. The proportion of worldwide film festival cumulative revenues sourced from the film industry itself is very small.

So-called 'runaway' screen production is typically regarded as the willing extension of cultural dependency and abject capitulation in the face of Hollywood hegemony. At the time, in the 1970s and 1980s, when Hollywood was beginning systematically to take production offshore, it would have been inconceivable for most national cultural policy and screen policy settings to support the development of facilities and creative skills to attract runaway Hollywood productions. Nevertheless, since that time, a growing number of cities have built studios, developed their creative human capital, and engaged in place-competitive bidding for large-budget Hollywood, but also Japanese and increasingly Bollywood, screen production: Wilmington NC, Orlando, Vancouver, Alicante, Montréal, Cape Town, Toronto, Louisiana, Rome, Wellington, the Barrandov studios in Prague, Babelberg in Berlin, and Budapest.

Goldsmith, Ward and O'Regan's *Local Hollywood: Global Film Production and the Gold Coast* (2010) tells the story of another 'local Hollywood', Australia's Gold Coast:

> *if we want to understand Global Hollywood, we need to attend not only to the design centre in Los Angeles, but also the many Local Hollywoods which have sprung up around the world. There is one Los Angeles; there are numerous Local Hollywoods. ... To get at these ordinary places we need a different attention ... these places and interests have not only transformed Hollywood but also transform themselves in the process. (2010: 29)*

Investing in such a volatile industry, the authors argue, was consistent with a city which had re-made itself many times over as it grew on the back of national and international tourism, itself a highly volatile industry. The key urgers, investors and decision-makers in this case were international studios (Warner Bros), commercial film exhibition interests, provincial government and city council. The strategy to attract offshore high-budget US movies and television and to justify this in terms of industry and skills capacity and infrastructure building set it resolutely apart from, and indeed directly at odds with, the intent of national cultural and screen policies designed to regulate for, and subsidise, only identifiable national content. It is inconceivable that such national policy settings would or could have supported the development of Warner MovieWorld Studios on the Gold Coast (and the associated major theme park).

Creative city as digital city: Seoul

Seoul is the most wired mega-city in the world, with around 80 per cent of the population having broadband and personal computers (MIC 2008).

Superfast broadband and digital saturation are everyday affordances; online, Seoul netizens are globally connected but come together in highly communal, locationally-specific *bangs* (ubiquitous communal online social spaces). Scott and Storper's 'large-scale agglomeration' occurs in games and film; national-cultural assertion is strong (although local film exhibition quotas are being wound back under the US Korea Free Trade Agreement); but also the new conditions of 'produsage' (production-consumption blurring) are played out through massive social investment in user-generated content and Web 2.0, a hyperactive blogosphere (OhmyNews), and massive multiplayer online games (MMOG) (Choi 2010; Hjorth 2008). This is all mediated by the Korean language, which is bound to act as a locative moderator of global-local flows. It is here in Seoul that many of most advanced experiments in connected living, in fostering 'smart and connected communities' for home, office, shopping, learning, wellness, sports, and also every other dimensions of social and personal activity, are being developed (Dignan 2010; Lindsay 2010).

The creative city fashioned out of dire circumstances: Lagos

It would be hard to think of a greater contrast to the pantheon of culturally creative cities extolled by Peter Hall than Lagos. Lagos is projected to be the fastest-growing city in the world, exploding from 288,000 in 1950, to 14 million in 2010, to 23 million by 2015. Lagos is one of the most chaotic, least planned cities in the world and yet out of it has grown the newest major film industry in the world: Nollywood. Evolving out of an informal economic base reliant on pirate networks that have gone commercial, with absolutely no state subsidy or other support mechanisms, Nigerian video is low-tech, low production quality, high-volume filmmaking servicing mostly the urban poor:

> *... thinking of Nollywood as an example of low-tech, informal innovation gives us a new understanding of what an innovative media production and distribution might look like. If we think of innovation in this way ... then Lagos would surely be the innovation capital of the world.*
> *(Lobato 2009: 194; and see Lobato 2010)*

The creative city as non-metropolitan: New Zealand, the Northern Rivers of New South Wales, and 'creative' suburbia

Much CCD has given rise to the widespread perception that the prototypical creative city is represented by inner urban milieux – dynamic, bohemian, innovative, and cosmopolitan – while that which exists outside, particularly the outer suburbs of large cities and smaller towns in predominantly rural landscapes, are dull, static and culturally backward.

The case of Aotearoa New Zealand makes this perception difficult to sustain. The successes of filmmakers such as Peter Jackson; the best-practice screen infrastructure he has built in Wellington (the WETA studio complex); design-led innovation into manufacturing and tourism; leading strategies for cultural and eco-tourism – these are all examples of world-class creativity on a very small national population base (4.3 million), with only three cities of significant size. Those seeking to understand the creative dynamics of the country gesture towards a 'giant creative village, in which social connectedness, trust and a sense of belonging form an ideal framework for creativity to flourish' (Smith 2010). This is in contrast of Florida's vision of highly mobile, footloose creative capital based on the strength of weak ties.

The Northern Rivers region of New South Wales, Australia, is a relatively sparsely populated non-metropolitan area but with a relatively high creative workforce and is a well-known lifestyle region, a classic 'sea change' destination. It is the only sustainable creative milieu outside the Australian capital cities. But what makes it 'sustainable' as a creative location is the high proportion of producers with prior track records of deal making and wealth creation and who have been drawn to the region, not for Florida's urban buzz, but for a specifically non-metropolitan lifestyle (Henkel 2010).

'Creative Suburbia' (see Collis et al. 2010; Felton et al. 2010; and see Flew and Gibson, this volume) is a project examining the motivations for creative workers to choose to live in the outer suburbs of major Australian cities. These motivations include: freedom from the distractions of the inner city, freedom from the inner city's perceived homogeneity of culture and the constraints of having to be 'groovy' in a specific way; provision of better value to clients because the costs of expensive inner-city offices are not being passed on to clients; and access to more physical space, including the ability to work from home in larger premises. An investigation of the location quotient, and use of an alternative statistical methodology for creative industries measurement, demonstrates that inner cities may not, in fact, be as important as it assumed in terms of the spatial disposition of creative workers.

The non-alignment of production and consumption policies: Brisbane

We noted at the start the problematic of production capability in Brisbane in the context of consumption-driven cultural growth. Production-centric policies seek to develop a stronger, more efficient and more talented workforce, which has implications not only for workplace, business and cluster conditions, but also education and skills. Policies on the consumption side instead tend to respond to demand from the professional class for more sophisticated cultural services. Florida's so-called bohemian 'creative core' tends to be less important than his creative professionals in this demand-driven scenario: it is the professionals who have more disposable income and seek to cultivate cosmopolitan and global rather than local tastes.

Brisbane developed a balanced consumption–production mix some years ago in its five-year cultural strategy, *Creative City* (Cultural Policy Unit 2003). At least half of its eight strategic 'platforms' sought to support production capacity. The others spoke of creating vibrant neighbourhoods, celebrating diversity and social opportunity. However, a change in government soon after saw the strategy shelved, and subsequent city visioning has focused on generic lifestyle amenities, and 'creative professional' (science-technology) industry and workforce agendas (Brisbane City Council 2005).

Conclusion: policy implications

As a general rule, in those jurisdictions which have reasonably developed cultural policies and programmes, direct support through major subsidy portfolios, as well as content regulation, occurs at the national level. These are production-centric policies. Smaller subsidy, and consumption-oriented, policies typically are found at the state, provincial

and municipal levels. One of the enduring policy challenges is for optimum coordination of these differing foci of public policy.

The opportunity costs of some consumption-oriented policies can detract from innovative production-oriented policies, especially place marking through major investment in iconic buildings. Political leaders are partial to the siren song of the 'edifice complex'. A recent UK report from NESTA (Chapain et al. 2010) strikes the right note about balancing production- and consumption-centric policies:

> *Although investments in the iconic public buildings that are seen to be the hallmark of creative cities can produce undoubted cultural and economic benefits, they also take money from other initiatives to support local creative businesses using an 'industry and innovation' approach ...*
>
> *Although the latter approach creates less immediately visible outputs, it might also be more conducive to developing a healthy and sustainable local creative ecosystem – one where creative graduates are able to gain employment when they finish their degree, creative value is captured locally, and local and regional innovative performance is improved. (Chapain et al. 2010: 45)*

This is particularly pertinent due to the degree to which, as this chapter has noted, the production and consumption of culture are blurring, and tomorrow's citizens/consumers will expect the two to be much more interdependent. Many policies, however, can be shaped to suit both production and consumption. Access and equity policies can open up cultural experience on both sides of the ledger for those hitherto excluded. Digitising national collections, while also addressing the vexed issue of copyright for re-use, makes the cultural heritage of populations available for both personal enrichment on the consumption side and creative expression on the production side. The myriad licensing, insurance, and zoning regulations that state and municipal authorities typically have control over impact the capacity both to produce and consume at the local level in ways that are often more significant than national subsidy programmes. As one activist argues, in the aptly titled 'Thoughts for politicians in search of a cheap arts policy':

> *Ever tried to rent a park, a hall, put on a gig or hold a show? The permits, permissions and red tape involved are where 90 per cent of the*

interactions between governments and the arts take place. For many artists, particularly those starting out, they are a killer. There is huge potential to lead here. Streamline the permits, slash the insurance requirements, offer meaningful exemptions for small projects and not-for-profit projects and events. Make it possible for communities to create events without the need for capital, lawyers and interminable time lost in the wheels of government. (Westbury 2010)

Balancing production- and consumption-centric policies will remain a challenge for all creative cities.

REFERENCES

Anderson, Benedict R. O'G. (1991) *Imagined Communities: Reflections on the Origin and Spread of Nationalism.* Revised and extended edition. London: Verso.

Brisbane City Council (2005) *Our Shared Vision – Living in Brisbane 2026.* Brisbane: Brisbane City Council.

Bruns, Axel (2008) *Blogs, Wikipedia, Second Life, and Beyond: From Production to Produsage.* New York: Peter Lang.

Chapain, Caroline, Cooke, Phil, De Propris, Lisa, MacNeill, Stewart and Mateos-Garcia, Juan (2010) *Creative Clusters and Innovation: Putting Creativity on the Map,* NESTA Research Report, www.nesta.org.uk/library/documents/Creative-Clusters-29Nov.pdf.

Choi, Jaz Hee-jeong (2010) 'Playpolis: transyouth and urban networking in Seoul', PhD dissertation, Queensland University of Technology, Brisbane.

Collis, Christy, Felton, Emma and Graham, Philip W. (2010) 'Beyond the inner city: real and imagined places in creative place policy and practice', *The Information Society,* 26(2): 104–112.

Cultural Policy Unit (2003) *Creative City: Brisbane City Council's Cultural Strategy 2003–2008.* Produced in collaboration with Brecknock Consulting and Comedia. Brisbane: Brisbane City Council.

Cunningham, Stuart (1992) *Framing Culture: Criticism and Policy in Australia.* St Leonards: Allen & Unwin.

Cunningham, Stuart (2011) 'Developments in measuring the creative workforce', *Cultural Trends,* 20(1): 25–40.

Cunningham, Stuart and Jacka, Elizabeth (1998) 'The continued relevance of the "national" as a site for progressive policy making', *Javnost: The Public* 5(4): 80–84.

Curtin, Michael (2003) 'Media capital: towards the study of spatial flows', *International Journal of Cultural Studies,* 6(2): 202–228.

Curtin, Michael (2008) 'Spatial dynamics of film and television' in Helmut K. Anheier and Y.R. Isar (eds) *The Cultural Economy. The Cultures and Globalization Series 3.* London: SAGE.

Curtin, Michael (forthcoming) *Media Capital: The Cultural Geography of Globalization.* London: Blackwell.

Davis, Mike (2006) *Planet of Slums.* London: Verso.

Dignan, Larry (2010) 'Cisco's Grand Telepresence Experiment in Songdo, South Korea', *ZDNet,* 3 June 2010, www.zdnet. com/blog/btl/ciscos-grand-telepresence-experiment-in-songdo-south-korea/35336.

Felton, Emma, Collis, Christy and Graham, Philip W. (2010) 'Making connections: creative industries networks in outer suburban locations', *Australian Geographer,* 41(1): 57–70.

Florida, Richard (2002) *The Rise of the Creative Class and How It's Transforming Work, Leisure, Community and Everyday Life.* New York: Basic Books.

Florida, Richard (2005) *Cities and the Creative Class.* New York: Routledge.

Florida, Richard (2006) *The Flight of the Creative Class: The New Global Competition for Talent.* New York: Harper Business.

Florida, Richard and Tinagli, Irene (2004) *Europe in the Creative Age.* New York: Basic Books.

Gibson, Chris (ed.) (2010) Special issue on 'Creative geographies: tales from the "margins"', *Australian Geographer* 41(1).

Gibson, Chris and Kong, Lily (2005) 'Cultural economy: a critical review', *Progress in Human Geography,* 29(5): 541–561.

Goldsmith, Ben, Ward, Susan and O'Regan, Tom (2010) *Local Hollywood: Global Film Production and the Gold Coast.* St Lucia: University of Queensland Press.

Hall, Peter (1998) *Cities in Civilization: Culture, Innovation and Urban Order.* London: Phoenix Giant.

Hamdi, Nabeel (2004) *Small Change: About the Art of Practice and the Limits of Planning in Cities.* London: Earthscan.

Henkel, Cathy (2010) 'From margins to mainstream: how screen and creative industries developed in the Northern Rivers region of NSW: 2000–2010', PhD dissertation, Queensland University of Technology, Brisbane.

Hermanson, Judith A. (2010) 'Principles for realizing the potential of urban slums', International Housing Coalition, Washington, DC, www.intlhc.org/docs/Hermanson_paper_on_slums.pdf.

Higgs, Peter L., Cunningham, Stuart and Pagan, Janet D. (2007) 'Australia's Creative Economy: Basic Evidence on Size, Growth, Income and Employment', Research report,

ARC Centre of Excellence in Creative Industries and Innovation. Available at: http://eprints.qut.edu.au/8241/.

Hjorth, Larissa (2008) 'Being real in the mobile real: a case study on convergent mobile media as domestic new media in Seoul, South Korea', *Convergence* 14(1): 91–104.

Huang, Angela (2010) 'Beijing as media capital', PhD dissertation-in-progress, Queensland University of Technology, Brisbane.

ID (2010) Brisbane City Council Community Profile: Brisbane LGA, http://profile.id.com.au/templates/profile/Clients/327Bris/PDF/10.pdf.

Infrastructure Australia (2010) *State of Australian Cities*. Produced by Infrastructure Australia's Major Cities Unit. Canberra: Commonwealth Government of Australia.

Jacobs, Jane (1961) *The Death and Life of Great American Cities*. New York: Random House.

Landry, Charles (2000) *The Creative City: A Toolkit for Urban Innovators*. London: Earthscan.

Landry, Charles (2006) *The Art of City Making*. London: Earthscan.

Lee, Richard E. (2010) *Knowledge Matters: The Structures of Knowledge and the Crisis of the Modern World System*. St Lucia: University of Queensland Press.

Lindsay, Greg (2010) 'Cisco's Big Bet on New Songdo: creating cities from scratch', *Fast Company*, 1 February, www.fastcompany.com/magazine/142/the-new-new-urbanism.html.

Lobato, Ramon (2009) 'Subcinema: mapping informal film distribution', PhD dissertation, University of Melbourne, Melbourne.

Lobato, Ramon (2010) 'Creative industries and informal economies', *International Journal of Cultural Studies*, 13(4): 337–354.

Markusen, Ann (2006) 'Urban development and the politics of a creative class: evidence from the study of artists', *Environment and Planning A*, 38(10): 1921–1940.

McRobbie, Angela (2005) 'Clubs to companies', in John Hartley (ed.), *Creative Industries*. Oxford: Blackwell Publishing, pp. 375–390.

MIC (2008) *Survey on the Internet Usage*. Seoul: Ministry of Information and Communication.

Montgomery, John (2008) *Survey on Internet Usage*. Seoul: Ministry of Information and Communication.

Mumford, Lewis (1961) *The City in History: Its Origins, Its Transformations, and Its Prospects*. New York: Harcourt, Brace and World.

Oakley, Kate (2004) 'Not so cool Britannia: the role of the creative industries in economic development', *International Journal of Cultural Studies*, 7(1): 67–77.

Peck, Jamie (2005) 'Struggling with the creative class', *International Journal of Urban and Regional Research*, 29(4): 740–770.

Sassen, Saskia (1994) *Cities in a World Economy*. Thousand Oaks, CA: Pine Forge Press.

Saunders, Doug (2010) *Arrival City: How the Largest Migration in History is Reshaping Our World*. Portsmouth, NH: Heinemann.

Saxenian, AnnaLee (1996) *Regional Advantage: Culture and Competition in Silicon Valley and Route 128*. Cambridge, MA: Harvard University Press.

Scott, Allen J. (2000) *The Cultural Economy of Cities: Essays on the Geography of Image-Producing Industries*. Theory, Culture and Society Series. London: SAGE.

Scott, Allen J. (2005) *On Hollywood: The Place, the Industry*. Princeton, NJ Princeton University Press.

Scott, Allen J. (2006) 'Creative cities: conceptual issues and policy questions', *Journal of Urban Affairs*, 28(1): 1–17.

Sinclair, J., Jacka, E. and Cunningham, S. (1996) *New Patterns in Global Television: Peripheral Vision*. Oxford: Oxford University Press.

Smith, Jason (2010) 'The creative country: policy, practice and place in New Zealand's creative economy 1999–2008', PhD dissertation, Auckland University of Technology, Auckland.

Storper, Michael and Scott, Allen J. (2009) 'Rethinking human capital, creativity and urban growth', *Journal of Economic Geography*, 9(1): 147–167.

Taylor, Peter J., Derudder, Ben, Hoyler, Michael, Huang, Jin and Witlox, Frank (2010) *Global Urban Analysis: A Survey of Cities in Globalization*. London: Earthscan.

Throsby, David (2010) *The Economics of Cultural Policy*. Cambridge: Cambridge University Press.

Westbury, Marcus (2010) 'Thoughts for politicians in search of a cheap arts policy', *The Age*, 2 August 2010, www.marcuswestbury.net/2010/09/27/thoughts-for-politicians-in-search-of-a-cheap-arts-policy/, 27 September.

CHAPTER 9

THE CREATIVE CITY: COMPELLING AND CONTENTIOUS
Charles Landry

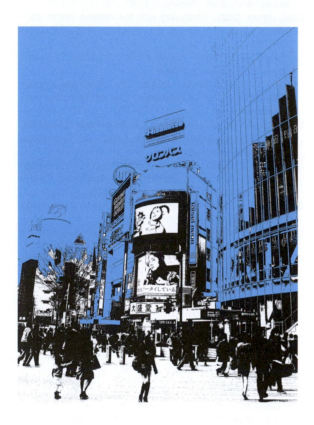

There have always been creative cities, but today we are trying to plan them. Is this possible? More and more cities call themselves creative and by this they often mean they have a strong cultural and creative economy infrastructure as well as a large creative class. This is a narrow definition as urban creativity has a far wider scope.

What is a creative place?

A creative place can be a room, a building, a street, a neighbourhood and a creative city or a city-region is a good amalgam of all these. The qualities of each are rather similar: a sense of comfort and familiarity, usually a good blending of the old and new, variety and choice and a balance between the calm and the invigorating or risk and caution.

A creative city is a place where people feel they can fulfil themselves – there are opportunities. Things get done. It is a place where people can express their diverse talents which are harnessed, exploited and promoted for the common good. These forms of expertise act as a catalyst and role model to develop and attract further talent in a self-reinforcing cycle. Here there are myriad, high-quality learning opportunities, formal and informal, where self-development is easy, where learning programmes are forward-looking and adaptable and highly connected. There are ladders of opportunity and choices and a sense that ambition and aspirations can be met. There is a 'can do' mentality. People see the city is an engine of possibilities. There are places to meet, talk, mix, exchange and play. There is multicultural colour and diversity as this implies distinctiveness and varied insights. Yet even better it is an 'intercultural' place where the focus is on mixing different cultures, attitudes and experiences and sharing ideas and projects together (Wood and Landry, 2007).

The confidence to be outward-looking comes from a sense of familiarity with people around them, in their family, their friendships or networks, their neighbourhood or workplace, or because of the physical landmarks in the city be that a street, a café or a set of facilities. This anchors their sense of safety and security. The feeling of community is important, but it needs to be an evolving one that adapts to changes and so is resilient. Once people have confidence, they want to explore, discover, be curious and be surprised. This implies that the city has rich layers that do not reveal themselves immediately. This creative place exudes crucially a sense of a 'higher purpose'. This means there are soulful places too, perhaps a gallery or a site of interest often taking the place of our religious centres.

The overall physical environment functions well for its inhabitants; it is easy to move around and connect with each other. Its high-level urban design inspires, stimulates and generates pride and affection. The architecture, old and new, is well assembled, and the street pattern is diverse and interesting. Webbed within the ordinary is the occasional extraordinary and remarkable or memorable. It is an environment in which creators of all kinds are content, but not complacent, and motivated to create, and where there are outlets and channels to communicate their ideas or research or sell their work. It is a natural marketplace, where people exchange ideas, develop joint projects, trade their products, or work in its advanced industries. It offers a rich register of vibrant experiences through, for example, gastronomy, the arts, heritage and its natural surroundings, including thriving mainstream and alternative scenes and a healthy network of third spaces. Opportunities abound: the place is welcoming and encouraging. Its dynamism makes it a magnet and so generates critical mass and attracts people from outside, and this guarantees longevity.

The political and public framework within which this exists has a clarity of purpose and direction, and understands the importance of harnessing the potential of its people. It is lean, clear and focused. Its workings are easy to navigate and it is accessible, open and encourages participation. Public employees here are focused on the job at hand regardless of departmental boundaries. Differences are a natural part of this discussion culture. They are debated, accepted, negotiated and resolved without rancour. Its leadership has vision and is strategically agile yet is grounded in day-to-day reality. It is respected and trusted and recognizes its vital role in continuously identifying new opportunities and future-proofing. The society it rules over has a high degree of cohesion, is relatively open to incomers and to new ideas, even though these can sometimes be uncomfortable – indeed, creative places are often not that cosy and can be somewhat edgy. Levels of crime are in general low, the place feels safe and standards of living are relatively high. It is socially alert and seeks to avoid ghettoizing its poorest. Social organizations are active, well-funded and constructive.

Industry is innovative and design aware, with a strong focus on new trends, emerging technologies and fledgling sectors such as developing the green economy or creative industries. It is well networked and connected and its commitment to research and development is well above average. Cross-fertilization across even the most diverse sectors occurs naturally. Public-private partnerships happen as a matter of course. The business community is entrepreneurial, has drive and is forward-thinking. It understands and utilizes well its natural resources,

it harnesses existing talents and acts as a breeding ground for new skills. Business leaders are respected figures in their community and give something back. The community in turn is proud of its products and the reputation it brings to the place. Good use is made of its effective communications systems, including local and international transport, high-speed internet access and connectivity to the world at large.

Overall, as in all creative places, this place is unlike any other. You can feel and sense the buzz; it is obvious to residents and visitors alike. It accentuates its distinctiveness in a relaxed and unthreatening way. It is at ease with itself. Its history, culture and traditions are alive, receptive to influence and change, absorbing new ideas which in turn evolve and develop its distinctiveness and culture. A creative place is therefore:

- a place of anchorage
- a place of connection
- a place of possibility
- a place of inspiration
- a place of learning.

Contentious or compelling

The creative city concept has become contentious. A danger is that the notion is becoming empty and hollowed out through overuse. Some worry it is too much of a fashion, thoughtlessly applied without detailed understanding of its potential. Consequently, people get bored as they think about the 'next big thing': 'the learning city', 'the liveable city' or 'the sensory city'. Simultaneously there is a paradox – the more we discuss creativity, the more we focus on a culture of risk aversion.

There is a proliferating global frenzy as places want to evolve as creative cities or simply to claim they are a 'creative city'. Some talk of a Creative City Movement. Everyone is responding to a world that has changed dramatically. It feels like a paradigm shift and while many things seem the same, their underlying operating dynamics are different. The Creative City notion seems like an answer to coping with this transition. The creativity focus is like a rash, it has spread everywhere. Often people want creativity to solve more problems than it can cope with. Many problems or opportunities do not necessarily require creativity *per se*. The central issue is to have a mindset willing to reassess things openly and so be creative when necessary.

Some criticize the notion, claiming it is only concerned with narrow groups like artists or those involved in the media, design and performance industries. While both spheres are important, the essential question is: what are the specific qualities of artistic creativity that might help establish a more creative city. Equally, impacts of the products, services and the methods of working within the creative economy make them a significant part of creative urban development.

Others say the notion fosters a city-making approach that helps to spectacularize the city to attract the 'creative class' – that raft of knowledge workers and researchers who are crucial to developing a more knowledge-intensive, driven economy. They say this reinforces divisions between rich and poor, taking away the focus from the less privileged, rather than looking at their entrenched problems in an imaginative way. While this segment of the population is crucial, representing perhaps 25 per cent to 30 per cent in a country's centrally located cities, they do not represent the totality of a city's creative forces.

The over-strong emphasis on those sectors in the creative city debate is unfortunate and very narrow. It has never been sufficient. Urban creativity is much more. I have stressed: 'what can the other 75 per cent of apparently "non-creative" people contribute to a more creative city that discovers imaginative opportunities to moving forward or inventive solutions to problems?' To be an urban success I argued, in 1995, that

cities have one crucial resource – their people. Human cleverness, desires, motivations, imagination and creativity are replacing location, natural resources and market access as urban resources. The creativity of those who live in and run cities will determine future success. Of course this has always been critical to cities' ability to survive and adapt. Cities when they became large and complex enough to present problems of urban management became laboratories to develop the solutions – technological, conceptual and social – to their problems of growth and change. (Landry and Bianchini, 1995)

A journey through creativity

My first Creative City project was in 1989 in Glasgow and it was called: 'Glasgow – the Creative City & its Cultural Economy'. This signalled an ongoing interest in how going with the culture of a place and its embedded resources can help reinvent a city in transition, help it readapt to changing circumstances and give it strategic advantage. Since then I have developed my ideas by practically working with several dozen cities. This work has focused on helping cities to identify and harness their assets in a fresh way, to assess how these can be used imaginatively, to think through their long-term aims and to suggest how they can be implemented.

The primary conclusions are that the creative capacity of a place is shaped by its history, its culture, its physical setting and its overall operating conditions. This determines its character and 'mindset'. I evolved a contrast between the 'urban engineering paradigm' of city development, focused on hardware, and 'creative city making', which emphasizes how we need to understand the hardware and software simultaneously. Today the essential element of the personality of many cities is their 'culture of engineering', which is reflected in their mentality. The attributes to foster creativity associated with this mindset are both positive and negative. It is logical, rational and technologically adept, it learns by doing, it tends to advance step by step and through trial and error. It is hardware focused. It gets things done. There is a weakness in that this mindset can become narrow, unimaginative and inflexible and forget the software aspect, which is concerned with how a place feels, its capacity to foster interactions, to empower people and develop and harness their skill and talent. Mindsets foster or hinder and block creative potential. The challenge is to embed an understanding of the soft into how a city operates. Developing a 'creativity platform' is a main strategic tool in establishing a comprehensive 'creative ecology' within a city.

Making the invisible visible

The idea of the Creative City emerged from the late 1980s onwards along a number of trajectories. When introduced, it was seen as aspirational; a clarion call to encourage open-mindeness and imagination (Landry, 1990, 2000; Landry and Bianchini, 1995). Its intention was to have a dramatic impact on organizational culture. The philosophy was that there is always more potential in any place than any of us would think at first sight, even though very few cities, perhaps London, New York,

Amsterdam or Berlin, have been comprehensively creative over time. Not every city is creative, but every city can be more creative than it currently is.

The notion of the Creative City posits that conditions need to be created for people and organizations to think, plan and act with imagination in harnessing opportunities or addressing seemingly intractable urban problems. These might range from addressing homelessness, to creating wealth or enhancing the visual environment. It is a positive concept; its assumption is that ordinary people can make the extraordinary happen if given the chance.

For a city to work well requires, for instance, competent, sensitive, even visionary hospital managers or innovative traffic engineers such as those who invented 'shared space', or social workers with the insight to lure, say, drug addicts off their addictions. There is a vast arena for creative action with nothing especially to do with the world of new media or arts, although they may use their techniques to achieve their aims. Imagination helps in principle to solve any problem or grasp potential. It has many expressions: physical things like great design or architecture, new kinds of eco-housing, transport systems, rethinking hospitals with better relationships between doctors and patients, establishing forms of seamless connectivity between groups in the city. Creative inputs add value to businesses which are not normally considered creative, such as engineering, facilities management or the hospitality industry as distinct from design, film or music.

Many expressions of creativity are invisible. How is a change in attitudes, ambition and courage expressed? How is a willingness to listen to citizens seen? How is organizing a bureaucracy afresh projected? Cities, therefore, need to show their intent. Public, private or community initiatives are put across in diverse ways and design has moved centre stage. A cliché is to see the café, bar or night club as a proxy for creativity. Some are interesting, combining excitement with tranquillity, perhaps even being a home from home. Another is the reuse of old industrial buildings. Worldwide, several hundred old warehouses, breweries; train, bus or fire stations; cement, coal, textile, tobacco or steel factories; old markets; or military barracks have been transformed into culture or experience centres, 'incubators' and company breeding grounds and as hubs for wider urban regeneration. Strangely, those same places with horrible working conditions are celebrated as places for the new and hip.

Why do they resonate? They exude memory and the patina of ages in an age where novelty erases memory increasingly. Physically their large spaces allow for flexibility and interesting structures. Architectural statements are increasingly the most visible markers of change and the travelling troupe of 'starchitects' scour the world for new projects, each outbidding the next with outrageousness.

Deepening the creativity agenda

I detect in my own work with cities a desire to look at deeper possibilities for creativity across all domains. From this emerged the concept of the 'creative bureaucracy'. This notion is not a plan, but a proposed way of operating that helps create better plans and better future ways of operating. It is an adaptive, responsive and collaborative organizational form that seeks to harness the initiative and full intelligences of employees responding to the changing demands of those they serve.

The bureaucracies we have, especially in the public domain, were developed to solve the problems of their time. They reflect the culture of their age. At their best, they sought systematic procedures to bring transparency, fairness and equity to decision-making. Yet as they evolved, weaknesses appeared. Bureaucracies were once seen as benign and modern if somewhat technocratic. Its latest focus on efficiency created a neo-bureaucratic centralism that needs to be reassessed, especially in the context of user-driven service innovation.

Changes are already afoot in the organizational practices of the public sector, commercial companies and the wider world. It includes a shift to involving users more, co-creating policies, products or solutions; a shift from hierarchical to network thinking, a breakdown in traditional disciplinary boundaries, and cultural cross-fertilization. These have implications for how bureaucracies need to operate. The twenty-first-century bureaucracy should combine the best of the twentieth-century bureaucracy and evolving lessons about what makes good organizations work.

Cities ever creative: past and future

There have always been creative cities – an important reminder. What distinguishes those from the past from those we deem to be creative today? The difference between now and then, when the creative nature of cities grew more 'incidentally', is that we are now self-consciously trying to plan and build in the chances for creativity and innovation by creating the hard and soft 'infrastructures of encounter'. Since the 1970s we have 'rediscovered' the city and its primary virtues. In the West at least, we let cities degrade by encouraging suburban exodus, creating satellite towns, outlying science parks and by segmenting land uses and functions. The effects began to strip cities bare and drain the lifeblood. The subsequent doughnut effect hollowed out city centres, leaving them empty and lifeless.

A great dilemma emerges for creative city-making: Can you physically plan it by developing science parks, incubator centres or creative quarters? Do you instead need to provide conditions in terms of attitudes, finance mechanisms and regulations with a few physical interventions to allow inventiveness, buzz and stimulation to flourish?

Casting our mind across history and the globe, let's take a broader view of cities going back to the past, into the present and towards the future. Throughout history the city has been the hub for transactions and exchange: of ideas, knowledge, buying and selling and bargaining, of commerce, of services. A place for connecting, mixing and interacting in spite of separations between classes, groups, the rich and poor, the powerful and disenfranchised. The city agglomerates power and politics, finance and economics, society and culture. Here influence is traded and power brokers reside, perhaps operating locally or on a national stage. In the city cultural products gained in importance, monuments to greatness were built to impress, the spectacular and dazzling were staged to excite and astonish. The city has diversity, choice and complexity. It attracts the hopeful, the gifted, the ambitious, the influential. They gathered, they gossiped, did business and built prestige. It entices too those with dark desires, the criminal fraternity and those who want to remain anonymous and melt into the crowd. The city enchants, charms and captivates as well as repels, disgusts and depresses. The city provides critical mass. It is an accelerator of opportunities and a generator of problems. It is a laboratory for what is good and bad about living together. Things cluster. Specialisms evolve, activities abound. It is a catalyst for the innovations and solutions for the problems it creates. Often, though, the city weighs you down with its entrenched problems of urban decay, unemployment and hopelessness, crime, drugs, seediness and ugliness.

The seeds for a creative city, however, are inherent in the city being a city. This is true for ordinary as well as extraordinary cities. Even cities not at the centre of affairs have greater energy, usually, than surrounding towns and villages, simply because there are more transactions, more opportunities to share, to learn and research.

A changing urban paradigm

The transformation of cities globally in the last two decades has been breathtaking if not electrifying, even though the results are not necessarily liveable or beautiful. Think of over-engineered highway systems, enclosed hermetic retail worlds or reflective glass-fronted office blocks giving nothing back to the public realm – lifeless at street level. Icon mania is everywhere and rarely does using icons work. Copenhagen's Oresund bridge linking to Malmo is one. A sweeping elegance and grace and the fluid line of wind turbines communicates the region's green intent. Arriving at the Malmo side, the Western Harbour is carbon neutral, it combines and blends well the ordinary and the iconic. There is the Turning Torso by Calatrava with ordinary apartments and you can see its green workings everywhere. This is creative urbanism.

Many cities have tried to move from commonplace to special in seeking to attract skilled people and those the city believes can help generate wealth, improve their image or give external credibility. Initially the large, more global cities entered this 'war for talent', and 'culture', seen as the arts, was part of the urban revitalization inventory. The cleverer ones, like Singapore, knew that this talent needed to be varied, including scientists, managers able to run complex organizations, as well as digital media wizards. Many of these people are in a conventional sense not necessarily exciting individuals, although extremely good at their jobs.

A city suitable for factory work looks and feels different from one wishing to encourage people to be curious and inventive. In one people are effectively units of mechanical production; in the other, key ideas and wealth generators. Their atmosphere is completely different. Yet the regularly patterned industrial buildings with their flexibility have an allure to new economy workers. The image and perception of cities is increasingly seen as crucial in generating global resonance. So the inner dynamics and priorities of cities have changed. This poses a dilemma: do you focus on the internal needs of the city or on the outsiders you want to attract?

The larger cities especially seek to develop and project themselves as hubs of rich, deep experience and potential, making you want to associate yourself with them, work there, visit and come back and stay. Amsterdam, Berlin and Singapore offer excellent examples of marketing programmes (see websites www.iamsterdam.com, www.be.berlin.de and www.talentcapital.sg) showing how cities seek to lure the young and gifted to make their city their home. Bilbao with its 'make your dreams come true' is another.

More educated people increasingly choose their city before deciding on the company within it. Previously they chose the company or job. This explains why urban quality of life, its attractiveness and liveability, have become crucial. They are considered the new competitive tools. Within this, cultural life is seen as more important, whether more highbrow or alternative. According to a study by CEOs for Cities (www.ceosforcities.org), nearly 70 per cent of higher skilled people in the crucial age bracket between 25 and 35 in developed countries choose the city first. Twenty years ago the figure was around 20 per cent. What attracts these people? First, in spite of virtual connections, they want to link with people they imagine to be like themselves. Second, perceived 'liveability' is key. This is assessed by a combination of subjective life satisfaction indicators, such as having choices, variety, low levels of crime, cleanliness, accessibility to facilities, good quality urban design, even beauty, as well as objective factors such as infrastructure and transport systems. Third, they want a 'creative milieu' which is an environment that engenders stimulation, potential and exploration. Lastly, they want cultural distinctiveness. Here, the dominance of English as the lingua franca is harming many first-tier cities, such as Paris, Tokyo and Shanghai, whose deeper cultural attributes the incoming knowledge nomads rarely understand.

The danger in this process is exclusion. These urban attributes also attract the majority of 'ordinary' people doing everyday jobs who may not be able to afford the facilities or feel they are not for them. This is the shadowy side. Not everyone can afford to buy and consume, and sharp distinctions between haves and have-nots is increasingly visible.

Every city wants to get on to a bigger stage and this needs a physical expression of their apparent creativity. There is an oft-repeated repertoire, with the city increasingly becoming like a temporary artistic installation with buildings created more for their momentary seduction than to have staying power. Gleaming glass towers, bold shapes breaking out of the traditional pattern of the square box; vast retailing, entertainment or cultural centres which try to bewitch, enchant and seduce you; skyscrapers exploding on to the landscape, some with good public spaces, are just some of their features.

The global network of starchitects seeks to outdo each other in this process as they move from one city to the next. Rem Koolhaas, I.M. Pei, Cesar Pelli, Herzog de Meuron, Santiago Calatrava, Zaha Hadid, Norman Foster, Frank Gehry, Stephen Holl are just a few. The Guggenheim, the Turning Torso, the Maxxi Arts Centre, the Gherkin, Kiasma, the Elbphilharmonie, the CCTV headquarters, the Pyramid or the Petronas Towers (see Chapter 7 by Davide Ponzini in this volume). Mostly they are cultural institutions, the cathedrals of the post-industrial age. Part of this strategy is to raise the bar on urban infrastructure as an element of overall urban design. As cities battle for centrality, a raft of new airports, such as in Madrid, Munich and Beijing, or railway stations such as Berlin, Vienna and even Liége, are taking shape. The aim is to make public transport a delight to use. Yet many ask: 'Do architects like people?' 'Do they understand people?' They say: 'The buildings may look fine from the outside, but what do they feel like to work and be in.'

How does a city show its more subtle intent? Freiburg, the green city of Europe, has used the naming of a place – such as *Das Sonnenschiff*, a carbon neutral settlement. Here housing, offices, research centres and retailing co-designed by artists and architects have been brought together in a way that you know 'this city wants to be green'. The ability for a city to express its higher ethical purposes is one of the challenges for the creative city. Done well this can provide motivation or engender confidence.

In spite of icon competition most cities look the same. Looking at a picture you would not know if you are in China, the United States, Brazil, Australia or India. The clusters of high rise buildings can feel lifeless, soulless and faceless, and without personality built to a repeatable plan and pattern that could be anywhere. These cities are usually planned more with cars in mind than walkability. Surrounded by wide roads that make walking difficult, the buildings can hit the street without engaging you, as if to say 'keep your distance'. The shiny, clean surfaces that might appeal and tempt you from afar or in a glossy brochure offer little as you close in. There is hardly a sense you are welcome or that you can be part of what is going on behind the façade. The entrances are enclosed and usually guarded, there are plants here and there looking somewhat out of place. You feel small and insignificant as an individual. These cities can have an empty, shallow feel, even though they are interspersed with the occasional magnet like a retail emporium. Increasingly, therefore, cities want to look deeper and draw on history or culture as a means to re-establish distinctiveness, which is that which makes places special, unique and different.

Ordinary and extraordinary places

Looking at the acknowledged creative places from the past, it is striking how many were hubs of empires, like Athens, Vienna or London, or the centre of trading routes, like Venice. Unsurprisingly, as poles of attraction they lured the best and the brightest from around their known worlds, which continually helped them reinforce their positions.

Can all the ordinary global places, such as 650 cities around the world with over one million inhabitants or the thousand or so over 500,000 become creative when perhaps their industries like producing large quantities of coal, steel and beer have been lost?

Yes and no. Athens gave us an intellectual heritage that fostered debate, analysis and critique. Venice highlights to us the importance of specialization, expertise and trade networks. Florence reminds us how important new business models are, such as its invention of banking systems. Vienna of the late nineteenth century shows us how a configuration of core ideas can affect a number of disciplines simultaneously. The rise of Paris as an arts and fashion leader was triggered and aided by royal sponsorship. London of the swinging 60s hit a global mood of change and the success of Silicon Valley helps point out the elements required, organizational, financial and legal, to turn ideas into reality.

So, no, most of these places will never be what Athens was, or London to some extent still is, and Shanghai is today becoming. They do not have the traditions, intellectual history and skills base as well as wide-ranging and renowned institutions and deep structures to draw on. They do not have the critical mass or global resonance to attract the diversified and profound skills to make an impact across a range of fields. They are not capital cities where economic, political and cultural power agglomerates.

Yet does that matter? Not many cities or quarters within them have all the ingredients and qualities required to be 'complete' creative places. These are places that in a virtuous cycle reproduce themselves over time. They have the hard and software infrastructures, from educational institutions, showcasing possibilities to social networks, to maintain their position and reputations and so attract the interesting. Collectively, these create a compelling story of place that helps drive forward momentum. These qualities can be seen, for instance, in the creative quarters of the Sohos of New York and London or rue Saint Honoré in Paris. The world is large and not every place needs to be centre-stage to globally connect. Places of regional or national importance can have impact and, indeed, in tight niches resonate globally. Places should measure themselves by their own ambitious standards, attempting to punch above their weight. They can set targets such as the Flanders region that is becoming a recognized hub for successful small-company entrepreneurship feeding off the skills and research of its network of universities.

Interestingly, places not in the media or political gaze can often innovate better as Peter Hall's magisterial work *Cities and Civilization* (1998) exemplifies. Think of places not at the centre of affairs, like Glasgow's rise as a shipbuilding innovation hub two centuries ago or Los Angeles' emergence as a centre for film in the early twentieth century or more recently Helsinki's impact on internet communications. The many gritty industrial places seeking to reinvent themselves may not have the glamour and image we now associate with a Milan or a Barcelona. Yet remember that design-conscious Barcelona, known for its mercantile tradition, was one of the earliest cities to industrialize and fashion-savvy Milan has a rich industrial tradition. The same applies to Lodz, Poland's historic textile city, which emerged as a centre for film teaching and filmmaking, or Liverpool and Manchester in music. There can be an honest, straightforward and a 'getting down to business' approach in those industrial places that those at the centre of finance or trade can lose. So, yes, each city can learn from the best.

Cascading waves of urban creativity

The urban creativity agenda is moving down the urban scale. It started two decades ago with the

25 largest global cities as recognition grew of the shift from nations as hubs of wealth creation to city-regions. Noticeably, urban amenities became more significant, such as cultural activities and facilities from arts to sports to recreation. Probably the first study was that of Harvey Perloff in 1979 which was encouraged by the not-for-profit organization Partners for Livable Places (Burns and Friedmann, 1979). It launched a programme documenting the economic value of design, cultural amenities and activities in Los Angeles. This triggered a significant array of economic impact studies of the arts with the arts community in the US beginning to justify their economic worth (The Port Authority of New York and New Jersey, 1983) starting with New York. Shortly thereafter similar comprehensive studies were carried out in the UK (Myerscough, 1988) and Australia (Throsby and Withers, 1979) and these have been followed up by as many as several hundred studies on the impact of the creative industries. The main point is that the strategies adopted by the largest cities, such as a focus on creative economy, the attempt to liven up the urban experience and the use of architecture were then followed up by those in the second rank, such as Manchester, Barcelona, Hamburg, Minneapolis or Rotterdam. Now even smaller cities are developing creativity-focused strategies. Often they are more interesting than those of larger cities; examples include Ghent and Genk in Belgium, Umea in northern Sweden (the first truly northern European Capital of Culture), Tilburg, Arnhem and Heerlen in the Netherlands, Penang in Malaysia, Nantes in France or Kanazawa in Japan.

The mission statement of Ghent, for instance, is: 'To harness all the creative forces in the city to increase our opportunities'. The take-up by the artistic community has been difficult since they saw this as an opportunity for further grant support. Instead Ghent has shifted focus and developed projects such as how to deal with child obesity in innovative ways. Umea, as an example, got its university design department to redesign over 30 services within the local authority from a design perspective. The city of Arnhem gave over a whole street of smaller shops to young fashion designers coming out of their arts school. This category of city has great potential since they are small enough to make it happen, if they are not parochial and inward-looking, but large enough to be taken seriously.

Even very small places are in on the act. I have over the last five years, supported by the Swiss government, been involved with ten towns in Albania, most with populations of below 30,000, who have been reassessing their cultural resources, from olive growing to a tradition of interculturalism, to see how they can use these assets as growth points. Equally, the Slow Cities Movement has been encouraging a welter of urban innovations (see www.cittaslow.net). The main lesson is that creativity is an all-pervasive attribute as important to urban development as electricity. In order to move on to this new terrain we need to shift the old intellectual architecture which has sedimented itself into our minds like a geological formation. To be creative in an urban context usually involves a challenge to existing ways of thinking about possibilities and a different assessment of what the resources of a city are. To do this well requires an open-minded environment. This means that the organizational culture of a city needs to foster a culture of creativity which by being embedded helps a city to rethink itself when necessary and to adapt to changing circumstances. This requires a willingness to look at issues afresh. Once done this might involve changing things, but on occasion, after an unprejudiced review, it might mean keeping things as they are. The primary task involves creating the soft and hard pre-conditions.

The journey towards creativity and beyond starts with being curious. If a city's culture encourages and legitimizes people, whether poor or well off, whether educated or unschooled, whether in traditional working sectors or more knowledge-intensive ones, to be curious this provides a launch pad. Then it is possible to be imaginative. With imagination we can envision possibilities and have creative ideas. Many may not work, but at least there is an ideas bank to work with. Once these ideas have gone through the reality checker, the few that are valid can become inventions and, when widely applied, innovations. Such an innovation can be an end product, a service, a technology, a technique and procedure, a process, an implementation mechanism, a problem redefinition or new professional attitudes or a change in mindset.

Creativity is context-driven. What is creative in one circumstance may not be in another. Whereas in the past we might have harnessed engineering prowess to solve urban infrastructure problems or public health issues, today, needs are different. Of primary importance is the ability to find new ways of empowering people, working through issues of co-creation, rethinking democratic processes, establishing ways for the urban collectives to create joint visioning and aims, integrated thinking, grasping the essence of different disciplines and finally understanding what the new urban resources are. What is deemed to be creative in a small Albanian city like Korca or Lezhe will be different from what we expect from a Melbourne.

Creativities: their qualities and characteristics

Creativity is both generic, a way of thinking and a mindset, and task-oriented in relation to particular fields. Creativity requires certain qualities of mind, dispositions and attitudes, including curiosity, openness and a questioning attitude. It involves fluency and flexibility and the ability to draw on ideas from across disciplines and fields of inquiry, to think laterally and blend concepts from seemingly unrelated domains. It is based on divergent thinking, which opens out possibilities, reveals patterns and helps find solutions before prematurely closing in on a specific answer.

Everyone is in principle creative, but not equally creative, yet everyone can be more creative than they currently are. The same applies to organizations, neighbourhoods and city-regions. Creative behaviour and the ability to innovate occur when two types of mind are present. One is the exploratory, opportunity seeking and connecting mind that can range horizontally across facts, issues and specialist knowledge. This is the enabling mind associated with being creative. This needs to be allied to the focused, vertical mind of someone who knows a subject in profound detail. This is the instrumental mind.

We can grasp quite easily what a creative individual might be like; for instance their capacity to make interesting connections and to have sparks of insight. But the priorities for creative organization are different, adding a layer of complexity. Such an organization probably has mavericks and creative individuals, but for the organization to work it needs other types too: consolidators, sceptics, solidifiers, balancers, people with people skills. The creative organization needs mixed teams. Indeed many may be quite 'ordinary' people, but because its spirit or ethos is open, exploratory and supportive, this maximizes potential.

Moving on to the next layer – the creative city – issues become very difficult as complexity rises exponentially as you involve a mass of individuals and an amalgam of organizations with different cultures, aims and attitudes. These can push in opposing directions. The challenge is to discover where the lines of strong agreement can flow and to build on these so that similarities become more important than differences, which need to be negotiated to move forward as in a mediation process. The overarching skill needed for a creative city is that of the connectors, enablers, and facilitators. These can be individuals or intermediary organizations who can stand above the nitty-gritty of the day to day.

REFERENCES

Burns, Leland S. and Friedmann, John (eds) (1979) *The Art of Planning: Selected Essays of Harvey S. Perloff*. New York: Plenum.

Hall, Sir P. (1998) *Cities and Civilization: Culture, Innovation and Urban Order*. London: Weidenfeld & Nicholson.

Landry, C. (1990) *Glasgow: The Creative City and its Cultural Economy*. Glasgow: Glasgow Development Agency.

Landry, C. (2000) *The Creative City – A Toolkit for Urban Innovators*. London: Earthscan.

Landry, C. and Bianchini, F. (1995) *The Creative City*. Bournes Green: Comedia/Demos.

Myerscough, J. (1988) *The Economic Importance of the Arts in Britain*. London: Policy Studies Institute.

The Port Authority of New York and New Jersey (1983) *The Arts as an Industry: Their Economic Importance to the New York–New Jersey Metropolitan Region*. New York: The Port Authority of New York and New Jersey.

Throsby, D. and Withers, G. (1979) *The Economics of the Performing Arts*. London: Edward Arnold.

Wood, P. and Landry C. (2007) *The Intercultural City: Planning for Diversity Advantage*. London: Earthscan.

CHAPTER 10

THE PRODUCTION OF CULTURE: ABU DHABI'S URBAN STRATEGIES
Yasser Elsheshtawy

This chapter investigates the urban strategies pursued by Abu Dhabi, capital of the United Arab Emirates, in order to attain world city status. It focuses on the ways in which the city is using culture-based urban development and spectacular architecture to attain this goal. By analyzing the Cultural District of Saadiyat Island, the author offers a comprehensive view of how the rhetoric of the various stakeholders masks the extent to which they are deeply embedded in a late-capitalist discourse, which views culture as a marketable commodity. The author also examines how such projects are used to establish regional dominance. He concludes by suggesting an alternative and more sustainable approach, which would lead to a locally inspired cultural development process, closely tied to the city's local populace.

Introduction: the curious case of Abu Dhabi

My aim in this chapter is to investigate Abu Dhabi's efforts to become a globally significant city, specifically through the creation of a cultural infrastructure that would help transform it into a center for culture: globally, locally and within the wider Middle East. Globally, world-class museums and centers of education, as well as being a media hub, would attract foreign talent and diversify its economy. Locally, these projects would affirm an Emirati identity in the face of a majority expatriate populace.[1] At a regional level, the focus on culture would legitimize the city, and in turn the entire Gulf, as a competitor to the Arab world's traditional centers (Egypt, Syria, Lebanon, etc.). In this way the 'flags with tribes' stigma would be overcome.[2]

To that effect, the city has embarked on an unprecedented construction drive and has allocated what seem like unlimited resources, in spite of the 2008 financial crisis, to develop cultural districts, host world-class universities, and engage in a massive urban transformation under what has been called Abu Dhabi Vision 2030. These visions are conceptualized as 'cultural infrastructure' and thus have not experienced any halt in their execution. Using a strategy of spectacular architecture and urbanism, these projects are intended to ground the city firmly within the ranks of global cities. In fact, by utilizing such a strategy, the city is no different from many others across the world, where culture is being used to attract investment and creative talent. Yet at the same time the Abu Dhabi case is unique in many respects – and these are of particular importance in the context of this book, as they pertain to issues related to urban governance, cultural politics and policy.

The uniqueness of the Abu Dhabi case stems from its geographical position, its recent emergence as an urban entity, population make-up, as well as government structure. With regard to geography, it is located in a region awash in oil and gas resources that will provide sufficient money to fund these projects for the next 100 years (at least). Moreover, its native population is a minority facing a massive expatriate influx that threatens to erase its local 'identity'. At the same time, this identity is in many respects illusive since the region did not have any substantive urban tradition to begin with and as such it lacks conventional cultural and artistic markers, e.g., a thriving local art scene, or a critically engaged, and artistically literate, local population. But more significant is its governmental structure, which impinges directly on cultural policy.

Abu Dhabi, like the rest of the Arabian Peninsula, is governed by a 'family'. While government institutions, advisory bodies, etc., give the appearance of a democratic system, the reality is different (Davidson, 2005, 2007). Invariably, governmental bodies are headed by a member of the ruling family, and major decisions are never taken without consulting royal princes or 'Sheikhs'. Public participation, debate and consultation with the local populace – both native and expatriate – almost never takes place. The two institutes in charge of implementing the government's cultural policy are the TDIC (Tourism Development and Investment Company) and the ADACH (Abu Dhabi Authority for Culture and Heritage). Both are wholly government bodies utilizing the expertise of cultural consultants – in many instances westerners.[3] At present they constitute the cornerstone for implementing the city's cultural policy.

In this chapter I will be looking at the extent to which these cultural policies resonate with city inhabitants, who are in fact essentially bypassed in this process. My treatment is grounded in a critical discourse that focuses on the use of architecture and urbanism as tools that further these cultural and political objectives. A main point of critique is that these developments will result in 'cultural enclaves' isolated from the local population and geared towards transient residents and tourists. I begin, however, with a brief overview of urban and architectural developments in Abu Dhabi.

Origins and urban development

A look at the city's origins in 1761 reveals a rather remarkable transformation. Its urban development started in earnest in 1962 following the discovery of oil. However, in these early phases urbanization efforts were tentative and did not gain momentum until 1966, when Sheikh Zayed assumed leadership. A frantic effort at catching up with the modern world ensued, aiming to transform a small, nomadic encampment into a cosmopolitan city (Fahim, 1995; Elsheshtawy, 2011a). Examining images taken by BP (British Petroleum) in 1962 and 1963 shows the desolate character of its built environment, mostly consisting of closely placed huts, narrow alleyways and a remote fort. Only a few structures along its waterfront had recognizable modern features – shops, houses for BP employees and a post office (Photo 10.1). For what could only be described as a village, whose inhabitants lived in medieval-like conditions, in dire need of improvement, mostly western consultants were hired to develop a masterplan. This led to the construction of a functioning road system, various municipal projects and services, appropriate housing, and so on. Yet things remained somewhat primitive.

The period from the late 1960s to the 1980s saw a surge in construction activity and the real emergence of Abu Dhabi as an actual city, recognizable internationally. A series of key events added to the city's significance: the withdrawal of British forces and the creation of the United Arab Emirates, which united seven existing emirates previously known as the Trucial States, with Abu Dhabi as its capital, in 1971. The current recognizable shape of the city emerged between the late 1980s and 2004, as a result of various policies pertaining to land distribution to locals, and the construction of iconic landmarks such as the Emirates Palace Hotel. Yet, up until that moment change had been slow. Indeed, the ruler attempted to shield the city as much as possible from globalizing influences that were exerting themselves in next-door Dubai. Moreover, through its architecture an attempt was made to develop an Arab-Islamic identity that would distinguish it from its neighbor, which relied on a spectacular mode of urbanism that unabashedly adopted western forms (e.g. Elsheshtawy, 2010).

But all that was set to change in 2004, which witnessed the death of Sheikh Zayed and the transfer of power to his son Sheikh Khalifa. In addition, a number of cabinet changes saw the introduction of young, western-educated ministers – most of them belonging to the ruling family. They were intent on transforming Abu Dhabi into a global player. A series of political and economical changes were to significantly shift the city's urban growth paradigm, through ambitious projects (Photo 10.2). These ranged from entire new residential and tourist complexes to vast malls and town-sized commercial and industrial developments, as well as the development of a vast number of islands surrounding the city (Elsheshtawy, 2011a). All this was done under a general vision dubbed *Abu Dhabi 2030*, operating

Photo 10.1   A market area in 1960s Abu Dhabi

(Source: © BP plc; ARC113279_222 BP archive. University of Warwick)

under the slogan that the city will be a 'contemporary expression of an Arab city'.

In the following sections I will focus on the cultural component, which on the face of it projects an image of sophistication and enlightenment. Yet it is nevertheless based on a shrewd calculation that exploits the worldwide trend of 'cultural commodification' and the emphasis on 'global culture'.

The late capitalist museum: a paradigm shift

As I have discussed in the previous section, Abu Dhabi has been engaged in a massive effort to transform the city from a 'laid-back' metropolis to one that is more assertive at a global level. For this purpose it is employing numerous strategies, which on the surface appear to be a unique response to globalizing conditions, and an understandable preparation for a post-oil future. However, these cultural endeavors are grounded in a global discourse dating back to the 1990s. It would be useful

to provide a brief overview of these theoretical underpinnings in order to help in both understanding and critiquing the developments taking place in Abu Dhabi today. My aim is to show that the city has become the perfect staging point for this paradigmatic shift, given its unique geographical and demographic characteristics and aided by unlimited financial resources.

Theoretical origins: towards a 'universal museum'

The efforts under way in Abu Dhabi are part of a worldwide trend in which the meaning and significance of the museum has been reconstituted as a result of globalizing influences and the shift toward a business-based model. Moreover, these trends suggest a redefinition of culture and its larger meanings within postcolonial and transnational systems. This process began in New York in the 1990s with many museums experiencing financial difficulties. Such developments were exacerbated following 9/11 and

Photo 10.2   Modern Abu Dhabi – a scene from the Central Business District (Photographer: Yasser Elsheshtawy)

the subsequent economic downturn (e.g. Ostling, 2009).[4] Moving museums towards a business-based model, and promoting an idea of culture as a commodity that can be sold, moved and exchanged, began to suggest a way out for these troubled cultural landmarks. This fundamental conceptual change was based on the ways in which the pre-monitory theoretical writings of such post-modernist writers as Fredric Jameson and Rosalind Krauss were applied to the museum as an institution.

Rosalind Krauss, in her 1990 essay 'The cultural logic of the late capitalist museum', sets out the main parameters of this shift. As she put it, 'the notion of the museum as a guardian of the public patrimony has given way to the notion of a museum as a corporate entity with a highly marketable inventory and the desire for growth' (Krauss, 1990: 5). Thus, according to Krauss, culture has turned into a commodity of sorts. She in turn acknowl-edged a debt to Fredric Jameson, who in a 1984 essay about post-modernism argued forcefully for the emergence of a 'global culture', one of whose characteristics is that '…aesthetic production today has become integrated into commodity production' (Jameson, 1984: 56). In more than one sense, this

debate actually harks back to the work of the Situationists in the 1960s, specifically the writings of Guy Debord (1970) and others, who dealt with the impact of media on everyday practices.

Krauss observed that there has been a change in the way a museum is designed and experienced, as well in how it is placed within a given city. This has led to a move away from what she termed the 'encyclo-pedic' museum – a collection of artifacts placed chronologically for instance with the objective of facilitating a grand narrative – to a 'synchronic museum' which 'would forego history in the name of a kind of intensity of experience, an aesthetic charge that is not so much temporal (historical) as it is now radically spatial' (Krauss, 1990: 5). Yet such procla-mations were merely meant to obscure or justify the notion that culture has become a form of capital and that museums can be treated as a business. And it is precisely because of this that museums have now become part of what has been termed a 'global expansionist model', a corporatization of culture (Mathur, 2005). What remains to be investigated is the impact of this new paradigm on urban space – the extent to which the city has been shaped and recon-figured – as a result of an 'urban cultural economy'.

Urban cultural economy

The developments discussed above need to be understood within the larger context of the idea of an 'urban cultural economy' triggered by the widely cited but now largely discredited work of Richard Florida, centering on the creative economy and the creative worker (Florida, 2002). Darla Decker has not only debunked this work, but has also identified the characteristics and problems associated with these new cultural clusters (Decker, 2008; also see Glaeser, 2005; Peck, 2005).[5] She strongly identifies with the work of Andrew Ross, who notes that one of the main outcomes of this new urban cultural economy is the 'cultural quartering' through which policy makers mark out an area within a city based on cultural products (Ross, 2007). This cultural quartering leads to fragmentation, gentrification and a loss of heterogeneity. The Guggenheim was right at the forefront of this trend, which served its global expansionist strategy ideally, manifested in its Bilbao branch (also see Fiss, 2009).

Another downside is the affirmation of class distinctions. Culture-based urban developments are considered to be both cause and effect of 'an uneven distribution of economic gains and cultural forms' (Decker, 2008: 231). Moreover, they reinforce existing power structures by catering to the interests of 'urban elites' who determine both the type of development as well as its location. In this sense, they confirm neo-Marxist theories dealing with the impact of capitalism on urban space (Harvey, 2006; Davis & Monk, 2008). Yet while no one can discount such critiques, they do not take into account agency – the extent to which citizens can resist or subvert change, for example. The notion of a passive consumer accepting helplessly what is presented in front of him/her underlies much of the discourse concerning the new 'urban cultural economy'. As Arjun Appadurai (1996) noted, an emphasis solely on the triumph of multinational corporations assumes a consumer complicity that denies individual agency and the various identity negotiations and altercations that occur as the consumer encounters the product. In the following sections I will elaborate on this.

Constructing cultural infrastructure: Saadiyat Island

How is the Saadiyat Island cultural project using iconic urban and architectural forms tactically in order to achieve the general strategy outlined above? I will discuss the spatial characteristics of this development as well as attempt to uncover the underlying rationale. I will show that the various stakeholders involved employ a rhetoric that is tied to a global discourse concerning the role of culture and museums in a globalizing (or late-capitalist) world. How is this cultural strategy being implemented through policies and various governmental organizations? What are the enculturation efforts that aim to provide a justification for an, arguably, disinterested local populace?

District origin or towards spectacular architecture

Harking back to its conservative and traditional role, Abu Dhabi always saw itself as the center of culture in the UAE. In the 1970s it hired a well-known architectural firm to design a cultural center and a national library. This would become a main venue for staging classical concerts, art exhibits, as well as a major book fair. It seemed only natural that the city's sights would eventually turn toward creating a more substantive venue for culture. Most significantly, in 2004, the newly formed Abu Dhabi Tourism Authority (ADTA) embarked on a project to develop Saadiyat Island – located 500 meters from the city's shoreline – into a 'world-class', 'environmentally sensitive' tourist destination that included as its centerpiece the creation of a new cultural district for Abu Dhabi and the UAE. In July 2006, an agreement was signed between TDIC and the New York-based Guggenheim Museum to establish a 'world-class' museum devoted to modern and contemporary art to be built as part of the cultural district, and designed by Frank Gehry. In a flurry of press releases, Sheikh Mohamed, Abu Dhabi's crown prince, claimed that the project 'will become an international cultural hub for the Middle East on par with the best in the world' (Ameen, 2006). In addition, the development included a classical museum by Jean Nouvel (affiliated with the French Louvre) and a museum dedicated to the life of Sheikh Zayed designed by Foster Architects (Photo 10.3).

Conceptually, all the architects involved provide vague and generalized contextual references for their buildings. Frank Gehry argues that his design alludes to the traditional alleyways of Arab towns. Nouvel fluctuates between recreating an image of an Arabian town, copying the waterways of Venice, the discovery of objects within a forest, and a rain of light resulting from perforations in the gigantic dome covering the entire complex. Interestingly, both buildings are projected out onto the water on an artificial island, thus away from Abu Dhabi proper. Foster's Sheikh Zayed Museum – unveiled amidst much fanfare during a visit by the Queen of England – suggests falconry through the creation of gigantic wing-like structure emerging from an artificial hill. These are indeed the physical characteristics of the district, but what still needs to be investigated is why this project was conceived in the first place – and in this particular location.

Beyond the spectacle: rationalizing the project

To rationalize the project, more or less two lines of argument are put forward: the first is a political argument, according to which it will contribute to 'cultural enlightenment'; the second is an economic one, which views the entire development from a profit-making perspective.

The notion of Abu Dhabi becoming a 'new' cultural center in the Middle East has occupied a central

Photo 10.3 **Saadiyat Island – Guggenheim in the foreground, and Nouvel's Domed Louvre in the back (Photographer: Yasser Elsheshtawy)**

position in justifying such a massive undertaking. This point has been put forward by officials in different formats. Journalist Judith Miller has suggested, based on encounters with various people involved in this endeavor, that such projects are being adopted so as to provide a counterpoint to fundamentalist tendencies. Such views were echoed recently in an article by Nicolai Ourossof (2010), who argues that rulers are using architecture and art to 'reshape their national identities.' Significantly, as officials have argued, these projects are seen as a way to educate and enlighten local citizens, instill a sense of national pride and provide local society with the necessary tools for global engagement.

The second line of argument in an economic perspective sees the cultural district as part of a larger phenomenon involving the role of the museum in a global world. The Guggenheim in particular, which occupies a dominant position within the island, has become symptomatic of the 'McDonaldization' of culture. It has in effect been turned into a brand that can be placed anywhere. Abu Dhabi, by acquiring this brand, is thus plugging itself into this global cultural network – becoming another stop on the world art circuit. However, the museum's former director argues that this is not about 'exporting a commodity' or 'setting up a franchise', but is being done rather in the spirit of communication – the museum would bring modern works of art to the local settings and help foster local talent.[6] There are many who observe, however, that the region lacks the necessary art scene to enable such museums to succeed.[7] Yet if such buildings are to be more than mere spectacle, or a pawn of some global cultural scheme, a local art scene is indispensable. I will examine this in the next section dealing with the notion of 'enculturation'.

Educating the public: enculturation and awareness-raising

A significant component in creating this 'cultural infrastructure' more or less from scratch is to engage the local population – particularly to counter the 'cultural colonialism' perspective and also to show that this is not just a matter of utilizing surplus capital generated from oil. As a first step, the local population needs to be given a framework within which they can view these projects. Thus, many

local commentators are portraying Abu Dhabi's foray into the world of culture as a source of pride, since it moves the Gulf from a position on the 'periphery' and wrests the lead from traditional centers of power in the region. Dissenting or alternative viewpoints are rare. There are a few exceptions, though, with some noting the need to maintain an independent identity, while others question whether a truly local culture can take hold in a society dominated by rampant materialism (White, 2010).[8] Such dismissive reactions are also present to varying degrees among Arab commentators, who focus on the importation of culture or observe that 'foreigners have been rented to design a future'.[9]

To counter these viewpoints, governmental organizations have been engaged in a massive effort that on the face of it aims at educating the local population but seems to be more concerned with giving the 'appearance' of a vital art scene. This is achieved through a series of events such as seminars, exhibitions and art fairs, which, according to officials, are meant to turn the public into a museum-going population.[10] There is also the Abu Dhabi Art Fair, organized by TDIC and ADACH, whose twin objectives are to 'plant the seeds of a local art market and bring into the region high-quality art worthy of the bare walls of its future museums'.[11]

More revealing are the seminars in which various art experts, academic scholars and stakeholders are invited to explain to the Abu Dhabi public the worthiness of these endeavors. Similarly, exhibitions and shows taking place in the grounds of the Emirates Palace Hotel – itself an exclusive enclave with controlled accessibility – have been for the most part geared towards an expatriate audience. These have included an elaborate Picasso exhibition, which for the first time showed (cubist) nude paintings (Photo 10.4). A show called 'The making of the Guggenheim', incorporating some key works from the collection, such as Matisse's *Nude in the Forest* (a barely recognizable figure in a miniature painting), was supposed to prove that Abu Dhabi will not censor art works. But these events have been sparsely attended by locals, or even for that matter resident Arabs from other countries. On Saadiyat Island itself, a large temporary exhibition center has been erected where exhibitions, film shows and seminars are held. According to media reports, these events are 'helping build expectation and knowledge of art in Abu Dhabi'.[12]

Photo 10.4 **Picasso Exhibition held at the Emirates Palace Hotel (Photographer: Yasser Elsheshtawy)**

So while the groundwork is being laid – top-down – for the emergence of a local art scene, it is geared for the most part to a westernized audience. At another level, agreements with various institutions aim at the transfer of knowledge and knowhow. The 'Louvre deal' is particularly telling in its details, as it is based on setting up an independent museum, not tied to the Louvre brand. Rather, French officials are interested in setting up an independent museum, and have detailed a process of transferring knowledge to their Emirati counterparts.[13] All this might suggest that there is a process in play that could ultimately lead to a vibrant local art scene. The reality maybe different though. Consider, for example, that the Guggenheim Abu Dhabi has a team of three curators working in New York to build a collection with a budget of up to $600 million, more than 200 times the annual acquisitions budget of the Guggenheim in Manhattan (Ourossof, 2010). The 'local' art scene is not being conceived locally but outside Abu Dhabi. Tellingly, Bruno Marquardt, former director of the French agency set up for the Louvre project, told me that when approached by Abu Dhabi officials, they were told that 'when you invite a museum you invite the devil'.[14] It is hard to see how this could lead to any local artistic revival.

Assessment: cultural enclaves and cultural colonialism

One particularly striking aspect of the Saadiyat Island cultural district is its distance from the city of Abu Dhabi (Photo 10.5). Indeed, one of the main characteristics of the new 'urban cultural economy' is the creation of cultural quarters that promote class distinctions and affirm the elite nature of these spaces. As such, these districts could be construed as cultural *enclaves*, which exclude the general population because they are far from the city center. Unlike Bilbao, where the Guggenheim has contributed to a revival of a derelict industrial site, in Abu Dhabi the mere location of the museums suggests an exclusionary spatial strategy.

The remoteness of these districts and their disengagement from the city both underscore the fact that they are meant to be displayed as precious objects, to be admired from a distance for the local population, and that ultimately they will serve transient residents and tourists. Rather than build inside the city, for instance next to the existing cultural center, a decision was made to develop an isolated district in the service of, and responding to, global capital. Thus Fares Braizat, a Jordanian professor at Qatar University, notes that in spite of the extraordinary buildings that are being built, a much more concerted effort needs to take place whereby

Labels on image: Saadiyat Island, Abu Dhabi Island, to dubai, to al-ain

Photo 10.5 Satellite view of Abu Dhabi Island showing the relationship to Saadiyat Island (Courtesy of NASA)

local people are persuaded that they have a stake in this future. Otherwise such endeavors may end up reinforcing 'cynicism about engagement with the West that brought down Western-style modernism in this part of the world decades ago' (Farhat, 2007). Physical infrastructure in and of itself will not be enough to contribute to cultural enlightenment. What is needed is a much broader social and cultural engagement, otherwise culture may simply be used to mask unpleasant socio-political realities.

One particularly potent argument alluded to earlier pertains to the notion of cultural imperialism, the sense that Abu Dhabi is succumbing to western influences. Such viewpoints are anchored in a belief that unequal and uneven forces of cultural representation operate in a globalizing world and that there is an attempt to impose a hegemonic order on the less advantaged and less developed. Yet as art historian Poulin (2010) observes, such views do not apply in the case of Abu Dhabi; it is not an undeveloped country that needs 'civilizing' – in other words, museums did not force themselves on the city. Indeed, the use of western institutions may

simply be a matter of adopting best practices. But while it may not be a matter of one country dominating another, as Poulin notes, another form of domination may be taking place – that of cash over culture. Thus, Abu Dhabi's money is being used to acquire cultural dominance, at least within a regional context. As Poulin puts it, 'not only is the Emirate acquiring knowledge through the use of their financial power, but it is also establishing itself as a veritable superpower of knowledge.' Thus, Abu Dhabi, through its adoption of pre-packaged cultural models, is encouraging a globalization of culture, which in turn – it is hoped – will lead to an assertion of cultural authority.

Eastern promises: the ascendancy of Abu Dhabi

Abu Dhabi's foray into culture is based on several integrated and interrelated factors: economic, educational and political. Yet it is also part of a much larger trend whereby an East–West realignment is

Photo 10.6 A street corner gathering in Abu Dhabi's Central Business District, used by its low-income South-Asian community (Photographer: Yasser Elsheshtawy)

taking place, with countries such as China, India and South-East Asia asserting their power not just economically but also culturally. Abu Dhabi and the larger Gulf region are important players in this realignment, which is seeing the rise of such cities as Mumbai and Bangalore, Beijing or Mumbai, which are major centers of trade and commerce, gleaming with newly built skyscrapers and shopping malls. Economist Ben Simpfendorfer notes that we are witnessing a 'global historic rebalancing' (Simpfendorfer, 2009: 154) as a result of three factors: the rise of the China growth model; the rise of Arab wealth funds; and the rise of what he calls an 'Islamic corridor'. Such economic dominance will inevitably lead to a focus on culture as well.[15] This shift is particularly visible in Abu Dhabi, which has taken advantage of the financial crisis in the west and positioned itself along with its neighbors, Doha and Dubai, as a center for the sale and exchange of art in the region.[16] In an essentially top-down manner, governments in the region are engaged in a process seemingly grounded in noble cultural and educational objectives, but in fact deeply embedded in a global capitalist discourse. Spectacular architecture and urbanism play a complicit role in furthering and promoting this vision – leading to 'geographies of exclusion'.

However, inclusive approaches are possible and may offer an alternative for these westernized visions. And, they do not have to be based on an illusive past but can be inspired by the rich urban tapestry characterizing cities such as Abu Dhabi (e.g. Tatchell, 2009; Elsheshtawy, 2011b). Thus, instead of urban cultural quartering, spaces may be set up in the margins, in industrial districts and in unremarkable sites (Photo 10.6). In such settings, a truly locally inspired art scene could flourish, which would ultimately make the city's forays into the realm of culture sustainable and more effective.

Notes

1 See Belkaid, Akram (2010). 'A cause for concern,' *Le Monde Diplomatique* (English edition). August, p.

2 A saying attributed to an Egyptian diplomat in the 1960s where he argued that 'Egypt is the only nation-state in the region – the others are tribes with flags.'

3 See TDIC website, http://www.adach.ae/en/portal/adach/about.authority.aspx.

4   See also Kimmelman, Michael (2002). 'An era ends for the Guggenheim,' *The New York Times*, December 6, www.nytimes.com/2002/12/06/arts/critic-s-notebook-an-era-ends-for-the-guggenheim.html (accessed February 7, 2011) and Kimmelman, Michael (2004). 'New York's bizarre museum moment,' *The New York Times*, July 1, www.nytimes.com/2004/07/11/arts/art-architecture-new-york-s-bizarre-museum-moment.html (accessed on February 7, 2011). Moreover, numerous commentators have taken to analyzing and documenting these troubles – financial and otherwise (e.g. Ostling, 2009).

5   Also for a thorough criticism see Jacobs, Karrie (2005). 'Why I don't love Richard Florida,' *Metropolis*, February 22, www.metropolismag.com/story/20050222/why-i-dont-love-richard-florida (accessed March 11, 2010).

6   Interview with Tom Krens on the *Charlie Rose Show*, aired January 3, 2006 on PBS.

7   See e.g., Poulin, 2010; also Hynes, F. (2006). 'The goog effect – American imperialism or visionary museum. practice,' http://blogs.usyd.edu.au/bizart/2006/08/the_goog_effect_american_imper_1.html (accessed, February 10, 2007); and Saltz, J. (2007). 'Downward spiral: the Guggenheim Museum touches bottom,' *Village Voice*, www.villagevoice.com/issues/0207/saltz.php (accessed March 29, 2007).

8   Miller, Judith (2008). 'Abu Dhabi: East leans West.' *City Journal*, 18(1), Winter, www.city-journal.org/2008/18_1_abu_dhabi.html (accessed February 1, 2011).

9   See for example, Abeer Mishkhas (2007); Youssef Ibrahim (2007).

10 Bloomberg (2009). 'Oil wealth, immigrants stir angst in U.A.E., exhibition shows,' *Bloomberg News*, February 24, www.bloomberg.com/apps/news?pid=newsarchive&sid=aCQjY7DoR9xY&refer=muse (accessed February 1, 2011).

11 Lankarani, Nazanin (2010). 'Art fair illustrates Abu Dhabi's commitment to culture,' *The New York Times*, November 10, http://www.nytimes.com/2010/11/11/arts/11iht-m11cart.html (accessed February 1, 2011).

12 Hughes, Ronald & Gillet, Nathalie (2009). 'An Emirati collection starts life in France,' *The National*, May 27, p. 4.

13 Also see Hughes, Ronald & Gillet, Nathalie (2009). 'An Emirati collection starts life in France.' *The National*, May 27, p. 4.

14 Personal communication, October 2010, Berlin – during a seminar at the ZMO (Zentrum Moderner Orient).

15 For instance, institutions such as The Tate Gallery in London – sponsored largely by wealthy Middle Eastern patrons – have begun devoting considerable amounts towards purchasing art from the region, which has become 'The Next Big Thing'. In Gornall, Jonathan (2011). 'The new medicis', *The National: The Review*, March 11, pp. 4–7.

16 Morris, Ian (2010). 'Here comes the East', *The New York Times*, December 21, www.nytimes.com/2010/12/22/opinion/22iht-edmorris22.html (accessed February 13, 2011).

REFERENCES

Ameen, A. (2006). 'Frank Gehry to design Guggenheim Museum,' *Gulf News*, July 9, p. 3.

Appadurai, Arjun (1996). *Modernity at Large: Cultural Dimensions of Globalization*. Minneapolis: University of Minnesota Press.

Davidson, Christopher (2005). 'After Shaikh Zayed: the politics of succession in Abu Dhabi and the UAE,' *Middle East Policy*, 18(1), pp. 42–59.

—— (2007). 'The emirates of Abu Dhabi and Dubai: contrasting roles in the international system,' *Asian Affairs*, 38(1), pp. 33–48.

Davis, Mike & Monk, Daniel Betrand (Eds) (2008). *Evil Paradises: Dreamworlds of Neoliberalism*. New York: New Press.

Debord, Guy (1970). *The Society of the Spectacle*. Detroit: Black and Red.

Decker, Darla (2008). 'Urban Development, Cultural Clusters: The Guggenheim Museum and Its Global Distribution Strategies'. Dissertation. New York University.

Elsheshtawy, Yasser (Ed.) (2008). *The Evolving Arab City: Tradition, Modernity and Urban Development*. London: Routledge (paperback 2011).

—— (2010). *Dubai: Behind an Urban Spectacle*. London: Routledge.

—— (2011a). 'Cities of sand and fog,' In Elsheshtawy, Y. (ed.), *The Evolving Arab City*. London: Routledge.

—— (2011b). '(In)formal encounters: the metamorphosis of Abu Dhabi's central market,' *Built Environment*, 37(1).

Fahim, Mohammed (1995). *From Rags to Riches*. London: The London Centre of Arab Studies.

Farhat, Maymanah (2007). 'The Louvre Abu Dhabi, exploitation and the politics of the museum industry,' *ZNet*, March 27, www.zcommunications.org/the-louvre-abu-dhabi-exploitation-and-the-politics-of-the-museum-industry-by-maymanah-farhat (accessed February 17, 2011).

Fiss, Karen (2009). 'Design in a global context: envisioning postcolonial and transnational possibilities,' *Design Issues*, 25(3), pp. 3–10.

Florida, Richard (2002). *The Rise of the Creative Class*. New York: Basic Books.

Glaeser, Edward (2005). 'Review of Richard Florida's *The Rise of the Creative Class*,' *Regional Science and Urban Economics*, 35(5), pp. 593–596.

Harvey, David (2006). *Spaces of Global Capitalism: Towards a Theory of Uneven Geographical Development.* London: Verso.

Jameson, Fredric (1984) 'Postmodernism or the cultural logic of late capitalism', *New Left Review.* 1/146, July–August 1984, pp. 53–92.

Krauss, Rosalind (1990). 'The cultural logic of the late capitalist museum,' *October*, 54, pp. 3–17.

Mathur, Saloni (2005). 'Museums and globalization,' *Anthropological Quarterly*, 78(3), pp. 697–708.

Ostling, Susan (2009). 'The global museum and the orbit of the Solomon R. Guggenheim Museum, New York,' *The International Journal of the Humanities*, 5.

Ourossof, Nicolai (2010). 'Building museums and a fresh Arab identity,' *The New York Times*, November 26.

Peck, Jamie (2005). 'Struggling with the creative class,' *International Journal of Urban and Regional Research*, 29(4), pp. 740–770.

Poulin, Taylor L. (2010). 'An oasis in the desert? Issues and intricacies concerning the Louvre-Abu Dhabi museum expansion,' *StudentPulse: Online Academic Student Journal*, February 22, www.studentpulse.com/articles/177/3/an-oasis-in-the-desert-issues-and-intricacies-concerning-the-louvre-abu-dhabi-museum-expansion (accessed on February 7, 2011).

Ross, Andrew (2007). 'Nice work if you can get it: the mercurial career of creative industries policy,' *Work Organization Labour and Globalization*, 1(1), January, pp. 13–30.

Simpfendorfer, Ben (2009). *The New Silk Road: How a Rising Arab World is Turning Away from the West and Rediscovering China.* London: Palgrave Macmillan.

Tatchell, Jo (2009). *A Diamond in the Desert: Behind the Scenes in the World's Richest City.* London: Sceptre.

White, Allison (2010). 'Cultural evolutions in the United Arab Emirates,' *E-merge: Journal of Arts Administration and Policy*, May 18, http://blogs.saic.edu/emerge/2010/05/18/cultural-evolutions-in-the-united-arab-emirates-by-allison-white/ (accessed February 7, 2011).

CHAPTER 11

AMSTERDAM: A MULTICULTURAL CAPITAL OF CULTURE
Simin Davoudi and Wil Zonneveld

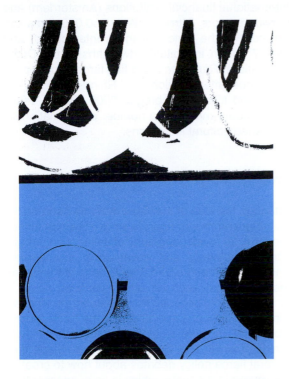

Amsterdam, with a population of under one million, is comparatively small. However, as part of the Randstad (a polycentric urban region comprising three other major cities of Rotterdam, The Hague and Utrecht with complementary functions) it can be comfortably positioned among the world cities. This chapter offers a profile of Amsterdam and its position in the wider metropolitan and regional context. Its authors explore the city's cultural profile in the context of Dutch cultural policy and governance, and discuss multiculturalism in Amsterdam and the way in which it has been accommodated in the Dutch housing policy and planning tradition. They conclude by highlighting the current neoliberal approaches to public policy and their implications for Amsterdam as a multicultural 'Capital of Culture'.

Introduction

There is an ethic in Amsterdam, based in centuries of benevolent activism by intermediate organizations, that comes to play in creating its diverse, egalitarian milieu. (Fainstein, 2007: 110)

Amsterdam offers a distinct case. On the one hand, the city rubs shoulders with the world cities by offering globally networked financial institutions, a cosmopolitan outlook, and around-the-clock attractions of a metropolis. On the other hand, it portrays a charming image of a provincial town with a well-kept historical urban fabric, no dominance of the automobile, a humanely scaled urbanism, and a sense of civic engagement. Behind these two faces is a long history which goes back to its seventeenth-century Golden Age, when Amsterdam could be comfortably qualified as a world city of mercantile capitalism. However, its top position in global trade was combined with what Simon Schama (1987) calls the 'embarrassment of riches', a defining feature of the Dutch culture in its Golden Age. 'Dutchness', he suggests, 'was often equated with transformation, under divine guidance, of catastrophe into good fortune, infirmity into strength, water into dry land, mud into gold' (Schama, 1987: 25).

Having emerged from the polders to become a vibrant city, Amsterdam is the epitome of efforts to 'moralize materialism', 'not through divine guidance as much as through secularized spatial planning and an extraordinarily committed civic consciousness that persists to the present' (Soja, 2007: 119), as well as a perceived engineering feat. Its strong civic consciousness is reflected in and reinforced by a generous welfare system, an egalitarian tradition, and a political culture of consensus-seeking, consultation and compromise (Hendriks, 2006: 935), all of which permeate the Dutch approach to cultural policies and governance, as will be discussed in this chapter. We will, however, show that not all is well, particularly after major changes that have been taking place in recent years. The remaining part of the chapter consists of four main sections. Section two discusses the position of Amsterdam in its wider metropolitan and regional context. Section three describes the cultural profile of Amsterdam with reference to Dutch cultural policy and governance. Section four discusses the extent and nature of multiculturalism in Amsterdam in the context of Dutch housing policy and planning tradition. The final section concludes the chapter by exploring the implications for culture of the current neoliberal approaches to public policy.

A decentralized 'world city'?

Despite several waves of restructuring, Amsterdam has remained among the higher ranks of cities to date, even with a population of less than one million. A contributing factor in maintaining this position is Amsterdam's relative proximity to three other major cities in the Netherlands – Rotterdam, The Hague, and Utrecht – and their actual and perceived complementary functions and cultural activities. Together, they form a densely developed polycentric urban region known as *Randstadt* (Davoudi, 2003). As Shachar (1994) suggests, *Randstad* often provides a substitute, albeit a contested one, for the lack of a single Dutch world city. The term was coined by the Dutch aviation tycoon, Alfred Plesman, in 1938 (Burke, 1966; Rossem, 1994). Looking at the distribution of population and cities in the west of the country, he argued that another location (apart from Schiphol which is close to Amsterdam) was needed for a national airport in the middle of the ring of cities that he called *Randstad* (or Rim City). Unusual for his time, he argued that the cities in *Randstad* would eventually coalesce and create an integrated urban area which would become Europe's fourth city in terms of population size – after London, Paris and Berlin – and third or even second city in terms of economic power. What Plesman argued, and many others echoed him, was that given the density, proximity and expansion of the cities in the west of the country, it is legitimate to consider the area as a single metropolis. This idea was later given international fame in the field of spatial planning when Sir Peter Hall (1968) put the *Randstad* alongside the premium league of seven 'World Cities'.

Most of the Randstad's constituent cities, which date back at least 400 years, have since expanded to the point where they are beginning to overlap. However, they have been kept apart, to some extent, by a system of green belts and a large protected area of water and agricultural land called the Green Heart, without which the *Randstad* would have become a Dutch Los Angeles. In addition to the four large cities, the southern part of the *Randstad* (the 'South Wing') is also an agglomeration of densely packed and sprawling cities (Kantor, 2006).

Randstad is therefore home to Europe's largest port (Rotterdam), its fourth largest airport (Schiphol), a major internet exchange hub, a large concentration of international justice and legal organizations (The Hague), and a major centre for international financial institutions (Amsterdam) and service sectors (Utrecht). With 350,000 firms (50 per cent of the Dutch business interactions) and over 7 million inhabitants (two-fifths of the Dutch population), *Randstad* is the fifth largest metropolis in Europe after London, the Rhine–Ruhr region, Paris and Milan (Lambregts, 2006; OECD, 2007; Wall, 2009), and hosts a number of internationally renowned cultural institutions.

Fragmented governance

Although the idea of the *Randstad* has been on the Dutch governments' agenda since Plesman coined the term, its exact geographical delineation, administrative authority and governance arrangement have not yet materialized. This is despite Plesman's insistence that such an urban complex needs a single authority because its constituent provinces – the middle layer of administration in the Netherlands – would not be able to work together efficiently, a foresight which has proved to be true. Since then several fierce policy debates about how to create a metropolis in a country which is so quintessentially polycentric have taken place but none has resulted in the creation of a single, pan-*Randstad* authority (Lambregts and Zonneveld, 2004). Attempts to forge alliances and coalitions under a new label of 'Deltametropolis'[1] (an area between the Rhine and Meuse rivers) have not been able to overcome the fragmented governance structure of the area,[2] as pointed out by the OECD review:

> *Official boundaries for the Randstad do not exist and it does not fit into one of the three government tiers in the Netherlands. It remains an almost abstract concept as no government policies are implemented using it as the geographical basis for intervention. (OECD, 2007: 6)*

The result has been continuous competition between the constituent cities, and particularly between Rotterdam and Amsterdam, over a whole host of issues including the location of nationally-subsidized cultural institutions. The rivalry goes back to the latter part of the nineteenth century (Kooij and van de Laar, 2002) when Rotterdam began to grow rapidly after the opening of the *Nieuwe Waterweg* in the 1870s. The new waterway gave the port an open access to deep water of the sea and provided the city with a growing number of wealthy merchants and ship owners who were keen to improve the cultural standing of Rotterdam. For example, a large part of the famous Old Masters collection of the Boijmans van Beuningen Museum was once owned by one of the 'harbour barons' (Kooij and van de Laar, 2010: 16). Nevertheless, Rotterdam's bourgeoisie was always smaller in size and had a somewhat different cultural orientation compared with its counterparts in Amsterdam, mirroring the distinction between 'new' and 'old' money, respectively. This, however, has not stopped Rotterdam from competing with Amsterdam over all aspects of public life, be it the ports, football clubs, 'high' culture, or attracting the 'creative class'. In the 1980s, for instance, there were major clashes between the two cities about the government's decision to locate in Rotterdam a national architecture institute created by the merger of three former Amsterdam architecture institutes and one based in Rotterdam. This was a deliberate political decision aimed at decentralizing the nationally-funded cultural institutes (Kooij and van de Laar, 2010: 16) in the spirit of Dutch egalitarian tradition, but at the expense of Amsterdam's metropolitan aspirations. Similar competition occurs over privately-financed development projects that can lead to lucrative revenue for the cities through increased land prices.

Lack of coordination is not exclusive to the *Randstad* scale; it happens at the level of cities too. A clear indication of this is the uncoordinated closure of some of Amsterdam's most important cultural institutes for renovation in the last decade. The Rijksmuseum, which will reopen in 2013, has been closed for about a decade now, with the exception of some rooms showing the most loved masterpieces. The grand-scale renovation and restructuring of this national institute has been severely hindered by a clumsy municipal administration. The Amsterdam municipality is split into seven districts (at the time of writing), one of which is responsible for the management and contested planning issues related to the renovation of the Rijksmuseum, a responsibility well beyond its capacity. Another tragic example is the closure of the modern art gallery the Stedelijk Museum, in 2003 with, as yet, no reopening

date. Its renovation has been hindered by poor management, budget overruns, construction problems and the bankruptcy of the developers in 2011. In spite of temporary exhibitions elsewhere in the city, the closure of the Stedelijk has had negative effects on the turnover of modern-arts galleries in the inner city; it seems that the city has lost its appeal as a centre for modern art. The third uncoordinated closure is that of the maritime museum, which took place around the same time. On a more positive note, the opening of the first foreign branch of the Hermitage in 2009, housed in a large, seventeenth-century nursing home, has been a major boost to Amsterdam's position as the cultural capital of the *Randstad*, as discussed below.

Amsterdam: the cultural capital of the *Randstad*

While the ideal of a polycentric region implies an almost equal distribution of cultural institutions across the four major cities, the reality begs to differ. According to Stam et al. (2008), the strongest concentration of creative industries (defined as arts, media and publishing, and creative business services) are in the North Wing of the *Randstad* (Amsterdam–Utrecht) which hosts the Dutch broadcasting industry in the Gooi region (where employment in creative industries is the highest in the Netherlands, at 22 per cent). Although Utrecht is particularly strong in publishing and media, Amsterdam boasts a concentration of all three types of creative industry as well as major cultural institutions. It is therefore not surprising that Amsterdam is considered as the cultural capital of the *Randstad* (Hendriks, 2006; Kantor, 2006). It has the largest historical city centre in Europe (with its large ring of canals protected as a world heritage site since 2010) and is home to more than 40 museums (including the Rijksmuseum, the Van Gogh Museum, the Rembrandt House and the first branch of the Hermitage), a large array of performing arts and music halls (including the National Opera, one of the two large classical ballet ensembles, the Netherlands Philharmonic Orchestra, and the Royal Concertgebouw Orchestra), a wide range of restaurants offering a variety of international cuisines, and around-the-clock entertainments. Many of the structures and institutions that lie behind Amsterdam's current cultural (as well as economic) pre-eminence were established during the Dutch Golden Age in the seventeenth century, which in turn was made possible partly through the influx of rich people, artists and craftsmen, especially after the siege of Antwerp by Spanish troops in 1584–85.

In comparison with other major cities, Amsterdam did not suffer much from the problems associated with a declining industrial base, with the exception of its northern residential quarters across the IJ river, where the workforce was highly dependent on the shipbuilding industry. These were concentrated at the north banks of the river and have now become regenerated into a focal point for creative industries. Its historical strengths in 'global trade, high caliber knowledge-rich services and the financial sector have once again replaced commodities as the key to economic development' (Musterd and Deurloo, 2006: 80). 'Cultural industries' – defined as 'publishing, advertising, radio and TV production, news agencies, the arts sector, film and video production' (ibid., 2006: 81) – are particularly important in such substitution. Amsterdam's success in attracting small, independent firms in advertising and creative industries from across the world is due to a number of factors, such as the city's overall image, the availability of a well-educated workforce (including a high number of students), a multilingual population, a high quality of infrastructure and amenities, legal and political stability, and low corporate taxes (Engelen and Musterd, 2010).

Much has been written about the role of the so-called 'creative class' in boosting city economies and the 'quality of place' as a key component of attracting creative people (see Florida, 2002). Drawing on this notion, a study undertaken by Trip (2007) has shown that in the first part of the 2000s, 27.2 per cent of the population could be considered as being employed in creative industries. It is argued that Amsterdam's economic resurgence in the second half of the 1990s was due to the fact that it was the only Dutch city in which there were measurable spill-over effects in terms of employment growth from creative to other types of industry (Stam et al., 2008). Distinguishing between three types of creative industry – arts, media and publishing, and creative business services[3] – Stam et al. (2008) argue that the latter are most dependent on economic cycles (and the least innovative) while the former (arts) are the least dependent, maybe due to arts' dependence on public subsidy.

Cultural policy

The above observation may be due to the cultural policy in the Netherlands which has been described as lying between the European tradition of government intervention and the Anglo-Saxons' 'arm's length' stance (Delhaye, 2008: 1304). The central government's subsidy has always been available to support the autonomy and quality of the arts on the basis of a value system that eschews profitability as a measure of success. However, if subsidy is reduced or withdrawn in favour of marketization, it remains to be seen how independent of economic cycles arts organizations will remain. Furthermore, recent changes in the taxation system may also affect the arts. The level of Value Added Tax (VAT) on the arts is to be increased from 6 to 19 per cent, which would in turn reduce the number of visitors, although of course the effect will differ from sector to sector because of difference in price elasticity.

Dutch cultural policy emerged in 1956 when the National Arts Council, a semi-independent body whose role was to advise government on the arts, was established. It began to thrive in the 1960s when advisory groups, interest groups, and consultative structures were put in place. In the 1970s, and in line with Dutch traditions mentioned above, a policy of disseminating culture to lower-income social groups was initiated and arts policy increasingly pursued intercultural dialogue and supported ethnic minority artists. Also at city level, the arts have been fostered by municipal councils, although in a patchy and sporadic way. Although Amsterdam's own cultural policy was initiated in the 1920s, it was not until the 1960s that it secured its own arts council, a local version of the National Arts Council, mentioned above, with a specific remit to advise the city on funding awards (Holleman, 2004, cited in Delhaye, 2008). From the 1980s onwards, the cultural policy moved from encouraging participation to inviting the involvement of the 'New Dutch' (migrants to the Netherlands). The present centre-right government has abandoned this objective because it does not believe in 'multiculturalism' (see below). In the 1990s, the city developed its first four-year plan (1997–2000) as a framework for cultural organizations to make longer-term projections.[4] This plan echoed the national policy – in terms of both content and structure – through which it was administered. The plan continued the trend of targeting a wider and more diverse public, and stipulated that arts institutes should be responsive to public demand. However, in the late 1990s an evaluation of the city's arts policy found that although audiences had been increased, their diversity had not; the employees and the appeal of the arts world in Amsterdam remained restricted to dominant social groups. A further 1999 report from the British cultural expert Trevor Davies found little awareness of diversity in Amsterdam's cultural institutions, despite the fact that half of the under-18 audience had an ethnically mixed background (Delhaye, 2008).

Amsterdam: a multicultural city

Take a seat by the window in a café, on one of the squares in Amsterdam Poort shopping centre on a Saturday afternoon, [...] and as you watch the ever changing scene outside, you may marvel at the way the public spaces of larger cities in western Europe and North America have become transnational commons, where white, black, brown and yellow people mingle. (Hannerz, 2007: 178)

Until the 1960s, there were very few (4 per cent of the population in 1967) non-native Dutch in the Netherlands (Delhaye, 2008). However, Dutch cities have always been particularly prone to settlement by 'foreigners', and Amsterdam has undergone continuous waves of immigration, attracting, for instance, French Huguenots in the seventeenth century, central and eastern European Jews in the eighteenth century and Indonesians and South-Moluccans after the independence of Indonesia in 1949. With the 1970s waves of immigration to the Netherlands from former Dutch colonies in Surinam and the Antilles came labour migrants from other parts of Europe, such as Turkey, and from North Africa, who were attracted by the high-performing post-war Dutch economy. Even after the contraction in labour migration due to the 1970s recession, relatives of Turkish and Moroccan migrants, for example, as well as asylum-seekers continued to arrive (Delhaye, 2008).

The four *Randstad* cities of Amsterdam, Rotterdam, Utrecht and The Hague have particularly high concentrations of ethnic minorities compared with the rest of the Netherlands. In Amsterdam, people who are classed as 'foreigner'[5] amounted to 41 per cent of the total population in 1994, rising to 49 per cent in 2004 (Musterd and de Vos, 2007). According to municipal figures, some 178 nationalities

are represented in the residential population of the city, making Amsterdam one of the most ethnically diverse cities in the world.[6] Those with highest numbers are Surinamese, Antillean, Moroccan, Turkish, and South Europeans. Between 1994 and 2004, Moroccans had grown from 6 to 8 per cent of the Amsterdam population and Turks from 4 to 5 per cent. More than half of the people of foreign origin have also acquired Dutch nationality, which means that 88 per cent of the Amsterdam population has Dutch nationality.

Immigration policy initially supported the labour migrants in maintaining their own culture and language on the grounds that this would ease their eventual return to their own countries – including children born of immigrant families in the Netherlands (Snel, 2003, cited in Delhaye, 2008). The first official immigration policy, put in place as late as 1983, promoted integration while retaining the culture of origin (van den Broek and van den Camp, 1983, cited in Delhaye, 2008). However, from the 1990s onwards, policy on minorities tilted towards an increasing emphasis on integration and away from the emphasis on retention of ethnic identities. This has been intensified since the prominent murders that took place at the beginning of the twentieth century: that of the right-wing politician Pim Fortuyn in 2002 by a left-wing extremist and of the film director Theo van Gogh by an Islamic extremist in 2004. In the aftermath of van Gogh's death, the reaction of Dutch politicians was to steer arts policy towards a reappraisal and instantiation of the Dutch canon, as reflected in the policy to complement the intercultural dialogue that it had hitherto supported.

If multiculturalism is defined as policies 'that value cultural difference, perceive integration as a two-way process, and consider intolerance and discrimination as serious obstacles to the emancipation of minorities' (Hajer and Uitermark, 2008: 8–9), then the above-mentioned assassinations seem to have marked a departure from multiculturalism. In its place, they seem to have ignited a 'new realist' discourse on immigration, putting greater pressure on immigrants to integrate with the culture of the country of habitation (Prins, 2002; Ghorashi, 2003). As a result, the concept of multiculturalism, especially popular on the left of the political spectrum, has become less popular or even suspect. However, if one uses a more neutral interpretation of multiculturalism, as a mere descriptor of a population characterized by a large variety of cultures and nationalities,

Amsterdam remains a multicultural city and to a much larger extent compared with all other cities in the *Randstad* and the country at large.

Social and spatial segregation?

The overriding question is whether the multicultural nature of the population has led to a segregated and divided city. The answer on the whole should be negative as Amsterdam seems to have been relatively 'successful in integrating its immigrant populations, socially and spatially, into the urban fabric' (Soja, 2007: 134). Social segregation along ethnic lines is much less apparent than, for example, in Rotterdam and The Hague. The latter has always been segregated and the former is experiencing increased segregation because of economic decline. Hence, by comparison, Amsterdam displays an exceptional heterogeneity (Kauko, 2009). Its 'Inner Suburbs', for example, include some of the best-appreciated and most expensive neighbourhoods as well as some of the cheapest and worst reputed. Furthermore, some of the areas with the lowest 'neighbourhood annoyance' levels can be found within *De Wallen*, the notorious red light district. Examining the changes in the Moroccan and Turkish make-up of Amsterdam districts between 1994 and 2004, Musterd and de Vos (2007) found that the emerging patterns are linked more to typical steps in the residential property ladder taken by immigrant families than to conscious or unconscious strategies of ethnic minority concentration. When people moved houses, their places were often taken by other low-income and ethnic minority movers, apparently attracted by what they could afford rather than by ethnic clustering. Analysis of the housing types preferred showed a link with these groups and post-war social housing. Those Moroccans moving in came from areas with smaller and older properties and with more private rented housing. The Moroccans moving out went to areas with a higher share of larger and owner-occupied properties. Even the new towns around Amsterdam, such as Purmerend and Almere, are part of this system of residential moves.

A major explanation lies in the housing and planning policies of the national government and the municipality. For nearly two decades central government has been supporting the building of new housing estates within or at the edge of existing urban agglomerations (through a planning policy known as

VINEX[7]) to prevent suburbanization and sprawl which have taken place in many other parts of the world, resulting in segregation at regional levels, with higher income groups and families leaving the central city. The municipality is the major landowner in Amsterdam and is therefore able to create owner-occupied housing for higher income groups in the less popular areas and social housing for lower income groups in more popular areas.[8] The policy has been to attain a level of 30 per cent social housing in every major housing project, using the profits earned by the municipality from the land developed for commercial and especially office uses. The office market has now totally collapsed and is unlikely to recover for at least a decade. Hence, the funding available for transfer from a commercial to a housing project is almost non-existent, making the 30 per cent doctrine untenable for the most expensive locations (the redevelopment of previously developed sites in the existing urban fabric is always more expensive than development on green fields). As a result, many building and restructuring projects have been put on the back-burner with large areas of land lying vacant. What this will mean for segregation remains to be seen, but it is already clear that the financial crisis, coupled with the election of right-wing politicians, has struck the Amsterdam planning strategy in the heart.

Conclusion

Amsterdam, once deeply divided between Catholics and Protestants, managed to reconcile its religious differences through the policy known as 'pillarization'.[9] While the religious rationale has been substantially weakened by decades of secular principles, the moral commitment to democracy and fairness is still alive and underlines the city's continuing prosperity, diversity, cultural values, practices and investments. It is true that polarizations and spatial segregations have been creeping in for some time, but it is also true that they have been fought back by a generous welfare state, a propensity to take decisions through consensus, and a 'moral code' which has continued to strive towards equality and egalitarianism.

The future, however, is uncertain. The current administration is a centre-right minority government supported in the Parliament by the right-wing PVV ('Party for Freedom') under the leadership of Geert Wilders. The extent to which they are committed to the long-standing moral principles which have guided previous actions remains questionable. Signs of divergence are already on the wall, as far as cultural policies are concerned. The dominant view in the current coalition government is that over the past years the arts and the cultural sector as a whole have become far too dependent on government subsidies and for the benefit of the cultural elite. They have therefore put in place plans for cutting down the national arts budget each year. It will be reduced to €200 million in 2015, a cut of some 20 per cent. Museums and cultural heritage will be spared from the cuts to a certain extent. So the sectors most likely to be hit (with a 50 per cent cut by 2015) are the performing arts: music, drama, dance and opera, all heavily concentrated in Amsterdam. The city will also be hit indirectly. After retreating from an initial plan of closing down the Netherlands Broadcasting Music Centre (which hosts two classical music orchestras: the renowned Netherlands Radio Choir and a large light music orchestra), the government is now planning to cut its budget drastically. These ensembles often play in Amsterdam halls, especially in the Concertgebouw and the Music Theatre, so their diminishing presence will have a profound effect on their revenues and on the cultural status of Amsterdam.

Budgets for the arts will be affected by another development as well. Within Europe, the Netherlands is at the bottom of the league in terms of taxes collected locally. Indeed, 94 per cent of all taxes are collected by the national government (Merk, 2004), leaving municipalities and provinces with little influence on their income through taxation. The bulk of the municipal and provincial budgets derive from the 'provincial and municipal funds'. These, too, are subject to cuts by the national government. The effects are already visible. For example, many municipalities are closing down libraries. However, so far, no major cuts in the Amsterdam arts budget of about €85 million per annum (about 10 per cent of the art budgets of all Dutch municipalities put together) are foreseen. There will be some shifts from larger to smaller cultural institutes to ensure their survival. Despite this, Amsterdam will be disproportionally hit by budget cuts because of its status as the cultural capital of the *Randstad*. In a country with little tradition of private sectors' financial support and individual philanthropy, the cuts in public sector support will be a major blow to cultural institutions. Amsterdam's cultural sector, which has thrived on government subsidies, is now confronted with a major threat. The sector has to reposition itself and come to terms with the disappearance of several groups, institutes, ensembles and the closure of music halls and galleries, which increasingly appears to be unavoidable.

Notes

1 Deltametropolis was established as an attempt at bottom-up network building, under the directorship and aegis of Dirk Frieling, Professor of Planning at Delft University. It consisted of the four main *Randstad* cities and eight smaller cities of 100,000 inhabitants and more. By 2006, the Association Deltametropolis had 32 members: 12 cities, five Chambers of Commerce, six Water Boards, four green institutional members, three housing corporations, employers and transport organizations (Hendriks, 2006).

2 The Netherlands has three levels of government: national, provincial and local. The Randstad covers four of the 12 Dutch provinces of: North Holland, South Holland, Utrecht and Flevoland. These comprise 207 of the 938 Dutch municipalities.

3 Excluding business services such as software and IT on the grounds that work in these industries is not always creative.

4 There is currently a fierce debate in the advisory infrastructure about cultural policies in Amsterdam. The 'alderman' in charge of these policies is pushing through a plan to appoint a personal advisor. There is a general fear that she is using this to bypass the municipal arts council and open the way for political influence on the content of arts, which goes against the prevailing doctrine going back to the 1848 national constitution.

5 A term used by the Dutch government based on oneself or one's parents born outside the Netherlands.

6 It should be noted that some nationalities are represented by only one or two people.

7 The acronym originates from a 1991 national policy document.

8 With the principal aim of avoiding speculation, the Amsterdam land lease system, started in 1896, gave to the municipality ownership of all the land outside the historical core and the nineteenth-century extensions. Amsterdam is the only *Randstad* city which applies this system on such a grand scale. Once becoming the property of the municipality, land is never sold again.

9 This concept, which became internationally known by the seminal work of Lijphart (1968), relates to societies such as those of the Netherlands and Belgium, in which different ideologies or faiths (in the Netherlands: Catholicism, Protestantism, liberalism, and socialism) have been institutionalized in 'pillars', each characterized by its own institutions in domains such as broadcasting, health care and education. To avoid large-scale clashes, a complex consensus-seeking structure evolved over the years. Pillarization is gradually fading away, although many of its organizations are still there.

REFERENCES

Burke, G. (1966) *Greenheart Metropolis: Planning the Western Netherlands*. London: Macmillan.

Davoudi, S. (2003) 'Polycentricity in European Spatial Planning: From an Analytical Tool to a Normative Agenda', *European Planning Studies*, 11 (8): 979–999.

Delhaye, C. (2008) 'Immigrants' Artistic Practices in Amsterdam, 1970–2007: A Political Issue of Inclusion and Exclusion', *Journal of Ethnic and Migration Studies*, 34 (8): 1301–1321.

Engelen, E. and Musterd, S. (2010) 'Amsterdam in Crisis: How the (Local) State Buffers and Suffers', *International Journal of Urban and Regional Research*, 34 (3): 701–708.

Fainstein, S. (2007) 'The Egalitarian City: Images of Amsterdam', in Deben, L., Heinemeijer, W., and van der Vaart, D. (eds), *Understanding Amsterdam: Essays on Economic Vitality, City Life and Urban Form*. Amsterdam: Het Spinhuis Publishers, pp. 93–117.

Florida, R. (2002) *The Rise of the Creative Class*. New York: Basic Books.

Ghorashi, H. (2003) 'Ayaan Hirsi Ali: Daring or Dogmatic? Debates on Multiculturalism and Emancipation in the Netherlands', Focal – *European Journal of Anthropology*, 42: 163–169.

Hajer, M. and Uitermark, J. (2008) 'Performing Authority: Discursive Politics after the Assassination of Theo Van Gogh', Public Administration, 86 (1): 5–19.

Hall, P. (1968) *The World Cities* (1st edn). London: Weidenfeld and Nicolson.

Hannerz, U. (2007) 'Cities as Windows on the World', in Deben, L., Heinemeijer, W., and van der Vaart, D. (eds), *Understanding Amsterdam: Essays on Economic Vitality, City Life and Urban Form*. Amsterdam: Het Spinhuis Publishers, pp. 179–197.

Hendriks, F. (2006) 'Shifts in Governance of a Polycentric Urban Region: The Case of the Dutch *Randstad*', *International Journal of Public Administration*, 29: 931–951.

Kantor, P. (2006) 'Regionalism and Reform: A Comparative Perspective on Dutch Urban Politics', *Urban Affairs Review*, 41: 800–829.

Kauko, T. (2009) 'Classification of Residential Areas in the Three Largest Dutch Cities Using Multi-dimensional Data', *Urban Studies*, 46: 1639–1663.

Kooij, P. and van de Laar, P. (2002) 'The *Randstad* Conurbation: A Floating Metropolis in the Dutch Delta', in van Dijk, H. (ed.), *The European Metropolis 1920–2000*. Proceedings of a Conference at The Centre of Comparative European History, Berlin, 2002, pp. 1–20.

Lambregts, B. (2006) 'Polycentrism: Boon or Barrier to Metropolitan Competitiveness. The Case of the *Randstad*, Holland', *Built Environment*, 32 (2): 114–123.

Lambregts, B. and Zonneveld, W. (2004) 'From *Randstad* to Deltametropolis: Changing Attitudes Towards the Scattered Metropolis', *European Planning Studies*, 12 (3): 299–322.

Lijphart, A. (1968) *The Politics of Accommodation: Pluralism and Democracy in the Netherlands*. Berkeley, CA: University of California Press.

Merk, O.M. (2004) 'Internationale vergelijking omvang decentrale belastingen: Nederland in middenpositie [International Comparison of Decentralised Taxes: The Netherlands Takes a Middle Position]', B&O, November: 21–23.

Musterd, S. and Deurloo, R. (2006) 'Amsterdam and the Preconditions for a Creative Knowledge City', TESG: *Tijdschrift voor Economische en Sociale Geografie*, 97 (1): 80–94.

Musterd, S. and de Vos, S. (2007) 'Residential Dynamics in Ethnic Concentrations', *Housing Studies*, 22 (3): 333–353.

OECD (Organization for Economic Cooperation and Development) (2007) *Territorial Review: Randstad Holland, Netherlands*. Paris: OECD.

Prins, B. (2002) 'The Nerve to Break Taboos: New Realism in the Dutch Discourse on Multiculturalism', *Journal of International Migration and Integration*, 3 (3&4): 363–379.

Rossem, V. van (1994) *Randstad Holland*. Rotterdam: Nai Uitgevers.

Schama, S. (1987) *The Embarrassment of Riches: An Interpretation of Dutch Culture in the Golden Age*. London: Fontana Press.

Shachar, A. (1994). '*Randstad Holland*: A "World City"?', *Urban Studies*, 31 (3): 381–400.

Soja, E. (2007) 'The Stimulus of a Little Confusion', in Deben, L., Heinemeijer, W., and van der Vaart, D. (eds), *Understanding Amsterdam: Essays on Economic Vitality, City Life and Urban Form*. Amsterdam: Het Spinhuis Publishers, pp. 117–143.

Stam, E., De Jong, J.P.J. and Marlet, G. (2008) 'Creative Industries in the Netherlands: Structure, Development, Innovativeness and Effects on Urban Growth', *Geografiska Annaler: Series B, Human Geography*, 90 (2): 119–132.

Trip, J.J. (2007) 'Assessing Quality of Place: A Comparative Analysis of Amsterdam and Rotterdam', *Journal of Urban Affairs*, 29 (5): 501–517.

Wall, R.S. (2009) 'The Relative Importance of *Randstad* Cities within Comparative Worldwide Corporate Networks', TESG: *Tijdschrift voor Economische en Sociale Geografie*, 100 (2): 250–259.

CHAPTER 12

CREATIVE CITY, CITY MARKETING, CREATIVE INDUSTRIES AND CULTURAL POLICY: CHALLENGES FOR ANTWERP

Annick Schramme and Katia Segers

A certain 'creativity hysteria' is abroad in Europe today, as exemplified by the choice of 2009 as the 'European Year of Creativity and Innovation'. The notion of the 'creative city' dominates the policy thinking of most European cities and regions. In Flanders, Antwerp leads the way in the elaboration and implementation of 'creative city' frameworks. But how relevant are such frameworks in the broader context of arts and culture policy? How has the city taken up 'creative city' thinking and how is this related to city marketing and cultural policy in general? Do these frameworks work to mutual benefit or do they hinder each other instead? To answer such questions, the authors analyze the rhetoric of Antwerp's policy discourse; they also compare the performance of the city with that of Stuttgart, Manchester and Rotterdam.

Introduction

The concept of the nation-state dominated the political system of the nineteenth and twentieth centuries. From the end of the latter, however, there has been a paradigm shift towards the urban system (as discussed in the Introduction to this volume). Scholars in various disciplines (Jacobs, 1993; Hall, 1998; Landry, 1995; Florida, 2002) have characterized cities as sources of creativity and innovation, where residential and occupational diversity, the concentration of knowledge, the presence of all sorts of facilities, etc. are thought to create a dynamic and superior social climate (Banks and Hesmondhalgh, 2009). Different theorists have sought to account for the continuing importance of place and community in economic and social life (Porter, 1998; Florida, 2002: 6, 219; Hospers, 2003: 261).

Not place in itself, but communities and people linked to places, are regarded as being the main motors of regional growth. Proponents of human capital theory argue therefore that the key to such growth lies not in reducing the costs of doing business, but in endowments for highly educated and productive people. The clustering of human capital is seen to be even more important to economic growth than the clustering of companies (Jacobs, 1993; Florida, 2002: 221). As a rich cultural offer appears to be a key precondition for attracting highly educated and productive people, linking creative city policy and cultural policy is thought to be beneficial. But is this really true? Does linking city marketing, creative city policy and cultural policy offer added value for the city and its inhabitants or is there a risk of a clash between different objectives?

Pitfalls of creative class thinking

'Right to the city!' With this slogan, a group of artists, architects, designers, managers, students, among others, in Hamburg protested a few years ago against the hype of the 'creative city'. This was a few years after a lecture given there by Richard Florida that inspired the city authorities of Hamburg to implement his ideas by regenerating a number of neighbourhoods in the city. As a result of this policy, a few years later, several parts of the city became more expensive. The group of protesters, all belonging to the 'creative class', felt that they had been used by the city authorities as a tool for gentrification. They advocated that the city belonged to everybody (Oehmke, 2010). This 'current event' reflects very well the paradoxes linked to 'the creative city'.

One of these is gentrification. In terms of social development, many authors agree that urban development based on Florida's frameworks tends to produce social inequalities (Waitt, 2009). The initial emphasis on 'cool' facilities, bohemian shopping centres and high-end establishments resulted in an economic revival of these creative places, but then transformed them into exclusive spaces. It also led to the displacement of low and middle income inhabitants (Scott, 2000). Five of the top ten creative cities in the USA are, not coincidentally, also among the top ten in terms of social inequality. So attracting more highly educated people tends to produce social inequalities (Scott, 2000; Waitt and Gibson, 2009).

The idea of the creative class as an innovative source of urban dynamism has therefore not surprisingly been subject to a great deal of criticism (Kotkin, 2001; Caust, 2003; Peck, 2005; McGuigan, 2008; Pratt, 2008; Catungal and Leslie, 2009; Throsby, 2010: 136). An important set of criticisms concerns the definition. According to Florida, the creative class consists of two components: the super creative core that is fully engaged in the creative process, and 'creative professionals' who work in a wide range of knowledge-intensive industries such as high-tech sectors, financial services, the legal and healthcare professions and business management (Florida, 2002: 69). Artists are the ultimate creative class, belonging to the super creative core. Their ideas are vital for innovation in other sectors of the urban economy (Jacobs, 1993), as technological and economic creativity are nurtured by and interact with artistic and cultural creativity: 'This kind of interplay is evident in the rise of whole new industries from computer graphics to digital music and animation' (Florida, 2002: 5).

Yet, among others, the Dutch cultural geographer Gerard Marlet states that is impossible to measure a positive effect of the presence of artists on economic growth of a city (Marlet, 2009: 172; see also Glaeser, 2001: 27). At the most, their presence helps to increase the international symbolic position and image of major cities (Marlet, 2009: 172).

Chicken or egg?

In fact, cities have always been creative and diverse. Yet a unilinear positive correlation between creative class theory-based policy and the rise of new urban economies is difficult to find. Conversely, creative class theory has even proved to be problematic to policymakers, city planners and managers looking for strategies to stimulate wealth and economic growth (Waitt and Gibson, 2009). As an ideal formula to attract creative people doesn't exist, according to several authors local policymakers can only try to create the right conditions. Hospers, for example, (2003: 266) doesn't believe in the manipulability of the city. Not every city has the capacity to become a 'creative city'. Not marketing, but the presence of a unique historical and creative environment, the distinct identity of a city, is the most important condition (Waitt and Gibson, 2009). When every city uses the same unique selling point (USP), distinctive attractiveness disappears and together with it any real competition between cities. Investing in culture is therefore not the right choice for every city. Smaller cities, for example, would do better to invest in a good accessibility (Waitt and Gibson, 2009).

Other authors, such as Peck and Marlet, point out the danger of using instruments such as creativity indexes to make rankings of 'most creative' cities. Creativity lists are not scientific; they are manipulative and make smaller cities worry unnecessarily about their attributes (Peck, 2005: 745–747). The same goes for indicators that try to link cultural and culinary indicators and the creative class. Marlet points out that it is very difficult to make out what came first: the creative class or the cultural and culinary offer (Marlet, 2009: 235). In the Dutch city of Utrecht, only one-third of the people belonging to the creative class mentioned the attractiveness of the city, namely the presence of history, performing arts and catering industry, as the main reason for their choice of residence (Marlet, 2010).

The role of cultural production in creative cities

The success of policies aiming at stimulating the local economy by attracting creative people, cannot be proved empirically, according to Marlet. On the basis of his research of the growth of the creative class in Dutch cities, he even found a negative correlation between the number of artists in a city and the growth of the creative class. Nor did he find a significant relationship between the presence of artists and the growth of employment. On the contrary, he revealed a clear link between the cultural offer and the degree a city is attractive to the higher educated part of the population. In sum: it is not the presence of artists residing in regenerated buildings that is a stimulus for the city, but the cultural production itself. A city's cultural offer tends to be an important factor, attracting highly educated people to it. According to Marlet, such cultural offer has to meet four important criteria to attract highly educated, creative people and to play a role in their residence choice. It has to be small-scaled and diverse, continuously available, placed in sophisticated locations and has to address principally the local population (not primarily tourists). Hence cities with a huge and diverse cultural offer also possess a greater stock of human capital (Marlet, 2009: 336). It is no longer the presence of industry that guides people's choice of residence (Florida, 2002: 104). Today, households are attracted by a diverse cultural offer and other facilities. Culture therefore plays an important role in the competition between cities. The most popular cities are 'walking cities', where people live at walking distance from the city centre, offering a wide cultural offer, restaurants and pubs and other attractions in the historical centre (Marlet, 2009). This means that in an indirect way cultural offer, and not the presence of artists as such, is the important driver.

The case of Antwerp

Since the publication of Richard Florida's book in 2002, the city of Antwerp – with its long cultural history tied to its role as one of the most important European ports – has also developed a creative city policy, together with an arts and culture policy. But do they really benefit the latter?

Arts and culture as drivers of urban generation?

After Brussels, Antwerp is the largest city in Flanders, with about 482,000 inhabitants, a high percentage of which are older than 65 years (20 per cent). Younger people make up 28 per cent and a large group of immigrants – about 50 per cent – live in the city centre. After Amsterdam, Antwerp is the European city with the largest number of different nationalities (over 170); it has a flourishing Jewish community and significant Moroccan, Chinese, Turkish and Eastern European communities. Being an important worldwide diamond centre, there is also a significant community of Indians and people from the Middle East. The City Council's yearly budget for arts and culture counts for about 4.83 per cent of the city budget (€62 million).

Most of the large cultural institutions of Flanders – such as the Royal Ballet of Flanders, the Flemish Opera and the Royal Museum of Fine Arts – are located in the city of Antwerp. Antwerp's international reputation is largely the result of the presence of internationally rewarded Belgian fashion designers, the sixteenth-century baroque painter Pieter-Paul Rubens, the Plantin Mosetus Printing House (a World Heritage site) and the diamond industry. Some 86 cultural organizations and companies employ around 2,500 people. The economic output of the cultural sector amounts to some €130 million. On a yearly basis, about 3.5 million people visit Antwerp's cultural organizations, of which 1.9 million attend performing arts events. It is therefore not surprising that art and culture are important aspects of the City Council's policy. This has been especially the case since 1993, the year in which the city was a European Capital of Culture. This event provided a significant boost to the city's culture.

In the last two decades, the city's deputy mayors in charge of culture have belonged to the Flemish Social Democratic party. The spread of culture, cultural participation and community building were, not surprisingly, the main goals of Antwerp's cultural policy. Today, the cultural offer is within the reach of all, as the city has five cultural centres and a network of public libraries, well spread over the city, and two community centres. Culture is considered or thought to have significant leverage: as an avenue of participation, for social and intercultural cohesion, for economic growth, for tourism and, of course, for urban regeneration.

According to David Throsby (2010: 134), cultural capital in some cities is so concentrated, that they qualify for the title of 'city of art'. This is a popular concept in Europe, and is used to describe cities whose entire character is defined by the presence of art and architecture. Despite the fact that Antwerp is not on the list, Flemish people are eager to describe Antwerp as 'a city of art'. According to Charles Landry (2006: 32), it is hard to find 'novel, vibrant roles and purposes for these more ancient European towns, beyond keeping them pretty for tourists. Nothing wrong with tourists, but when there are too many of them the lifeblood of a city can be sucked out. A place can fossilize.'

Aware of the dangers of investing only in tourists, the Antwerp City Council has set in motion two large heritage projects, which aim to both attract tourists and find new ways to involve the local population. The city government is building a new museum of local heritage (called 'MAS'), which means 'Museum at the River', which opened in 2011 and will be the first newly constructed museum building in 150 years. The Dutch firm Neutelings Riedijk Architects was awarded the assignment after an international competition. The building's concept refers to the history of Antwerp as a port city, since it is conceptualized as a 'warehouse' consisting of stacked spaces, and ties in best with the location's historic function and atmosphere. According to its USP, 'Antwerp in the world, the world in Antwerp', the museum exhibits the city's collection of local heritage and the heritage of all the different nationalities that have lived in Antwerp over the centuries. It is located in Antwerp's old port district, called the *Eilandje*, which has become a bustling neighbourhood. Creative people are moving to this district and companies are setting up their offices here. Although the government is not expecting a Bilbao effect, it does hope that the museum will attract a lot of visitors – first of all local inhabitants – to enjoy the city and the river. In the same area, a second (intangible) heritage project, called the Red Star Line Memorial, will open in 2012. This is the site from which more than 3 million people left for America at the beginning of the twentieth century. The citizens of Antwerp are closely involved in these two projects. Although both aim to show that

arts and culture can be drivers for urban generation, will the dynamic created by these projects lead to the sustainable development of the city? Only the future can tell...

City making or city marketing?

To determine whether the 'creative city' concept is an important aspect of Antwerp's city marketing activities, we have analyzed the discourse of Philip Heylen, the present (Christian Democrat) Deputy Mayor for Culture and Tourism, who in speeches and interviews often refers to Antwerp as a 'creative city'. He strongly emphasizes the link between culture and economy, between a rich cultural heritage and the port of Antwerp. He makes abundant reference to the most famous historical and contemporary city icons, such as Pieter-Paul Rubens, the fashion designers, the diamond industry as well as the contemporary art scene.

Yet, there is little coherence between this discourse and the official city marketing campaign started in 2004 (and still running in 2011) by the Mayor of the city, who is a former marketer. This campaign's strap line is '*It's everybody's city*'. The campaign logo displays the bright character 'A' (Antwerp). This 'feel good' campaign was aimed, first, at restoring the trust of the local population after a corruption scandal and, secondly, at checking the rising popularity of the extreme right *Vlaams Belang* party through investing in community work. But there has been no coordination, let alone communication, between the Mayor's city marketing policy and the Deputy Mayor's efforts to promote Antwerp as a creative city of arts and history. The international promotion of Antwerp as a creative city is not part of a broader city policy. This lack of coordination seems to offer an explanation of why the city of Antwerp has not surfed the waves of 'creative city' hype until today.

Antwerp as 'a creative city'?

Next we took a close look at the city's efforts regarding the creative industries. Only very recently (in 2009) the Department of Economy and Employment developed a creative industries policy. A first policy paper was approved by the City Council in June 2010 (Voorhamme, 2010). Urban development is the main goal of this policy. Specific areas of the city were identified as suited for economic development and regeneration. In these areas, efforts have been made to attract

Figure 12.1 Evolution of the added value in Creative Industries sub-sectors in Antwerp, 2000–2007

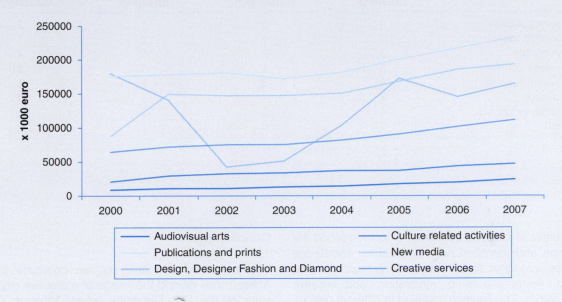

small enterprises of creative workers. A SWOT analysis was carried out in order to measure the diversity of the city's labour market, its lifestyle characteristics, its social interactions, etc., based on Richard Florida's 3Ts model: tolerance, talent and technology (Florida, 2002). The findings and conclusions of this report were rather positive. (see Figure 12.1)

This commissioned research shows that around 12,000 people work in the creative sector in Antwerp, whose added value was €800 million in 2007, or 39 per cent of the total added value of all major cities of Flanders. In comparison to the other major Flemish cities, the creative potential of Antwerp is rather high. Moreover, Antwerp has the best creativity index. The number of settlements in the creative industries grew spectacularly (by 45 per cent up to 86.362 in the period 2003–2008), and 34 per cent of the employment in the creative sector in the major Flemish cities is concentrated in Antwerp. Nearly all sub-sectors grew in the period between 2000 and 2007, except for design, fashion design and the diamond industry, which have stagnated because of their high market dependency. The most remarkable difference between Antwerp and the other Flemish cities is the diversity and the versatile nature of the creative industries.

'So far so good', one could conclude from this analysis. Yet, it is necessary to take a closer and more critical look at the concepts used. The indicators do not provide a complete picture of the reality. According to Florida's theory, the city of Antwerp is supposed to be a very tolerant city. Antwerp is indeed, after Amsterdam, the European city with the largest number of different nationalities. Yet, if one looks closely at the political reality since the 1991 local elections, the picture is totally different. In 1991 the extreme right-wing party became the largest in Antwerp. One-third of the Antwerp voters voted for the extreme right. Only since the latest local elections in 2006, has this right-wing party lost its leading position.

Secondly, Antwerp is supposed to be a 'diverse' city, according to the report. Diversity is, as described above, a key goal of the still ongoing city marketing campaign of the Mayor. Yet the Antwerp case also shows that gentrification can hamper diversity: indeed, today it is under pressure in Antwerp, since only small segments of the population can afford to live in these trendy locations (Catungal and Leslie, 2009: 703). This goes for artists as well, since studio space is becoming more and more expensive. After the first report, the city commissioned a second inquiry on the economic impact of Antwerp as a

Table 12.1   Benchmark results of Antwerp, Rotterdam, Stuttgart and Manchester

	Antwerp	Rotterdam	Stuttgart	Manchester
Knowledge base	4	3	1	2
Economic base	3	4	2	1
Environment	3	2	1	4
Business context	3	1	4	2
Entrepreneurship	4	3	2	1
Innovation	2	4	1	3
Creative industries	4	3	2	1
Total	3	4	1	2

'creative knowledge economy'. This broadened the scope and identified seven indicators: knowledge base, economic base, environment, business context, entrepreneurship, innovation, and creative industries. The findings revealed in different picture. Antwerp finds itself only in the third slot, when compared with Rotterdam, Stuttgart and Manchester (see Table 12.1).

But this report presents several methodological shortcomings. First, no data were available about the 'independent workers' (yet, most creative workers are independent workers, or nano-firms of one or two people). It is weakened by a lack of recent data sets (e.g. the latest Urban Audit dated from 2004). Also, the concept of 'innovation' is used in a limited sense, namely 'technological innovation'. The most remarkable shortcoming, however, is the relative scantiness of data on the role of arts and culture within the indicator 'creative industries'.

Antwerp's policymakers were thus confronted with two different reports, pointing to different, even contradictory conclusions. There was obviously an urgent need for new, more robust data. Especially with regard to artists and other members of the creative class, the City Council found itself lacking evidence. Its Department of Economics has therefore decided to conduct further research and has created several working groups in order to elaborate policy measures for the creative industries, while trying to link the different aspects of the city policy: creative industries, creative city, city marketing, arts and cultural policy, and community building.

Conclusions

In the light of our analysis, we conclude that Antwerp has gained the image of a creative city in spite of the City Council's policy. Although the 'creative city' rhetoric and policy is relatively new to the city, it possesses many strengths: it has a strong identity, a historical and aesthetically pleasing city centre, the presence of important heritage properties, a dynamic artistic scene, a large and diverse cultural offer, and some new interesting architectural projects. Yet, in Antwerp, Charles Landry's creative city turns out to be work in progress.

We have to be alert to how difficult it can be to reconcile economic and cultural goals. The traditional legitimations of cultural policy could be put at risk by this new economic approach, especially in economically difficult times. A creative city strategy would attend not only to the attraction of the creative class, but also to the development of cultural infrastructure, local cultural participation and involvement, the development of a flourishing and dynamic creative arts sector, community-oriented heritage conservation, and support for wider creative industries that are fully integrated into the local economy (Throsby, 2010: 140). A lot of work needs to be done in Antwerp in order to coordinate and integrate the different policy goals and instruments. Linking creative industries, creative city, city marketing, arts and cultural policy, and community building could indeed contribute to a policy in which artists, arts, culture, heritage and creativity are central, to the benefit of these actors and, especially, to the people of Antwerp themselves.

REFERENCES

Banks, Mark and Hesmondhalgh, David (2009) 'Looking for work in creative industries policy', *International Journal of Cultural Policy*, 15 (4): 415–430.

Boonstra, B. et al. (2009) *Wijken die werken – de relatie tussen stedenbouwkundige kenmerken en wijkeconomie.* Delft: TNO Information and Communication Technology/ Ministries of Education, Culture and Science, Economic Affairs and Justice, The Netherlands.

Catungal, John Paul and Leslie, Deborah (2009) 'Contesting the creative city: race, nation, multiculturalism', *Geoforum,* 40: 701–704.

Caust, Jo (2003) 'Putting the "art" back into arts policy making: how arts policy has been "captured" by the economists and the marketers', *International Journal of Cultural Policy*, 9 (1): 51–63.

Florida, R. (2002) *The rise of the creative class.* New York: Basic Books.

Glaeser, Edward L. et al. (2001) 'Consumer city', *Journal of Economic Geography*, 1: 27–50.

Hall, P. (1998) *Cities in Civilzation.* New York: Pantheon Books.

Hospers, G.J. (2003) 'Creative cities in Europe: urban competitiveness in the knowledge economy', *Intereconomics*, 38 (5): 260–269.

Jacobs, Jane (1993) *Life and death of the American city.* New York: The Modern Library.

Kotkin, J. (2001) *The new geography: how the digital revolution is reshaping the American landscape.* New York: Random House.

Landry, C. (1995) *The creative city.* London: MPG Books.

Landry, C. (2006) *The art of city making.* London: MPG Books.

Marlet, G. (2009) *De aantrekkelijke stad.* Utrecht: VOC Uitgevers.

Marlet, G. (2010) *Muziek in de stad. Het belang van podiumkunsten, musea, festivals en erfgoed voor de stad.* Nijmegen: VOC Uitgevers.

McGuigan, J. (2008) 'Doing a Florida thing: the creative class thesis and cultural policy'. Paper presented at the International Conference on Cultural Policy Research, Istanbul.

Oehmke, P. (2010) 'Who has the right to shape the city?', *Der Spiegel*, 7 January.

Peck, J. (2005) 'Struggling with the creative class', *International Journal of Urban and Regional Research*, 29: 740–770.

Porter, M. (1998) *On Competition.* Boston, MA: Harvard Business School Publishing.

Pratt, A. (2008) 'Creative cities', *Urban Design Journal*, 105: 35–38.

Roodhouse, S. et al. (2007) *Read this first: growth and development of creative SMEs.* Utrecht: Libertas, Bunnik, pp. 42–48.

Scott, A. (2000) *The Cultural Economy of Cities.* London: SAGE.

Throsby, D. (2010) *The economics of cultural policy.* Cambridge: Cambridge University Press.

Voorhamme, R. (2010) 'Antwerp: an open city where creative and talented people meet'. Unpublished Policy Paper, City of Antwerp.

Voorhamme, R. (2010) 'Antwerp: innovation in creativity: stedelijk actieplan voor innovatie in de stedelijke creatieve economie'. Unpublished Policy Paper, City of Antwerp.

Voorhamme, R. (2010) 'Antwerp: innovation in knowledge: stedelijk actieplan voor innovatie in de stedelijke kenniseconomie'. Unpublished Policy Paper, City of Antwerp.

Waitt, G. and Gibson, C. (2009) 'Creative small cities: rethinking the creative economy in place', *Urban Studies*, 46 (5): 1223–1246.

CHAPTER 13

'CREATIVE GOVERNANCE' IN BERLIN?

Janet Merkel

Since the reunification of Germany in 1990, Berlin has undergone massive social, economic, political and urban transformations. While the city's economy is still precarious, culture has become a key asset and is being mobilized for a wide range of developmental purposes. Unfortunately, however, the city lacks an appropriate cultural policy and governance framework to meet these challenges. In fact, the Berlin case highlights the serious overburdening of cultural policy that can result from the prominence and complexity of culturalist approaches in current urban development.

Introduction

For urban sociologists who have lived in the 'New Berlin' for longer than the past decade, the city provides a great real-life laboratory in which every walk and every day presents something new to discover and understand. Formerly peripheral neighbourhoods have become central and have undergone extensive redevelopment and gentrification. A massive in and out migration has taken place, whereby half of the population has been exchanged. The Berlin Wall and its death strip, once the symbol of the Cold War, and a city divided between two competing world systems, has almost disappeared from the urban landscape. And finally, Berlin has again become a capital city and an important element in the creation of a (re)united Germany.

This (re)construction process involved massive material and symbolic changes most obviously apparent in the new Regierunsgviertel or the Potsdamer Platz. It also triggered the search for new images as well as a redefinition of Berlin's place in the world (Marcuse, 1998; Cochrane and Jonas, 1999). The city that for 40 years had had a special status under the Four Power Agreement, with both the East and the West heavily subsidizing their respective parts as showcases, was now catapulted back into the real world, a world which in 1990 was characterized, and still is today, by a profound macrosocial trend: globalization or, to be more precise, a multiplicity of globalization processes 'that have marked the urban condition in novel ways' (Sassen, 2000: 145). In a broad sense, by globalization we mean increasing interconnections and interdependencies through the worldwide movement of objects, meanings and people (Anheier and Isar, 2008). In this chapter, we focus on the cultural dimension of globalization in cities, and how cultural policy and politics are affected by it in Berlin.

Globalization diversifies, enriches, stretches, and connects, but also standardizes urban cultures and lifestyles, especially the reactions of urban policy makers towards globalization. We have seen the rise of the 'entrepreneurial city' (Harvey, 1989) and the 'creative city' (Landry, 2000) as major worldwide formulas. In terms of culture, the conditions of globalization have set off at least two broad developments in cities that challenge cultural policy in a profound way: the recognition of the *economic and social value of culture*. Culture has been mobilized and instrumentalized to achieve all sorts of objectives in order to support growth and competitiveness. Additionally, inner cities have become a preferred site for cultural and creative production. And in the same way that cities support cultural heritage or high-art institutions in order to promote the culture-based redevelopment of urban spaces and economies, policy makers also have to acknowledge citizens and the specific meanings they attach to a place, as well as their collective memories, shared histories, and the diversity of artistic and cultural expressions. Consequently, a contemporary cultural policy has to take all these different aspects of urban culture(s) into account.

All this means that cultural policy today is only imaginable in a complex governance structure that caters to these diverse interests. How does Berlin manage to address this challenge? What is the role of cultural policy in the city, and what specific issues arising out of the Berlin case can enrich our understanding of the interrelatedness of globalization, culture and governance? The argument put forward in this chapter is that with the increasing awareness and valorization of the importance of culture(s), there is a significant decrease in *actual* cultural policy in Berlin. While this decrease can be explained by specific economic and institutional reasons as well as a general shift towards a more economistic cultural policy, it also points to a serious overburdening of cultural policy that stems from the prominence and complex meanings of culture in current urban development thinking. In our eyes, therefore, an alternative model is needed and we shall present such a model in our conclusion.

The current state of cultural policy in Berlin

In Germany, cities and municipalities have always been the places where cultural policy is made and implemented. Even though the major responsibility for cultural policy rests with the *Länder* (cultural devolution principle) because of the federal structure of the German political system, it is the municipalities that contribute more than 50 per cent of the overall cultural budget (Städtetag, 2008). The responsibility for culture is part of local autonomy, but municipalities are required to provide only a 'basic cultural spectrum'. Everything over and above is voluntary and varies drastically among cities. This rather vague notion of local cultural policy has come under additional criticism since it has been recognized that the public sector alone need not be the sole supplier of culture, but rather that economic

and civic involvement is not only encouraged but necessary (Städtetag, 2008). But this shift towards a *governance perspective* in cultural provision is still searching for good working models.

Nevertheless, cultural policy in Germany has a long tradition, strong advocates and high priority. It is deeply rooted in educational values and the notion of individual and societal well-being (Wesner, 2010). While cultural policy once had a strong focus on artistic and intellectual activity, it ultimately addressed only a privileged minority that was literate enough to value it. It was not until the early 1970s that the concept of 'socioculture' was introduced to cultural policy by the German Assembly of Municipalities. Under the motto 'culture for all', it centred on questions of access and participation, cultural competence, empowerment, and education, and how the basic cultural spectrum could be provided for all people. Today, there is a further broadening of objectives for cultural policy in cities: on the one hand, emphasis is placed on its economic values in terms of branding for boosting tourism, investments and in supporting creative industries. On the other hand, its social values are emphasized in regard to countervailing socioeconomic polarization, fostering social cohesion, and stimulating intercultural dialogue between an increasingly diversified population. In this context, we shall explore four issues as specific challenges that call for local policy answers. However, these challenges are deeply linked with conditions of globalization and illustrate the excessive demand for culture policy that we mentioned earlier.

Cultural policy as multi-level governance

Since Berlin is a so-called 'city-state', which simultaneously makes it a municipality as well as a *Land*, its cultural policy is a concrete example of multi-level governance. The three important layers are the boroughs, the federal state level (referred to as the Senate or *Land*), and the national level. The boroughs are administrative districts that work under the principle of local autonomy but do not have the status of a legal entity as a municipality. They fulfil local administrative tasks, are led by district mayors, have their own 'cultural affairs offices' and enjoy a certain degree of independence in their expenditures and interpretations of specifications by the city. The 12 boroughs are responsible for providing such basic infrastructure as local libraries, music and adult education schools, sports facilities, cultural education and empowerment projects for children and youth development. Almost 50 per cent of their budgets are bound to voluntary sociocultural purposes and referred to as 'district-related cultural work', i.e. projects supporting specific social or ethnic structures in the borough, its local history, or inspiring more civic involvement. This decentralized cultural policy in the boroughs fulfils important tasks with respect to the quality of life, finding one's identity, social cohesion, equal opportunities, the promotion of young talents and it significantly contributes to Berlin's overall cultural diversity. However, precisely these voluntary provisions are constantly endangered by the Senate's financial cuts and constitute a permanent source of public contestation over the value of voluntary provisions and their sociocultural functions in cultural policy debates.

In contrast, the Senate level is the more strategic one, as it defines the overall key themes for cultural policy in Berlin, provides the funding for artists and cultural groups, and is responsible for supporting Berlin's 'cultural beacons', such as the major museums, theatres, opera houses, orchestras, concert halls and several public foundations.

The German government supports cultural projects that are either of importance to Berlin as the country's capital or have an international impact. In 1999 a 'capital-culture-treaty' between the federal government and Berlin was introduced, clearly stating the responsibilities arising from Berlin's capital city status and indicating who has to cover the costs. With almost €10 million at its disposal, the 'capital culture fund', responsible for the promotion of artistic projects, has nearly the same annual budget as Berlin's own current artist and project fundings. Furthermore, the government supports particular institutions with €83 million per year. Unlike Paris or London, however, the most important player in Berlin's cultural policy and supporter of the cultural infrastructure is the Senate, not the federal government. This specific structure gives shared responsibilities to the boroughs and the federal government, but also different sets of ideas on what is of cultural value, to whom and what makes an object viable for cultural policy. Berlin's dire financial state is an additional cause for major debates about these responsibilities and leaves cultural policy as the city's most contested policy field. Furthermore, Berlin is highly dependent on EU funding.

The economic value of culture

Berlin has made culture its 'primary industry'[1] and economic asset – whether through cultural consumption in tourism or in cultural production through the growth of cultural and creative industries.[2] This development has been promoted by both top-down (political) and bottom-up movements, while Berlin's unique cultural infrastructure served as the basic nexus. Besides its relatively moderate living expenses, stories about the city's empty spaces and its in flux situation after reunification have greatly appealed to artists from around the world. This reputation has promoted a lively cultural scene ever since, making Berlin a favourite playground for all kinds of creative people, mostly in subcultural terms (Grésillon, 1999; Stahl, 2008). But, in recent years, Berlin has become a centre of gravity that draws upon on economic resources and challenges cultural and creative industries in other cities around the world. Publishing houses are moving back, while film production companies, advertising agencies, designers, architects and galleries are setting up their offices in the city. Young creative people come to study in and/or afterwards to set up businesses in this experimental, low-cost environment. Currently, creative industries account for more than 21 per cent of Berlin's gross domestic product and 10 per cent of overall employment (Senatsverwaltung für Wirtschaft, 2008). The significant number of self-employed people working below the VAT line of €17,500 per year with their small businesses are not included in official data. Even though they are deeply intertwined with the city's public cultural infrastructure, creative industries are treated mainly as an economic issue and responsibility lies with the economic department. Cultural policy showed no great concern for them but continues to concentrate instead on the 'old' cultural industries where arts professions are the core.

However, common themes have been acknowledged, e.g. in film support, and a steering group, which also includes the planning department, has been set up. In most cities, cultural policy and creative industries policy have been mixed, even though they are two unlikely siblings. Although they have a lot in common, they should be treated separately due to distinctive modes of production, institutional bases and aesthetic contents (Cooke and Lazzeretti, 2008). They do, however, call for more cross-governmental coordination, a reorganization of competences, and clearer definitions of policy objectives for both.

Furthermore, the growing convergence of cultural and economic policy can also be seen in the case of tourism, which is a strong growing economic sector in Berlin, especially with budget travellers. More than 9.1 million 'official' visitors were counted in 2010, an increase of 9.5 per cent from 2009 (see press information on offical statistics for tourism in 2010 at www.statistik-berlin-brandenburg.de/). In order to promote tourism, the marketing of culture has gained priority and inner-city districts like Mitte or Prenzlauer Berg have been swamped with newly built hostels and hotels.

Cultural policy and urban branding

Using culture for urban (re)branding and global marketing initatives is one of the major trends to be found in cities all over the world. Under the banner of 'urban competitiveness' a stronger emphasis is being placed on locality, authenticity and local cultures for distinctiveness and place-based promotion to attract tourists and to boost investments. Associated with that is a stronger mobilization and exploitation of culture for the (re)development of urban spaces: setting up cultural quarters and districts, often in disused former industrial sites such as ports or warehouses, branding museum clusters, preserving cultural heritage, celebrating all kinds of public events, and labelling oneself as a multicultural and creative city (Evans, 2001). During the last few years, Berlin has been involved in all of these developments and has gained an impressive increase in tourism as well as in new investments. While most of these measures can be critized on several levels, e.g. their outward perspective, their economic impact, or the consumption focus, the most important question they raise is that of representation or, as Sharon Zukin famously asked, 'Whose culture? Whose city?' (Zukin, 1995). More accidentally than intentionally, however, the most successful branding slogan for Berlin has come from its Mayor, Klaus Wowereit: 'Berlin is poor, but sexy'. It sums up the city's main contradictions: a low socioeconomic profile and a high unemployment rate, but a diverse and rich cultural geography. The distinct urban lifestyles that have emerged can be interpreted as creative solutions to Berlin's post-reunification economic meltdown. But these 'artistic lifestyles' in the inner city only show one side of Berlin; they overshadow the huge number of long-term unemployed and social welfare recipients, the elderly and, of course, the quite different situation that obtains in the outer boroughs. These groups are not represented and do not fit in the urban imagery of a culturally vibrant city. Even worse, their low socioeconomic profile is turned into an advantage in public discourse.

Cultural policy and cultural diversity

The debate about cultural diversity and intercultural dialogue is at a very early stage in Berlin. Even though Berlin has a relatively low rate of foreign population as compared to elsewhere in Germany (13 per cent, mostly from Turkey and Eastern Europe), migration has recently been officially acknowledged as the 'lifeblood' of the city. Berlin's first migration policy was not established until 2005, however, despite a long-term migrant population with high density rates in certain districts. An important role is played here by the boroughs since ethnic and cultural diversity are reflected in the social practices, distinct norms, values, and routines in the everyday life in a neighbourhood. It is in the context of the borough that a shared sense of place, belonging and tolerance can be developed. For this reason, a more socioculturally oriented local cultural policy approach in the boroughs is of particular importance. Some boroughs, like Neukölln, are already very much engaged in supporting ethnic cultures, but as mentioned earlier, their budgets are under constant threat. Moreover, recognizing migration as a productive force for urban life calls for renegotiating representation, since cultural diversity and, especially, the idea of a multi-ethnic society, imply reconsidering cultural empowerment and education, as well as access and participation to cultural infrastructures (from local libraries to high art). It also creates the need to adjust programmes for artist funding, which until now were reserved primarily for German artists. It is also necessary to reach a clearer understanding of how difference can become a source of social renewal and economic innovation (Ash and Graham, 1997). Cultural policy in Berlin has yet to take on this challenge.

Cultural policy and identity politics

A further challenge lies in the recreation of a united city, after more than 40 years as a divided one, while, at the same time, having to deal with remnants of the past (such as the German empire, the Weimar Republic, Nazism) that have left their marks on the city's material and symbolic infrastructure. Former national borders during the Cold War have also meant that cultural boundaries still prevail between the Eastern and the Western part of the city, even despite the dramatic in- and outward migration, as well as high rates in intra-urban mobility. Berlin still has two city centres, which stand as symbols for the dual cultural structure in the city and date back to before the Second World War, although they were intensified through subsidization during the period of division (Grésillon, 1999). They also exemplify two distinct cities with their own peculiarities that have evolved, and still live on, in daily practices for many citizens.

Since reunification, there have been several attempts to invent new images and a common identity for a united 'New Berlin'. Mostly, because of its unique geopolitical position, Berlin had been envisioned by its political elite as a centre of Central Europe, a gateway to the East, a European Metropolis or a Global City (Molnar, 2010). This repositioning of Berlin, however, came within an existing structure of a polycentric city system in Germany, a growing 'Europe of the Regions', and a more globally connected world. While globalization processes gave cities a new strategic importance (Sassen, 2000), Berlin lacked the economic infrastructure to gain the necessary 'connectivity'. Only in cultural terms has Berlin gained worldwide recognition and been able to attract a global art and culture crowd. Therefore, culture has become not only important for Berlin, it has an existential meaning as *the* most important asset.[3] This was reflected not only in the last coalition agreement between the ruling parties, where Berlin was designated as *Germany's one true metropole*, but also in the city's place-making strategies.

The current 'be Berlin'-campaign can be seen as the latest attempt to construct a new identity for the city. Interestingly, this campaign was initated to address the local population first and to create new narratives by citizens themselves. It was only afterwards that it was used as a global marketing campaign with the slogan 'The place to be'. The campaign explicitly deals with the contradictions, differences and variety of meanings that co-exist in the cultural heterogeneity of a city. It embraces this diversity by emphasizing, not one, but many perceptions and by giving its citizens the opportunity to express their own ideas about what 'be Berlin' means for them. The official sign for the campaign is an empty speech bubble into which anyone can put their thoughts in the form of a three-part phrase such as 'be open, be free, be Berlin'. A central element is a website where everyone can share his/her stories, ideas and personal phrases (see www.be.berlin.de/). The campaign has gained huge support from the local population. It presents the city as a constant breeding ground of ideas, identities, meanings, practices, lifestyles, and makes visible the unavoidable negotiations of intersecting trajectories and multiplicities that Doreen Massey (2005) described as the 'throwntogetherness' of place. Hence, this campaign resembles more of a strategy in identity politics than plain place-marketing. It is less an attempt to construct new 'we-identities' than a calling for a shared sense of place. Nevertheless, it is mobilized story-telling that can also be read as part of neoliberal place-branding activities for the sake of urban competitiveness.

A lesson in governance?

The case of Berlin clearly shows a considerably greater awareness of the cultural dimension in urban development processes and its interelatedness with conditions of globalization that have affected the city on various levels. Culture is used to consume, distinguish, instrumentalize, mobilize and more, but does cultural policy provide the appropriate framework for all these objectives? Probably not. Thus, most of the key themes in the cultural dimension of Berlin's urban development are not strategically linked or reflected in its cultural policy, and responsibilities are scattered between different Senate departments. There are several institutional and financial reasons for this.

First, the restructuring of Senate departments between the ruling parties after the last election led to the abolition of a separate Senate department for culture and resulted in a chancellory for cultural affairs, which is situated in the mayor's office. While the mayor justified this decison by making culture a top priority and therefore under his jurisdiction, it resulted in more dissemination than coherence. Ever since, culture policy has taken a back seat and become almost unvisible in the public realm. The coordinating, administrative and steering role of a designated Senator for Culture is sorely missing in the overall governance structure for cultural policy – whether regarding the coordination with the other *Länder*, the German federal government, the boroughs, the different Senate departments with their specific responsibilities that constantly criss-cross culture politics, and, of course, the diverse range of quasi-public, private and not-for-profit stakeholders in Berlin's cultural infrastructure. A particular role is played by publicly owned but privately operating companies, which deliver specific parts of cultural policy, e.g. for tourism marketing, for project funding in creative industries, and for cultural projects such as huge festivals.

A second reason for the decline in cultural policy is Berlin's dismal financial state. Since the financial crisis of the late 1990s, there have been severe cutbacks in all Senate departments. With a €60 billion debt, and the national government's refusal to help out, the overall aim is to save costs. Culture in particular has always been a field in which costs can be saved easily, since the promotion of culture is based on the will of the municipalities. In Berlin, the financial crisis has led to nearly 90 per cent of the budget being spent on the preservation of the 'high culture' infrastructure.

To sum up, while Berlin has been very entrepreneurial in developing, marketing and instrumentalizing its cultural assets, it also presents a highly fragmented cultural governance landscape which is not supported by a coherent cultural policy framework. There is no *steering group for culture* across the different Senate departments or government levels, nor does a *comprehensive cultural strategy* for the city exist which defines clear responsibilities for all the different actors involved, nor is there a discussion about the usual funding policy, the underlying values, nor has cultural policy's overall role in urban development been reassessed. So far, Berlin has not developed a solution on how cultural policy can integrate its economic, social, educational and urban developmental goals into a coherent policy framework, or how all the different stakeholders can be actively engaged. Therefore, culture as a policy field has been dissolved into a complex governance structure with dispersed responsibilities and diverse stakeholders who barely take notice of each other.

Conclusions

As Janet Ward (2004) suggested, Berlin is a city where the image-making campaigns project a virtual global city that by far outstrips the real city through its lack of economic conditions for such visions. During the past 20 years, Berlin has undergone massive transformations from the icon of Cold War division to a cultural metropolis. While the reunification of Germany has left Berlin with massive structural fractures and new segments in economic, social, cultural and political terms, globalization additionally forced the city to adjust on different scales – among others, in recognizing its economic insignificance in national and international comparison. Although culture and creative industries provided a way for the city to 'reconnect' with the world and become part of the 'global space of flows' (Castells, 2001), it remains to be seen whether this will have lasting impacts on the economic restructuring process.

However, the Berlin case also exemplifies a current development that can be observed in many cities: culture has turned into an almost unmanageable policy field, that cuts through nearly all policy areas and whose responsibility can no longer be clearly allocated to one department. Instead, it needs more decentralized steering and cross-sectional coordination. Widening the notion of culture and valorizing its multiple roles in diverse urban development purposes raises questions about objectives for cultural policy and how cities can gain the capacity to act with such a multidimensional concept of culture. Taken seriously, cultural policy would become 'culture mainstreaming',[4] whereby culture is not seen as a separate policy field but as a relevant dimension in all other policy fields. Every policy then has to be checked for the cultural dimension: a complex and challenging task that presupposes an appropriate definition for the cultural dimension – which is not as easy to nail down as in the case of gender mainstreaming. Therefore, it is more likely that we will see different cultural policies emerge in cities. At best, these different cultural policies will be combined into a coherent cultural strategy for the city. But the regulation will be decentralized and supplied by public, private and civil organizations in a complex governance network that requires a high degree of coordination and cooperation. A strategy would identify all the relevant actors in the city, define priorities and responsibilities, and would make active use of interdependencies, instead of just acknowledging them, as in the case of creative industries which cut through economic, planning, education and cultural politics. A cultural strategy would differ from cultural policy as it integrates more objectives and stakeholders in a productive but also flexible framework, whereby current cultural policy could be redefined as 'arts policy' in its traditional sense. Such an approach would allow *cultural diversity in the widest sense to be the centrepiece of an urban cultural policy* and not only 'high culture' infrastructure, as is the case in Berlin.

Notes

1   See the statement of Dieter Kosslick, director of the Berlinale film festival in a recent interview (www.hollywoodreporter. com/news/berlin-became-coolest-city-planet-97748) (accessed 10.02.2011).

2   In Berlin, the German classification of the term 'cultural and creative industries' is used to combine all activities that have the 'creative act' at their core. While 'cultural industries' relates to the arts professions and the publicly subsidized cultural sector, the term 'creative industries' covers more the market-oriented activities in cultural production.

3   A personal note: much to our regret as social scientists, the incredible scientific diversity of Berlin's university and research landscape is never given the attention it deserves by policy makers and in public discourse.

4   'Culture mainstreaming' is an approach that can be found in the Lisbon Treaty of the European Union. Article 167, paragraph 4 states that: 'The Union shall take cultural aspects into account in its action under other provisions of the Treaties, in particular in order to respect and to promote the diversity of its cultures' (European Union, 2010: 121).

REFERENCES

Anheier, H.K. and Isar, Y.R. (2008) Introducing the Cultures and Globalization Series and the Cultural Economy. In: Anheier, H.K. and Isar, Y.R. (eds), *The Cultural Economy. The Cultures and Globalization Series 2.* London: SAGE Publications, pp. 1–12.

Ash, A. and Graham, S. (1997) The Ordinary City. *Transactions of the Institute of British Geographers, New Series* 22: 411–429.

Castells, M. (2001) *Die Netzwerkgesellschaft.* Opladen: Leske und Budrich.

Cochrane, A. and Jonas, A. (1999) Reimagining Berlin. *European Urban and Regional Studies* 6: 145–164.

Cooke, P. and Lazzeretti, L. (2008) Creative Cities: An Introduction. In: Cooke, P. and Lazzeretti, L. (eds), *Creative Cities, Cultural Clusters and Local Economic Development.* Cheltenham: Edward Elgar, pp. 1–22.

European Union (2010) *Consolidated versions of the Treaty on European Union and the Treaty on the functioning of the European Charter of Fundamental Rights of the European Union.*

Evans, G. (2001) *Cultural planning, an urban renaissance?* London: Routledge.

Grésillon, B. (1999) Berlin, Cultural Metropolis: Changes in the Cultural Geography of Berlin since Reunification. *Cultural Geographies* 6: 284–294.

Harvey, D. (1989) From Managerialism to Entrepreneurialism: The Transformation in Urban Governance in Late Capitalism. *Geografiska Annaler. Series B. Human Geography* 71: 3–17.

Landry, C. (2000) *The Creative City: A Toolkit for Urban Innovators.* London: Earthscan.

Marcuse, P. (1998) Reflections on Berlin: The Meaning of Construction and the Construction of Meaning. *International Journal of Urban and Regional Research* 22: 331–338.

Massey, D. (2005) *For Space.* London: Sage.

Molnar, V. (2010) The Cultural Production of Locality: Reclaiming the 'European City' in Post Wall Berlin. *International Journal of Urban and Regional Research* 34: 281–309.

Sassen, S. (2000) New Frontiers Facing Urban Sociology at the Millennium. *British Journal of Sociology* 51: 143–159.

Senatsverwaltung für Wirtschaft TuFB, Der Regierende Bürgermeister von Berlin, Senatskanzlei – Kulturelle Angelegenheiten, Senatsverwaltung für Stadtentwicklung (2008) *Kulturwirtschaft in Berlin: Entwicklungen und Potenziale.* Berlin.

Städtetag, D. (2008) Kultur in Deutschland aus Sicht der Städte. Positionsbestimmung zum Bericht der Enquete-Kommission 'Kultur in Deutschland' des Deutschen Bundestages. Beschluss des Hauptausschusses des Deutschen Städtetages in der 196. Sitzung am 05. November 2009 in Berlin.

Stahl, G. (2008) Cowboy Capitalism. *Space and Culture* 11: 300–324.

Ward, J. (2004) Berlin: The Virtual Global City. *Journal of Visual Culture* 3: 239–256.

Wesner, S. (2010) Cultural Fingerprints – The Legacy of Cultural Values in the Current Cultural Policy Agenda in Germany. *International Journal of Cultural Policy* 16: 433–448.

Zukin, S. (1995) *The Cultures of Cities.* Malden: Blackwell.

CHAPTER 14

BRAZZAVILLE: A GLOBAL VILLAGE OF AFRICAN CULTURE

Patrice Yengo

This profile tracks popular culture in the city of Brazzaville in the second half of the twentieth century. Once a colonial capital and capital of Free France, Brazzaville bears the imprints of a rich cultural heritage and ceaseless innovation in literature, music, theater, and dance. After a decade-long genocidal civil war (1993–2002), Brazzaville has been weighed down by a chronic disjuncture between an incapacitated central state and a vibrant popular culture. Congolese artists have remained resilient, however. Galvanized by the war, they have found new paths to creativity, ultimately showing that the devastating impact of globalization has resulted in both homogenization and renewal.

Introduction: the weight of recent history

With its rich tradition of French language literature, theater, and music, Brazzaville, the capital of the Republic of the Congo (known also as Congo-Brazzaville) remains among the most culturally vibrant cities in Africa. At the same time, there has never been a wider gap as there exists now between public policies that are centralized, ill-managed, and habitually trapped in bureaucratic morass and predatory political snares on the one hand, and the vibrant popular initiatives that are fragmented and often abortive, but still bold and innovative on the other. In order to understand this discrepancy between the official and the popular levels, we must first consider the historical significance of the city of Brazzaville, and its place within the very core of the nation's cultural politics. It is Brazzaville that epitomizes the chronic disjuncture between the rich artistic activities of the local neighborhood youth and the city's politics of cultural management. The artistry of the young, which pulses with creativity in painting, sculpture, comic strips, and the performing arts, which is fully open to innovations from the outside world, presents a contrast to the city's public initiatives. The latter consist mainly of such stunted projects as those run by the School of Art and Painting in Poto-Poto (Ecole d'art et de peinture de Poto-Poto) or the biennial celebrations of the Pan-African Music Festival (FESPAM).

Before going further, we must understand the saliency of Brazzaville in the annals of the country's past, beginning with the historic convulsions that gave birth to the Congolese state in 1960. Since independence, the history of Congo-Brazzaville can be divided into three major periods: the first begins with independence; the second period opens with the founding of the one-party system in 1963 and all of its popular organizations, including the National Union of Congolese Writers and Artists (UNEAC), an all-inclusive gathering of artists; the third period can be said to begin with the institutional changes unleashed by the democratization process led by the National Conference. The democratization process would entail crippling social tensions and would lead ultimately to a decade-long genocidal civil war (Yengo, 2006). The war would eventually set in motion the exodus and exile of numerous Congolese writers and artists toward Europe where they would either meet with quick success and for-tune in some cases, or with unexpected fallout in others. Europe, with its various capitals, thereby became the multifocal antipode of Congolese cul-ture. Members of this cultural community in exile would gain international recognition as belonging integrally to the broader culture of the African diaspora. Beneficial as European exile may have been in material terms for these artists, the political haven in Europe could not shield them from the ineluctably homogenizing forces of the global market.

The Liaison years and the Poto-Poto school of painting

Brazzaville's centrality in all of this is hardly accidental. The city's importance derives directly from its former status as the former capital of Equatorial French Africa (AEF) and as the headquarters of the Gaullist resistance to the Nazi occupation of main-land France. Brazzaville thus became the capital of Free France in 1940 following the armistice with Germany. It was on the basis of this status that the city hosted the 1944 'Brazzaville Conference,' in which Charles de Gaulle delivered his famous speech announcing the changes to come in French colonial politics. It was also as the capital of France that Brazzaville gradually came to reflect the new cultural politics of the empire, which soon offered up fresh opportunities to the African elite. These elite individu-als would 'come together in the cultural associations created by the Social Services of the Governor General of the AEF in 1948, which had in mind to provide a literate African public in the various urban centers and county-towns a general framework for cultural activities such as public lectures, sports and recreation, music, and cinema' (Diazinga, 2008: 7).

The voice of these cultural associations was the review, *Liaison*, whose serial publication first began in 1950 and continued until 1960 just after independ-ence. The contributors to and staff of *Liaison* were selected among Africans who had attained a certain level of education, such as instructors, teachers, and functionaries, otherwise known as the *évolués*, or 'evolved', originally a colonial label for the native elite. The editorial board was headed by Paul Lomani Tchibamba, and was made up of African as well as French members. Since 1957, two women have been made contributing members: Yvonne Cabon, a Frenchwoman, and Céline Yandza, a Congolese

woman, both of whom were members of the Association of Women of the French Union or AFUF. Very quickly, there emerged within the ranks of *Liaison* a small community of writers whose member-ship has since continued to grow. The most cele-brated among the members has been the novelist Jean Malonga (1907–1985), whom historians and literary critics have long considered the father and doyen of Congolese contemporary literature (Kadima-Nzuji, 2010). Two of his novels, *Heart of the Aryanne* [*Coeur d'Aryanne*] and *The Legend of Mfumu Mâ Mazono* [*La légende de Mfumu Mâ Mazono*] appeared in 1953 and 1954 respectively, demonstrat-ing the profound and unique voice of the African elite. These writers sought to return to their African roots in order to relay the customs and traditions of their culture. At the same time, they wished to remain open to outside influences and currents. Their works bore the double stamp of oral tradition and innovative ver-bal intervention. The most important representatives of this literary community included not only Jean Malonga, but also Patrice Lhoni, Leyet Gaboka, Letembet Ambily, and Sylvain Mbemba. Soon others followed in their footsteps: Martial Sinda, for example, whose novel, *The First Song of Departure* [*La pre-mier chanson du depart's*], was inspired by the writ-ings of Léopold Senghor and Aimé Césaire, and also Tchicaya U Tam'si who acquired name recognition with his first collection of poems, *Bad Blood* [*Mauvais sang*] (1955).

It was during this time that Pierre Lods, a French officer who had been posted to the Congo, left the army to relocate to Brazzaville as a painter. He found room for a studio in a disused hangar located in a popular quarter of Poto-Poto, in one of the 'black Brazzavilles' famously described by anthro-pologist Georges Balandier. Lods' first students and collaborators were none other than his domestic servants. With their help, he transformed the studio into a veritable center for African art. Lods followed a simple dictum: no classes, no instruction; in a word, no method. For him, it was enough to let the brush run over the canvass to express the painter's own fantasy and imagination, which artists often cautiously bridled at when they came in contact with the outside world. Also, Lods encouraged his students to turn away from the influence of Western art, and thus prohibited them from reproducing works by others. He wanted students to concen-trate on themes of African art. The result was a style that was schematic, rudimentary, and reduced to the bare essentials with expressiveness and fantasy of movement. These works showed not only scenes of genre painting, but also dance scenes and market scenes; in short, scenes of everyday life. Albert Bandila, François Iloki, Nicolas Ondongo, Félix Ossali, Philippe Ouassa, François Thango, and Jacques Zigoma came to best represent this school, which soon gained renown during the first grand exposition held in Brazzaville. The school became known internationally, and expositions followed one after another: 1952 Galeries de Palmes in Paris; 1954 in South Africa; 1956 in the Museum of Modern Art in New York (ADEIAO, 1991).

Painting was not the only art form to have interested the colonial authorities. We must not forget the sculptures that incited a real fad in colonial Brazzaville, notably by such artists as Roger Lelièvre (otherwise known as Roger Erell), an architect who gave to his city a real 'look' with exceptional and monumental artworks from the 1940s to the 1960s. Among these was the famous Basilica of Saint Anne of the Congo. The essential idea for Erell was to combine the technique of Western art with local materials and native artistic inspiration. He took under his wing a young Congolese sculptor Benoît Konongo, whom he had brought over to the Applied Arts section of the Colonial School Edouard Renard of Brazzaville around 1945. There Konongo refined his own technique, especially in the finishes that Europeans had long perfected. Konongo's mastery earned him a special commission from the Catholic Episcopate for the Church of Saint Anne, consisting of three votives, each with depictions of Christ and the Virgin Mary (Obenga, 2010).

In 1960, with the disintegration of the AEF, the review *Liaison* fell out of print. Pierre Lods left the Congo at this time and moved to Dakar, taking with him the school he had founded in Brazzaville but transforming it into a type of cooperative for artists, which it still functions as today. If the demise of the AEF brought an end to the monopoly held by Brazzaville over cultural activities in Central Africa, then it also permitted other countries to profit from the city's cultural legacy and heritage, notably in music and in literature.

The one-party regime and the pluralism of creation

The decade prior to independence was also marked by vibrant cultural exchanges between Brazzaville and Léopoldville (now Kinshasa). The two cities had always been home to the same human communities who shared several common languages and cultural innovations. In fact, modern Congolese music can be considered the fruit of the frequent voyages made by musicians between the two banks of the Congo. The musical pioneers of this fusion often found themselves in Léopoldville to record their works. Among the best known were the Brazzaville musicians Paul Kamba and Kinois Wendo Kollosoy (Gondola, 1996).

The post-independence music scene, however, saw a decline in the cultural fusion between Brazzaville and Léopoldville that had been so lively during the previous decade. This slump was due to the nationalist politics of the new states that had once made up the AEF. These governments not only let fester social tensions that emerged disguised as intra-ethnic confrontations, but they also imposed new nationalisms that tore apart the various nations that had coexisted throughout the region prior to colonization, and who had maintained peaceful trans-border ties during the colonial period. Such political and social tensions soon became impediments to the antecedent development of regional dynamism and cultural fusion between Léopoldville and Brazzaville. With this dissolution of the cultural fusion between the two cities, many musicians from Brazzaville origins who had been active in Léopoldville returned home to continue with their music. Some had come back to Brazzaville on the eve of independence in the wake of the violent anti-colonial uprisings of Léopoldville in January 1959, when the city spiraled into political turmoil. Most notably among the repatriates to Brazzaville were those who founded the Orchestra *Bantous of the Capital* in August 1959. With the support of the authorities and placed under the artistic direction of Jean-Serge Essous, the *Bantous of the Capital* effectively formed the third wave of modern Congolese music. (The first wave was begun by the Democratic Republic of the Congo's African Jazz group founded by Joseph Kabaselé, otherwise known as the Great Kallé, and the second wave had been launched by the OK Jazz group of François Lwambo, otherwise known as Franco). But it was the *Bantous* that became the pride and standard-bearers of modern Congolese music in Brazzaville and across greater Africa after independence. The *Bantous* also livened up the first celebrations of independence of many Central

African countries and, in 1966, garnered huge success during the First Festival of Black Arts in Dakar. Their tours across the world, notably in Europe, South America, and Cuba were incredibly successful and made Congolese music famous around the world. After several years, the orchestra *The Bantous* became, in effect, a kind of 'school of music' where young musicians could experiment and take their first steps (Bemba, 1984).

The veritable 'revolution' in culture, however, occurred with the advent of the one-party system in 1963. Between 1960 and 1963, Congo-Brazzaville was governed by the conservative Abbé Fulbert Youlou, a Catholic priest whose controversial ascent to power was sustained by the colonial administration. Youlou's leadership thus provoked widespread popular unrest. On August 15 1963 Youlou was overthrown by a popular insurrection led by trade unionists who were openly socialist and who, after seizing power, formed the one-party government. The life of the party can be divided into two major phases: the first lasted between 1964 and 1968, and was under civilian rule. The party of this first phase was known as the National Movement of the Revolution (MNR) and was headed by Alphonse Massamba-Débat, a former schoolteacher who was elected President of the Republic. The second phase lasted from 1968 to 1991, and was led by radical factions that had taken over the army. The one-party system thus turned increasingly radical, adopted a Marxist-Leninist ideology, and took on the title of the Congolese Workers' Party or the PCT. Three military officers came in turn to hold the reins of power: the first was Commander Marien Ngouabi (1968–1977), the second was General Yhombi-Opango (1977–1979), and the third was General Denis Sassou-Nguesso (1979–1991).

In the course of this period, civil society was brought under the heels of the mass organizations. These were the Revolutionary Union of Congolese Women (URFC), the Movement of Pioneers, made up of youngsters between the ages of 10 and 14, and the Young Socialist Union of the Congo (UJSC), a youth organization that gathered members between the ages of 14 and 29. With respect to the unions, the multi-union system disappeared and there emerged in its place a single-union system led by the Labor Union Confederation of the Congo (CSC). Artists and writers at this time were assembled within the National Union of Congolese Writers and Artists (UNEAC).

One of the paradoxes of the one-party system in Africa in general and in the Congo in particular since the 1960s has been the discrepant policies relative to each of the political, social, and cultural realms. Politically, the period of the one-party system was marked by repeated coup d'états – there were no less than 12 in all between March 1964 and February 1979 – and by political assassinations that followed one after another, exposing the deadly rivalry that persisted within the party. With respect to the sphere of culture, however, artists were given great leeway. If musicians and songwriters were keen to pepper their lyrics with apologetic couplets addressed to political leaders, the majority of artists were less inhibited and felt free to create. It was within the interstices of creative freedom tolerated by the state that Congolese writers actively cultivated their writing. Those who have known Brazzaville during the 1970s and 1980s could well attest to the cultural fermentation that enlivened the city. Under the impetus of writers such as Sony Labou Tansi (*La Vie et demie*, 1979; *L'État honteux*, 1981; *L'Anti-peuple*, 1983; *La Parenthèse de sang 1981…*) and Sylvain Bemba (*L'Enfer, c'est Orféo*, 1970; *Le Soleil est parti à M'pemba*, 1984) or Emmanuel Dongala (*Un fusil dans la main, un poème dans la poche*, 1974; *Jazz et vin de palme*, 1981; *Le Feu des origines*, 1987), a camaraderie of authors sprouted and fertilized the terrain of African literature with their irreverent works. At the same time, following in the path of the Kenyan writer Ngugi wa Thiong'O, who abandoned the English language to write in his native Kikuyu, a different brotherhood of writers emerged and severed their ties with the French language to contribute dramatic works in their native Congolese languages with rare subversive force.

Why the literary and theatrical effervescence?

Several reasons can be adduced for this creative effervescence under the one-party system.

First was the valorization of national culture as an ideological affirmation of the party. From 1963 onward, the Congolese government encouraged artistic and literary production. Across all literary genres, Congolese writers denounced colonization and brought to the theater such themes as generational conflict, while they also exalted the memory of national heroes. Many at the time gained international acclaim. For example, Guy Menga was awarded the Grand Prix of Literature in the field of Francophone literatures of Black Africa in 1969, and was followed by Henri Lopès who repeated the honor three years later. Yet another writer, J.-P. Makouta-Mboukou became laureate just one year after Lopès. In the tracks of these pioneers, other renowned writers followed – Emmanuel Bounzéki Dongala, Sony Labou Tansi, Tati-Loutard, not to mention such women writers as Marie Léontine Tchibinda, who asserted herself as one of the country's most prolific authors. These and others heightened the literary reputation of this small country and instituted a true spirit of emulation. All of this was achieved without the help of the central government, which had not even bothered to establish a proper publishing house.

This literary effervescence can also be explained by the impact of mass education throughout the country. Congo-Brazzaville has to this day the highest rate of education in all of Africa with a literacy rate of over 82 per cent. This superior level of schooling would also account for the strong appetite for reading and writing among the Congolese, a phenomenon that cannot be explained otherwise given the high cost of books and the lack of any real distribution circuit for print materials. There are still very few libraries in the country, while literary works continue to sell at exorbitant prices unaffordable to the average Congolese. The scant number of libraries and reading centers, the most notable of which has been the *Centre Culturel Français*, hardly suffices to satisfy the strong passion for books among the Congolese population.

Finally, the sheer aura of the intellectuals and the fascination for writing of the political leaders might also explain the relative liberty enjoyed by a wide range of authors at this time. Presidents Fulbert Youlou and Massamba-Débat were known to have edited works of ethnology and political history. Marien Ngouabi was immersed in poetry. Former Prime Minister Henri Lopès and former Minister of Culture J.-B. Taty-Loutard were first-class Francophone writers.

Another factor worth noting is the impact of the oil industry on the behavior of the political leadership. Oil brought high levels of profit to the country, which through a prebendary distribution network enriched the pockets of political leaders. Politicians therefore were more interested in safeguarding their revenues than they were in monitoring non-political forms of social contestation and protest.

The Center for Training in Research in the Dramatic Arts (CFRAD) also played a prominent role in boosting the country's cultural dynamism. Before 1965, Brazzaville had but two theater troupes. These later fused to become the National Congolese Theater in 1965, which then became the main stage for pieces by Guy Menga, Sylvain Bemba, Maxime N'Debeka, and Tchicaya U Tam'si. The CFRAD was founded in 1969 just after the first Festival of the Arts of the Congo, and served immediately as a rallying point for young cultural animators and actors during the years between 1970 and 1990. Theatrical creativity reached its apex at this time. Acclaimed playwrights accompanied and supported the theatrical production of new performance troupes: the *Rocado Zulu* Theater of Sony Labou Tansi, the artistic *Troupe de Ngunga* of Matondo Kubu Turé, and the *Théâter de Emmanuel Dongala* were just some of the examples. Amateur troupes were not to be outdone: the Tchang Brothers, the Theater of Friendship, for example. Middle schools and high schools also formed theater groups, and held competitions during the festivals that marked the end of the school year. The international interest in and recognition of Congolese theater soon propelled the country's troupes on to the global scene. There was also a parallel movement in Brazzaville to restructure the theater troupes. Efforts were made to improve their management and to enhance scenographic research. The actor and director Matondo Kubu Turé, for example, founded the Association of New Art (*Association de Nouvel Art*) which struggled to promote budding artists.

A multifaceted culture

Independently of the international export and worldwide recognition of Congolese Francophone literature and theater, there also flourished a domestic literary culture rooted in the local languages. With hardly any editorial or publication support, enactors of native language theater and culture discovered the power of oral transmission. While Congolese authors writing in French were garnering distinctions abroad, songwriters who wrote in the local languages composed songs and declamations set to expressive rhythms, and achieved success with a popular audience at home. It was on these fertile domestic grounds that new musical currents flowed and traditional music also was revived. Among such musical currents that surged in the aftermath of the fall of President Fulbert Youlou were choral works. These were performed by local vocal groups. It was in 1964, in Brazzaville, that the first vocal groups were formed by the movement of the National Youth Organization. This musical current would amplify and explode on to the Brazzaville stage during the two weeks of cultural festivities organized in the city from 7 to 16 August 1967 and from 8 to 16 August the following year. It was also in the course of these two national cultural assemblies that saw the rise of several remarkable vocal groups.

The Angels, directed by the Kimbolo brothers, was one of the rare groups to have survived the first wave. After having criss-crossed the world and collected numerous prizes, The Angels were transformed into a ballet company. Casimir Zoba, one of the original members of the vocal group, took on a new name to become the celebrated singer Zao, famous for his anti-military song, 'The Veteran'. Les Echos Noirs, later the Mbamina Orchestra, was directed by Samba Ngo, who eventually made a successful career in the United States. The Elus, directed by Georges Taboueya, performed brilliantly with the Bantous of the Capital at the first cultural Panafrican Festival in Algiers in 1969 where the group won the Bronze medal. Les Cheveux Crépus, directed by Jacques Loubelo, was famous for popularizing traditional anti-colonial songs.

Politically committed songs would find their most important vocal organ and interpreter in Franklin Boukaka, whose career took off at the tender age of 15 in 1955. He became one of the most passionate African musicians after independence. He had always been a committed participant in anti-colonial political circles since an early age. Boukaka made his actual debut in Léopoldville but subsequently returned to Brazzaville where he played first with the Cercul Jazza before launching a solo career. As a solo artist, he performed with the semi-traditional orchestra The Sanzas, with which he launched an international career. It was with The Sanzas that he headed to Algiers in 1969, then on to Conakry, to Paris, and finally to Cuba. His greatest hit recording was, without question, the album entitled Le Bucheron (Lumberjack), arranged by Manu Dibango. The eponymous title song of the album depicts the misery and suffering of the lower classes. In the same album, he also celebrated the 'Immortals', by paying homage to the revolutionary heroes of Africa, Latin America, and Asia. Boukaka was a true African resistance fighter, and his songs fearlessly flayed the political regime, which ultimately cost him his life. In 1972, at the still very young age of 32, he was assassinated by a military gunman following a coup d'état. With Boukaka, the Sanza, also known as the Likembé, a traditional instrument with nine steel strips attached in a row on to a hollow wooden casing, retrieved its bygone glory, relaunching the career of past pioneers of this instrument, such as Antonie Moundanda. An unquestionably exceptional composer and singer, Moundanda founded the group Likembé Géant, with which he has traveled to all four corners of the globe. Other much younger musicians soon found in traditional music their source of inspiration, which would bring them instant recompense. This was especially the case of Zongo Soul.

This cultural profusion would last until 1990. During the atrocious decade that followed, however, African societies would suffer the tumultuous contingencies of democratization pursued under the National Conferences. Central Africa would ultimately descend into unprecedented violence and armed conflict.

The civil war and exile of artists: the globalization of Congolese culture

In the wake of the political disruption that broke out in the North with the disintegration of the Soviet Union, African nations weighed down by the one-party system tried little by little to introduce elements of political pluralism. The process of democratization took effect after the speech given by François Mitterrand in 1990 in La Baule, where he urged African leaders to incorporate reforms in their respective countries. In the francophone nations, democratization processes unfolded under the auspices of 'National Conferences', vast conventions bringing together the entire gamut of political and social forces in each country. These conventions took on the character of constituent assemblies and as such they were compelled to reach a peaceful democratic consensus. The process, however, was less than appeasing. Elections that were held with the intention of reaching a consensus were all too often heatedly contested, providing ample opportunities for the junta to instigate armed conflicts marked by unimaginable levels of violence. Congo-Brazzaville was at the center of this political history. After the 1991 National Conference and the elections that delivered victory to the partisans of Pascal Lissouba, elected President of the Congo in August 1992, violent conflicts ensued. During his term, President Lissouba faced three sequential civil wars that pitted his militia against the opposing faction, and set Brazzaville to fire and sword (Dabira, 1998). The end result was the return to power of the former President Denis Sassou-Nguesso. Far from bringing in political stability, this led to an even more murderous conflict (1998–2002) that not only took the lives of almost 30,000 people, but also forced into exile the vast majority of the survivors in the country. Some of these survivors were exiled internally, having taken refuge in the forests, and were forced to endure the most inhumane conditions, while others fled the country (Le Pape and Salignon, 2001). Those who were more fortunate found refuge in nearby African countries and in the West. Over time, these exiles were imbued with a transformative energy that was in fact derived from their personal experiences during the civil war. This energy allowed them to discover a new path to creativity. The diaspora thus came to manifest itself as a major pole in the regeneration of Congolese culture and creativity.

The new flight of Congolese literature in the French language

Emmanuel Dongala was among the Congolese writers whose literary destiny was remade by exile. He found himself in the United States, thanks to the help of the Pen Club. At the request of the writer Philip Roth, Dongala produced one of the most profound works of literature on the civil war in Congo-Brazzaville. His novel, *Johnny, chien méchant*, later adapted for the cinema by director and actor Mathieu Kassovitz, was a gripping testimony to the situation and warring lives of child soldiers. Maxime Ndebeka took refuge in France and found there conditions that allowed a literary renewal. His latest works were unflinching denunciations of the misdeeds and crimes of the African leaders. One of the most important revelations among these writers in exile was Alain Mabanckou,

whose nostalgic account of the Congo prior to the civil wars won him endless international honors. The experience of exile also influenced writers of dramatic works. Most notable was the work of Julien Mabiala Bissila, who directed plays with the Nguiri-Nguiri company at the *Theatre des Argonauts* in Marseilles. There he directed a dramatic episode of the civil war, the 'missing persons of Beach'. Another actor and director, Dieudonné Niangouna, was discovered in France by the *Francophonies* company in Limousin, and became a familiar name in the staging of dramatic stories throughout Europe. In 2005, one of his pieces, the *Vieux Colombier*, was chosen to represent the new African theater at the *Comédie française*. The piece also brought triumph to his collaborator, the young author Wilfried N'Sondé, whose first novel, *Le Coeur des enfants léopards*, won the *Prix des Cinq Continents* in francophone literature and the Senghor Prize for Literature (Steinmetz, 2009).

It should be noted, however, that within the Congo itself, artistic creativity did not altogether disappear, and that the theater still beats its wings, prefiguring the changes to come. At the fiftieth 'Global Day of the Theater' held in Brazzaville on 24, March 2011, the *Négropolitain des 3 Francs* theater company organized a large festival, where a number of directors participated and animated the stage. These were the directors of the *Théâtre du Scorpion* (founded in 1990 by Antoine Yirrika), a former member of the *Ngunga* troupe, and also of the *Salaka* company and the *Théâtre de la francophonie*, the TF. But the most delightful projects were by those bearing messages of solidarity, such as the *Compagnie Zacharie* theater troupe, made up of hearing-impaired children from Congo-Brazzaville whose achievements and successes have been steadfast and uplifting.

Cultural dynamism and popular innovation amidst bureaucratic sluggishness

Congo-Brazzaville was not the only country in Central Africa to have endured political violence. Its neighbor, the Democratic Republic of the Congo (DRC) also experienced violent regime changes, from Mobutu Sese Seko to Joseph Kabila. Every political shift in power erupted into violent conflagrations. It was against the backdrop of incessant war that a restructuring of Congolese music unfolded.

Galvanized by the war, music found new sources for inspiration. Above all with respect to dance, the *ndombolo*, which imitated the waddle associated with the politician Joseph Kabila, burst on to the popular scene and spread like wildfire across Africa. Its 'prophets' were Papa Wemba, Kaffi Olomidé and *Wenge Musica* for Kinshasa; *Extra Musica*, *Watikanya* and *Patrouille* for Brazzaville. But it was in the structure of the music, which accompanied the dance, that the most significant changes could be detected. Played at a tempo that grows quicker and quicker, the portions of the dance music played by the guitarist used gimmicks and sudden breaks never heard before, making the guitarist not just a simple accompanist, but also a real animator of the music. This role of animator is constantly relayed between the guitarist and a singer who is designated as the *atalaku*. The *atalaku* enters immediately at the beginning of the music, directing the percussions, animating the audience, and reinforcing with his maracas the aggressive rhythms that follow. Throughout the dance, he calls out to the audience and cries out words of war, and lists the names that await execution. The *atakalu* displays and exercises hypnotic power over the public, and is sustained throughout the playing of the music by untimely jolts of the guitar and drums that in turn sound out noises that imitate bombs, explosions, and other reverberations of war. The *atalaku* is therefore the real pivot upon which the rhythm turns as its energetic beats recount the violence of society and war. It is not by chance that the titles of the musical pieces are borrowed from military operations: Desert Storm; Ultimatum; Embargo; Attack; Let Pass; Pentagon; X Files; The Blow of Hammer; Law; Staff Headquarters, etc. Just as it is with globalization, the music and *ndombolo* feed on the violence constantly in mutation in a world marked by international conflict. The *ndombolo* invites the dancer to take the position of the firing squad for an eventual attack and is told to take cover because 'hélico eza ko ya, eza na likolo' (The helicopter of the battle has arrived; it is above your heads); or to take off on the path of exile because 'obus kanga bissaka' (the shells are flying; take up your bags). The images of war abound and are carried over by the hypnotic beat of the music. The ultimate irony, however, is manifest in the nickname given by the militia to their canons: the *Ndombolo*.

A fresh resurgence of faith has also offered up a response to the distress of the war. Places of worship are full of people again and Pentacostal churches have become big winners; they have also provided new venues for music-making, with audiences for these eclectic songs, which are a *mélange* of blues, rumba, gospel, *soukouss*, or *ndombolo*. They have invaded the CD market and have found their way into funeral services.

It was on yet another register that the civil wars have nourished the creativity of Congolese artists. Whereas, until recently, Congolese dance had been confined to the choreography by traditional figures, it has grown into a source of unlimited creativity for a renewal of Congolese culture. No less than seven dance companies have been created to perform a uniquely Congolese style of contemporary dance. Among these, we must note the *Yela Wa* company, and the *Envie-Scène* Company, which performed the WA-Zingou, and the *Zonzama* company of Dethmer Nzaba, *Studio Maho*. The initiator of this adventure was the choreographer Chysugone Diangouaya, who founded the *Centre d'Expression corporelle, Arts dramatiques, de Contes, de Percussions et Chants Africains* in 1992. It was from within this Center that the first contemporary dance company of the Congo emerged, *the Ballet-Théâtre Monana*. Two years later, in 1994, the Association of Young Creators of Brazzaville [*Association des Jeunes Créateurs de Brazzaville*] was founded. In 1996, the Association participated in the staging of the first Festival of Choreography in Brazzaville, 'Mabina Dance' [*Mabina Danse*], which would inspire the founding of numerous companies. DeLaVallet Bidiefono, another choreographer, founded the *Compagnie Baninga*, which became a sensation during the *Francophonie* festival in Limoges. The performance, entitled 'Imprints... Words will come later...' [*Empreintes. On posera des mots après*] rested on choreography whose theme was the post-traumatic pain of the civil wars. Critics instantly took note: 'three men and a woman dance on a precipice of an abyss, in the land of the prey who fall victim to the civil war. Their bodies shake in panic-ridden jolts. They throw themselves on to the ground in time with the explosive strums of a rock guitar and then stand at attention, baton in hand. From the piece emanates a somber rage that sets the entire stage' (Steinmetz, 2009).

This rage perhaps vindicates the disinterestedness of the Congolese authorities for a culture they cannot possibly contain. It is surprising to see how much this dynamism is at odds with the decrepit and feeble cultural infrastructure and the almost non-existent subsidies for artists and rehearsal halls. With the exception of the CFRAD, where renovations have gone on for more than 15 years, artists have no choice but to use the rooms offered by the cultural section of the French Embassy in the Congo to hold rehearsals for their performances. It is thanks to these services that the theater troupes and dance companies have financed their tours. And if their fame has rebounded in the country, it is not because of cultural politics but against them! Officials have not refrained from taking full advantage of the international credit of the artists. The Congo has obtained the prestigious right numerous times to host the Pan-African Festival of Music (FESPAM), a coming together every two years of more than 2,000 musicians from all over the continent. But the FESPAM has been debilitated by inadequate management and lack of support for the artists despite the colossal investments poured into the festival by the country's authorities. Even with the colossal investments put into the festival by the country's authorities, the FESPAM has not been able to match other continental events of similar scale, such as the MASAA (Market for Arts and Performances of Abidjan) or the Pan-African Festival of Cinema of Ouagadougou (FESPACO). The FESPAM has always been surrounded by suspicion regarding political corruption and fraud. It is as if in the countries rich in oil, the only culture that has been worth preserving has been that of waste.

Conclusion

Brazzaville has always been at the crossroads of global cultural interchange in Africa. With its rich multi-lingual communities and spirit of openness since pre-colonial times, the city has always had a tradition of drawing on the past while nourishing creative energies in the present, and pursuing innovations for the future. Brazzaville has thus demonstrated a long history of cultural resilience that has allowed it to survive not only the colonial period, but also one of the most destructive civil wars in modern times. The biggest enemy of Brazzaville's cultural development remains the inept political leadership whose main interest has been the profits of its globalized petrol industry. Yet, Brazzaville's culture thrives from below and it is this popular energy that will be the key to its cultural survival and continued rejuvenation amidst the pull of globalization's homogenizing forces.

REFERENCES

Association pour la Défense et l'Illustration des Arts d'Afrique et d'Océanie (ADEIAO) (1991) 'Congo-Zaïre, Thango de Brazza à Kin', *Cahier de l'ADEIAO*, 10. Paris.

Bemba, S. (1984) *50 ans de musique du Congo/ Zaïre, 1920–1970*. Paris-Dakar: Présence Africaine.

Dabira, N. (1998*) Brazzaville à feu et à sang, 5 juin 15 octobre 1997*. Paris: L'Harmattan.

Diazinga, S. (2008) 'Regards sur la jeune fille de l'Afrique équatoriale à travers la revue *Liaison,* (1950-1960)', *Annales de l'Université Marien NGOUABI*, 9 (1): 77.

Gondola, Ch. D. (1996) *Villes miroirs: migrations et identités urbaines à Kinshasa et Brazzaville, 1930–1970*. Paris: L'Harmattan.

Kadima-Nzuji, M. (2010) *Jean Malonga, écrivain congolais (1907–1985)*. Paris: L'Harmattan.

Le Pape, M. and Salignon, P. (eds) (2001) *Une guerre contre les civils. Réflexions sur les pratiques humanitaires au Congo-Brazzaville (1998–2000)*. Paris: Karthala.

Obenga, T. (2010) *Histoire générale du Congo des origines a nos jours: Tome 3, Le Congo au 20e siècle.* Paris: L'Harmattan.

Steinmetz, M. (2009) 'Congo, douleur dansée', *L'Humanité*, 28 September.

Tchicaya U Tam'si (1955) *Le Mauvais Sang*. Paris: P.J. Oswald.

Yengo, P. (2006) *La guerre civile du Congo-Brazzaville, 1993–2002. Chacun aura sa part*. Paris: Karthala.

CHAPTER 15

SPECTACULARIZING FÈS

Justin McGuinness

This profile explores two cultural initiatives in Fès: a major music festival and a series of urban design projects. The first attracts large local as well as European and North American audiences; it also features an intellectual forum that aims to 'give a soul to globalization'. The second, in contrast, has been piloted by the populist Mayor. Both have transformed the city's profile and represent a form of proto-urban branding. But with the rise of popular protest via social media in Morocco, which is critical of the excessive expenditure on festivities and the events' supposed elitism, the time of visitor-focused urban spectacle may be over. More accountable forms of cultural initiative may emerge, rooted in local society and displaying more obvious benefits for the local population.

Introduction

In the early 1990s, Morocco's cities were far from being hives of cultural innovation. Cinemas were closing or run-down, bookshops were few and far between, and cultural spectacle – art-house films, dance, theatre – were largely in the form of events programmed by the cultural services of foreign embassies, in particular the extensive network of French cultural centres. By the end of the 2000s, however, a sea-change had occurred: every major city had an annual cultural event. Marrakesh's autumn international film festival had taken that city's notoriety beyond that of tourist destination while Casablanca had *L'Boulevard*, an annual celebration of new urban music[1]. New cultural infrastructure was on the drawing boards, including a 'starchitect' designed theatre for the capital, Rabat, and the restoration of Casablanca's historic neo-Oriental abattoirs as a setting for live performance and exhibitions. Tangier's historic *Teatro Cervantes* was set for restoration as well. The new cultural infrastructure – a combination of a sound logistics base, thematic week-long events, a high level of official and private sponsorship and restored or redesigned spaces – was not, however, largely piloted by the Ministry of Culture. Rather, para-governmental agencies, high-profile individuals and regional and municipal authorities took the lead in establishing and maintaining festivals which quickly gained loyal local – and in some cases foreign – followings. The annual week of entertainments, both free and paying, spectacularizes Moroccan cities and is looked forward to by all. The biggest festivals – the Festival *Gnaoua d'Essaouira* and *Mawazine* in Rabat – attract audiences from across the country, largely as their budgets allow them to bring in major international stars. In the case of Morocco's spiritual capital, Fès, the annual festival, generally referred to in French as the *Festival de Fès des musiques sacrées du monde*, now balances small-scale, elite concerts of religious music in historic buildings with jumbo events, including rap, out on the urban edge. A sleepy provincial capital, which usually only gains media attention for student demonstrations, collapsing slum housing and violent *faits divers*, every June becomes the site of multiple daily concerts and a high-level colloquium linking the global, the local and the spiritual. The usual urban rhythms are transformed; for those with time to race from con-cert to concert, all of Fès is a stage. In the pages that follow I will examine the development of festive public spaces and events in contemporary Fès, focusing on two figures who have been crucial to the development of spectacle in the city. The aim is to portray something of the interrelationship between culture, politics and space in the city.

The Festival de Fès goes back to the early 1990s. Along with the *Festival Gnaoua* held in Essaouira, a beautiful Atlantic coast town, it is a forerunner of the current slew of festivals. Both were founded with global intent. While world music inspired by the *Gnaoua* tradition, rooted in a form of ecstatic traditional practice, was the focus in Essaouira, the founder of the Festival de Fès, deeply imbued with the values of Sufism, saw staged music from the world's major religious tradi-tions as a way to transcend political divisions. The growth of the festival – and the development of smaller events focusing on jazz, Andalusian music and local cuisine, chiefly held in the old city or *médina* – has accompanied efforts to end Fès's relative poverty (official discourse in Morocco runs that cultural events are a good lever in poverty reduction). I will now attempt to situate the city in the Moroccan urban system before discussing some-thing of its particularities.

Fès: historic city of the extremes

Arguably, of all Moroccan cities, Fès is the one with the most extremes: symbolic, ecological, demo-graphic, socio-economic and heritage-wise. The first Islamic city in Morocco was founded in Fès in the year 808. The visual focus point of the historic city is the mausoleum of Moulay Idriss II, the city's founder. Although rebuilt many times, the mauso-leum-mosque, along with the nearby great *Mosquée Qaraouiyine*, are focus points for Moroccan Islam and the imaginary of the Moroccan nation-state. These are sites visited by Morocco's sovereign who bears not only the title of king, but also that of *amir al-mu'minine*, commander of the believers. The symbolic charge of Fès is reinforced by the fact that the Manifesto for Independence was drafted and signed here. In ecological terms, the city is at the edge of an earthquake zone. Tremors from the 1994 quake at Al Hoceïma were felt in the city. An argu-ment goes that the abandoning of the city's traditional

water supply system has been extremely detrimental. The drying out of the ground has rendered fragile the poorly maintained brick and rubble-stone build-ings which compose the majority of the city's built fabric. The city is also one of demographic and socio-economic contrasts, a phenomenon recog-nized since the 1970s (El Kohen Lamghili 1976; PNUD/Ministère de l'Intérieur 1991). Parts of the old city have around 1,000 inhabitants to the hec-tare. Since the city's heyday in the 1920s and 1930s, when elite families built themselves large and comfortable courtyard homes, the housing stock has decayed under the multiple pressures of rural in-migration and the need for cheap workshop space. The importance of Fès as heritage was rec-ognized at international level in 1981when the city was listed as a UNESCO World Heritage Site, the first place in Morocco to achieve this status. Major historic buildings, most notably the mediaeval *med-ersas* and the fortified gates, have been restored. The housing problems of large numbers of low-income residents in the old city have remained unsolved, however, as a recent report by the gov-ernmental housing and urban development corpo-ration recognizes (Al Omrane 2009). Nevertheless, it would seem that demographic pressure in the old city is declining. And unexpectedly, the historic built-fabric was given a boost in the early 2000s with the arrival of a small but relatively wealthy cohort of foreign home-buyers, possibly as many as 300 (McGuinness 2007). This new contingent in Fès has bought large city residences as premises for up-scale tourist ventures (hotels and restaurants). A similar trend among Moroccan investors can be observed too. The old city, setting for most of the Festival de Fès's concerts, is thus characterized by a highly contrasted pattern of property use, with wealthy micro-pockets of retrofitted buildings sitting alongside swathes of poorly maintained or unsafe housing and polluting craft activities.

Fès in the Moroccan urban context

In terms of the nexus of relations between built-fabric, culture, heritage and tourism in Morocco, the only comparable city to Fès is Marrakesh, also a former imperial capital and now a UNESCO World Heritage Site. Both have populations of around 1.5 million, a strong historic identity, landmark architec-tural monuments and, in terms of urban form, a contrast between the dense *medina* and the twentieth-century, French-built, modern city or *ville nouvelle*. In Marrakesh, foreign-led gentrification began in the mid-1990s (Escher et al. 2001). There the climate and the immediate eco-system (an extensive oasis and the nearby High Atlas Mountains) also proved attractive to tourist ventures. Like Fès, Marrakesh has a concentration of craft industries producing goods largely for the tourist market.

Moving more broadly, all of Morocco's cities have witnessed massive urban expansion since the end of the 1990s. Land held in communal ownership of various kinds or belonging to state agencies and local government has been released for housing and commercial development on a large scale. The national '*ville sans bidonvilles*' ('cities without slums') initiative of the mid-2000s has produced extensive zones of low-rise apartment blocks, while private developers are producing gated-estates of various kinds. Fès, like other cities, has seen the development of business parks. A better housed, more prosperous population is thus ready to take part in urban entertainments of a broader character than the 'traditional' male-dominated football-stadium and café culture. As compared to the early 1990s, the population of Fès is now globally connected, watching television from across the world – or at least the Arab world, if the number of satellite dishes on the *Médina*'s roofs are anything to go by.

To turn now to another nexus, that of culture, urban spaces and governance, the situation in Fès is complex and can only be handled in broad brush terms in the space of a short article. Two thematic areas, two figures may allow us to sense something of the dynamics at work in Fès where a form of place-promotion (not labelled as such in any of the documents I have seen) has emerged through a redefinition of certain urban spaces and the creation of events, of which the Festival de Fès is by far and away the most important. The persona of university professor Faouzi Skali, qualified by some as a cultural entrepreneur, was crucial to the city's star cultural event, the *Musiques sacrées* (Berrada and Miyara 2006: 80); the colourful figure of Hamid Chabat, currently Mayor of Fès, is central to the redevelopment of public space. Both Skali and Chabat have their place in the broader picture of Moroccan public life: Skali as occasional public intellectual (El Azizi 2003; Zouari 2005), Chabat as populist politician (Anon 2010; Boudarham 2010).

The initiatives taken by both run with a key global urban trend: the heightened use of cultural spectacle and space in its various manifestations to achieve visibility for a city.

To move back a step, it should be stressed at this point that numerous institutions and social actors are at work in Fès – just as they are in other cities. Briefly, there are two administrative hierarchies, one designated by the central authorities (the governors, caïds, etc.), the second the product of local elections (the municipal council and the communes) (Barrou 2006). Semi-independent bodies such as the *Conseil régional du tourisme* work to promote the city, while at least three actors work to enhance heritage and improve the historic built-fabric. In addition to these, there is a further layer of civil society organizations. To outside observers, the precise areas of responsibility of the governmental and para-governmental bodies is opaque, to say the least.

Spectacularizing Fès through urban space: the political factor

Returning to urban spectacularization under the impetus of political actors, the current Mayor, Hamid Chabat, is the key player – or at least proclaims himself as such (Nafaa 2010). Istiqlal Party MP for Fès since 1997 and secretary general of the *Union général des travailleurs marocains* (UGTM), Chabat first became Mayor in the 2003 municipal elections. Re-elected for a second five-year term in 2009, he is something of a case apart in Moroccan municipal politics. On the whole, city mayors are not high-profile figures at national level. At local level, they tend to work in tandem with the Ministry of the Interior's designated representatives, the regional governors and prefects. Chabat, however, is a media-friendly, populist politician whose public statements, however controversial, regularly make the news. While previous municipal presidents in Fès have come from major Fassi families, Chabat is an *aroubi*, a man of the countryside, and certainly not a 'real Fassi'. Nevertheless, according to Chabat, under his mandate 'Fès had taken on a different appearance', with real transparency in the management of municipal affairs. Under the leadership of the *Union des forces socialistes populaires* (USFP), local management was marked by a high level of corruption.

If the city had stagnated under the socialist-led council, this was in part due to the general context of 1990s Morocco, where the ageing King Hassan II put all his efforts into assuring a smooth handover to his son, Sidi Mohamed, who came to the throne in 1999. Mohamed VI brought the technocrats to power, and as reforms and the pace of economic growth picked up in the mid-2000s, Chabat benefited from the ambient dynamism – Fès acquired a new railway station, an improved airport, and new areas of low-income housing. A series of sales of municipal land and property brought new funds into the municipal coffers. While he was (obviously) not directly responsible for any of the changes in the second half of the 2000s, he was able to *claim* ownership of them in his frequent public statements. Chabat has generally proved adept at managing cultural symbols. (His declaration in 2009 that the foundation of Fès was predicted by the Prophet Mohamed in a *hadith* was variously mocked and greeted with stupefaction.) Political capital was made during the run-up to the 1,200th anniversary of the foundation of Fès in 808. Roads were widened, 1,200 palm trees and 1,200 plane trees were planted, and an itinerant public exhibition (organized by the Ministry of Culture) started from the recently refurbished Place Baghdadi (Saad-Alami 2008). In preparation for the 2009 municipal elections, a major refurbishment of the public spaces of Fès was announced, including 12 new major fountains and 1,200 small ones. In real terms, this translated into the transformation of the city's main street, the Avenue Hassan II, into a sort of Moroccan Ramblas, popular on summer evenings. Other streets, on the edge of the poorer districts, were repaved, planted and generally upgraded. Dusty public space became urban salon were public events could be held; the effect on Chabat's popularity was guaranteed.

Chabat has not, however, sought to gain political capital from the *Festival de Fès des musiques sacrées du monde*, the city's lead annual event. It may be that the festival was felt to be off-limits, its logistics being under the direct supervision of Mohammed Kabbaj, a former royal advisor and high-level public servant who was also president of the Association Fès-Saïss, about which more later. Or perhaps given that the Festival de Fès has been qualified as elitist, targeting in part a foreign audience, Chabat felt that involvement was unlikely to win new voters. There would seem to be limits to the Chabat-brand of

urban spectacularization, however, as a recent report for the Municipality, commissioned by Chabat himself, indicates (Bami 2010).

Spectacularizing Fès through religious music: the spiritual appeal

Whatever the case, spiritual communion, the core concept of the Festival de Fès, stands a long way from Hamid Chabat's brand of populist politics. The underpinning idea, that music, and in particular music related to mystic practice from traditions that would otherwise rarely, if ever, meet, was the brainchild of a local intellectual, Faouzi Skali, back in the early 1990s. Unlike the municipal achievements of Mayor Chabat, for the moment poorly documented, the development of the Festival de Fès can be followed – thanks to the large amount of media coverage, orchestrated by the event's efficient press office. The Festival de Fès can be seen as another agent of urban spectacularization, arguably at least as important as Chabat's projects in that it wins attention both local and global for the city. Nevertheless, like the urban improvement works, there is an underlying political dimension – as is only to be expected in an event which is tied up with religious and cultural symbols.

It should be stressed that back in 1994 there was no indication that Fès would be home to a successful annual event based essentially on religious music (the city had seen major urban riots in 1990). The catalyst was an unusual one: the mediation of war and its effect on an individual. An appalling military adventure in the Middle East, the 1991 Iraqi occupation of Kuwait and the subsequent Western reaction, was witnessed globally thanks to the new medium of satellite TV. Moroccans, like many other peoples in the Arab and Muslim world, were shaken by the images of violent conflict pouring into their homes via satellite news networks. The reactions to the images had a particularly sharp impact on Faouzi Skali, then a lecturer at the city's teacher training school and a follower of the *Boutchichiya* Sufi way. In reaction to the American president's Operation Desert Storm, Skali was to put together a rather different operation, down in the south-east of Morocco at the dunes of Merzouga and then in Fès: ten film-makers were invited to Morocco to present their work on different spiritual traditions from around the world. The visual image, used as an arm of war, was to be used in the service of peace. The event, dubbed *Voies de la paix et enseignement du désert: vers la rencontre des grandes traditions du monde*, was a success, the wordy title notwithstanding.

In fact, a colloquium organized in Fès as part of the *Voies de la paix* event proved to be the founding moment: participants were invited to an evening of *samaâ*, Sufi chanting, which generally only takes place in saints' shrines or private homes. This *samaâ* 'performance' turned out to be the most memorable part of the whole initiative. Skali thus turned to a different concept, a festival based on spiritual music. As luck would have it, the then ruler, King Hassan II, was willing to be patron. In 1994, the first season of the *Festival de Fès des musiques sacrées du monde* was held; Skali was to remain festival director for 12 years. Music from across the great religious and spiritual traditions was the central element of the programme. Subsequently, the festival was to link up with the Association Fès-Saïss, one of a number of 'unofficial' regional organizations established in Morocco in the late 1980s and early 1990s.[2] Funded by the Ministry of the Interior, the brief of such institutions was to develop projects which the slow-moving Moroccan civil service was unable to implement. The new associations provided a given region's 'great and good' a framework within which to act. Headed by Mohammed Kabbaj, and like Skali, a scion of an old Fassi family, the Association Fès-Saïss was no exception. The headquarters were established in elegant premises, the early twentieth-century Dar Tazi, in the Batha district of the Médina; the *Festival des musiques sacrées* was soon to be its best-known initiative. Over the years, the number of venues expanded. All were of strong aesthetic impact. The great fortified courtyard of Bab Makina, built in 1886 and once home to the Moroccan mint, continues to host the more expensive concerts (the acoustics are good). A large public space, the Place Baghdadi, close to the northern bus station, and Bab Bou Jloud, the main access point to the upper, western end of old Fès el Bali, was used for larger-scale, cheaper or free events. A tradition of free late-night Sufi events at Dar Tazi developed. By the early 2000s concerts were also being organized on the vast race course[3] in *Fès ville nouvelle* and out at the Roman site of Volubilis, close to Meknès.

By 2004, the Festival de Fès was clearly a success – or perhaps victim of its success. A large number of major specialized musicians had performed at Bab Makina, all classical in their respective traditions. Among artists to have marked the festival in recent years are Mohamed Reza Shajarian (2003), the 85-year-old Ravi Shankar (2005) and Jordi Savall and Hespérion XXI (2006). Recently unearthed Baroque music has found a place alongside acapella singing from Tibet. While the organizers stressed in the mid-2000s that quality was central to their choice of artists, the Festival's programming had undoubtedly begun to cater to a wider range of tastes than at its beginnings. In 2005, for example, the hugely popular Iraqi singer Kadhem Essaher attracted an audience of over 30,000 at the Place Baghdadi – while a more courtly performance by the Tokyo dance company, the Ensemble Gagaku, was given at Bab Makina. The decision to hold the festival in late May or early June, outside European and Moroccan school holidays, proved to be no obstacle to the event's development.

The Festival de Fès: global cultural event?

In addition to the musical groups from across the world, in what sense is the Festival de Fès global? It certainly attracts a huge number of journalists, putting the city on the world's media map: the most desultory of web searches will produce articles full of praises for the festival in outlets as diverse as *The Guardian* and *travelintelligence.com*, *Jeune Afrique*, *Le Monde*, *Le Figaro* and *Témoignage chrétien*. However, while building understanding through spiritual music, a space of communion through shared aesthetic pleasure was one of the Festival's original aims; providing a global space for dialogue was another.

Back in 1994, the Festival's first year, the parameters of world communication were different: the global North mastered satellite television and the Net was limited to the universities; Huntington's 'clash of civilizations' thesis had gained popular currency. There was a need for other voices to be heard in public space. And so the Festival sponsored a programme of debates led by thinkers and specialists with global – or at least European – reputations. Each morning in festival week, these discussions, open to all, were held under the great holm-oak tree in the garden-courtyard of the Musée Batha. The tone was one of transnational engagement, ethical, intellectual and spiritual; a space of communion through shared aesthetic pleasure had emerged. From 2001, these discussions were labelled the *Rencontres de Fès*. The aim was now to give 'a soul to globalization'. The reach of the *Rencontres* can be felt in *L'Esprit de Fès*, a book published in 1994 to celebrate the Festival's tenth anniversary (Calmé 2006). The appendix listing participants shows that by that year a very particular psychographic was in attendance, including academics, high-profile journalists, inter-faith dialogue builders, NGO activists, performance artists, French and Moroccan politicos and functionaries from global institutions. Their writings published in *L'Esprit de Fès* call for a juster, more spiritually grounded world order. This is an interpretative community, characterized by a humanist ethic, working to escape both literalist religious positions and perhaps to create a new, spiritual coherence. In this concentration of personal statements linked to the Festival, a particular sense of belonging to the social world is expressed, a normative 'what-should-be', a consensus with which it is difficult to disagree.

A reaction to a war mass-mediated at global level and a poorly formulated theory of world conflict had been at the root of the Festival de Fès. Other global events were reflected in the debates and music of later sessions, through which a fusion of the Festival's cultural aims and intellectual positioning took place. In 1996, for the third session, Skali managed to get the Philharmonic Orchestra of Sarajevo over to Morocco, its first performance abroad since the end of the Bosnian War (1992–1995). Flown in on an aircraft placed at the Festival's disposition by King Hassan II, the Orchestra included musicians from all the city's communities, Bosnian, Croatian, Muslim and Serb, and was seen to represent a hope for reconciliation and peace. Subsequently, Afghans, Iraqis, Israelis and Palestinians have participated. By 2005, this desire to build transnational dialogue out of conflict was clearly the Festival's distinguishing mark – and it enabled Skali to gain global recognition. World Bank adviser Katherine Marshall promised US$100,000 for the *Rencontres*, without strings attached – an important gesture, it was felt, towards an event which was a potential platform for radical *altermondialistes* and others critical of the Bretton Woods institutions.

The global cultural side of the Festival de Fès plays out in other institutional ways, too. It has enabled the city to acquire a further mark of global cultural distinction, in addition to a UNESCO World Heritage listing. The longest established festival of sacred music, at least in Europe, is the *Festival de musique sacrée de Perpignan*, founded in 1987.[4] In 2003, the Perpignan Festival, along with those of Fès and Dijon, was one of the founding signatories of the Charter of World Sacred Music. In June 2007, at the Fès Festival, nine festivals came together to establish the *Association Réseau international des musiques sacrées du monde*.[5] Apart from Bangalore and Fès, all network members are European. As one of only two festivals in the global South, the Festival de Fès thus acquired further kudos. Thanks to the organizational committee's skill and commitment, the event has clearly won mind-space for Fès at global level.

Political implications of a city-wide cultural event

The Festival de Fès, as portrayed so far, seems as unproblematic as Mayor Chabat's programme of urban projects transforming loyal voters' daily lives. Creating as it does, for a brief time-slot, a network of social relations around the collective enjoyment of music and performance, it is an event around which there can be little disagreement – apart from occasional salvoes in the local press about the high price of some concerts and complaints about elitist programming (Zizi 2003, 2004) – now largely resolved thanks to the big side-events. There is a further layer of politico-cultural complexity to be explored, however, tied up with the growth of conservative Islamist political parties and the staging of Sufi practice at the Festival (Cook 2001). In its first years, one of the biggest challenges was how to bring the chants of the religious brotherhoods, whose members had no experience of public performance, on to the stage. That this was accomplished successfully was in no small measure due to Faouzi Skali's interpersonal skills – and inside experience of *Boutchichiya* practice.

However, *tariqa* (Sufi brotherhood) presence in the Festival can be read in more ways than performance. It may be seen to reflect in a diffuse way the growth in interest in *tariqa*-based Islam both in Morocco and abroad since the early 1990s. As a method to counter the rise of militant *salafist* Islam and its potential to develop a radical challenge to the Moroccan government, the regime opened up to the *tariqas*. The Minister of Religious Affairs, Ahmed Taoufik, was a Boutchichi adept, as were certain other high-placed officials. By the mid-2000s, the annual celebrations of the *mouled* (Prophet Mohammed's birthday) at Madagh, the *Boutchichiya tariqa*'s chief centre, in eastern Morocco, had taken on the appearance of a pilgrimage. Thousands of adepts travelled from across the country and abroad to participate and perhaps acquire a measure of *baraka* (blessing) from moments in the presence of the *Boutchichiya*'s guide, the venerable Sidi Hamza (Ramdani 2007).

The Festival de Fès' energetic press office has never focused specifically on the Sufi angle. The diversity of approaches in the cultivation of the soul has always been the theme, whether from the monotheistic or other traditions. However, a fine line was being trodden by Festival organizers. In the first place, it was a bold step to stage non-monotheist performers in a city as conservative as Fès. For many *salafists*, idol-worshipping non-monotheists are pagans and nothing more, while Sufi practice is not far from godlessness. Happily, conservative religious criticism has targeted the festivals in general, arguing against the inappropriateness of staging 'decadent' Western popular music (Allali 2006) (the singer Elton John played to huge crowds at Rabat's *Mawazine* festival in summer 2010, despite Islamist criticisms). At another level, this festival received criticism from the Left, given the close implication of palace cronies in the organization (Semlali 2009).

The Sufi aspect of religious-cultural practice has grown stronger, if anything, since the mid-2000s. Both the key protagonists of the present article have played a role. In 2008, Faouzi Skali, who had given up his position directing the Festival de Fès, founded a new *Festival de la culture soufie*, to run every spring. Spiritual music, mainly Moroccan, and intellectual debate was the formula, representing a return to the first festival experiment back in the early 1990s. At a more political level, Hamid Chabat regularly refers to a *triangle sacré* in the central Médina, with its points defined by the Shrine of Moulay Idriss II, the Qaraouiyine Mosque and the Shrine of Sidi Ahmed Tijani, eighteenth-century founder of a *tariqa* which became – and still is – highly influential in west Africa. *Tijaniyyah* adepts have long travelled to Fès – and the local tourist board in various publications referred to the importance of spiritual tourism, with the *Tijani* visitors obviously in mind. In 2008, a

major operation upgrading the façades in the vicinity of the three main religious monuments was launched. In 2011, the King launched restoration works on the Shrine of Moulay Idriss.

The successful expansion of festivals and the refurbishment of public spaces – both under the guidance of the public authorities – go hand in hand in Fès. For the global visitor, visiting monuments, perhaps taking in a festival, the city has a clear heritage-preservation and cultural-promotion agenda, at least in the *Médina*. For informed residents, a largely opaque agenda informs festivities and architectural refurbishment. Cultural and heritage initiatives are interwoven with political undertones. *Tariqa* adepts, *salafists*, local notables and tourist investors observe developments as projects emerge. Urban spectacularization takes place against a complex politico-cultural background. The two major examples of urban cultural practice explored here, while broadly similar to initiatives elsewhere, bear all the marks of the 'Moroccan paradox', theme of many a café discussion: the ability to undertake large-scale operations with wide impact, while many key essentials of urban life – access to reasonably priced drinking water for all, secure housing, universally available quality primary education – remain unsatisfactory.

Interestingly, in spring 2011, in a context of growing political protest against corruption and nepotism levelled at both the Moroccan bureaucracy and central government, the web-based *Mouvement du 20-Février* called for Rabat's *Mawazine* music festival to be cancelled. The 19,000 members of the anti-*Mawazine* Facebook group took the line that the sponsorship funding mobilized in support of *Mawazine* would be better used to complete more solid cultural projects – the national contemporary art museum and the national dance institute – rather than the temporary urban fireworks of the festival (Benmehdi and Cherkaoui 2011). Whether the Festival de Fès, often criticized for elitism, would come under attack remained to be seen at the time of writing.

Notes

1 See www.boulevard.ma.
2 The Association Fès-Saïss was established in 1988. Officially, its mission is 'to contribute to the cultural, economic and social development of the city of Fès, and to

preserve and promote the Médina of Fès, a mediaeval city which has been declared part of the World Heritage by Unesco'. See www.fesfestival.com (2006 website, consulted in December 2009).

3 The race course or *Champ des courses* was unfortunately sold off for private property development, yet another element in the rushed sale of public land which marked urban growth in the mid-2000s across Morocco.

In 2009, major free events were moved to dusty open ground in the new suburb of Aït Skato.

4 See www.mairie-perpignan.fr.

5 See www.wsm-network.org. Of the nine founding festivals, four have websites – Brighton, Dijon, Fès and Perpignan. The remaining *five* festivals are Bangalore, Banska-Stiavnica (Slovakia), Czestohowa (Poland) Florence and Lodz (Poland).

REFERENCES

Allali, Réda (2006) 'Les nouveaux fascistes', *Le Journal hebdomadaire*, 24 June, 44–52.

Al Omrane (2009) *Al Omrane. Dix ans d'intervention en médinas.* Rabat: Al Omrane Holding.

Anon (2010) 'Les rois de la provocation' (special feature), *Le Soir*, 12 June 2009, 16–18.

Bami, Rachida (2010) 'Fès peu attractive malgré ses atouts', *Le Matin*, 26 May, 14.

Barrou, Brahim (2006) *Fès, de la gestion urbaine normative à la gouvernance.* Rabat: Institut national d'aménagement et d'urbanisme.

Benmehdi, Hassan and Naoufel Cherkaoui (2011) 'Les voix s'élèvent pour l'annulation du Festival Mawazine', *Magharebia* (online magazine), www.magharebia.com/cocoon/awi/xhtml1/fr/features/awi/features/2011/04/14/feature-02.

Berrada, N. and L. Miyara (2006) 'Fès en quête de vision et de synergies: entretien avec Faouzi Skali, directeur-général de la fondation Esprit de Fès', *Labyrinthes*, April–May, 80–82.

Boudarham, Mohammed (2010) 'Qui peut arrêter le roi Chabat?', *Tel Quel*, 27 February, 18–19.

Calmé, Nathalie (2006) *L'Esprit de Fès. Dédié aux générations futures.* Monaco: Editions du Rocher.

Cook, Bruce (2001) 'The 2001 Fez Festival of World Sacred Music: an annual music event in Morocco embodies and reflects Sufi traditions and spirit', *International Journal of Humanities and Peace*, 17 (1) 54–61.

El Azizi, Abdellatif (2003) 'L'islam politique est une hérésie', *Maroc Hebdo International*, 560, 30 May, 13.

El Kohen Lamghili, Ahmed (1976) 'Comment sauver Fès', *Lamalif*, 78, March, 18–20.

Escher, Anton, Sandra Peterman and Birgit Clos (2001) 'Le bradage de la médina de Marrakech', *Actes du 6 éme colloque maroco-allemand de Paderborn 2000*. Passau: Maghreb-Studien 14, 217–232.

McGuinness, Justin (2007) 'A cosmopolitan turn in the Médina', in Susan Ossman (ed.), *Places We Share: Migration, Subjectivity and Global Mobility*. Lanham, MD: Lexington Books, 121–141.

Nafaa, Mohammed (2010) *Le phénomène Hamid Chabat.* Rabat: Editions et impressions Bouregreg.

Ossman, Susan (ed.) (2007) *Places We Share: Migration, Subjectivity and Global Mobility* Lanham, MD: Lexington Books.

PNUD/Ministère de l'Intérieur (1991) *Sauvegarde de la ville de Fès: rapport phase 1.* Groupe 8/Urbaplan/SIDES en collaboration avec ADER – Fès et UNESCO, June, 203 pp.

Ramdani, Redouane (2007) 'Soufisme ou idolâtre? Voyage au royaume du Cheikh Hamza', *Tel Quel*, 83, 7 June, 22–25.

Saad-Alami, Younes (2008) 'Fès, 1.200 platanes pour le 1.200ème anniversaire', *L'Economiste*, 17 January, 20.

Semlali, Aïda (2009) 'Saison festivals: quand la politique s'en mêle', *Le Journal hebdomadaire*, 23 May, 20–25.

Zizi, Yassine (2003) 'De mon âme à ton âme', *Tel Quel*, 83, 21 June, 32–34.

Zizi, Yassine (2004) 'Berrada et Aït Qihho, de sortie à Fès', *Le Journal Hebdomadaire*, 12 June.

Zouari, Faouzia (2005) 'Faouzi Skali, un mystique dans la cité', *Jeune Afrique*, 10 June.

CHAPTER 16

RESHAPING, INSTALLING, PIONEERING, SPEARHEADING... REALIGNMENT OF ISTANBUL

Asu Aksoy and Kevin Robins

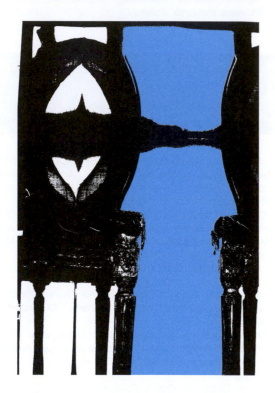

This profile of Istanbul explores recent developments that bear on cultural policy and cultural regulation in the city. Istanbul is a rapidly developing metropolis seeking to position itself in the context of the world system of 'global cities'. As with all such cities, neoliberal dynamics hold sway. The authors analyze the new dynamics in one particular municipality, Beyoğlu, located at the very heart of the city, whose cultural, leisure and historical composition make it central to the developments that have brought such slogans as 'cool Istanbul' into circulation. They focus on the strategies the Municipality, run by the conservative and religiously-oriented Justice and Development Party (AKP), has adopted to deal with urban cultural policy issues. By uncovering the contradictory dynamics in play, they argue that the process of change is strongly associated with a weakening of local democracy.

Introduction

'The atmosphere of a city is simply the way that life takes place in it' (Böhme 2006: 132). A productive metaphor: the atmosphere of a city, the changing atmosphere of an urban culture. Atmospheres are phenomena that we commonly – and spontaneously, inescapably even – associate with our *experience* of a place, or of a situation, or an encounter. 'You sense an atmosphere, on the one hand,' says Gernot Böhme, 'only by way of your own feelings, and yet, at the same time, as what emanates from another person, from objects, or from the environment' (2006: 132). Atmospheres concern the everyday lived relation to one's surroundings, and they translate into the complex array of moods, tones of feeling, emotions – and also mindful awareness – associated with this always ongoing situated and implicated relation. Atmospheres are 'affective powers of feeling, spatial bearers of moods' (Böhme 1993: 119). In an important sense, one knows the city by way of the moods that it evokes, through an 'awareness of my state of being in an environment, how I feel here' (1993: 120). Strange as it may seem, we want to argue that urban governance can only work effectively when it entails an awareness of how policy-making is, as much as anything, about the production of atmospheres. Urban democracy can mean very little without a democratic *feel*. The quality of atmosphere and mood in a city is a key measure of the relative success or failure of urban governance initiatives.

In the following account, we are concerned with Istanbul. Our focus will be on recent developments in cultural policy and governance in contemporary Istanbul, and with regard to what is distinctive about these developments. And, since we cannot straightforwardly consider this vast city as a whole to be a unitary or a coherent urban space, our reflections will be specific, addressing some of the key issues of urban cultural governance in just one municipality, Beyoğlu. Through a detailed discussion of the newly initiated planning-cum-cultural strategy in this one part of the city – though, no doubt, its culturally the most vital zone – we draw attention to what we consider to be problematical in contemporary urban governance strategies – seeming to be symptomatic of what is going on in general in Istanbul.

Many recent observers of contemporary urban transformation and of affiliated developments in urban governance have a rather positive scenario to project. Thus, for example, Erik Swyngedouw (2010: 232) writes of what he calls the 'glocal' city in terms of 'new urban possibilities', involving the production of spaces in which 'all manner of new urban social and cultural practices emerge, where new forms of urbanity come to life'. What he – entirely abstractly – refers to as the 'new governmentality', or 'stakeholder urban governance' (2010: 218), is said to involve emergent 'institutional or quasi-institutional arrangements that are organized as horizontal associational networks of private, civil society and state actors' (2010: 220). And so on... Our reading of the atmosphere and the mood in Istanbul today is quite contrary to what Swyngedouw regards as somehow inherently potential in a posited new urbanity (in the 'creative city', as it is commonly termed these days). We can see no evident signs of new institutional arrangements, or of associational networks, or of processes of creative enactment. What we see instead is a city being 'renewed' that is at the same time a city being diminished.

This is in alignment with a characteristic, and no doubt indispensable, Istanbul urban narrative. Consider, *inter alia*, the anger of the renowned architect Sedat Hakkı Eldem (1979: xxi–xxii), who, some 30 years ago, judged that 'Istanbul possessed with real value and beauty has long passed', lamenting 'the extent of the errors and neglect committed at the present day'. What remains? This is a question that cannot be avoided here; see Aksoy and Robins 2011.

Consequently, there is now a charged mood in the city – an underlying disposition of frustration, of resentment, and of resented fatalism. It is the disturbed mood of those who are the co-producers of the city's life – who have been the co-producers of its vitality and its vivid atmospheres – as they now find the nature and the terms of the co-production ever more unequal, uncreative, undesirable, and stressful.

Why Beyoğlu?

Looking immediately across the Golden Horn to the 'old city', the now so-called 'historic peninsula' of Istanbul, Beyoğlu is at the very heart of the cultural city of Istanbul. In the Ottoman period, and particularly during the nineteenth century, when it was known as Pera, Beyoğlu was the distinctive preserve of the European populations living in the city (French, Germans, Austrians, Italians, British, etc.) and of non-Muslim Ottoman citizens (Greeks, Armenians, Jews). Effectively it was a city within a city. Along, and in the immediate vicinity of, the Grande Rue de Péra, which ran the length of the district, were embassies, hotels, churches and chapels, arcades, markets, theatres, stylish cafés and brasseries ('Strasbourg', 'Viennoise', 'Suisse', 'Koutoulas'), cabarets, couturiers and milliners, jewellers, elegant restaurants and patisseries – all reflecting the then contemporary European paradigm of urban sophistication (Naum-Duhani 1947, 1956). The Italian traveller Edmondo De Amicis, who visited Istanbul in 1874, characterized Pera as 'the "West End" of the European colony [he was evoking the West End of London]; the centre of pleasure and elegance' (2005 [1877]: 41). With its thoroughly 'European' character, Pera had the complex atmosphere of a cosmopolitan space – within the Ottoman capital city, it was a space of ethnic, linguistic, religious and cultural diversity (Tischler 2006). In the early twentieth century, however, during the period in which the Empire was breaking up and the new Turkish nation state was being brought into existence – and when Pera was consequently driven to become monocultural Turkish-national Beyoğlu – this cosmopolitan ethos was forcibly demeaned and diminished. And yet we can say that there always remained a residue of cosmopolitan sensibility, maybe even a certain persistence of cosmopolitan disposition, in Beyoğlu. And now, as Istanbul takes on the imposed challenge of re-branding itself as a new-century global city, this cosmopolitan residuum, the cosmopolitan legacy of Pera, has once again become activated, albeit in a different modality, instrumentally, tactically, and nostalgically. 'Cosmopolitan Beyoğlu' has become an invaluable image and advertising resource, a newly exploitable symbolic asset in the cause of global-city positioning, solicitation and marketing. And 'Pera', with all of its appreciated, accumulated connotations, has become a valued trading brand for local businesses. (And, interestingly, the real significance of this cosmopolitan local history has not entered the discourses of more critically minded constituencies of interest within the Municipality.)

Aspects of cultural governance

In addressing questions of cultural governance within its jurisdiction, there are a number of challenges that Beyoğlu Municipality has to address, according to an order of priorities that it must establish within the frame of its strategic initiatives.

First, there is the question of the rich but decaying historical legacy, now at the disposal of the Municipality. The potential for Beyoğlu as a distinctive, late-Ottoman heritage zone (quite distinct from – albeit very close to – Sultanahmet) has recently come to figure highly on the local authority's policy-cum-enterprise agenda. On the one hand, there is the renewal of what has become a valuable stock of nineteenth-century buildings – buildings that have been re-evaluated, and have now come to seem to be worthy of listed status. The urban fabric of Beyoğlu is characterized by a predominantly neo-classical architectural style (Çelik 1986: 133–137), and has many decent, if not classic, examples of Art Nouveau (Batur 2005). And, on the other, and in parallel development, there is the potential to exploit the image of historic Pera that has now evolved in the form of Pera-nostalgia. 'The name "Pera" started appearing on a number of shop signs, alongside names reminiscent of Greek, Armenian, Jewish or Levantine inhabitants and business owners of a century earlier' (Eldem 2006: 23). Both the inherited built environment of Pera, then, and its memorialized image have become crucial factors to be taken account of in the Municipality's new-generation strategies for city projection, promotion and marketing.

A second issue that the Municipality has to negotiate is also a consequence of the historical legacy of the district, namely its non-Muslim character and lifestyle, which once translated into its distinctive 'West-End' ethos. This is the 'non-tangible' legacy of its *fin-de-siècle* days of restaurants and beer halls, theatres and music halls – the key aspect of Beyoğlu's twenty-first century global-city posturing. These days, the night-life culture of restaurants, bars and clubs is booming as never before. In August 2005, *Newsweek*'s front cover ran the headline 'Cool Istanbul', dubbing it 'Europe's hippest city' (Foroohar and Matthews 2005: 32). And, at the beginning of 2011, the UK *Observer* newspaper

characterized Istanbul as 'the new party capital of Europe', replete with 'boutique hotels, fusion eateries and world music clubs' (Finkel 2011). It is this 'cool' and 'vibrant' Beyoğlu way of life and lifestyle that most closely, and 'classically', corresponds to the ethos of the by now hegemonic (secular, materialistic, commercial) global-city paradigm, nesting, we should emphasize, within a city that is also a pious city.

A third issue concerns contemporary artistic and cultural creativity, for this is also, in the rapidly transforming Istanbul context, what Beyoğlu has come to stand for. It is the locus of a new cultural ferment and inventiveness. In her recent book *Istanbul: Stadt unter Strom* – the sub-title is roughly translatable as 'Electric City' – Sibylle Thelen (2008) observes that, in the recent period, a new generation of artistic and cultural practitioners (from Orhan Pamuk to Nuri Bilge Ceylan to Elif Shafak; from Mercan Dede to Kutluğ Ataman or Fatih Akın) has radically transformed the city's profile, and not least in a wider European and international context (and she is absolutely right to draw attention to the extensive transnational connectedness of Istanbul's new creative milieu). In creative-artistic terms, in terms of the lease of 'new energies' and a newly unleashed 'creative chaos' (2008: 13, 15), Beyoğlu has come to assume a vanguard role in the city. This is where Istanbul's latest generation of cultural practitioners is to be found; it is the district where artists want to be found, and to be found working. As such, *Istanbul: Stadt unter Strom* is effectively, though implicitly, a celebration of Beyoğlu – the district in the city that most evidently fits the bill as 'electric city'. But there is far more to the Beyoğlu artistic phenomenon than this narrative of individual creative presence tells. The Beyoğlu 'arts scene' is a cultural-business scene, too, and has a powerful institutional presence. With their museums, art galleries, research centres, performance spaces, most of the powerful conglomerates of Turkey have their cultural foundations located in Beyoğlu: it is here that we find Istanbul Modern, Pera Museum, the Atatürk Cultural Centre (presently, and controversially, closed for restoration), the Borusan Culture and Arts Centre. Then there are independent enterprises, such as the Babylon music venue, and many, many smaller and flourishing commercial music halls, performance spaces, and avant-garde venues. And, of course, there has been the major coup of the prestigious award of

European Capital of Culture status to Istanbul for 2010 – not just a Beyoğlu achievement, but certainly an achievement that would have been inconceivable without the cultural resources of Beyoğlu. Beyoğlu is, by far, Istanbul's major cultural-artistic asset, with the capacity to generate whatever it is that a twenty-first century global city has the obligation to produce, promote and project. But, it needs to be stressed that a significant portion of the cultural capital of the area accrues from the investment and commitment of private philanthropy and corporate projects of social responsibility, which by their very nature have their own visions and norms about aesthetic and artistic work. They are autonomous players embedded in all kinds of transnational networks of arts and culture thus commanding huge international following. Their power is such that they are able to call the shots in cultural creativity and thus shape Beyoğlu's image.

This takes us to the fourth challenge for cultural policy, which concerns the question of identity. And this is quite a complicated question, particularly in the Beyoğlu context. Two distinct logics are in play. On the one hand, Istanbul has to acknowledge that one of the requirements of a global city is to be cosmopolitan; tourists demand cosmopolitan experiences. And, in the Istanbul context, it is Beyoğlu that stands for the cosmopolitan history and culture of the city. On the other hand, there is a certain official resistance to such an urban identity, and a desire to construct something more 'authentically' Turkish for the new Istanbul. This is most apparent in the conservation-cum-renewal projects in the historic neighbourhoods, and, in Beyoğlu, the Tarlabaşı district presently demonstrates most clearly what is happening. Listed buildings are being targeted to be demolished, to then be replaced by *historical-looking* ones. To be replaced, that is to say, by new structures, with façades remaining intact and the whole interiors modernized. With these urban renewal projects a new style is emerging, which we may call neo-Ottomanism, whereby, through 'façade retension' or 'façadism', a newly-conceived variant of the 'old' is reified and valorized as more acceptable, and marketable, than the dilapidated but nevertheless living 'old' that survived from Beyoğlu's actual past.

Now – our fifth point – we come to the most formidable and, as we will go on to argue, the most decisive aspect of the new urban cultural governance agenda, which is the real-estate side of the cultural economy. Things are in fact more serious and 'for real' than the catchy slogans of 'cool Istanbul' or 'electric city' allow for. Until quite recently, the Istanbul real-estate boom was taking place in the outlying districts of the city, with the construction of shopping malls, office buildings, gated communities and high-rise residential projects. In the recent period, however, we have seen a booming escalation of gentrification developments in the core, historic areas of Istanbul, notably in Sultanahmet, Beyoğlu and Şişli (İslam 2010). Land and property prices are soaring (Sotheby's real-estate arm, International Realty, is presently buying up property in the Galata district of Beyoğlu, until recently a run-down historic neighbourhood). And in this buoyant new economic context, the Beyoğlu Municipality has become extremely proactive and entrepreneurial, pursuing the cause of urban renovation, in the name of both gentrification and the promotion of tourism. With the recently approved Beyoğlu Conservation Plan, there will be a hefty boom in the amount of real-estate investment in the district putting pressure on the city fabric, its identity and its socio-economic character. This is a massive challenge to the Municipality in terms of balancing public and private interests and in being able to ride the storm of private capital influx.

The real life of governance

The concept of 'local governance' has come to take on a positive connotation in the recent literature of urban cultural policy. Somehow this keyword, 'governance', has come to be associated with possibilities of political devolution and decentralization, with a valorization of local civic autonomy, with the advocacy of a new political conduct that is responsive to local access, engagement and participation. We have to say, however, that the recent Beyoğlu experience – in terms of both substantive policy decisions and mode of political operation – belies such constructive anticipation. In the contemporary Istanbul context, the real life of urban governance is a far cry from the democratic possibility.

The everyday real world of local administration here in Istanbul (and, no 'here' is unique any more) is unfortunately a compromised reality. 'Globally-localized', of course you can think of it as such – globalization as experienced at the local level – but this doesn't automatically or necessarily translate into a politics of local democracy. Indeed, it can be said that the conditions of globalization seem now, if anything, to be inhibiting local democracy in the case of Istanbul. There are also active logics of constraint at work, democracy-impeding logics, we have to say. Democracy must always, in some way, be about openness; in principle, at least, it stands for autonomy, choice and attendant possibility. Beyoğlu, in stark contrast, may be taken as a case of a governance system in which decision-making processes have been subordinated to the governing logics of political affiliation and global enterprise, in close collaboration (a system in which local autonomy is occluded, and localization is quite compatible with authoritarianism).

How does cultural governance take shape in Beyoğlu, then, in the real-world context of contemporary, 'globalizing' Istanbul? How is the Beyoğlu local government dealing with the challenges we outlined above? According to its ambitious Mayor:

We are reshaping whole Beyoğlu from one end to the other. We are installing street lighting; we're pioneering in restoration of civil structures and monumental works. Beyoğlu is a district which has spearheaded change in Turkey since the day of its inception. From fashion to banking, from recreation to culture, literature to cinema, architecture to sculptures with a broad spectrum approach it has renewed itself through history, has been a source for the renovation of the country. Beyoğlu once again owns up to this innovation spirit which it has stayed behind. We are preparing hundreds of projects for Beyoğlu. (Beyoğlu Municipality n.d.)

Reshaping, installing, pioneering, spearheading... This is all about the marketing of 'brand Beyoğlu'. In understanding the nature of this response, there is a structural aspect to be addressed, concerning the nature of the relation between the local and the central and between public and private interests.

First, the logic of political affiliation has a clear significance. The local authority of Beyoğlu is under the control of the conservative and religiously-oriented AKP (the Justice and Development Party), which also controls the Metropolitan Municipality, and which for some eight years now has been the ruling national party of Turkey. The logic of ideological and cultural affiliation operates within

a powerful and decisive logic of globalization, and characterized by global-city formation. As a party committed to neo-liberal economics, the AKP is fully committed to globalization and its consequences, as its leader, Recep Tayyip Erdoğan, has made abundantly clear. Committed, therefore, to making Istanbul a fully operational global metropolis (Aksoy 2008). We see that local authorities governed by AKP are equally engaged in the globalization agenda, and in the context of the devolution of power to the local level since the arrival of AKP to the central government, local municipalities have been embellished with more power to put into effect their visions (Aksoy 2009). The vision of local politicians these days is articulated in terms of making their cities competitive, branding and marketing them as attractive locations for investors, tourists and consumers – entrepreneurialism in local government is now a readily accepted, and indeed expected, practice. At every level of government, then, from the district of Beyoğlu to the metropolitan level of Istanbul to the central government level, Istanbul's strategy to become a global city is being shared and put into action. Culture, of course, takes on a whole new significance in this new environment of local enterprise. Cultural heritage and cultural industries have now come to be acknowledged as forces of attraction, as projectors of identity, and as generators of wealth. (And, of course, in this domain of operation, in terms of both the ancient and the modern, bountifully-endowed Beyoğlu no doubt sits in prime position.) Local entrepreneurialism receives support from the state in the form of legal and regulatory changes, including a controversial new law for the 'renewal' of historic areas (Law No. 5366), in addition to well-financed programmes for the development and promotion of the city's cultural and tourism infrastructure, as it was the case in the Istanbul 2010 European Capital of Culture programme where central government committed an investment equivalent to the Ministry of Culture and Tourism's annual budget towards the restoration and regeneration of the city's cultural heritage. Law No. 5366 (for the 'Preservation by Renovation and Utilization by Revitalizing of Deteriorated Immovable Historical and Cultural Properties') is a good example here to demonstrate the determination of local and central governments to push the agenda of urban regeneration for the purposes of city marketing and the ensuing result of the arrival of very powerful new players into the stakeholder map of the city. This law gives extraordinary powers to local authorities to declare urban renewal areas, and to implement development plans in run-down areas within historic – and often, indeed, 'deteriorated' – cultural sites.

The structural position, then, in which Beyoğlu Municipality finds itself is actually one of demo-cratic inhibition and restriction. On the political side, there is pressure from central government and from the Istanbul Metropolitan Municipality to carry out large-scale renewal projects. Pressure to conform, that is to say, to what has become a standard, imposed model for urban development. It would be politically unthinkable for Beyoğlu to buck the trend. And, to add to this, there is now pressure and con-straint from economic and entrepreneurial inter-ests, too. A great deal of potential development, a great deal of money to be made – and, for the Municipality, economic development possibilities (and prestige, too). In this complex force field of motivations and invested interests, there is minimal room for manoeuvre. Exceptionalism has no place in the overall planning logic in play. Local autonomy is not an issue to be addressed.

We come now to a second aspect of the way in which the actual dynamics of globalization are shaping, and determining, cultural politics, govern-ance and policy in Istanbul. This concerns how the structural relations and forces that we have just been outlining become translated into a rationale of purpose, a programme of action, a determination of priorities. This is to shift from structural to substan-tive issues. What has taken shape under the present administration? What logics of develop-ment have come into play as a consequence of the new political and economic partnerships and alli-ances? What has happened in the real world of cultural policy and governance in Istanbul and Beyoğlu?

The Beyoğlu Conservation Area Plan

Let us draw attention to the core constellation of objectives that seem now to be most central to the urban cultural initiative of Beyoğlu Municipality (they are not the only concerns of the Municipality – but we suggest that they are the primary ones). These privileged objectives are all direct outcomes of the AKP's overt globalizing ambitions, in which Istanbul

is to be made the principal stage for demonstrating to the world Turkey's global status. First, and funda-mentally, there is the emphasis on upgrading the district. This amounts to extensive gentrification projects, and the only way to achieve this objective seems to actively involve big-league private-sector interests and resources. And, at the present historical moment, given the long neglect of Istanbul's historic, inner-city districts over decades, there are massive 'cleaning-up' opportunities to be had. The modernization 'delay' in Istanbul – Çağlar Keyder (2010: 32) characterizes it in terms of the 'final commodification of land' – turns out to now provide a major opportunity, in terms of twenty-first century investment and development opportunities. The pursuit of gentrification, conducted in the name of revitalization and upgrading goes hand in hand with the desire for image transformation. That – urban image re-design – is a second cultural objec-tive, presented as an imperative: to make Beyoğlu look, as the mayor Ahmet Misbah Demircan has put it, like Champs-Élysées (*Hürriyet* 2009) – rather than the dilapidated relic of a weary old Ottoman city that Orhan Pamuk (2005) has, all too graphi-cally, and famously, and globally, depicted. A cam-paign of strategic image-projection, in order to correct, or to vanquish, decades, at least, of per-ceived image-deficit in the eyes of the outside world.

Second is the new identity and function attributed to Beyoğlu. The Beyoğlu Conservation Area Plan (actually prepared by the Metropolitan Municipality), which was made public at the beginning of 2011 (Beyoğlu Municipality 2011) – made quietly public (we say this because the Plan was initially avail-able only at a seriously prohibitive price, and only made reasonably accessible after public protest) – re-affirms the local government's new vision of Beyoğlu. It is a plan that makes apparent the priori-ties of the governing political mindset – by now conventional global-minded priorities.

So, just what are the points of priority in this Plan? What are the points of emphasis? The first and essential point to be made is that the Plan indeed has a pre-eminent emphasis on real-estate development, across a premium zone of three square kilometres of this inner-city municipality. The detailed, parcel-level focus is intended to maximize real-estate investment possibilities in a neighbourhood that cannot expand because of its very central location (Ünlü Yücesoy 2008). Thus, out of the total 10,000 or so properties in the area, the ones which are not listed, 5,800 of them become potential targets for real-estate development with no conservation restrictions attached. Hence the size of new construction activity that will be descending on the district is evident.

The Plan clearly aims to create gentrified, cleaned out, and upgraded built environments that are deemed to be attractive for tourists and for moneyed classes. This new class of users and residents are what the Municipality is after and the Beyoğlu Plan has been very clearly shaped by this prerogative. Greater commercialization and the promotion of tourism as engines of economic growth constitute, then, the main gist of Beyoğlu Municipality's vision for the area. According to this new image, all the functions that do not fit in with the projected new identity of the Municipality are targeted to be moved out, and in their place new functions that are in harmony with this identity are to be installed. What this amounts to is the removal of all the established manufacturing activities and warehouses that came to inhabit different parts of the district, and which gave it its social character. Lighting equipment producers, household appliances producers, furniture-makers, jewellery-makers, the wholesale of construction materials and of car parts, etc. – these are all set to move (or, rather, be moved) out of the area. In their place will be new, up-market leisure and consumption spaces, to compete with the many others that have been proliferating all across Istanbul in the last ten years.

Upgrading of historical stock, so imagined, will also serve to 'improve' the image and identity of the district. The themes of tourism, consumerism, image and identity are tightly interwoven. In this same cause of image improvement, and with the same eye on tourism, the Plan identifies specific areas for cultural establishments to be situated. The most important of these are the Haliç Shipyard Area, the Tepebaşı district and Tophane. What is significant is that Haliç Shipyard area and Tepebaşı areas are both being transferred to major private groups. Haliç Shipyard area has been given to the Koç company, to be turned into an industrial museum complex; and the Tepebaşı area was earmarked to another major industrial conglomerate, the Suna and İnan Kıraç Foundation, which has explored the possibilities – without success as yet – of a Frank Gehry-designed opera house there. Tophane is the only district in which there are small and individually-run art establishments in operation – also, of course, part (a small part) of the gentrification moment. However, considering that Tophane is in the catchment area of Galataport – a major cruise ship development close by, on the Bosphorus – it is likely that there will be a huge rent increase in Tophane, eventually driving the small galleries out. This is, of course, the logic of the big gentrification – the logic of the Conservation Area Plan that seeks to override the piecemeal (disorganized) everyday life of the citizens of Beyoğlu – what Alan Blum (2010: 66–67) calls the vital 'sense of continuity and consequentiality' necessary to their lives in the city, vitally necessary for them to be able 'to imagine themselves as mattering'.

Civic atmosphere

We are by now a long way from 'cool' and 'electric'… We come to the real heart of the matter – the crucial heart: to the social realities of Beyoğlu, which have no place in the scheme of urban renewal as developed in the Plan. We have already suggested that the new developments in Beyoğlu – from cultural and heritage installations through to shopping centres and leisure spaces – are intended primarily for visitors, for consumers and tourists. We want to reflect now on the implications of this prioritization, with its consequent and effective disavowal of the realities – the aspirations and the demands – of the populations living in the Municipality. These demands include a sense of continuity, to pick up again on Alan Blum's (2010: 66) formulation, but also the more ambitious ideal of 'being of consequence, of ambition, expectation, and opportunity…' For Blum, a creative urban environment is one that can sustain 'the image of a normal life that is treated inspirationally as the exemplary life, valued as a life worth living and that matters and that makes a difference at any present defining moment'. An idealistic formulation: that urban citizens would demand a future of consequence. And, in the new Beyoğlu context, this aspiration has been disturbed and unsettled, and in its place there is now a sense of impermanence and vulnerability – of radical inconsequentiality.

Some 15 years ago, Stéphane Yerasimos (1997: 213) characterized the then occurring processes of gentrification in Beyoğlu in terms of a 're-conquest of the centre' by the middle classes. Since the 1960s, many parts of the then abandoned centre had been occupied by migrants from Anatolia, driven from the land and looking for a foothold in the city. What developed in the process was an informal, and invariably illegal, settlement pattern and economy. It was chaotic, and at times precarious, but it worked as a functioning system, creating its own distinctive mechanisms and drawing upon its own collective and patrimonial resources. The beginnings of the middle-class 'reconquest' of that time, mostly in the Cihangir district, were also, in their own way, informal – Eda Ünlü Yücesoy (2008: 38) writes of 'the amorphous, individual-driven character of the gentrification process'. Composed for the most part of what are frequently referred to as bourgeois-bohemians (those working in the creative and social professions – media, advertising, design, fashion, architecture, NGO activists, etc.), these were individual gentrifiers, drawn by the attractive housing stock of Cihangir, but also concerned with the improvement of the social and cultural environment. These incomers had a strong sense of the virtues of informal association and of the vital significance of public space and culture. Over time, then, Beyoğlu developed a very mixed demography: poor Anatolian migrants, the creative-professional middle classes (of cool Istanbul), as well as Roma/Gypsies, Kurdish refugees, transnational migrants (including many Africans). A heterogeneous population that came together over time, each group finding a place according to its means, all of them finding some means to coexist, even to acknowledge their place in the overall diversity and complexity that had taken shape. Over time, the gathering of different social and cultural constituencies, creating in the process a kind of contemporary cosmopolitanism – the elements of a cosmopolitan potential, at least. They are the co-producers of a distinctive urban atmosphere – of the mixed atmosphere of Beyoğlu.

But the re-conquest of the centre has now taken a new proportion and character. No longer the affair of individual gentrifiers, now it is a question of the moneyed middle classes, and of a more systematic takeover, driven by systemic corporate and political interests. Then there is the conquest of the idea of Beyoğlu: that is, the generalization of chosen styles of building types and urban fabric from the Ottoman period, and their reification as the 'authentic' culture of Beyoğlu. What this amounts to is that the whole area becomes ossified as a museum piece and a new norm is set, what we

may term 'neo-Ottomanism', in architecture and design. In the end, this it what the Beyoğlu Plan is all about. The consequences of this next phase of the re-conquest for Beyoğlu – in social, cultural, and human terms – are immense. First, there is the continued marginalization and exclusion of the poor and of those marked as undesirable (Yardımcı 2010). Their vital interests suppressed, they are to be driven from the urban centre and thereby from social visibility. Second, what we are seeing at the same time is a calculated assault on the principle of informality, which has been a significant factor, a social and organizational resource we can say, in the practices of daily life in Istanbul. Informality may readily translate into autonomy, partial at least. The new re-conquest is clearly about the extensive assertion of control over the urban space. And, third, what is now being deconstructed is the social ecology that has developed over the years in Beyoğlu, accommodating a diversity and complexity of groups. Let us not idealize it, but let us acknowledge the establishment of a certain *modus vivendi*, a manner and idiom of coexistence of different ways and trajectories of life, the exercise of what we might call reasonable association. What is happening with respect to architecture and urban design – standardization, that is to say – is also being applied as a corresponding principle of modernization and homogenization in the social and cultural domain. What is required is a demographic profile in keeping with the objectives of the Beyoğlu Plan.

A case in point

Boğazkesen Street runs down from İstiklal Caddesi, the former Grande Rue de Péra, to the neighbourhood of Tophane, and from there you can walk on in just a few minutes to the Istanbul Modern. Tophane is a poor inner-city district, the living space of conservative and religious migrants from Anatolia. However, given its recent corridor status between cultural spaces, it has recently become the location of around a dozen small, commercial art galleries. On the evening of 21 September 2010, an attack occurred on a number of these galleries, in which visitors to gallery openings were assaulted and injured by locals wielding sticks, knives, broken bottles and pepper spray. Why? It was quickly argued that this was a conflict between religious and secular cultures, with religious conservatives objecting to young gallery visitors drinking alcohol on the street outside the galleries, and/or to being disrespectful to women in the street wearing headscarves. And it was also said that some of the 'taboo-breaking' gallery exhibits were offensive to both Islam and to Mustafa Kemal Atatürk, the founder of the Turkish Republic. On the basis of a further reflection, it was suggested that a major factor of provocation had been the logic of rapid gentrification in the neighbourhood: that local inhabitants were becoming agitated and concerned by the newly opening galleries, and also by the proliferation of alcohol-serving restaurants and apartment hotels, all of which were conspiring to push up rents, and were creating anxiety among the established residents about their ability to maintain their hold on livelihood in Tophane.

It was a street confrontation, a localized conflict. But it turned out to be much more too: to be a resonant event, a symbolic encounter – concerning dispossession, enforced displacement, the uncivil force of urban enclosures. It proved to be an event conveying the fact of a deep divide of interests, and the fact, too, that there is no longer trust among the vulnerable populations of the city. One artist recalled an assailant shouting out 'You don't want us, so we don't want you'. Two days after what he dubbed the 'incident', the Turkish Culture Minister visited Tophane and called for 'tolerance'. 'Those who present the incident in Tophane as a panorama of Turkey are engaged in an extremely stale game', declared the Prime Minister of Turkey, no less. Clearly the Ministers, Cultural and Prime, were quickly aware that the 'incident' had a swirling gravity. What happened in Tophane actually is clearly telling us something significant about what is going on in Istanbul generally these days. It is telling us something about the atmosphere of the city, the sensed atmosphere, about the city's grave mood at this time.

REFERENCES

Aksoy, A. (2008) 'Istanbul's choice', *Third Text*, 22(1): 71–83.

Aksoy, A. (2009) 'The Atatürk Cultural Centre and AKP's "mind shift" policy', pp. 191–212 in Ada, S. and İnce, A. H. (eds), *Introduction to Cultural Policy in Turkey*. Istanbul: İstanbul Bilgi University Press.

Aksoy, A. and Robins, K. (2011) 'History, memory, debris: Sulukule, don't forget', pp. 222–230 in Anheier, H. K. and Isar, Y.R. (eds), *Heritage, Memory & Identity. The Cultures and Globalization Series 4*. London: SAGE.

Batur, A. (2005) 'Art nouveau architecture and Istanbul', pp. 141–166 in editor? *Art Nouveau from Europe to Istanbul, 1890–1930*. Istanbul: Tarih Vakfı.

Beyoğlu Municipality (n.d.) 'Beyoğlu as a brand', available at: http://en.beyoglu.bel.tr/our_brands/default.aspx?SectionId=1680 (accessed 10 February 2011).

Beyoğlu Municipality (2011) *Beyoğlu Kentsel Sit Alanı Koruma Amaçlı Uygulama İmar Planı Raporu* [Beyoğlu Urban Conservation Area Building Works Implementation Plan for Conservation], published on the website of the Beyoğlu Municipality, www.beyoglu.bel.tr/beyoglu_belediyesi/haber_default.aspx?SectionId=143&ContentId=31698.

Blum, A. (2010) 'Reflections on the platitude of the "creative city"', pp. 65–95 in Boutros, A. and Straw, W. (eds), *Circulation and the City: Essays on Urban Culture*. Montreal & Kingston: McGill-Queen's University Press.

Böhme, G. (1993) 'Atmosphere as the fundamental concept of a new aesthetics'. *Thesis Eleven*, 36: 113–126.

Böhme, G. (2006) *Architektur und Atmosphäre*. Munich: Wilhelm Fink.

Çelik, Z. (1986) *The Remaking of Istanbul: Portrait of an Ottoman City in the Nineteenth Century*. Seattle, WA: University of Washington Press.

De Amicis, E. (2005) [1877] *Constantinople*. London: Hesperus.

Eldem, E. (2006) 'Ottoman Galata and Pera between myth and reality', pp. 18–36 in Tischler, U. (ed.), *From 'Milieu de Mémoire' to 'Lieu de Mémoire': The Cultural Memory of Istanbul in the 20th Century*. Munich: Martin Meidenbauer.

Eldem, S. H. (1979) *Istanbul Anıları/Reminiscences of Istanbul*. Istanbul: Aletaş Alarko Eğitim Tesisleri.

Finkel, A. (2011) 'Istanbul thrives as the new party capital of Europe', *Observer*, 2 January.

Foroohar, R. and Matthews, O. (2005) 'Turkish delight', *Newsweek*, 29 August: 31–34.

Hürriyet (2009) 'Istikal caddesine Şanzelize modeli', 3 August.

İslam, T. (2010) '30 Jahre Abenteuer: Gentrifizierung in Istanbul', pp. 69–80 in Pschera, M., İlk, Ç. and Bacık, Ç. (eds), *Intercity Istanbul–Berlin*. Berlin: Dağyeli.

Keyder, Ç. (2010) 'Istanbul into the twenty-first century', pp. 25–34 in Göktürk, D., Soysal, L. and Türeli, İ. (eds), *Orienting Istanbul: Cultural Capital of Europe?* London: Routledge.

Naum-Duhani, S. (1947) *Vieilles gens, vieilles demeures: topographie sociale de Beyoğlu au XIXème siècle*. Istanbul: Editions du Touring et Automobile Club de Turquie.

Naum-Duhani, S. (1956) *Quand Beyoğlu s'appelait Péra: les temps qui ne reviendront plus*. Istanbul: Edition 'La Turquie Moderne'.

Pamuk, O. (2005) *Istanbul: Memories of a City*. London: Faber and Faber.

Swyngedouw, E. (2010) 'City or polis? Profitable politics... or the end of the political', pp. 214–233 in Buijs, S., Tan, W. and Tunas, D. (eds), *Megacities: Exploring a Sustainable Future*. Rotterdam: 010 Publishers.

Thelen, S. (2008) *Istanbul: Stadt unter Strom*. Freiburg: Herder.

Tischler, U. (2006) 'Retour aux sources: indicateurs identitaires à Péra comme *milieu de mémoire*', pp. 38–58 in Tischler, U. (ed.), *From 'Milieu de Mémoire' to 'Lieu de Mémoire': The Cultural Memory of Istanbul in the 20th Century*. Munich: Martin Meidenbauer.

Ünlü Yücesoy, E. (2008) 'Contested public spaces vs. conquered public spaces: gentrification and its reflections on urban public space in Istanbul', pp. 29–47 in Eckardt, F. and Wildner, K. (eds), *Public Istanbul: Spaces and Spheres of the Urban*. Bielefeld: transcript.

Yardımcı, S. (2010) 'La face cachée de la métropole', *Urbanisme*, 374: 71–73.

Yerasimos, S. (1997) 'Istanbul: la naissance d'une mégapole', *Revue Géographique de l'Est*, 37(2–3): 189–215.

CHAPTER 17

JOHANNESBURG: INVESTING IN CULTURAL ECONOMIES OR PUBLICS?

Edgar Pieterse and Kim Gurney

In the dramatic governance reforms Johannesburg has undergone since 1994, the metropolitan government has sought to play a key transformative role in a context where the formal economy served mainly the white middle classes and undermined the prospects of the black majority, structurally excluded during the apartheid era. The potential of urban culture as part of a larger tourism and development strategy was identified in the early stages. The strategies subsequently implemented included the development of a 'cultural arc' sweeping through the inner city, with the area of Newtown at its core. The authors' analysis of this flagship initiative articulates tensions in urban regeneration between economic development with a cultural bent and its externalities, social and otherwise. It shows how global policy trends have been followed locally, revealing the contradictions arising from a 'creative cities' discourse and related boosterism strategies. Because these have created an enabling environment for property

investors, exacerbating lines of exclusion, the authors advocate a shift in emphasis to socio-cultural and ecological frames and newly imagined publics.

Introduction

South Africans are adept at negotiating the vicissitudes of globalization. The advent of democracy took place in the wake of the collapse of the Berlin Wall and within just a few years, the national liberation movement had to find its political feet in a world of ideological flux and deep-seated uncertainty. This was a profound challenge given the long-term imbrication of African nationalism and Soviet-style socialist ideas that marked the body politic of the liberation movements. The much celebrated South African Constitution (circa 2003 and finalized in 2006) and relatively peaceful transition to majority rule in 1994 reflect the capacity for localization of numerous global political and development discourses in circulation at the time. The political deal and associated developmental project post-1994 was an astute combination of liberal democratic, free market, social democratic and participatory democratic tenets, institutions and policy ambitions (Pieterse and van Donk, 2002). It worked relatively well to provide a framework for effecting the political transition from racist apartheid rule to democratic governance but remained unproven as a viable approach to deal with economic and cultural inclusion.

The city of Johannesburg is at the heart of the Southern African economy and unsurprisingly boasts the wealthiest metropolitan government. 'Joburg metro', as it is colloquially known, is also one of the most ambitious and interesting components of the state when it comes to figuring out how to position the city in relation to complex and dynamic regional and global flows of people, finance and ideas. Thus, since the inception of a unified metropolitan government in 2000, this metro has been actively engaged in carving out an endogenous set of policies to deal with tough competing pressures. For example, the wealth of the city resides in the northern suburbs with the new finan-cial hub, Sandton, at its economic core. Owing to unprecedented private investment in commercial, retail, and private estates, Joburg metro (also referred to as the City) is confronted with massive infrastructural investment pressures to accommo-date and reinforce this growth, manifested most acutely in garish commercial and retail property developments (Murray, 2008). This growth pressure is reinforced by the fact that the City derives 75 per cent of its revenue from property taxes and other local tariff streams. At the same time, the City is also confronted with the massive apartheid legacy of inadequate and slum housing to the south that, due to existing levels of poverty and economic isolation and sustained in-migration, also requires massive infrastructural investments. Due to high levels of unemployment (30 per cent) and poverty, many households within these constituencies cannot cover the full costs of these investments and effec-tively represent a permanent drain on the City's fiscal resources. However, the ruling ANC draws its electoral support from constituencies in these sub-urbs (known colloquially as townships and informal settlements) and therefore tries to find a magical balance by making expensive capital investments in both the north and south of the City. This triggers all manner of political and social conflicts and a variety of unintended consequences such as sprawl, which entrench severe social and class divides.

Equidistant to the north and south lies the old soul of the city: the Johannesburg inner city. This is the site where the city found its voice with the dis-covery of gold and other minerals at the end of the nineteenth century and where the colonial project was anchored during the heady decades of mod-ernization and industrialization. It hosted the origi-nal central business district and all the largest financial interests that grew up and wealthy around the mineral-industrial economy that continues to underwrite the South African economy (Parnell and Pirie, 1991). As the cradle of urbanism, the inner city also reflects the tumultuous socio-cultural his-tory of racial, ethnic and class conflicts as waves of migration and fierce political contests played them-selves out on the streets of the inner city (Parnell, 2003). Fast-forward to the dawn of democracy in the early 1990s and this same site had become the embodiment of both capital and white flight leaving the debris of deindustrialization and long-term pub-lic neglect in its wake (Beall et al., 2002).

In the first few years of democratic local govern-ment, the City had no choice but to confront the challenges and opportunities that the inner city represented; not least because the headquarters of the Council resided there. In some ways, the inner city became the litmus test for the new City govern-ment because if it were incapable of reversing decline in this area, it had no chance of turning around the fortunes of the larger metropolitan area. The urgency and potentiality of the inner city ben-efited from an interesting and idiosyncratic set of dynamics that has been playing out on the ground since the 1980s, which reinforced the potential for imaginative and meaningful urban renewal.

In this chapter, we provide a highly stylized account of the efforts by the Joburg metro and associated public bodies to use a cultural lens to drive an ambitious area-based urban renewal strat-egy during 2000–2010. This policy agenda was heavily influenced and shaped by globalized dis-courses on 'creative cities', but also profoundly rooted in local processes, struggles and agendas of strong-willed actors. We draw attention to a cen-tral dilemma that the City faces: How does one use cultural-based approaches to urban regeneration and not simultaneously worsen social divisions and lines of exclusion? We further enquire whether the experiences of Johannesburg demonstrate that the globally pervasive creative cities discourses on urban renewal are fundamentally flawed because they fail to address how underlying social and eco-nomic inequalities need more than just an agglom-eration of talent and creative firms plugged into inviting streetscapes, ICT clouds, social networks and engaging cultural infrastructures. By posing this question we assume that global symbolic (and financial) flows are not uni-directional but always the product of both localization and re-export – a dynamic that is part and parcel of the multi-dir-ectionality of global ideas and cultural practices (Appadurai, 1996; Clifford, 1994; Hall, 1991).

The next section provides a synoptic overview of the institutional architecture that surrounds the regeneration of the inner city and a specific geo-graphic swathe within it dubbed the 'Cultural Arc'. Thereafter, we shift register and tone and provide a stylized sense of the various agendas, actors, co-incidences and tensions that bubbled to the surface as the state endeavoured to bring the arc to life through substantial public investment into various precincts and infrastructures. This covers the period during 1998–2010, with a few historical references that reach back into the 1980s when Newtown in particular (a key node in the arc) was identified as a site ripe for cultural renewal. We conclude this inevitably partial account with a set of reflections on what this case study means for our broader search for the dynamics of cultural politics in the context of intensified processes of globalization. But first it is essential to locate this narrative with some institutional contextualization.

Institutional architecture

Inner city regeneration is a complex and multidisciplinary task, requiring a range of skills and a high level of coordination across functional departments. The City of Johannesburg has established a core capacity to manage this complex process. This capacity comprises a dedicated Member of the Mayoral Committee, two dedicated Inner City committees, the Johannesburg Development Agency (JDA), and a Region 8 Task Team. (City of Johannesburg, 2006: 193)

To make sense of this assertion by the City, it is important to explain in brief the overall institutional architecture of the metro. Joburg metro, as a single-tier structure, came into legal being in December 2000 under the Mayorship of Amos Masondo. Before this restructuring of local government, Johannesburg was governed by a two-tier metropolitan system, which reflected the earlier round of institutional amalgamation to incorporate the asymmetrical, racially-defined local government structures from the apartheid era. The two-tier system was unwieldy and caused a financial collapse of the city's finances in 1997/1998, which in turn sparked a period of intense structural adjustment and institutional reform with strong neo-liberal overtones (Gotz et al., 2011). In more practical terms, the two-tier system also made area-based integrated development programming impossible. For example, the inner city was sliced into three sections by virtue of the boundaries of the sub-metropolitan councils that governed the area (City of Johannesburg, 2006). With the establishment of a single-tier metropolitan government at the end of December 2000, there was a powerful drive to streamline and rationalize the service delivery functions of the Council.

Thus, one of the key features of the newly established metropolitan municipality of Johannesburg was the inauguration of a number of arms-length service delivery entities or special purpose vehicles. These 'utilities', or 'municipal-owned entities', have been set up as private companies, albeit ones wholly owned by the City and that operate under the mandate of City leaders to achieve clear service-delivery objectives. At the same time, the entire metropolitan area was divided into 11 regions to promote more effective urban management. Significantly, these regions are not independent substructures, with their own budgets and powers. The inner city correlated more or less with Region 8, which reinforced the possibility of a more coherent development approach to the territory.

The governance and implementation authorities represented a complex mosaic of actors, networks and counterveiling dynamics. The lead political body was a Section 80 committee, dedicated to the inner city, made up of Joburg councillors. This political committee was formally advised by a Section 79 committee that comprised 'the Member of the Mayoral Committee responsible for the inner city; relevant Ward Councillors and PR [proportional representative] Councillors; the Johannesburg Inner City Business Coalition; the Johannesburg Inner City Community Forum; representatives from the Council's utilities and agencies, the Metropolitan Trading Company (Pty) Ltd and the Johannesburg Development Agency (Pty) Ltd; representatives from the Association of Social Housing Organizations and other relevant NGOs; representatives of Provincial Government; and representatives of the Provincial Legislature' (City of Johannesburg, 2006: 194). At a more technical and operational level, another structure was brought into being: the Region 8 Inner City Task Team. Across these different bodies, a single 'Inner City Regeneration Business Plan' was produced to underpin and guide the investments made to translate the inner-city vision and strategy into material realities with generative effects. The pivotal player in this soup bowl of actors and interests was the Johannesburg Development Agency (JDA), which took the lead in conceptualizing and driving the catalytic investments contained in the plan (interview, Gotz, 17 March 2011).

The JDA took the lead in identifying a range of substantial investment projects to lay the foundation towards the realization of a vision that sought to transform the inner city into the following:

[A] Dynamic city that works; is liveable, safe, well-managed and welcoming; is people-centred, accessible and celebrates cultural diversity; is vibrant and operates 24-hours a day; a city for residents, workers, tourists, entrepreneurs and learners; a city focused on the 21st Century and is truly global; a city which respects its heritage; and a city which is a trading hub of Africa, thriving through participation, partnerships and the spirit of Ubuntu. (City of Johannesburg, 2006: 195)

An easy but lazy move could be to zoom in on all the policy clichés in this statement that confirm discursive consistencies with various free-floating ideas about becoming a 24/7 mixed-use, vibrant nerve centre for creativity and talent. On the basis of the data we have collected, one is indeed able to tell a compelling story about the oppressive and exclusionary impacts the projects that seek to advance this vision have had over the course of the past decade. However, this is not the occasion for that line of argument and others have made it in compelling ways (Dinath, 2006: 151; Gaule, 2005; Matlaba, 2007: 112–113; Murray, 2008; Virasamy, 2010: 34, 74–75). Instead, we now turn to one element in the over-arching inner-city renewal strategy that sought to turn around a very depressed and run down area with rich historical, heritage and cultural layers and institutions – the Cultural Arc, anchored in Newtown.

Fostering renewal along the Cultural Arc

A powerful animating notion gave form and focus to the desire of many actors and groups to salvage Newtown and associated nodes across the inner city. This was the idea of a Cultural Arc that arose in Newtown, extended across the railway track to Braamfontein, taking in the University of Witwatersrand (Wits) and following up Braamfontein hill to Joburg Theatre (renamed in 2009 from the Civic Theatre) and the Constitution Hill precinct that abuts the notorious Hillbrow area, but contentiously stopping short of the Johannesburg Art Gallery in the city's eastern district (see Figure 17.1). The conceptual framework behind the Cultural Arc was initiated by a Wits academic Carolyn Hamilton. A key architect who worked in this space during this period, Monica Albonico, says the concept was comprehensive, motivated in part by the City's recognition that Newtown's public-sector regeneration driver would require a broader cluster of dynamic support, including private investment and the educational

Figure 17.1 Detail of the 'Cultural Arc' in the inner city of Johannesburg (Newtown)

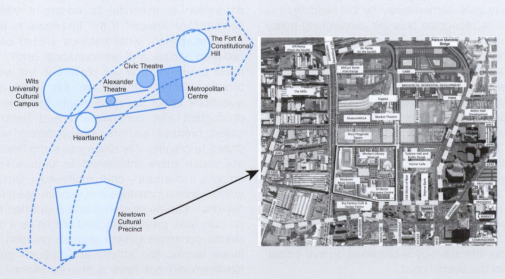

institutions based in Braamfontein (interview, 2 March 2011). Stephen Hobbs, co-director of The Trinity Session, which has managed public art projects with the JDA, says the arc was a powerful way to rethink the inner city as a new millennium project and it tapped into an existing consciousness to set up a dialogue between Newtown and Constitution Hill: 'It was always nodally focused with public environment upgrades that facilitated pedestrian access, with transport infrastructure to improve that experience, and with linkages like the [Nelson] Mandela bridge' (interview, 22 February 2011).

The Cultural Arc resonated well with a related study by Avril Joffe on the prospects for a creative economy cluster in the inner city (Creative Strategy Consulting, 1999). She suggested that:

> *Newtown ... could stand out as South Africa's premier example of urban regeneration and as a metaphor for our ability to transform the old and the dying into the new and the alive. The vision we have arrived at for Newtown is inspired by the many successful 'cultural quarters' around the world. Underpinning this vision is a detailed examination of the Creative Industries and their growth and potential in the greater Johannesburg region. Included here is the film and television, music, multimedia and craft industries. (Creative Strategy Consulting, 1999: 6)*

This assertion underscores the fact that global discourses were very powerful in shaping the policy imaginary about how to understand, read and potentially recast the potential of the territory. But before one gets carried away by this reading, it is important to recognize how the overarching policy framework for inner-city renewal came to overdetermine the calculus about what should happen in Newtown and, most importantly, how to sequence investments. In appreciating the sequencing of investments, one can get some sense of the underlying logic of renewal efforts.

In brief, the Inner City Renewal Strategy operates on the following series of policy tenets. The overriding goal is to 'raise and sustain private investment leading to rise [sic] in property values' (City of Johannesburg, 2006: 196). Since the primary objective is to raise property values, the supporting elements of the strategy centre on reducing the risk associated with investing in this area. Concretely, the strategy is premised on five 'pillars' to achieve the overall goal:

1 Effective urban management, which boils down to by-law enforcement, managing informal trade, and keeping the public realm safe and pristine.
2 Infrastructure maintenance and upgrade to raise the investment viability of the area.
3 Support for existing and latent economic sectors.
4 Identification and removal of so-called sinkholes, which refer to buildings and properties that are in disrepair, overcrowded, abandoned, or poorly maintained, because these are seen as toxic to overall property values.
5 Targeting ripple-bond investments, which represent public investments, to coincide with private investments to make these more secure and surrounded by a favourable environment (City of Johannesburg, 2006).

It is against this policy mindset and economic considerations that the culture-based strategy for the Cultural Arc needs to be considered.

Interviews with key informants and various policy documents of the JDA, Blue IQ and the City's Department of Arts, Culture and Heritage all confirm that Newtown was seen as an ideal location for a culturally-focused renewal strategy because of the existing artistic institutions and spaces and earlier histories of it being a bohemian convergence point of sorts even during the apartheid years. However, how best to promote and embed a cultural hub was and remains deeply contested. For example, how much artistic institutional density and practice needs to live at the core of the broader cultural frame? Also, how much of the artistic production is essential to ensure a vibrant art consumption space? If the emphasis is primarily on consumption, what balance should be struck between visual and performance arts? Beyond these questions that vex players in the art world, broadly defined, there are the much tougher questions about the relationship between artistic production and consumption and broader so-called creative sectors. Policy actors who are drawn to creative city discourses and frameworks are much more interested to understand how creative industries – craft, multimedia, film and television, music industries and various design-related sectors – can be clustered and supported to scale up their size, productivity and output as a driver of overall economic growth and job creation. Amidst these issues, the artistic and cultural groups in Newtown did not have a shared vision. And as tends to happen with cultural organizations, the dynamics between these actors and organizations were marked by fragmentation, minor competition and often disconnect (Shand, 2011).

The first major intervention into the Cultural Arc geography was to facilitate mobility and access. Thus, key to activating these 'nodes' along the arc was building the Nelson Mandela Bridge in 2003, in addition to two on- and off-ramps that allowed ease of access from the inner ring road that circumscribes the inner city. The priority was turning the highly symbolic and resonant Mary Fitzgerald Square at Newtown's centre into a public events space. According to the JDA's former CEO Lael Bethlehem, the next pillar was the establishment of a commercial office development, 1 Central Place. This facilitated attracting A-grade private investment into Newtown, which was, significantly, led by mining group AngloGold Ashanti. It redeveloped the Turbine Hall, a derelict former power station, that became the group's new inner-city headquarters. The other early investment was into a major social housing project, called Brickfields, which was targeted at upper working-class and professional groups who could not access public or private housing markets. In light of the tenets of the overall inner-city renewal strategy, Bethlehem confirms that these initiatives created a favourable platform for attracting particular kinds of investment:

What happens when there is urban decline is you have a break in the normal property cycle. ... People stop reinvesting in the buildings and nobody will buy them. So basically the public environment upgrade and the various interventions are to create a platform so that private property owners will come back in. (Interview, 17 February 2011)

Bethlehem is clear that investment is the JDA priority. When questioned about the criticism that Newtown is sometimes perceived as having lost an edgier cultural programming along the way, she reposts: 'I suppose sometimes the edgier cultural elements come in with an edgier environment. And the truth is from the city's point of view, our aspiration was also to regenerate the area and bring investment in. There is a bit of a tension I think between those two things' (interview, 17 February 2011).

There is also an underlying tension between regeneration and heritage. As City-owned infrastructure became available for development, legislation put the brakes on the process. For instance, Newtown's original Market Building (now housing a museum) was protected because of a unique engineering feature. The building could not be knocked down so the Market Theatre came in and arts-oriented rejuvenation in the area arguably began. Steven Sack, Johannesburg's director of Arts, Culture and Heritage, believes insertion of such heritage legislation in a sense causes market failure: 'It creates enormous limitations of what you can and can't do in terms of new development plans. And so classically cities all over the world with those kinds of buildings start looking for cultural tenants' (interview, 22 February 2011).

Intensified intervention by the South African Heritage Resources Agency (SAHRA) began with a public outcry at the destruction of Newtown's cooling towers in 1985, and a series of inhibitors on commercial development followed (Shand, 2010: 28–29). The government later promulgated the National Heritage Resources Act (No. 25 of 1999) to succeed the National Monuments Act. It protects, among other things, structures older than 60 years – no part may be altered or demolished without a permit. Empowered by this Act, SAHRA more recently obtained a provisional heritage declaration for the core of Newtown, adding another complexity. The inhibiting impact of heritage provisions is regarded as a major damper on inward investment since it scuppered the property development ambitions of the Newtown Urban Design Framework (interview, Harrison, 25 February 2011).

Despite these constraints, various indicators are encouraging in terms of the inner-city renewal strategy approach. Visitor statistics for the area as measured by the Newtown Improvement District show total evening visitors doubled from 79,626 in 2003 to 149,472 in 2009, while daytime visitors tripled from 83,087 to 243,382 (Shand, 2010: 71). Total visitor numbers, with events taken into account, more or less doubled over this same timeframe from 224,713 in 2003 to 457,804 in 2009. But evident in the breakdown is how poorly the events space fares in recent years, dropping from a peak of 177,651 in 2005 to 107,520 in 2008 and just 64,950 in 2009. This might have informed the current revamp of Mary Fitzgerald Square. It is being refurbished, for the second time in a decade, in a R15-million project to better accommodate large events, improve pedestrian flows, create space for relaxation and soften the hard landscaping (JDA, 2011).

The impact of the JDA's public-sector regeneration on private-sector investment is also positive, according to research it commissioned in 2009. The analysis included Newtown projects, executed between 2001 and 2007, totalling R188.7 million, looking at factors like vacancy rates, rentals and transaction levels. It concluded that the JDA had a 'significant' effect on resurgence in specific areas and consequently the reversal of fortunes of the inner city as a whole, 'a key contributing factor to the physical upliftment, change in perceptions and the resultant change in investor confidence, leading to increased rates of property purchase and refurbishment in the inner City' (JDA, 2009: 12).

The news for Newtown is forward-looking on the economic regeneration front: the property developers Atterbury have already broken ground on a previously derelict land parcel for a new R857-million development called The Newtown Junction. When complete in 2014, the 50,000 square metre complex will comprise a hotel (City Lodge), a retail shopping centre (The Potato Sheds) and an office block (The Majestic). Sue Parke of Atterbury Property Developments says Newtown has a rich but limited cultural offering:

> By having a retail shopping centre there – the movies, more restaurants, more coffee shops, more activity and a place for people to shop – it's going to draw more feet and ultimately those feet will start staying and going back to the theatre and taking advantage of the cultural offering within the area. So it's really giving the visitor a more diverse offering in terms of what they can do there rather than going just for a show. (Interview, 1 March 2011)

The underlying assumptions upon which such flagship developments rest have their detractors. Preston points out how culture industries as catalysts for inner-city rejuvenation can be problematic: Newtown 'openly and unabashedly' operates within a world city discourse (2006: 67), predicated upon specific Western capitalistic assumptions, leaving little room for alternative African city models. Bethlehem, however, says she is 'unconvinced' about such Eurocentrism debates – 'To me, what matters is two things: one, to regenerate the area. And the second is that you truly generate opportunities for cultural industries to thrive' (interview, 17 February 2011).

Lipietz (2004) argues that the City's pursuit of prestige projects in the name of urban regeneration has less to do with the whole-hearted application of neoliberal precepts than with the rather desperate attempts at reaching some kind of control in an inordinately confused, fluid and chaotic environment. But the end result, as Virasamy (2010: 98) argues, is an undeclared competition for space in Newtown with arts and culture organizations fearing they will get pushed out to make way for income-generating businesses. It remains to be seen what impact Newtown Junction will have on the area. The hope is that it will act as tinder to the dormant potential of Newtown to fulfil its ambitions as the cultural heart of Johannesburg.

Because the general consensus among Newtown's past and present role-players is that the area has failed to live up to its potential and there is a notable disjuncture between a 'big vision' imposed on the area from policymakers and the daily reality of the cultural precinct. That, however, is where agreement ends: the reasons proffered for this shortfall are multifarious. They range from poor planning to missed opportunities, inner-city perception problems, an inadequate public-private sector mix and lack of a residential spine to poor public transport and inadequate infrastructure commitment. Others include unrealistic scoping, by benchmarking against the successful Waterfront development in Cape Town, and failing to grasp the fragmentation of Johannesburg and its nature of neighbourhood formation and the notion of the local. According to Sack:

> [Johannesburg] has a range of business districts across the city, it has shopping precincts, it has cultural precincts scattered across the city. It doesn't really have a centre. … If you look at what happened in the World Cup: where did the big gatherings happen? In Sandton. Where do the big union marches happen? In the city. So it's like many particularly American cities – it doesn't really have a centre and a heart. And I think in a way the vision was somehow that Newtown would become that centre. Maybe it's just inappropriate to think that there is going to be a centre to Johannesburg – a cultural heart or cultural centre. (Interview, 22 February 2011)

Others, like the former director of arts and culture in Johannesburg, Christopher Till, critique the switch to a highly politicized space: 'What's crept in is more of an economic aspect to it where there is a financial opportunity or return which is seen in the first instance rather than encouraging what that economic return can be realized by' (interview, 2 March 2011). In the meantime, the Newtown approach is being challenged by its neighbour, Braamfontein, which is also the second node in the overall Cultural Arc. Over the past year, a cultural hub has consolidated along Juta Street: it comprises commercial art galleries, a creative precinct hosting various art, design, food and retail enterprises in a popular complex '70 Juta', a rejuvenated hotel that doubles up as a popular live music venue and a growing number of arts and cultural producers who have decided to base themselves in the area. Cultural institutions are moving there too, raising the spectre of displacement – for instance, the French Institute of South Africa (IFAS), formerly an anchor tenant in Newtown. And Wits university is building a flagship new art gallery in the precinct. As Hobbs says of Braamfontein, '*that* is effectively the materialization of the Cultural Arc, with or without calling it the Cultural Arc' (interview, 22 February 2011). He calls what is happening in Braamfontein the result of 'a very intelligent urban design framework' from a consultation process that began several years ago and coalesced; it engaged politicians, private stakeholders, public institutions and cultural networks, to see how they could benefit from a public environment upgrade that materialized four years ago (interview, 22 February 2011). In contrast, he says Newtown struggles because it doesn't have the same public-private sector make-up or residential spine. He adds: 'It's a suburbanization of that part of the CBD as opposed to the residential densification of an inner city streetscape … they are very different economic interactions' (interview, 22 February 2011). Property developer Adam Levy is one of the leaders of the Braamfontein resurgence. Mary Corrigall writes that Levy and others believe the City never followed through on its pledge to Newtown, forcing the artistic community to shift its commitment:

Newtown has failed as a cultural hub. So much of what goes on in Joburg is about hype: you can brand anything. With Newtown the City identified the most low density place it could turn with the least amount of investment and got interesting tenants but then left it to its own devices. (Quoted in Corrigall, 2010: par. 12)

And Braamfontein is not the only competitor: a new 'Arts on Main' development in the east of the inner city, with galleries, studios and residential development,

has also taken off on the back of private development. As Sack puts it, 'it partly has to do with the failings of Newtown that those precincts become possible' (interview, 22 February 2011).

The final node in the Cultural Arc is the Constitution Hill precinct, which houses the country's Constitutional Court. It is built on the site of the Old Fort prison, better known as 'Number Four', and the Women's Jail. It was opened in 2004 as a mixed-use complex that includes elements of law, heritage, museums, exhibitions and performance spaces acting together as a site of conscience. Law-Viljoen writes that the Court caused something of a stir in the architectural community when it opened: 'It was an unorthodox building but despite debates stirred up by such features as the angled columns in the Foyer and the incorporation of old bricks from the demolished Awaiting Trial Block, the warmth and openness of the building were undeniable' (2006: 8). Very significantly, the site is not fenced despite its location at the edge of Hillbrow. It is beyond the scope of this chapter to discuss its significance, suffice to state that it works reasonably well as a visitor centre but is also uncannily docile.

Conclusions

The investment into the boosting of the Newtown Cultural Precinct in Johannesburg is clearly consistent with much of the tenets in the globalized policy discourses on creative boosterism strategies. In some ways, Newtown had all the prime characteristics to succeed as a cultural hub anchoring the regional creative economy: it boasts a rich treasure trove of architectural, symbolic and institutional heritage; it contained substantial buildings owned by the public sector and land that could be deployed for renewal efforts; it already contained a considerable mix of economic activities, possibilities, social uses and residential population, albeit small. It is therefore understandable that it emerged as the focus of multi-level governmental efforts to effect a creative renaissance in the inner city. As demonstrated earlier, it has been partially successful, at least in terms of visitor numbers, and the role the Mary Fitzgerald Square fulfils as the mass congregation point for public screenings of mega sporting events such as the soccer World Cup or mass public concerts on public holidays, and so on. Yet, almost all of our informants suggested that there was something amiss. Newtown lacks alacrity. Newtown struggles to ignite as a space of cultural dynamism, artistic production, social integration and imagination. For many commentators and informants, this can be ascribed to the fact that Newtown is over-designed and over-engineered, and as a result it has displaced organic creativity and resonance, which effectively mutes invention and innovation that in turn depends on a critical mass of diversity. In the South African context, diversity by force has to reference class, race, nationality, gender, occupation, religion, ethnicity, economic status (i.e. formal or informal) and sector. However, narrow commercially-driven renewal efforts, by definition, gloss over structural differences and inequalities and rather seek to stage diversity as a source of economic potential.

The urban renewal approach of the inner city that operates on the basis of creating an enabling environment for property investors is singularly inappropriate and misplaced to foster open-ended dynamics to draw on the latent interests and desires of resident and (informal) economic groups in the node and the financial ambitions of potential investors. The question that should have been asked is what a creative cluster would comprise if one recognized and validated the low-end, informal, transitory and fluid populations and interests that made up Newtown when renewal efforts got underway. This goes to the heart of the broader conceptual and theoretical imperative to redefine the nature and dynamics of African urbanity that is rooted in extreme economic inequality, deep lines of inclusion and exclusion, and intensified cultural identities because these markers play such vital roles in structuring access to all kinds of urban opportunities (Simone, 2004). In reviewing the policy documents on Newtown that gave flesh to the renewal desires in the Cultural Arc concept, it is clear that government, design firms and private sector actors never paid much mind to who was living in the inner city, what they were doing, and how they and their cultural needs and aspirations could be placed at a centre of a renewal strategy. We are not arguing that one can fashion a mainstream economic renewal effort through such an approach, but we are convinced that the notion of culture-based renewal needs to shift its gaze beyond the narrow determinants of creative clusters and industries to appreciate the possibility of imagining public life and cultural publics in profoundly different ways (Mbembe and Nuttall, 2008).

This implies a reordering of perspective where economic infrastructures become secondary to ecological and social-cultural infrastructures. In recent years, the city of Medellín in Colombia (see Chapter 21 by Octavio Arbeláez Tobón in this volume), with acute social and economic problems, has demonstrated how a systematic and concerted investment into education, leisure, social, public and low-key economic infrastructures within poor neighbourhoods but connected through a city-wide accessibility grid, can in fact dramatically improve the quality of life for large numbers of people without falling victim to some idealized notion of the power of the creative industries to catapult the urban poor into vibrant economies (United Cities and Local Governments, 2010). This approach also resonates with the intimations of Steven Sack (interview, 22 February 2011) that it may be more suitable to explore and understand the City at a much finer grain, and rather explore how best to foster a latticework of (often informal) emergent energy, connectivity, collaboration and vibrancy as ordinary people depend on social infrastructures to make do, get by and access rich cultural lives. These cultural registers may not be readily commodifiable, but at least they are central to the lives of the majority of urban citizens. It may also be that it is actually in such seemingly mundane and unvarnished settings that true artistic spark can best emerge because it rubs up against the visceral pain, pleasure and desire lines of the real city.

REFERENCES

Appadurai, A. (1996) *Modernity at Large. Cultural Dimensions of Globalization*. Minneapolis, MN, and London: University of Minnesota Press.

Beall, J., Crankshaw, O. and Parnell, S. (2002) *Uniting a Divided City. Governance and Social Exclusion in Johannesburg*. London: Earthscan.

City of Johannesburg (2006) *Reflecting on a Solid Foundation: Building Developmental Local Government 2000–2005*. Johannesburg: City of Johannesburg.

Clifford, J. (1994) Diasporas. *Cultural Anthropology*, 9(3): 302–338.

Corrigall, M. (November 4, 2010) *What Happens when the Pioneers set up Artistic Enclaves?* Retrieved from http://corrigall.blogspot.com/2010/11/what-happens-when-pioneers-set-up.html [Last accessed: February 28, 2011].

Creative Strategy Consulting, SQW (SA) (1999) *The Creative City: Johannesburg and the Creative Industries*. (Report prepared for the DBSA Gauteng Strategic Development Initiative Programme.) Johannesburg: Creative Strategy Consulting.

Dinath, Y. (2006) Re-generating the Culture Factory: Deconstructing Interpretations of Culture in the Hybrid City. (Published Master's dissertation.) University of the Witwatersrand, Johannesburg, South Africa.

Gaule, S. (2005) Alternating Currents of Power: From Colonial to Post-apartheid Spatial Patterns in Newtown Johannesburg. *Urban Studies*, 42(13): 2335–2361.

Gotz, G., Pieterse, E. and Smit, W. (2011) Desenho, limites e perspectivas da governança metropolitana na África do Sul [Design, Limits and Prospects of Metropolitan Governance in South Africa], in Klink, J. (ed.), *Governança das metropoles: conceitos, experiências e perspectivas*. Sao Paulo: Annablume.

Hall, S. (1991) The Local and the Global: Globalization and Ethnicity, in King, A. (ed.), *Culture, Globalization and the World-System*. London: Macmillan.

Johannesburg Development Agency (2009) *Analysis of the Impact of the JDA's Area-based Regeneration Projects on Private Sector Investments*. Johannesburg: JDA. Retrieved from www.jda.org.za/keydocs/2009/impact_investments.pdf [Last accessed April 4, 2011].

Johannesburg Development Agency (2011) *JDA Sculpture Competitions in the Inner City* (Press Release March 2011). Johannesburg: JDA.

Law-Viljoen, B. (ed.) (2006) *Light on a Hill: Building the Constitutional Court of South Africa*. Johannesburg: David Krut Publishing.

Lipietz, B. (2004) Muddling-through: Urban Regeneration in Johannesburg's Inner City. Paper presented at N-Aerus Annual Conference, 15–16 September 2004, Barcelona. School of Oriental and African Studies, University of London. Retrieved from www.n-aerus.net/web/sat/workshops/2001/papers/Lipietz.pdf [Last accessed: February 7, 2011].

Matlaba, S. (2007) Assessing Economic Empowerment in the Newtown Cultural Precinct. (Published Master's dissertation.) University of the Witwatersrand, Johannesburg, South Africa.

Mbembe, A. and Nuttall, S. (2008) Introduction: Afropolis, in Nuttall, S. and Mbembe, A. (eds), *Johannesburg: The Elusive Metropolis*. Johannesburg: Wits University Press.

Murray, M.J. (2008) *Taming the Disorderly City: The Spatial Landscape of Johannesburg after Apartheid*. Cape Town: University of Cape Town Press.

Parnell, S. (2003) Race, Power and Urban Control: Johannesburg's Inner City Slum-Yards, 1910–1923. *Journal of Southern African Studies*, 20(4): 307–314.

Parnell, S. and Pirie, G. (1991) Johannesburg, in Lemon, A. (ed.), *Homes Apart: South Africa's Segregated Cities*. London: Paul Chapman.

Pieterse, E. and van Donk, M. (2002) Incomplete Ruptures: The Political Economy of the Realisation of Socio-Economic Rights in South Africa. *Law, Democracy and Development*, 6(2): 193–229.

Preston, L. (2006) Johannesburg as World City: Arts and Culture Policy in the Urban African Context. (Published Master's dissertation.) University of the Witwatersrand, Johannesburg, South Africa.

Shand, K. (2010) Newtown: A Cultural Precinct: Real or Imagined? (Unpublished Master's dissertation.) University of the Witwatersrand, Johannesburg, South Africa.

Simone, A.M. (2004) *For the City yet to Come: Changing African Life in Four Cities*. Durham, NC, and London: Duke University Press.

United Cities and Local Governments (2010) Policy paper on urban strategic planning: Local leaders preparing for the future of our cities. Barcelona: UCLG.

Virasamy, B. (2010) Cultural Bandwagon to Cultural Brand-wagon: A Study on the Cultural Branding and Influence of Culture-led Regeneration and City Branding on Resident Arts Organisations in Newtown, Johannesburg. (Published Master's dissertation.) University of the Witwatersrand, Johannesburg, South Africa.

Interviewees

Albonico, M. 2 March, 2011. Personal interview. Newtown, Johannesburg.

Bethlehem, L. 17 February, 2011. Telephone interview.

Burnett, R. 11 March 2011. Personal interview. Rosebank, Johannesburg.

Gotz, G. 17 March 2011. Personal interview. Braamfontein, Johannesburg.

Harrison, P. 25 February 2011. Personal interview. Newtown, Johannesburg.

Hobbs, S. & M. Neustetter. 22 February 2011. Personal interview. Jeppestown, Johannesburg.

Parke, S. 1 March 2011. Telephone Interview.

Sack, S. 22 February 2011. Personal interview. Newtown, Johannesburg.

Till, C. 2 March 2011. Telephone interview.

CHAPTER 18

RICH BUT DIVIDED... THE POLITICS OF CULTURAL POLICY IN LONDON

Kate Oakley

In the United Kingdom, cultural policy has become closely entwined with the use of culture as a resource for economic development, particularly under the 'creative industries' discourse. The promotion of such economic arguments at the city level could be seen as the triumph of neoliberal urban governance models but is more complex than that, as it blends social democratic approaches with more neoliberal-inflected urban entrepreneurialism. Traditional policy concerns of access, identity or education have never disappeared, though they have often been remade in other guises and with different language. The author explores this mix of urban governance models and its impacts on the cultural politics of London today.

Introduction

This chapter explores the dual role London has been made to play as both national capital and world city through an analysis of the last 30 years of cultural policy-making.[1] As a national capital, London has, over that time, functioned as a crucible for the UK's cultural policies; from the Greater London Council-led cultural industries approaches of the 1980s, via 'Creative London', to a recent return to a more traditional arts-based approach under its current Conservative administration. The assumptions guiding these polices, while shaped within the particular social and economic context of London, have subsequently been exported, both nationally (Schlesinger, 2009) and, in the form of 'creative industries', internationally (Cunningham, 2007).

At the same time, London's politicians have sought, both explicitly and at times implicitly, to transcend its role as national capital, to stress its status as a World City and its core role within the international circuits of capital and ideas that make up the global cultural industries (Massey, 2007). In the fine art market, fashion and architecture, to name but three, London's cultural practitioners address themselves to a constituency, not only beyond, but at times exclusive of, the rest of the UK. This duality is reflected in the cultural policies adopted by London's various administrations over recent years, which have moved between a focus on the local (neighbourhood-level regeneration, small-scale workspace developments, concerns with inequality in access to culture) and the global (festivals, trade fairs and overseas missions). A notable example of this duality was of course the successful Olympic bid, which stressed London's multiculturalism and diversity, and the claims of Olympic-level spending to be able to regenerate historically impoverished East London (Livingstone, 2005; Massey, 2007).

It is in part a story of 'fast policy' (Peck, 2002), the rapid development and rapid redundancy of policy approaches, developed both in London and imported from elsewhere. This reached its most extreme form in the years 2003–2008, when three distinct policy formations were adopted and dropped by the then economic development organisation, the London Development Agency (LDA).[2] As this took place under the New Labour period in Britain, and under a Labour, though not particularly 'New Labour' Mayor, it is possible to see this in the light of the somewhat frenetic nature of New Labour policy-making, with its fondness for short-term initiatives and policy innovations over longer-term approaches. But, as this chapter argues, it is also indicative of the tensions, contradictions and conflicts that underlie cultural policy-making in a city like London.

It is tempting, and indeed persuasive, to characterise London in the last 30 years as a fairly straightforward story of neoliberal urban governance models (Peck et al., 2009), particularly given the disastrous dominance of its financial elites. But that would be to underestimate the complex political provenance of London's recent cultural policies, blending as they do social democratic 'cultural industries' approaches, which sought to reshape the state–market relationship, with liberal cosmopolitanism[3] (Beck, 2006) and urban entrepreneurialism. In an attempt to bridge what the Introduction to this volume describes as the gulf between cultural policy and politics, this chapter sets out to explore this complex political legacy and its manifestations in cultural policy.

The Greater London Council and the cultural industries

This period of London's government, from 1981 to 1986, has been well covered in the literature but is nonetheless a crucial part of the story of London's approach to cultural policy (Bianchini, 1987; Garnham, 2005; O'Connor, 2009). In particular, this chapter argues that its legacy influenced later 'creative industry' interventions, particularly in terms of assumptions about the opportunities offered to ethnic minorities and working-class people by the expansion of cultural labour markets. While the political *differences* between cultural and creative industry approaches have been thoroughly examined (Hesmondhalgh, 2005; O'Connor, 2007) and are acknowledged here, what is less often acknowledged are the *continuities*.

What became the Greater London Council's (GLC) cultural industries polices arose out of a mixture of arts and economic policy, in the context of a broader political strategy which was trying to reconstruct the Left of British politics, at that time stunned by the success of Thatcherism (Bianchini, 1987). The fracturing of Labour's traditional working-class voting bloc (Hobsbawm, 1981) was to be countered by a broader appeal to ethnic minorities, women and

the young, an appeal which took cultural political form in the embrace and support of commercial popular culture. Ethnic minority, or black arts as they were called at the time, were, for the first time, the subject of particular public interventions in cinema, theatre and festivals, while training schemes aimed at improving the representation of ethnic minority workers within the cultural sectors were established and funded (Bianchini, 1987).

At the same time, the GLC's Industry and Employment committee, under the influence of figures such as Robin Murray and academic Nick Garnham, was developing approaches to the 'cultural industries' which sought to break down distinctions between subsidised and commercial culture, as well as notions of high and low. As most people's cultural consumption was hugely shaped by market forces, cultural policy needed to take account of this, they argued, and could thus include public investments in commercial enterprises such as recording studios, publishing houses and magazines, as well as traditional arts organisations.

As Bilton (2010: 257) has argued, the GLC's marriage of democratic arts policies and support for cultural enterprises was grounded in a social democratic politics that, while not reflected at national level, produced a 'paradoxical alliance between left-wing local authorities and right-wing central government – which laid the foundations for Britain's influential creative industries policies more than 10 years later'. If later creative industry policies placed much greater emphasis on entrepreneurial individualism than on questions of identity and representation, those earlier concerns did not disappear altogether. What did fade, however, was an active concern to reshape the market, particularly in questions of distribution of cultural goods. By the time 'creative industries' was taken up in London over a decade after the GLC's experiment, the willingness of public administrations to intervene in market *structures* was considerably diminished. Those who were excluded by the market remained a concern of public policy, but equipping them to compete *within* the market was the aim, not changing the rules of the game altogether.

Creative London

The creative industries discourse was well established at national level and, indeed, had been taken up by other cities and regions, by the time the Mayor's Commission on Creative Industries was set up in London in 2002 (O'Connor and Gu, 2010). In his second incarnation as London's senior politician, this time as elected Mayor, Ken Livingstone set up the Commission. It was described as 'business-led' (LDA, 2002) and comprised around 15 representatives of media and cultural firms, universities and community arts organisations. The Mayor's Economic Development Strategy, published the previous summer, had laid stress on the importance of the creative and cultural industries to the London economy, an importance re-enforced by *Creativity: London's Core Business* (LDA, 2002), which identified the creative industries as the fastest-growing sector in London's economy, and the source of one in every five new jobs.

The Commission's remit was constructed primarily in terms of economic development, and is peppered with terms like 'faster balance sheet growth', 'cluster development' and 'models of business finance', but it nevertheless shows elements of a common heritage with the GLC's cultural industries approaches (LDA, 2002). Particular emphasis is placed on the importance of ethnic-minority-led economic development and the need to develop specific measures to help BME[4] businesses. Over the lifetime of the Commission, the theme of 'regeneration' became more significant, so much so that in his Foreword to the final report (*Creative London*, published in 2003), Ken Livingstone spoke of the need for stimulating the cultural and creative industries themselves, for their jobs and growth potential, 'but also in terms of their ability to enhance London's regenerative capacity' (LDA, 2003: 12). It was a question of asking not just what London could do for the creative industries, but what the creative industries could do for London.

The Commission met over a six-month period between 2002 and 2003 and took evidence from academics, policy-makers and practitioners, before publishing its report and recommendations. These were to be acted on by a unit within the London Development Agency, now branded as 'Creative London'. One distinctive element of these interventions, which included measures such as providing intellectual property (IP) advice, and working with universities on small business incubation, was the strongly spatial flavour. While the Commission was a pan-London undertaking, and as London is home to the majority of the UK's cultural and creative industries, hence had national implications, a good deal of focus was placed on creating a new administrative

geography for London, a series of localised 'hubs' which concentrated support for cultural enterprises.

These hubs were to be established just outside the main concentrations of cultural sector employment in London – in areas such as Lewisham, Haringey and King's Cross – which combined high levels of creative industry activity with high levels of social deprivation. This co-location was not an accident. The Commission was strongly influenced by the belief that creative industry employment could benefit those from marginalised groups, and even, with adequate training and investment, those who had been unemployed. Initiatives were to be 'particularly targeted at disenfranchised groups', and London's 'rich but divided' legacy of social polarisation was to be 'actively challenged' (LDA, 2003: 15). Hubs were sometimes developed from existing community development or community arts organisations, some of which had been around in one form or another since the GLC days or before and, with the opportunism necessary to survive changing political fortunes, had rebranded themselves in the contemporary language of economic development. But the hub strategy was also an attempt to cut across existing administrative boundaries – the hub at King's Cross in north London, for instance, lay on the boundary of two London boroughs – Camden and Islington.[5] Rather than place creative industry funding-programmes support within these boroughs, and hence within existing local government structures, an attempt was made to bring new actors into the delivery of public services, an attempt both brave and fraught with subsequent problems.

In a sign of both the rapidity of policy development and deployment in the New Labour years, and of the conflicting politics that underlay it, Creative London, in its original incarnation, lasted all of three years, from 2003 to 2006. Although funding for individual hubs and particular programmes, such as 'Own It', the intellectual property advice service, continued for some years afterwards, the spatial elements of the programme and the concern with regeneration and combating deprivation were soon under attack from various quarters.

'Drop the regeneration baggage'

From its earliest days, New Labour's answer to those who felt that its creative industries polices stressed economic goals above all others had been to stress their role in promoting social inclusion, particularly via employment. This argument drew directly, not only on cultural industry strategies, but also on the activities of arts organisations in the UK over the previous decades (Chelliah, 1999). Social exclusion was firmly within the remit of the Department of Culture, Media and Sport (DCMS), almost from its creation in 1997, and led to much of what was later derided as the 'instrumentalism' of New Labour's cultural policies (Mirza, 2006) with their explicit concerns with questions of access and the potential for ameliorative social impacts.

The role of the creative industries in creating employment for young, unemployed people was also seen as important. The fact that the creative industries were growing meant that they could be, and were, explicitly linked to regeneration efforts. At times it was suggested that not only could the growth of these sectors produce work opportunities, but they could also develop citizenship, 'the personal confidence, flexibility and self-reliance on which success in the changing employment market increasingly depends' (DCMS, 1999: 29). Yet by 2003, criticism of New Labour's 'instrumentalism' in cultural policy was growing – often from arts organisations themselves. In some cases, this was traditional cultural conservatism (Tusa, 2000), but in other cases, concern came from the ranks of those viewed as sympathetic to New Labour (Holden, 2004). At the same time, economic development agencies that had capitalised on creative industries, both as a source of public funds and as an apparently compelling policy narrative, were learning that the purported links between the development of the creative sector and employment opportunities for the marginalised were weak. And still others were asking questions about the type of employment that the creative sectors offered (McRobbie, 2002).

As data on the creative and cultural industries improved, it became clear that such employment offers generally poor prospects for young people lacking relevant social contacts or unable to support long periods of unpaid work (Oakley, 2009a). Far from offering opportunities to the socially excluded, in fact women, ethnic minorities and the working class were strongly under-represented in the labour force. In London, ethnic minorities make up between a quarter and a third of the workforce, yet in broadcasting, music and publishing, by 2007, the proportion of ethnic minority workers was less than half that of London's workforce as a whole. Around 35 per cent of the cultural and creative industry workforce in the capital is female, compared with

43 per cent in the rest of the economy and, while changes year on year are slight, these proportions tend to be worsening, not improving (Freeman, 2010). The nature of cultural labour markets, with an over-supply of graduate labour, very small firms, strong social networks and a suspicion of formal qualifications, makes direct 'equal opportunity' interventions difficult. Thus public policy continues to struggle with questions of representation in cultural labour markets, amid rising concern in some Western countries about declining social mobility (Cabinet Office, 2009).

In London, in the mid-2000s, the combination of concern about instrumentalism, the lack of evidence that creative industry polices could 'deliver' on social inclusion, and pressure from the sectors for a more industrial policy, focused on more promotion and exports and less on social inclusion and regeneration, led to a rapid change of direction.

Showcasing, festivals and city promotion

If the early part of the 2000s saw echoes of the 1980s in London's cultural policies, after 2005 a much more conventional approach to creative industry support was adopted. In place of a focus on neighbourhoods and spatial redistribution, polices were directed towards particular sub-sectors of the creative industries where London was perceived to have competitive strengths, such as film, design and fashion.

Support for exports, festivals and events like London Fashion Week became the focus for policy-makers. 'Creativity', increasingly decoupled from particular association with artistic activities, became the new mantra, celebrated somewhat uncritically via events such as the 'World Creative Forum', the self-styled 'Davos' of creativity, which took place as part of London's Design Festival.

Although he was arguably less influential in terms of London policy-making, as the city was more sure of its attractiveness to the 'creative class' than other cities more desperate for economic turnaround (Peck, 2005), the influence of Richard Florida can nonetheless be detected in some London policies of that time. To the extent that there was concern with place, spatial strategy for the creative industries began to concern itself with consumption, not production. A proposed national film centre for the South Bank of the Thames and a permanent home for London Fashion Week were among ideas proposed as part of the UK government's relatively short-lived plans to make Britain 'the world's creative hub'.

At this point, rather than pursuing a distinctive path, London's policy increasingly resembled that set at national level. Ten years after the creative industry mapping documents, the Department for Culture, Media and Sport was rethinking what it now termed its 'creative economy' policy, and was also shifting from locally-focused economic development (easily dismissed as 'creative anywhere') to policies that emphasised the wider role of 'creativity' and its links to innovation (Oakley, 2009b). Particular sub-sectors were the focus of attention for policy-makers and there were tax breaks for the film industry, support for designers in manufacturing and mooted (though never really delivered) help for videogames. Instead of the focus on entrepreneurial start-ups and new policy actors that had dominated the early years of New Labour, larger firms and cultural institutions were increasingly the trusted vehicles of public policy. In London, this meant long-established cultural organisations such as the Tate and the British Museum, both of which extended their central London presence. Ironically, the one major move outside the capital in this period – the relocation of part of the BBC to Salford in the North West of England – was also a testament to shifting policies. Instead of hoping for an economic miracle from independents, regional economies were seen to need a boost from the big players.

London, World City

In July 2005, to surprise in some quarters, London was awarded the 2012 Olympic Games, an event which almost single-handedly determined the direction of its cultural policies and, more importantly, funding, for the next seven years. In his speech at the Singapore Presentation to the International Olympic Committee, Mayor Ken Livingstone stressed London's multiculturalism, 'a city in which 300 languages are spoken every day, and those who speak them live happily side by side' (Livingstone, 2005). London's pitch was unashamedly, and effectively, the 'world city', and indeed the later years of Livingstone's terms of office saw London increasingly act as sort of city-state (Hunt, 2007), with the Greater London Authority opening its own 'overseas offices' in Delhi, Mumbai, Beijing, Shanghai and Brussels.

When Kevin Robins spoke of London as 'that great provocation to the clarity and coherence of British national culture' (2001: 77), he saw it as a way to rethink citizenship beyond the burdens of national, in the case of the UK, post-imperial culture. This version of 'city air makes you free' is often beloved of the inhabitants of great metropolises, particularly those keen to disassociate themselves from what they see as the reactionary elements of national cultures. Such sentiments were clearly key to Livingstone's presentation of London as a World City, but as Doreen Massey has so coherently argued, these arguments also need to be seen alongside London's role as a producer of inequality, 'a heartland of that socio-political economic formation that goes by the name of neo-liberalism' (2007: 8).

Before (and even after) its own spectacular crisis, the financial services sector of London's economy demonstrated this phenomenon perfectly. In 2005, it was estimated that of the approximately 1 million jobs in London's economy dependent on finance, over 700,000 were related to London's role in the global economy, rather than domestic markets (Corporation of London, 2005). And the wealth generated in financial services did its bit to help maintain London as the UK's most unequal region: high salaries, bonuses and house prices drove a concentration of wealth in the capital that not only sharpened inequality, but threatened to detach London from the rest of the UK in ways that could wreck any claims of the city as a progressive alternative to the national state. Historian Tristram Hunt warned of a new 'Edwardian' age in London, whereby London would continue to break away from the rest of the country, investing its wealth anywhere but in its own, national backyard (Hunt, 2007). Again, this had a cultural political resonance. The more London drifted away from the rest of the UK, the less its cultural production reflected the reality of life there, and the more its metropolitan media and political conversation failed to resonate beyond its border.

Back to basics – the global financial crisis and the collapse of 'creative industries'

While the financial crisis and its aftermath are still having an effect on London and the UK's economy, evidence has emerged that even during the boom, London's cultural economy had not perhaps been quite as healthy as sometimes portrayed. Following the 'dot com bust' in 2001, total cultural employment in London fell for three successive years, only rising again 2005. It took until 2007 for both employment and output to rise above the 2001 peak, which, while it suggests an underlying growth trend, also suggests creative jobs may take a long time to recover after downturns. Those parts of the creative and cultural industries dependent on business-to-business and public spending – notably, advertising, architecture and design – all took hits in terms of both employments and turnover (Freeman, 2010). Growth resumed in 2007 and 2008, and London's creative workforce now stands at nearly 800,000 (Freeman, 2010), but the political climate has changed utterly. The election of a Conservative Mayor, Boris Johnson, in May 2008, saw a move away from any lingering concern with both urban regeneration as a goal for cultural policy and other forms of instrumentalism.

More surprisingly, perhaps, it also signalled a move away from the strong promotion of the creative industries as a vital part of London's economy. In part this was practical. The national election of a Conservative-Liberal coalition in May 2010 saw the biggest public spending cuts in many decades in the UK, and the infrastructure of economic development, built up by New Labour, was largely dismantled. Regional development agencies, the bodies that had perhaps done most to promote the creative industries via a variety of funding schemes, grants and capital developments, were abolished. This included the London Development Agency, which had spearheaded Creative London, funded the hubs and other interventions and, for a while, acted as the primary source of policy and expertise in this field. Sub-sectoral agencies such as the UK Film Council were also abolished at national level, and, as in the boom time, many of these changes had greater impacts in London than elsewhere, as London is generally the home of public agencies for culture as well as the bulk of employment in the sectors themselves.

However, the greater threat to London's role as a centre of the creative and cultural industries perhaps comes in the proposed changes to Higher Education, introduced in late 2010 by the Coalition government. The proposed ending of public funding for undergraduate education in all arts, humanities and social science subjects raised genuine alarm in a city where Higher Education is recognised as the primary feeder of the creative economy (Vasagar, 2010). Indeed, London's strength in arts education had formed part of its claims to be a centre of global cultural production. In a report commissioned in 2007, the city had sought to 'benchmark' its cultural assets against other world cities, namely New York, Paris, Tokyo and Shanghai (LDA, 2008). The report considered a wide range of indicators, from number of museums to number of bookshops, but also stressed that London's large student population, together with the internationalism of that student body, provided a major fillip to both cultural production and consumption in the capital. Figures provided by the Higher Education Statistical Agency (HESA) showed that there are approximately 50,000 students studying at specialist arts universities and colleges, around twice the number of those in New York, and far outstripping the other cities.

Given this wholesale dismantling of 'creative economy' infrastructure, therefore, Conservative Mayor Boris Johnson's cultural policy, when released in November 2010, could do little more than promise to try to 'keep the flame alive' during a period of intense contraction. Again, as Livingstone had done earlier, the Mayor liked to set himself against national government on occasion, notably over changes in welfare payments to tenants (Roberts, 2010). The threat to 'cap' welfare paid to poor and unemployed people in private rented accommodation raised the spectre of Parisian-style (or in the Mayor's rather more dramatic terms 'Kosovo-style') 'social cleansing', with poor people being removed from their traditional homes in inner London's mixed neighbourhoods to cheaper housing outside the capital. This was a threat to London's cosmopolitan identity, in a city which prided itself on the cheek-by-jowl living arrangements of its citizens, even if, in practice, economic polarisation means that their lives were conducted with little reference to one another (Massey, 2007).

Yet in cultural policy, while again trying to take a more pro-arts line than that taken by central government (LDA, 2010), lack of public funding this time gave the city relatively little room to manoeuvre. The Mayor's role was reduced to advocacy and seeking to encourage other public bodies to take the arts seriously. Central government was stressing the potential for private philanthropy to fill the gap left by public funding cuts, a move which could only entrench London's superiority in funding terms over the rest of the UK, given that the city receives almost 70 per cent of all private investment in the arts in the UK (Mermiri, 2010). Yet, despite this, it was hard to avoid the feeling that London in 2010 was cannibalising previous investments in culture faster than it was creating new ones.

Conclusions

As Hesmondhalgh (2005: 96) has commented, what often seems to be forgotten in discussion of cultural policies is that 'these are areas of public policy more generally'. As such, an examination of them can tell us much about the overall public policies and, indeed, politics of a city. In London's case, its World-City status, the dominance of its financial services industries, its history as an ex-imperial capital and continuing role as a national capital, combined with its relative openness to migration, have all been more significant factors in the success of its cultural and creative industries than its cultural policies alone have been. Equally, despite the whiff of managerial consensus that has often accompanied debates about 'creative cities', in fact the politics that shape creative and cultural policies are no less conflicted, adversarial or complex than those of any other area of urban life.

It has been the argument of this chapter that London's cultural polices over the last 30 years can provide a useful lens with which to view the most significant political battle of that period: that between neoliberal urban governance models and the remnants of a social democratic settlement. For much of that period, and particularly in the New Labour years of 1997–2008, an attempt was made to argue that one could be made to serve the other; an entrepreneurial economy could be harnessed to serve the needs of the poor and the excluded, if only they could be made ready for the competition. The expansion of the cultural and creative sectors, with their potential for creating jobs, allied to instrumental arts policies, with their potential for creating citizens, offered ways to do this. While the economy grew and public spending remained high, this 'double-shuffle' (Hall, 2003) could be made to work, albeit never quite as well as some advocates

claimed. But when the real motor of London's economy imploded in the financial crisis of 2008, and public funding collapsed, these tensions were laid bare and often exposed as contradictions.

The 'alliance between left-wing local authorities and right-wing central government' (Bilton, 2010), which had characterised the birth of explicitly socio-economic policies for the cultural sectors in the 1908s, has broken down. The New Labour attempt to fuse social and economic ends in cultural policy has been discontinued. The distinction between commercial 'creative industries' and 'the arts' is being re-enforced, undoing the policy direction of several decades. And a philanthropic and voluntaristic model of cultural support is being reintroduced, albeit with little immediate success. The attempt to accommodate neoliberalism within a social democratic settlement is at an end. And London's politics and its cultural polices seem likely to be more fragmented, more contested and more conflictual in the years to come.

Notes

1 By 'cultural policy', I mean both policies specifically aimed at the arts, media and design sectors and those policies that use culture towards other social and economic ends.

2 The London Development Agency was one of the Regional Development Agencies set up in England under New Labour. Unlike the others, which reported to central government, the LDA reported to the Mayor of London and the elected London Assembly.

3 By this I mean the combination of social liberalism with the desire for a cosmopolitan, post-national identity that the global city appears to offer.

4 By the time of the Creative Industries Commission, the favoured term for what had been called black arts was BME (Black and Minority Ethnic), later BAME (Black, Asian Minority Ethnic).

5 Each of the 32 London boroughs has its own elected government.

REFERENCES

Beck, Ulrich (2006) *Cosmopolitan Vision*. Cambridge: Polity Press.

Bianchini, Franco (1987) 'GLC R. I. P., 1981–1986', *New Formations*, 1: 103–117.

Bilton, Chris (2010) 'Manageable Creativity', *International Journal of Cultural Policy*, 16(3): 255–269.

Cabinet Office (2009) *Unleashing Aspiration: The Final Report on Fair Access to the Professions*. London: Cabinet Office.

Chelliah, Ramani (1999) *Arts and Regeneration*. London: Local Government Unit.

Corporation of London (2005) *The Competitiveness of London as a Global Financial Centre*. London: Corporation of London.

Freeman, Alan (2010) *London's Creative Workforce: 2009 Update*. London: GLA Economics.

Garnham, Nick (2005) 'From Cultural to Creative Industries', *International Journal of Cultural Policy*, 11(1): 15–29.

Hall, S. (2003) 'New Labour's Double Shuffle', *Soundings*, 24: 1024.

Hesmondhalgh, David (2005) 'Media and Public Policy as Cultural Policy: The Case of the British Labour Government', *International Journal of Cultural Policy*, 11(1): 95–108.

Hobsbawm, Eric (1981) 'The Forward March of Labour Halted?', in M. Jacques and F. Mulhearn (eds), *The Forward March of Labour Halted*. London: Verso.

Holden, John (2004) *Capturing Cultural Value*. London: Demos.

Hunt, Tristram (2007) 'A new Edwardian Age is Dawning', *The Observer*, 4 March.

LDA (London Development Agency) (2002a) *London Creative Futures: Creating Competitive Advantage through London's Creative Industries* (Unpublished). London: Creative Industries Commission.

LDA (2003) *Creative London*. London: London Development Agency.

LDA (2008) *London: A Cultural Audit*. London: London Development Agency.

LDA (2010) *Cultural Metropolis: The Mayor's Cultural Strategy – 2012 and Beyond*. London: London Development Agency.

Livingstone, Ken (2005) Singapore Presentation speech. Available at: www.london2012.com/documents/locog-publications/singapore-presentation-speeches.pdf (accessed 11/11/10).

Massey, Doreen (2007) *World City*. Cambridge: Polity Press.

McRobbie, Angela (2002) 'Clubs to Companies: Notes on the Decline of Political Culture in Speeded-up Creative Worlds', *Cultural Studies* 16(4): 516–531.

Mermiri, T. (2010) *Arts Philanthropy: the facts, trends and potential*. London: Arts and Business.

Mirza, Munira (ed.) (2006) *Culture Vultures: Is UK Arts Policy Damaging the Arts?* London: Policy Exchange.

Oakley, Kate (2009a) *Art Works: A Review of the Literature on Cultural and Creative Labour Markets*. London: Creativity, Culture and Education.

Oakley, Kate (2009b) 'The Disappearing Arts – Creativity and Innovation after the Creative Industries', Special Issue of *International Journal of Cultural Policy*, 15(4), November: 403–413.

O'Connor, Justin (2007) *The Cultural and Creative Industries: A Review of the Literature*. London: Creative Partnerships.

O'Connor, Justin (2009) 'Creative Industries: A New Direction?', *International Journal of Cultural Policy*, 15(4): 387–402.

O'Connor, Justin and Gu, Xin (2010) 'Developing a Creative Cluster in a Post-industrial City: CIDS and Manchester', *The Information Society*, 25(3): 169–174.

Peck, Jamie (2002) 'Political Economies of Scale: Fast Policy, Interscalar Relations, and Neoliberal Workfare', *Economic Geography*, 78: 331–360.

Peck, Jamie (2005) 'Struggling with the Creative Class', *International Journal of Urban and Regional Research*, 29(4): 331–360.

Peck, Jamie, Theodore, Nik and Brenner, Neil (2009) 'Neoliberal Urbanism: Models, Moments, Mutations', *SAIS Review*, 29(1): 49–66.

Roberts, Laura (2010) 'Boris Johnson Demands Exemption from Housing Benefit Cap', *The Daily Telegraph*, 28 October.

Robins, Kevin (2001) 'Becoming Anybody: Thinking against the Nation and through the City', *City*, 5(1): 77–90.

Tusa, John (2000) *Art Matters: Reflecting on Culture*. London: Methuen.

Vasagar, Jeevan (2010) 'Jeremy Deller and College Leaders Warn of Cuts' Impact on Young Artists', *The Guardian*, 15 November.

CHAPTER 19

THE CULTURAL MAPPING OF L'VIV
Ihor Savchak and Linda Knudsen McAusland

This chapter examines the recent experience of the city of L'viv through the prism of an activist 'cultural planning' exercise initiated by a local non-governmental entity, the Centre for Cultural Management. The goal was to provide a framework for cultural policy development in the city. The method and process through which this goal was pursued are described, together with the main challenges and opportunities that were laid bare. The recommendations that resulted, now being gradually implemented, hold out many useful lessons for a renewal of the ways in which the governance of culture is tackled in cities such as L'viv.

Introduction

L'viv is a city in western Ukraine, with a population of around 1 million inhabitants. Throughout the twentieth century, its people lived through constant change. Between 1900 and 1999 there was no single generation that lived continuously within the confines of a single country, as the city belonged successively to the Austro-Hungarian Empire, the West-Ukrainian National Republic, Poland, the USSR, and, finally, the independent nation-state of Ukraine. Living through this period and facing the constantly renewed challenges that came their way, people learned to be patient, persistent, flexible, tolerant and creative. As a result, current global changes do not threaten to undermine L'viv and Ukraine in the same way they may do in societies with more apparently stable ways of life. As there has been little stability here, current transformations are simply another layer in our history of change. The people of the city see them as opportunities for development.

But L'viv has always been a centre of Ukrainian culture and identity. It remained so despite Soviet oppression and persecution, and this role was especially evident in the late 1980s and early 1990s, when many cultural initiatives invigorated a sense of national awareness. After the proclamation of Ukrainian independence in 1991, some members of the city government became interested in strategic planning. Because of culture's strong presence in the city (if only in terms of its architecture), it was thought that this sector could play a key revitalizing role. Simultaneously, members of the cultural community were struggling to exist in the changing environment of post-Soviet L'viv. Old systems and old perspectives had been stretched to the maximum. To take significant steps forward, new ways of thinking and being were indispensable.

These converging circumstances provided the context, motivation and resources for the Centre for Cultural Management to initiate a 'cultural planning' process in L'viv. By the term 'cultural planning', we understand a process of inclusive community consultation and decision making that helps local government identify cultural resources and think strategically about how these resources can help a community to achieve its civic goals. In 2007, with support from the European Cultural Foundation, we inaugurated the very first such process in Ukraine.

Cultural mapping: our credo

The Centre believes cultural activities have to be viewed more broadly than just from an artistic perspective. It is both difficult and artificial to try to separate culture from other aspects of life, such as the new economy, justice, human rights, social transformation, and politics. All these domains are interconnected, impact each other and form the basis for who we are. We also are convinced that cultural expression may be the resource that can most effectively catalyze change. Culture is the heart and soul of who we have been, who we are now and who we will become – as individuals, as communities, and as a nation. It is what gives life meaning. As a result it is important to everyone. Because, as an issue, it has less potential to be divisive at a core level, it can play an important role in creating a model for how diverse perspectives can come together to articulate shared values and find common ground. Cultural workers *are* members of the community. They live in neighbourhoods, send their children to school, need health care and worry about their economic future. Cultural policy should reflect and embody this reality and be linked with other policies and other incentives. Working 'in sync' with each other, they can produce the results we are struggling for.

When we launched the planning process in L'viv, we certainly focused on its cultural aspects; however, we also tried to keep this bigger picture in mind. We were aware that we could not strengthen the local cultural community and create more and better opportunities for it if we used a narrow understanding of the arts that did not embrace their interconnectedness with other aspects of life. In addition, we considered that cultural expression can be an important platform from which to broader issues. Directly challenging legal, regulatory and political systems via traditional avenues can be controversial because these entities are political hotbeds, ripe for corruption. Culture is much more accessible, much less threatening and, as a result, much more likely to produce durable patterns of change models that can be applied in other sectors. Additionally, the cultural community has the capacity to catalyze such processes in non-traditional and dynamic ways. Cultural workers are recognized as creative individuals who embrace innovation, as they are often poised at the cutting-edge of whatever they become involved in. They are acknowledged as having the ability to speak to the key issues of their time through the metaphor that is their work. As such, cultural workers and the cultural community have much to contribute to the shaping of their community and nation. We believed the problems in L'viv and Ukraine were due not just to bad laws, bad politicians, or a lack of entrepreneurship, but also to the culture of our community, as broadly defined. So, if we really want changes, we should start there – with a democratic approach – working from the bottom up and tapping into our most creative elements.

The cultural mapping process

The goal for our mapping project was to engage the residents of L'viv in a community exercise that would identify the cultural resources of the city, together with problem areas in the field of culture, thereby creating a preliminary framework for future cultural policy development. We wanted the process to be transparent and accountable, to provide the opportunity for each person to be heard, and for each participant to see him/herself reflected in the outcomes. We designed it to be inclusive, accessible, interactive, participant-driven, and intergenerational.

When we began, there already had been many training sessions, workshops, roundtables and conferences on the issue of culture in the city. The consensus appeared to be that these meetings had been boring, not useful and not credible, as they had produced few tangible outcomes. Participants included policy makers, media, business people, religious and community leaders, educators, funders and other community members interested in or impacted by culture. Each category of participant was invited to engage in a series of project activities, respond to questionnaires and participate in interviews. Surveys were distributed to cultural organizations, tourist agencies and members of the general public in order to solicit input from both cultural provider and cultural consumer perspectives. Events included an initial introductory conference that convened prospective cultural planners from around Ukraine and leaders in the field from around Europe. They also featured a series of focus groups, held to explore the status quo of the cultural sector, its abilities for capacity development and its vision for the future.

Among the new forms of meetings we considered for our gatherings was World Café methodology, which is based on the informal interactive generation of ideas for community development processes. Though the concept was born in the US, it fitted our needs perfectly. Living under the Soviet regime for many years, our society had been artificially fragmented and bordered. Policy makers and officials rarely communicated informally with the public, who were never treated as an important player in policy development. World Café focused on small group conversations; it engendered comfort and trust while encouraging meaningful communication. For many of our 32 participants, it was the first time they had been treated as constructors of a process. In total, we conducted four Cafés, positioning them as socially productive leisure time for the participants. In addition to World Café, we also analyzed announcements and advertisements in the city; advertisements, announcements and articles in local newspapers; the content in local *Yellow Pages* and on internet sites; and participation in cultural events.

What the exercise was to map

We designed our cultural map to include both the 'hardscape' (bricks and mortar) and the intangible dynamics (power and influence) of the cultural community. Key elements were:

1 *Types of cultural organizations*. We found it difficult, however, to draw clear margins around the cultural sector and often consulted to resolve this and linked issues with local university faculty and others who specialized in cultural issues.
2 *Location of cultural organizations*. As L'viv is a big city, this element was especially important to understanding challenges in accessibility to cultural activities.
3 *Key cultural players*. It was important to identify these individuals and entities and to understand how they interacted, so that they could be brought in as partners in the process.
4 *Available space and funding for cultural activities*. The only other resource more important to a dynamic cultural community than the previous two are cultural workers themselves and their outputs, so it was vital for us to know what was available for this purpose.

5 *Overall capacity in organizational development and planning*. It was imperative in identifying a baseline condition to understand clearly where the community's strengths and needs lie.
6 *Challenges*. Challenges always exist. Knowing about them means they can be addressed. Not knowing about them allows them to remain as active impediments.
7 *Opportunities*. Often opportunities are found in unexpected forms and places. They can leverage success, so it is vital to know about them.
8 *Critical points of action*. Based on analysis of all of the information gathered during the process, we then could identify important next steps as well as who should take them.

Findings

Demographics

The cultural sector of L'viv is comprised of state institutions, NGOs, private commercial companies and individual artists, as shown in Table 19.1 (further information on these institutions and their contact details are available online at www.kultura.org.ua – but in Ukrainian only). The vast majority of these are located in the centre of L'viv; most professional and organized cultural activities happen there as well. As a result, the city outskirts and 'dormitory suburbs' have limited opportunities to engage in professional, cultural life close to home, the exception being church or neighbourhood-organized festivities. The key cultural players in L'viv included the Municipal Department of Culture, the Regional Department of Culture (including regional institutions located in L'viv), cultural entrepreneurs (including galleries), culturally-focused non-governmental organizations (in all disciplines), parishes/religious communities, schools, students and youth circles and individual culture enthusiasts.

Existing resources

State cultural institutions generally have their own premises and receive a guaranteed share of the state, regional and/or municipal budget. Their seemingly more financially secured position is both an advantage and a challenge; while they receive guaranteed support, the organizations had become dependent, rigid and, as a rule, engaged less initiative in innovation and exploration – managerially and artistically. As the level of state funding has

Table 19.1 The cultural assets of L'viv

Archives [8]	Musicians [182]
Architectural institutions [41]	Cultural heritage organizations [17]
Libraries [87]	Relative educational institutions [30]
Houses of culture [23]	Monuments [25]
Publishing houses [80]	Parks [13]
Galleries [78]	Professional associations [42]
Media [64]	Design studios [62]
Cafés, restaurants [104]	Audio recording studios [10]
Film production [15]	Choreographic institutions [29]
Cinemas [11]	Theatres [29]
Clubs [140]	Tourism agencies [174]
Culture heritage [285]	Festivals [82]
Cultural centres [189]	Foundations [103]
Literature magazines/site [10]	Photo studios and organizations [89]
Studios [59]	Churches [104]
Arts agencies [19]	Other [5]
Museums [59]	

slipped, some have taken to renting out a part of their facilities for income. NGOs are dependent on project grants, usually from international foundations and, more recently, from the city council. This lack of guaranteed financial resources has forced them to be creative in both production and fundraising. Despite these obstacles, the quality of their projects is often high. Private, commercial, cultural initiatives are supported through their own revenue-for-service programming.

Challenges

Many challenges were found in the areas of financing, attendance, housing and management. While these issues are common to arts organizations around the world, they are especially problematic in Ukraine and L'viv because of the continuing legacy of the Soviet era. Within this overall context, two particular challenges need to be underlined: resistance to change and the problem of accessibility. As regards the first, L'viv's cultural community is on the cusp of change, yet continues to operate with a skill base and a retrograde mindset. For the most part, established organizations are attempting to operate in a new context using skills and tools relevant to another era. And there is resistance to learning and operating with the new skill set. Added to this is an apparent disconnect between expectations based

in the past and realities based in the present. In such a situation, no amount of well-intentioned activity will result in positive outcomes. Symptoms of this challenge include rigidities in the bureaucratic system of administration and financial support; the cultural institutions, themselves; community leadership and community members. There is a decided unwillingness and/or unreadiness to decentralize on the part of state authorities and cultural institutions. As Vita Susak, an active cultural player in L'viv, told us, 'City authorities and cultural institution administrators should feel the necessity and have the desire to intensify their activities. The question is how we can make them think in those terms.'

Corruption appears to exist anywhere that anyone has control over the means of resource allocation. It is a threat because it allows one individual or a few individuals to control access to resources both for the cultural provider and consumer. This effectively limits or eliminates opportunities to spark cultural innovation and appreciation, both of which are essential to further development. There is also an unwillingness to cooperate; scant recognition of the importance or value of cooperation for catalyzing ideas, leveraging resources, or learning new methods, whether within the sector or with others; and there is little cooperation with international professional associations and networks.

There is a lack of leadership, for in most sectors there is passive recognition or little awareness of the need for leadership in service to the community rather than in service to one's own agenda, and the cultural community is no exception. The majority of people expect positive changes will come from outside; they are not aware or convinced that they themselves are the drivers of change in their lives and their community.

We also found that while traditional sources of funding have diminished or disappeared, the expectation of financial dependency on state, regional or local budget continues. There is a continuing assertion that art and culture should be supported because they exist – the idea of 'art for art's sake'. At the root of this phenomenon is the perception that the museum or the theatre is not a provider that needs to be alert to the issues of the consumer. Many artists believe their role is to concentrate on their art and that it is therefore someone else's responsibility to finance their activities. There is a lack of recognition for or interest in the role of social entrepreneurial activity, marketing or any other means to build revenue from other sources. Quite often, when an artist or organization does attempt entrepreneurial activity to raise funds, their efforts result in frustration for all involved – for the artists, their managers, their audience and the community in general. This is probably due to inexperience and lack of training, but the frustration reinforces negative perceptions about change.

The challenge of accessibly exists on two levels: the cultural provider and the cultural consumer. The challenge for culture providers lies in insufficient access to information on existing resources. Cultural workers do not know where to go for ideas on management models, funding sources and colleagues. There are few or no capacity-building or organizational development services available locally, and most cultural workers are not used to thinking of the internet as a tool for finding such opportunities. Inexperience with the rest of the world can complicate matters, resulting in unrealistic expectations. When someone does use their initiative to locate information or services or potential partners, often they are stymied by language barriers or are ill-prepared to make strategic choices and/or to leverage their minimal resources.

The challenge for consumers is in finding out what's happening, getting to it, or being able to afford it. At the time of the mapping process, there was no centralized, publicized calendar of events for the city. The media was unreliable in this regard. And it is difficult to contact cultural organizations directly – our research showed that only state institutions were well represented in the *Yellow Pages*; commercial cultural institutions and services were partially represented, and there was practically no information on culture specialists, the primary elements of the culture infrastructure, or on culturally-focused NGOs. Moreover, public transport is limited, especially if one lives in the suburbs. Regular public transport service ends at eleven at night; anyone living in these areas and wanting to attend an event in the Centre would have to return by taxi, making the total cost unaffordable. A further impediment for older and physically impaired consumers is that events are often physically inaccessible. In addition, over the last two decades, the bulk of the population has struggled simply to feed their families. As a result, there has been a gradual atrophy of perceived cultural need accompanied by a slow provincialization of L'viv. As Myroslav Marynovych (Vice-Rector of the Ukrainian Catholic University) told us:

Many people do not participate in cultural events. However, this does not mean they are completely degraded human beings. When it comes to prioritizing use of the limited financial resources they have, cultural activities, unfortunately, are not often in the winning position. What we need to do is to make the majority of city dwellers aware of the importance of cultural activities in their life, so that they make it a priority for themselves at least once a month. This would be a beginning.

Finally, we learned there are few or no venues for alternative voices, especially for the young and the experimental artist. As a result, there are few or no opportunities for the cultural consumer to explore and support these perspectives.

Opportunities

The cultural mapping process also revealed opportunities that we (the community) can leverage:

• New legislation and regulations to catalyze development could be launched.
• Long-term as well as short-term planning and goal-setting could be created.

- Active cooperation and exchange inside the sector and beyond could be catalyzed.
- The current world focus on Ukraine could be exploited, especially from Europe and in light of the preparations for the 2012 European soccer championships to be jointly held in Poland and Ukraine.
- Current federal and local interest in cultural planning could be leveraged.
- The residents' loyalty to and pride in their city could be proactively engaged.
- (Both domestic and international research shows that L'viv residents love their city and are proud to live here. Acording to the most recent survey, conducted by GfK Ukraine (www.gfk.ua) in the autumn of 2007, the L'viv population's loyalty to its city is very high (4.23 points on a five-point scale). L'viv residents love their native city (4.80) and they are convinced that L'viv is the best city for them (4.34). This loyalty to the city should be acknowledged and used by policy makers, local authorities and civil society leaders. There should be more space envisaged where inhabitants of the city can participate in the strategy development of the city they live in.
- The Ukrainian diaspora could be tapped for expertise, partnership opportunities and financial support. Ukrainians have moved all over the world, but no matter where they are they retain an emotional and very real connection to their homeland. There are significant Ukrainian communities throughout Europe and North America, each with a new understanding based in their own experiences of life elsewhere of the potential for development in Ukraine. In these communities there exists a desire waiting to be leveraged to positively impact conditions in their homeland.

Key issues

As a result of all of the information gathered, we identified several key issues and critical points of action.

First, we need to build closer working relationships between the cultural community and policy makers, between municipal and regional Departments of Culture, and among state, public and private cultural institutions. At the moment there is neither good communication nor cohesive activities among them.

There are several options for additional resource development for the cultural community. First, the current distribution and use of public funds by governments and authorities is no longer effective, and it is necessary to develop and introduce new legislation, as well as improve local administrative regulations that can catalyze as well as support the cultural community. National laws and local administrative regulations have not been updated since independence in 1991, if at all. In most cases they are out of date and are no longer relevant. As Andriy Pavchyshyn, a local cultural activist, told us: 'We need to change the legislative background for the development of culture. Many concrete suggestions have been elaborated, however there is not enough awareness in the Parliament to vote for them.'

We could enact new laws on charity donations to cultural institutions, implementing a contract basis of employment, improving management skills, improving marketing techniques, introducing adjunct commercial services on site – such as bars, cafés, miscellaneous merchandise – investing in capital and/or capital upgrades which will increase competitiveness, and new grants. Those who can and should initiate the resolution of these issues are the local cultural operators and the local cultural community. We will be able to do this when there is a critical mass wanting these changes and who are willing to create the public pressure necessary to make them happen. This is where capacity-building projects can help.

We need to secure greater support for the overall development of the cultural community, including but not limited to professional infrastructural development – with an emphasis on growing a new generation of cultural managers, modernizing cultural facilities, creating the conditions that will catalyze public and private initiatives (legislation, local decrees) and increasing funding opportunities. Grants for one-time artistic projects alone will not help the cultural community be more productive and useful. There is a need for systemic initiatives with a broader vision on the application of culture. In the long run such a strategic approach will turn out to be cheaper and much more effective. Working in a local community to build its capacity to cope with new challenges has always been more useful than one-time injections into separate projects, which often are dispersed and not strategically connected. In order to make change and bring cultural activities up to date, there is a need to converge existing financial and human resources and make them work for this change together. This convergence, or at least communication and coordination of activities, should happen on different levels: foundations, local cultural agents, authorities, and individuals.

A combination of training sessions, regular face-to-face and online communication, and involvement of various cultural players in the same initiatives could lay the ground for serious renewal, gradually building local capacities to engage in new market realities, as well as improve the community's relationship to authorities, public funds, audience, etc. Similarly, we need to build opportunities for cultural self-expression and debate. The cultural infrastructure of the city is archaic and monolithic. The city does not have enough spaces for contemporary art explorations and manifestations. We need to create centralized access to a wide range of timely, meaningful, supportive information for both the cultural community and the cultural consumer. At the moment, there is a huge informational gap between the two.

We need to build opportunities to learn and experience what is happening in other parts of Europe and the world. Owing to strict visa regimes, imposed by many countries towards Ukrainian citizens, it is difficult to work internationally. On the other hand, local cultural managers can be more proactive and use internet opportunities, as this digital tool is being used more and more in international projects. We need to be more engaged in active cooperation and exchange inside the sector and beyond. Gradually, more and more cultural institutions and individual artists realize that they can achieve much better results though cooperation with others and not by competing with each other. According to Andriy Pavlyshyn, a reputed local analyst of civic issues:

Globalization processes might give the city a good chance. Already now we can see some benefits out of that as. For example, there are some Russian and Chinese film companies coming here to shoot their films in a natural environment they cannot easily find in other places. It could be a good chance for us; however, we need to improve our cultural infrastructure to exploit it.

We need to preserve our rich cultural heritage and use it for the development of the city in more creative ways. Investments into heritage preservation should be gradually covered by the income generated by a robust creative tourism industry yet to be developed.

We need to build community awareness of and appreciation for culture, including engaging in a community-wide cultural planning process that includes a community-driven visioning component. It has become abundantly clear that local people want to be stakeholders in city development, and they are ready to contribute their time and ideas. Engaging them will help us re-orient our expectations and activities towards long-term goals as well as short-term benefits. We will not achieve better results without strategic planning, currently absent. Building long-term strategies will help us to secure short-term results that support our intentions and vision. As Myroslav Marynovych, Vice-Rector of the Ukrainian Catholic University, puts it:

We need to build our activities on the basis of local people needs and needs of each residential area of the city. Each quarter of the city is unique; having their needs in focus, we can initiate many innovative and unique cultural activities there. The diversity of these activities will help us to revitalize the cultural humus of L'viv to grow the 'orchids' we are striving for. It cannot be realized vice-versa.

Recommendations

In the light of our findings, we made the following recommendations to the L'viv community:

- *Continued cultural planning.* The cultural mapping process is a beginning. It should be followed by a fully-fledged, community-driven cultural planning process that culminates in a clearly articulated cultural vision for the city, identifying long-range goals as well as the strategies and objectives for achieving them. These goals and objectives then should become the backbone of strategic choice-making about the allocation of governmental resources, including funding, legislation, permitting, capacity-building, planning for accessibility, etc.
- *Municipal, regional and state-level cooperation.* An individual or a cultural organization exists not only in a municipality but also in a region and a state; the cultural sector is impacted by all three. There are multiple incidents where

governmental processes and laws actually work at cross-purposes with their own stated goals. This is amplified when one layer of government establishes policies that not only contradict their own laws, but conflict with those of other governmental structures. If different levels of government work at cross-purposes with each other, they compromise both individual initiative and meaningful growth – and they create confusion and opportunities for corruption. If any single governmental entity works at cross-purpose with the needs of the community, it compromises first the individual and, ultimately, the community they are charged to support.

• *Access to information.* During the cultural mapping process we heard over and over again that people wanted/needed access to information about opportunities; that if they had it, they could help themselves. This access applies both to cultural providers and cultural consumers. For cultural providers, it is very important that they have access to information about all aspects of cultural management, including new models, training opportunities, exchanges, professional networks, etc. At the minimum, cultural consumers need access to dependable, timely and accurate information on the calendar of events.

• *Capacity development.* L'viv's cultural managers must be exposed to the best new models for management and planning as well as for artistic development. This information, which often stresses the benefits of cooperation and collaboration, will catalyze both growth and creativity. This information includes new models and best practices that can broaden perspectives, colleagues – regional, national and international – who can share experiences and potentially create partnerships, and new thinking on art and creativity.

• *A city where all voices can be heard.* The city needs to support and encourage a full spectrum of options and opportunities to create and experience the arts and culture; this recommendation applies in all venues, including education. A dynamic cultural environment is such because it embraces its diversity; creativity is rooted in the energy that results when multiple voices have the chance to be heard. Historically, it is this 'conversation' around differences that sparks new ideas and new ways of thinking. New

research indicates that these types of creative centre have a positive impact beyond the cultural sphere. L'viv had it once; it deserves to have it again.

Conclusion and next steps

The cultural mapping of L'viv was carried out in 2007–2008. Since then we have been constantly encouraging everyone in the city to view the exercise as a first step towards change. The Cultural Map is a baseline assessment as well as a guide for future action, and we encourage policy makers to see it as an opportunity to start the process of exploration and integration of L'viv's cultural environment into public policy development and planning. Since the Map's publication in the autumn of 2008, there have been concrete responses to some of its recommendations. For example, in 2009, the city of L'viv began publishing a monthly, comprehensive calendar of cultural activities (*OT-OT*), available in hardcopy and on the internet. This action directly addressed the issue of centralized access to information for the cultural consumer.

When we completed the process, we did not consider our work done, leaving it only to others to act. Instead, again with the support and cooperation of the European Cultural Foundation, we launched new initiatives for development of individuals and organizations, directly addressing the key issue of building the capacity of the cultural community to work more effectively. An initially unexpected result of this work is the development of a growing network of cultural workers, brought together through the mapping process and subsequent programming. This network is catalyzing its own actions, including collaborative ventures among cultural workers from L'viv and with others around the country and in Europe. In 2010, these capacity development initiatives were expanded to include six other cities in Ukraine. One goal for this initiative now is the creation of a formal, national network of cultural providers, who ultimately can find a common voice that will impact public policy development. Accompanying this expanded initiative will be a web portal that serves both as a repository of information and a catalyst for partnership and collaboration. Finally, cultural providers in L'viv are realizing a greater number of successful grant submissions, more audience-friendly projects and higher audience numbers. And, we are seeing a reframing of the role for the Centre's work in L'viv – a result of a clearly growing appreciation for its relevance to stakeholders in the city and around the country.

So, overall, our situation does appear to be improving, albeit slowly. We continue to encourage the cultural community to see opportunities both for individual and civil sector initiative and growth. We hope the Cultural Map will play a part in increasing public awareness of the value of and role for culture in our community. This is its true value – as a catalyst for further creation. The city of L'viv is regaining its former status as cultural capital of Ukraine, and the city's numerous cultural festivals are attracting more visitors from other cities and countries. We have revealed that ongoing globalization brings us more chances for the development than threats. While there remain obvious obstacles to be overcome, we know our goal is absolutely realistic – we can do it!

CHAPTER 20

MARSEILLE–PROVENCE 2013: CULTURAL CAPITAL, BUT FOR WHAT KIND OF EUROPE AND UNDER WHICH GLOBALIZATION?

Ferdinand Richard

This account of the cultural process in Marseille focuses on the challenges, opportunities and tensions within the preparations that are being made by the city-region 'Marseille–Provence' to become a 'European Capital of Culture' in 2013 (together with Košice in Slovakia). This collection of Mediterranean municipalities has rich cultural assets and an enviable geo-cultural position. In the context of globalization, however, notably migratory flows and worldwide transcultural connections, the author discusses how these preparations present a range of challenges, tensions and perhaps some missed opportunities.

Introduction: the potential

Strategically placed at the centre of the western Mediterranean – but facing strong competition – Marseille seeks to capitalise on and harness its creative talents. To begin with, Marseille can boast of a considerable number of such talents, based on the wide variety of artistic groups found there, together with a solid infrastructure of artistic provision, even if the latter is neither as rich nor as well endowed as those of other major French regional cities, such as Lyon or Bordeaux. Over decades of regular relations with other centres of the arts in the southern Mediterranean, particularly in the Arab countries, Marseille has also greatly increased its cultural exchanges of individual artists, teams or groups.

Built up by many different ethnic communities over 26 centuries of history (an exceptionally long life-span for a city, even in Europe), the heritage of Marseille, both tangible or intangible, is a fountain of life where, directly or indirectly, consciously or unconsciously, a myriad of artists quench their thirst, whether they are established or nascent, either originating from the various sections of the city's population or hailing from other shores and attracted by this extraordinary location. Even if their motives are sometimes little more than fantasy, their 'artistic assimilation' is often both rapid and definitive. It is often said that the artistic career of an artist from Marseille who has 'gone up to the capital' (i.e. Paris) continues to show characteristic and indelible signs that a discerning eye can rapidly detect. It goes without saying that this has nothing to do with either the artist's accent or their physical appearance. It should, however, be noted that, after the 1990s, 'the golden age of the Marseille *movida*', there followed a slowdown or maybe even a moderate decline in the arrival of European and non-European artists. Incidentally, in this context, one might easily imagine Marseille–Provence 2013 playing the role of a flow regulator.

Conventionally, Marseille's industrial image is seen only as a negative aspect and this obscures its more attractive features. Its tag graffiti and its strong smells can be seen as the flip-side of that other, summery Provence: full of festivals, bathed in the scent of rosemary and the blue of the lavender fields. Two opposite worlds indeed… The city therefore seeks to overcome this difficult starting point and, in this sense, becoming European Capital of Culture in 2013 is a blessing that none of the city's leaders can afford to disregard. However, taking advantage of the blessing will depend on the city's ability to harness its creative talents and this goal will not be attainable through local measures alone. Indeed, the more the mechanisms of globalisation gain ground, the more a gap emerges between two ideologies or cultures across the European continent.

The first option, which might seem obvious, relates to a rationalisation or a uniformity of 'cultural consumption' and logically implies a concentration of power among an ever-decreasing number of global monopolies, giants of the 'entertainment industry', who industrialise artistic production in 'top-down' flows. Here – where we might also question the contradiction in terms between 'creative' (a singular and experimental act which cannot be considered 'industrial') and 'industry' (essentially, the act of duplication which, by definition, is not 'creative') – the concept of 'creative industries' is deliberately interpreted in a particular way which is in principle divergent from 'cultural diversity' (cf. Anheier and Isar, 2010). Works are mass (re-) produced, are highly entertaining, with a short life-span and low production costs, making them accessible to the resources of the private mass market. The target is the world market. The source is concentrated in a few cultural 'Golden Triangles' of an all-consuming attractiveness.

The second option proposes globalisation in the form of instantly multilateral, multilevel, multicultural production networks (therefore 'bottom-up'), within which power is shared, equally or not, between different geographical extremes and varying weights. There is a kind of expanding profusion of initiatives that leaves more room to the commercial balance of power than to global industrial planning. This balance of power is never definitive: everything about it is negotiable. Working within it, priority can be given to works of a more singular, lasting nature, which have a low turnover and a strong power of influence, clearly identified by their 'territory' of origin, possibly costly and unlikely to exist without public funding. Driven by specific population centres, they 'communicate' a shared, proclaimed identity. Targets appear through a fluctuating network of local markets, which are more or less interconnected. Every individual is a potential source of cultural production.

As usual, the ever-changing reality lies somewhere between these two extremes. However, the two options influence cultural decision-making in radically different ways. For the simple fact of raising any city or any group of towns or cities to the rank of 'European Capital of Culture' obliges it to place itself, consciously or unconsciously, in line with one of them.

Marseille–Provence 2013

Marseille–Provence, one of two cultural 'capitals' for 2013, will obviously not escape this rule, although, in this respect, the city has not as yet expressly chosen either option in an undisputably clear fashion. Yet its candidacy is unique, which may in some respects represent a pause for thought in Europe's 'cultural journey' at the dawn of the European Commission's new 2014–2020 planning period. Unique indeed, because of a novel combination of diverse factors: the large number of towns involved, the area's geostrategic position in the Mediterranean, i.e. at the junction of Europe and its neighbouring zones, and the long-term cultural structure of the area. Will culture remain a vaguely identifiable object, floating above us, the preserve of certain specialists isolated in a 'protosphere'? Or will it undergo a radical 'mainstreaming', swarming with experts in all administrative services, in all departments of private enterprise, involving itself in public health, in education, transport, security and even in the search for social cohesion? It is clear that, for the programme directors of the European Commission, what happens today through the creation and management of the Capitals of Culture serves as research and development for the long-term ambition of integrating Europe's different regions.

We will not enter into any critique here of the themes to be explored during Marseille–Provence 2013.[1] They are all the more legitimate in that they structured the decisive line of argument that led to the success of this candidacy. A visit to the website of 'MP13' (as we shall choose to call it from now on) is enough to understand the thematic expectations of its backers (be they the European Commission or the French State) and the strategic intelligence of Bernard Latarjet, who directed the candidacy and then became the principal director of the entire operation. Latarjet is a senior government official, having served in the French Ministry of Culture, notably as an adviser to Jack Lang and, subsequently, as an aide to President François Mitterrand, finally as the director of the *Grande Halle de la*

Villette in Paris.[2] No quarrel, then, with the overall aims of the project, yet there is a slight frustration regarding its artistic daring, which is somewhat restricted by an almost 'miserabilist' context that weighs down MP13: the city is seen to be needy and therefore deserves to be chosen over Lyon, Bordeaux or Toulouse. This kind of 'positive discrimination', barely defensible and of little instructive value, opens the door to all sorts of exaggeration and reflects an unflattering image that the city's residents would willingly leave behind them, once and for all.

Nor is it useful to dwell on the destructive effects of the worldwide financial crisis which has hit businesses very hard, both here and elsewhere. However, we should rapidly take up an entrepreneurial sociology of Marseille which is seen, contrary to cities like Lyon or Lille, to have somehow become consolidated around businesses that are more family-based than industrial and whose international influence reflects an older, trading-post style of commercial policy, rather than global monopolies, international alliances or multinational networks. The hopes of finding business sponsorship have also been significantly reduced from the level they were pitched at when the bid was made. In terms of artistic programming, therefore, MP13 must make certain choices which will limit it financially and which, if Bernard Latarjet's line is not sufficiently supported, could well attain the very basis on which the bid was won, namely that the project would put in place sustainable cultural infrastructure and provision, investment for the long term rather than showy events and public relations. Unfortunately, there are already signs that such processes are taking place…

We need to discuss further certain specific predispositions of the city that complicate the process. Belonging to both Provence and to Marseille, as I have done for 46 years now, I must at the outset make it clear that it is not at all my intention to damage either the bid or its success, but rather to restore to it all the dignity that it has the right to expect.

Uniqueness and atavism, overcoming problems

To ensure this dignity, several obstacles have to be overcome. First, there are several internal political restrictions. Examining the city's geography in terms of concentric circles, we see that first – from Arles to La Ciotat, taking in the town of Aix-en-Provence – shows immediately that MP13 is primarily a partnership representing more than 130 municipal districts surrounding Marseille, with a total resident population of about 1.5 million. A great team effort… Sadly, this team effort is increasingly hampered by a major event in the political calendar: in 2014, barely a year after the event, each of these 130 municipalities will hold elections and each incumbent mayor will be counting on the dynamism of 'MP13' to lure voters to re-elect her or him. This manipulative exploitation of the event could go so far as to severely call into question the notion of the 'common pot' (or central fund), a symbol of the unity at the heart of the bid. Some mayors have even gone so far as to declare that their financial contribution will only be confirmed on condition that it will be exclusively used within their own territory, a condition impossible to manage for the visionary and demanding artistic programme planner that MP13 seeks to be.

We also have to bear in mind the position of the 'second circle' of municipalities, which are not integrated into the main bid but belong to the regional community that also contributes financially. These municipalities have legitimate expectations of a 'return on investment', although they are geographically distant from the regional capital. Finally, the fast-approaching prospect of the Euro-region's plan becoming operational requires this bid to echo it. Note that the Euro-region to which we belong – made up of PACA (Provence–Alpes–Côtes d'Azur), Rhône–Alpes, Piedmont, Liguria and Aosta – aims to be first off the starting-block. But in view of the kinds of ongoing programmes, negotiations and alliances that can be observed, this seems to be still no more than just a declaration of intent.

Another major political constraint is the proposed reform of the local government authorities that is currently being debated in the country. This reform, expected to enter into force in 2012, would mean that municipal responsibility for cultural matters could become either optional, obligatory or even might be done away with. Certain outcomes would cruelly deprive the municipalities concerned not only of major additional resources that they have the right to expect from the Regional Council and also from the administration of the *Département*, but also the indispensable 'political advocacy' that these major local government authorities could provide. Even though, with the exception of Marseille and Aix, the towns do not really have the capacity for external cultural relations (and what would a European Capital of Culture be without international relations?), one might have expected an effort in this respect from the Region or the *Département* Council at the international level. But will these entities even still exist after 2012? What direction will a collective bid involving more than 130 towns take if two shared levels of administration (the *Département* and the Region) were to disappear and if the new structures that replace them do not acquire sufficient competencies for cultural affairs?

Currently erratic French cultural policy

The European project increasingly calls the country's established models of cultural policy into question. These inward-looking models have aimed traditionally to achieve national prestige and influence, to propagate an official state culture. Until now the prerogative of the central state, the making of official cultural policy followed a single model, possibly reproducible at the local level, with every town seeking somehow to be yet another 'Paris in miniature'. And if we are to believe the directives set out by the then Foreign Minister Bernard Kouchner in December 2009 – where no mention is even made of local authorities and even less of any decentralised cultural cooperation – France's cultural diplomacy remains a domain reserved for a 'diplomacy of influence' [sic], essentially aimed at strategic goals which have little to do with cultural rights. Let us not forget that the French Government is one of the most stubborn in its refusal to ratify, for constitutional reasons, the European Charter for Regional or Minority Languages adopted under the aegis of the Council of Europe in 1992. In view of Marseille's polyglot population, this is a strikingly incoherent position.

More or less painfully, but irreversibly, a transfer of cultural sovereignty from the European nation-states to their local power structures is taking place and gradually finding its own limits. We believe that, within the French Ministry of Culture itself, certain voices are making themselves heard, evoking a reversal of the principle of 'Culture for All', whose record is far from positive, in favour of a move towards the principle of a 'Culture *of* All' – in other words from a model of cultural 'democratisation' to that of cultural 'democracy', encouraged by the recent ratification of the 2005 UNESCO *Convention on the Protection and Promotion of the Diversity of Cultural Expressions*. The national debate about culture, or rather the glaring absence of a true debate, creates confusion in the governance of cultural affairs. It has created a vacuum that some local government authorities are trying to fill, especially the larger towns and cities. It is a difficult period, but also an exciting one, because multilevel governance of culture is coming into play, from the local to the pan-European, as shown by the public debate on this subject in the European Parliament in June 2010.

Therefore the French State will soon have to harmonise its international commitments, bringing the more instrumentalising orientations revealed by the Foreign Ministry's directives referred to above into line with the ideas it adopted when it ratified UNESCO's 2005 Convention. On the face of it, the two sets of principles are incompatible and this ambiguity will resonate throughout the world of the arts, including the European Capital of Culture project.

Two great challenges

In this context, it requires considerable daring on the part of a French city to seek to become a European Capital of Culture and is bound to create innumerable pitfalls. If the political elites have the vision and the courage, and if Mr Latarjet (or his successor) understands the full extent of local knowhow, then MP13, the 'anti-Parisian' rebel, could succeed with dazzling cultural innovation, and could take advantage of the candidacy to launch a renovation of its cultural policy, to be extended well beyond 2013. Or else it might sink down to the lowest common denominator of average European cultural mediocrity, based from one end of the continent to the other on the same works, the same communication, and the same places and venues, and it may possibly suffer from Byzantine political struggles. In any case, it will be essential to ratify a certain number of seminal texts, especially the UCLG's *Agenda 21 for Culture* (as discussed in Chapter 5 of this volume by Duxbury, Cullen and Pascual), something which no participant in MP13 has yet done, with the exception of the City of Aubagne, which deserves our compliments for doing so.

Accepting its internal diversity

Although it owes its survival and its pride to its dazzling indiscipline, occasionally mixed with indolence (which, besides, renders it so human), our city-region must finally accept the reality of its own patterns of immigration. Let's admit it, the greatest militants for Marseille's cause are to be found among its innumerable immigrants, as is to be expected, but also among 'Parisians', northerners, not necessarily the inhabitants of the most affluent quarters, sometimes those who are audaciously un-French, who humbly adopt the cause, thereby becoming 'more Marseillais than the people of Marseille themselves'. Conversely, it is enough to read the self-satisfied, quasi-populist phrases, the 'Pagnolesque' clichés, dished out by the national press, including (above all?) the 'progressive' press, in order to understand the extent to which Marseille suffers from a negative image in the minds of French people, especially where the life of the mind is concerned.

It's an old cliché, but also the reality, that the city of Marseille welcomes children from all over the world into its schools, with no hesitation concerning their colour, their accent or their material wealth or lack of it. No one comments on your origins. We wait to see your work! This redeeming principle ought also to be applied to the cultural field in general and to MP13 especially, provided that the project actually succeeds in including everyone from the humblest to the most boastful of the Provençal people. The moral contract which should link MP13 to its inhabitants will operate within this delicate balance: trust artistic innovation, trust the people, because, in Marseille, the one should not prevail over the other. Breaking this contract could well be one of the principal causes of the failure of MP13, should that come about.

Going beyond its geostrategic heritage

Marseille was the chief port of the French Colonial Empire. It always was and still is one of the main transit points of immigration and emigration, especially within the 'Mediterranean backyard'. Toulon, which could have been the other big city in the bid, had its municipality not chosen to dissociate itself from it, is the home port of the French naval forces and their allies. Marseille recently welcomed a department of the World Bank and is also claiming a leading role in the Cultural Council of the Union for the Mediterranean as in other areas of influence. Therefore purely 'heritage' reasoning means pushing MP13 to adopt an inward-looking attitude of 'self-segregation', one that also remains within the French sphere of influence, which some outspoken commentators would see as pure neo-colonialism.

In fact, nobody in this city dares to question the sometimes stifling clause of a kind of obligatory 'Mediterraneanism', which would tend to suggest that there could be no justification for deploying the cultural expertise of MP13 outside the Mediterranean. Quite apart from the fact that the concept of a 'dialogue among Mediterranean cultures' is above all a western idea (for the Arab world, the Mediterranean is not necessarily a place of convergence), it is obvious that others have already forcefully claimed the 'Mediterranean' label already. Competition is fierce and we could hope that, intelligently, we might enhance the visibility of MP13 in the world, well beyond the Mediterranean (but not without it), through certain specific attributes and skills that our geocultural region possesses more fully than others do. These include the range of cultural activities, places of artistic creation, public sector support for culture, integration of contemporary creation with local heritage, gradual improvement of a formerly devastating cultural tourism, interdisciplinary cross-fertilisation, decentralised cultural cooperation, etc. These are all areas of expertise or works in progress already recognised the world over – and not just in the Mediterranean 'neighbourhood' area – as belonging to the region. These could integrate its 'Mediterranean sound' into a truly global concert… MP13 could achieve such results for itself but also for its neighbours, both European and North African, especially as, in some ways, it already does so, quite naturally.

There is another painful problem: the lack of coordination (even the competition) among the Cultural Council of the Union for the Mediterranean – largely led by France and chaired by Renaud Muselier, deputy Mayor of Marseille – the Anna Lindh Foundation – which is an emanation of the 'Barcelona Conventions' and the 'armed wing' of the European Commission for Dialogue between Mediterranean Cultures – and the initiatives of the Spanish International Cooperation Agency (AECID). In addition, there are other circles of power that confuse the Mediterranean theatre even further. Obviously, every player plays its pawns according to its own interests and, to my knowledge, the new external relations services of Baroness Ashton (High Representative of the EU for Foreign Affairs and Security Policy) have not yet issued even the slightest element of doctrine which could allow us to envisage a minimum degree of cohesion, of clarity or of alignment. The image given by this diplomatic confusion is abysmal, and the project is suffering accordingly. Seen from Algiers, from Istanbul or from Ramallah, of what kind of Europe will MP13 be a Cultural Capital?

Conclusion

In conclusion, the evidence suggests that MP13 will be (or is already) in the eye of a hurricane whose unpredictable movements could either pass it by or do it serious harm. It is not entirely clear whether, when they brought the bid to the baptismal font, its creators had indeed measured the dangers ahead. Yet this problematic context is in itself a challenge, and we will certainly see if the intrinsic cultural resources and the life-blood of MP13 are capable of joining forces once more against misfortune. They are strong, deeply rooted, and not always visible, and they occasionally reside in the strata of population where we least expect them. For over 2,600 years, the people of Marseille have demonstrated an astonishing capacity for resistance–resistance that has been passive to varying degrees. Centres of population that have shown such a capacity for synthesis, and who therefore bear witness to very real richness of culture, are rare in Europe. Furthermore, it will be necessary to give every one of them good reasons for identifying with this project and making it their own. This is one of the political frameworks which still needs consolidation.

Finally, as has already been said, the timing of this project makes it a full-scale test for the European Commission's approach to culture at the dawn of the 2014–2020 planning period, especially regarding the capacity of local government authorities to at least partly assume key policy challenges. It is, of course, at the level of European institutions that the future equilibrium between local development, continental harmonisation, global fair trade and cultural diversity will be established. The member states of the European Union, which until now have been leading players in making these choices, will have to deal as much with the growing autonomy of local power as with a European institutional reality that brings them all inexorably closer together. Certainly, MP13 will experience the joys and the horrors of cultural renovation but, like a mirror, will reflect to its backers all the fundamental questions that such an event will not fail to raise. But are they ready to answer these questions?

Notes

1 'Le partage des midis: création et créateurs en Euroméditerranée'; 'Migrations, exiles, voyages'; 'Partage et conflits de mémoires'; 'Racines et actualités religieuses'; 'Masculin-féminin'; 'Valeurs et figures communes: Athènes et Jérusalem'; 'Les 100 ans de Camus'; 'Gastronomie Nord-Sud', 'Partage de l'Eaux'; 'La cité radieuse: l'art dans l'espace public'; 'Promeneurs et nomades', 'Chemins de traverse'; 'Mille et une nuits'; 'Cities on the edge'; 'Nouveaux commanditaires: nouvelles écritures, tous acteurs'.

2 Soon after this chapter was drafted, however, Bernard Latarjet stepped down from the post of Director but will continue to be a key player in the project, with major functions of oversight and supervision. We do not know why he chose to do this but it is certain that his decision was not the result of any kind of management or political crisis.

REFERENCES

Anheier, H. and Isar, Y.R. (2010) *Cultural Expression, Creativity and Innovation. The Cultures and Globalization Series 3*. London: SAGE.

UNESCO (2005) *Convention on the Protection and Promotion of the Diversity of Cultural Expressions*. Paris: UNESCO.

CHAPTER 21

MEDELLÍN: TALES OF FEAR AND HOPE[1]
Octavio Arbeláez Tobón

How richly people have always dreamed … of the better life that might be possible. Everybody's life is pervaded by daydreams: one part of this is just stale, even enervating escapism, even booty for swindlers, but another part is provocative, is not content just to accept the bad which exists, does not accept renunciation. This other part has hoping at its core, and is teachable. (Ernst Bloch, 1986: 3)

Introduction: the city and its fears

Two decades ago, Medellín could have been described as a city without nuances, which prayed devoutly in its churches, laboured unremittingly in its factories, workshops and offices, respected authority, read the same newspapers and listened to the same music and voted for the same conservative politicians: a calm and silent city, ideally placed for the preservation of traditions and privileges. But then, abruptly, things began to change.

On the heels of the strident cries of the student movements of the 1970s, which had marked the first ruptures of the city's routines, came a set of new players – people who flourished in the shadow of drug trafficking, a commerce so profitable that in the space of a few years it had transformed the map of rural and urban wealth and penetrated the mindset of the entire country. This was particularly the case in Medellín, which Pablo Escobar, the most famous of the new rich, made his base of operations, demonstrating that it was indeed possible to transform the narrative hitherto imposed by those who had traditionally held the levers of economic and political power.

With the brutal car bomb attack on the offices of the newspaper *El espectador* and the killing of its editor, the so-called 'time of the bombs' ('*epoca de las bombas*') made its brutal entry into public awareness. The streets of the city were taken over by terror. Faced with the random risk of an explosion that would take their lives, people took refuge in the safe silence of their homes. By the close of this 'Pablo Escobar chapter' in the life of the city, Medellín had become known the world over as the city of drug traffickers. Fernando Botero's small painting of the moment at which bullets penetrated the drug lord's bloated body, now in the Museum of Antioquia, had already become part of the visual public memory of that period. The period also generated a range of sociological and literary analysis exploring the deep wounds it caused to the city. It spawned novels such as Fernando Vallejo's *La virgin de los sicarios* and Jorge Franco Ramos's *Rosario Tijeras*, both made into movies, as well as several journalistic accounts. All these works document the period and must be read if its history is to be properly understood.

Yet, contrary to all expectations, Paulo Escobar's death did not free Medellín's streets of violence. Armed bands offered themselves to the highest bidders and the city found itself caught up once again in a war that resembled its predecessor and that, like the latter, threatened to continue indefinitely. Young men were recruited in their respective neighbourhoods by the first comers. Those who used to play football in the street fashion of all against all, now found themselves armed, organized into opposing militias and ordered expressly to wipe out their enemies. In all the country's cities, a conflict that had begun on the margins of society was now brought to its heart.

During the reign of Pablo Escobar, the armed groups that entered the drug trade had considerably enriched themselves, mainly through the protection of cocoa cultivation and the clandestine processing laboratories that sprung up in jungle tracts. Guerrilla and paramilitary movements were paid to deploy either tolerance or vigilance; and now, they also inherited the labour force of the different city neighbourhoods. A struggle for the control of these city districts ensued, with each zone taking on the colouring of the group that controlled it. The fighting spread to other city zones as a premonition of what was to come. The nights were full of violent explosions, kidnappings, disappearances, extortion and massacres. Fear entered into our hearts anew and once again we began to shut ourselves up in our homes at the fall of darkness.

The violence of drug trafficking and armed conflict are not just chapters to be forgotten, however. For they also triggered the appearance of what is today called the city's 'cultural resistance'. The nights of terrors stimulated the search for what might bring us together and unify our forces, and these we found in the quotidian dimension of cultural practice. In the neighbourhoods suffused with conflict, the old *casas de cultura* were still there, those cultural entities that brought together whole communities around story-telling, theatre performance, dance and music. They kept hope alive.

The Medellín of today assumes the identity of a multicultural city in the sense that it contains different views of the world, yet it cannot be discussed in the abstract, as if urban reality were a theoretical construct. In various parts of the city more than 50,000 people of African descent live, work and dream; their different cultures surely enrich the ways of their neighbours. Like their peers everywhere in the world, young people are constructing a new urban imaginary to replace the image of the assassin who once preyed upon and killed them; exile is no longer the default option for them and they are no longer ashamed of their city before visitors from elsewhere. The new symbols of the city in this new age are its parks and its libraries, for

indeed it is the cultural sector that has led this process of symbolic transformation.

Urban culture and public policy

The role culture has played in the transformation of Medellín has been recognized internationally. In effect, the educative dimensions of the city's urban culture are considered to be more than the work of a single administration. Rather they are to be embedded in the practice of citizenship and as *politicas de Estado*[2] that must be nurtured and transformed in accordance with the city's future needs. It can be affirmed that Medellín sees itself today as a space of transformation in the habits and ways of life of its citizens, whose long-term goal is to attain a more equitable, participative and tolerant intercultural society. It is also as the staging ground for a range of cultural wealth, in which different sectors of society address different clusters of issues related to difference – economic, gender and sexual preference – in order to convert the city into a space of expression for the autonomous development of its cultural traditions, both material and immaterial, and for the sharing of its public memory, whether oral, visual or written, while also tackling the asymmetries intrinsic to the dynamics of contemporary cultures.

Nevertheless, and as we indicated earlier, the previous climate of violence and its sequels of social fear have occupied a central place in the life of the city for three decades, albeit in different forms depending on the particular historical moment. Although it is clear that this phenomenon is the result of many different factors and has to be analyzed through a range of prisms, and linked to the different forms earlier conflict has taken, one of the principal causes has been the process of urban population growth itself. In other words, the characteristic feature of recent history, in which peasants have flocked to the cities, violently displaced from their rural origins, and now occupy urban zones that remain irregular, informal and sometimes illegal. And these are places that recreate conditions for conflict, poverty, marginalization and inequity – in a word, places that exclude their inhabitants from the benefits of urban living. In a different perspective, manifestations of urban violence are linked to the drug trade, which has corrupted key social actors, eroding the moral fibre, perverting with the promise of easy cash an entire generation of young people who, bereft of either opportunities or expectations, turn to illicit practices as the only alternative for the future. The end result is a perpetuation of the vicious circle of stigmatization and exclusion. It is important to mention also that the drug trade also brought about a form of violence directed against people in the cultural sector itself, as well as social and community leaders, all of whom, despite everything, continued to pursue alternatives and more inclusive social models. There is also the latent perception of lingering tensions in the everyday life of the *barrios*, where many of the problems that brought about the terrible realities described above remain as alive as ever.

This was the context in which the concept of 'citizen culture' propagated by Antanas Mockus, a former mayor of Bogotá, made its appearance. This notion, that its author has introduced into the public policy discourse in Colombia, pertains to a whole made up of that minimum of shared customs, actions and rules that together generate sentiments of shared belonging, facilitate urban conviviality (*convivencia*), lead to a respect for the shared heritage and promote the recognition of the rights and duties of citizens. The aim behind the deployment of this concept was to trigger off and coordinate a mix of public and private initiatives to directly influence the manner in which citizens perceive, recognize and use their social and urban environments, as well as the way in which they relate to each other in each of these settings. To belong to a city is to recognize these contexts and in each context to respect the relevant rules of the game. To appropriate the city is to learn how to use it, while valorizing and respecting its order and its public goods character. The patterns of citizen participation in the planning of the cultural development of the city were the innovative outcomes of the adoption of this discourse, and these were matched by significant budgetary outlays for cultural development, which hitherto had been residual.

This notion of urban citizenship, taken up as a public policy framework, and the participation that accompanied it together gave new meaning to the relationship between culture and local development. As stated in the city's first draft cultural development plan for 2010–2012:

Culture contributes to the achievement of convivencia based on participation, in the spirit of pluralism in the public sphere. But in addition, in the case of Medellín it has been an element of citizenship of the last two city administrations in two ways. First, the space it has created, with the recovery and/or creation of public spaces and the construction of cultural facilities and infrastructures that facilitate the emergence of individual, group and community projects, in the extent to which these spaces promote the circulation of information, they also promote creativity and privilege dialogue. The second is the strengthening of citizenship by deliberative democracy and active participation, the mounting of group projects build up the public sphere as an arena of encounter with the Other.

In this sense, two key issues must be kept in mind: the path traced out by the reinforcement of the public space as the core of citizenship and its fundamental contribution to the promotion of exchanges and dialogue and, the fact that for this reason, difference has become constitutive of the socio-historical and contributes to our capacity to respond to new challenges and adopt options and reasoning that are adaptive.

The participatory dimension is crucial not only because it is part and parcel of the planning process, but also because it is integral to budgetary decision-making. Furthermore, the creation of public facilities in the spirit of 'social architecture' became a priority of the architect in charge, Alejandro Echeverri, who stressed 'the positive impact it would have in the city and its role in improving the quality of life, above all in poor neighbourhoods' (2010: 137). This positive impact was secured through ensuring the cultural sustainability of these public buildings, while community appropriation allowed the transformation of the city to be converted into a focus of interest and point of reference,

placing value on the role assigned to culture as an urban fact, on the idea of the public good and the increasingly close relationship which has been created between the technical domain, understood in the broad sense as the disciplinary, and the political, understood also in the broad sense as the construction of civil society. (Echeverri, 2010: 137)

Sergio Fajardo, who was the mayor from 2004 to 2007, observed that this effort was

the most appealing to the most humble and the people's pride has resonated with us all.

Architectural beauty has been a key element: where earlier there was death, fear and disjuncture, today we have the most impressive buildings of the highest quality where we can all be brought together by culture, education and peaceful convivencia. Thus we are sending a political message about what the dignity of space means to all citizens, and this supposes recognition, it reaffirms self-esteem and creates feelings of belong. Our buildings, parks and avenues are beautiful and modern.[3]

For the current mayor, Alonso Salazar, what has been achieved is to have 'mobilized the power of aesthetics as an engine of social and cultural change' (see Boxes 21.1 and 21.2).

Box 21.1 Living infrastructure in Medellín

Medellín, the second largest city of Colombia, with a population of 3.5 million people in its metropolitan area, has undergone remarkable industrial progress in recent years and today has an increasingly service-oriented economy. But in 1991 it was the most violent city in the world, with 381 violent deaths per 100,000 citizens, which was equivalent to an alarming rate of 20 deaths each day of the year. Most of the victims were young people killed by gunshot. Today, Medellín is transformed. It is no longer the most violent city in the world: in 2007 violent deaths dropped to a 20-year low, amounting to just 26 deaths per 100,000. Two outstanding individuals led this political, social, educational and cultural transformation: Sergio Fajardo, who was Mayor from 2004 to 2007, and his successor, Alonso Salazar (2007–2011). Fajardo was a mathematics professor with no political experience when he was elected and Salazar was a prestigious intellectual and researcher.

Education and culture were the key elements in the transformative process, and the policy framework this represented was backed up with effective political and financial decision-making: 40 per cent of the budget was allocated to education and 5 per cent to cultural affairs. Entry to the major city museums, which are managed by foundations, is free for all citizens throughout the year. These include the Museum of Antioquia, the Museum of Modern Art and the **Casa Museo Pedro Nel Gómez**. This entry policy, subsidized by the city budget, has caused museum attendance to increase significantly: there were 800,000 visitors to these three museums in 2010. Through the Open Hall Programme and agreements reached with theatre companies, entry to the 21 theatres in Medellín is also free one day a month for the whole population. A 50 per cent discount is also offered to students, the elderly and the handicapped throughout the year. In addition, in the 23 libraries of the city's Public Library System, people have free access to almost 2,500 computers, including free wireless connectivity. More than 12,000 young people have free access to cultural networks: 4,500 are pupils in 26 symphonic music schools and polyphonic choirs, located in low-income neighbourhoods; 600 children and youngsters take part in two symphony orchestras and two choirs; 5,000 students make up the Literature Network; 1,000 youngsters are part of the Theatre Network; 300 belong to the Dance Network; and 800 to the Visual Arts Network.

In the cultural project of Medellín, cultural infrastructure plays a vital role. This includes Library Parks, cultural centres, the **Casas de la Cultura**, music schools, theatre halls, museums and public spaces. This infrastructure consists of much more than physical structures, for it includes fundamentally social elements: each site has a social team that is constituted before construction begins, even before it has been designed! Quick participative diagnostics (known as DRP) are conducted to collect people's perceptions regarding what the cultural buildings should signify. These social teams meet with the community, and roundtables are organized to generate proposals about the future sites. They hold talks with architects and engineers during the construction phases. Once the new venues are inaugurated, the members of the roundtables become part of the management team and organizational committees, helping integrate them with the community at large and enliven these new spaces. The end result is that these spaces are essentially appropriated by the community.

'Social City Planning', the component that has had the greatest impact, basically entails substantial investment in specific urban projects targeted to low-income neighbourhoods. It is based on the premise that the city has a historical debt to pay with regard to these forgotten neighbourhoods and it does this through the construction of high-quality architectural projects which have both aesthetic and social impact. These projects range from the 'Metrocable' transport system to educational and cultural sites, including public space improvements. The jewel in the crown is the well-known Metrocable public transport system, consisting of cable cars in the air, which is also connected to the Metro system of the city. This idea took shape in the mid-1990s, leading to the first cable car line in 2004, the second in 2008, and others which will begin to operate shortly. The innovation here was that a technology commonly used in skiing slopes and touristic sites was adapted as a low-cost transport system for low-income sectors of the city, where the topography is particularly craggy. As in all the projects, effective communication and active local community participation have played a vital role. Though their transport capacity is limited to 25,000 to 30,000 passengers per day, the Metrocables contribute significantly to improving mobility in the nearby zones, without any cost to citizens, given that an ordinary Metro ticket includes the Metrocable ride. They have allowed poor neighbourhoods to be part of, and feel part of, the rest of the city. The 20-minute ride from the periphery, at the top of the mountain, 10 kilometres away and 350 metres in altitude, to the city centre has enabled access to previously unknown and 'dangerous' areas, and has contributed to the increase of local, national, and international tourism. The scheme has also contributed in stimulating local transformations: the first Metrocable (line K) led to the construction of the Juan Bobo housing project, recognized among 'best practice' projects in the Dubai 2008 Contest: it offers its inhabitants, in difficult and unstable terrain surrounding a small river, better accessibility, better organized public space, re-positioning and improved housing, all contributing to reduce environmental risk.

The Library Parks idea, initiated in Bogotá a few years back, was adopted and further developed in Medellín for low-income areas. These Library Parks offer the community a range of services such as computers, skill-based courses, cultural activities, recreational and sport sites, social programmes, and support in the creation of small businesses. The city is similarly present in the very architectural form of six new high-quality schools built by Colombian architects for the low-income areas: monotonous brick-built neighbourhoods have been replaced by buildings whose shape, size, material and colour contrast strikingly with their surroundings. These buildings are even the envy of privileged sectors of the city! The Centro Cultural de Moravia, for example, was the last work of the best-known Colombian architect of recent times, Rogelio Salmona. The quality of such projects has brought worldwide recognition to both the city and the architects.

Box 21.2   Transformation through civic culture

How does one transform the attitudes of the citizens of a city that is called the most violent in the world? For a true transformation has indeed taken place in Medellín over the last decade, taking it from a city notorious for fear and violence to one with a growing reputation for cultural contributions from internationally-renowned residents or **paisas**, such as artist Fernando Botero or the singing sensation Juanes. Noteworthy elements of this transformation include many concrete elements such as increased security, higher investments in education, and of course the dramatic enhancement of city infrastructure.

The policies adopted and implemented by Medellín's mayors, specifically Sergio Fajardo, all point to a more important principle: trust. In a situation where security seemed unattainable, citizens found

(Continued)

themselves suffering a punishment they did not deserve, that of living in a city without lively communal life in public spaces – a natural reaction to fear of crime and violence. Therefore a commonly used excuse for not investing in these spaces in cities with major security issues is that violence and crime must decrease before the people can or will utilize major public spaces. Medellín, like Bogotá under Mayor Antanas Mockus, put in place public policies and investments based on the reverse: that when there is trust, the community will want to reclaim public identity, and to come together under an ethos of shared citizenship, common spaces and a commitment to access and inclusion. And the cornerstones of these policies were transparency and education.

The investment in public spaces and the focus on instructing and empowering the people of Medellín to use them was an education in civic culture. Any reduction in violence, Fajardo argued, must be immediately followed by social intervention. The backbone of the plan involved huge investments in building a welcoming and accessible city. Major funding was given to education, and the showcase projects of that investment were five grand Library Parks. Each features state-of the-art library facilities and a park for readers to enjoy Medellín's eternal spring weather. As of 2010, the Library Parks were reporting usage from more than 70 per cent of the city's population, functioning not only for education, but also as community centres offering free programmes such as business training, civics lessons, computer labs, and art galleries.

The slogan displayed at each Library Park – 'A space for the human spirit to join together, in freedom and in dignity' – embodies the philosophy employed by Fajardo to bring the community together. Another major project undertaken during his time in office was the Metrocable transportation system described in Box 21.1. These costly projects were paid for by tax money and, during Fajardo's term as mayor, Medellín, a city with a history of struggling to get residents to pay tax in the first place, saw a more than 20 per cent increase in collection. Posters were put up at building sites that read 'Here are your taxes': by clearly demonstrating to citizens that when they care for their city, living conditions can improve, the municipality was able to foster participation in civic activities.

In the 2010 Colombian presidential election, Fajardo ran as the running mate to another visionary candidate, Antanas Mockus, the former mayor of Bogotá. The two gained a strong tide of popular support in their 'Green Wave' campaign, running on the message they had both demonstrated in their cities that power is not only exercised by governments but also by citizens. Though they lost, the transformation of Medellín is an inspiration to the country, which has long been plagued by drug-trade and paramilitary violence. The city's experience has shown that by policies of social and educational investment, trust can be restored, civic culture can flourish and quality of life can improve dramatically.

Laura Collier

The story of hope

When interrogated about the 'formulas' underpinning the remaking of Medellín, Fajardo replied: 'The answer is easy to provide: reduce violence and convert all of that reduction immediately into social opportunities. It was as simple as that.' But it was also evident that the recognition of diversity understood as the encounter between differences was the first building block in the construction of a public discourse on culture. In the case of Medellín, diversities and asymmetries had so far never been sufficiently brought to light and analyzed, in a context in which difference was closely related to the inequities intimately bound up with the conditions of poverty, violence and displacement in which a large percentage of the population is obliged to live, constrained within certain zones of the city, whether for cultural, family and economic reasons. These conditions had made for a reality marked by territorial marginalization and exclusion. Again, as identified in the cultural development plan:

This is of singular significance since unequal access to the benefits generated in the city reduces the force of interactions, limits the spread of dialogue and limits opportunities to achieve an inclusive mode of development. For this reason, recognizing differences means not just making the vulnerable more visible, but also reinforcing actions that would enable all to participate in equal terms in the different circuits, flows and intercultural interactions.

Second, the search for 'a place in the sun'. As the plan put it, 'the city can no longer set aside the flows through which we are connected with the rest of the world and that brings the city face to face with issues to responses must be supplied'. Hence, while Medellín is not a major global city, it is nevertheless directly impacted by the tensions that face all cities today, obliging each of them to navigate between a degree of relative autonomy that allows it to decide on its future vocation and a reduced margin of manoeuvre as it has to address the needs of its inhabitants, young and old, serving an ever-increasing and ever more diverse population, which is also ever more aware of its rights. This connection to and insertion within the global system requires a far greater degree of acceptance and indeed of integration as regards diversity and the processes of interculturality. At the same time, it calls for a reconceptualization of what is specific and what is local in relation to a globalized cultural scene.

Finally, it is important to underscore interventions in and on physical space that are carried out on the assumption that the improvement of infrastructure and other material conditions generate synergies that have a positive impact on other dimensions of development. However, these physical interventions require adequate contextualization, with the participation of their users, the city's inhabitants. Yet there is also a significant popular claim that is mentioned in the cultural development plan as well: 'Our city must expand its public and semi-public spaces that contribute to improving the quality of life of its inhabitants and the consolidation of equitable development, particularly in those sections of the city that have been excluded from modernization processes.'

The continuity of the public policies formulated for Medellín have been threatened by subsequent political developments in the country. For this reason

they need to be consolidated by a culturally active citizenry that is able to invoke and defend the progress that has been achieved. Hence we need to bear in mind certain key reference points – all subject to revision – for a critical discourse that sustains the process:

- Despite the progress achieved by recent city administrations and private bodies, the cultural rights of Medellín's inhabitants, as well as their responsibilities in relation to both the public sphere and the state, remain in need of consolidation.
- Although different ways of life and cultural expressions co-exist in the city, their relations remain asymmetrical, exclusionary and discriminatory, whether on the plane of social relations or in the practices of public and private cultural institutions.
- Although we have progressed on the road towards a democratic culture, the latter is threatened by the 'democratic pessimism' generated by the fact that urban spaces of congregation for conflict resolution are so little recognized and used and because citizens are still so ill-informed about the mechanisms and avenues of participation.

In the domain of culture, as Ernst Bloch indicated, wherever there is a surplus that in a transformed society can yield a dividend, 'the problem of ideology is broached from the side of the problem of cultural inheritance, of the problem as to how works of the superstructure progressively reproduce themselves in cultural consciousness even after the disappearance of the social bases' (Bloch, 1986: 154). It is not just in times of social flourishing that we encounter cultural production that transcends mere political management. It also happens whenever there are certain cultural manifestations that are transcendental conditions in the form of art, science and philosophy and that create the spaces capable of generating the horizon of hope that is so clearly discernible in Medellín today.

Notes

1 Translated from the Spanish by Y.R. Isar.
2 Latin American analysts often make a distinction in the Spanish language between the notion of *politica de gobierno*, which is more or less the policy followed for a limited

period of time by a given city or national administration, and the *politica de Estado*, which is the durable, long-term political vision of an entire society or state.

3 From his speech entitled *Medellín: del miedo a la esperanza*, which he has delivered on many occasions in many different settings.

REFERENCES

Bloch, Ernst (1986) *The Principle of Hope*, Vol. 1. Cambridge, MA: The MIT Press.

Echeverri, A. (2010) *Medellín medio ambiente urbanismoy sociedad*. Medellín: Centro de Estudios Urbanos y Ambientales.

CHAPTER 22

MELBOURNE AND BRISBANE: THE CLAIMS OF SUBURBS

Terry Flew and Mark Gibson

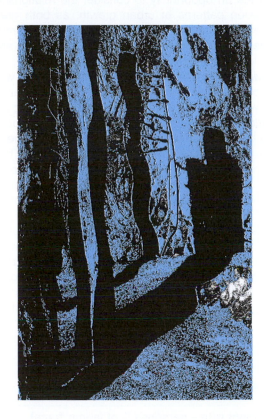

This chapter critiques the imagined geography of creative cities and the creative industries, which presumes that inner cities are densely clustered hubs of urban culture and creativity while suburbs are dull, homogeneous dormitories from which creative people must escape in order to realize their potential. Drawing upon a study on creative industries workers in Melbourne and Brisbane, the authors argue that these workers are as likely to be located in the suburbs as in the inner city, and that they clearly identify advantages to being in outer suburban locations. Their findings provide a corrective to dominant urban cultural policy narratives that stress cultural amenity in the inner cities.

Introduction: globalization and suburbanization

Australian cities provide an interesting historical perspective and contemporary lens through which to debate the question of whether the twenty-first century urban form should be based on mega-cities and global city-regions, or be more decentralized and suburban. Australia was described as the 'world's first suburban nation' as early as the 1960s (Horne, 1964), and its suburban roots are in fact much deeper. From the first European settlement of Sydney Cove in 1788 onwards, considerable attention was given by both urban planners and social reformers to developing patterns of lower-density housing than those found in European cities (Davison, 1995). By the 1920s, consistent governmental support for home ownership had ensured that the main planks of Australian suburbanization were in place, and land-based capitalism was giving more and more Australian workers a 'stake in the country' (Johnson, 2006). Trends towards suburbanization were intensified in the post-Second World War era, with favourable tax policies for home ownership, highway and freeway construction, the decentralization of government service delivery, and the development of enormous shopping centres. It is only from the 1970s onwards that significant counter-trends towards urban consolidation and the repopulation of inner cities have gained momentum, and even here it occurs alongside the development of many new housing tracts on the outer suburban fringe, as part of what are known as Master Planned Communities (MPCs), with quasi-privatized forms of local governance.

Australia is one of the most urbanized countries in the world. Almost 75 per cent of the Australian population lives in 17 major cities with populations over 100,000, and over 50 per cent live in five cities with populations over 1 million (Infrastructure Australia, 2010). Australia's population is forecast to grow from 22 million in 2010 to 35 million by 2050, and much of this new population will be concentrated in the major cities or in surrounding 'Boomburb' regions such as the Gold Coast and Sunshine Coast areas around Brisbane, and the Central Coast region north of Sydney. Much of this urbanization will in fact be suburbanization, with an estimated 2 million new dwellings required by 2031 in the cities of Sydney, Melbourne and Brisbane alone, with associated pressures arising from the growth of outer suburban and peri-urban regions, including the provision of transport and infrastructure and the question of future jobs.

The period from the mid-1980s to the mid-1990s saw uneven development between the manufacturing heartland states such as Victoria and South Australia that experienced relative decline, and the 'sunbelt' regions such as South-East Queensland that experienced rapid growth, as well as significant population movement out of rural and regional Australia (Fagan and Webber, 1994). This is also the period where Sydney emerges as a world city, and a leader of business and financial services. Writing in 2000, the year of the Sydney Olympics, Daly and Prichard (2000: 167–168) argued that 'Sydney has become the unquestioned corporate and financial capital of Australia, and is poised to become a leading financial centre for the Asia-Pacific region'. By contrast, the period from the mid-1990s to the late 2000s, which has been described as the age of *new prosperity* (Fagan, 2002) based around the global resources boom, saw a substantial diminution in the differences between Australian states in unemployment rates, and a narrowing of the gap between Sydney and other capital cities (see Table 22.1).

It is in this context that it becomes relevant to consider the rise of Australia's 'second tier' cities – Melbourne and Brisbane – and the urban renaissance that both experienced in the 2000s. Both cities also provide an opportunity to consider the relationship between patterns of urban growth, as both grew inner cities and peri-urban fringe communities simultaneously, the provision of cultural amenities, and the location of their creative workforce.

Melbourne is Australia's second largest city with a population of just over 4 million. Its early character was set by an extraordinary boom following the discovery of gold in Victoria in 1851. For a period in the late nineteenth century, Melbourne was one of the richest cities in the British Empire and had grandiose ambitions of rivalling the great metropolises of Europe and North America. It has suffered, however, from deeper than usual periods of depression. It recovered from its first major 'bust' in the 1890s by establishing a manufacturing base, but by the 1980s this too was in serious decline. Having also lost much of its finance and media industries to Sydney, Melbourne suffered a period of stagnation and unflattering comparisons with other 'rust-belt' cities around the world. However, the last 20

Table 22.1 Unemployment rates by state/territory, Australia*

State/territory	Unemployment rate – persons (% of labour force)		
	June 1992	June 2001	June 2010
New South Wales	9.6	5.8	5.2
Victoria	11.1	6.1	5.3
Queensland	10.4	8.1	5.2
South Australia	11.4	7.2	5.0
Western Australia	10.0	8.0	4.1
Tasmania	11.4	8.8	6.0
Australian Capital Territory	7.1	5.6	2.9
Northern Territory	6.0	7.2	3.2
AUSTRALIA	10.3	6.7	5.0
Mean (unweighted)	9.6	7.1	4.6
SD	0.707	0.461	0.353

*The unweighted mean varies from the weighted mean because of different population sizes. In particular, the two Territories (Australian Capital Territory and Northern Territory) have much smaller populations than the other states. This does not affect the overall argument, since the variation between their unemployment rates and those of the other states is high in June 2010, indicating that the SD would be even lower in June 2010 if they were not included.

Source: Australian Bureau of Statistics, Report 6202.0 – Labour Force, Australia, July 2010.

years have seen another renaissance, based particularly on lower costs relative to Sydney and attractions in lifestyle, culture and sport. It has a calendar of major events, an active live music scene and a reputation for stylish bars, restaurants and cafés, as well as a strong history of multiculturalism: it is the major destination in Australia for international migration and has seen a population growth since 2001 of 4.1 per cent (DPCD, 2008: 5).

Brisbane is a city of just over 2 million situated in the sub-tropical north of Australia. As the southern capital of the vast state of Queensland, it was often seen historically as a 'big country town' primarily servicing the agricultural and mining industries, or as a destination point for those travelling to major tourist destinations such as the Great Barrier Reef. Over the past 30 years, Brisbane and the South-East Queensland region (which includes the Gold Coast and Sunshine Coast) have been the fastest growing parts of Australia, with population growth driven by large-scale internal migration. It is a highly decentralized city, and its city council is the largest local government authority in Australia. Since the 1990s, there has been a focus on developing high-technology sectors and the creative industries in Brisbane and South-East Queensland, as part of the Queensland state government's 'Smart State' initiatives.

Creative workforce

The greatest concentration of creative workers in Australian cities is still in the city and inner suburbs. Concentration should not be confused, however, with total volume. Australia has witnessed a significant suburbanization of employment over the last 20 years, similar to that noted by Edward Glaeser and co-authors in the United States, where the median employee now works seven miles (11 km) from the city centre (Glaeser et al., 2001: 2). According to figures compiled recently on Melbourne by planning consultant Alan Davies (2010b), the average distance of jobs from the city centre is now 15.6 km, a 26 per cent increase over the 25-year period from 1981. While the single greatest concentration of jobs is in the city, a clear majority of jobs in most sectors are in the suburbs, not only in manufacturing and retail, but also for the general category of 'Culture and Recreation'. Jobs in 'Sport and Recreation' are, unsurprisingly, strongly biased to the suburbs, but even in 'Motion Picture, Radio and

Television Services' and 'Libraries, Museums and the Arts', nearly half of all jobs are now suburban.

There is relatively little data available on the finer breakdown of suburban creative employment, but what there is suggests a somewhat different profile from inner-urban areas. Our research indicates, for example, that average ages are somewhat higher. Across a total of 128 creative workers surveyed across selected outer suburbs of Melbourne and Brisbane, 64 per cent were aged over 40. Many were found to be combining creative work with raising children or caring for ageing parents or relatives. These figures present a rather different picture of creative workers from the one popularized by Richard Florida's work on the 'creative class' and also represented in much of the literature on creative cities: that of unattached creative workers in their 20s or early 30s, inhabiting 'bohemian' downtown areas and experimenting with alternative experiences and lifestyles. It would be a mistake to set 'young urban' and 'family suburban' creative practitioners against each other as mutually exclusive categories: many individuals inhabit both modes at different stages of their careers. But there is perhaps insufficient attention given in policy development to older creative workers. Many are at periods of peak earning capacity and are also often key figures in maintaining networks and professional organizations.

It is often assumed that suburban creative practitioners are generally 'hobbyists', and cultural policy in relation to the suburbs is more often placed in the basket of community development than industry development. Our research suggests, however, that these assumptions may be anachronistic, with an increasing number of fully commercial businesses locating in the suburbs. A majority (55 per cent) of suburban creative practitioners surveyed depended on their creative work for their primary income. There are some differences in fields of creative practice in the suburbs, with a bias towards 'artisanal' practices that can be pursued independently of large organizations. A comparison, using census data, of the suburbs we surveyed with national averages (Table 22. 2) indicates, for example, that Architecture, Design and Visual Arts are strongly represented in the suburbs, whereas Film, Television and Radio are less so. Advertising and Marketing were surprisingly well represented in the suburbs, but the Software and Digital Content industries less so, which would

Table 22.2   Breakdown of suburban creative industry employment against national averages (per cent)

	Advertising & marketing	Architecture, design & visual arts	Film, TV & radio	Music and performing arts	Publishing	Software & digital content
Creative industry employees in suburban Statistical Local Areas (SLAs)	16	39	3	5	17	20
National average 2001	10	26	8	7	18	31

Note: National average is 2001 data; SLA data is from 2007 census. SLAs include: Dandenong, Frankston, Melton East, Ipswich East, Redcliffe-Scarborough and Doolandella-Forest Lake.

Source: Analysis by ARC Centre of Excellence for Creative Industries & Innovation using customized extracts of ABS Census data on employment and incomes 1996, 2001 and 2006.

seem surprising given the decentralizing capabilities of broadband infrastructure.

It is also often assumed that suburban creative practitioners are relatively dependent, with an 'umbilical' relation to the inner city for cultural nourishment and institutional support, but this assumption is also questionable, and associated with an out-dated characterization of the suburbs as commuter dormitories for city-based employment. In the Melbourne case, less than 10 per cent of total workers in the suburbs of our research commute to the city (Davies, 2010a). An analysis of transport patterns and residential longevity of creative practitioners reinforces a picture of a fairly high degree of local orientation. Only 37 per cent of those we surveyed visited the inner city 'regularly' (at least once a month) and almost a third (32 per cent) accessed it 'rarely' (fewer than three times a year). The average length of residence of creative practitioners, at least in established suburbs, was significant, ranging between 14 and 19 years, and the degree of satisfaction with the suburb as a place to live and work was also high. These findings are consistent with increasing evidence of a 'polycentrism' in cities around the world (Glaeser et al., 2001; Knapp and Schmidt, 2003; Soja, 2010). In fast-growing, medium-sized cities such as Melbourne, there are strong policy incentives to work with this tendency

as a way of managing problems of transport and excessive demand on urban infrastructure. The Victoria State Government now favours a decentralized urban structure for Melbourne with the designation of six 'Central Activity Districts' outside the CBD (DPCD, 2008).

Another significant development in the relation between city and suburbs has been changing patterns of immigration. Australia has seen a substantial increase in immigration over the past decade. In 1999–2000, there were 70,200 admitted under the formal migration plan; at the peak in 2008–2009, this had risen to 171,318 – one of the highest per capita formal migration rates in the world (DIC, 2010). Historically, new migrants have generally settled in the city and inner suburbs of the major cities, giving the latter a cosmopolitan character and increasing their claims to cultural vibrancy against the relative monoculture of the suburbs. However, this pattern has been dramatically reversed over the last 20 years, as spiralling rents have forced lower-income populations out of the inner city and led new migrants to settle in the suburbs. It is now increasingly the inner cities that are prone to being seen as monocultures, while the suburbs have become the major arena for new experiments in Australian multiculturalism (Wise, 2005; Lee, 2006).

Box 22.1 Multicultural Dandenong

Dandenong, 30 kilometres south-east of Melbourne, is one of the most culturally diverse localities in Australia, with residents from 156 different birthplaces, including Vietnam, Cambodia, Sri Lanka, India, China, Italy, Greece, Bosnia and Afghanistan. Some 56 per cent of the population was born overseas and 51 per cent from countries where English is not the main language. Dandenong has a longer history of multiculturalism than many Australian suburbs, as it was an important manufacturing centre in the post-war period. Established in the nineteenth century as a centre for agricultural industries east of Melbourne, its population trebled in the 1950s following the development of factory employment in agricultural machinery (International Harvester), motor vehicles (General Motors-Holden) and food processing (Heinz), with many of the new workers coming from war-torn Europe (Alves, 2005). Since the decline of manufacturing in the 1970s and 1980s, it has had persistent problems of unemployment, which has also meant that it has some of the cheapest residential property. When combined with good transport connections and established migrant support services, this has made Dandenong one of the leading local government areas in Australia for the reception of new migrants.

Despite its recent economic problems, Dandenong has some of the elements for a revitalization. Business opportunities continue to be offered in relatively cheap land, good transport and access to a growing population in eastern Melbourne. It has recently been designated by the Victorian State Government as one of six 'Central Activity Districts' to become a focus of future employment growth and public investment outside the CBD. In 2005, the urban development authority VicUrban commenced a $290 million programme, in partnership with the City of Greater Dandenong, for a regeneration of the central area. The multiculturalism of the city has increasingly been seen as an important part of this renewal. The Dandenong market, for example, an icon of the region since its establishment in 1866, is now celebrated for its 'vibrant cosmopolitan atmosphere' and array of food, clothing and handicrafts from all over the world. While many recent migrants are concerned primarily with basic needs associated with resettlement, there are also significant numbers who have sought to maintain or develop creative practices as writers, artists, designers and musicians. Dandenong does not offer quite the opportunities for making this work known as the inner suburbs of Carlton and Fitzroy did for previous generations of migrants. There is also a tendency among some groups, particularly those from traumatized backgrounds, to 'keep to themselves'. But migrant creative practice nevertheless has considerable potential to contribute to the future development.

Paradoxical geographies of Australian suburbia

Australian suburbs occupy a paradoxical place in the nation's cultural identity. While they are the places where most people live, this reality is derided by many intellectuals, cultural critics, political radicals, urban planners and social scientists, who view the suburbs as mundane, consumerist, spiritually empty, politically conservative and environmentally unsustainable. The degree to which suburbia is 'an idea whose meaning is unstable and whose connotations continue to oscillate between dream and ... nightmare' (Craven, 1995: 48) is captured in a rich vein of Australian satirical comedy, from Barry Humphries' Dame Edna Everage character, first developed in the 1950s, to situation comedies such as *Kath and Kim*, which make fun of the aspirational *gaucheness* of families in the outer suburbs of Australian cities (Turnbull, 2008). Our own research found that the distribution of creative workforce in Melbourne and Brisbane does not fit the stereotyped image of diverse, hip and culturally rich inner urban areas existing alongside the suburbs as boring, culturally homogeneous and lacking in urban amenity (Collis et al., 2010).

It was clear that those creative industries workers in Brisbane and Melbourne who lived in suburban locations largely did so out of personal choice, rather than being forced out by the high cost of housing in the inner city, and that in many cases the relative serenity of the suburbs was preferred over the clustering, dense networks and 'buzz' commonly associated with the inner city. Such findings

239

are consistent with a growing body of work on the appeal of intangible elements associated with lower-density places to creative workers (Drake, 2003; Chapain and Communian, 2009; Brennan-Horley et al., 2010), and run counter to commonly held assumptions about the appeal of inner-urban creative clusters and high levels of agglomeration to the so-called 'creative class'. It also runs counter to what might be termed the 'suburban realism' thesis propounded by some political conservatives, which counterposes the 'common sense' of socially conservative working-class suburbanites to the cause-driven politics of inner-city elites (Allon, 2008). More generally, the trends in suburban creative industries employment in cities such as Melbourne and Brisbane challenge the representational geography of cities that presents the inner cities as sites of clustered creativity and productivity, and suburbs as purely consumption-oriented zones (Collis et al., 2010). There is instead what Gibson and Brennan-Horley (2006: 461) have called a 'more complex mosaic of suburban employment and diversified labour markets' in the creative industries, suggesting that while location can be a source of creative inspiration, this can involve other kinds of location than inner-urban creative clusters (Drake, 2003).

Conclusion and policy implications

The 2000s proved to be a lively time for urban cultural policy debates, with the renewed focus upon cities and nodal points in globalization intersecting with a growing body of work on the sources of growth and differentiation among global city-regions (Scott, 2008), and the role that culture can play in urban regeneration (Evans, 2009). Some of this work was animated by Richard Florida's thesis on the rise of the creative class (Florida, 2002, 2008), and the view that urban planners needed to focus upon providing cultural amenities to secure highly mobile knowledge workers, while others observed the role played by the *soft infrastructure* of interpersonal networks in the formation of successful urban creative clusters (Kong, 2010). There is, of course, considerable scepticism about the transferability of the creative cluster/creative class concept as a general framework for urban cultural policy (Oakley, 2004; Peck, 2005; Wyszomirski, 2008; Kotkin, 2010), and our own research questions the

empirical realities lying behind the imagined geography of creative cities.

At the same time, a notable feature of both the supporters and critics of the creative class thesis tends to be its focus on inner cities and its relative neglect of suburbs. Grodach and Loukaitou-Sideris (2007) look to progressive urban cultural development strategies designed to redistribute resources to underserved communities as an alternative to creative class or entrepreneurial city strategies, but fail to consider whether suburban populations may themselves be such underserved communities warranting new forms of cultural investment. Similarly, critics of 'top-down' urban cultural planning often oppose it to more organic, 'bottom-up' sources of creativity and/or revolt deemed to be lurking among the more marginalized communities of the inner city (O'Connor, 2004; Harvey, 2008). Again, in so far as the suburbs appear at all in such discourses, it is as fetters on progressive urban cultural politics and incubators of conformity and conservatism. David Harvey (2008) associates the suburbs with possessive individualism, the oppression of women, soulless design and architecture, and 'pacification by cappuccino' (2008: 32) in shopping malls and multiplexes, in a discourse that bears striking family resemblances to earlier anti-suburban traditions in Australia.

In developing urban cultural policy and governance strategies that better serve the more spatially dispersed creative workforce, it will not be enough to transplant strategies designed for the inner city to the suburbs. It cannot be simply a matter of building more arts and cultural centres in suburban regions, or trying to emulate creative cluster models premised upon imagined geographies of inner-city bohemianism. There is a need, first, to identify and map the cultural resources already available in these areas and, second, to undertake more grounded analysis of how forms of networked sociality are maintained among creative workers outside inner cities. It was notable from our studies that suburban creative workers are not well served either by professional associations, which tend to prefer early evening meetings in the inner city, or by suburban business and commercial associations, which tend not to understand the risk profiles and the shorter time horizons of small firms in the creative industries. We suspect that suburban university campuses may be an underutilized resource in the development of suburban creative clusters. Productive comparisons might be made with the way that 'college towns' have evolved as major cultural hubs in the United States (Flew, 2010; Florida et al., 2010).

Two final issues that arise from recognition of the dispersed and suburbanized nature of the creative industries workforce in major Australian cities relate to the need for more dispersed and decentralized approaches to cultural policy and cultural funding, and to investment in digital infrastructure. Westbury and Eltham (2010) have argued that Australian cultural policy generally, and the funding practices of the Australia Council as the peak arts funding body in particular, have failed to adequately address and respond to the increasingly dispersed and decentralized nature of creative work and cultural production and consumption in Australia:

Immigration, demographic change and new technologies and communications media have transformed the spectrum of cultural choices available. The large-scale infrastructure and mass subscription model that underpins the logic of many funded arts organizations is poorly equipped to respond to the plethora of new artists, art forms, audiences, genres, and subcultures emerging in a rapidly changing cultural dynamic. (Westbury and Eltham, 2010: 42)

Flagship arts organizations tend to be concentrated in inner cities, and in so far as arts and cultural funding is tilted towards them and away from newer forms and practices, this will act to maintain socio-spatial inequalities in the distribution of cultural resources. The issue is not one of building more arts and cultural centres in the suburbs; it is about being more open to the diversity of cultural practices emerging out of Australian suburban communities. What a more suburban cultural policy may look like in practice is clearly a matter that warrants further research, as it has the potential to substantially reshape the priorities of arts and cultural organizations.

The other key issue relates to access to high-speed broadband services. At present in Australia, there is an unhelpful divide between communications policy that deals with broadband infrastructure on the one hand, and arts and cultural policy on the other. As a result, discussion of the National Broadband Network (NBN) is largely driven by questions of cost, access, speed and the most suitable public/private sector investment mix, while questions of digital content for these high-speed networks, and the scope to lever new forms of competitive advantage in the creative industries based upon distributed access to these networks, is dealt with as a second order policy issue. Any national cultural policy for the twenty-first century also needs to be a digital communication policy, and vice versa. Such a focus would provide considerable support for those working in the suburbs in creative industries and occupations.

REFERENCES

Allon, Fiona (2008*) Renovation Nation: Our Obsession with Home*. Sydney: UNSW Press.

Alves, Lesley (2005) 'Dandenong', in Andrew Brown-May and Shurlee Swain (eds), *Encyclopedia of Melbourne*. Melbourne: Cambridge University Press, pp.194–195.

Brennan-Horley, C., Luckman, S., Gibson, C. and Willoughby-Smith, J. (2010) 'GIS, ethnography and cultural research: putting maps back into ethnographic mapping', *The Information Society*, 26 (2): 92–103.

Chapain, Caroline and Communian, Roberta (2010) 'Enabling or inhibiting the creative economy: the role of the local and regional dimensions in England', *Regional Studies*, 44 (6): 717–734.

Collis, Christy, Felton, Emma and Graham, Phil (2010) 'Beyond the inner city: real and imagined places in creative place policy and practice', *The Information Society*, 26 (2): 104–112.

Craven, Ian (1995) 'Cinema, postcolonialism and Australian suburbia', *Australian Studies*, 9: 45–69.

Daly, M.T. and Pritchard, B. (2000) 'Sydney: Australia's financial and corporate capital', in J. Connell (ed.), *Sydney: The Emergence of a World City*. Melbourne: Oxford University Press.

Davies, Alan (2010a) 'Are the suburbs dormitories?', *The Melbourne Urbanist*, http://melbourneurbanist.wordpress.com/2010/09/21/are-the-suburbs-dormitories/. (accessed 8 November, 2010).

—— (2010b) 'Jobs in the suburbs – the structure of suburban employment in Melbourne', Pollard Davies Pty Ltd,

Presentation to *Creative Suburbia Symposium*, Queensland University of Technology, 29–30 September.

Davison, Graeme (1995) 'Australia: the first suburban nation?', *Journal of Urban History*, 22 (1): 40–74.

DIC (2010) *Fact Sheet 2 – Key Facts in Immigration*. Canberra: Australian Government (Department of Immigration and Citizenship), www.immi.gov.au/media/factsheets/02key.htm#e (accessed 12/11/2010).

DPCD (2008) *Melbourne 2030: A Planning Update – Melbourne @ 5 million*. Melbourne: Victorian State Government (Department of Planning and Community Development).

Drake, Graeme (2003) '"This place gives me space": place and creativity in the creative industries', *Geoforum*, 34: 511–524.

Evans, Graeme (2009) 'Creative Cities, Creative Spaces and Urban Policy', *Urban Studies*, 46 (5/6): 1003–1040.

Fagan, Bob (2002) 'Dealing with the new prosperity: implications for work and workers', *Australian Geographer*, 33 (3): 353–358.

Fagan, Bob and Webber, Michael (1994) *Global Restructuring: The Australian Experience*. Melbourne: Oxford University Press.

Flew, Terry (2010) 'Creative clusters and universities: the cluster concept in economics and geography', in M. Peters and D. Araya (eds), *Education in the Creative Economy*. New York: Peter Lang, pp. 75–90.

Florida, Richard (2002) *The Rise of the Creative Class*. New York: Basic Books.

Florida, Richard (2008) *Who's Your City: How the Creative Economy is Making Where to Live the Most Important Decision of Your Life*. New York: Basic Books.

Florida, R., Knudsen, B. and Stolarick, K. (2010) 'The university and the creative economy', in M. Peters and D. Araya (eds), *Education in the Creative Economy*. New York: Peter Lang, pp. 43–74.

Gibson, Chris and Brennan-Horley, Chris (2006) 'Goodbye pram city: beyond inner/outer zone binaries in creative city research', *Urban Policy and Research*, 24: 455–471.

Glaeser, Edward (2000) 'The new economies of urban and regional growth', in G. Clark, M. Feldman and M. Gertler (eds), *The Oxford Handbook of Economic Geography*. Oxford: Oxford University Press. pp. 83–98.

Grodach, Carl and Loukaitou-Sideris, Angelika (2007) 'Cultural development strategies and urban revitalization', *International Journal of Cultural Policy*, 13 (4): 349–370.

Harvey, David (2008) 'The right to the city', *New Left Review*, 53: 23–40.

Horne, Donald (1964) *The Lucky Country*. Melbourne: Penguin.

Infrastructure Australia (2010) *State of Australian Cities 2010*. Canberra: Infrastructure Australia Major Cities Unit.

Johnson, Louise (2006) 'Style Wars: revolution in the suburbs?', *Australian Geographer*, 37 (2): 259–277.

Knapp, W. and Schmidt, P. (2003) 'Restructuring competitive metropolitan regions in north west Europe: on territory and governance', *European Journal of Spatial Development*, 6: 1–42.

Kong, Lily (2010) 'Creative economy, global city: globalizing discourses and the implications for local arts', in H. Anheier and Y. Raj Isar (eds), *Cultural Expression, Creativity and Innovation. The Cultures and Globalization Series 3*. London: SAGE, pp. 166–175.

Kotkin, Joel (2010) 'Urban legends', *Foreign Policy*, 181: 128–134.

Lee, Terence (2006) 'Creativity and cultural globalisation in suburbia: mediating the Perth–Singapore "Network"', *Australian Journal of Communication*, 33 (2/3): 21–42.

Oakley, Kate (2004) 'Not so Cool Britannia: the role of the creative industries in economic development', *International Journal of Cultural Studies*, 7 (1): 67–78.

O'Connor, Justin (2004) '"A special kind of city knowledge": innovative clusters, tacit knowledge, and the "creative city"', *Media International Australia*, 112: 131–149.

Peck, Jamie (2005) 'Struggling with the creative class', *International Journal of Urban and Regional Research*, 29 (4): 740–770.

Scott, Allen J. (2008) *Social Economy of the Metropolis: Cognitive-Cultural Capitalism and the Global Resurgence of Cities*. Oxford: Oxford University Press.

Soja, Edward (2010) *Seeking Spatial Justice*. Minneapolis, MN: University of Minnesota Press.

Turnbull, Sue (2008) 'Mapping the vast suburban tundra: Australian comedy from Dame Edna to *Kath and Kim*', *International Journal of Cultural Studies*, 11 (1): 15–32.

Westbury, Marcus and Eltham, Ben (2010) 'Cultural policy in Australia', in M. Davis and M. Lyons (eds), *More than Luck: Ideas Australia Needs Now*. Sydney: Centre for Policy Development, pp. 40–44.

Wise, Amanda (2005) 'Hope and belonging in a multicultural suburb', *Journal of Intercultural Studies*, 26 (1/2): 171–186.

Wyszomirski, Margaret (2008) 'The local creative economy in the United States of America', in H. Anheier and Y.R. Isar (eds), *The Cultural Economy. The Cultures and Globalization Series 2*. London: SAGE, pp. 199–212.

CHAPTER 23

MEXICO CITY: CULTURAL POLICIES, GOVERNANCE AND CIVIL SOCIETY

Lucina Jiménez

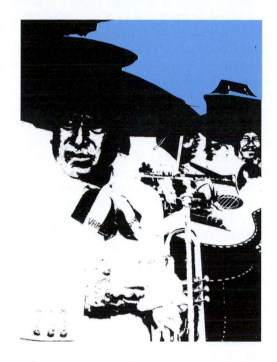

In Mexico City, one of the world's most socio-economically fragmented and unequal urban agglomerations, cultural democracy needs to be constructed for a highly diverse civil society. But the city's policies are shot through with inadequacies and contradictions. Its public management culture is too weak to enable participation or to harness the creative energies and entrepreneurial spirit of its citizens. To be sure, a strong business sector based on culture exists already, but small-and medium-sized initiatives in the cultural sphere are unable to progress and Mexico's citizens need the chance to take advantage of the opportunities of globalization and become full players in translocal cultural processes.

Local cultural governance challenges

Mexico City is truly a city of cities, a gigantic conglomerate which is impossible to capture in a single photograph or moving image. Ancient Tenochtitlan, the pre-Hispanic city densely populated by native peoples either swept away or in fierce resistance to the Spanish colonization, was destroyed and rebuilt several times over the course of five centuries to finally become, at the beginning of the twenty-first century, a chaotic, disorderly megalopolis. Over time, Mexico City became the centre of economic, political and religious power, reproducing and multiplying both the diversity and the inequality which characterizes the country as a whole. According to the population census of 2000, there is now a 'megalopolis around Mexico City, with the metropolitan areas of Querétaro, Pachuca, Tulancingo, Puebla-Tlaxcala, Cuautla, Cuernavaca and Toluca all linking to it both functionally and territorially'.[1] This vast conglomeration occupies only 5 per cent of the country's territory and yet generates 42 per cent of national GDP. In this chapter, however, I will be focusing on Mexico City itself rather than on this broader megalopolis, which, as it stands, has been little studied in terms of cultural policies.

Despite being one of the world's largest cities, Mexico City does not constitute a legal entity in itself. It is made up of 51 administrative and political units belonging to two different bodies: the so-called Federal District (16 boroughs) and the 35 municipalities of the State of Mexico. Together, they make up what is known as the Mexico City Metropolitan Area, which concentrates together 18.3 per cent of the national population with 17,844,829 inhabitants, of which more than 50 per cent are women (INEGI, 2011). The influence of the country's capital on national economic development is high, contributing as it does 26 per cent of its Gross Domestic Product.[2] Although the growth rate of the central boroughs is actually negative, the urban sprawl is spreading out towards the 10 municipalities on the border of the Federal District at a rate of 1.4 per cent per year and towards the other 25 non-bordering so-called 'conurbations' at an annual growth rate of 3.7 per cent.

Unlike cities such as Bogotá, Buenos Aires, New York or São Paulo, Mexico City does not enjoy political or managerial autonomy in a number of diverse fields relating to local development, having been created in 1824 as a territory to house the federal authorities, which made it into an urban monster where the citizens, up until very recently, were not entitled to choose their governors. Mexico City is rich in diversity, being the seat of multidimensional, changing identities built by indigenous and native peoples, teenagers, young people, men and women, all of whom give life to hybrid manifestations with links to oral traditions, different cultures of the body, and musical and visual cultures. It is the home of cultures which express the passage of historic migrations and the contemporary transit of national and Latin American migrants towards the United States, those forced into exile by the dictatorships of South America, and the social revolutions and natural disasters of the Caribbean. But above all it is the result of the mixture and translocal character brought by cultural globalization. Managing this diversity through cultural policies, with a view to development and democracy, is today one of the central challenges for the city.

In the big city, there is room for everyone and everything. It is multi-seasonal, eclectic and contradictory. Even in the midst of the inequality that leaves 67 per cent of the population in poverty, its cultures develop as a catalyst for multiple social relationships, and do so in dialogue, clashing or – in the majority of cases – separate or indifferent to the cultural policies of the institutions, which still largely concentrate on book culture, museums, the performing arts and the formal mechanisms for arts education.

A contradiction of local cultural governance here, contributing to weak interaction with civil society and poor public participation, is that it involves bodies from several different levels of government, each of which has its own distinct political agenda and cultural policy priorities, since each is conceived by a different political party. There are no true State cultural policies as such at the federal or metropolitan levels. As such, cultural governance in Mexico City operates through the micro-worlds of the public federal, state or local institutions themselves, along with the infrastructures, programmes and venues created by major universities such as the Universidad Nacional Autónoma de Mexico (UNAM) – the largest public university in Latin America – and the Autonomous Metropolitan University (UAM). These also contribute to giving a sense of cultural dynamism to the city.

Another set of governance challenges consists of the public policy needs raised by the growth of civil society initiatives, which have increased significantly in recent decades, but which have done so without any legal base which regulates their relationships with institutions, or support, or financial incentives or clearly established sources of funding. Hence many of them are in a particularly fragile condition which results in their emerging and then disappearing again and again, before the indifferent gaze of the federal and local public institutions.

In spite of the programmes and lines of work promoted by the federal government and the governments of the Federal District and of the State of Mexico, none of these has taken the form of a metropolitan cultural *policy* which is capable of mobilizing the creative energy of a city whose society is highly fragmented and unequal, where the skyscrapers, the large financial centres and the luxurious commercial districts coexist within the same territory with extensive areas suffering segregation and exclusion. The chaotic urbanization favoured by land speculation has created 'dormitory' towns across an enormous peripheral area, where the urban landscape, infested with metal rods with their soft drink bottles placed to form lightning conductors, is a metaphor for a multitude of antennas all pointed towards an uncertain future.

The federal State of Mexico, with its 35 municipalities, forms a belt surrounding the city, and threatening to devour it or to squeeze it to the point where its borders are broken, but without bringing with it any cultural policy which is capable of attending to all of these diverse populations. In the city of Nezahualcóyotl alone, more than a million inhabitants live without any cultural infrastructure or communal spaces. The concentration of cultural activities in the centre and the south of the city, where the bulk of the cultural infrastructure is focused, is in stark contrast to boroughs such as Iztapalapa, where almost 3 million people live without access to a single theatre, museum or library of any note, despite its being one of the focal points of a tradition involving millions of citizens, through different schemes for community participation and representation, around the annual Holy Week celebrations.

The neighbourhood cultural policies which aim to involve local populations have operated in the city through the so-called 'Casas de cultura', institutions conceived under the conventional models of education in the arts and in some cases in trades

Figure 23.1   Organizations playing a role in the cultural policies of Mexico City

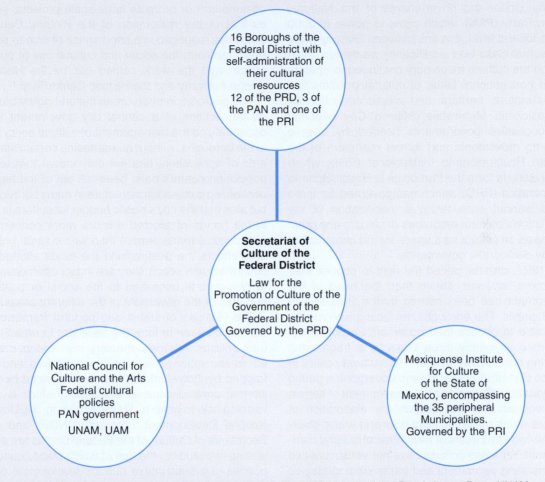

16 Boroughs of the Federal District with self-administration of their cultural resources 12 of the PRD, 3 of the PAN and one of the PRI

Secretariat of Culture of the Federal District
Law for the Promotion of Culture of the Government of the Federal District Governed by the PRD

National Council for Culture and the Arts Federal cultural policies PAN government UNAM, UAM

Mexiquense Institute for Culture of the State of Mexico, encompassing the 35 peripheral Municipalities. Governed by the PRI

PRD – Democratic Revolutionary Party; PAN – National Action Party; PRI – Institutional Revolutionary Party; UNAM – Universidad National Autónoma de Mexico; UAM – Autonomous Metropolitan University.

and handicrafts, rather in the spirit of artistic processes proper, lacking as they do both professionally trained teachers and training templates built on contemporary designs. The professional arts schools are mostly federal, although the city also has some which, at the time of writing, are clearly insufficient to meet the demand of young people and children.

Mexico City has thus created a new form of social exclusion caused by the distance between the federal or local cultural infrastructure and more than 80 per cent of the population (CONACULTA, 2004). Furthermore, the educational system in Mexico City, centralized at the federal level, does not include any cultural or aesthetic education. All of this creates new forms of aesthetic illiteracy and offers little possibility for the sustainable development of cultural entrepreneurship within civil society.

Democracy and local cultural policies in transition

During the government of the Institutional Revolutionary Party (PRI), Mexico City promoted two cultural policies: one related to performances in public parks, and the other to a policy for civil celebrations less frequented by the public on a voluntary basis. At the federal level, the ties with intellectuals and artists granted the regimen additional legitimacy. Under the governments of the National Action Party (PAN), which came to power in 2000 at the federal level, this link between State and the intellectual class was significantly weakened, even though the cultural machinery continued to operate in the conventional fields of cultural policies: fine arts, literature, heritage and artistic education for professionals. Meanwhile, Mexico City was led by successive governments headed by diverse left-wing movements and former members of the Partido Revoluciónario Institucional (PRI), which broke away to form the Partido de la Revoluciónario Democratica (PRD), which has governed for three terms without contributing a mobilization of the population's cultural resources or placing any great emphasis on culture as a space for the construction of new democratic governance.

In 1997, citizens gained the right to choose their governors, whereas before that, the head of the government had been named by the President of the Republic. The boroughs, as local governments, were able to choose their governors up until 2000. Governed for nearly three terms by a fragmented left-wing represented by the PRD, cultural politics in Mexico City have in the process undergone a period of gradual structuring and the development of certain initiatives which point towards the elaboration of policies which make the local level and ethnic diversity the two key thrusts of new forms of cultural management. Yet these policies have not yet succeeded in generating permanent and transparent strategies of civil society connection and participation.

In 2003, the Government of the Federal District, through the Assembly of Representatives, issued a Cultural Development Bill that promised to allot 2 per cent of public resources to culture. The corresponding regulations were not published until 2010, however, and to date that percentage of public expenditure has not been reached. The agency created for cultural policies was first an Institute which later became a Secretariat of Culture, although it did not receive either a structure or a significant budget in accordance with what the bill envisaged. It is important to point out that in the logic of a left-wing government which pays close attention to the trends of its public service leaders, the Secretariat of Culture is not the only agency involved in the cultural policies of the city, since so many other local government agencies (e.g. for Environment or Social Development) realize cultural activities, manage the main cultural infrastructures of the city (the federal government) or promote large-scale projects, such as that of the restoration of the Historic Centre, which has managed in a short space of time to positively transform the social and cultural use of public space, with the work carried out by the Historic Centre Authority and the Historic Centre Trust.

The elaboration of an urban cultural policy based on the actions of a central city government that decentralized the management of cultural policy out to the boroughs, without guaranteeing certain standards of application, has not only meant that large population centres have been left out of the highly centralized cultural infrastructure in many boroughs, but also that the city's public budget for culture is left in the hands of elected officials more concerned with political management than with cultural policy. This affects the destinations the funds allotted to culture actually reach: they are in fact often devoted to non-cultural uses tied to the social or political priorities of the governors of the different areas.

The vestiges of statist and populist frameworks can still be seen to form the backdrop to urban cultural policies. At times, the very instruments created for the management of new initiatives end up trapped by individual relations or influenced by the internal contradictions of a left-wing which is still learning how to govern. At time of writing, the United Nations Development Program (UNDP) and the Secretariat of Culture of the Federal District are supporting two studies, the first of which places cultural policies in a sustainable human development context in the perspective of cultural consumption and the formation of intellectual capacities (Nivón Bolán, 2010), while the second measures culture's contribution to the city's wealth as 9.3 per cent of the GDP – including the so-called shadow economy that generates no tax revenue (Piedras Farías, 2010).

Mexico City is a place where the use of public space is disputed between political parties, private advertising companies, youth graffiti movements, the transit needs of millions of citizens who make use of the city for work, family, entertainment and the pursuit of underground activities which have little to do with the official cultural infrastructures, with which only approximately 15 per cent of the urban population engage. The use of space and the construction of the urban order, understood as the rules which, legally or pragmatically, involve the use and abuse of public space (Duhau and Giglia, 2004) fall outside the boundaries of any formally defined cultural policies.

All this originates in the complexity of the political culture of the governing left, with constant dialogue between federal powers and local ones, the latter establishing their legitimacy and visibility through a game of contradictory relationships negotiated with the federal executive level, in which there exists a very weak capacity for interaction with and between citizens. The participation of citizens, highly influenced by the old power structure of the defeated PRI, is based more on clientelism and proximity to power than on any authentic democratic participation. To a large degree, it is this political culture that conditions the city's need to constantly negotiate for resources and rules, as governance strategies, while cultural policy, located outside the issues of urban development, remains on the peripheral edges of the left-wing governments.

In Mexico City, neither the federal government nor the local government have created clear, transparent and public mechanisms for the generation of new forms of funding or incentives for citizens' cultural initiatives. There are no incentives or sponsorship laws and the sole funding strategy continues to be that of direct or indirect subsidies, which are exercised most of the time on a case-by-case or even discretionary basis. Although community projects are financed by the Secretariat of Culture of the Federal District, this funding does not guarantee the continuity of cultural processes, nor the possibility of creating cultural networks which can contribute to the strengthening of social cohesion and governability.

Thus the cultural policies of the city are fragmented and poorly articulated. The only coherent effort has been that of the late writer and promoter Alejandro Aura, who set up the *Faro de Oriente*, a cultural infrastructure located in one of the most impoverished urban areas in the city and which has become an emblematic site for the development of creative and collective projects which create, produce and distribute their own cultural products, and whose model has been reproduced in Milpa Alta, Tláhuac and other peripheral areas of Mexico City.

The monumental city and the anonymous policies of pleasure

Despite Mexico City's motto of 'Intense Cultural Movement', local policies are built on a fragile institutional structure which does not receive more than 400 million pesos ($31 million) per year. These funds are provided within a strict regulatory framework and have little chance of trickling down to the community level, not because of any lack of interest or desire, but rather because these policies have inherited the musty old structure of a system designed to promote weekend performances, civil programmes which characterized the cultural policies of the PRI governments. The influence of heavily monopolized television structures and the growth of cable systems also fail to offer the possibility of building participative populations. The communication city establishes forms of governance that are articulated through the powers that be. Any encouragement of social participation comes via political or commercial marketing strategies and messages, in reality TV shows or in entertainment game shows which citizens can attend in the television studios. However, it has been the media arena where disputes between political forces, electoral battles and the legitimization strategies of the different movements have been settled and here the citizens are only a subtext.

Historically, Mexico City has been considered the city of palaces. The name was not unwarranted, since this is a city where modern and contemporary architecture coexist with that of colonial times, with that which gives testimony to the force of ancient times, represented not only by the archaeological sites of Templo Mayor, the Plaza de las Tres Culturas or Ciucuilco, but also by markets where traditional knowledge and foundation myths are mixed with plastic and synthetic fibres in an explosion of colour that astonishes any visitor. It is also a very theatrical city, featuring more than 150 sites, including theatres, auditoriums, bars and other venues where performing arts events are held, with ticket sales increasing particularly at the beginning of this century, following a series of severe downturns in audience numbers. The museums and art galleries of Mexico City are also numerous and even include some (if not as many) where electronic art is on show, these being more visited by young people familiar with these trends and with direct connections to galleries and artists in Barcelona, Berlin, New York, Paris or São Paulo, alongside the more classical spaces exhibiting colonial art or modernist murals, the work of the generation of the 1960s or those dignifying popular art and handicrafts, not so often afforded the prestige of

Figure 23.2   Performances in Mexico City (Federal District)

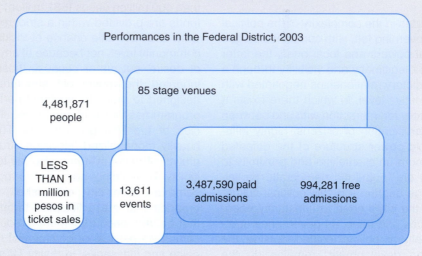

Performances in the Federal District, 2003

85 stage venues

4,481,871 people

LESS THAN 1 million pesos in ticket sales

13,611 events

3,487,590 paid admissions

994,281 free admissions

Source: INEGI (2005)

so-called fine art. Mexico still maintains this distinction between 'fine art' and 'popular art'.

Although it has been more than a decade since the creation of any new cultural infrastructures, with the exception of the Contemporary Art Museum of the UNAM, Mexico City still swings between the torpor of daily life and the pleasures not recorded in any cultural statistic: from boxing and wrestling to horse racing and the nightclubs, raves, and underground pits lit up by the colours of the DJ. Or the neighbourhoods where the steps of the new 'duranguense' or 'cumbia' are danced, or the latest hits from Ibiza's club scene boom out, right down to the new places, legal or otherwise, where thousands of young people who have nowhere else to go other than a shopping centre congregate and indulge their pleasures. Similarly, within the space of just a few years, the city has earned itself a place within the ranks of the global showbusiness economy, thanks to the emergence and consolidation of large companies promoting Broadway-style musical theatre, massive rock and pop concerts, electronic music and all the other shows that can also be found in Madrid, New York or Buenos Aires. This sphere rarely appears in the cultural statistics of the city, which consider the institutional infrastructures, practically unknown to the bustle of a fragmented city which prefers to lock itself at home to watch pirated movies or television or to listen to black market CDs.

The fractures of urban space and civil society

The organized civil society that emerged following the earthquake which tore apart the city in 1985 created a number of diverse agencies for participation, and urban and cultural intervention. The first organizations were created spontaneously by citizens, who weaved webs of solidarity and provided a catalyst for the demands of the popular urban movement: the Association of Residents and Victims of 19 September, the associations of seamstresses, the Neighbourhood Assembly, Mexican Dance, the Forum for Mexican Culture, the Mexican New Song Committee, the Mexican Film Federation, among others. Most of these died out in the 1990s, following the wearing down of their working mechanisms and, above all, the absence of support strategies.

The decade of the 1990s saw the growth of large companies operating in the world of large-scale showbusiness, of the previously mentioned global musical productions, themed exhibitions, fairs and other events, while the small cultural centres and creative companies still lacked support and financial viability. For this reason, a Network for Independent and Alternative Cultural Spaces (RECIA in Spanish) was formed – a network of young people at the helm of independent cultural centres joining forces to drive forward a change in local legislation so as to achieve equal treatment in terms of financing, applications and permits for cultural centres. The dialogue with the city's cultural authorities has been long and intermittent. There are no censuses of autonomous initiatives or creators, nor any diagnoses of production chains for the different creative sectors.

In 2006, the Secretariat of Culture drew up, for the first time, a training programme in cultural management and support to artists for the setting up of cultural companies: 'Imagination in Movement'. However, the weight of certain ideological factors, internal contradictions and differences of opinion with regard cultural entrepreneurship together put paid to the programme, which trained 58 cultural companies before coming to a halt. This is one of the initiatives most widely accepted among those citizens who are convinced that culture can be a field which contributes to well-being and the social economy.

In 2010, the Secretariat of Culture celebrated the city's being named 'Latin American Capital of Culture'. This created an opportunity to once again take up autonomous initiatives and take advantage of the potential of the organizational experience acquired by the small publishing houses, management companies, art schools, audiovisual production companies, design firms and performing arts companies that drive urban creativity. One of the challenging tasks remaining will be to consolidate this field of cultural policy together with civil society, which could bring about a substantial change in terms of the limited subsidy schemes that still characterize urban cultural policies. Consensus mechanisms and the establishment of public dialogue are being built through the increasing use of social networks, in which citizens readily express their disagreements and their initiatives. It is no surprise that Facebook and Twitter are serving as catalysts and amplifiers in the absence of other forums and other ways to construct democratic governance. Communication over digital and electronic networks has done away with the traditional broadcaster–receiver relationship in order to create new forms of participation which, although still not the norm, do contribute to the generation of new spaces for expression.

The recent demonstrations held in various cities around the country in March 2010 in protest at the killing of several young people in Morelos was organized from within the cultural sector via these new communication channels, without including the political parties. It is the unstructured civil society that takes to the streets and protests, amidst drums, performances and spontaneous music, demanding 'ni un muerto más' ('no more deaths') in the face of the 40,000 casualties of the war against drug-trafficking.

Conclusions

The main contradiction facing cultural governance in Mexico City is the lack of coherence among the different levels of government involved and the lack of a contemporary and participative vision of cultural policies within institutions, since none of them has the capacity to have an effect in a truly metropolitan sense. This is not due only to the sheer degree of political and administrative fragmentation, or the heterogeneous nature of the vast urban population. In fact it exists primarily because territoriality has lost ground as the core of cultural politics due to the impact of migration and the trans-local character of urban cultural identities.

Strengthening the institutional aspect of the city's culture, by granting its management agencies with their own structure, by fulfilling budget pledges, generating cultural legislation and professionalizing the public management of culture, are all conditions which, although they do not offer any guarantee of radical change, could have an influence on a medium- and long-term process to reverse the conditions of vulnerability that predominate in the everyday exercise of citizens' cultural rights, especially in the case of teenagers and young people, native peoples and the various minority groups.

What are required are policies that convey a vision which is more closely linked to sustainable cultural development, looking beyond traditional activities: book promotions, the organizing of festivals, the creation of entertainment options for children and the extremely worthy promotion of leisure activities, such as the installation of ice rinks in the Zócalo and artificial beaches at different points around the city. Mexico City needs to establish diversity, sustainable development and social participation as basic transversal criteria of its cultural policies. Unlike cities such as Medellín, Bogotá, São Paulo or Buenos Aires, where citizens actively participate in the structuring of new public spaces and the creation of cultural action networks for citizens, in Mexico City civil society often acts outside the operations of the institutions, which do not set down a truly democratic and participative relationship for the management of the population's cultural resources. Government initiatives operate in a fragmentary manner, failing to coincide with the practices of the citizens with regards the management of urban space and urban order in terms of the environment, public space and coexistence in diversity. Educating for coexistence in diversity becomes a priority once again, faced with the symptoms of intolerance and the growth of different forms of social violence.

The recovery of public space, establishing links for the metropolitan management of cultural policies, specifying the cultural competencies of the city's boroughs, creating cultural ties and stimulating civil participation are all priorities for the generation of a new cultural governance. Although the regulations of the Law of Cultural Development suggest that the programmes of the boroughs be connected

to the Secretariat of Culture of the Federal District, this would require the establishment of micro-regionalization criteria or sector priorities which are tied to proposals for well-being and social participation. Democracy and the consolidation of new governance scenarios based on culture would help generate sustainable conditions for the development of initiatives by citizen, youth and resident organizations, communities and indigenous peoples, and for the social management of social creativity in a city which today stands – contemporary, hybrid and chaotic – atop its own contemporary memories.

Notes

1 INEGI, Press Release, 29 January 2001.
2 See www.inegi.gob.mx/prod_serv/contenidos/espanol/
bvinegi/productos/integracion/sociodemografico/medio
ambdf/2002/archivo14.pdf, consulted September 2010.

REFERENCES

CONACULTA (2004). *Encuesta de Prácticas Culturales y Consumo Cultural en México*. Mexico City: CONACULTA, p. 273.

Duhau, Emilio & Giglia, Angela (2004). 'Conflictos por el espacio y orden urbano'. *Estudios demográficos y urbanos*. El Colegio de México, May–August, 2004, pp. 257–288.

INEGI (2005). *Cuadernos de Cultura*. Mexico City: INEGI.

INEGI (2011). Population Census for 2010. Available at: www.censo2010.org.mx/, consulted in April 2011.

Jiménez, Lucina (2010). 'Empresas Culturales y economía de la creatividad en México', Ábaco: *Revista de Cultura y Ciencias Sociales*, (Asturias, Spain) 2/3 (64–65): 49–59.

Nivón Bolán, Eduardo (2010). *Desarrollo y Cultura en la Ciudad de México*. Mexico City: United Nations Development Programme PNUD, p. 52.

Piedras Farías, Ernesto (2010). *Economía y Cultura en la Ciudad de México*. Mexico City: United Nations Development Programme PNUD, p. 39.

CHAPTER 24

MUMBAI: HISTORIC PRESERVATION BY CITIZENS
Abha Narain Lambah

This chapter explores a particular aspect of cultural policy in Mumbai: the challenges that beset the city's historic fabric urban heritage and of saving this urban heritage for the future. The author takes stock of the existing framework for heritage preservation in the context of urbanization and development pressures and shows how concerned individual citizens (of whom she has been one) and citizens groups, rather than the municipal authorities, have taken the lead in enforcing these regulations and breathing new life into the historic stock. On the basis of Mumbai's experience in this area, she also recommends ways in which this experience can be consolidated into a fully-fledged policy for heritage preservation in the city.

Introduction

Bombay (renamed Mumbai) is the quintessential multicultural Indian city, India's financial capital and a bustling melting-pot of various ethnic, religious, cultural and regional groups. The city developed from a group of swampy islands in the seventeenth century into a nineteenth-century cotton trading hub to finally emerge as the busy metropolis of 19 million people in the twenty-first century.[1] Colonized first by the Portuguese and then the British, it owes its economic growth in large measure to immigrant populations of Zoroastrian Parsis, Bohra Muslims, Ismailis, Konkanis, Kannadas, Gujaratis, and after Partition, refugees from Sindh and West Punjab.

The urban fabric of Mumbai is held together by the tenuous warp and weft of historic architecture and modern infills, strained with the needs and aspirations of its millions. The narrow promontory of South Mumbai marks the footprint of the old British Fort, playing the dual role of commercial centre as well as historic core of the city. In this bustling metropolitan city, virtually bursting at the seams, where the historic fabric is also the centre of the downtown business district, the up-market residential areas and the focus of dizzying real estate values, the pressures of urbanization constantly influence the fundamental equation between the old and the new, threatening to change the delicate balance between conservation and development. This dichotomy of the past and present is an unavoidable reality and yet, it is this interface between the past and the present, the historic and the modern, that makes for the intriguing dynamics within the city.

Given the position of Mumbai as the financial nerve centre of India, India's economic liberalization policies of the 1990s and the resulting real estate boom could have had tremendous repercussions for the Fort precinct and many such historic quarters located in South Mumbai. These areas had the highest real estate prices in the country and thus were under the greatest pressure of urban transformation, with modern skyscrapers, threatening to entirely engulf, if not obliterate the fragile historic fabric.

A national pioneer in Heritage Regulations

The *Heritage Regulations for Greater Bombay* were framed and gazetted on 20 February 1991.[2]

This was the first government notification in India for inviting objections and suggestions for framing a heritage policy towards the 'non-monumental' urban heritage of a city. An official notification of the Government of Maharashtra (No. DCR 1090/3197/RDP/UD – II of 21 April 1995), issued as a publication entitled *Heritage Regulations for Greater Bombay*, enumerated buildings, structures, fountains, open spaces and precincts under various categories of Grade I, II and III as heritage. The regulation came into force on 1 June 1995 and, with subsequent notifications, now includes 574 buildings, one public open space, 14 milestones and 18 precincts that qualify for protection under the regulation.

Mumbai thus became the Indian pioneer in the field of urban conservation as this made it the first city to establish urban heritage regulations. Before this, there was no protection policy for built heritage outside the ambit of the federal government's Ancient Monuments and Archaeological Sites and Remains Act of 1958. So, beyond the 5,000-odd monuments protected by the Archaeological Survey of India or by the governments of the respective Indian states, the requirement that a monument had to be at least 100 years old to qualify for protection left most of Mumbai's colonial nineteenth- and early twentieth-century heritage unprotected. Moreover, 'monument-centric' policies largely focused on ancient and medieval sites, excluding most of Mumbai's Victorian and Art Deco structures as well as vernacular residential neighbourhoods.

The 1995 *Heritage Regulations for Greater Bombay* included cultural landmarks ranging from monumental public buildings to private bungalows and neighbourhood landmarks, protecting them from demolition and regulating the developmental interventions to their built fabric. The city fabric was further delineated into heritage precincts – the Victorian Neo-Gothic Fort area, the Art Deco Marine Drive, the temple precincts of Mahalakshmi and Banganga, the East Indian Christian villages of Khotachiwadi, Bandra and Matherpakadi, and other historic neighbourhoods were deemed to be areas of urban significance and historic value. This was a paradigm shift, moving away from the established approach of viewing monuments in isolation and introduced the idea of urban conservation into the planning vocabulary and policy. The regulation did not place a complete freeze on listed structures, but allowed for a grading procedure whereby structures

placed in the elite Grade I list merited 'strict preservation' both to their internal and external features, those under the Grade II category allowed for some internal modifications while Grade III structures had a greater degree of flexibility for alterations. To monitor these changes, the Heritage Committee, an advisory body consisting of multidisciplinary experts from a range of fields such as urban history, conservation, archaeology, engineering and architecture, was established to judge each case on its merits, with reference to the grading and significance of each structure.

This heritage legislation was successful in accomplishing a colossal task, that of enabling the preservation of a considerable amount of historic building stock that would have been lost to the pressures of urbanization. It was also successful in acknowledging the colonial heritage and urban grouping of buildings as worthy of preservation. With a gradation in the levels of intervention allowed to heritage structures based on the listing criteria, it recognized the need to preserve and yet reconfigure a city. The Heritage Regulations acknowledged the reality of Mumbai's living and functioning public structures, such as railway stations, courts and libraries, in a bold departure from prevalent policies which had confined monuments to museum pieces, dead, stratified and fenced off from the urban matrix. Soon other cities such as New Delhi and Kolkata were to follow the Mumbai model in addressing their urban heritage.

From regulation to action: citizens in the lead

Heritage listing not only helped protect historic sites and properties in the city, but also opened up tremendous opportunities for the urban revival of historic areas such as Ballard Estate, Horniman Circle, Kala Ghoda to reinvent themselves as business and art districts. In the past decade and a half, citizens groups and local area associations have led urban conservation and cleanliness drives, e.g. that pertaining to the historic cricketing ground of Oval Maidan, where through the efforts of the Organization for Verdant Ambience & Landscape (OVAL) local residents managed to raise more than US$300,000 in corporate funding and sponsorship to restore the vast urban green in the heart of the city and clean up the area around it.

In 1998, the Kala Ghoda Association, a local citizens' group, launched the idea of combining art events with heritage buildings, launching a two-week art festival with open air concerts, artists workshops, heritage walks, poetry readings, street-side galleries and open air cafés to bring to life the historic buildings and streets of a Victorian heritage precinct in the downtown area of Mumbai. The festival raises funds through public and corporate sponsorship and the money generated helps undertake physical improvement of the historic district, such as the restoration of Elphinstone College, sidewalk improvement and the provision of street furniture. The festival has emerged as an iconic contemporary art event on the national calendar.

The case of Dr Dadabhai Naoroji Road is another such model of citizen participation in heritage management. Characterized by arcaded bazaars and neoclassical buildings, this street is among the busiest commercial areas within Mumbai's Fort precinct. It connects major urban landmarks such as the Crawford Market, the *Times of India* Building and the World Heritage Site of Victoria Terminus (renamed Chhatrapati Shivaji Railway Terminus), to the elegant Flora Fountain at the southern end and is one of the primary arterial linkages within the Fort area, catering to a phenomenal influx of pedestrians that flow out of the old Victoria Terminus building each day. By the very fact of its existence as a dynamic commercial spine and nerve centre of the city, as well as being perhaps the busiest pedestrian thoroughfare in the entire country, it plays a very critical role in the public perception of Mumbai.

The entire stretch of Dadabhai Naoroji Road was declared a heritage streetscape of Grade IIA significance, and acknowledged as an important architectural ensemble within the Fort heritage precinct. In 1998, I was appointed by the Heritage Conservation Society of the Mumbai Metropolitan Regional Development Authority (MMRDA) to prepare a documentation and design handbook for the historic streetscape that aimed to provide for a regulated streetscape with well-designed shop fronts and sensitively designed street furniture, so as to best present the architectural heritage of the area. The project was completed in 1999, documenting each of the elegant façades and conducting extensive surveys of signage and street furniture as well as detailed, measured drawings of the fine architectural façades lining the street edge. Extensive surveys and building inventories led to the collection of statistical data on the number of buildings in need of restoration.

Our *Design Handbook for a Heritage Streetscape: Guidelines for Signage and Street Furniture* was presented to the city's Municipal Corporation in 1999. Beginning in July 2000 and for a year thereafter, the Municipal Ward office of the Brihan Mumbai Municipal Corporation conducted monthly meetings with the occupants of the heritage road, creating awareness about the guidelines and enlisting public support. By 2001, a majority of the shop fronts on the street had conformed to the shop front guidelines and a citizens' group representing a public initiative towards conserving this streetscape was formed. A pilot project for street furniture to blend with the historic ambience of the precinct was also initiated along the *Times of India* building stretch, to be replicated through the entire street. Today, the Heritage Mile Association has formed a body of the local stakeholders, occupants and shop-keepers to collectively fund the street improvement initiatives. This has happened without any government funding and is a model of a truly participatory system of local stakeholders working towards the improvement of their heritage precinct, contributing financially towards streetscape improvement.

There are specific local reasons for this. Unlike the colonial cities of Delhi and Calcutta that were built as capitals of the British Empire, Bombay is a city built by private enterprise. Thus, many of its nineteenth-century public buildings, cultural and educational institutions were built through the generosity of its many philanthropists. The generosity of the Parsi merchant Jehangir Jeejeebhoy helped establish the historic J.J. School of Art and J.J. Hospital, whereas iconic structures such as the Elphinstone College and University Convocation Hall were funded by the famous philanthropist Sir Cowasjee Jehangir, also a Parsi. David Sassoon, a Baghdadi Jew, contributed to the establishment of a library and synagogue, while the Gujarati merchant Premchand Roychand funded the construction of the university library and clock tower.

So what we see happening today, 100 years later, is that most of the conservation initiatives for Mumbai's public buildings have also seen public partnerships take shape. In 1999, a local citizens' group called the Horniman Circle Association raised funding through neighbourhood banks to undertake shop-front regulation and façade restoration of rent-controlled buildings in the neoclassical sub-precinct of Horniman Circle. In 2001, the Kala Ghoda Association funded the restoration of the Victorian heritage building of Elphinstone College. In 2004, a group of eminent citizens and artists formed the Friends of J.J. School of Art, a citizens' initiative to help revive and restore the Arts School and conserve its historic building. Funds were raised through a combination of corporate sponsorship, art auction and music concert to support the project, which won a UNESCO Pacific Award for Heritage Conservation. In 2006, the Convocation Hall of the University of Mumbai was restored, with funding from the state government as well as through the Jamshed Tata Trust.

Over the decades, the government too has moved gradually towards establishing a fund for the conservation of the heritage buildings in public use. An annual budget of US$3 million has been allocated to Victorian public buildings in the city for their specialized conservation.

Joining the dots...

Yet, while individual acts and patterns of conservation have shown great success, it is time to join the dots. Much remains to be done to make the conservation movement a success in the city when we take stock of the situation a decade and a half into this pioneering regulation. Today we have a well-structured regulation in place, but what seems most lacking is the establishment of economic incentives and a strong political commitment to support this regulatory framework. Heritage listing protects listed buildings from demolition, but it cannot prevent a building from ruination through sheer neglect, if not wilful destruction. The Heritage Regulation acknowledges and protects the vernacular built heritage and private buildings, but there are no economic policies to support heritage, nor any fiscal incentives to help private owners restore and maintain their heritage properties. While the Heritage Committee is an advisory body to review development proposals concerning heritage buildings, it does not have budgetary allocations to make financial grants in support of deserving projects of conservation in the city and can be merely overruled by the will of the Municipal Commissioner. And, though guidelines for heritage

precincts such as Khotachiwadi, Bandra, Marine Drive, Opera House and Mahalakshmi were prepared years ago, bureaucratic red tape has prevented these from being notified to make them operational and effective. So whereas heritage listing was successful in saving heritage buildings from demolition, it has not been able to ensure that buildings do not fall victim to dereliction, abandonment or wilful neglect. A classic case is that of the old Watson's Hotel, a nineteenth-century cast-iron structure that was once an elite hotel, now verging on structural collapse due to the inability of the private owner to pay for the restoration and a host of tenants and sub-tenants who refuse to vacate the building, or contribute to its restoration due to outdated Rent Control laws.

For any conservation policy to be effective, it is imperative to create a balance between issues of architectural concern and those of urban infrastructure through the coordination of various involved agencies, planning and legislative bodies and government organizations. This also needs to have an amply broad public base to ensure its implementation at the grass-roots level, supported by sound economic policies.

What seems to be most lacking today, however, is the political will and administrative backing to support this regulatory framework. In 1999, an amendment to Development Control Regulation 33(7) aimed at addressing the issue of old Rent Control buildings and removed nearly 300 Grade III buildings on the Heritage List and precincts from the protective ambit of the Heritage Regulation. Such buildings could henceforth be demolished without Heritage Committee clearance and replaced with modern edifices with a higher floor space index (FSI), thereby severely threatening the survival of historic areas such as Khotachiwadi and Marine Drive where a large bulk of the buildings are still protected.

While other cities such as New Delhi, Kolkata and Hyderabad have followed the Mumbai example and framed strong heritage policies, since 1999 a strong builder–politician nexus in Mumbai has resulted in new government policies systematically chipping away at the Heritage Regulations. Nearly 41 per cent of the listed heritage structures protected under the ambit of the *Heritage Regulations for Greater Bombay* 1995 are under private ownership and most fall in the Grade III category and can therefore be demolished under the new Development Control

Regulation DCR 33(7). And, whereas this percentage in the prime Grade I category is negligible, nearly half of the Grade III structures, and nearly 70 per cent of structures in most heritage precincts, are privately owned. Repeal of this amendment, along with sensitive repair guidelines adopted by the MHADA Repair Board, would give a new lease of life to the hundreds of vulnerable buildings threatened by imminent destruction today.

Policy recommendations

A vision for the city's heritage would begin in fact with the way development plans are sanctioned in the city. Transparency in civic governance should be the first priority that would ensure a clear transparency on what building is proposed to be demolished, which new addition is coming up in an old area, whether this will impact the infrastructure of that locality, or the aesthetic quality of that streetscape. Strengthening of Heritage Regulations, tailormade Architectural Controls for individual precincts, fiscal incentives and tax benefits for conservation of heritage buildings and proactive government policies for culture are the need of the hour.

Better vigilance and implementation of existing policies would ensure the reduction of much of the urban chaos we witness today. The city is no stranger to handsome neoclassical façades obliterated by the clutter of shop signs and unchecked encroachment. Merely implementing signage guidelines for historic areas and regulating the sizes of sign-boards is a simple task for the Municipal Corporation's licensing authority, and would help achieve an urban facelift without costing the government a penny – all that is needed is stricter vigilance and honest enforcement.

Political will and vision among the politicians and the bureaucracy is needed to finally publish and notify the many urban conservation guidelines prepared by MMRDA's Heritage Conservation Society that have been gathering dust in the labyrinths of the municipal offices for years. Nearly ten years after the Heritage Regulation of 1995, most historic precincts, such as the Fort area, Mahalakshmi, Marine Drive, etc., are yet to implement precinct-specific bylaws that would ensure sympathetic development, leaving them vulnerable to developmental pressures. Though MMRDA commissioned the preparation of precinct guidelines for areas such as

Marine Drive, Mahalakshmi, Bandra Village, Khotachiwadi and Mahatharpakadi years ago, they still gather dust and are yet to be notified. Prompt notification and implementation of these urban controls would ensure that these remaining vestiges of historic areas survive for future generations and that new development is well regulated and sympathetic to the historic context.

A critical next step will be that of incentivizing heritage preservation and creating economic policies to support conservation. Innovative tax incentives for restoring heritage buildings, funds for heritage preservation and financial mechanisms such as soft loans are the need of the hour for the vast bulk of the city's buildings constructed before 1947. The idea is to understand that historic stock is an asset, not a liability, and merely requires innovative financial mechanisms to make it economically sustainable. Tax breaks for restoring private buildings and financial tools for restoring and retaining heritage would ensure a greater public involvement in restoration and a trend towards innovative reuse of heritage properties rather than demolition and reconstruction.

Innovative urban-level schemes and pilot projects are also needed to revitalize the city's urban assets. Iconic urban plazas, such as those around Flora Fountain, Horniman Circle and Nagar Chowk, offer a tremendous opportunity for pioneering urban innovations and pilot schemes for revitalization. The historic Crawford Market has a remarkable potential for adaptive reuse and revival along the lines of Boston's Quincy Market, and schemes of reinvigorating areas such as Ballard Estate after office hours should be taken up on the anvil for a holistic economic revival of the historic inner city. Innovative urban solutions such as night bazaars in heritage precincts, illumination of Victorian streetscapes and well-designed hawker plazas are possibilities that require considerable brainstorming and public debate but could also offer solutions for economically sustainable urban solutions. Initiatives in the field of alternative transport systems and pedestrian zones in areas such as Bora Bazaar, Rampart Row and Banganga should be explored and pilot projects to assess their viability should be initiated.

In a city such as Mumbai where each square inch of open space is a luxury, we fail to exploit the potential of areas such as the Parel Mill lands – hundreds of acres of land in the central district of Parel where cotton mills once operated. This vast expanse could have been Mumbai's solution for a planned urban renewal. Instead of short-term gains from parceling off pockets of land to private builders and fragmenting this prime area in the centre of the city, the implementation of a holistic vision for the mill lands with provision of an 'urban green' for the city, integrated development models for new construction along with rehabilitation and adaptive reuse of the surviving mill structures as public landmarks could do for Mumbai what Boston's Charlestown or San Francisco's Presidio National Park achieved for these cities. The integrated development of the Eastern Waterfronts is another such idea being explored by the Urban Design Research Institute. If implemented, it could open up a completely new avenue for the future growth of the city. It is time we revisited the concept of incorporating open spaces into the city fabric, and thought of reintegrating historic sites and expansive open spaces such as Mahim Fort, Sion and Sewri Forts, Worli Fort and Bandra Fort into the urban mileau and giving them back to the city as vital green spaces.

While cities like Shanghai, Bangkok and Kuala Lumpur in Asia have adopted an aggressive, all-out policy to woo tourists and tourism dollars, Mumbai is still rather laid back in tapping this immense economic potential. Even with its two World Heritage sites of Victoria Terminus and Elephanta, the city is still largely perceived as a financial and business destination, unlike other cities that use a UNESCO World Heritage Site listing as a major advertising and earning opportunity through heritage tourism.

The decentralization and *Panchayati Raj* models are perhaps best suited for our metropolitan city, at least in the field of civic improvement.[3] Local Area Management Committees and citizen associations such as Kala Ghoda Association, Bandra Welfare Association, D.N. Road's Heritage Mile Association, and Horniman Circle Association have demonstrated the efficacy of community-driven models in fund-raising, maintaining, restoring and improving local neighbourhoods. So why not give them greater powers to coordinate efforts of the various service providers in the area and strengthen this system with adequate legislation?

Notes

1 According to the Mumbai Metropolitan Regional Development Authority (MMRDA), the population of the Metropolitan Regional Development Area is 19 million people as per the 2001 census. Whereas Greater Mumbai has a smaller population at 11.9 million as per the 2001 figures, daily commuters to the city converge from the entire metropolitan regional area as the workforce in the financial capital.

2 The British term 'gazetted' refers to an announcement in an official journal.

3 *Panchayati Raj* is the ancient Hindu system of village self-government that the Indian government has revived by decentralizing a range of governance functions to the village level. The word *panchayat* literally means an assembly (*ayat*) of five (*panch*) wise and respected elders chosen and accepted by the village community.

CHAPTER 25

NEW YORK CITY: CITY CULTURE AS PUBLIC DISPLAY
David Halle and Louise Mirrer

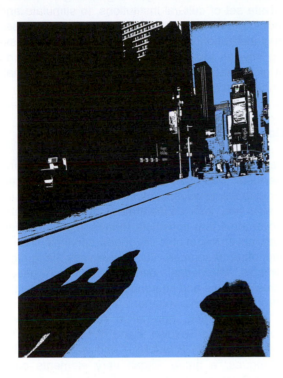

Cultural policy in New York City has evolved from a time when rapid movement between the city and the world brought diverse cultural expression to New York, to a time when new technologies have so compressed time and space that the expression of global cultures requires no movement at all. This chapter speaks to New York's shifting cultural priorities over nearly 400 years, asking how well suited – or not – the city's cultural priorities may be to its current stage of globalization.

Global from the start

Founded in the early 1600s as a Dutch trading post, New York from the start has been a cultural 'mixing bowl' – attracting people and goods from Europe, Africa, and Latin America. These early beginnings appear to have motivated a peculiarly 'New York' definition of culture, which to this day often means the public expression and/or display of the customs and artifacts of others. In this sense of the term, culture has nearly always been the object of official policy in New York, sometimes regulated to be constrained, but more often promoted. In the late seventeenth and early eighteenth centuries, for example, the cultural expression of the city's diverse populations (i.e. basically its customs – especially those seen as distinct from the dominant Dutch and English groups) were subject to a complex web of rules and regulations intended to constrain. People of African descent, Spanish Jews, and Catholics were a particular target of early cultural policies, with sanctions and proscriptions affecting activities that spanned modes of, and venues for, worship, holiday celebrations, and parades.

Later on, in the nineteenth century, when globalizing inventions such as the packet, clipper, and steam ship dramatically increased the speed of movement across the Atlantic, the city developed a set of cultural priorities and policies to advantage itself of the newly-compressed world. This involved promoting the acquisition and display of culture (basically artifacts) imported from abroad as a way of 'branding' New York as a 'world' city, every bit as culturally sophisticated as London, Paris, or Rome. The city's elite, now regularly embarking on what was called the 'European Grand Tour,' returned home from their travels to Europe, the ancient Mediterranean, and around the world with huge caches of souvenirs that ranged from Egyptian mummies and papyruses to stuffed birds and religious relics from Latin America and the Philippines. The curious treasures brought back to New York from abroad were often deposited in, and formed the basis of, the city's increasingly robust collection of encyclopedic museums, which by the end of the nineteenth century included the New-York Historical Society (founded 1804), the American Museum of Natural History (founded in 1869), the Metropolitan Museum of Art (founded in 1804), and the Brooklyn Museum (founded in 1897).

From the organizational point of view, three of these four early museums were created as the result of a highly original and successful idea that continues to mark the structure of many of New

York's cultural institutions to this day, and goes a long way to explaining their dynamism. This is a partnership between public and private sectors that takes the form of privately-led cultural institutions housed in city-owned buildings on city-owned land. This model was driven by the desire to promote institutions displaying prized artifacts from selected foreign cultures. In so doing, it combined American values of independence and enterprise with European traditions of public support for the arts. Public–private partnerships in this specific form (city-owned buildings and land housing privately-led organizations) would eventually support the creation of 34 institutions, all members of the city's Cultural Institution Group, as well as hundreds of other private cultural institutions that would eventually also benefit from city funding.

Starting in the 1960s, the collections, exhibitions, plays, and concerts of New York's cultural institutions came to be influenced by, and to reflect the desire to display, a new kind of diversity: that of the foreign origins of the residents of the city itself. This diversity reflected, though now in a new way, the city's distinct concept of culture as basically the customs and artifacts of others. Between 1850 and 2009, 19,460,962 immigrants arrived to stay in New York. Starting with El Museo del Barrio (founded in 1969), brand new cultural institutions such as the Museum of Chinese in America (founded in 1980), the Italian American Museum (founded in 2001), Jazz at Lincoln Center (founded in 1996), the Tenement Museum (founded in 1992), and the Museum of Jewish Heritage (founded in 1997), all were built to tell this 'glocal' story.

Today, then, cultural policy in New York has come full circle, focusing, as in its very earliest days, on its own, diverse population. But this time around, the city's efforts tend to be centered on promoting and celebrating the cultural expression of others, rather than limiting and constraining as it was in the late seventeenth and early eighteenth centuries. More recently still, since the 9/11 terrorist attack on the World Trade Center, this effort has been endowed with a new and urgent motive. Superimposed on the aim of celebrating the distinct cultures of local ethnic/foreign groups, which was often politically motivated by the goal of garnering the latter's support and especially its electoral votes, has been the urgent mission of fostering tolerance and mutual cultural respect for other peoples in a context where the absence of such respect can foster acts of terrorism with potentially catastrophic consequences for the entire city.

This chapter speaks to these shifting cultural priorities over time: how the city government has endeavored, often using its highly original public–private set of cultural institutions, to stimulate and promote the city's cultural life over various phases of globalization. The chapter concludes by assessing how all this is changing in the current stage of globalization, which includes some major challenges and uncertainties.

Going more global

New York was a global city from the start, and thereafter was usually in the forefront of each earlier globalizing wave, containing elements, albeit far slower and less concentrated, of the flows and movements that constitute today's 'highly accelerated movement of objects (goods, services, finance and other resources, etc.), meanings (language, symbols, knowledge, identities, etc.) and people across regions and intercontinental space' (see the Introduction to this volume).

The city's first, non-native American resident came from the Spanish island of Hispaniola – today's Dominican Republic – and was called 'Jan Rodrigues,' a name whose very elements combined Dutch and Portuguese. Rodrigues, who was of African ancestry although free, was dropped off by a Dutch ship in 1613 with instructions to engage in commerce with Manhattan's natives. Thirty-four years later, when Peter Stuyvesant took charge of what was then called New Amsterdam on behalf of the Dutch West India Company, he was given the title, 'Director-General of New Netherland, Curacao, Bonaire and Aruba.' As Mike Wallace points out (2010: 22), this title instantly linked Manhattan to a Caribbean archipelago. Eighteen different languages could be heard on the streets of New Amsterdam in those days, a settlement of only 1,000 people. The English took over New Amsterdam in 1664, renaming it 'New York.' The former Dutch outpost quickly became the center of a network of global trade: timber and grain exported to England; manufactured goods carried from England to Africa; molasses, rum, and slaves shipped from Africa and the West Indies to New York. When the Erie Canal opened in 1825, connecting the American continent, New York became the new fulcrum of global trade and soon the busiest port in the world.

Culture, in the city's earliest days, was closely linked to religious expression, and cultural policy at that time, as mentioned earlier, was mostly about determining which religious groups from abroad would be admitted and which excluded. When, for example, 23 Sephardic Jews fearing the Inquisition arrived from Brazil after its recapture by the Portuguese, Peter Stuyvesant tried to turn them away. But the Dutch West India Company, lobbied by Dutch Jewish investors, overruled him. These Spanish Jews went on to establish New York's first synagogue, in lower Manhattan nearby the three other denominations permitted houses of worship in New York: a Dutch Reformed church, a Presbyterian church, and a Baptist church. Catholics, on the other hand, were barred from the city under the Dutch and were denied a place of worship under the English – except for a brief period of time (1683–1688) when the Duke of York appointed Thomas Dongan, a Catholic, as governor (Wallace 2010: 24).

Early cultural policy in New York was also linked to regulating the global phenomenon of slavery, and protecting the very existence of slavery in New York until 1827. It involved the establishment of rules governing the public cultural expression of enslaved people which, not surprisingly, was strictly limited. Yet the city's enslaved Blacks did manage to wrest some opportunities for public cultural demonstration, which by this time mixed European, American, and African customs and beliefs. For example, owners in late eighteenth-century New York permitted their slaves several days of release to celebrate 'Pinkster,' a holiday modeled on the Dutch celebration of Pentecost but transformed into a preserve of African-American culture, with music, dance, and games. (Rael 2005: 136). Another form of intermittently-sanctioned cultural expression for African Americans in early New York was the parade, in which free Blacks commemorated events important to their history, for example the abolition of the slave trade in 1807.

From the early nineteenth century on, New York, which as Kenneth T. Jackson notes, owed 'its location, its growth, its prosperity and even its very existence, to its port' (Jackson 1999), benefited from the development of increasingly faster modes of sea transportation. Indeed, every major innovation in travel from the early nineteenth through the mid-twentieth centuries, which propelled the world into new stages of globalization, gave New Yorkers new opportunities for commercial and cultural exchange. Packet ships, which unlike other ships operated on a regular schedule, began leaving the Port of New York for Liverpool in 1818, keeping to a disciplined timetable which made it possible for the city's business and cultural elite to come into increasingly frequent contact with the rest of the world, and especially to bring back artifacts that formed the basis of the city's great museums, as described below. Clipper ships in the mid-nineteenth century 'clipped' days off the time required for travel abroad. In 1849, the clipper ship 'Sea Witch' broke all records when it returned to New York City from China in just 75 days carrying tea and other goods, as well as people, from ports of call that included Valparaiso and Callao. The opening of the Erie Canal in 1825 connected New York with Midwestern grain and hence enabled it to profit from, among other things, the export of flour to Europe. The development of increasingly faster steamships in the 1920s cut travel time between New York and cities abroad, thus cementing its commercial reach globally; and the establishment in 1927, of Pan American World Airways – which used the word 'clipper' in its aircrafts' names – by New York entrepreneur Juan Trippe, transformed the speed and ease with which New Yorkers and others could travel the globe.

These early innovations, together with the dramatic increase in new immigrants to the city – especially at the turn of the century when New York's population tripled in a single generation (1880–1919) – enlarged and enriched the culture of New York, with, among many other examples, art and artifacts brought back from abroad and made accessible to the public in museums; distinctive new buildings designed and built by immigrants based on old-world models (e.g. the Guastavino vault, brought to the city by an immigrant from Valencia, Spain); and new ideas about culture's civilizing role imported from great European cities.

The public–private partnership model

In the nineteenth century, the project of establishing New York as the world's cultural center was seen to be as much the city's 'manifest destiny' as westward expansion was the nation's. Indeed, there is abundant evidence in exhibition reviews, criticism, and discussions of taste, of a cultural agenda for New York that was intended to make it an equal, if not greater, cultural center than the old European centers of empire. In his 1816 'Address before the American Academy of the Fine Arts' in New York City, New York's then Mayor DeWitt Clinton declared that 'A Republican government, instead of being unfriendly to the growth of the Fine Arts, is the appropriate soil for their cultivation' (Ferber 2011: 95). Though Clinton addressed the American Academy of Fine Arts, and alludes to the United States in his phrase, 'Republican government,' it was clear at that time that American culture had its seat in New York.

New York had always linked commerce with culture, but as New Yorkers became increasingly prosperous the will to develop the city as a great cultural capital sharpened. The city's elites increasingly saw 'culture,' defined here as acquiring and displaying prestigious art and artifacts from the world's great civilizations, as a crucial way to make New York a great global city, the equal of cities such as Paris or London. In 1854, for example, the city's first museum, the New-York Historical Society, whose province at that time included all of art history, vigorously set to work raising funds to acquire ancient art that would rival the collections of the British Museum and the Louvre. Eventually the Society's galleries showcased one of the world's great Egyptian collections – consisting of over 1,100 pieces of sculpture, jewelry, and other works of art and archaeology, including three large mummies of the Sacred Bull, Apis, the only specimens known in the world (Vail 1954: 109).

With increasingly frenzied collecting on the part of tycoons like Henry Clay Frick and J. Pierpont Morgan, who sought to develop New York as a repository for all the cultural riches of the world with the explicit agenda of making the city comparably important to Europe's greatest cities, the 'great migration' of Western European art to New York got underway. This migration produced the Metropolitan Museum of Art's spectacular 'Old Master' collection, assembled by Frick, Morgan, and others, including Henry Marquand, the railroad and banking magnate and a founder of the Met.

The ambitions of wealthy New Yorkers to live in a great world city motivated the establishment, in 1869, of the city's unique and unprecedented cultural policy: the public–private partnership. The deal

was that the city government would construct and maintain museum buildings – just as government did in Europe – but a private board would build the collections and operate the institution – a hallmark of American private enterprise. By the end of the nineteenth century, the American Museum of Natural History, the Metropolitan Museum of Art, the Staten Island Institute of Arts and Sciences, the New York Botanical Garden, and the Bronx Zoo had all been created according to this model of public–private partnership.

Thus New York City's basic policy direction with respect to the arts was launched. This distinct, and basically highly successful, partnership has been and remains a major reason for New York City's prominence as a cultural city, allowing it to channel the efforts of some of its richest residents into publicly accessible cultural institutions that are also huge tourist draws.

Still, the model of public–private partnership was bound to subject cultural institutions to the vagaries of political winds – both for both better and for worse. On the positive side, New York's political leadership has typically seen the benefit of cultural pre-eminence, which helps the city generate revenue from tourists and also attract commerce, for example corporate headquarters, whose CEOs and employees favor New York for its cultural appeal. Other, somewhat related factors have led to a steady stream of public funding for culture, even in difficult economic times. For example, despite the current real estate downturn, which has led to the freezing or cancellation of many private construction projects, several major New York cultural institutions are proceeding with city-funded building projects. And there has been an incentive for politicians to see innovative ways of meeting the city's funding obligations, for example LaGuardia's Municipal Art Committee, which stimulated the city's cultural life during the Depression, and 'Percent for Art,' which nowadays 'taxes' developers in support of the creation of public art for city buildings, often by local artists. Also important and positive have been the responsiveness of politicians to their less wealthy constituents, which has generated the development of venues such as City Center that provide affordable music and theater experiences and the ability of the city to control, and keep modest, admissions prices to city-supported cultural institutions.

Among the negative features of the public–private partnership is the ability of city government, via its control of funding to cultural institutions, to censor or suppress art and other forms of cultural expression. The only major actual instance of this, at least in recent times, was Mayor Rudy Giuliani's 1999 attempt to withdraw city funding from, and cancel the lease of, the Brooklyn Museum of Art for mounting the show *Sensation*. This exhibition featured the work of young British artists in Charles Saatchi's collection, and in particular a sculpture by artist Chris Offili which featured the Virgin Mary with breasts and feet made of elephant dung, and surrounded by 'obscene' images (human anuses). Giuliani claimed the image was 'disgusting' and an 'insult to Catholics,' an important voting block in the city to whom Giuliani was clearly pandering (Halle 2001). Although the Mayor's attempt to punish the Brooklyn Museum and to close the show both failed, the event definitely had a chilling effect on the willingness of cultural institutions in New York to mount risky shows, especially shows that might incur the wrath of local politicians.

Going 'glocal'

This [old immigration] system violates the basic principle of American democracy, the principle that values and rewards each man on the basis of his merit as a man. It has been un-American in the highest sense, because it has been untrue to the faith that brought thousands to these shores even before we were a country. (Lyndon B. Johnson, on the signing into law of the Hart Cellar Act)

The Hart Cellar Act, passed in 1966, radically altered the course of United States history, reforming immigration policy so that huge waves of new immigrants from Asia and Central and South America were now welcomed to its shores. Before Hart Cellar, immigration was based on a regionally-based quota system that favored immigrants from Western Europe and strictly limited those from Asia, Latin America, and Africa. This was replaced by a system that basically guaranteed admission for close relatives of any already present US residents, so that the immigrant composition of the United States now became much more globally representative and also mushroomed. Between 1965 and 1970, immigration to the United States doubled; it doubled again between 1970 and 1990.

New York was a major recipient of these new immigrants. Given the city's long-standing propensity to define culture as about *other/foreign* customs and artifacts, existing museums and cultural institutions now began to seem increasingly one-sided and excessively focused on presenting a few privileged 'cultures'. One result of this newly perceived deficiency was an explosion of ethnic museums, which were also a major departure from the early American view that forms of cultural expression smacking of 'selfish' or 'interested' motives were distasteful (Wallach 1998: 305). Cultural institutions, particularly museums, were now central not only to the city's great cultural pantheon, but also – and perhaps, above all – to the assertion of the city's newly-numerous ethnic groups' political and economic clout, with politicians vying to take credit, and hoping for reward at election time from members of the ethnic group at issue, for directing public funds toward their establishment. As a result, it became possible to see much of the world without ever leaving the city: the ultimate time–space compression (Berger 2003).

New York now has more than 25 ethnic museums, including the African Museum, the Asian American Arts Center, the Asia Society, El Museo del Barrio, the Garibaldi Memorial, the Hispanic Society of America, the Italian American Museum, the Japan Society, the Kurdish Heritage Foundation of America, the Lower East Side Tenement National Historic Site, the Museum of Chinese in America, the National Museum of the American Indian, the Polish American Museum, Scandinavia House, the Studio Museum in Harlem, Tibet House, and the Ukrainian Museum, among others. Unlike earlier institutions such as the Metropolitan Museum of Art, whose cultural diversity on view was the consequence of collectors importing treasures from Europe and the ancient world, these institutions often focused on the lived experience and/or voices of non-European ethnic communities in New York. As Susanna Torruela Leval (1995: 2) writes:

Museums like El Museo del Barrio and The Studio Museum in Harlem came into being because there was an urgent need for them to represent particular cultural communities neglected by major institutions like the Metropolitan Museum and the Museum of Modern Art. These traditional institutions had not fulfilled that need because their early history was predicated on a romance with Europe – that continues to this day.

The present: opportunity and uncertainty

The very latest stage of 'globalization,' heavily defined by and involved in new technologies, especially the internet, is only starting to unfold but is likely to have huge implications at least for some sectors of culture (here 'the arts'). For example, for nearly 400 years, the engagement in, and enjoyment of, culture in New York required people to be physically present in a particular, localized, physical space: parade routes and houses of worship, for example, in early New York; museums, concert halls, botanical gardens, and so on in the nineteenth and twentieth centuries. But technology has now begun to suggest that physical presence in a particular location may be obsolete. Are we now in another breakthrough phase *vis-à-vis* globalization/time–space compression or is this a quantitative change? The answer so far seems to depend on which components of culture are at issue, as the following two very different cases of opera and fine art show.

For example, on October 10, 2010, the Metropolitan Opera debuted a High Definition (HD) production of Wagner's *Das Rheingold* in movie theaters all over the US – and the world. Everyone could now enjoy the Met without ever stepping foot in its Lincoln Center home – with better views than in the Opera House's best seats! Virtual exhibitions produced today by nearly every major museum make it possible to compress Berger's few daytime hours even further, visiting the sites of slavery in New York, hearing Lincoln's speech at Cooper Union, and learning the story of Elizabeth Evans Hughes, one of the first children to be successfully treated for diabetes – to name a few currently available on the New-York Historical Society website – with the click of a mouse.

On the other hand, the internet and associated technologies may be less able to replace the physical experience of directly viewing art (Stallabrass 2004). Consider the case of commercial art galleries. Since the end of World War II, New York has been the acknowledged center of modern and now contemporary art. Chelsea, on Manhattan's Far West Side, is the most important contemporary art gallery district in the world with well over 250 galleries.

The internet – and the massive, still unfolding, revolution in retail selling it has triggered – is a seemingly potent challenge to the commercial gallery model on which Chelsea is based and which has dominated the art world for over a century. The use of the internet that offers this threat involves selling art, viewed on a dominant website, directly to purchasers without the mediation of a gallery. Yet constraining the internet's triumph over physically located, commercial galleries is the fact that art works are highly differentiated – almost every work is unique – and many of the factors that differentiate them often cannot be adequately grasped unless the work is viewed directly, in person, allowing far more detail than the internet currently makes possible. As a result, the internet has so far mostly complemented, not undermined, New York's commercial galleries as a way of selling art.

This is apparent in the most important recent attempt to sell art over the internet. Charles Saatchi's famously innovative gallery in the renovated Duke of York's Headquarters building in Chelsea, London, allowed on its website, starting in 2005, any artist, free of charge, to display up to eight works of art, and field email inquiries from, and negotiate directly with, any potential buyers. By 2009 the art of 65,000 artists was viewable on the site, which aggressively promoted the fact that it takes no commission fees, proclaiming: 'Buy Art Free of Commission from Artists Around the World.' The logo also stressed that buyers could shop around the clock for contemporary art made anywhere in the world, using a PayPal-assisted, click-and-buy feature. In 2007 Saatchi decided to find out whether the site's artists were achieving any real-world sales. So the staff asked a randomly selected 1,000 artists on the site how much they sold on the site per week. The 41 per cent who responded said their combined sales amounted to $30,000 a week – an average of roughly $75 per week for each artist. This was not a lot per artist, a tiny fraction of the world market for contemporary art, and certainly not yet a major threat to the main commercial galleries.

The Saatchi experiment revealed a further problem – a single mega-site might offer too many choices, overwhelming the viewer. Saatchi's site took to an extreme the viewer's desire to see a wide range of products, flooding viewers with artists and works. Totally democratic in accepting all art, it lacked the filtering mechanism provided by galleries and museums, which pick and choose which artists to display. At the same time the viewer, unable to see the works in person, lacked the ability to properly judge for him/herself between this mass of works. This is clearly a problem any website selling art will face if it starts to be successful in presenting a large number of works.

In summary, Saatchi Online did not sell enough art, or the work of well-known artists, so did not seriously threaten the commercial galleries. By December 2010 the Saatchi Online Saleroom was gone. The entire Saatchi Gallery website was franchised out to a Los Angeles-based entrepreneur, Bruce Livingstone, who, in January 2011, said he planned to recreate Saatchi Online, but now as a profitable site for selling art by charging a commission whose profits would go to a group of investors. Anyway, the new Saatchi Online seems unlikely to take more than a tiny share of the overall art market or undermine the traditional commercial gallery model, although it had yet to be tested. At this point, New York's commercial art galleries still seem safe.

There is a final factor complicating the question of the future of New York's cultural institutions built on the requirement that the audience be physically present in a particular space such as a museum or concert hall, and so on. This factor revolves around the social experience long associated with engaging in culture. It has long been established that people seldom attend cultural institutions alone: they go in pairs or in larger groups. In this sense, experiencing culture has been an intrinsically social event, which suggests that it may be quite hard, for example, for virtual exhibitions to adequately replace the experience of physical attendance. Whether people can adequately recreate this 'social experience' by Twittering and Facebooking about their virtual cultural experiences is unclear.

Conclusion

In the first decade of the twenty-first century, this city, which was a 'cultural mixing bowl' from the start, has become a place where culture – defined in its peculiarly New York way as the public expression and/or display of the customs and artifacts of others – can be experienced anytime, anywhere. Though some forms of culture – fine art, for example – may be less susceptible than others to the transformations that new technologies have wrought, the consequences of this latest stage of globalization/time–space compression for the city's cultural policy could be huge. For nearly 400 years, New York focused almost obsessively on the physical spaces within which culture might be practiced or displayed – museums, parade routes, houses of worship, zoos, gardens, concert halls, and so on. Indeed, the city's very identity as a 'global city' began with the establishment of museums: beautiful spaces housing cultural 'gems.' Today, city support for cultural institutions' capital projects, such as renovation and new construction, is at an all-time high. Whether the new technologies driving the latest stage of globalization render these physical space as straitjackets or, on the contrary, allow them to become re-energized centers for solidifying New York's cultural pre-eminence, will be interesting to find out.

REFERENCES

Berger, Joseph, 2003. 'Ethnic Museums Abounding,' *New York Times*, July 4.

Ferber, Linda S., 2011. 'Nature's Nation: American Taste and Landscape Painting, 1825–1876.' In Barbara Dayer Gallati (ed.), *Making American Taste*. London: D. Giles.

Halle, David, 2001. 'The Controversy over the Show *Sensation* at the Brooklyn Museum, 1999–2000.' In Alberta Arthurs and Glenn Wallach (eds), *Crossroads: Art and Religion in American Life*. New York: The New Press.

Jackson, Kenneth T., 1999. As quoted in Ric Burns (ed.), *New York: A Documentary Film*. New York: Steeplechase Films.

Rael, Patrick, 2005. 'The Long Death of Slavery.' In Ira Berlin and Leslie Harris (eds), *Slavery in New York*. New York: The New Press, 11–146.

Stallabrass, Julian, 2004. *Art Incorporated: The Story of Contemporary Art*. Oxford: Oxford University Press.

Torruela Leval, Susana, 1995. 'Coming of Age with the Muses: Change in the Age of Multiculturalism.' Paper in series entitled *Arts, Culture, and Society*. New York: Andy Warhol Foundation for the Visual Arts. http: /www. warholfoundation.org/grant/Paper5/Paper.html.

Vail, R.W., 1954. *Knickerbocker Birthday: A Sesquicentennial History of the New-York Historical Society*. New York: The New-York Historical Society.

Wallace, Mike, 2010. 'Nueva York: The Back Story.' In Edward Sullivan (ed.), *Nueva York: 1613–1945.* New York: Scala, 19–51.

Wallach, Alan, 1998. 'Long-term Visions, Short-term Failures: Art Institutions in the United States, 1800–1860.' In Andrew Hemingway (ed.), *Art in Bourgeois Society 1790–1850*. Cambridge and London: Cambridge University Press.

CHAPTER 26

PARIS: A PROCESS OF METROPOLITANIZATION

Stephen W. Sawyer and Mathias Rouet

While Paris has been at the heart of globalization for centuries, the current phase of globalization provides a new context for thinking about the city's cultural policy and governance. Focusing on the wider metropolitan region, this chapter introduces some of the dominant contours of these transformations. Its authors claim that Parisian culture is increasingly defined by new territorial fault lines. The traditional policies of decentralization have been confronted by new spatial logics. The development of cultural goods and practices in the metropolitan region has generated new ideas about their production and consumption, and the contexts within which the two processes are possible.

Introduction

Globalization is a historical process and as such the place of Paris as a 'capital' of culture in the world is not a new phenomenon. Since the sixteenth century, the rise of Atlantic commerce, the emergence of a dominant court culture, the state construction of the Academies and the expansion of the French empire throughout the early modern and modern periods forged this central place in these earlier phases of globalization.

Today, as our current round of globalization has created a more competitive field among cities that increasingly strive for a place in the global cultural economy, Paris still stands as a model for state cultural planning. Moreover, because of its prominent place in the process of globalization over the last four centuries, the city's experience is particularly pertinent for understanding how the relationship between globalization, culture and the urban has been transformed in recent decades. In the postwar period, the establishment of UNESCO in Paris was one of the great symbols of its role as a center of world cultural governance. In many other ways, Paris remains at the core of the world's urban cultural network. In 2010, Paris was the third most visited city in the world, with 77.1 million passengers passing through Roissy-Charles de Gaulle Airport and 60.6 million nights of hotel stays in the Ile de France region. Similarly, the Louvre remains the most visited museum in the world (8.5 million visitors in 2010) and the Pompidou and Orsay museums were not far behind in eighth (3.5 million) and ninth places respectively (3 million) (INSEE-DGCIS-CRT, 2010). It is also noteworthy that Paris contains the highest concentration of cinemas in the world.

And yet, the current phase of globalization presents a fundamentally different context for thinking about Parisian cultural policy and governance. While the French state remains a powerful force in shaping city policy and governance (50 per cent of spending on culture by the French state goes to Paris!), the city is increasingly shaped by local, European and global forces that escape the national scale of policy tools. Our profile seeks to introduce some of the dominant contours of these transformations by offering a broader perspective of Parisian metropolitan culture in the global context of the early twenty-first century. We focus on the Paris metropolitan region, which includes the city of Paris proper and the three neighboring *départements*: Hauts de Seine, Val de Marne, and Seine St Denis – what has been alternatively referred to as the Grand Paris, Paris Métropole and Région Capitale, depending on which authority is speaking (as well as planning and paying). It is in this larger metropolitan context that questions of cultural policy and governance have become essential issues for Parisians as well for the local, national and global authorities. Our approach in this profile works with a broad definition of culture, including the traditional-institutional meaning such as museums, theaters and music halls, but also, in particular, as an experience or as a *scene* (Clark, Navarro, Silver) that extends the notion of urban culture out into the varieties and types of amenities (everything from *boulangerie* to tattoo parlors) that one finds in the neighborhood and to creative and cultural industries (like video-games and the cinema industry). Using this broader definition, we also argue that metropolitan culture in global cities (and no doubt elsewhere as well) is being rapidly redefined both in its content and its relationship to urban space.

Spatial logics of Parisian culture: a cultural donut hole?

The aggressive cultural politics of past kings, emperors and republics have left a rich cultural heritage in the heart of Paris. But as rich as they may have been in times past, they have been greatly accelerated in the last three decades with the *Grands projets*, in other words, a new National Library, the Grand Arche at La Défense, the I.M. Pei additions to the Louvre, a new Opera House, and a vast Park to the north (le Parc de la Villette). All of these have been erected since the 1980s while their historical counterparts were constructed over almost 400 years! The acceleration of large-scale cultural projects has taken yet another new turn in the last decade through the franchising and export of major Parisian institutions like the Louvre, the Pompidou Center and the Sorbonne. Thus, while Paris has long sat at the center of a world cultural network with an overwhelming density of major cultural institutions, these cultural resources have been transformed into export brands, both within France, as with the Louvre outpost in the city of

Lens and the Pompidou Center's Metz branch, and abroad – the Louvre Abu Dhabi and the Sorbonne Dubai. What was once an exclusively Parisian experience has moved increasingly towards a franchised model that transforms the vast resources of Parisian cultural heritage into an exportable experience. The net result, then, of these transformations is a greater density and prestige for cultural institutions in the center of Paris and greater exposure in more distant and different regional and international contexts.

This process has been accompanied by an increasingly rich local cultural movement in the suburbs which also has regional, European and international echoes. Parisian suburbs continue to serve as vibrant sites for cultural innovation, both within institutions such as the cultural campus around *MC93* in Bobigny (the *Maison de la Culture* for the 93 *départements*) and in less formal artistic networks and spaces such as the new artistic terrains (*les nouveaux territoires de l'art*). Street artists as well as other grass-roots initiatives that function on low budgets and thrive in contexts of low infrastructural resources are aided by artists' networks such as *C.A.R. Sud-est* that bring together troops of street artists, *MADD 93* that specializes in contemporary amplified music in Seine St Denis, and the *Zebrock* network that supports the development and diffusion of music as well as professional and amateur support for music making. These artistic programs are built on a close connection to the suburban social and cultural landscape. The Laboratoires d'Aubervilliers and the Musée Précaire are particularly good examples of the connection between spaces of cultural innovation and the suburban territory (Hirschhorn and Chapuis, 2005). In 2004, the artist Thomas Hirschhorn built a temporary museum with the help of the neighborhood residents. Over the course of three weeks, youth created a temporary space made up of recuperated and other non-permanent materials like cardboard in the neighborhood of Landy in Aubervilliers. By an interesting process of reversal, they were then exchanged with artworks from the Pompidou Center in the heart of Paris. Hirschhorn described this process, stating: 'The concept of cultural heritage [*patrimoine*] – a collection of either material or non-material "goods", inherited or belonging to a person or persons, but most often tied to the state, is precisely what is called into question by the Musée Précaire (Haidu,

2004). Other examples of grass-roots artistic initiatives abound, for example, the *TRAM* network that ties together sites of creation and exhibition for contemporary art in Paris and in the near suburbs. One Saturday a month, the *Taxitram* proposes to visitors the discovery of artistic sites that are not easily accessible. Similarly, the region of Ile de France, which focuses on contemporary music, tries to link musical experiences across the suburban territory. These networks reveal an essential aspect of artistic production in the suburban milieu, namely, frequent inaccessibility, both for financial reasons and in terms of housing cost, and a preferred isolation and marginality within the larger urban environment which have been fertile ground for the display and production of culture.

The spatial logics of metropolitan culture are in part shaped by state cultural policy. Institutions in inner-city Paris, for example, receive approximately 50 per cent of all cultural spending distributed by the state (more than €2 billion dedicated to Parisian arts within the €4.1 billion allotted to culture in 2005 (*Chiffres clés de la culture*, 2007) – note, for example, that the Opéra National de Paris represents by itself 20 per cent of the budget for *spectacle vivant* in France and half the music budget).[1] However, as a result, the suburbs benefit less directly from this massive spending in culture while the distant provinces benefit far more from the other 50 per cent of cultural spending in France – the creation of Parisian cultural antennas in the Middle East is similar in that the 'Parisian' cultural experience will be available to those in distant lands. Thus, in spite of the fact that the Parisian metropolitan area also contains cities such as St Denis, Montreuil, Boulogne-Billancourt, with more than 100,000 inhabitants, they directly receive a relatively small share of the cultural budget.[2] This has been part of a radial logic of massive cultural investment focusing on the city center that understands democratization and access to culture as the ability to attend cultural events and institutions of international notoriety in the center with occasional investments in the suburbs and then larger state efforts in the provinces. This builds on the tradition of the state cultural planning model developed by André Malraux in the context of Jean-François Gravier's influential *Paris et le Désert Français* that denounced an excess of Parisian centralization. In this context, territorial equality in the access to culture became a priority for his

ministry. This approach has dominated for more than 30 years and is perhaps best captured by the decentralization of theaters designed to support cultural production and diffusion of performing arts throughout France.[3]

The result, however, has not been a lack of culture in the suburbs. Rather, it has meant that the metropolitan region as a whole has developed around the twin poles of state investment and international notoriety in the center and vast new artistic terrains in the suburbs. This process has generated what might be referred to as a *cultural donut hole* with very different types of cultural production, consumption and industries in the center than those throughout the Paris metropolitan region. Broadly speaking, world-recognized traditional and institutionalized forms of culture dominate in the center, while the surrounding suburbs have developed vibrant artistic networks and sites of cultural production of a different type, largely below the radar of massive state investment, but that have in many cases developed a national and even international reputation by means other than century-old traditions of state investment.

The territorial logic has been somewhat different with the creative industries that are often used as markers of the success of cultural development. Cultural industries are concentrated in the Ile de France region surrounding Paris. Some 48 per cent of all *creative* jobs in France are located there while it only contains 25 per cent of all French jobs. Within the metropolitan region, inner-city Paris contains 43 per cent of the total while the rest is located in the periphery with the *département* of Hauts de Seine not far behind with 33 per cent. In these cases, the industries are primarily concentrated in a few *communes*, such as Issy-les-Moulineaux and Boulogne-Billancourt, adjacent to Paris to the southwest. Similarly, as a result of the concentration of the tertiary sector, much like other global cities in London, New York and Tokyo, all the *départements* within the metropolitan region have increased their share of cultural industries over the last 15 years. Paris, however, has gained less quickly than the Hauts de Seine and the Seine St Denis (currently 6 per cent of all cultural industries). In particular, the video-game, audiovisual, and advertising sectors have developed at a very rapid pace (IAU IDF, 2010). In recent years, Paris's share of the creative job sector decreased in Ile de France by 11 per cent between 1994 and 2007, while those in the Hauts de Seine increased 7.5 per cent and Seine St Denis by 2.5 per cent.

Beyond these trends in creative industry, there would also seem to be a progressive separation between traditional measures of culture production and creative industrial clusters. For example, while the wealthy communes in the Hauts de Seine, such as the cities of Issy-les-Moulineaux and Boulogne-Billancourt, are home to a large share of creative industries, they are relatively weaker in cultural associations. For example, while they are situated above the mean for cultural associations for the metropolitan region as a whole (the mean is 6,175 inhabitants per association and Issy contains 5,123 inhabitants per association and Boulogne-Billancourt contains 5,213), they are less well endowed than other cities, such as Aubervilliers with 4,083 or Bobigny with 2,812 – both relatively poorer communes in Seine St Denis. It is reasonable, then, to propose a weak correlation between the local cultural milieu and cultural production in creative industries.

Beyond the center–periphery dynamic of culture in the metropolitan area, there are also broader territorial trends of cultural production and consumption. In particular, metropolitanization has been responsible for increasing a west-side and east-side distinction within cultural institutions and practices. The west side has remained more largely defined by traditional and institutionalized forms of culture, including museums, fine restaurants, luxury stores, and hotels. The west continues to benefit from recent projects. In the seventh *arrondissement*, the Quai Branly Museum for what the French call *arts premiers*, designed by Jean Nouvel, opened in 2006 in the presence of Jacques Chirac. Moreover, there have in recent years been increasing ties between the cultural forms of western Paris and the luxury industry, such as exhibitions at the Grand Palais or Orsay that either feature luxury brands or are sponsored by them. There was also a recent agreement signed between the *Comédie Française* and Christian Lacroix. Similarly, one of the most expensive and glamorous projects in the Paris region of the early twentieth-first century, the *Fondation LVMH* designed by Frank Gehry, is being constructed in the Bois de Boulogne to the west of the city. On the other hand, the eastern regions have witnessed the transformation of a Communist red belt. It is primarily in these areas that a policy geared toward the 'creative

class and precarious intellectuals has taken place. These new cultural territories have also been the great benefactors of the wave of state-sponsored projects that has existed since the 1980s and 1990s – such as the Opera Bastille, the Parc de la Villette, the Cité de la Musique, the National Library, the Cité de l'Immigration, Mac Val, etc.

Outside a loose east–west distinction, as the metropolitan region has become more culturally integrated, it has also placed a new emphasis on the waterways. The Seine has been traditionally tied to cultural production on a local, national and global scale with such events as the Universal Exhibitions in the nineteenth and early twentieth centuries, but on the metropolitan scale it has taken on a renewed importance in cultural planning. Both major rivers of the metropolitan area, the Seine and the Marne, as well as the canal system have become of greater importance in structuring the cultural landscape of the Paris metropolitan region. There have been multiple cultural and artistic festivals such as the *Festival de l'O* or *Rock en Seine*, river- and canal-front planning efforts, such as the jogging and cycling paths along the Canal St Martin and the Seine, and the new center for dance in Pantin just off the Canal St Martin. The construction of a new line of museums and cultural destinations along the eastern portion of the Seine, beginning with the L'Institut du Monde Arabe, the new museum of design, and the National Library, as well as the string of universities and institutions of higher learning that follow toward Ivry, also attest to the renewed importance of water in building cultural institutions in Paris. As another strong symbol of the renewed cultural importance of the river, the city has recently proposed the creation of a floating cinema. Thus, many of the projects proposed for the reflection on the Grand Paris sponsored by the Ministry of Culture have given renewed vigor to one of Napoleon's famous statement on the capital: 'Paris – Rouen – Le Havre, one city for which the Seine is the main street.'

From suburban access to resistance: the case of the Comédie Française

The cultural policy that has governed Parisian cultural development on the local, regional, national and European levels has no doubt been successful in generating 'access' to cultural institutions in the center of the city. But the variety of cultural production on the metropolitan scale has generated a different, and perhaps even more fundamental reframing of the relationship to culture in terms not just of who has access, but also who produces cultural objects and contributes to the cultural scene of the metropolis.

The attempt in the fall of 2008 to move a part of the august *Comédie Française* to the vibrant cultural campus of MC93 in Bobigny with the support of the Ministry of Culture was a strong example of the complexities of the dynamics involved in a metropolitan cultural landscape. The ambition of the move was clearly stated by the director of the *Comédie Française*, Murielle Mayette: 'Stuck in the centre of Paris, the premier dramatic company of France risks cutting itself off from a growing audience which will not come to it if it doesn't go to them. The aim [of the project] is to create an artistic and dramatic utopia' (Burke, 2008). The *Comédie* sought a suburban audience as part of a broader position in Parisian arts. The territorial logic of cultural 'decentralization' has pushed theaters into new areas of the metropolitan region in order to 'democratize' culture. As Laurent Fleury (2008: xxx) suggests, this type of 'cultural democratization' can be understood 'as a technique for social change of which the decentralization of theaters is one example. It is an attempt to "cover the entire territory," in order to win over the public in the provinces that were compared to a dessert after WWII.' The move to Bobigny was to provide a similar outlet. As Christine Albanel stated: 'Yes, it is a question of giving the *Français* [the *Comédie Française*] a new mission of decentralization' (Liban, 2009).

Without insisting on the paradox, it is of course striking to note that with the radial organization of the Parisian transportation network, the latter's location in the heart of the city makes it no doubt one of the most accessible theaters in the entire Metropolitan region. The move to Bobigny, which is not well served by public transportation, actually pushes the theater into an area that is difficult to access. This problem has already been an essential part of the Nanterre theater's programming, as they have been forced to create an intermodal regional train–bus service that links the suburban theater to the center of Paris. Thus the move to Bobigny, or the construction of many of the suburban theaters, is not necessarily a question of access.

The logic of cultural decentralization of the *Comédie Française* in the metropolitan region is part of a broader trend that has guided Parisian cultural institutions and elites. There are already many examples of such metropolitan decentralization in the realm of theater, such as the *Théâtre des Amandiers* in Nanterre and almost a dozen others throughout the suburbs. Similarly, the Bobigny project was part of a process of pushing French/Parisian culture into the backyards of a portion of the Parisian population that, as Mayette argued, would never come to see the theater in the center of Paris – not necessarily because they could not make the trip, but because of the 'scene' surrounding it.[4] The move then built on the complexities of the metropolitan cultural space that has assumed an opposition between 'high' culture in the center that needs to be 'decentralized' out into a space where it has not yet penetrated.

It is no doubt in part for this reason that the project met with such a violent reaction on the other end of the suburban ring, in Bobigny itself. Patrick Sommier, director of MC93, likened the move to the cultural imperialism of the Second World War: 'Never in a time of peace have we seen one theatre make another one disappear in order to expand.' He then quoted Primo Levi, 'as described in [Levi's] *If This is a Man*, the feeling of revolt comes when you feel you have no identity and that anything can be done to you without your accord' (Burke, 2008). Sommier's reaction was clearly a revolt against what was perceived as cultural imperialism. The sharp reaction to the opportunity to host one of the most famous cultural institutions in French suggests that more was at stake than a simple attempt to enlarge the theater's audience. It was also a conflict about who should be making decisions about cultural production and practices in the metropolitan region.

Towards a Greater-Parisian culture: specifi-cities

Thus, cultural planning on the metropolitan scale has faced issues that far outstrip a narrow definition of culture as such. From redefining 'local' identities, to improving integration and decreasing social inequalities, cultural initiatives reveal both tensions and the variety of definitions of culture that reign across the city.

A recent article in the *Le Monde* insisted: 'Like Shanghai, New York or Berlin, the strength of Paris is in its specificity. In the competition between cities (*métropoles*), singularity, or singularities, must be exacerbated instead of attempting to apply old models such as tall towers, business districts, financial poles or Silicon Valleys' (Burgel and Chemetov, 2010). Indeed, local specificities have become an essential part of global cultural development. In response, cities throughout the Paris region have begun searching for and developing a particular cultural identity – an attempt to define their specificity as a sign of what they have to offer the Paris metropolitan region in their singularity. A series of examples provide insight into this process. The EPADESA (consortium for planning the area around the *Défense* suburb of western Paris) has developed a vast marketing strategy designed to focus on a cultural lifestyle by branding and inventing the area as a 24-hour city that never sleeps. They have also created the Défense Jazz Festival and the Festival Chorus. A consortium for planning the Orly–Rungis–Seine Amont area has requested from the *Institut d' Aménagement Urbain de l'Ile de France* (IAU IDF) a study that would allow them to draw similar cultural traits between the 12 collectivities that have not traditionally been culturally bound (IAU IDF, 2011).

Clichy and Montfermeil, two of the poorest municipalities in the metropolitan area, have proposed an ambitious project for urban regeneration through culture. The mayors have projected the coupling of recent urban renovation and the arrival of the tramway with a major cultural event: the creation of a branch of the *Villa Medici* in Clichy-Montfermeil. The project for creating a *Villa Medici* in the suburbs fits somewhere between a centralized state initiative like the *Villa Medici* in Rome and the *Villa mais d'ici*[5] in Aubervilliers, Seine St Denis. While Rome's *Villa Medici* promotes French artists recognized by the state and the international artistic community, the suburban *Villa mais d'ici* is a dynamic socio-cultural association that emerged out of an industrial and abandoned area without state support. Building up from the grassroots, this modest association has become one of the more important cultural sites in its commune. The mayors' project for Clichy and Montfermeil is thus interesting, and no doubt telling, in the metropolitan context: they look to build on France's international cultural capital, captured by the *Villa Medici*, at the same time that they seek to generate the kind of local support and networks that

have made the *Villa mais d'ici* a key contributor to the suburban cultural scene.

Meanwhile, a similarly ambitious project for the arts in the poorest *arrondissement* in central Paris has revealed tensions about alternative artistic spaces within the inner city. The '104', a building of 34,000 square meters created in 2008 in the nineteenth *arrondissement*, is a new artistic establishment created by the City of Paris designed to bring together all the arts. Inspired by the industrial warehouses of Berlin, it hosts residents of young European artists who must in turn keep their studios open to the Parisian population. This establishment is designed to promote contemporary artistic creation and as such has been labeled a success. This has not, however, prevented critiques that local residents never go there whereas it is above all a destination for 'bobos' from central Paris.

Other debates have raged on how Paris, 'the ultimate urban destination,'[6] has become a victim of its great cultural success. The question 'Is Paris Dying?', strangled by its internationally acclaimed museums, tourists and the rapid gentrification of the inner city, comes back like a common refrain in planning cultural events. Parisian authorities have been particularly keen to discard the reputation of a museum-city since a series of polls published by *Le Monde* showed that French youth preferred London, Barcelona and Berlin for night-life. In response, a petition circulated in nightclubs and other areas of the late night cultural scene entitled 'When the night dies in silence.' The city has since decided to respond by insisting on its 1,000 establishments staying open until 5 am. It has also organized the White Nights festival, attempting to draw attention to Parisian night culture.

While the city and region have generally fostered local initiatives through festivals, local theaters and exhibition centers, the state has increasingly been perceived as an outsider, especially outside the city center. In this context, the national government has focused on maintaining the city's global cultural competitiveness. For example, recognizing the economic and tourist impact of staging movies in Paris, the state put into place in 2009 a new tax credit for making films in Paris. This resulted in more than 20 film productions in Paris during the summer of 2010, from Woody Allen to Martin Scorsese. Similarly, in response to what was perceived as the lack of a centralized location for classical music in Paris, along the lines of the Berlin Philharmonic, the state has decided on the construction of a new Paris Philharmonia. The state will be the principal financial supporter of the project, but it is expecting support from local governments, an expectation that has led to debates and delayed the project.

While Paris, then, remains a major cultural capital of the world, the current process of globalization has shifted the scales, the sites and many of the key actors in the Parisian cultural scene. Generating new local artistic terrains and cultural actors as well as tensions about what role culture should play in a city with a strong cultural mission, these competing definitions of culture on the local, national and international scales will be essential to defining the cultural landscape of the Paris metropolitan region in the continuing globalization of culture.

Notes

1   The *député* Yann Gaillard of the UMP (conservative political party) cited IFRAP (2007). It is worth noting that in France, the state names the director of the Paris Opera.

2   Versailles is one exception. It hosted more than 5.8 million tourists in 2010. It also receives an exceptional amount of state subsidies for a suburban site. However, the recent move on the part of the state to reduce these subsidies has pushed the Château to strive for greater financial self-sufficiency in the years to come. It is worth noting that the cultural identity of the city of Versailles has resisted larger trends in the metropolitanization of Parisian culture. Endowed with the tremendous cultural resource of the palace and other historical infrastructures, the city remains a cultural exception within the Grand Paris.

3   The French state delineates three types of public location for performance: there are five national theaters that are almost entirely under the authority of the state, 34 centers for drama and 68 national stages that were substituted for the *Maisons de la Culture* in the 1980s.

4   As the debate took form around the move to Bobigny, Muriel Mayette announced '… la mission ne change pas. C'est l'interprétation qu'on en fait qui change. Il faut s'adapter au monde, comme nous le faisons déjà avec les captations télévisées ou l'édition de DVD. Il faut aller vers un public qui ne viendra jamais salle Richelieu, parce que c'est trop loin, parce qu'il est trop impressionné pour cela.' Moving the theater in the eyes of Mayette was a means of pulling out of a neighborhood that was too 'impressed' by the Palais Royal. The comparison to putting the *Comédie's* performances on television or on DVD is telling as the push out to the suburbs was perceived as reaching out into the backyard of the people that would not otherwise make the trip to the theater.

5   The *Villa Medici* and the *Villa mais d'ici* are homonyms in French. *Villa mais d'ici* could be translated as 'the Villa that is here' as opposed to the *Villa Medici* in Rome. This play on words reinforces the idea that one does not have to travel to a well-financed distant location to enjoy culture.

6   Marketing phrase used by the *Office du tourisme et des congrès de Paris*.

REFERENCES

(2007) *Chiffres dés de la culture 2005*, direction du budget, mai.

(IAU IDF) (2010) "Le tourisme en ile de France, un élément majeur de l'aménagement du territoire," Institut, d'Aménagement Urbain, Île de France, *Notes rapides*, n° 511.

Bardon, A., Guigou, B., Montillet, P., Sallet, C. (mars 2011), "Orsa: reconstruire l'identité socioculturelle du territoire," Note rapide, *Territoires*, n° 540. Paris: IAU IDF.

Burgel, G., Chemetov, P. (2010) "L adoption du texte de loi sur le Grand Paris: une victoire à la Pyrrhus," *Le Monde*, June 3.

Burke, J. (2008) October 19, 'Paris underdog battles bastion of elite culture: Theatre merger leads to conflict in the arts world. *The Observer* (England). (http://www.guardian.co.uk/stage/2008/oct/19/theatre-france-mc93)

Camors, C., Soulard, O. (mars 2010) "Les industries créatives en Ile de France, un nouveau regard sur la métropole," Paris: IAU IDF.

Fleury, L. (2008) *Sociologie de la culture et des pratiques culturelles*. Paris: Armand Colin.

Gravier, J.F. (1958, 1947 1st ed.) *Paris et le désert français*. Paris: Flammarion.

Haidu, R. (2004) "Les Utopies précaires de Thomas Hirschhorn," *Le Journal des Laboratoires*, n°3, December.

Hirschhorn, T., Chapuis, Y. (2005). *Musée Précaire Albinet, quartier du Landy, Aubervilliers 2004*. Paris: Xavier Barral.

Liban, L. (2009) 'À quoi sert la Comédie- Française?' L Express, N°. 3006, 12 Février.

Panerai, P. (2008) *Paris Métropole, formes et échelles du Grand Paris*. Paris: éd. de la Villette.

Silver, D., Clark, T., Navarro Yanez, C.J. (2010). "Scenes: Social Context in an Age of Contingency." *Social Forces* 88: 2293–2324.

Zimmern, B. (2007) "Angleterre vs. France: le match des entreprises," *IFRAP. Société Civile* n° 74.

CHAPTER 27

SÃO PAULO: RICH CULTURE, POOR ACCESS
Maria Carolina Vasconcelos-Oliveira

This chapter analyses cultural policy and governance in yet another city that combines rich and diverse cultural production with great inequality of access. In São Paulo, cultural dynamism and inequality are two sides of the same development process. Adopting a cultural democracy perspective, the author reflects on the challenges involved in elaborating cultural policy in this context, which involves multiple actors, strategies and cultural contents. On this basis, she poses some general questions with a view to suggesting guidelines for planning and evaluating cultural policies in São Paulo and similar settings.

Introduction

Like other very big urban areas in the global South, São Paulo is a huge city that seems to have been built by putting together many smaller cities. Today, its population exceeds 10 million (IBGE, 2010). The metropolitan region encompassing the city proper and 38 adjacent cities has more than 19 million inhabitants, about 10 per cent of Brazil's population. Graph 1 (in Part 2 of the volume) shows that from the 1980s on, the tendency has been a more stabilized growth (SPTuris, 2008). The city is responsible for almost 13 per cent of the national GDP (IBGE, 2010) and is the Brazilian capital of knowledge (and certainly one of the most important centres of Latin America too), concentrating a highly qualified labour force and knowledge-intensive economic activity (see Comin and Vasconcelos-Oliveira, 2010). Most of the leading educational institutions of the country, including schools, universities and R&D laboratories, are also located in the city.

Naturally, São Paulo also offers a highly diverse infrastructure for culture, leisure and entertainment, as well as for sophisticated consumption – it is probably the largest capital of culture/entertainment of South America too. The availability of cultural goods/activities is definitely one of the reasons why some researchers define São Paulo as a 'global city'. According to the municipality's register of cultural facilities, in 2009 there were 240 theatres or sites for theatre performances, 124 museums, 74 cinemas with 325 film screens, 85 cultural centres and almost 300 concert halls or sites for music performances (SMDU/Dipro, 2009). São Paulo Turismo (SPTuris), the agency responsible for managing tourism and events in the city, adds 64 parks or green areas, seven soccer stadiums, not to mention 79 shopping malls and 50 specialized shopping streets (Cidade de São Paulo, 2010). Featuring among the top 15 cities in this regard, São Paulo also holds almost 300 international events each year, e.g., *Carnaval* (Carnival party), the São Paulo Fashion Week, the *Bienal Internacional de Artes de São Paulo* (Brazilian's largest visual arts events), the *Virada Cultural* (an all-night festival with hundreds of free cultural attractions), the *Parada Gay* (one of the largest gay pride marches in the world) and the *Mostra Internacional de Cinema* (Brazilian largest international film festival).[1]

Its rich cultural life has made São Paulo a major tourism destination and in 2009, 11.3 million people visited the city, 9.7 of them Brazilian and 1.6 million foreign. Although most tourists still mark 'business' as their main reason for visiting, SPTuris (2008) observes that even they use the cultural and consumption infrastructure of the city in their free time. The image of the city is constructed upon its ethnic diversity, especially in its consumption dimension – something like a 'find here all that you could ever want' approach, which guarantees that if someone searches for German or Lebanese cuisine at 11pm, or for a Iranian film festival for the weekend, she will find it. Multicultural and global (at least in a cultural sense) have already become commonly used adjectives when talking about São Paulo.

We shall begin by tracing aspects of the historical development process that have determined today's cultural diversity. Then we shall move to the other side of the story, to how some of the main cultural and leisure activities offered by the city are highly concentrated in a small area, the central zone, which means that most of the city population does not have access to them. Finally, we shall offer some reflections on the cultural policy challenges this situation presents, illustrated by some good practice initiatives.

The construction of a 'mixing bowl'

The notion presented in the Introduction to this volume that large urban spaces are the cultural 'mixing bowls' of globalization fit perfectly with the case of São Paulo. Yet this diversity, indeed its whole development trajectory, is not just the outcome of 'local' processes, but of national dynamics and policies as well (Comin and Vasconcelos-Oliveira, 2010). We will argue that the same development processes that created São Paulo as a rich, multicultural and vibrant scenario also generated the many types of inequality seen here.

São Paulo is diverse in both the sociological and the anthropological senses.[2] The two dimensions are obviously related since the diversity and richness in terms of cultural production (the palpable culture, to be consumed or practised) reflects diversity in habits, traditions, values and signs. This multiculturalism is largely the result of migratory flows, especially during the last 100 years. As suggested in Comin and Vasconcelos-Oliveira (2010), unlike most European and Asian cities, which appeared long before the nation-states they belong to, in the Americas most cities are the product of multiple migration processes. In Brazil, and particularly in São

Paulo, the big waves of European and Asiatic migration during the two twentieth-century world wars and several rounds of internal migration, not to mention the earlier Portuguese colonization and the import of African slave labour, contributed fundamentally to the ethnic and social composition of the city. These migrations were crucially important to the city's economic development because of their impacts on the labour market. It would be no exaggeration to say that São Paulo, physically, economically and culturally speaking, is a city largely built by foreigners (including migrants from other parts of Brazil). The early formation of a free urban labour market was a decisive factor for the development of industrial activities in the city, as important as the accumulation of capital from coffee exports.[3] Many of the European immigrants, already used to urban life and skilled in commercial or even factory activities, became engaged in small business and commercial activities, transforming the economic and cultural landscape of the city.

Economic development surely contributed to the increase of cultural production by creating and attracting more qualified workers to the city. But more than that, we could argue that economic development was related to the cultural diversity of the city as both a cause and a consequence (see Arruda, 2001; and Bruno, 1984). We note periods of great changes in both economic and in cultural life, suggesting they were different sides of the same process of modernization. For example, around 1930, during the development of industrialization through import substitution, the city's effervescent cultural context also hosted important events such as the *Semana de Arte Moderna* (1922) (symbolizing the beginning of artistic Modernism in Brazil), the establishment of the University of São Paulo (1934) or of the first department of culture in the municipality (1935). During the 1950s, when the city entered a long cycle of economic growth (that led it to be credited for 50 per cent of Brazilian industrial production between the 1950s and the 1970s), the 400-year celebrations also took place, with events that included the foundation of Oscar Niemeyer's Ibirapuera park.

Since the last century, São Paulo has also symbolized the promise of economic progress in Brazil and has been its main locus of cultural diversity and excellence in the arts. The 'cosmopolitan air', the multiculturalism and the availability of cultural and entertainment options in the city are the results of its diverse social composition, of capital accumulation, of higher levels of education – all made possible by choices made at the municipal, state and federal levels along the years. But the development processes also resulted in many inequalities. Within the country, the state of São Paulo came to concentrate political and economic power in an irreversible way. Within the city, São Paulo's abrupt growth has created inequalities of access to its benefits and to urban space itself.

Economic development and migration combined resulted in an exponential demographic increase.[4] In the 1940s, the side-effects were already visible in the peripheral areas: problems concerning housing and health services, and insufficient public efforts to solve them. With no successful urban planning, the city has grown chaotically, in the direction of its peripheries, as the costs of living in central areas have always been too high. However, most of the city's benefits are still restricted to the central zones. Combined with an expensive and insufficient transport system, this results in serious inequality of access to employment options, to specialized health services, and to other benefits, including cultural services. These multiple inequalities were the worst side-effects of the hyper-concentration strategy sponsored by the national government that has made São Paulo one of the richest cities of the world, in economic and cultural terms.[5]

Unequal access to cultural infrastructure

In this section we analyse some data about the distribution of cultural facilities in the city. We shall adopt the familiar 'cultural democracy' paradigm (as opposed to the notion of 'cultural democratization') in which 'culture' is not restricted to artistic production. That the infrastructure for the most legitimate forms of culture is concentrated in the central region does not mean that 'there is no cultural life' in the peripheral zone. But it would be much better if citizens living in the peripheral zones could include more types of activity in their list of cultural options. In the same way, from a cultural democracy perspective, our position is not that they must like or prefer the arts over other kinds of culture, for we refuse any notion of cultural hierarchy and see access in terms of possibility, not of obligation.

Physical availability is also far from being the only or the most important factor restricting the access to cultural services/products, especially art-related ones. From a cultural democracy perspective, physical proximity is not enough to trigger appropriation and appreciation of cultural goods and services, especially those involving complex languages and references. Educational processes – formal or informal – are essential to guarantee effective access. But in a survey on cultural practices and the use of free time in the metropolitan region of São Paulo, Botelho and Fiore (2005) concluded that beyond educational level and income, household location is among the most important factors influencing cultural practices. This may be explained by the finding that people living in the peripheral zones are the ones with low access to quality education. In view of this, and since cultural practices are not only outputs of but also inputs to the educational process, they also mobilize cognition mechanisms (see Vasconcelos-Oliveira, 2009) – the problem of unequal access becomes even more perverse.

We have mapped the spatial distribution of certain cultural facilities in the city of São Paulo in order to show how they are concentrated and to indicate the lack of coverage in the peripheral zones. Our maps include only types of cultural option that have a mappable physical structure.

The polygon highlighted in the maps refers to the expanded centre, the area around the historic centre and surrounded by some of the most important car routes of São Paulo. It concentrates the most important economic activities and jobs of the city, especially the most qualified ones. It is also where people with higher income and educational attainment live. The peripheral districts have higher rates of population growth and young people. The maps show that, except for libraries and parks, all of the cultural infrastructure considered is concentrated inside the polygon. This corresponds to one of Botelho and Fiore's (2005) most impressive findings, namely that a person who lives in the expanded centre had 160 per cent more chance of becoming a heavy cultural practitioner (defined in terms of number and diversity of cultural practices). This could be explained both by locational and by educational and income factors, since the inhabitants of the peripheral districts have lower schooling and income levels.

The concentration is even more impressive if we look at private cultural facilities, notably art galleries and concert halls. It is also interesting to look at the distribution of concert halls (private, in general) in

Map 27.1 Cinemas in São Paulo (2009)

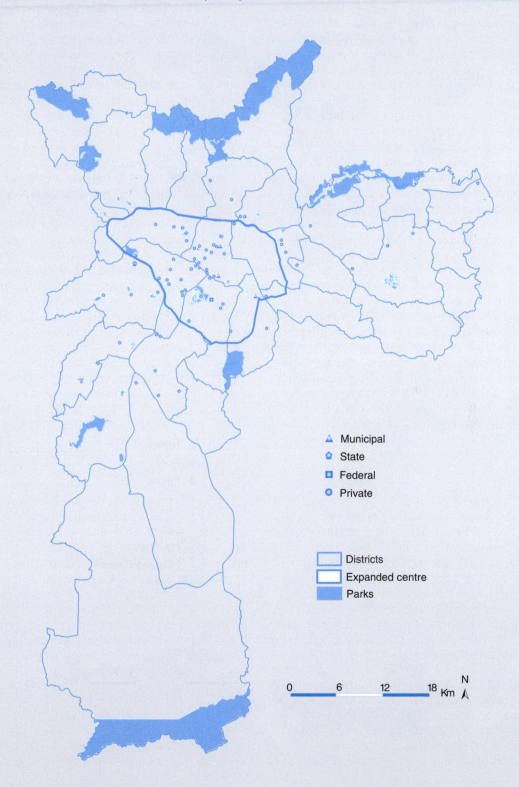

△ Municipal

⬠ State

▣ Federal

◯ Private

▭ Districts

▭ Expanded centre

▮ Parks

0   6   12   18 Km   N

Map 27.2 Theatres and spaces for theatre performances in São Paulo (2009)

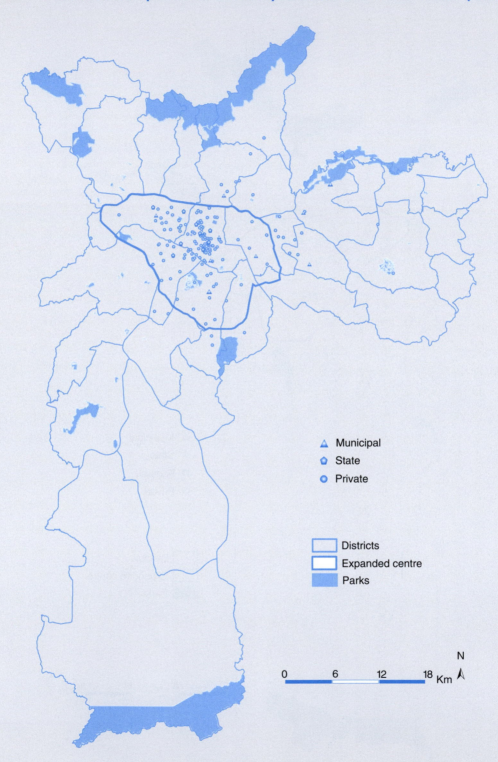

△ Municipal

⬠ State

○ Private

☐ Districts

☐ Expanded centre

▧ Parks

0   6   12   18 Km

N

Map 27.3   Concert halls and spaces for music performances in São Paulo (2009)

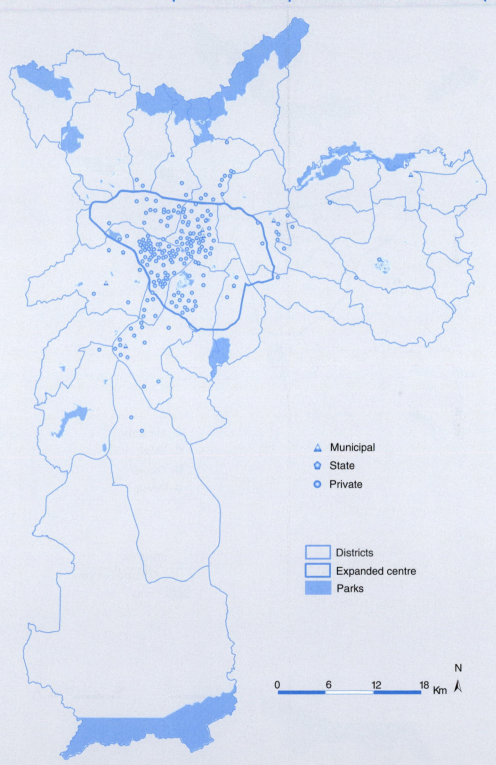

△ Municipal

⬠ State

◉ Private

☐ Districts

☐ Expanded centre

■ Parks

N

0   6   12   18 Km

Map 27.4   Cultural centres in São Paulo (2009)

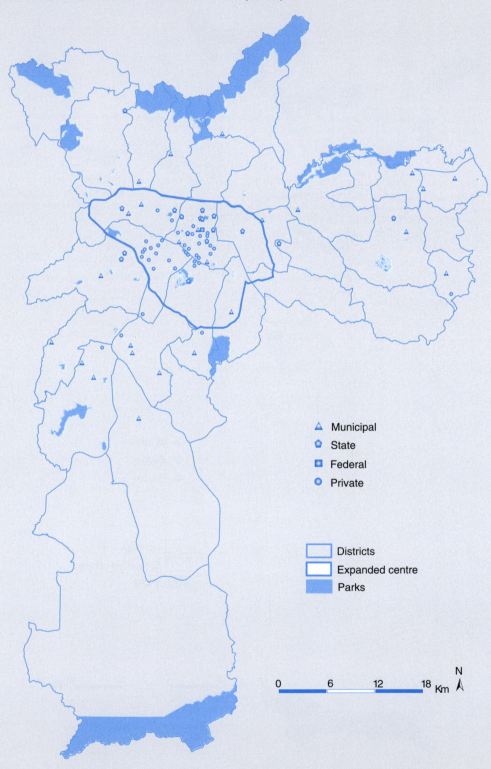

△ Municipal

⬠ State

▣ Federal

◯ Private

▢ Districts

▢ Expanded centre

▮ Parks

0   6   12   18 Km

N

Map 27.5   Museums in São Paulo (2009)

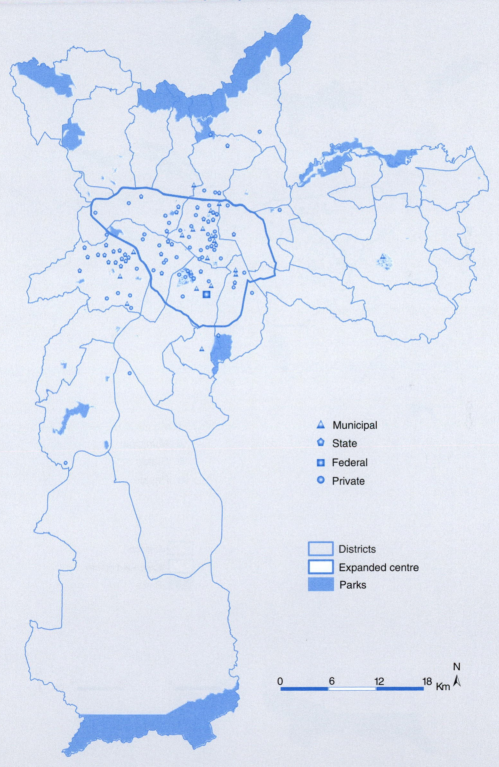

Municipal

State

Federal

Private

Districts

Expanded centre

Parks

0   6   12   18 Km

N

Map 27.6   Art galleries in São Paulo (2009)

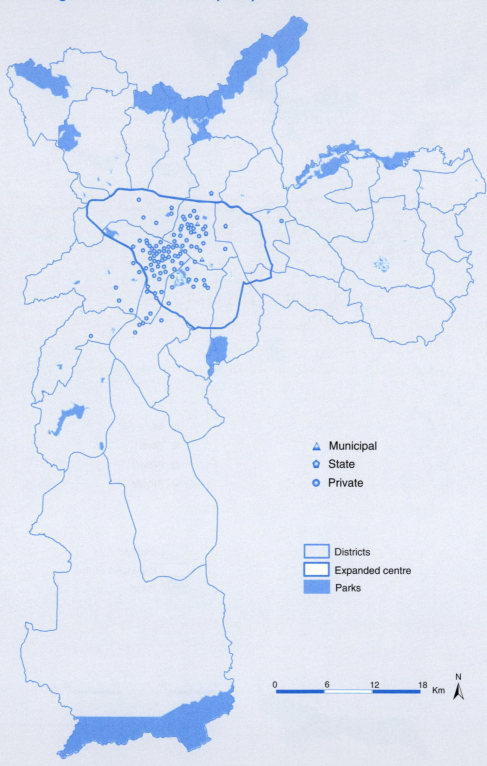

△ Municipal

⬠ State

⬡ Private

▢ Districts

▢ Expanded centre

▮ Parks

0   6   12   18 Km

N

Map 27.7   Libraries in São Paulo (2009)

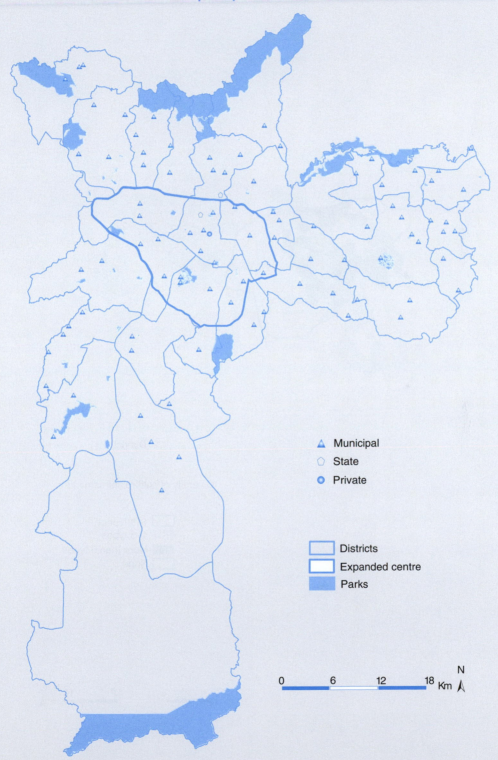

△ Municipal
⬠ State
◉ Private

☐ Districts
☐ Expanded centre
▨ Parks

0   6   12   18 Km

N

Map 27.8 Diversity of cultural infrastructure in São Paulo (2009)

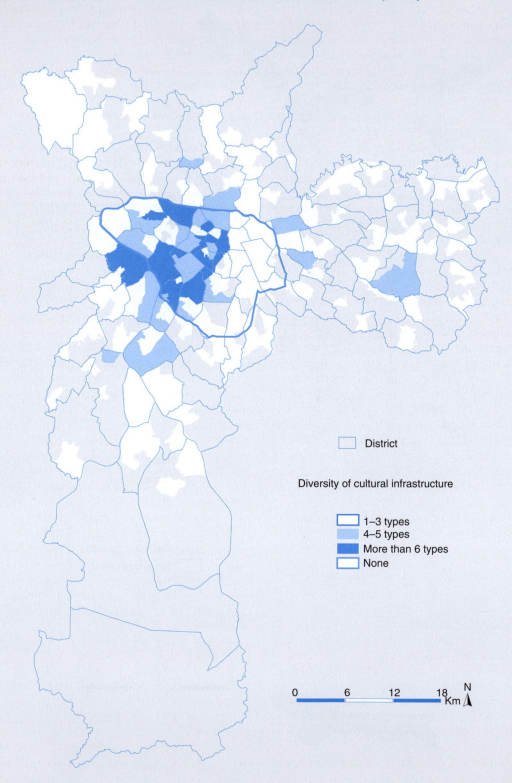

District

Diversity of cultural infrastructure

- 1–3 types
- 4–5 types
- More than 6 types
- None

0 6 12 18 Km

N

the light of Botelho and Fiore's observation that, although most respondents have declared listening to music as very common home practice, almost half of them had never been to a popular music concert, and almost 90 per cent had never been to a classical music concert. As regards cinemas, it is interesting to note that the more dispersed distribution is related to the presence of film screens in shopping malls or commercial centres, increasingly frequent in the peripheral areas of the city. As Rolnik and Frugoli Jr (2001) point out, shopping malls have become the most common places for leisure and sociability among young people in peripheral districts – owing precisely to the lack of public spaces. Botelho and Fiore (2005) also find 'going to the cinema' the most popular external practice (excluding home practices). The screens located in shopping malls usually show commercial films, almost never including alternative production.

Theatres and spaces for theatre performances are abundant in the city. São Paulo is Brazil's theatre capital and one of the most important theatre poles in Latin America, with more than 600 performances per year (SPTuris, 2008). There is a strong presence of alternative groups and troupes, many of them having their own performance spaces. Going to the theatre or other performing arts events, such as dance, were nevertheless among the less declared practices in Botelho and Fiore' survey (2005), since these practices are especially sensitive to income and educational levels. Map 27.8 summarizes the differences among the districts, showing the amount of types of cultural facility available. The darkest areas are more diverse in terms of types of cultural infrastructure: not surprisingly, the central area prevails again.

Cultural policy and the challenges of inequality

The inequality of access to cultural options in the city of São Paulo poses many challenges. We shall discuss three governance-related issues: targets, coordination and the scope of cultural initiatives.

First, we argue (cf. Chapter 8 by Stuart Cunningham) that attention should be paid equally to production and consumption. This means bringing in plural and heterogeneous audiences, and not only in an abstract way. Policy-makers, then, must at the same time support the production of cultural

goods and services (the authorities act as patron here) and provide consumption opportunities to citizens. According to Jiménez (2006), cultural policy during the twentieth century tended to privilege the production rather than the consumption side. Although the author was writing about the Mexican context, the same judgement applies to Brazil. We could refer to this as a target-related problem. Cultural policies have been disconnected from the educational dimension, ignoring important issues such as audience formation and the sharing of specific languages and references. This is reflected in the great distance between cultural (especially artistic) production and citizens (Jiménez, 2006).

Botelho (2001) suggests that prioritizing the production side is a consequence of adopting an old 'democratization' paradigm that promotes 'erudite' or 'high' culture. According to her, this usually triggers two patterns of policy action: the sponsorship and promotion of artists and producers and the implementation of art centres in peripheral zones, aiming at 'bringing culture' to the population by providing physical access to it. But cultural policy must also take into account the attributes of audiences and the dynamics of art consumption. A step forward would be to give the citizen the possibility to effectively make and live culture. This would mean blurring the boundaries between creator and audience, empowering every citizen to adopt a more active position in the face of cultural production. In Jiménez's words (2006), rather than conceiving artists (creators) and audiences as distinct categories, it would be better to see every citizen as a potential creator. This would give 'audiences' the means to increase their possibilities of expression or their capacity to reconstruct of the public spaces, through initiatives exploring, for example, practices of amateur art. In this ideal picture, cultural practices are tools for exercising citizenship in a broader sense, rather than only for audience development.

Another important governance issue is related to who is in charge of cultural affairs in the city. In São Paulo, there are various players: the municipality, state and federal government and private actors – not only NGOs or associations, but also enterprises and conglomerates which invest in cultural initiatives in order to obtain tax credits. We shall focus on the last, which is part of a national trend. The liberal governments leading the country during the 1990s dismantled the few and rather weak structures and institutions in the cultural field, restricting policy to tax exemption laws designed to induce corporate investments in culture (Rubim, 2007). The budgets of public cultural departments were so small that the public institutions themselves (museums, for example) had to compete with cultural producers for private funding (Botelho, 2001). Guided by market aims, these investors usually follow a cost-benefit logic, prioritizing initiatives that seem more promising in terms of financial and brand-related revenues, that is, successful cultural attractions. This has been demonstrated by an increase in the volume of cultural initiatives in places where consumption rates were already high (such as São Paulo), and involving cultural contents that were already legitimized, thus offering more cultural options to those who were already heavy consumers. But surely the policy goal should be to go further. The participation of multiple actors, including businesses and civil society, in funding cultural initiatives is desirable, but it does not mean that public cultural policy loses importance. On the contrary, governments are challenged to articulate coherent strategies to link the investments made by different actors.[6]

Fortunately, from the 2000s on, the national government has been committed to more effective cultural policy, although the main tax-exemption law dating to 1991 (the Rouanet law) is still a highly controversial topic. Yet culture is given low priority at all levels of government, especially by municipalities. Less than 60 per cent of the country's municipalities had some kind of cultural policy in 2006, and usually this was entrusted to departments working on several areas and without specifically qualified staff (Calabre, 2009). Even in São Paulo, the resources allocated to culture are meagre when compared to expenditures in other areas (see Graphs 3 and 4 in Part 2), although recent data show that municipal expenditures in culture evolved from 1.1 per cent of the budget expenditures in 2005 to 1.5 per cent in 2008 (Secretaria Municipal da Cultura, 2009). Comparing this with the national level, Barbosa (2007) shows that over 60 per cent of Brazilian municipalities are unable to achieve 1 to per cent level of funding for culture.[7]

The last aspect we wish to discuss is the question of scope. The idea of policy-making at local level matches the cultural democracy paradigm, which presupposes no hierarchy among the different types of culture, and ideally guarantees the right of every citizen to practise, consume and live different 'types' of culture. In times of multiplicity – of actors involved in policy-making, of initiatives and actions, of audiences and of cultural production – acting at the local level would be a means for the policy-maker to be aware of the real needs of the community and to be within reach of the citizens. But in such a huge and diverse city, is the local level really the municipal one? Sometimes large and unequal urban settings such as São Paulo require action at the district or zone level, especially if the aim is to achieve effective interaction with the population. This choice may imply giving autonomy to institutions at the district (or sub-city) level.

Good practices in São Paulo

This last section illustrates the discussion presented above with some empirical data, presented here not as complete case studies, but in order to emphasize some of the aspects we have just addressed.

First, we choose to mention the São Paulo Sesc (Serviço Social do Comércio), a private organization whose budget is provided through a compulsory contribution (tax) paid by commerce and services workers and companies.[8] It is one of the main cultural actors in the city, thanks not only to its large budget, but also to its presence in many different districts and to its diverse and rich cultural programme. Each of its 17 branches in the metropolitan region is a complete cultural facility on its own, with infrastructure and programmes for sports, arts, leisure and other activities.[9] Sesc uses a non-hierarchical conception of culture, as all of the activities and attractions offered are considered 'cultural'. The myriad of possible points of appropriation favours the development of strong ties among visitors and the institution at the branch level. And this proximity to the institutional context makes it easier to deliver specific cultural products/services (including art-related ones).[10] Sesc places culture in a wider educational project. Every item in the programme is conceived under the rubric of so-called informal education. The institutional objective is not restricted to offering cultural activities or developing audiences. Education is an abstract guideline that permeates the entire programme, not involving specific training programmes, but general purposes, concerning citizenship and the urban space, for example.

Each branch has its own atmosphere and identity, which is strongly related to the way the branch, the district and the audiences have structured their relations. Each one has autonomy. This decentralization, while it may generate some costs and difficulties for the whole organizational structure, enables more effective interaction with local audiences, although this does not take place with equal effectiveness at all branches. Sesc's commitment to cultural production sometimes seems to count more than the institutional goal of increasing access to cultural activities and of articulating culture in an educational project – and here we return to our earlier point about the double function of the cultural policy-makers, of supporting cultural production but also guaranteeing access. Activities such as courses and workshops are part of Sesc's programme, but shows, performances and other cultural attractions tend to prevail.

The educational guidelines sometimes appear to be too abstract, using a conception of the 'audience' that is also too generic. Its events are attended more by people who are already heavy cultural consumers (or producers) than by people who visit it for sociability or leisure activities. Fortunately, there are many exceptions, which suggest the potential of the institution to propose 'new' cultural practices to visitors. But the promotion of art and other cultural-related education activities could be increased, in order to complement the programme's artistic attractions, particularly in view of the inequality of access we observe.

There are some other institutions that appear to privilege audiences, sometimes even providing access to production facilities. The Centro Cultural da Juventude Ruth Cardoso – a fully-equipped municipal cultural centre focused on young people – is a good example. The Centre, founded in 2005 in a semi-peripheral zone of the city, despite being committed to the performing and visual arts, also promotes amateur cultural practices and hosts artistic/cultural groups that already exist in the region. Some street dance groups use the Centre to rehearse and practice, which symbolizes an interesting pattern of interaction with the existing cultural context at the local level (Secretaria Municipal da Cultura, 2009).

Projeto Vocacional, led by the Department of Culture of the São Paulo municipality is also an interesting model, totally focused on the audience. For more than ten years the project has been engaged in making creative processes flourish in peripheral communities, conceiving the participants as potential artists, through actions including amateur practices. The project is implemented in public schools or cultural centres and is an interesting example of cultural policy decentralized to the sub-city level. The organization of the project is also special since the artist who conducts each group (during cycles that usually last one year) is free to propose the programme, but is supposed to share with the other instructors the project's main pedagogical strategies. Regular meetings of the artist-guiders and coordinators guarantee this coherence and unity. This flexible structure favours effective interaction with people at the local level.

Among the several weaknesses related to Projeto Vocacional and Centro Cultural da Juventude, we mention the fact that, as governmental institutions, their guidelines and planning are susceptible to politics-related changes.

Conclusions

We have argued that cultural policy-making in cities such as São Paulo becomes more complicated as the actors, the variety of actions and strategies and the cultural contents diversify. All these processes challenge old hierarchies and oppositions (high versus low culture, popular versus erudite, emancipatory versus mass-produced). In our view, co-ordinating actors are extremely necessary in order to define minimal parameters and guidelines and to organize a myriad of existing initiatives in this context of relativism and loosely defined boundaries that surely also represents new and positive possibilities.

On the basis of our empirical data and reflections, we are able to formulate three general questions, each of which may be useful elsewhere, especially in large urban spaces combining cultural wealth and socio-economic inequality. These questions are: Which culture? Culture for whom? Culture for what?

Which culture? Thinking about this question involves not only challenging the established definitions of 'culture', but also reflecting about the extent to which the cultural policy or strategy will include several 'types' of culture in its scope. It may also involve making choices about when it is more interesting to foster 'native' cultural values and preferences, and when it is better to suggest (and provide real access to) new cultural references, for example, as part of an educational process.

Culture for whom? Cultural policy-makers and researchers must acquire fuller knowledge of the beneficiary – or potential beneficiary – of any proposed initiative. This may require some effort in order to comprehend the process of appropriation of (or attendance to) the particular cultural activity, and the factors influencing consumption. Institutions that do not ask such questions risk falling into an empty or naïve discourse; for example, when their job is providing access to complex cultural forms, they may simply end up providing physical access. We suspect that strategies using educational actions – aiming at sharing languages and references – would end up merely providing more cultural options to people who are already consumers, which is not exactly broadening access.

Finally, culture for what? The answer we give presupposes ideas about the functions of culture, in its sociological dimension (and, even before that, the issue of whether culture is supposed to have functions). We could list some of the most common ones: to complement educational processes; to transform the relationships of the citizen with space and community; to generate economic returns; to construct and preserve heritage and collective memory; or simply to increase community well-being. The question is crucial in choosing between a democracy or democratization paradigm, or in setting priorities for supporting the arts (because art is important) or establishing policies to increase and diversify the cultural options open to all citizens (because the citizen is important). In this extremely simple example, of course both sides are important, and this is why the decision processes are so complex and require so much reflection.

We believe that it is essential to ask such questions when we organize processes of elaborating, evaluating and coordinating cultural policies and initiatives, especially in times of relativism and diversity. The answers to such questions, which will certainly vary with each city context, are bound to yield sound guidelines for policy-making and may be a step towards the overcoming of inequalities of access.

Notes

1 See Graph 8a, in Part 2 of this volume, for an evolution of these events in time.

2 The cultural disciplines usually analyse two dimensions of culture. The sociological dimension frames 'culture' as a specific type of production, socially organized to construct symbolic contents and targeting a particular audience. It is a visible and palpable dimension, which commonly refers to legitimated cultural activities/manifestations, such as the arts (Botelho, 2001). In the anthropological approach, all activities related to self/group expression can be considered 'culture' as well, including habits and values (see Botelho, 2001; Coulangeon, 2005; Vasconcelos-Oliveira, 2009). Here we use the anthropological meaning, while emphasizing a sociological dimension in certain instances.

3 The successive waves of foreign immigration represented a possible way to face the scarcity of labour in the country after the abolition of slavery in 1888. During the industrialization process starting in the 1930s, migrant labour played a crucial role.

4 From 1950 to 2000 São Paulo city grew from a little over 2 million inhabitants to more than 10 million.

5 Many of the public investments made at the national level benefited the state and the city since the end of monarchy, either by explicit actions to support the coffee economy in the beginning of the twentieth century, or by policies to foster industrial production from the 1950s on (see Comin and Vasconcelos-Oliveira, 2010).

6 Lucina Jiménez argues in the present volume that despite the plurality of actors proposing cultural initiatives in Mexico City, there is no *metropolitan cultural policy* able to mobilize and organize the fragmented initiatives. It is the same in São Paulo.

7 The Brazilian Congress is currently discussing the possibility of developing a constitutional amendment to ensure that 2 per cent of federal expenditures are allocated to culture, as well as 1.5 per cent at the state level and 1 per cent at the municipal level. The proposal was first put forward in 2003. Another proposal put forward in 2010 would allocate 3 per cent of the budget to culture at the federal, state and municipal levels.

8 Sesc is a national institution created in 1946 as a parastatal organization. Despite having considerable autonomy in defining its governance structure and in executing its budget, the institution uses public funds derived from taxes collected on specific activities. Sesc São Paulo is the state-level organization and it has a high degree of autonomy from the national Sesc. Here we consider only the actions and programme that Sesc implements in the city level.

9 Despite having some branches in peripheral zones, most of them are concentrated in a relatively central area.

10 The author conducted Master's level research on the institution, aiming to understand its ability to influence visitors' cultural practices. Proximity, confidence and the construction of strong ties between visitors and the institution at the local level are among the most important factors revealed.

REFERENCES

Arruda, Maria Arminda (2001) *Metrópole e cultura*. Bauru: EDUSC.

Barbosa, Frederico (2007) *Política cultural no Brasil 2002–2006: acompanhamento e análise*. Brasília: Ministério da Cultura.

Botelho, Isaura (2001) 'As dimensões da cultura e o lugar das políticas públicas'. *São Paulo em Perspectiva*,15 (2), Revista da Fundação SEADE, www.scielo.br/scielo.php?script=sci_art text&pid=S0102-88392001000200011 (acessed May 2011).

Botelho, Isaura and Fiore, Maurício (2005) *O uso do tempo livre e as práticas culturais na região metropolitana de São Paulo*. Report of the first stage. São Paulo: Centro de Estudos da Metrópole, CEBRAP.

Bruno, Ernani Silva (1954) *História e Tradições da Cidade da São Paulo: São Paulo de Agora (1919–1954)*. São Paulo: Hucitec.

Calabre, Lia (2009) 'Gestão cultural municipal na contemporaneidade'. In: Calabre, Lia (ed.), *Políticas culturais: reflexões e ações*. São Paulo: Itaú Cultural Rio de Janeiro and Casa de Rui Barbosa Foundation.

Cidade de São Paulo (official tourism site for the city of São Paulo) (2010) São Paulo em números. Available at: www.cidadedesaopaulo.com/sp/br/sao-paulo-em-numeros (acessed May 2011).

Comin, Alvaro and Vasconcelos-Oliveira, Maria Carolina (2010) 'Southern cities: locomotives or wagons of national development?' *Economic Sociology: the European Newsletter*. 11 (2) March: 31–9. Available at: http://econsoc. mpifg.de/archive/econ_soc_11-2.pdf (acessed May 2011).

Coulangeon, Philippe (2005) *Sociologie des pratiques culturelles*. Paris: La Découverte.

Instituto Brasileiro de Geografia e Estatistica IBGE (2010) Cidades@ – São Paulo. Available at: www.ibge.gov.br/cidadesat/topwindow.htm?1 (acessed May 2011).

Jiménez, Lucina (2006) 'Por que hablar de cultura?' In Berman, Sabina and Jiménez, Lucina (eds), *Democracia cultural: una conversación a cuatro manos*. Mexico: Fondo de Cultura Económica.

Rolnik, Raquel and Frugoli, Jr, Heitor (2001) 'Reestruturação Urbana da Metrópole Paulistana: a Zona Leste como território de rupturas e permanências'. *Cadernos Metrópole*, 6, 2nd semestre de 2001: 43–66.

Rubim, Albino (2007) 'Políticas culturais no Brasil: tristes tradições, enormes desafios'. In Rubim, Albino and Barbalho, Alexandre (eds), *Políticas culturais no Brasil*. Salvador: EdUFBA.

Secretaria Municipal da Cultura (2009) *Relatório anual gestão 2005–2008*. São Paulo: Secretaria Municipal de Cultura.

Secretaria Municipal de Desenvolvimento Urbano SMDU/ Dipro (2009) *Cadastro de Equipamentos Culturais, 2009*. São Paulo: SMDU/Dipro.

SPTuris – (São Paulo Turismo) (2008) *Tourism indicators and research in the city of São Paulo*. Available at: www.cidadede saopaulo.com/sp/images/stories/observatorio/1_indicadores_ pesquisas_do_turismo_2008.pdf (accessed May 2011).

Vasconcelos-Oliveira, Maria Carolina (2009) 'Culturas, públicos e processos de aprendizado: possibilidades e lógicas plurais', *Políticas Culturais em Revista*, 2 (2).

CHAPTER 28

SHANGHAI: IMAGES OF MODERNITY
Justin O'Connor and Xin Gu

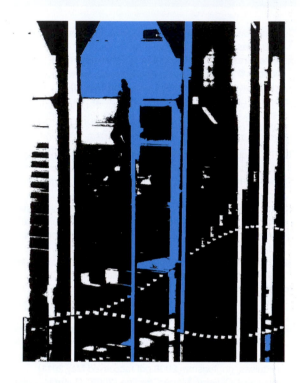

This chapter examines Shanghai's use of culture to position itself as a global city and how a particular narrative has informed western commentators and Shanghai policy-makers alike. They also analyze the development of cultural infrastructure and the parallel separation of art and entertainment, with contemporary art as an unexpected challenge, but one the city successfully negotiated. They look at the marketization of culture, tracing the connections between market reforms in culture and those in the wider economy. They argue that the half-formed or distorted use of western concepts such as 'creative industries' or 'creative clusters', rather than indicating a duplicity or an incomplete modernity, actually highlight some of the complicities of canonical cultural policy.

Introduction: development and cultural policy in China

China is still a developing country, and to understand it we usually look to its trajectory (coming from somewhere and going to somewhere else) and its energy (mass multispeed). China is very big and moving very fast. But we are no longer in the Newtonian world. Its trajectory may not be assimilated into our regulated system and its sheer gravitational mass may bend the space–time of western modernity. The question of culture and its governance in China cannot be viewed as the on-site assembly of a pre-fabricated system, or as a gradual approach to a norm – whether this be tardy, or chaotic, or with local idiosyncrasies. In China the technical apparatus of western cultural policy as practised by the West is brought face to face with itself, not by the political critique of cultural academics, but by its encounter with a system of governance which refuses to accept its foundational ideas as universals. The confrontation thus reveals cultural policy as precisely a cultural politics – a cultural politics frequently couched in the depoliticized form of technical specifications for competent governance underpinned by the unassailable language of human rights.

The idea of development implies a historical narrative and a set of normative concepts around modernization that are highly politicized. The 1980s witnessed the disappearance of most socialist-inspired modernization programmes and the dominance of the free market/liberal democratic model known as the 'Washington Consensus'. From around the same time western (and indeed worldwide – see Isar in this volume) notions of cultural policy moved away from an arts-centric perspective towards a wider view of culture as a 'way of life' and its governance (itself a new term) as necessarily involving the active participation of the private sector and 'civil society'. The emphasis within cultural policy on the cultural and communal dimensions of social development challenged 'neo-liberalism', and acted as an alternative model for many left-of-centre development organizations and individuals. At the same time, its opposition to the use of arts and culture solely for nation-building, its emphasis on the involvement of private sector and civil society, and its demand that everyone should have access to global flows of art and culture – all under the banner of cultural diversity – allowed it to make common cause with more right-of-centre agencies against 'closed' authoritarian regimes of all persuasions. In this context a depoliticized language of cultural policy finds itself promoting 'good' governance in terms of administrative competence for a cultural sector whose social benefit and already-existing separation from other spheres of governance (economic, legal, political) is simply taken for granted as a sign of modernization.

China's modernization, always ambiguous, sits on a major fault-line. On the one side, its rapid development is welcomed or bemoaned as the final triumph of global capitalism, and quizzed for its potential to promote or resist democracy. On the other side, its rise is seen to break the unipolar world order, to usher in the Asian century, and thus in some way to fundamentally transform the narrative of world history begun in eighteenth-century Europe and exemplified by Hegel's lectures of the 1820s. Across such a fault-line the depoliticized language of cultural policy finds itself at a loss. Too big to be accommodated as a local anomaly, China persists as an unspoken question indefinitely postponed.

It is Chinese cites that offer a better promise of cultural policy traction – where the former's modernizing narrative seems more self-evident and pragmatic, and the latter's technical assistance more appropriate and transferable. Overarching national narratives do not disappear at city level, but they are inflected by local narratives rooted in specific histories and circumstances. City policy-makers are much more directly involved in detailed operational decisions 'on the ground' and – in contrast to the more 'abstract universal' interventions at national level – stand directly to benefit, or suffer, from their consequences. City policy-makers thus tend to have more direct contact with domestic and international intermediaries who, representing a wide range of different interests, bring very concrete experiences and perspectives, concepts and techniques to the policy-making process. Where better to explore this than in Shanghai – rapidly modernizing, economic giant and glamorous pin-up: China's 'most western city'.

As in Saussurian linguistics, cities frequently acquire meaning from what they are not. San Francisco is not LA; Manchester is not London; Milan is not Rome; Rotterdam is not Amsterdam; Shanghai is not Beijing. If Beijing carries the tradition-soaked weight of the nation-state narrative, then at first sight Shanghai is unburdened, open, fleet-footed, future-oriented. Shanghai, announced a wide-eyed Paris Hilton, 'looks like the future'. But on second glance, the Shanghai future is also a return, a rerun, of a previous future. Shanghai is where nineteenth-century modernity made landfall in China. As the 'Paris (or New York) of the East' it represented a particular vision of Chinese modernity. The first question, then, is what kind of a return was this and how was it managed? Symbolized by the vertiginous corporate cityscape, it is certainly a future set for doing business and going shopping. But as an aspiring global city Shanghai will also need 'culture' – as brand image and multivalent economic resource without doubt, but what else? The second question is how, if at all, is it possible to mobilize the economic resources of culture without somehow buying into its (relative) autonomy or into its emancipatory, democratic promise?

Shanghai: historical background

The outlines of Shanghai's history are now well known – see Sergeant, 1991; Bergére, 2009; Wasserstrom, 2010). Until 1850 it was a small city on the edge of China's leading economic region. It was transformed by the arrival of the maritime powers of Britain, France and shortly thereafter, the USA. They used the powers confirmed by the 1842 Treaty of Nanking to assert their control of the north bank of the Huangpu River (tributary to the huge internal waterway of the Yangtze), carving out a new territory ('concessions') adjacent to the old Chinese walled city. Here they established their own legal and administrative systems, an enclave of modernization on the edge of the Qing Empire. The city rapidly developed into one of Asia's biggest ports, using Chinese intermediaries to expand its trade up the Yangtze into the huge interior. Jerry-built mass housing provided accommodation for Chinese labour and great profits for the colonial owners of some of the most expensive real estate in the world. As Chinese landowners and merchants relocated to the city – especially after the mid-century ravages of the Taiping uprising – an entrepreneurial Chinese 'middle class' began to emerge. By the end of the nineteenth century these took advantage of foreign technology, expertise and capital to participate in the industrialization of the city and its hinterland. The foreign municipal councils embarked on a thorough-going 'Haussmanization' of the city, giving it water, sewerage, transport, electric lighting and gas-supply infrastructure to rival any city on earth. By the 1920s, Chinese capital – still impenetrably organized outside the western banking system – began to move into the new consumer economy of leisure, entertainment and shopping which gave Shanghai its distinct identity as capital of Chinese modernity.

Modernization created an embryonic Chinese capitalist, entrepreneurial middle class – the classic development script in microcosm. They were actively involved in the reform movements in the late nineteenth and early twentieth century, combining calls for rational and scientific administration with strong nationalist and anti-colonial sentiments. Given that they were a small minority caught between the bulk of the Qing Empire and the might of the foreign powers, there was, however, no question of 'bourgeois revolution'. They were also increasingly caught between their nationalist and democratic aspirations and the militancy of the trade unions and the Communist Party after the First World War. After dispatching the Communists from Shanghai and other cities in 1927, the Kuomintang increasingly took nationalist aspirations in an authoritarian direction, and by the time of the Japanese invasion of 1937 had more or less nationalized Chinese capital. The arrival of the Communists at the end of civil war in 1949 merely set a seal on the decline of that entrepreneurial Chinese capitalism that had seemed to be emerging in the wake of western modernization.

But Shanghai did not just stand for modernization – an emphasis on industry-led economic growth and scientific administration also embraced in its non-entrepreneurial and state-directed version by the Communists (and the Kuomintang). The city also stood for modernity. It is where the word 'modern' first entered the Chinese lexicon. The creation of a Chinese enclave – they represented over 80 per cent of the population in the foreign concessions – free from the constraints of the Qing state and open to the ideas and energies swirling around Shanghai produced a new kind of Chinese urban culture. Although immigrants were initially brought under the tutelage of regional associations and their landowner/merchant patrons, by the end of the nineteenth century new customs, values and identities were emerging, along with an urban

leisure and consumption economy. By the end of the 1920s, Shanghai's popular cultural infrastructure was comparable with New York, London and Berlin. Shanghai had the first cinemas in Asia, a popular press, bookshops (which soon also sold records), a commercial film and music industry and was China's publishing centre. The era witnessed an explosion of tea-houses and dance halls, hotels and restaurants, bars and night-clubs; department stores, popular entertainment centres; and a resurgence of urbanized (often feminized) Chinese opera – many funded by Chinese capital. These provided opportunities for Chinese entrepreneurs and consumers, as they also did for the multinational population that thronged the concessions. They were serviced from an urban proletariat who mostly lived in abject poverty, creating a spectacle of squalor and riches few writers could resist. Prostitution, gambling, drink, opium: Shanghai acquired a distinct image of glamorous, amoral, rank decadence.

For the Chinese Communists – Mao building on the image of the peasant more than the urban working class – this urban decadence was an index of the destruction imperialism and capitalism had wrought on China. Shanghai remained the industrial powerhouse of China into the 1970s, providing huge inputs into the national coffers but receiving very little investment in return. When Deng Xiaoping began his opening-up campaign in the late 1970s, it was to the south that he first turned, transforming the fishing village of Shenzhen and the Pearl River Delta into a free trade zone to rival Hong Kong. Only after 1989 did Shanghai belatedly get the green light. Starting in 1991 it began its meteoric rise with the development of the flat rice fields of Pudong, transforming them within a few years into the global financial cityscape of the new Shanghai. It is now the biggest city in China, its biggest port and its economic powerhouse. It is set to replace both Hong Kong as the financial capital of Asia, and Tokyo and as the preferred Asian location for multinational headquarters.

Heritage, culture, image

When Shanghai fell in 1949 to the Chinese communists a door was shut. During the cultural revolution the door was bolted for good. A world had gone … [C]ommunism has fallen on the city

*like a sandstorm, burying and preserving. …
Communism has mummified Shanghai's
appearance in a manner inconceivable to a
Westerner. Shopping centres, over-passes and
subways are all missing. So, despite carefully
preserved wrappings, is Shanghai's spirit. … To
write about a spiritually dead city presents
difficulties. (Sergeant, 1991: 5–6)*

*After years of stagnation, the great metropolis of
SHANGHAI is undergoing one of the fastest
economic expansions the world has ever seen.
The skyline is filling with skyscrapers; there are
three thousand now, more than New York, and
another two thousand are coming soon. Gleaming
shopping malls, luxurious hotels and prestigious
arts centres are rising alongside. Shanghai's 21
million residents enjoy the highest incomes on the
mainland, and there's plenty for them to splash out
on; witness the rash of celebrity restaurants and
designer flagship stores. In short, it's a city with a
swagger, bursting with nouveau riche exuberance
and élan. (Rough Guides online, 2011)*

Shanghai's own popular narrative is of an heroic return; at last unfettered, its energy and entrepreneurialism are given full reign, returning it to
its rightful pre-eminence. As such, the fortunes of
Shanghai *vis-à-vis* Beijing have often stood – for
citizens and foreign observers alike – as proxy for
the wider fate of western-style commercial development in China. Leaving aside for now how this seriously misinterprets what is actually taking place
in Shanghai, even at face value this narrative is
fraught with ambiguities and political pitfalls. It is a
narrative that taps into the bedrock of local Shanghai
identity but it also reactivates some powerful historical images long dormant in the West. This is
image capital too valuable not to be mobilized within
the global circuits of city-to-city competition; but,
touching as it does on the very trajectory of Chinese
modernization (coming towards the West or headed
somewhere else?), it requires careful management.
In its relationship with Beijing, Shanghai can certainly play the card of global commercial connections; it cannot (nor, as we shall see, would it ever
want to) represent some kind of repudiation or
rectification of the 1949 revolution. Further, its
association with a previous incarnation of western
urban modernity certainly does not represent some
embodiment of June 4th 1989 and the aspirations
to a Chinese democracy. Quite the contrary.

This is the broad context within which the arrival
of 'cultural policy' is to be understood. I say 'arrival'
because the conceptual toolkit in what is now
termed 'cultural policy' was elaborated principally in
Europe in the 1970s and 1980s (and has been
propagated worldwide by UNESCO). Up to the end
of the 1970s, art and culture in China were conceived as a combination of national heritage and
propaganda – and sometimes indeed 'health'.
During the Cultural Revolution (in parallel with the
growing attacks on the idea of the historical tran-
scendence of the aesthetic in the West) any residual autonomy of art (derived from a Soviet-style
competition in excellence with the West, especially
in ballet and classical music) was abolished. Unlike
Mao, however, Deng was notoriously indifferent to
art and cultural questions, and moved them away
from centre stage. In the late 1970s he oversaw the
creation of a new Ministry of Culture, separate from
that of Propaganda (leaving each side to bitterly
contest the borders), and in line with the general
thrust of his reforms he broke up the big state monopolies and encouraged the introduction of the
market. As in the Soviet Union – though less drastically – cuts in state funding rapidly transformed the
landscape of official culture (Kraus, 2004). We will
discuss this more below. One consequence was to
give city governments more autonomy in the funding of culture, gearing this much more directly to
their own concerns.

For most Chinese cities, expanding exponentially
across the space of a decade, cultural policy (where
it existed) was restricted to the preservation of historical monuments, the upkeep of museums and
the provision of venues for state-funded performers.
Cultural policy made its first connections in relation to this preservation of national heritage, which
was linked to the growing tourist market. UNESCO's
listing of World Heritage sites was increasingly
important for the growing cultural tourism trade
across Asia (Winter et al., 2008). After the ravages
of the Cultural Revolution, UNESCO, the Beijing
government and a range of other domestic and
international agencies were keen to restore, preserve and index the national patrimony. In Shanghai
this presented some specific problems of how to
deal with a modern heritage – that is, one marked
by the hand of imperialism – and how this would link
to its ambitions to become a new global city.

For development was rapidly demolishing the
preserved ruins of *Shanghai Moderne*. Becoming

global meant becoming Manhattan in quick time; but a telescoped process also meant that concerns about historic preservation also appeared sooner. International cultural policy norms combined in the 1990s with local architects, historians and artists to convince the Shanghai government that a preserved built heritage would be crucial to its future global image. The grand commercial buildings on the Bund and the opulent villas and art deco blocks of the French Concession were rapidly listed and given official plaques (Abbas, 2002). But rather than this being read as a return to a thwarted entrepreneurial past, it was instead an act of surpassing; the burgeoning cityscape of Pudong incorporated the ruins of colonialism as an index of its achievements. Indeed, Shanghai's adoption of western cultural policy norms would henceforth operate in a dual register: the glimpse of return (to the thwarted path of western modernity) used to strike out into a very different future.

As always, what counted as heritage was a political question. In general, the imperialist heritage was not a problem, so obviously had it been repudiated (and standing in for what the Communists *had* so successfully repudiated); more problematic were other shreds of the city's past. Thus while the imperialist heritage was preserved, the old workers' housing, the *Shikomen* blocks so distinctive to the city, were torn down and the residents relocated. The industrial heritage of this rapidly deindustrializing city was also destroyed – only latterly did 'creative clusters' save some of these. It was not the decadence that was the problem – of which more shortly – but the remnants of those Chinese reforms movements not incorporated into the Communist narrative. Those currents of industrial and political reform, such as the 'self-strengthening movement', which suggested that the Qing Empire was not entirely feudal, were ignored. The 2010 Expo development destroyed the late nineteenth-century arsenal site, which was a key testimony to the Empire's reforming zeal in Shanghai. Indeed, the distinct qualities of a *Shanghai Moderne* – not simply 'Imperialism meets Feudalism' but the opening of a liminal space in which alternative Chinese modernities might emerge – are much more suspect to the official narrative than is the city's glamorous decadence. In Shanghai not only did 'East meet East' – Japanese responses to modernization were profoundly important for China – but the oppositional currents of European radicalism and Asian

anti-colonialism encountered a Chinese intellectual culture eager to learn and adapt (Yue, 2006; Liang, 2010). In fact it is the very restricted image of *Shanghai Moderne*, as 'divine decadence' rather than a fecund cultural and social meeting place, that has fuelled the ambiguous process of 'back to the future' that the city learned to do so well.

Learning to embrace decadence

How did the Shanghai government learn to see itself from the outside and gain the skills necessary to present a coherent image to that outside? How did its officials learn that this was not just a question of presenting themselves as 'open for business' – such as in Shenzhen – but that the cultural resource of Shanghai's history could be transformed into global image-capital of great power? This learning process took place elsewhere than in the technical expertise of heritage preservation. It was to be found in the more amorphous space of 'culture-led regeneration' that had coalesced around a range of economic, social and cultural transformations in the deindustrializing cities of the developed West.

Mao's revolution had cleansed Shanghai not just of capitalists but also of urban decadence. In parallel with the modernization of European, Soviet and North American cities in the same period, the chaotic mess of the nineteenth-century city was to be replaced by a rationally planned modern industrial city. Shanghai's return not only brought back the imperialist past but its decadent memories – prostitution and opium, the very symbols of Chinese degradation. However, the resurgent city of skyscrapers might incorporate the now surpassed imperial buildings, but not so (or not immediately) its degraded past. For example, one of the first tourist redevelopments in the new Shanghai was around the sixteenth-century *Yu Yuan* Gardens and the eighteenth-century *Hu Xin Ting* teahouse. While pulling down much of the historic Chinese city, they built an ersatz or 'Disneyfied' 'Chinatown' around these two monuments, assuming this would be required by tourists. But this was not the image of Shanghai in the minds of western tourists or ex-patriates. These images of *Shanghai moderne* could be found in the emerging market for old adverts for soap, cigarettes and other nostalgic early modern merchandise; for old postcards and memorabilia; and for art décor furniture and fittings of a very different stamp from traditional *chinoiserie*. These images and objects found their way into the décor of bars and restaurants opened by or for 'ex-pats', often in the ex-foreign concession areas of the city whose atmosphere of nostalgic charm had been abandoned or resolutely ignored by the local Chinese.

The sign that the potential of these images had been recognized came in 2004 with the opening of *Xintiandi*, an office, retail and bar/dining complex near a major shopping street. It was constructed from the elements of the old *Shikumen* housing blocks, but made fit for modern use and provided with open 'piazzas' in trusted *po-mo* fashion. It was telling that the development company was from Hong Kong, and equally so that the architect, Benjamin Wood, was a protégé of Benjamin Thompson, whose 1979 transformation of Faneuil Hall in Boston represents a foundational moment of heritage-led urban regeneration. The Hong Kong developer was asked to incorporate the old Girls' School which hosted the first meeting of the Chinese Communist Party; rather than the burden this would represent for most of the Shanghai developers at that time, such historical patina was a godsend. So much so that the developers reconstructed a *Shikomen* house as a period museum over and above the brief (Liang, 2008).

Sharon Zukin's work on 1970s New York charts a protracted and fraught decade across which artists and historical preservationists resisted a modernist development process in SoHo and transformed a dirty old area of Manhattan into one of its most sought after (Zukin, 1982). She uses the notion of cultural intermediaries to describe the cultural work of revaluation, of transforming urban junk into new cultural capital through its historical associations. The frisson of buried memories, reactivated through memoires, histories, novels (e.g. Ballard's *Empire of the Sun*) and photographic collections animated the thousands of young foreigners who flocked to the city from the mid-1990s. The first wave of ex-pats had walled up well outside the old centre (Ross, 2009); increasingly, the new ones moved to the historical districts and brought with them the cultured leisure infrastructure latterly made famous by Richard Florida.

The lead cultural intermediaries were no longer Zukin's artists and bohemian wanabees but international developers and architects, ex-pat 'What's On' magazines and travel and lifestyle journalists. It is through these that the city learned to mobilize its decadent past. The western nostalgia for the chaotic and vital world of the nineteenth-century metropolis had by now produced a non-threatening consumption landscape in its regenerated Postfordist cities. The completion of *Xintiandi* indicated that the city government had also learned that the image of old Shanghai, whose corruption and degradation were so essential to the Communist narrative, could be safely repackaged to provide the cultural capital for up-market leisure and retail (see He and Wu, 2005; Liang, 2008).

Building a cultural infrastructure

What of the governance of the production of culture? We noted above Deng's creation of a Ministry of Culture covering areas previously reserved for that of Propaganda. This was of a part with Deng's 'demobilization' of Chinese society. In broad outline for cultural policy, this meant the gradual separating out of 'art' and 'entertainment', a process that had happened *de facto* in European countries since at least 1945. At the same time Deng introduced a process of market reform which applied – albeit differentially – to both of these, discussed below. In this division, art was deemed to be 'sensitive'. On the one hand, it concerned national heritage and identity and, on the other, it was where intellectuals were to be found – and intellectuals were the traditional thorn in the side of the socialist state. Entertainment was mostly safe, though as a popular form, it needed careful scrutiny.

Arts policy more or less covered traditional Chinese arts and crafts – calligraphy, painting, sculpture, opera, theatre, dance, poetry and so on – along with western-oriented arts including classical music, ballet, literature, oil painting and (to some extent) film. The former concerned national heritage and identity; the latter involved that international public sphere of intellectuals and artists that had been both courted and held in suspicion by the Soviet Union and, to a lesser extent, the People's Republic. In particular, the autonomy of art, central to western cultural theory and policy, was a moot point in socialism. In order for the Chinese government to 'normalize' art (that is, respect its autonomy) it would need to negotiate its traditional threat, associated with the autonomy of literary intellectuals (Wang, 1996). The most immediately threatening was literature and film, which had verbal, explicit meaning; the least threatening was classical music (whose abstractions had allowed Shostakovich to play cat and mouse with Stalin). Classical music was also highly internationalized, traditionally providing a stage on which the Communist world could show its artistic superiority. But other developing Asian countries – such as Japan and South Korea – also invested heavily in classical music as a sign of the modernization of culture.

The first urban cultural policy initiatives in China, from the second half of the 1990s, saw the building of a cultural infrastructure that focused on museums, traditional arts and craft, and the performing arts. Many cities in China began this process but the redevelopment of People's Square clearly announced Shanghai's intention to compete on a global scale – an intention realized most comprehensively in its huge expo site in 2010. A new museum (1996) to house an important collection of classical Chinese artifacts stands opposite the Urban Planning Exhibition Centre (2000), a mix of planning and Shanghai urban history. But the centre piece of the performing arts infrastructure was not to be Chinese opera but classical music. This came at a time of the boom in piano learning as a sign of modern educational and social aspiration with seemingly universal currency (Kraus, 1989). A new Grand Theatre was built in 1998 and in 2007 they completed the (very expensive) refurbishment and relocation (by a few metres, to make way for a highway) of the old 1930s concert hall. At the heart of the new Pudong district they built an enormous park, a Science and Technology Museum (2001) and the huge Shanghai Oriental Arts Centre for the performing arts (2005). Such an assemblage of cultural infrastructure indicated Shanghai's ambitions and formed a part of similar efforts in East Asia – as in Singapore, Hong Kong, Seoul and Taipei (Wu, 2004). It was the cultural equivalent of 'catch-up' and required the infusion of technical support from western experts – architects, consultants, curators and so on (the scale of the task can be seen in comparative terms in London Development Agency, 2008). But this arts infrastructure, focused on touring productions and performers, rarely spoke to local concerns and interests (Kong, 2009) and reproduced most of the basic problems raised internationally since the 1990s about the imposition of arts-led regeneration projects on 'ungrateful' local populations.

Some of the tensions within the project to build a globally oriented arts infrastructure were revealed as it became clear that classical music had rapidly declined as a form of international cultural capital. The value of touring productions of *Swan Lake* and international conductors and soloists was being replaced by something Chinese policy-makers had not expected – 'contemporary art'.

The transformation of 'modern' into 'contemporary art' is a story we cannot tell here, apart from suggesting that its 'post-modernist' phase uncoupled artistic innovation from any overarching historical narrative (Foster et al., 2005). It was a transformation that happened in highly telescoped fashion in the Chinese art world since the mid-1980s (Smith, 2005). Underground for most of that decade, the 1993 Venice Biennale saw 'contemporary Chinese art' hit the world stage, becoming since then almost a genre in its own right. 'Contemporary art' was where – in the view of the Chinese (and earlier the Soviet) government – the autonomy and radical uselessness of the modernist tradition was most concentrated. It was also an area of culture that had emerged from the art schools in direct contradiction to the formal curriculum and the ideological stance of socialism. The history of individual repression and censorship, the closing of independent art spaces and shows, is well known – and it continues today, most notably with Ai Weiwei.[1] What is less acknowledged is the patience and acumen by which this radical autonomy (and indeed the frisson of censorship for a world now indifferent to the shock of the new) was accommodated within Beijing and Shanghai's cultural policy-making.

As with the task of recognizing the image of *Shanghai Moderne* dispersed among visitors and returning nationals, understanding the attraction of contemporary art took some time and sensitivity. Why was it that, rather than the official galleries, western visitors were making their way to old factories, still covered in oil and machine parts, to look at art works produced outside the official system? In Beijing, Park 798 was the most famous; in Shanghai, their version was an old textile factory on Morganshan Road – M50. Starting in 1998 with the management letting out vacant space to artists, by 2004 it had attracted private galleries and foreign art businesses. At that point it was on the verge of demolition, the city hovering between its dubious ideological content and unofficial status and the growing recognition that the international art market was not only worth billions in itself but was a major source of cultural capital for cities. It is now central to its promotional offer as happening city of culture (Zhong, 2009).

The last five years have seen tentative, pragmatic, exploratory ways of bringing contemporary art within the cultural offer of the city, and isolating its radicalism from the wider cultural context. This is always difficult. Ai Weiwei is the latest example of how easy it is to step over the mark and the consequences of so doing. But all in all the international contemporary art framework of biennials, exhibitions, white cube galleries, private small-scale galleries, curators, magazines and books, happenings, openings, press releases and in-flight features are all now in place in Shanghai. We talk of the skill required for the Chinese transition to a market system, but the rapid acquisition of this level of skill and sophistication in handling the complex and allusive code of the international art market is also a major achievement. This is not just at the municipal government but also at district government levels, many of whom have identified and use intermediaries well connected in this world. It indicates that the 'radical autonomy' of contemporary art might be equally compatible with regimes other than those of neo-liberalism, as Julian Stallabrass (2004) charges.

On the other side, entertainment was considered more or less safe. The state-controlled media content in news, current affairs and documentaries was always wary of the more direct content of novels and films. But it actively promoted the consumption of urban culture and leisure commodities and worked hard to transform these from state-run bureaucracies into cultural industries. On the other hand, some elements always escaped. In Shanghai especially it was 'rock' music that continually strayed over the line from safe entertainment to the more edgy areas associated with contemporary art. In China, this music was associated since the 1980s with western 'spiritual pollution'; 'rock' clearly associated with the individualistic, anti-social behaviour proclaimed (though no longer really believed) by its western exponents. It was also a function of its low barriers to entry; 'Here's three chords, now form a band' could be a radical slogan in a culture governed by highly disciplined art forms and large state cultural organizations. In response, the state at all levels tended to move from outright repression in the 1980s to the more proactive creation and control of access to media space. It promoted a form of non-challenging pop/rock, creating a market, the exclusion from which meant not notoriety but oblivion (Baronovitch, 2003).

Therefore the impact of digitalization on music was somewhat attenuated in China. The separation of recorded pop and live, semi-official 'rock' was never particularly tied to questions of access to a big market (as in the mainstream/indie division in the West) because of lax copyright controls both before and after World Trade Organization (WTO) access. It was a division more constructed by state media gatekeepers. Digitalization (as elsewhere) meant 'live' was even more at a premium, but such live music gatherings were always somewhat edgy for the authorities. Rock music in Shanghai, like in many other cities, is thus still heavily policed despite the income and brand potential it might have. Only in Beijing does it proliferate. Shanghai has not learned (yet) how to link – as in art – the edginess of pop/rock to the city's cultural capital, and the music scene is never part of Shanghai's in-flight offer.

The real challenge to the art/entertainment division lies in two areas. First, in the internet, where both the state and large commercial conglomerates are challenged by new forms of access to production and distribution. Second, in the dispersed and fragmented urban cultures emerging around new forms of cultural production and consumption made possible by both the communication possibilities of the internet and the new legitimation given – if sometimes only as by-product – through the new discourse of 'city of culture'.

Cultural industries

Market reforms in the cultural sector were a key objective for Deng. We need to say something about the introduction of the market because this is often equated with 'modernization' *per se*. Markets are not the same as capitalism and as such we have to take seriously the claims by Deng and his successors that China has a socialist market economy. Often characterized as a face-saver, in fact this description has more truth than many give it credit for (Arrighi, 2007). Deng's reforms between 1978 and 1989 were frequently justified in terms that echoed Lenin's introduction of the *New Economic Policy* in 1921; that is, recognizing both the advantages and dangers of the market. In this transitional decade Deng's introduction of market reforms in the countryside and the explosion of small-scale businesses and entrepreneurs in the town and village enterprises (TVEs) produced a rapid growth in agricultural and light-industrial produce but brought two problems. First, it was clear that – as with the *Third Italy* – there were real limits to the ability of such small 'Smithian' market economies (Arrighi, 2007) to grow in a world dominated by multinationals. At some point very large national champions, as in Japan and the Asian Tigers, would be required. Second, the events of June 4 1989 made the political threat identified by Lenin (that is, a resurgent capitalist class) seem very real. Many small-scale entrepreneurs were supportive of the demonstrators (Tsai, 2007; Huang, 2008; Andreas, 2010; Chen and Dickson, 2010). Post-1989 there was a sense that large-scale capital intensive industries and market reforms had to take place, but also that such large-scale development could not take place outside the orbit of the party. In very general terms, post-1989 the party took the lead in promoting this industrial development; it did so by a gradual transition to market pricing, but also by the creation of large-scale 'private' conglomerates under the control of the party. It was a policy of 'let go the small, control the big', and it characterized Chinese economic development until the present (Naughton, 2007; McGregor, 2010).

This is the context for market reforms in culture. Though the introduction of market pricing was central to this, it did not necessarily mean 'privatization' in the way it was understood in the West. Within the specific area of 'art' – as in most western countries – there was also the national cultural heritage dimension which acted as an 'exception'. The main lines of the reforms in the arts were a reduction in direct state employment across all art forms and an expectation that more revenue would be generated by those that remained. These reforms were felt hardest by writers and visual artists who had previously worked within the state guilds and now launched into the world of 'freedom to write, freedom to starve' (Kraus, 2004). The performing arts troupes were rationalized – that is, there was a reduction in numbers, and the remaining troupes were expected to perform fewer but bigger productions, with higher quality production values in bigger auditoriums, generating more ticket income. As with many other areas of reform, these state companies

were expected to run on market prices but had many restrictions on number of productions, employees, etc. The sort of arts ecology existing in Britain – a tripartite state-sponsored-edticket-funding model – does not exist in China. Indeed, this is rarely recognized among policy-makers who regularly present western policy in terms of a privatization to which they should aspire. This results in a state-funded sector made up of large, quite bureaucratic organizations whose activities are regulated and a purely commercial 'private' sector that is expected to survive in a market that tends to be regulated in favour of these large state companies. This produces an ecology in which experimentation and small-scale companies – especially in the Chinese forms of opera, music and theatre – are quite peripheral to mainstream cultural policy concerns.

In the cultural industries – a term adopted in the late 1990s – the situation was somewhat different. If entertainment was safer and less related to 'national identity' than art, it was also a huge potential market; reforms meant a shift to market pricing but market entry was restricted. As elsewhere, the state divested direct control (allocation of funding based on bureaucratic targets) while also creating large conglomerates that would integrate the cultural production value-chain and provide a consolidated market presence. This meant decentralization – for Shanghai a real benefit (even if it led to duplication of production elsewhere). It set up committees (mirroring those at national level) to manage some very large 'private' media and publishing conglomerates – expanded by the later addition of new media, games and animation companies. The size of the potential regional market coupled with this local state control and the small numbers of dominant market players meant that very quickly there was a market monopoly organized around clientele or *guanxi* systems (Lee and Huang, 2007).

The situation grew out of three policy objectives. First, to introduce market discipline and efficiencies; second, to retain a degree of control over the ideological content; third, to ensure a strong domestic sector. All these combined to suggest that a large-scale foreign investment in this field – such as Rupert Murdoch or Time Warner – was not acceptable. However, while ideological control is often emphasized by western commentators, the protection of domestic markets from far more advanced global competition, while growing the necessary local expertise and market sophistication, is a common strategy in developing countries. The pursuit of these three objectives led to certain problems, exacerbated at the local level. First, as with other sectors, economic growth in these circumstances meant that it was the controlling influence, the party members and their clientele networks who enriched themselves. Leaving aside questions of corruption, there have been persistent problems around low-level market entry, leading to monopoly abuse and increased economic inequality. Second, it has tended to restrict experimentation and innovation. These are exacerbated at local levels because city governments have much closer direct stakes in the local economy over which they preside and therefore – other than in Beijing, with its multiple routes to competing power centres – the possibilities of control over entry are greater.

Shanghai combines both of these tendencies in the context of a highly scrutinized local party/government apparatus (a legacy of the Cultural Revolution and later power struggles with Beijing) and the huge potential local market with aspirations to the global. The result is that much of the cultural production sector in Shanghai suffers from the worst of both worlds. They operate in a very market-oriented, short-term commercial environment, driving them towards big audiences and away from risks. But they do not have any real competition outside the large conglomerates. In some ways the city's media sector mirrors the monopoly dominance of the private sector in countries such as Italy. This has produced an ecology very similar to that of the arts sector – a well-financed but culturally conservative sector dominated by large organizations and a marginalized, small-scale, more experimental sector entirely dependent on private finance, ticket sales, etc. (Schilbach, 2010). The two have rarely come into contact with each other until recently.

Creative industries

In this context the introduction of the idea of creative industries was inevitably multivalent. Though arriving slightly later than in other East Asia countries, the UK-inspired revamping of the cultural industries agenda had great attractions for policy-makers, especially in a commercially oriented city such as Shanghai. Indeed, following on from Hong Kong, the city was the first to espouse the new terminology in 2005. There was a background concern with moving up the value chain, from 'made in China' to 'created in China'; the absence of major Chinese brands despite their pre-eminence in global manufacture; and a more general emphasis on human capital and creativity which remains important for the government (Keane, 2007). More directly, the term suggested a post-WTO interest in intellectual property and in high value-added production suited to a post-industrial city such as Shanghai. As in the other East Asian countries, creative industries was associated with high-tech 'ideas-driven' industries, not just arts and cultural industries – nanotechnology, software development, R&D, business consulting and so on. All of these, bar the first, were adopted within Shanghai's definition of the term. To these were added design (fashion, industrial, new media) along with advertising and animation. These were then 'creative' and ideas-driven but more or less 'safe'.

In this sense the previous policy models of promoting high-tech industries through science parks (Ross, 2009) could very quickly be transplanted to the idea of 'creative clusters'. But it was not so straightforward. There were political questions. First, how did 'creative' square with 'cultural'. This is a big debate in the West, with many arguing that this ambiguity led to an overly economic emphasis (O'Connor, 2010). In China the distinction was mapped on to the division between 'safe' and 'sensitive' (in the sense of political and national patrimony/identity). The older opposition of art and entertainment was now expanded to include 'design' and 'lifestyle'. If it was that the creative industries – animation, new media, design, fashion, games, business consulting, marketing – could be defined as safe, then these might then fall within the purview of the economic development committee and also allow more local autonomy. Shanghai as a city thus pushed the creative industries as part of its economic development; and the economic committee sought to uncouple these sectors from the control of the cultural committee. Beijing (state and city) was much more circumspect, hovering between cultural, creative and 'cultural-creative' (Hui, 2006). On the face of it this was again commercial Shanghai and traditionalist Beijing, and this is clearly the image intended by the Shanghai government. But this is to ignore another key aspect of the creative industries agenda – that is, its emphasis on small and medium-sized enterprises (SMEs) and the idea of a creative ecology.

In fact Shanghai's agenda remained very much 'control the big, let go the small'. Market entry was very controlled – and so were the activities of the SME sector. This sector tends to be economically and politically marginal in Shanghai. It is Beijing, with its multiple sources of power and influence, its plethora of arts and cultural institutions, and paradoxically its very closeness to power ('hiding in the light'), that has the sort of marginal risk-taking experimental scene so crucial to the creative industries agenda in the West. Thus while Shanghai wanted the creative industries as part of an economic agenda, the promotion of experiment and risk taking among an ecology of SMEs with more access to the market, this was not on the cards. Or rather, it has tried to develop ways of integrating the innovation effects of the micro-sector within its larger corporate structures. This is part of the rationale behind creative clusters (which we discuss below) but also a more general search to find ways of integrating the 'learning effects' generated by SMEs and independents within the larger corporate structures – those with more capital, more *guanxi*, more sophisticated management and global links. The 'Trojan horse' model of the creative industries promoted by some commentators in the West, where the economic need to introduce 'creativity' and 'innovation' into the production and consumption of cultural goods would inevitably break or transform the shackles of state control (a view shared by many neo-liberal economists in China), needs much closer examination (see Hartley and Montgomery, 2009a, 2009b; Keane, 2010; Potts, 2010). Indeed, this attempt is not so different from similar tendencies in the West where the creative businesses that employ over 50 people (10 per cent of total businesses in the sector) account for over 60 per cent of sector profits (Evans, 2009).

This brief account should indicate the complexity of policy-making in China. It is easy for western observers to identify the outer form of a policy – often a direct translation of an English term such as 'creative industries' – as the adoption of an international policy norm when quite other things are happening. The sorts of public agencies that emerge in these fluid policy fields can also be very difficult to pin down. For example, the clear separation of public and private is often not possible in China, giving rise to those 'amphibian institutions' identified by John Friedmann (2005). Creative clusters are a case in point.

Adopted in 2005 as part of the city's new creative industries strategy, cluster policy combined the two elements of culture-led urban regeneration and the promotion of highly networked physically proximate creative businesses drawn from frequent fact-finding trips to the West. It did so in a specific context of socialist industrial-base planning and highly controlled public-private urban development. Identifying the city's reserve of old industrial spaces as a developmental resource (see above), the government used them to promote this new creative sector. It owned the land but leased it, with tax breaks, to private investors – though these investors often had close links with the local state. The model was a success in that very quickly there were over 80 such clusters with the number of new and unofficial clusters growing all the time. The authors' own investigations[2] suggest that these developments represent a complex mix between the need to gain rent from old buildings; demands to pay pensions to displaced workers; the promotion of the creative industries; the possibilities of generating profits through related non-creative, often residential developments; commitments to industrial heritage preservation; and exercising scrutiny over any sensitive cultural production. Increasingly it is clear that, with a few exceptions, the driving force is commercial office development aimed at the high-end of the sector (western designers and architects at a premium) and real estate development – a loss-making creative cluster acting as anchor for up-market 'urban villages' and/or leisure and retail offers. Indeed, as an amphibious organization, Shanghai's lead creative industries agency is at the forefront of such real estate development. Chinese creatives – at least the sort of small-scale, experimental entrepreneur-intermediaries expected by western observers – operate in more fluid virtual-physical spaces very different from official clusters (Hee et al., 2008; Wang, 2009). Again, it might be noted that this is frequently the case in the West.

Conclusion

Despite its glamorous hype and its enthusiastic embrace of both culture and creative industries, Shanghai's is not an innovative urban space but a highly controlled one. Paradoxically, this control has gone hand in hand with its hyper-commercialization. Indeed it is traditional, nation-state-heavy Beijing where much of the cultural innovation takes place. Shanghai, they say, is all about money. In this sense Shanghai's modernity has been neutered, turned into spectacle. The 2010 Expo tried to relaunch a heroic modernity long since abandoned by the West; in the end its focus was overwhelmingly on the modernization of urban infrastructure, albeit with some green tinges. *Better City, Better Life*: though a crowd puller, its attempt to relaunch a twenty-first-century urban modernity was a failure (Connery, 2011).

We have tried to show how Shanghai has adopted many canonical cultural policy concepts and techniques, but that they are put to work within a very different system, one quite distinct from the normative expectations of the policy paradigms elaborated in the West. But in highlighting these disjunctions we are not simply pointing to the duplicity behind the façade of compliance. As Zizek has shown on many occasions, attempts at subterfuge can reveal the truth of the appearance. In this case, the way in which the Shanghai government has put western cultural policy norms and techniques to work for itself reveals a truth about these policy norms in the West. That is, their own very real ability to accommodate the programme of neo-liberalism.

The recognition that the trajectory of Chinese development might not just be lagging – when will capitalist liberal democracy come? – but going someplace else has been registered by the recent accounts of China as a distinct form of capitalism. No longer is economic development to be restricted to those countries adopting western norms – what Hutton (2007) calls 'enlightenment values' and Ferguson (2011) 'freedom' (a difference that tells a lot about the West's current political *agon*). We are now told there is 'good' and 'bad' capitalism, and that China is the latter (Tsai, 2007; Huang, 2008; Chen and Dickson, 2010; McGregor, 2010). That China might not be either, that it might represent an alternative future however attenuated, is rarely aired in these discussions, but it forms part of the Chinese new left approach (Hui, 2003, 2009). This western-centric view misses another possibility, perhaps buried deep in Shanghai's notorious headquarters of the Gang of Four: that of a residual socialist past which might yet be used to construct an alternative future.

Notes

1　A well-connected artist with studios in Beijing and Shanghai, and showing (among other places) in the Tate Gallery's prestigious Turbine Hall, he was arrested in March 2011 and currently is still under house arrest at time of writing.
2　The authors lead an Australian Research Council-funded project 'Soft Infrastructure, New Media and Creative Clusters: Building Capacity in China and Australia' (see www.creativeasia.co.uk).

REFERENCES

Abbas, A. (2002) 'Play It Again Shanghai: Urban Preservation in the Global Era', in Gandelsonas, M. (ed.), *Shanghai Reflections: Architecture, Urbanism, and the Search for an Alternative Modernity*. pp. 33–55.

Andreas, J. (2010) 'A Shanghai Model?' *New Left Review* 65: 63–86.

Arrighi, G. (2007) *Adam Smith in Beijing: Lineages of the Twenty-First Century*. London: Verso.

Baronovitch, N. (2003) *China's New Voices: Popular Music, Ethnicity, Gender and Politics, 1978–1997*. Berkeley, CA: University of California Press.

Bergère, M.-C. (2009) *Shanghai: China's Gateway to Modernity*. Stanford, CA: Stanford University Press.

Chen, J. and Dickson, B.J. (2010) *Allies of the State: China's Private Entrepreneurs and Democratic Change*. Cambridge, MA: Harvard University Press.

Connery, C. (2011) 'Better City, Better Life', *boundary 2* 38(2) (forthcoming Summer)

Evans, G. (2009) 'Creative Cities, Creative Spaces and Urban Policy', *Urban Studies* 46: 1003–1040.

Ferguson, N. (2011) *Civilization: The West and the Rest*. London: Allen Lane.

Foster, H., Krauss, R., Bois, Y.-A. and Buchloh, B. (2005) *Art since 1900: Modernism, Antimodernism, Postmodernism*. London: Thames and Hudson.

Friedmann, J. (2005) *China's Urban Transition*. Minneapolis, MN: University of Minnesota Press.

Hartley, J. and Montgomery, L. (2009a) 'Creative Industries Come to China', *Chinese Journal of Communication* 2: 1–12.

Hartley, J. and Montgomery, L. (2009b) 'Fashion as Consumer Entrepreneurship: Emergent Risk Culture, Social Network Markets and the Launch of Vogue in China', *Chinese Journal of Communication* 2: 61–76.

He, S. and Wu, F. (2005) 'Property-led Development in Post-reform China: A Case Study of Xindiandi Redevelopment Project in Shanghai', *Journal of Urban Affairs* 27 (1): 1–23.

Hee, L., Schroepfer, T., Nanxi, S. and Ze, L. (2008) 'From Post-industrial Landscape to Creative Precincts: Emergent Spaces in Chinese Cities', *International Development Planning Review* 30 (3): 249–266.

Huang, Y (2008) *Capitalism with Chinese Characteristics: Entrepreneurship and the State*. Cambridge, MA: Harward University Press.

Hui, D. (2006) 'From Cultural to Creative Industries: Strategies for Chaoyang District, Beijing', *International Journal of Cultural Studies* 9 (3): 317–331.

Hui, W. (2003) *China's New Order: Politics and Economy in Transition*. Cambridge, MA: Harvard University Press.

Hui, W. (2009) *The End of Revolution. China and the Limits of Modernity*. London: Verso.

Hutton, W. (2007) *The Writing on the Wall: Why We Must Embrace China as a Partner or Face It as an Enemy*. London: Little, Brown.

Keane, M. (2007) *Created in China: The Great New Leap Forward*. London and New York: Routledge.

Keane, M. (2010) 'Great Adaptations: China's Creative Clusters and the New Social Contract', *Continuum: Journal of Media & Cultural Studies* 23 (2): 221–230.

Kong, L. (2009) 'Making Sustainable Creative/Cultural Space in Shanghai and Singapore', *The Geographical Review* 91 (1): 1–22.

Kraus, R.C. (1989) *Pianos and Politics in China: Middle-Class Ambitions and the Struggle over Western Music*. Oxford: Oxford University Press.

Kraus, R.C. (2004) *The Party and the Arty: The New Politics of Culture*. Lanhan, MD: Roman and Littlefield.

Lee, C.-C., He, Z. and Huang, Y. (2007) 'Party-Market Corporatism, Clientelism, and Media in Shanghai', *The Harvard International Journal of Press/Politics* 12 (3): 21–42.

Liang, S.Y. (2008) 'Amnesiac Monument, Nostalgic Fashion: Shanghai's New Heaven and Earth', *Wasafiri* 23 (3): 47–55.

Liang, S.Y. (2010) *Mapping Modernity in Shanghai: Space, Gender and Visual Culture in the Sojourners' City, 1853–98*. London: Routledge.

London Development Agency (LDA) (2008) *London: A Cultural Audit*. London: LDA. Available at: www.static.london.gov.uk/mayor/culture/docs/cultural-audit.pdf.

McGregor, R. (2010) *The Party: The Secret World of China's Communist Rulers*. London: Allen Lane.

Naughton, B. (2007) *The Chinese Economy: Transitions and Growth*. Cambridge, MA: MIT Press.

O'Connor, J. (2010) *The Cultural and Creative Industries: A Review of the Literature* (revised edition). London: Creative Partnerships.

Potts, J. (2010) 'Do Developing Economies Require Creative Industries? Some Old Theory about New China', *Chinese Journal of Communication* 2 (1): 92–108.

Ross, A. (2009) *Fast Boat to China: High-Tech Outsourcing and the Consequences of Free Trade: Lessons from Shanghai*. New York: Vintage Press.

Rough Guides online (2011) *Rough Guide to China*, www.roughguides.com/travel/asia/china/shanghai.aspx (accessed 28/4/11).

Schilbach, T. (2010) 'Cultural Policy in Shanghai: The Politics of Caution in the Global City', *Journal of Policy Research in Tourism, Leisure and Events* 2 (3): 221–235.

Sergeant, H. (1991) *Shanghai*. London: John Murray.

Stallabrass, J. (2004) *Contemporary Art: A Very Short Introduction*. Oxford: Oxford University Press.

Tsai, K.S. (2007). *Capitalism without Democracy: The Private Sector in Contemporary China*. New York: Cornell University Press.

Wang, J. (1996) *High Culture Fever: Politics, Aesthetics and Ideology in Deng's China*. Berkeley, CA: University of California Press.

Wang, J. (2009) "Art in Capital": Shaping Distinctiveness in a Culture-led Urban Regeneration Project in Red Town, Shanghai', *Cities* 26: 318–330.

Wasserstrom, G. (2010) *Global Shanghai: A History in Fragments*. London: Routledge.

Winter, T., Teo, P. and Chang, T.C. (eds) (2008) *Asia on Tour: Exploring the Rise of Asian Tourism*. London: Routledge.

Wu, W. (2004) 'Cultural Strategies in Shanghai: Regenerating Cosmopolitanism in an Era of Globalization', *Progress in Planning* 61: 159–180

Yue, M. (2006) *Shanghai and the Edges of Empire*. Minneapolis, MN: University of Minnesota Press.

Zhong, S. (2009) 'From Fabrics to Fine Arts: Urban Restructuring and the Formation of an Art District in Shanghai', *Critical Planning* 16: 118–137.

Zukin, S. (1982) *Loft-living: Culture and Capital in Urban Change*. London and Baltimore, MD: The Johns Hopkins University Press.

CHAPTER 29

TORINO: A CHANGE OF SKIN AND MORE
Luca Dal Pozzolo

This account of Torino focuses on the city's strategy of combining urban renewal with huge investments on heritage and culture. To transform an industrial, Fordist city into a cosmopolitan 'Capital of Culture' requires a good deal more than a change of skin; and how quickly the 'more' can be attained depends on changing the minds of a large number of city inhabitants. It is a cultural process that affects individual and collective identities, longings, hopes and fears, and scenarios for the futures. These processes, which have been largely successful in Turin, need to be maintained as well as renewed. The current economic downturn requires a rethinking of the previous strategy and a new vision that can be shared not only among the most powerful stakeholders, but also by the majority of the citizens.

Introduction

Starting from the early 1990s, Torino began a long transformation process in order to overcome the image of a grey, one-company town, dominated by car manufacturing and beset by a major industrial crisis. Urban renewal, improving quality of life and re-discovering art and culture are among the strategic directions the city authorities chose to conquer a new position on the map of European regional capitals. In 1995 the new Urban Plan was finally approved, entailing huge infrastructural investments and considerable urban renewal, in the city center, along the earlier tram lines, which were replaced by a new underground ring. Great attention was paid to restoring public spaces, giving back to citizens a brilliant and baroque city center. In the mid-1990s, investment in cultural heritage involved particularly the museums of the metropolitan area and it became an explicit strategy shared with the region, and with bank foundations, especially the Compagnia di San Paolo and the Fondazione Cassa di Risparmio di Torino, which were active partners and provided considerable funds for arts and culture in general. The cultural heritage was identified as a key asset for tourism and hence for local development; thus huge investments were made on heritage preservation. The baroque Residences system of the royal house of Savoy was inscribed on the World Heritage List and became the object of a major restoration project, focused on its biggest structure, the Venaria Castle, not far from the city center. In spite of the scale of investment, until the end of the 1990s cultural demand grew but slowly. Yet the process was confirmed by a Strategic Plan approved in 2000. This template was shared by all stakeholders and envisaged effective inter-institutional governance and cooperation, notwithstanding the divergent political loyalties of the local and regional administrations.

In this context, the need to improve urban renewal for the assigned Olympic Winter Games of 2006 acted as a powerful 'social glue' among actors and stakeholders. Starting from 1999–2000, the impacts of these efforts became clearly visible:

museum visitorship grew constantly, due to events both big and small, while museum offerings were continuously expanded and improved. The focus was on providing an attractive cultural infrastructure with long-term projects such as the restoration of the Savoy Residences, new and/or refurbished museums, especially in Torino and the Metropolitan area. Likewise, hundreds of historical places and castles were restored in the region with the clear objective of climbing the European ranking of cultural cities. Torino and the Piemonte region actually increased their outlay in the cultural field, unlike other Italian cities and regions. Yet the sustainability of this growing supply of cultural infrastructure became problematic, as attention was focused exclusively on the winter Olympic Games.

Actually, the year 2006 was the real turning point, as it was during the Olympic Games that a large part of the city population, previously almost skeptical about the policy of investing in culture and tourism, realized how much the city had changed, saw the degree of increased international media exposure, the growth of touristic flows as well as changes in the everyday such as the heightened vitality of night life. The grey, industrial, one-company town now seemed definitively a memory of the past…

But 2006 was a turning point also because economic resources began to diminish and the very scale of cultural offer began to clearly reveal its unsustainability. Great projects, such as the Savoy Residences circuit, were still under way while the economic crisis that started in 2007 threatened to endanger the whole cultural system. A new skepticism emerged in the media and among the social groups that were diffident about the strategy of investing in culture, tourism and immaterial resources; claims emerged for more structural investments. Huge cutbacks in cultural budgets at every level – state, region, province, city – and the impossibility of obtaining more funding from the banking foundations generated, especially in 2009–10, serious difficulties for the large majority of cultural institutions, including even the capacity to cover their normal running costs. This downturn obscured the positive economic effects of the previous phase. At this point, economic sustainability became the priority, but a rationalization of costs was not enough. A new vision and a new strategy were clearly needed, taking into account the redefinition of the role of culture in the future of local society and of the city proper, and these were broader than economic impact concerns.

The beginnings

The city of Torino has a long tradition of innovation in cultural policies. Starting in 1975, the city gave birth to important cultural policies, inventing, among other features, the *Punti Verdi* (Green Points: public places, squares, gardens and parks with an intensive free access program of theatre and music performances) or organizing new festivals as *Settembre Musica*. In 1984 the opening of Rivoli Castle, bought by the region and restored to host the first Contemporary Art Museum in Italy, demonstrated the interest of the city and the region for contemporary visual arts. However, it was only in the early 1990s among the majority of policy makers that there arose a new awareness that culture, heritage and the arts could play an important role in the economic development of the city and of the region, rather than being only a sub-sector of welfare policies or quality of life. Arts, culture and tourism, neglected in the past as regards their economic and innovatory potential, began to be seen as strategic assets. Major research projects on the metropolitan area highlighted the economic impact of cultural activities and the benefits that could emerge from a synergistic, integrated policy for museums and heritage. For example, in 1995 and 1997, the Giovanni Agnelli Foundation commissioned Fitzcarraldo to carry out and publish research on the economic impact of arts and culture on the metropolitan area of Torino and on the Museum Metropolitan System and its contribution to the economy of the city. In point of fact, museums and heritage were the first sub-sector to receive large-scale funding from the city administration and from the region, and subsequently from the foundations created in the banking sector. Thus the Compagnia di San Paolo experimented with a partnership strategy, restoring the Egyptian Museum with the State's *Soprintendenza*. The Fondazione Cassa di Risparmio di Torino perpetuated the bank's policy of widely sponsoring and supporting restoration activities in the region and invested heavily in the restoration of the Savoy Residences. Notwithstanding this new season of interest and investment in museum and heritage, between 1990 to 1994 audiences actually sunk to their lowest level since the mid-1960s (see Figure 29.1). Indeed, one of the major concerns was

Figure 29.1 Audience attendances in the Metropolitan Museum System, 1952–2009

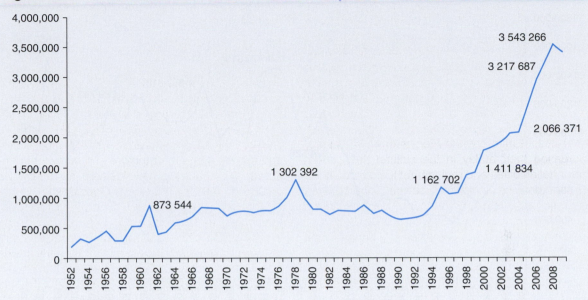

Source: Osservatorio Culturale del Piemonte (OCP)

the scant local demand *vis-à-vis* the goal of attracting big flows of cultural tourism.

Skepticism among opinion leaders and population on the economic role of culture and heritage was another sign of the gap between the new strategy and civil society; the economic crisis and the de-industrialization process seemed so massive as to rule out investments in culture. A large debate in the press and various other fora mirrored this concern, sometimes in simplificatory terms, as if it had been contended that culture and heritage could simply replace the economic role of industry. The apparent disinterest of the local audience was also a serious obstacle to overcome. New policies were put in place specifically to address local demand, e.g. the introduction of a museum season-ticket at a very competitive price in a cluster of museums. Trends in the performing arts sector were marked by different peaks of audiences, most of them induced by great pop music events and live concerts. On the contrary, theater, classical music, dance and opera showed almost stagnant demand, with little variations during these years, without profiting from increasing resources as did museums and heritage (see Figure 29.2).

In 1997 the Residences of the Royal House of Savoy were inscribed on the UNESCO World Heritage List and a major cultural tourism project based

on the most important Residences was envisaged. The Venaria Castle, supported also by EU structural funds, became the biggest heritage restoration site in Europe (Dal Pozzolo and Benente 2006). Again in 1997, the region, the city, the province of Torino, the Compagnia di San Paolo, Fondazione Cassa di Risparmio di Torino, the Regional Institute for Economic and Social Research (IRES), the Italian National Agency for Cinema and Performing Arts, and the Fondazione Fitzcarraldo signed an agreement to establish and fund an independent Observatory of Culture with a regional scope to study, support and contribute to cultural policies, in which all these different actors are involved. Growing investments, access to EU funds and programs, and shared responsibilities in the cultural system required a reliable data set and tools able to support a complex governance system.

In 1998, Torino – after a gap of 20 years – once again organized the public showing of the Holy Shroud, attracting about 2 million visitors, while audience figures in the city's museums jumped to the same level as 20 years before, showing how much tourism was contributing to visitorship. But the city was changing fast, and the impression was that a sort of threshold had been passed, that the audience was no longer just related to big events

Figure 29.2   Audiences for the performing arts in Torino, 1990–2009

The Figure concerns the city of Torino only, not the whole Province

Source: Osservatirio culturale del Piemonte based on data SIAE

like *Italia '61* – the Centenary of the founding of the Italian State with Torino as its first capital – or the exhibition of the Holy Shroud. Thus, a higher level of audience also began to be expected. This feeling was confirmed by facts, and a new interest for heritage and cultural activities was among the reasons for the growing audience, which was more explicitly in museum and heritage than in performing arts.

In 1999 Torino won the competition for the XX Winter Olympic Games of 2006, and this was a really structural turning point. Previous cultural investments were seen as being the assets needed to win the competition and to face the new challenges. This result, obtained with the cooperation of the city and the region, notwithstanding their political differences (the former was center-left, the latter center-right) acted as a powerful glue, and reinforced local governance involving the private sector and the banking sector foundations, giving a new impulse for the strategy of urban renewal based on the cultural and artistic sector. In 2000 a new showing of the Holy Shroud repeated the previous success and in the same year the Strategic Plan for the metropolitan area was approved. In its major infrastructural

programs, the cultural sector, museums and heritage occupied a big place in view of the explicit objective of attracting larger numbers of tourist visits.

Olympic enthusiasm

The Olympic Games represented a major objective that could focus strategies and projects on the part of the main social actors, from public bodies to private operators, especially the Italian banking sector foundations. A new impulse was given to local governance, giving continuity to already established cooperation among the state, region, city, province and the foundations. This long period of inter-institutional cooperation will be acknowledged later as one of the main success factors in the city strategy. Increased expenditure for art and culture (see Figure 29.3) was also acknowledged. It was particularly meaningful because other major investments, such as in the Venaria Castle, were funded not only by the cultural budget shown in Figure 29.2, but also from other budget lines, such as 'Public Buildings'. This great effort was well represented by the marked growth in the number of museums, castles, exhibition centers that were restored, built, or reopened: 41 in the metropolitan area between 1994 and 2009. The large number of building sites is the result of important funds specifically devoted to investments, while resources for running costs did not grow at the same pace. It was possible, therefore, to foresee the rise of sustainability concerns for the future, at the end of the growth phase. However, pressure to complete the cultural and infrastructural system focused attention on present activity, pushing these concerns towards a future scenario. In this period demand for the performing arts grew more slowly and did not keep pace with the increased supply, focusing especially on festivals spread across the region.

The new Museum of Cinema opened in 2000 inside the Mole Antonelliana, the most important landmark of the city skyline, and – thanks to its impressive impact – jumped immediately to the top of the audience figures, together with the Egyptian Museum. In 2001, the Palazzo Madama, the medieval castle in the main square of Torino with a baroque façade designed by Juvarra, reopened with the new display of the Ancient and Decorative Art Museum. In 2003, for the first time, the Metropolitan Museum System attracted more than 2 million visitors. While the number of museum venues was more than doubled since the early 1990s, visitors more than trebled but curiously there was no apparent increase in tourism. The museum season-ticket available to residents was the tool that increased local audiences and also made people aware of the existence of a coordinated system and a common exhibition policy. In a few years the season-ticket and the tourism card gave access to more than 100 museums in the region, producing more than 10 per cent of the total audience. It was clear that these investments had succeeded in changing cultural habits, in involving larger numbers of local people and in enlarging audiences. In addition to this, thanks also to the great work of the Film Commission, Torino came to be used for the shooting of many different national and international films, allowing a large

Figure 29.3 Public and private expenditure for the cultural sector in the Piedmont region and in the Torino province, 1999–2008

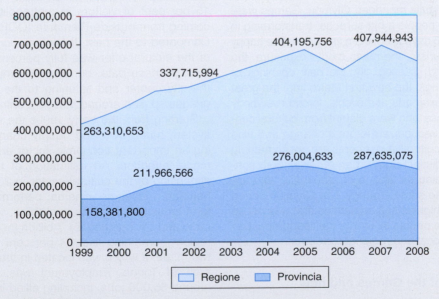

Note: These figures include the resources of the whole Piedmont region, provinces, municipalities above 15,000 inhabitants and bank foundations.

Sources: Osservatorio Culturale del Piemonte on data MIBAC, Regione Piemonte, Province, Fondatzioni Bancarie Peimontesi, Consulte

number of residents to understand the big change and letting the great cultural infrastructure emerge from the old image of the city. At the same time also the supply of performing arts and music grew slightly, though in a fragmented way, with the increasing importance of festivals and events.

On the eve of the Olympic Games two main issues emerged. The first was very clear and shared among the main stakeholders and the city and regional administration: the long phase of investments was not yet completed but it was strongly visible; it had led to an unprecedented level of cultural supply, but the challenge remaining was to market this internationally and attract those great flows of cultural tourism that were among the most important expected results of the city's strategy. The second issue was more hidden and subtle, and it was related to the new image of the city: what was the vision underlying this great urban and cultural transformation? What would be the image of the city at the end of the process? And how to share this vision at the local level? In the seventeenth century, the building of Torino was marketed among the European courts by the *Theatrum Sabaudiae*, a book of engravings describing the impressive urban and military transformations that effectively demonstrated the power of a little kingdom. A contemporary *Theatrum Sabaudiae* seemed to be needed to represent in a synthetic way the new cultural metropolis.

The successfully managed Olympic Games were for many local people a big surprise, transforming in the space of 15 days skepticism into pride. The happy invasion of tourism, the mass media exposure, the enlightened and glittering city, the new openings of Olympic buildings, the new first Metro line, the great offer of performing arts and events, forced everybody – including those who were distant from cultural consumption – to recognize the great change and also to realize that cultural investments are not something different and distinct from urban renewal; both contribute to shaping the image of a new city, and are two arms of the same strategy. The Olympic period succeeded in highlighting something that was not so clear for all the people in Torino: the reappropriation of the city by local and regional residents.

The legacy of the Games and new challenges

There is no doubt that the city of Torino and the metropolitan area profited greatly from the Olympic Games, much more than the actual mountain venues where they took place. The new strong point in these Winter Games was precisely their urban and cultural dimension, and the exposure of a city previously not so well known internationally, apart from its industrial heritage. The historical city, the baroque center with its splendid long articulation of arcades and the museums were all surprises for the media, promoting high-level international exposure. At the same time, customer satisfaction, measured through different surveys (Fondazione Cassa di Risparmio di Torino 2006; OMERO n.d.) was very high, especially because of the vitality of the city and the global offer, including the cultural, made possible through an intensive program of events and performing arts, hosted both in the main open public spaces and in the traditional and institutional venues. One of the first obvious results was the increase of tourism flows, especially in the city center, in 2008 and 2009 (see Figure 29.4). Visitor numbers to museums and heritage sites also increased, to around 3.5 million in the Museum Metropolitan System in 2008 and 2009, versus less than 3 million in 2006, the year of the Olympic Games. But the real news was that more than 50 per cent of visitors come from outside the region, and more than 15 per cent were foreigners; the same enquiry carried out in 2001 registered only 15 per cent of visitors in metropolitan museums coming from outside Piemonte (OCP 2001, 2008). Compared to the past, the international dimension of the cultural offer was fully perceivable not only through these data, but also by simply walking in the city center and listening to the different languages spoken around museum entrances.

Starting from the early 1990s the whole cultural system has grown and deeply changed, becoming an important economic sector and in terms of media attention. An estimation of the economic dimension of the cultural sector in 2007, including heritage, museums, cinema, performing arts, cultural industries such as publishing, video making, radio and TV, reached €1.7 billion for the Piemonte region (something like 1.4 per cent of the GDP), two-thirds of which was located in the metropolitan area of Torino. Employment was estimated at around 35,000 jobs, including allied industries and activities in the region (OCP 2009). Notwithstanding the long phase of investments in culture (estimated at more than €1.5 billion in the region, mainly on museums and heritage, over 15 years), the cultural

Figure 29.4 Tourism in Torino: attendances and arrivals, 2000–2009

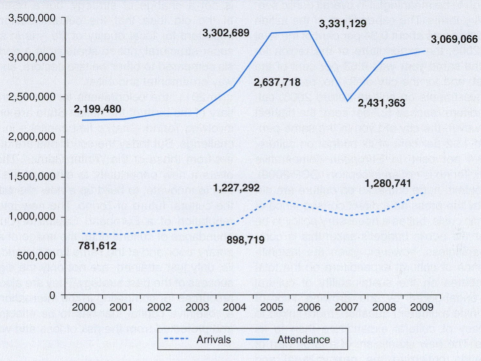

Source: Osservatorio Culturale del Piemonte based on Sviluppo Piemonte Turismo

infrastructure is not yet complete. The biggest project and investment, the Savoy Residences, is still ongoing and is not ready to be marketed as the most important cultural attraction of the region. In 2007, the Venaria Palace was opened to the public, attracting around 700,000 visitors in 2008 and 2009, but as a single venue, without playing the role of the portal of the whole system. Other residences are still under restoration and there is no investment to build up a coordinated tourist circuit through all the presidences. Many other venues and castles in the region face similar conditions, at a time when the economic crisis is having a seriously adverse effect on the cultural sector.

These effects are particularly severe as a result of the overlapping of different phenomena. First, the *Pax Olimpica*, the consequence of the sharing of objectives and goals by public and private actors, ended after the Winter Games. There is no longer a shared vision or a common agenda for future developments in the cultural sector, nor is there any new vision for the future of the cultural city after the turning

point of the Olympics. This has led to a weakening of the governance pattern established previously through the inter-institutional cooperation of the public and the private sectors. The principal actors in the cultural field now follow new individual strategies, oriented to the containment of cultural expenditure.

Another important factor in the crisis is the great expansion of the cultural infrastructure, driven by the large amount of money available for investment, some of which is supported by the State and by the European Union structural funds, while the amounts allocated for running costs has not increased at the same rate. On the contrary, since 2006 funding for culture diminished dramatically. The effects of the global economic crisis, added to the difficult economic and financial condition of the city of Torino after the Winter Games, are considerable. How sustainable are the current levels of cultural expenditure? The crisis has been a detonator of different contradictions and paves the way for new public polemics in the press on precisely the issue of sustainability. Yet, while every sector has seen cuts, the cutbacks on cultural spending are not large enough to be meaningful in overall public sector budgetary terms. The expenditure of the Italian State for culture was about 0.34 per cent of the total budget in 2008; the expenditure of the region for culture in the same year was 0.63 per cent of the total budget; and for the city of Torino, particularly active in investments on culture before 2006, cultural expenditure reached 5.7 per cent, the highest in Italy. However, the city of Lyon in the same period invested 13.2 per cent of its budget on culture, Valencia 9.4 per cent. In European comparative terms, then, Torino is not an exception (OCP 2009).

In this context, huge cutbacks on culture are not only seen by the press as a direct consequence of the economic crisis, but as a necessary policy to be adopted for the public budget's sake: this is completely meaningless, however, given the insignificant incidence of cultural expenditure on the total budget. Debates on the sustainability of cultural activities, endangered by the growing lack of resources, hide a different question, more linked to the legitimacy of cultural expenditure than to its dimensions. The new skepticism of a large part of the population criticizing the new cultural and innovative dimension of urban renewal is a mix of longing for the ancient industrial city, mistrust for immaterial activities, the impact of some scandals affecting the cultural sector, as well as a reaction to the economic impact of the culture that gave room in the pre-Olympic period to a dangerous rhetoric, which was irrational in terms of the expected results. This reaction reveals how dangerous economic impact justifications can turn out to be, for the winds of crisis were enough to obscure the positive impacts that are still visible. Trends in 2009 and 2010 show a split situation: on the one hand, audiences are increasing or stable, despite a radical reduction of all temporary activities, first of all exhibitions that were one of the main attractions for local visitors, while cultural tourism was growing in Torino and in the region. The direct expenditure on cultural tourism in the city of Torino, without counting the induced effects, is estimated to be more than €130 million. On the other hand, cultural institutions have become increasingly difficult to run and are having to progressively reduce their activities. The positive 'Olympic effect' is still alive, yet although its positive consequences remain, there is less and less capacity to sustain investments on culture and tourism to a degree that can exploit all

the positive effects over the long term. The real risk is not a change of strategy, but a re-emergence of the old idea that the cultural sector – albeit important for local quality of life – is in some way super-structural, not so strategic in a period of crisis compared to other welfare sectors, and in some way ornamental and elitist.

In 2011, the celebrations for the 150th anniversary of the birth of the Italian State are once again involving Torino – Italy's first capital – in a cultural challenge. But today the conditions are quite different from those of the Winter Games. The present offers a new opportunity to evaluate past strategy and to innovate, to build up a new shared vision of the cultural future of Torino. The new international reputation of a European Capital of Culture, the abundance of cultural offer, the image of a contemporary 'cool' and at the same time historic metropolis, only just attained, are not only the signs of the success of the past strategy. They are also precious resources for competing in the international arena, a collective capital that has to be effectively used and protected from the risk of loss and waste.

Conclusions

The case of Torino shows very well the importance and the 'long wave' of local culture, the way residents perceive themselves and their city, the way the city is used to represent itself. In this perspective, changing its image is for a city a long and deep process that affects its soul far more than the surface of the buildings. Memories and stories are not only incrusted in stones, but hosted in individuals, cemented by years of dreams and hopes about possible futures, giving room to contradictions and conflicts about collective destinies.

During the Celebrations of the Centenary of the Italian State in 1961, all the emphasis was placed on a vision of the future as the marvelous progress produced by human industry: a new modern quarter was built (*Italia '61*) paying special attention to the innovation. The first Chamber of the Italian Parliament in the Palazzo Madama was restored with funds made available at the last minute, as well as other very important and historical places for the history of the Italian State. This vision paid little heed to the historic and architectural heritage. Fifty years later, the pre-industrial historical city is rediscovered, restored and brilliant, as a new foundation, both material and immaterial, for local development, including arts, culture and knowledge as strategic assets and new functions for millions of square meters of abandoned industrial plants. But at the same time, this new vision meets with skepticism among many people, who see in it an attempt to turn the city's working-class memories into an archive, together with the city's industrial history itself, both parts of a city still alive, productive and able to contribute importantly to the future.

Torino's experience shows the complexity of a policy geared to image change, and the cultural content of a process that involves people in their roots and memories as well as in their expected futures. To harmonize these different strata, to compose them in a shared vision, respecting and giving room to each different cultural dimension, is the object of specific cultural policies that can also have different time horizons compared to a changing of image and a new territorial market strategy. If the Olympic Games provided a medium-term objective that was very effective in implementing coordination and common policies among the major stakeholders, in some way it constrained the vision of the next step. The global crisis worsened the situation, foregrounding the economic situation. From a previous – sometimes rhetorical – concern with economic impact, there was a forced shift toward economic sustainability. This has posed a real challenge to all institutions and individuals involved in arts and culture production and management: they can no longer remain dependent on public funding and must build new alliances with the private sector and directly with different audiences. But it is also necessary to go beyond the economic and build a new vision for a cultural city facing new global challenges.

Some of these challenges are very clear. There is a new intercultural dimension that, apart from some interesting experiences, has not yet been integrated as a powerful resource for the future of the city or made into a central object of cultural policy, despite the increasing number of new citizens coming from non-EU countries (see Chapter 3 by Phil Wood in this volume). This dimension is linked to the growing importance of others. The international and European dimension, envisaged in older times by the Savoy dynasty for their local unsustainable policy of great building yards and Residences, needs to be re-elaborated on the basis of a metropolitan dimension involving closer relationships with Central and Eastern Europe and, in the Mediterranean perspective, on links with Marseille, Barcelona and the southern shore, redesigning the geographic scope of new alliances and new synergistic policies for the future. Today's European context requires a new strategic vision for all its cities, Torino included.

REFERENCES

Dal Pozzolo, L. and Benente, M. (2006) *Baroque: 300 Years Old and as Young as Ever*. Torino: Umberto Allemandi Editore.

Fondazione Cassa di Risparmio di Torino (2006) *Visiting the City*. Torino: research realized by Fondazione Fitzcarraldo.

Fondazione Fitzcarraldo (2002) *Il pubblico di mostre e musei in Piemonte*. Torino: Città di Torino e Fondazione Fitzcarraldo.

OCP (2001) *Il profilo dei visitatori e il marketing delle mostre a Torino*. Torino: Osservatorio Culturale del Piemonte.

OCP (2007) *Relazione Annuale 2006*. Torino: IRES Piemonte.

OCP (2008) *Relazione Annuale 2007*. Torino: IRES Piemonte.

OCP (2009) *Relazione Annuale 2008*. Torino: IRES Piemonte.

OCP (2010) *Relazione Annuale 2008*. Torino: IRES Piemonte.

OMERO (Olympics and Mega-Events Research Observatory) (n.d.), www.omero.unito.it/?Omero.

CHAPTER 30

VANCOUVER: THE ENIGMATIC EMERGING CULTURAL METROPOLIS

Catherine Murray and Tom Hutton

This chapter explores the recent growth of Vancouver as a classic case of the post-Fordist economy that is deeply insinuated in local-global flows of capital and immigrants. A sophisticated system of cultural governance, combined with a self-conscious design doctrine of 'Vancouverism' have enabled a diversified cultural economy to emerge. The hyper-pluralist, trans-local cultural milieu is characterized by small to medium-sized enterprises, a progressive ensemble of regulation and redistribution, and pockets of aesthetic excellence. Vancouver has evolved impressively as a place with both limitations and vital cultural potential, despite its systemic marginalization by the federal government.

Introduction

Vancouver celebrated its 125th anniversary in 2011. Its metropolitan area population is now the size that the 'global cities' of New York and Paris were in 1900, similar in scale to others in the Pacific Northwest like Seattle. The economy is now estimated at $90 billion in 2010, placing it 64th among global city-regions. What niche will Vancouver occupy within the global hierarchy of cities and transnational societies in 2100? Optimistic projections foresee a population of some 5–6 million by 2085, the size Hong Kong is today (Hume, 2011) but such visions are easily contested (Andrew and Smith, 1999). Shaped by 'place luck' as much as exogenous global forces which are characterized by opportunism and flexible accommodation, Vancouver's growth has been moderated by a thick democratic regime, characterized by organized municipal parties representing neo-liberal growth and social democratic coalitions; grass-roots consultative processes; and multicultural adaptation (Lightbody, 2006; Brunet-Jailly, 2008; Good, 2009). Despite its loose federated structure (quite different from the defensive response of amalgamation pursued by Montreal and Toronto in global competition), we argue this regime has been relatively successful in balancing global and local social, economic and political forces to produce a hyper-pluralist face, with the second highest incidence of immigrant visible minorities on the continent, and trans-local cultural milieux, as measured by dual passports – 14 per cent and rising among recent immigrants (Statistics Canada, 2001b).

Historical economic narrative of the city-region

Up to the 1960s, Vancouver presented the classic features of the 'regional central place'. The Vancouver region was tightly bonded to an expansionist provincial natural-resource staple sector by means of administrative functions, major resource processing installations along the Fraser River and around False Creek, and the export functions of the Port of Vancouver. The metropolitan region was largely 'monocentric' (i.e. dominated by the higher-order services and advanced industries of the City of Vancouver), but was already experiencing increasing suburbanization of population and new industrial investment. The Vancouver economy thus functioned largely as a specialized 'core' to the provincial 'periphery', with relatively weak connections with the national and international markets in the period (Davis, 1976). Vancouver was seen by some as 'downtown British Columbia', experiencing a dramatic expansion of higher-order office employment which created over time a 'new middle class'

(Ley, 1996). The spatial mismatch between downtown office development and employment growth and an increasingly suburban residential orientation led in large part to the first modern regional plan, the *Livable Region 1976–1986,* predicated on a classic urban containment model (Bourne et al., 2011). This plan favoured the development of new regional town centres, investments in regional transit, and stronger development controls over the downtown, but was soon abandoned with a sharp global recession.

Box 30.1   Granville Island Cultural District

In the 1970s, visionary city and federal politicians developed one of the first revitalization projects in Vancouver to develop a cultural precinct based on mixed use. It features heavy industry (a cement factory), residential development, 53 art galleries, the Emily Carr Art School, the oldest craft co-op in Vancouver, and a thriving public market which is at the epicentre of the 100-mile *diet* launched from Vancouver (where all foods consumed are sourced from a 100 mile radius). Granville Island attracts more than 10 million visitors annually, making it among the most used cultural destinations in Canada. Such urban revitalization efforts were closely tied to the theories of noted urbanist Jane Jacobs, and followed on successful protests among downtown residents of Chinatown, which stopped a proposal for a major urban expressway. Today, Vancouver is unique among North American cities for its absence of these obvious blights on the landscape.

The 1980s was the major, redefining decade of wrenching changes in Greater Vancouver's development path. A serious commodity price shock in the early 1980s, experienced initially in the resource-dependent British Columbia interior and 'periphery', was rapidly transmitted to metropolitan Vancouver. Unemployment in Vancouver reached almost Depression era levels of 13–14 per cent. The depth of this recession produced profound structural as well as cyclical effects in the regional economy, including the closure of resource-processing operations. A series of corporate mergers and acquisitions began to shift the locus of control for British Columbia's resource economy from downtown Vancouver to Toronto and higher-order international business centres, further modifying Vancouver's linkage structures and provincial roles. But by the mid-1980s global processes and experiences drove recovery and restructuring and originated a long period of growth for the region, which has persisted through to today.

Some illustrative components of Vancouver's globalization experience over the 1980s included (1) large international immigration, notably from Hong Kong and other regions of the Asia-Pacific; (2) foreign direct investment (FDI) in Vancouver's property market, with the example of the Hong Kong Bank of Canada's symbolic head office building on West Georgia; (3) 'hallmark events', notably Expo '86, which attracted major federal government investments in Vancouver's infrastructure and international marketing; (4) urban mega-projects (described by Kris Olds (2001)), as exemplified by Li Ka-Shing's purchase of the former Expo site for the Concord Pacific Place project; and (5) external market reorientation of Vancouver's businesses. With regard to the latter, a series of empirical studies demonstrated an increasing international (and more specifically Asia-Pacific) market orientation, both for many of Vancouver's services and manufacturing industries (see Edgington and Goldberg, 1989; Hayter and Barnes, 1990; and Davis and Hutton, 1991).

But the most influential drivers of growth and change in the 1980s included international immigration, the private sector, and senior government investments and policy initiatives. These federal and provincial investments included housing, infrastructure, higher education, the Skytrain, and especially Expo '86.

Box 30.2 The Expo '86 gamble

Vancouver's bid to host over 50 nations at the Expo '86 World Fair to mark its centennial attracted chief architect Bruno Freschi to open up the industrial lands of the North Shore of the False Creek, and netted 22 million visitors. Expo '86 left an indelible mark on Vancouver's built landscape, with a geodesic dome as Science Museum, the imitation Sydney Sails for Canada Place (a convention centre and not Opera House) and Plaza of Nations. Losses were estimated at over $300 million, but the event marked Vancouver's coming of age as a landing strip for international capital (Berelowitz, 2005), persuading powerful Hong Kong investor Li Ka-Shing to invest in the Concord Pacific development which started the revitalization of Yaletown today. It is also attributed, falsely, for the growth in the cultural tourism industry, which began to accelerate in the 1990s (McMartin, 2010). The impact of Expo '86 was mixed in the arts and culture sector, causing a short-term loss of revenues for many cultural organizations, but not long dampening the ensuing decade of explosive growth.

The crucial role of local governments in shaping a positive environment for development should, however, be acknowledged, as seen in the quality of local services, recreation and amenity provision, and community planning.

The last decade of the twentieth century saw a consolidation of the redefining changes of the 1980s, including (1) a new sequence of immigration (but with diminished inflows from Hong Kong, and increasing emphasis on China and South Asia as 'donor' societies); (2) the growth and maturation of major employment clusters in suburban municipalities (such as Vancouver International Airport [YVR], the port expansion, Simon Fraser University, British Columbia Institute of Technology, and several regional town centres in Richmond and Surrey), as well as considerable dispersion of investment and jobs; and (3) the comprehensive reshaping of Vancouver's downtown with over 150 high-rise towers. Arguably, the signature strategic policy initiative of the post-war era in Vancouver – the seminal Central Area Plan (approved in 1991) – reallocated land resources through comprehensive re-zoning to privilege high-rise housing in the core beyond a smaller, consolidated CBD, and also reserved significant spaces in the inner city for a mix of activities under the 'choice of use' nomenclature, enabling the emergence of a new palette of specialized production districts and sites. Second, official heritage designation for buildings and landscapes in (notably) Yaletown, Victory Square and Gastown indirectly at least preserved the crucial built environments for new media industries.

The region's economic trajectory took on a pervasive *knowledge-intensive* quality, observed in the focus on educational standards and skills of the workforce, emergence of downtown university hubs, and growth of the international education market. The growing ascendancy of creative industries and of information-based, contact-intensive industries and the 'technological deepening' of production processes were readily seen in the concentrations in the downtown area. But the 'knowledge-based economy' was also increasingly a feature of the new spaces research and development, and advanced-technology manufacturing in suburban communities, notably in Burnaby, Richmond and North Vancouver, and it is this sector which produces a rate of patent production on par with Toronto (Agrell et al., 2011; Conference Board of Canada, 2011). Yet Vancouver has little in the way of high-end technology capacity in the new knowledge economy, as symbolized by its main rival Seattle in the Pacific North West (lacking the city's multinationals like Weyerhaeuser, Boeing, Microsoft, Starbucks and Amazon).

More emphasis in the 1990s was placed on the quality of urban design in the downtown (and in the City and region at large), and on the emergence of an 'experiential', high-amenity urban core and sub-urban centres (Punter, 2003). This new emphasis on design quality was intended to cater to the tastes and preferences of a rapidly-growing Central Area residential population and to the increasingly multi-cultural suburban communities, as evidenced by the incorporation of Asian design principles in a growing number of commercial centres in Richmond, Surrey, and elsewhere. The emergence of this distinctive civic design culture in Vancouver (called Vancouverism) also appeals to sophisticated international tourists and visitors, underscoring the centrality of amenity to the twenty-first-century urban economy. Part city marketing ploy/self-aggrandizement, and part ideo-logy, Vancouverism denotes a development ethos marrying private capital development with social economy innovations.

Box 30.3   Vancouverism

Vancouverism is a planning design ethos which incorporates a participative, responsive and design-led approach to urban regeneration and development. It features an innovative approach to mega-project planning, a system of cost and amenity levies on major private sector development schemes which have contributed over 18 cultural facilities, and other important social spaces, a participative CityPlan process to underpin active neighbourhood planning and extensive design guidelines. (See Punter, 2004; Berelowitz, 2005; Boddy, 2004).

After 2000, the emergent new cultural economy has produced distinctive new spaces and land-scapes of specialized production, together with aff-iliated consumption, opportunities for spectacle, and patterns and forms of housing. The principal bastions of the cultural economy in Vancouver include major clusters of key industries within the (former) obsolescent wholesaling districts of the CBD Fringe and the heritage districts of the inner city. These concentrations of new media and other emergent industries within the high-integrity con-servation districts and neighbourhoods of the inner city can be read as following the well-established patterns of other significant centres of the cultur-al economy, including, notably, London, New York, Toronto and San Francisco. While to some ana-lysts, notably neo-Marxists, the infiltration of these areas can be attributed principally to rent differen-tials and to the operation of capitalist property markets, there is an at-least equally cogent litera-ture which emphasizes instead the affinity for highly-textured heritage areas among artists, designers, and other cultural workers. But in the Vancouver case, the long-running attrition of the City's corporate head office sector since the 1990s (ceding predominance on this indicator to Calgary, which has half the population) has provided oppor-tunities for the re-colonization of CBD office space for many (broadly-defined) creative firms, inclu-ding videogame producers, computer graphics, and other new media. Thus here we see a critical intersection of the city's post-staples and post-cor-porate development trajectories within an emergent new economy of enterprises and labour engaged in the production of semiotic outputs.

New media firms now number over 600, clustered within a new space-economy constructed on the ashes of the obsolescent staples built environment of the inner city, including, notably, greater Yaletown, as well as Gastown, south of Granville Island, and Mount Pleasant and generating over $2 billion in revenues (Vancouver Economic Development Cor-poration, 2010). Its film production sector is now the third largest in North America, predominantly pro-ducing for the global market, with highly val-ued labour for pre- and post-production, generating another $1.3 billion (British Columbia Film, 2010). Vancouver has succeeded in attracting the highest proportion of artists, cultural workers and creators in any major Canadian city (Hill Strategies, 2010), and these workers are less centralized than in Toronto or Montreal. Finally, it is the last decade when cultural tourism made its power visible in this province. In 2004, the most recent data available, Vancouver received 8.53 million visitors, 41 per cent of whom attended a cultural event: a proportion significantly higher than either Montreal or Toronto, at 29 per cent respectively (see City of Vancouver, n.d.). While it may be argued that most cities of the 'West' experienced industrial decline and a shift to service-based production and lifestyles in the last decades of the twentieth century, Vancouver stands out as a paradigmatic exemplar for both the totalizing quality and rapidity of its transformation. As we have seen, it was the temporal intersection of its staples economy collapse and inflows of international immigration and capital, notably from the Asia-Pacific, that enabled change that occurred over longer periods in many other cities.

At this point in the city's economic narrative, Vancouver 'punches above its weight' despite its modest population (576,000 in the city and 2.1 million in 22 municipalities in the surrounding region, according to Statistics Canada's 2006 census (cited in City of Vancouver, 2008b)) and truncated corporate sector, similar to a Stockholm or Vienna today, but eclipsing them in competitive city discourses. Global city processes regularly recognize the city as the world's most liveable place by the Economic Intelligence Unit (Mason, 2003). Selective efforts to attract mega-events by its community leaders have insinuated Vancouver into international discourses on the improvement of human settlements and urban sustainability, such as Habitat 1976, the Second World Urban Forum of 2006, and the City has won sustainability awards (Marchington, 2011). Also, aggressive courting of international exhibitions to attract tourists and investment, such as the opportunities of Expo '86, have left a lasting imprint on urban transport and local development, and the City is now poised to exploit the legacy of the 2010 Winter Olympics. Vancouver has constructed a global reputation around architectural and landscape design (with locals Arthur Erickson, Bing Thom), lifestyle fashion (with Mountain Equipment Co-op, Arcteryx, Lululemon) and especially aboriginal visual arts markets (Emily Carr, Bill Reid, and contemporary aboriginal artists like Brian Jungen: see Sacco et al., 2007; Cernetig, 2010; Griffin, 2010). It has achieved very high international 'brand recognition': like Lady Ga Ga, it can go by its own name, without a national identifier (Cernetig, 2008).

Cultural governance and policy style

Detailed cultural planning has somewhat constrained this local–global growth coalition since the 1970s. Predicated initially on a growing self-recognition as a Western Canadian art centre of considerable significance (see MacDonald, 1992) Vancouver's civic cultural policy has evolved to a self-conscious blend of entrepreneurialism and social innovation (Brunet-Jailly, 2008; Weiler and Mohan, 2009). Quite unlike Toronto's close alliance with a creative class approach, Vancouver's cultural policy emerged from the social policy department of the city bureaucracy, and endorsed participatory values, which are entirely consistent with social progressivism[1] and neighbourhood development as expressed in a motion adopted by Council in 1987. Separation of the administrative body for the Office of Cultural Affairs (OCA) from social planning was achieved in time for Expo '86. The first Canadian city to tie participatory cultural democracy to an explicit 'creative city' aspiration in 1986 (Duxbury, 2004), Vancouver led the inception of the Creative City Network of Canada, a national professional network of cultural planners since the late 1990s, and became twice recognized as a cultural capital of Canada in the past decade (in 2003 and 2011).

In general, the Vancouver cultural economy is marked by a well-developed urban professional ethos, a relatively 'un-steered' set of provincial tax incentives to grow the cultural industries in the face of federal marginalization, a mature system of municipal cultural governance and instruments to protect the high and lively arts and a stable set of values which persists despite partisan political difference. An important measure of the robust nature of public cultural governance is continuous attention, and widespread community consultation. There have been repeated revisions to Vancouver's cultural policy goals in each decade of growth (1983 Arts Means Business; 1987 Cultural Plan; 1992 Vancouver Arts Initiative; 2006 Creative City Conversations; 2008 Cultural Plan; 2009 Cultural Infrastructure Plan); widespread consultation (most recently with an arts-sponsored summit in Surrey in 2010); and the emergence of fully-fledged programme evaluation methods conducted by third parties (Ference Weicker & Company, 2008; Artscape, 2008). Within the city, cultural impacts are now considered horizontally and integrated as far as possible across all planning processes, including economic ones.

The goal of Vancouver's 2008 Cultural Plan was to 'reflect the aspirations of a 21st century creative city ... on the leading edge of cultural activity and development, a city of learning where connectivity is the hallmark, building on the unique identity of its vibrant neighbourhoods' (City of Vancouver, 2008a). Today, the City has an extensive repertoire of cultural programmes, appointed a colourful Poet Laureate,[2] introduced annual Arts Awards, including a Vancouver Book award, and, together with the powerful Parks and Recreation Board, created 22 lively community centres in its various neighbourhoods. The policy tools of public ownership, regulation, peer-based public art programmes and finally direct cultural operating grants are extensively used. The OCA employs 21 staff in 2011, surpassing its provincial counterpart (Murray, 2009) and equivalent to Seattle. It has elicited donations of public space from private developers in return for more density in development and in turn then leases it long-term to some 13 'chosen cultural instruments', such as the Scotia Bank Dance Centre, the Arts Alliance, ArtStarts in Schools or Vancouver International Film Festival, built since 1990, and most recently with the Vancouver Symphony for a new community music school, popular with Asians – what some have called public works through negotiated planning agreements (Cupa, 2007; Artscape, 2008; MacDonald, 2010).

Box 30.4   The neighbourhood strategy of multi-use centres

The Roundhouse is an anchor in the new Yaletown, which is typical of the City's approach. At any one time, the Roundhouse can house a theatrical showing of a mime performance of the city's development, a photo exhibit, and an intense soccer game among Somali and Saudi youth in the adjacent gym. Such multi-use recreation centres indicate a powerful Parks Board, attuned to the use of public and green space to maximal cultural effect.

The city has also advanced imaginative public art programmes and supported the projects of some 341 arts, culture and heritage organizations between 2001 and 2006 (Ference Weicker & Company, 2008).[3] In 2007, the most recent year for which data are available, the City disbursed $10 million in grants to some 200 organizations, or per capita some $16 dollars.[4] Most of the money is concentrated among flagship municipal cultural institutions of the Vancouver Art Gallery, the Vancouver Symphony, Vancouver Museum, the HR MacMillan Planetarium and its Civic Theatres programme. About half (45 per cent) of its grants are under $10,000. A comparative survey of arts groups and creators reported that 'Vancouver is seen as a model in the delivery of arts and culture programs' (Ference Weicker & Company, 2008: 32), suggesting cordial relations between city-state and clientele despite persistent income precarity among cultural workers.[5]

Despite a city fiscal base sorely constrained by the Canadian Constitution to property and related tax raises, then, Vancouver spends 25 per cent more on recreation and culture than the Canadian average (Smith and Stewart, 2009).[6] It has also sought and received provincial support for imposing a 2 per cent hotel tax to reinvest in cultural tourism related projects (Burkheimer, 2008; Smith and Stewart, 2009). A sore point in Metro Vancouver has been the imbalance in local investment, with very little cultural support forthcoming from the other 22 municipalities of the region, despite the fact that over half of the regular theatre patrons in the civic-owned theatres come from the surrounding municipalities. The fastest-growing edge city, Surrey, is involved in developing its own cultural plan and creating a downtown core with flagship public institutions such as a library and proposed multi-use performance centre (Murray, 2008). North Vancouver and Port Moody have explicitly both developed arts plans, with the latter, the first terminus of the railroad, now calling itself a 'City of the Arts'. There is slow recognition in metropolitan governance of coordinating cultural initiatives or potential for scale economies.

As an emerging cultural metropolis, we argue, Vancouver is a poster child for the eclipse of the nation-state as the organizing focus of cultural policy.

The level of federal per capita cultural spending in Vancouver's home province, British Columbia, is among the lowest in Canada, proof of decades of systematic marginalization by national cultural policy. The federal government locates no other national cultural institution or museums here.[7] Without a large capital partner from the senior government or corporate sector, Vancouver's Cultural Facilities Plan 2008–2025 advocates an integrated planning approach to its many neighbourhoods, and in a mixed-use development intended to restrain gentrification, moved some of its offices into the new Woodward's downtown development in Vancouver's

'poorest postal code'.[8] Noticeably absent was any mention of the needs of the Vancouver Art Gallery, which has outgrown its location, or any new cultural precinct – which has involved the imagination of noted architect Bing Thom. Unlike Toronto, Vancouver has not constructed major iconic architectural places of cultural archive or consumption in the past decade, preferring instead to sink over a billion dollars into a major marine-side Conference Centre and refit its centre city Stadium. A recent decision to reject a half-billion dollar casino development, in hot downtown oppositional politics, suggests the struggle remains lively.

Box 30.5 Vancouver 2010 Winter Cultural Olympiad

The legacy of the most recent multilevel flagship project, the Cultural Olympiad of 2010, is mixed at the time of writing. Hampered by a subsequent provincial cut to cultural budgets, it is not clear that the Olympiad worked either to attract much international media attention, infuse local organizations with tourism revenues, commission new works (except for Lillian Alling by the Vancouver Opera), or keep the promises of the bid for importation of marquis international artists (Low and Hall, 2011). Local arts groups were pitted against each other in a competition which left winners (the Vancouver Art Gallery) and losers (the Scotiabank Dance Centre's conflict with the preferred Olympic Sponsor Programme with many organizations returning to pre-2007 revenue levels, suggesting a weak track record for mega-events in the local cultural economy. The City is expected to absorb losses of at least 5 per cent from the Athlete's Village housing complex.

If official multiculturalism may be said to have three stages – demographic, symbolic and structural – Vancouver's cultural economy is evolving to the third (Uyesugi and Shipley, 2005). In 2006, Statistics Canada found 41.7 per cent visible minorities in the Metro Vancouver Census Metropolitan Area (CMA), placing it just behind the Greater Toronto Area (Statistics Canada, 2010b). Today, the Vancouver scene attracts 150,000 international students annually, again, mostly from the Asian Region. Built places like the Chinatown/Strathcona district's Sun Yat-Sen Gardens, its heritage gates, and Arthur Erickson's major Sikh temple on Marine Drive which later became a magnet for the emergence of the Punjabi Market in the South Main (SoMa) District are testament to a broad public–private 'Pacific Rim consensus' (Good, 2009) that crosscuts ideological differences across the municipal parties. As early as 1988, the City Council passed

a multicultural equal opportunity programme, which launched the Hastings Institute and designed the Collingwood Neighbourhood House to promote the intercultural interaction that can occur in a mongrel city (Sandercock, 2003). The City devotes more resources to community integration (and especially service agencies like SUCCESS or MOSAIC) than other municipalities, and this may be one reason why racialized conflicts have been relatively few (Hiebert and Ley, 2003). The 2010 Olympics, unlike Expo '86, represents a crucial but as yet incomplete cultural symbol of a partnership with the aboriginal population – of which Vancouver has the second largest in Canada outside Winnipeg. The Olympiad featured the local Vancouver Olympic corporation (Vanoc), the City, and the Four Host Nations (Lil'wat, Musqeum, Squamish and Tsleil Waututh) as full partners in the Cultural Olympiad. Proposals for a national aboriginal art gallery to be located in Vancouver – already the site of a thriving commercial aboriginal art market estimated at some $100 million – represent a further important step in aboriginal integration and reconciliation, but these fall on deaf federal ears.

By its 125th anniversary, Vancouver has become a centre of intercultural, transnational fusion, combining 'Wet' coast ecology, Asia Pacific and First Nations signs, symbols and practice. Chinatown, Little Italy, Indian markets, cricket pitches, Korean restaurants in Coquitlam, South Asian housing cooperatives, and mosques are all part of Vancouver's neighbourhoods.[9] Richmond is predominantly Asian, but ethnic enclaves of Iranians in North Vancouver, Koreans in Coquitlam and South Asians in Surrey demonstrate how such 'ethnoburbs' can offer the social ties and networks that help locate shelter and jobs while avoiding segregation. Vancouver is often exploited by Richard Florida as an exemplar of cosmopolitan values attractive to the creative class (Florida, 2009). In a word play derived from Richard Florida's formula, *T* for *t*olerance stands for *t*roubling or contesting gender norms, establishing the West End and Commercial Drive areas, well known as gay and lesbian enclaves respectively, which are spreading across the cities now with the passage of gay marriage laws (Bouthillette, 1997). Vancouver also was home to the first Canadian Gay parade in 1971, which has grown to become one of the largest in North America, attracting over 500,000 in 2008 (Christie, 2009). It also stands for translation or interpolation of Cantonese, Mandarin, Punjabi, Farsi, Korean and a myriad of aboriginal mother tongues in cultural production. A recent study of local third or non-English/non-French language media found over 144 local and mostly unregulated print media and a surprising incidence of new venture start-ups among the rapidly growing South Asian (33), Iranian (8) and Korean language publications (22), one-third of them launched since 2000 (Murray et al., 2007). What is moot is the extent to which this cosmopolitanism is superficial lifestyle or a successful graft producing a hyper-plural, hybrid cultural animus with generative potential.

Sharp fault-lines pose intractable challenges for the next millennia. As Vancouver's partisan political model of governance might predict, there is discord in Eden. A growing social gap between urban aboriginals and others occupying the unceded territory of the Coast Salish; a seemingly inexorable cycle of gentrification and geographically and class-segregated poverty in hotspots across the Metro area, and the weakening in rates of economic inclusion of recent immigrants are posing intractable challenges for the twenty-first century, especially if the neo-liberal forces of economic rollback of the state continue to gather. The City Cultural Plan is signalling a change of language about changing its role from planner/enabler to facilitator/catalyst – what some fear is a code word for retreat from its formula for social progressivism.

Conclusion

Vancouver represents an enigma to its settlers and sojourners: the image of a postmodern boom town-city, increasingly uncoupled from its own hinterland, floating in the global imaginary, whose material processes of production are masked with a sign 'Under Construction' – a city constantly in the (re) making, physically, socially, culturally and economically. Vancouver remains an enigma among cultural geographers and policy-makers, widely accepted as having a well-developed 'sense of place' among residents and visitors alike, but dubbed variously 'Fantasy Government' (Persky, 1989; Hannigan, 1998), 'Dream City' (Berelowitz, 2005), 'Postmodern City' (Delaney, 1995) and 'A city of glass' (Coupland, 2010). The visual images of the city pose it like a simulacrum of staggeringly beautiful natural sea and mountain-scape, vulnerable at any time to a major seismic shock. Among the most puzzled by the Vancouver art scene was the Italian analyst Pier Luigi Sacco (see his chapter on Venice in this volume), for whom 'Vancouver seems to lack a consistent cultural identity' and shows 'no evidence that her creative industries are overall taking a leadership role in defining a competitive creative economy model' (Sacco, 2006: 35) intimately linked to its historical heritage. Yet its citizens report a sense of belonging (68 per cent) which is higher than Toronto and Montreal (Vancouver Foundation, 2010), showing a strong likelihood that Vancouver will remain a 'sticky place' (Markusen and Gadwa, 2010). In cultural form, Vancouver excels in the visual arts, aboriginal arts and crafts, and contemporary arts led by early photo-conceptualists (Griffin, 2011). Ken Lum's installation *House of Realization* alone has shown in Beijing, Dubai, Vienna, Berlin, and Barcelona, suggesting that the fact that Vancouver does not yet have a strong commercial art market has endowed the city with more experimental genres (as have the vital artist-run centres that put artists in the roles of presenters as well as creators: see Graves, 2008). To be sure, there is no artistic super-brand yet, like that gestated by the Robert LePage theatre company or the *Cirque du Soleil* from Quebec. Instead, there are individual stars.

The challenge is to continue to grow that Vancouver frontier predilection for experimentation into a critical mass of talent and expertise that can drive intellectual properties locally and export them to the world. Vancouver represents a case for small to medium-size enterprise and a socially balanced model of cultural development in the global city circuit. Its cultural scene is polarized by healthy dialogue between its detractors and fans, who would like to see a concerted global city model more like Berlin, or Toronto, and applaud the ambitious curator of the Vancouver Art Gallery imported from Los Angeles for the next generation of arts ambition and iconic place-building (Berelowitz, 2005; Dwyer, 2008). Will it continue to rise in the global hierarchy? As the US loosens its immigration laws, and India and China both grow and provide sufficient stability that the migration of moneyed investors slows to a trickle, the competitive advantages may decline. Property values may experience a sharp correction, further weakening the middle class, and the lack of local 'big capital' may perpetuate a build-to-sell mentality among many of the current cultural enterprises (Barnes, et al., 2009). On the other hand, natural limits to cultural growth for a metropolis of Vancouver's size and provenance may be reached and be eminently self-renewing, innovative and sustainable. We conclude that Vancouver is a place that enjoys both vital cultural potential and serious limitations. Like the encounters of its first pioneers, Vancouver's next cultural century will unfold by act of will, collectively and decisively leaving behind its legacy of colonialism, racism and exclusion.

Notes

1   A social and economic strategy of 'embedded liberalism' is described by Canadian policy analyst Keith Banting (2006), emphasizing the development of a new variant of the welfare state in parallel with economic growth quite at odds with American midwest traditions. See Grodach and Loukaitou-Sideris (2007).

2   The current Poet Laureate, Brad Cran, is a spare-time tax accountant who wears an earring. He refused to participate in the 2010 Olympics, protesting against the exclusion of the female ski jumpers, and an injunction for all participants to refrain from derogatory remarks. Cran also protested against the decision by the provincial government to cut back cultural spending to arts groups by 90 per cent after the recession, since mostly, but not completely, restored.

3   The public art programme lagged Seattle's (established in 1990 rather than 1973; Stevenson, 1992). Initially opposed by the Urban Development Institute, the mandatory 1 per cent rule is extracted through private developers' commitment. It has recently supported Eagles in the City (Gloria Mass), the Laughing Man by (Yue Minjun) and Blue Trees (by Konstantin Dimopoulos) in the Vancouver Biennale 2011. The new Vancouver Convention Centre is the home of a massive series of art installations.

4   By contrast, Seattle invested $2.2 million to support 275 artists and cultural organizations in 2008 at a level of about $7.50 per capita (see www.seattle.gov/arts/funding/default.asp). Seattle has no overall cultural plan at the time of writing. Only San Francisco is similar to Vancouver in its level of public investment in culture on the West Coast. A Cascadia Arts Summit in 2008 provided the first Pacific Northwest policy exchange about cultural economy measures.

5   Vancouver is a festival city, second only to Quebec in attracting 3 million citizens. It is known for its Children's Festival, Folk Festival, Vancouver International Jazz Festival, Vancouver Film Festival, and edgy multimedia PuSH Festival, but has been hurt by the recent federal funding strategy to privilege size and market value. Overall, Vancouver cultural workers report average earnings which are relatively higher than most other cities at $29,400, an earnings gap of some 14 per cent below the general workforce (Hill Strategies, 2006) but weakest for dance and visual artists.

6   The federal spending per capita in 2002–2003 was $44 compared to an average of $109 across Canada, and $154 in Quebec (see Hill Strategies, 2005).

7   The regional office of Canada's national public broadcaster, the Canadian Broadcasting Company (CBC) in Vancouver has been systematically stripped of local TV programming to barely sustainable levels over the past two decades. The CBC has nonetheless cooperated with the city in a downtown revitalization of its federally owned facility, creating a public square abutting the Vancouver Public Library. In a move of quiet corporate insurrection, Vancouver CBC staff led the national launch of an online independent music service (Radio 3) based in Vancouver which has developed a reputation for tremendous innovation and alternative music distribution, forging one of the first podcast public radio deals with Apple iTunes.

8   The city has 14 sites of social housing and before the Olympics tried to reclaim over 1,000 single-room occupancy residences from ageing housing stock. Woodwards is a $330 million development designed by local architect

Gregory Henriquez, with 536 high-end condos, 200 soc-ial housing units built to Leadership In Energy and Environmental Design (LEED) standard, a public cultural amenity housing a new media start-up called W-2 which served as the alt.media hub in the Olympics, a depart-ment of the Office of Cultural Affairs, and Simon Fraser University's School for Contemporary Arts.

9   There is also growing awareness of the changing social composition of immigration: recent immigrants are less likely to be integrated in the workforce than their earlier counterparts. Researchers are speculating that there is growing social risk of a persistent urban immigrant underclass. Nearly four out of ten immigrants who landed between 1996 and 1999 have low incomes or live in families with low income – that is, income below one-half of the median. For very recent immigrants, average income was a little more than one-half of that of the Canadian-born, and for those who immigrated during the 1986–1995 period it was close to two-thirds of that of the Canadian-born. But during the period 1995–2001, the average income of very recent immigrants increased by one-third, showing some signs of social mobility (see Statistics Canada, 2001). A recent study of low-income hotel work-ers in Seattle and Vancouver found better quality of life and more social mobility in Canada; the study attributes these findings to more financial resources, better access to health care, a more effective urban infrastruc-ture, and relatively lower stress among workers. (See Zuberi, 2006; Pendakur and Pendakur, 2007; Paperny and Dhillon, 2011).

REFERENCES

Agrell, S., Ebner, D., VanderKlippe, W. and Perraux, L. (2011) 'Why Canada is Late to the Tech Party', *Globe and Mail*, March 29.

Andrew, Caroline and Smith, Patrick (1999) 'World Class Cities: Can or Should Canada Play?' In Caroline Andrew, Pat Armstrong and Andre Lapierre (eds), *World Class Cities: Can or Should Canada Play?* Ottawa: University of Ottawa Press, pp. 5–26.

Artscape (2008) *Cultural Facilities Priorities Plan: Final Report.* May, http://vancouver.ca/commsvcs/cultural/policy/plan/pdf/CulturalFacilities.pdf.

Banting, Keith (2006) 'Dis-embedding Liberalism? The New Social Policy Paradigm in Canada'. In David A. Green and Jonathan R. Kesselman (eds) *Dimensions of Inequality in Canada.* Vancouver: UBC Press.

Barnes, Trevor, Holbrook, Adam, Hutton, Tom and Smith, Richard (2009) 'Creativity and Innovation in the Vancouver City Region', paper for the Innovation Systems Research Network, November 5–6, Toronto.

Berelowitz, Lance (2005) *Dream City: Vancouver and the Global Imagination.* Vancouver: Douglas and McIntyre Publishing.

Boddy, Trevor (2004) 'New Urbanism: The Vancouver Model', *Design Observer*, 16(2).

Bourne, Larry S., Hutton, Tom, Shearmur, Richard and Simmons, Jim (2011) *Canadian Urban Regions: Tra-jectories of Growth and Change.* Toronto: Oxford University Press.

Bouthillette, Anne-Marie (1997) 'Queer and Gendered Housing: A Tale of Two Neighbourhoods in Vancouver'. In Gordon Brent Ingram, Anne-Marie Bouthillette and Yolanda Retter (eds), *Queers in Space: Communities, Public Spaces and Sites of Resistance.* Seattle, WA: Bay Press, pp. 213–233.

British Columbia Film (2009) *Annual Activity Report 2009–2010.* Accessed April 17 2011. www.bcfilm.bc.ca/down-loadables/ActivityReport_0910_Web.pdf.

Brunet-Jailly, E. (2008) 'Vancouver the Sustainable City', *Journal of Urban Affairs*, 30 (4): 375–388.

Burkheimer, Ian (2008) 'Cultural Planning, Tourism and the 2010 Olympics', part of Proceeding for the Symposium on the Cascadia Region Cultural Planning and Development. Centre for Community Arts and Cultural Policy, University of Oregon, November 7, Oregon.

Cernetig, Miro (2008) 'Vancouver Surpasses Toronto and Montreal in City Brands Index'. Accessed April 2 2011. *Globe and Mail*, March 17. http://urbantoronto.ca/showthread.php?6253-Vancouver-Surpasses-Toronto-and-Montreal-in-City-Brands-Index&p=147641.

Cernetig, Miro (2010) 'Extract a Dividend from Metro Vancouver's Building Boom', *Vancouver Sun,* April 26.

City of Vancouver (n.d.) *Culture Plan Implementation I: Cultural Tourism.* Accessed April 10 2011. http://vancou-ver.ca/ctyclerk/cclerk/20080626/documents/csb6.pdf.

City of Vancouver (2008a) Creative City: *Culture Plan for Vancouver 2008–2018*, report of the Creative City Taskforce. January, http://vancouver.ca/creativity/pdf/CulturePlan2008_%202018.pdf.

City of Vancouver (2008b) *2008–2023 Cultural Facilities Priority Plan: Final Report.* May, http://vancouver.ca/commsvcs/cultural/policy/plan/pdf/CulturalFacilities.pdf.

City of Vancouver (July 6 2008c) *Update on Cultural Precinct.* Accessed April 10 2011. http://vancouver.ca/ctyclerk/cclerk/20080724/documents/csb4.pdf.

Conference Board of Canada (February 2011) 'Metropolitan Outlook: Winter 2011'.

Coupland, Doug (2010) *City of Glass: Doug Coupland's Vancouver* (revised edition). Vancouver: Douglas and McIntyre Publishing.

Cupa, Daniel Robert (2007) 'Amenity Bonuses: Bridging Cultural Production and Consumption in Vancouver City Centre'. MA Thesis Urban Studies, Simon Fraser University, Burnaby.

Davis, Craig (1976) *An Interindustry Study of the Metropolitan Vancouver Economy*. Urban Land Economics Report No. 6. Vancouver: Faculty of Commerce and Business Administration, University of British Columbia.

Davis, Craig and Hutton, Thomas (1991) 'An Empirical Analysis of Producer Services Exports from the Vancouver Metropolitan Region', *Canadian Journal of Regional Science*, XIV: 375–394.

Delaney, Paul (ed.) (1995) *Vancouver: Representing the Postmodern City*. Vancouver: Arsenal Press.

Duxbury, Nancy (August 2004) *Creative Cities: Principles and Practices*. Background Paper F 47. Ottawa: Canadian Policy Research Network. Accessed April 2 2011. www.cprn.org/doc.cfm?doc=1083&1=en.

Dwyer, Victor (2008) 'Vancouver Doesn't Need to Try to be Other Places', *Globe and Mail*, May 10, T5.

Edgington, David and Goldberg, Michael (1989) 'Vancouver: Canada's Gateway to the Rim'. In Edward J. Blakely and Robert Stimson (eds), *New Cities of the Pacific Rim*. London: Routledge.

Ference Weicker & Company (2008) 'Evaluation of the City of Vancouver's Cultural Grant Program', prepared for the Office of Cultural Affairs, May 26, Vancouver.

Florida, Richard (2009) *Who's Your City?* New York: Basic Books.

Good, Kirsten (2009) *Municipalities and Multiculturalism: The Politics of Immigration in Toronto and Vancouver*. Toronto: University of Toronto Press.

Graves, Jen (2008) 'The Vancouver Problem: Why is Vancouver Art so Much Better than Here?' *The Seattle Stranger*, April 7. Accessed April 4 2011. www.thestranger.com/seattle/the-vancouver-problem/Content?oid=1220602.

Griffin, Kevin (2010) 'Beyond the Mask and Totem Pole: Vancouver is the Hub of a $100 Million a Year Market in Contemporary Northwest Coast Native Art', *Vancouver Sun*, October 9, F1.

Griffin, Kevin (2011) 'Reflections on Ken Lum', *Vancouver Sun: Arts and Life*, February 12, D1.

Grodach, Carl and Loukaitou-Sideris, Anastasia (2007) 'Cultural Development Strategies and Urban Revitalization', *International Journal of Cultural Policy* I, 13 (4), 349–370.

Hannigan, John (1998) 'From Fantasy City to Creative City'. In G. Richards and J. Wilson (eds), *Tourism, Creativity and Development*. London: Routledge, pp. 48–72.

Hayter, Roger and Barnes, Trevor (1990) 'Innis's Staples Theory, Exports, and Recession: B.C., 1981–86', *Economic Geography*, 66: 156–173.

Hiebert, Daniel and Ley, David (2003) 'Assimilation, Cultural Pluralism and Social Exclusion among Ethnocultural Groups in Vancouver', *Urban Geography*, January/February: 24(q).

Hill Strategies (July 2005) 'Government Spending on Culture in Canada 1992–2002', report prepared for the Canadian Conference of the Arts. Accessed April 19 2011. www.hill-strategies.com/docs/Government_spending2002.pdf.

Hill Strategies (March 2006) 'Artists in Large Canadian Cities', in *Statistical Insights in the Arts*, accessed August 27, 2011. http://hillstrategies.com/dos/Artists_large_cities.pdf.

Hill Strategies (February 2010) 'Mapping Artists and Cultural Workers in Canada's Large Cities', study prepared for the Cities of Vancouver, Calgary, Toronto and Montreal, based on 2006 census data.

Hume, Stephen (2011) 'A Goodness Risen from the Pulp Mill Haze', *Vancouver Sun*, April 2, A11–12.

Ley, David (1996) *The New Middle Class and the Remaking of the Central City*. Oxford: Oxford University Press.

Lightbody, James (2006) *City Politics*. Toronto: Broadview Press.

Low, Duncan and Hall, Peter (2011) 'The 2010 Cultural Olympiad: Playing for the Global or Local Stage?', *International Journal of Cultural Policy*. Available online 19 May, 2011.

MacDonald, Bruce (1992) *Vancouver: A Visual History*. Vancouver: Talon Books.

MacDonald, Chris (2010) *A Guidebook to Contemporary Architecture in Vancouver*. Vancouver: Douglas and McIntyre Publishing.

Marchington, Erin (2011) 'Fifth Annual Sustainable Cities Ranking', *Corporate Knights*, Winter 34: 21–24.

Markusen, Ann and Gadwa, Anne (2010) 'Arts and Culture in Urban and Regional Planning: A Review and Research Agenda', *Journal of Planning Education and Research*, 29(3): 379–391.

Mason, M. (2003) 'Urban Regeneration Rationalities and Quality of Life: Comparative Notes from Toronto, Montreal and Vancouver', *British Journal of Canadian Studies*, 16(2): 348–362.

McMartin, Pete (2010) 'Expo '86 and 2010 Olympics: Welcome to the Future Again', *The Vancouver Sun*, 15 January, http://communities.canada.com/vancouversun/blogs/mewritegood/archive/2010/01/15/expo-86-amp-the-2010-olympics-welcome-to-the-future-again.aspx. (Accessed April 23 2011).

Murray, Catherine (2008) 'Edge Cities: Competitive and Collaborative Creative Economy Strategy for Surrey', white paper for the Surrey Economic Summit, Centre for Policy Studies on Culture and Communities, August 31, Surrey.

Murray, C. (2009) 'Place-Making and Place Taking: Cultural Policy in BC', in Michael Howlett, Dennis Pilon and Tracey Summerville (eds), *British Columbia Government and Politics*. Toronto: Emond Montgomery. pp. 371–392.

Murray, Catherine, Yu, Sherry and Ahadi, Daniel (2007) 'Cultural Diversity and Ethnic Media in BC', report for the Department of Canadian Heritage, Western Region, SFU: Centre for Policy Studies on Culture and Communities. Available at: http://www.bcethnicmedia.ca/.

Olds, Kris (2001) *Globalization and Urban Change: Capital, Culture, and Pacific Rim Mega-Projects*. Oxford: Oxford University Press.

Paperny, Anna Mehler and Dhillon, Sunny (2011) 'Poverty Looks Like This', *Globe and Mail*, January 8 Section S.

Pendakur, K. and Pendakur, R. (2007) 'Minority Earnings Disparity across the Distribution', *Canadian Public Policy*, 33(1): 41–62.

Persky, Stan (1989) *Fantasy Government*. Vancouver: New Star Books.

Punter, John (2003) *The Vancouver Achievement*. Vancouver: University of British Columbia Press.

Sacco, Pier Luigi, Williams, B. and del Bianco, Elvy (2007) 'The Power of the Arts in Vancouver: Creating a Great City', Vancity Report. Accessed 24 August 2011. www. theholmteam.ca/votewendy/media/PowerOfTheArts.pdf.

Sandercock, Leonie (2003) *Cosmopolis II: Mongrel Cities in the 21st Century*. New York: Continuum.

Smith, Patrick and Stewart, Kennedy (2009) 'British Columbia'. In Andrew Sancton and Robert Young (eds), *Municipal Government in Canada's Provinces*. Toronto: University of Toronto Press, pp. 282–313.

Statistics Canada (2001) 'Recent Immigrants in Metropolitan Areas: Vancouver – A Comparative Profile Based on the 2001 Census'. Accessed April 11 2011. www.cic.gc.ca/english/resources/research/census2001/vancouver/parte.asp.

Statistics Canada (2001c) 'Trends and Conditions in Census Metropolitan Areas, 89–613-MWE', Canada's Global Cities: Socio-economic Conditions in Montreal, Toronto and Vancouver, No. 10. Accessed April 11 2011. www.statcan.gc.ca/pub/89-613–m/2006010/4054717-eng.htm.

Stevenson, Susan (1992) 'The Politics of Local Culture: The Evolution of Municipal Government Arts Policy in Vancouver.' MA Thesis, Simon Fraser University, Burnaby.

Uyesugi, Joyce Lee and Shipley, R. (2005) 'Visioning Diversity: Planning Vancouver's Multicultural Communities', *International Planning Studies*, 10(3&4): 305–322.

Vancouver Economic Development Corporation (2010) 'Vancouver as a City Region in the Global Economy, Outlook 2020 Project', March. Accessed April 4 2011. www.vancouvereconomic.com/userfiles/file/news/BCBC%20Report_Marchper cent202010.pdf.

Vancouver Foundation (2011) *Vital Signs*. Accessed April 4 2011. www.vancouverfoundationvitalsigns.ca.

Weiler, Joseph and Mohan, Arun (2009) 'Catalyst, Collaborator, Connector: The Social Innovation Model of 2010 Legacies Now: Case Study Commissioned for the International Olympic Committee'. Vancouver: 2010 Legacies Now Corporation. Accessed August 24, 2011. www.2010legaciesnow.com/media-centre-downloads/?tx_2010media.

Zuberi, Dan (2006) *Differences that Matter: Social Policy and the Working Poor in the United States and Canada*. New York: Cornell University Press.

CHAPTER 31

VENICE, RELOADED? A TALE OF URBAN LIFE (AND DEATH)
Pier Luigi Sacco

This chapter explores the situation of Venice in the broader context of the Veneto region of Italy, showing how the city is steadily evolving into a big theme park, as its residents, forced out by high real estate prices, move in ever larger numbers to the mainland city of Mestre, or to nearby towns. Pressures to maintain the status quo are very strong, driven by the high rents generated by the tourist trap of the island city. But, as the author argues, this pattern is unsustainable; it condemns the city to disappear. In its place, the author argues, the need is for a revitalization strategy that could turn Venice into a world-class specialized hub for cultural and creative production. This could in turn ensure its long-term sustainability within the surrounding Veneto region production system.

What is the 'real' Venice? Facing the urban oxymoron

Venice is an unicum in the global context for its historical, socio-economic, urban and demographic characteristics. But in fact, although the name is so widely known, it is somewhat under-recognized that the actual city of Venice is made up of three distinct segments: the world-renowned lagoon-city; Mestre, the large urban cluster on the mainland, so far mostly overlooked by tourists and often said to be grim and charm-free; and finally Marghera, a 'dirty' industrial town dominated by a large petrochemical complex, one of the biggest in Europe. Any analysis of the case of Venice therefore needs to keep this urban oxymoron firmly in its sights.

Today, despite their long history of coexistence, the three pieces are more separate entities than components of a whole urban body. Over time, the issue of the administrative separation between the island and mainland cities has been taken up several times, but always inconclusively. The three pieces, however, are barely kept together by the administrative borders, but each one follows its own urban discourse. The insular city is steadily evolving into a big theme park (Kay, 2008), with its millions of yearly visitors that represent a sumptuous rent to be extracted through the over-pricing of every good and service sold. Residents are being expelled because of high real estate prices, and tend to move to the mainland city, Mestre, or to nearby towns. Former residential houses in the island city are either transformed into bed & breakfasts or are bought by global real estate investors. The Venice that everybody has in mind, therefore, is losing the characteristics of a proper city and is becoming more like a service center, dismantling its social fabric and running the risk of turning into a 'ghost town' in the low season of tourism.

Mestre, on the other hand, is becoming the 'real' Venice, as far as actual urban life is concerned. It suffers, however, from a strong dualism with respect to the insular city, in that it is commonly seen as an anonymous conurbation, in spite of its secular history. Currently under way is the construction of a very ambitious museum, M9, which aims at reconstructing the history of the city during the twentieth century through state-of-the-art display techniques, but the project is very controversial as it directly concerns the central question of what should be the cultural identity of Mestre. What Mestre seems to be really evolving towards is an anonymous tertiary, directional city that ought to be the region's capital but lacks the charisma to really fill this role compared to cities with a much stronger identity and similar or greater socio-economic weight, such as Verona or Padua.

Marghera remains mainly a heavy industry hub, although its residential parts are now being slowly rejuvenated and, most interestingly, it is being increasingly colonized by creative professionals. This could be an early sign of a season of massive urban renewal, but the big 'if' regarding the future of this piece of the city is the renovation of the industrial brownfield, and the huge costs to be borne to de-pollute the area and make it inhabitable again. Ideally, if properly converted to private residences and creative businesses, Marghera could become a vital and complementary counterpart to the island city, but there is huge uncertainty as to whether the needed resources for this to happen will ever become available.

Thus, in a sense, Venice is at a crossroads. On the one hand, the insular one is a global city, visited yearly by millions of tourists, and attracting periodically world-class VIPs and opinion makers for cool, exclusive events, and especially so during the Venice Biennale top dates, such as the opening of the Visual Arts and Architecture Biennials, and the red carpets of the Cinema Festival. But if, on the other hand, the current trend is left to itself, this global stance will end up killing the city completely, turning it into a shining but empty urban shell. At that point, even the physical preservation of the city will be at risk unless the city is properly managed as a theme park – which seasonally turns into a city-wide VIP lounge. Alternatively, the city could take a different turn and rework its socio-economic development model under an ambitious and far-sighted local governance vision. But this second option would imply a sharp discontinuity with the recent (and not-so-recent) past, which has been characterized by a substantial institutional inertia that has caused the city to be governed essentially by day-to-day micro-bargaining on the part of local stakeholders and interests. As a consequence, and rather surprisingly, the city is unable to attract outside capital and resources outside the narrow realm of real estate speculation. It is as if the only good reason to invest in Venice is to find a spot to observe its magnificent decadence from

a convenient vantage point. If this conclusion has to be countervailed, however, it is necessary that the three cities begin to join up their urban discourses into one – a brand new one, in fact, which may work out a credible and viable urban identity for a post-industrial city of the twenty-first century. The aim of this short essay is to flesh out one such possible discourse, and to connect it to the ongoing tensions and transformations of the Venetian metropolitan area.

It's the economy, stupid! Why Venice is what it is (and why it will not change) ... probably

In the current debate, be it with a local focus or be it conducted in the context of some international conference, the reason why any serious reasoning about the reworking of the Venice development model is inexorably mocked as naïve is that the reigning economic forces keep the city stuck in the current status quo. On the one hand, being a perfect tourist trap, it generates a safe and very profitable rent, which nobody would be willing to give up easily, and this settles the island city issue. On the other hand, the petrochemical pole warrants a considerable number of blue-collar jobs, which could possibly not be absorbed in the short run by the urban renewal process, the latter being in turn very unlikely to be affordable in either the public or the private sector perspective – and this settles the Marghera issue. And as to Mestre, it is the part of the city where the real investments are being made, and whose well-being is partly supported by the rent collection of mainland-dwelling island landlords who find it more profitable to rent their house in the lagoon rather than continuing to live there, in an increasingly expensive, deserted and uncomfortable urban context – perfect for a romantic weekend but extremely unpractical for everyday life. So it doesn't look as if things will ever change...

On the other hand, if one looks at Venice from the perspective of the mid-Veneto-city region – which embeds the city within a large conurbation which includes major centers such as Padua and Treviso, plus a dense web of smaller towns in between – it turns out that it is at the center of an area which is subject to steady economic and social change, as revealed by the recent local OECD survey (2010), which also underlines how such change is actually driven by a deep, ongoing restructuring of the local productive system caused by global competitive pressures. The main issue that seems to emerge is that the very factors that have generated the economic success of the area so far are likely to jeopardize its future adaptability. If, on the one hand, the area has reacted to external shocks by developing a specialization on innovation and knowledge-intensive activities, this change has not been supported by the development of a fully-fledged knowledge society. The consequences of this gap are serious. The region has been unable to educate and/or to attract enough highly qualified workers, whereas the average levels of educational attainment lie at the lower ranks of OECD metro areas, apart from Istanbul and Izmir. Expenses in R&D are insufficient to be globally competitive, also because of both the resilience of a too narrow-minded entrepreneurial attitude based on the cost-effectiveness of small-sized firms that still make up a considerable part of the economy, and the metro region lying well below the average OECD levels in terms of innovation performance. Population is quickly ageing, whereas rates of female participation in the labor force remain low and the relative weight of informal workers high. Moreover, episodes of social hostility toward immigrants are not infrequent – and this is also due to the fact that, as the city is not competitive enough to attract qualified immigrants, it basically attracts unqualified ones. And this process ends up feeding the informal economy. Environmental quality has been seriously compromised by ineffectively regulated urban development which in the short run has favored economic activity and production costs reduction, but in the long run is compromising a key local asset, by favoring urban sprawl, pollution and territorial deterioration. In a nutshell, then, the metro area has moved toward a post-industrial level of development while at the same time maintaining a transitional culture that is mostly rooted in the self-referential family culture of the small-sized firm, which is in turn still very reminiscent of its rural and crafts background. This contradiction clearly leads to disruptive effects in the medium–long run, and the deep global crisis has only exacerbated this criticality.

On the other hand, the metro area also suffers from historical limitations in terms of key governance choices. The infrastructural endowment, which has been critically low for years, is now improving but at a pace that does not match the transformation of the economy. The metropolitan transport network is underdeveloped, and this causes constant street congestion due to excessively high levels of private traffic. At the same time, the main transportation hubs (the airport, the railway stations and the port) are inadequately interconnected. What is more, the issue of the physical deterioration of the insular city is far from solved, and there is a substantial uncertainty about its long-run sustainability – whose prospects are likely to be further worsened by the current trends of global climate change, and by the constant stress on the city's carrying capacity caused by the inasion of tourists. The continuing activity of the petrochemical pole is further damaging the fragile lagoon ecosystem, and pollution from heavy metals and other poisons is substantial. At the same time, the city has attempted several times to address all these issues through various rounds of strategic planning. These have been entirely inconclusive, however, because of the reciprocal vetoes of different organized local interests.

Seen in this light, a laissez-faire approach to the development of the metro area looks less and less practical and viable by the day. Even a cursory analysis clearly shows that this territory cannot survive another long spell of lack of governance. The present developmental vision is simply unable to tie the loose ends together, based as it is upon an obsolete conception of the role of human and social development in determining the economic performance of an advanced economy. Crucial decisions and consequent actions will have to be taken in terms of urban planning and soil protection, of infrastructural development, of labor market and industrial policies, of social cohesion and gender policies, and so on. The real issue, then, is that of nurturing a transformational vision that may sustain this discontinuity, and to serve as a platform that may aggregate consensus and resources toward a more adequate local development model.

Taking culture seriously in Venice? And if so, 'what' culture?

My main argument is that the key ingredient on which an effective transformational vision for Venice can be built is an appropriate model of culture-led local development. When associating Venice and culture, the spontaneous reaction is to think in terms of tourism. But for the reasons that have already been explained above, touristic flows as they are, at the moment, are part of the problem rather than of the solution (Russo, 2001; Caserta and Russo, 2002). Mass tourism in cities with a substantial cultural heritage, if not properly embedded in a more articulate value chain of cultural production and dissemination, seriously endangers the cultural identity of the city, by compromising its cultural vitality and yoking it to the consumer sovereignty of the tourist, who seems in general much more interested in following a pre-defined performative scheme (Edensor, 2001), based on the recognition of well-known landmarks and of their symbolic appropriation in terms of compulsory rituals, rather than in exploring a complex and mostly unknown and unfamiliar cultural ecology (Light, 2010). The design of tourist policies has to take these aspects into account, in order to integrate properly the tourist experience into a more sensible experiential framework of authenticity and meaning (Cohen, 1988). In the case of Venice, the dimension of the touristic ritualization of the experience of the city is so quintessential as to be inescapable, as the classic text of Mary McCarthy (1963: 7–8) puts it:

> ...there is no use pretending that the tourist Venice is not the real Venice. ... The tourist Venice is Venice: The gondolas, the sunset, the changing light, Florian's, Quadri's, Torcello, Harry's Bar, Murano, Burano, the pigeons, the glass beds, the vaporetto. Venice is a folding picture-post-card of itself.

Therefore, if tourism cannot (and should not) be turned down, at the same time it is not from here that one can move toward a cultural revitalization of the city. On the contrary, what is needed is to revamp Venice as a site of cultural *production*. The fact that the insular city is progressively losing inhabitants creates a 'social void' that tourist occupancy can fill only improperly, as its quick turnover causes the dismantling of the city's social fabric. On the other hand, this 'social void' would lend itself quite well to be colonized by cultural producers – who often tend to consider Venice, and with reason, to be a particularly suitable place for creative thinking and production. Although there is a strong global trend that leads cities to characterize themselves more and more intentionally as 'creative fields'

(Scott, 2001), there are few cities like the insular Venice that offer such ideal material conditions to be literally reshaped as a cultural and creative hub. What is even more interesting is the fact that in the city there is already an urban neighborhood that is only meant for cultural purposes, which remains unused for most of the time and is fit to become a residential center of production. This is the Giardini di Castello, the area of the city that hosts the national pavilions of the countries that participate in the Venice Biennale (or better, of those countries that were lucky enough to secure such a privilege while space in the Giardini was still available). Most of the pavilions are currently not equipped to host residential cultural activities throughout the year, but making the necessary adaptations for this to be possible would require relatively minor investments, which would probably be undertaken willingly by most (if not by all) the represented countries. Even this relatively small and straightforward action would be enough to give a strong turn to the social logic of space use of a relevant part of the city, by securing a permanent critical mass of outstanding creative professionals coming from a rich and diverse range of countries and cultural environments and working in the city on a medium–long term basis. The Giardini, moreover, sit in a relatively remote location, that is far away from the beaten tourist tracks around San Marco and Rialto, and that really becomes attractive to non-residents during the periods of Biennale events. Therefore, the installment of a creative community in the area would not initially clash that much with tourist flows, while at the same time it could demonstrate an alternative way of living the city. The financial sustainability of the project could be secured by the various countries (the pavilions maintain the territoriality of the country to which they belong), who would thus be able to take part in a unique, world-class, exceptionally prestigious residential program, as well as by supra-national institutions (one might think, for example, of EU-funded cultural programs). The countries not having a pavilion in the Giardini but willing to participate in the program could partner with countries with a pavilion, thus further contributing to the project's viability. Even if not all pavilions would be activated, a program such as this could easily become the largest and most important cultural residential project at the global scale, and would be likely to attract many potential partners and investors willing to take advantage of such a concentration of creative talent and of the unique physical and social milieu that hosts it, according to the dynamics singled out by Currid and Williams (2009).

The idea of 'colonizing' the Giardini with a cultural residential project is particularly apt in the Venice case in that it implies a minimal level of public intervention and therefore does not conflict with the currently low governance capacity of the local administrations. This said, there are of course several different unused facilities, both in the insular city and in the minor islands of the lagoon, which could be equally easily refurbished to host cultural and creative production activities with a relatively small investment. Simply limiting attention to now abandoned islands with adequate size and hosting reusable facilities, one can list many possible interesting candidates. Focusing on a specific quadrant of the lagoon, such as the Southern one, one finds, for example, a most interesting potential system of five islands with such characteristics: San Giorgio in Alga, Sant'Angelo della Polvere, Sacca Sessola, Sant Spirito, and Poveglia (Carletti, Pesavento and Solmi, 2011). In the case of such minor islands, cultural residential use is possibly the only one that can restore present patterns of permanent occupation, but what is of particular interest, again, is the fact that such patterns are not minor, isolated attempts, but components of a larger cultural regeneration plan. Such a plan would of course entail the provision of basic infrastructure such as regular transportation systems between the reactivated islands and the main island city, and so on.

An urban regeneration plan for Venice based on cultural production could thus be launched in a relatively painless way by simply re-using existing, unused spaces that already exist and would be difficult to re-use in other ways. It would therefore be possible to benefit from this alternative mode of using urban space without having to subvert the currently prevailing modes altogether. But there are also other unused pieces of the city which could be at least partially amenable to such uses. The first example that comes to mind is the large complex of the Arsenale, which already partially hosts activities of the Venice Biennale, including some new, temporary pavilions of countries such as China (and Italy itself), and which could at least partially host more cultural and creative production activities. The future use of large areas of the Arsenale complex is still undecided, and no clear alternative

plans have been presented so far. In turn, other promising locations, where one could again re-use facilities that are currently abandoned and with no clear prospect of utilization, could also be found on the mainland, starting with the large, fascinating Forte Marghera, a former military complex strategically located on the border between the mainland and the lagoon.

Availability of space, therefore, is far from being the issue, and compatibility with the already existing patterns of space use is in turn less critical than one could think at first glance. But the absence of major obstacles does not mean, of course, that the route is worth pursuing. What is the rationale behind the creative urban renewal of Venice? Once again, to understand this point, we must switch back to the larger territorial perspective, that of the city-region.

Venice as a (cultural) global gateway for the Veneto meta-system of production districts

Focusing on cultural production residencies may be dismissed as a purely tactical action, incapable of bringing about serious socio-economic change in a large metropolitan area. But such reasoning would amount to seriously underestimating the effects that massive cultural reactivation may have on the context with the characteristics of Venice. Moreover, it would mean failing to understand how this stimulus could carry over to various sectors of the economy, from the rejuvenation of traditional production (starting with Murano glass), to the implantation of new, creativity-based specializations. The leap from creative residency to creative entrepreneurship is shorter than one might think (Rosenfeld, 2004; Hutton, 2006).

As we have noted earlier, although the Veneto region is one of the most important industrial regions in Europe, it is at the same time burdened today by the consequences of an imperfect and too narrow-minded transition from a traditional manufacturing economy to a knowledge-intensive economy (and society). In order to complete such a transition more effectively, the region must develop in the direction of the now socially ubiquitous processes of knowledge generation and dissemination. Cultural production and access may be the factors that enable such a structural change (Sacco, Tavano Blessi and Nuccio, 2009). In fact, focusing on the narrow perspective of the cultural and creative industries alone, the Veneto region is among the top 25 in Europe in terms of volume of workforce, but this ranking is not matched in terms of relative economic size (Power and Nielsén, 2010). This is a clear indication of the fact that culture-led development is an under-recognized option in the current local model. In this context, on the other hand, the ongoing dynamics of cultural production shows that the 'hot spots' of cultural research and innovation are at the moment far away from Venice on the regional scale (Buscema, Sacco, Ferilli and Terzi, 2011) – another clear sign of the fact that, in the absence of any countervailing policy, the weight of Venice (and possibly that of the whole region) on the global cultural map is likely to diminish further.

But to understand the real potential of the cultural regeneration of Venice, one has not only to consider the 'internal' dynamics of the cultural creative sector, but also, and most notably, its potential complementarities with other, non-cultural, production and value chains. As in other regions with similar economic fundamentals, the manufacturing sectors of Veneto are decentralizing part of their production to countries with lower labor costs, while maintaining locally directional and creative/styling functions, and some of the innovation functions. But the latter are beginning to be relocated in turn in foreign regions with better innovation performance. For these production domains that do not belong to the cultural and creative sectors but are nonetheless increasingly aware of the competitive potential of sophisticated design-oriented approaches to production, distribution, marketing and communication, a substantial interaction with processes of production of creative ideas, contents and products may be extremely rewarding in terms of transforming their organizational culture (Aage and Belussi, 2008). In this perspective, then, Venice may become the 'cultural gateway' which is able to concentrate a world-class critical mass of creative talent that can then become available for creative and innovative interaction with the whole regional manufacturing system, thereby opening up further routes for the sustainability of the cultural program. At the same time, the further global visibility of Venice as a cultural hub would create a very important platform for the quality productions of the regional manufacturing system, opening up new markets and winning new clients by attracting

them to their home territory rather than having to travel to a myriad of potential market outlets. Attraction of potential clients to their own territory is, for Veneto firms, more than simply saving on travel costs: it is a unique opportunity to demonstrate the local, highly idiosyncratic mix of highly specialized skills, breath-taking heritage, and sophisticated lifestyle which lies behind the regional culture of production (and consumption) and that has made the Veneto one of the top manufacturing regions in Europe. In a nutshell, then, the economic sustainability of the cultural regeneration of Venice is an endeavor in which the whole regional productive system has a stake. This is so in terms of a much needed knowledge-intensive societal transformation as well as in order to open up a highly specialized global gateway where cultural production and creative innovation gradually overtake mass tourism as the main drivers of the local economy. And in fact, this changing balance in the productive specialization of the local economy would be likely to gradually transform the city's tourist market toward more knowledge-intensive (and possibly technologically supported) forms of touristic experience. Heritage itself could provide a powerful basis for the development of technologically mediated, heritage-related content that would be highly valuable for all kinds of content platforms with a global standing.

A major leap forward in the cultural regeneration of the city could thus bring about an effect that the existing local weaknesses in the more conventional economic fundamentals have prevented so far. This has to do especially with attracting major investment flows, the lack of which has contributed to slowing down the pace of economic growth and social transformation. Cultural regeneration, on the other hand, has the advantage that it can be implemented gradually, and with relatively modest levels of investment when compared to more traditional alternatives based upon high-tech innovation or on massive infrastructural change. Of course, if the development dynamics are properly sparked, both high-tech innovation and massive infrastructure development would follow, but the difference here is that they are seen not as the cause, as it is commonly understood, but as the consequence of the socio-economic revitalization of the city. And this means, in particular, that the possibility to decontaminate the Marghera brownfield, and to make Mestre the main directional hub of the region – that is to say, the successful integration of the three segments of the city in a coherent urban body – go hand in hand with the return of the insular city to proper urban life. Specifically, Marghera was once Europe's largest industrial area. Properly reclaimed, it could aspire to become Europe's largest creative hub, bringing the local capacity for workspace and residences to another order of magnitude, which at that point could be functional not only to the needs of the regional economy, but globally as well. If places like the Silicon Valley or Route 128 have become world references for technological innovation, couldn't the Venice area occupy an analogous slot for creative production?

And as for Mestre, the ongoing project of the M9 museum, which will be centered on the industrial history of the city, and which will establish itself as a state-of-the-art twenty-first-century display, could finally allow the 'grim' part of the city to reclaim a cultural identity of its own. It would also encourage further cultural participation from residents and foster culture-oriented renovation of unused or misused fragments of the city, while at the same time mixing them with advanced public and private directional functions. The urban oxymoron could thus be reconciled under the unifying transformational vision of culture-led local development, addressing some of the structural contradictions and at the same time exploiting a unique factor of comparative advantage that could really put the metro area on the global map in a truly sustainable way (in all senses).

A new birth as a city?

What is, ultimately, the primary effect that a cultural revitalization of Venice would have on its sustainability? Simply put, it would allow it to become a city again. The long-term residency perspective would allow cultural and creative producers to inhabit the city with their families; it would allow a new generation of children to be born and grow up in the insular city; it would mean the return of everyday neighborhood services to revive the local urban fabric that is now colonized by fast-food outlets and souvenir shops. We cannot forget that Venice is thought and felt to be the heritage of all humankind. Can we allow its cultural identity to be destroyed and its physical environment to be consumed for the sake of the local rent positions of a few interest groups that are willing to sell out the city to their private, narrow-minded advantage? Are we willing to renounce the possibility of trying an alternative, experimental route through the re-use of spaces now abandoned without a cause? If our replies are negative, then we are willing to believe in the possible rebirth of Venice as a city; we are capable of envisioning it as an exciting twenty-first-century urban center. The symbol of Venice's most important concert hall, *La Fenice*, is the phoenix, the mythological animal that is constantly reborn from its own ashes. One cannot choose a better metaphor for the new future we wish to see for the city – a future that is no longer a nostalgic replica of the past, but a visionary demonstration of the transformational potential of culture in a post-industrial socio-economy.

REFERENCES

Aage, T. and Belussi, F. (2008) 'From Fashion to Design: Creative Networks in Industrial Districts', *Industry & Innovation*, 15(5): 475–491.

Buscema, M., Sacco, P.L., Ferilli, G. and Terzi, S. (2011) 'The Geography of Cultural Production as a Pseudo-Diffusion Process: A TWC Approach to the Case of Regione Veneto, Italy', Working paper, IULM University, Milan.

Carletti, T., Pesavento, F. and Solmi, L. (2011) *Isolae. Tra astratto e concreto. Una proposta di riattivazione per alcune isole della Laguna di Venezia*. Unpublished dissertation, University of Ferrara.

Caserta, S. and Russo, A.P. (2002) 'More Means Worse: Asymmetric Information, Spatial Displacement, and Sustainable Heritage Tourism', *Journal of Cultural Economics*, 26(4): 245–260.

Cohen, E. (1988) 'Authenticity and Commoditization in Tourism', *Annals of Tourism Research*, 15(3): 371–386.

Currid, E. and Williams, S. (2009) 'The Geography of Buzz: Art, Culture, and the Social Milieu in Los Angeles and New York', *Journal of Economic Geography*, 10(3): 423–451.

Edensor, T. (2001) 'Performing Tourism, Staging Tourism: (Re)producing Tourist Space and Practice', *Tourist Studies*, 1(1): 59–81.

Hutton, T. (2006) 'Spatiality, Built Form, and Creative Industry Development in the Inner City', *Environment and Planning A*, 38(10): 1819–1841.

Kay, J. (2008) 'Welcome to Venice, the Theme Park', *The Times*, March 1. Available online at: www.timesonline.co.uk/tol/travel/article3454108.ece (last accessed April 30, 2011).

Light, D. (2010) 'Performing Transylvania: Tourism, Fantasy and Play in a Liminal Place', *Tourist Studies*, 9(3): 240–258.

McCarthy, Mary (1963) *Venice Observed*. New York: Harcourt Brace.

OECD (2010) *OECD Territorial Reviews: Venice, Italy*. Paris: OECD.

Power, D. and Nielsén, T. (2010) *Priority Sector Report: Cultural and Creative Industries*. Brussels: European Cluster Observatory.

Rosenfeld, S.A. (2004) 'Art and Design as Competitive Advantage: A Creative Enterprise Cluster in the Western United States', *European Planning Studies*, 12(6): 891–904.

Russo, A.P. (2001) 'The Vicious Circle of Tourism Development in Heritage Cities', *Annals of Tourism Research*, 29(1): 167–184.

Sacco, P.L., Tavano Blessi, G. and Nuccio, M. (2009) 'Cultural Policies and Local Planning Strategies: What is the Role of Culture in Local Sustainable Development?', *Journal of Arts Management, Law, and Society*, 39(1): 45–64.

Scott, A.J. (2001) 'Capitalism, Cities, and the Production of Symbolic Forms', *Transactions of the Institute of British Geographers*, 26(1): 11–23.

CHAPTER 32

CULTURES AND CITIES: SOME POLICY IMPLICATIONS
Yudhishthir Raj Isar

This chapter brings together a selection of messages in the volume that bear on how policy is either implemented or envisioned. As regards implementation, it focuses on three issues: long-term vision and continuity, transversality and robust cultural mapping. As regards 'vision' issues, it warns against the perverse outcomes of cultural infrastructure-led urban regeneration policy, it argues for cultural democracy rather than cultural democratization, it urges caution in the use of the 'creativity' paradigm but far greater audacity with respect to the challenges of cultural diversity and sustainable development. As the experience of the city of Barcelona is both exemplary and emblematic – displaying a range of noteworthy policy positions, as well as some negative outcomes – it is highlighted in the form of a separate box on pp. 331–333.

Rationale

This penultimate chapter recapitulates several of the messages regarding cultural policy and governance in cities contained in the present volume. Some of them, but not all; for the chapters reflect a diversity of city experiences and situations in the context of globalization that is far too great to summarize in a single short essay. Underlying that diversity, there are two common threads of recognition: that the cultural dimension is central to urban policy and governance in general, and that the number one policy priority is to increase the resources allocated to the culture in all senses of the term and deploy these resources more effectively. Yet, as Oakley writes in regard to London, the politics that shape cultural policies 'are no less conflicted, adversarial or complex than those of any other area of urban life', a point echoed in Richard's evocation of Marseille, as it prepares itself to be a European Capital of Culture, and confirmed by the experience of many other cities.

All the chapters take up overarching strategic or 'how to' questions of method, procedure and coalition-building for city policy-making in the cultural domain. But they do so by adding the globalization perspective, a new twist that is bound to enrich the already considerable literature that tells city leaders – as well as cultural activists – why the design of a cultural strategy is important and advises them on how to get those strategies right.[1] Some chapters tackle broader issues of deontology or ethos – in other words the visions that ought to shape the strategies. We shall emphasize these vision issues here. But before we do so, it would be appropriate to say a few words about the 'nuts and bolts' questions.

Implementation strategies

The contributors to this volume endorse many generic policy principles that have been recommended to nations and cities alike – in particular three of them.[2]

First, they all advocate the need for a long-term forward-looking vision that would allow urban policymakers to stay 'ahead of the curve', capable of anticipating coming changes in urban demography and in patterns of cultural production and consumption.

But the play of city politics makes the long-term orientation essential for such continuity a pipe dream, although there are exceptional cases such as that of Barcelona, where one party remained in power for 32 years (see Box 32.1). As Oakley reminds us in connection with the experience of London, developments in any particular cultural domain are determined by far more than cultural policies alone.

Box 32.1 Barcelona: a policy paragon?

Many observers see the recent refashioning of Barcelona as an exemplary set of cultural responses to the challenges of globalization that are also emblematic of the blessings and pitfalls of entering the great global game. Urbanists and culture mavens in general extol the 'Barcelona model' (Marshall, 2004) as a clearly envisioned long-term strategy of culture-led urban regeneration served by notable architects and urbanists, professionally managed over the years, deliberately designed to position the city in global cultural flows, implemented by a mixed-sector coalition of committed local actors and based on an apparent local consensus.[3] This strategy has deployed cultural projects of all kinds as the core components of a city rebranding process that is generally perceived to have operated for the commodity and delight of both local citizens and tourists alike.

These successes, it must be said, have been based in large part on ideal preconditions, beginning with a long-standing awareness of Catalan distinctiveness going back to the twelfth century, which, because it was so embattled under the Franco regime, re-emerged with considerable force in the late 1970s and was then legitimized by the devolutionary stance of the Spanish state. There has also been the strong commitment to the local cause of the city's socio-economic and intellectual elite. Finally, as a major port city, Barcelona has a long practice of outside connections, whether with the rest of Spain, the Mediterranean or the whole world. The city authorities have capitalized on all these assets in a manner that gives a look of coherence, a 'joined-up' quality, to the city's cultural strategy, despite certain tensions, notably divergent meanings attached to Barcelona's new place in the world, that have emerged between the larger Catalan nationalism of the Generalitat de Catalunya and the more focused logic of competing as a city in the post-industrial global economy of both cultural goods and services and prestige. Assuming a spirit of global interdependence, the city has also taken on an international leadership role, as illustrated by the 'Agenda 21 for Culture' presented in Chapter 5. In point of fact, the 2004 'Universal Forum of Cultures', at which the latter was officially launched, placed the city's cultural ambitions at the heart of reigning transnational tropes such as dialogue, solidarity, rights, civil society and sustainable development.

The ways Barcelona has remade itself as a sort of 'ideal' global player have earned it many fans, including the present writer, as over the last three decades the city has shown off its architectural and artistic heritage as well as the vitality of its contemporary cultural production to ever increasing numbers of visitors and tourists. As early as the late 1980s, the City Council elaborated a strategic framework for city development based on a careful diagnostic assessment of strengths and weaknesses. The 1992 Olympic Games – clearly a global mega-event – were both an integral part of the strategy and a major catalyst for it; they left a positive legacy. The strategy adopted in their wake aimed to enhance the city's international connectivity and quality of life, while achieving post-industrial transformation. Similar motivations fed into the subsequent 'Strategic Plan for Culture 1999–2010', elaborated and monitored since then by the Barcelona Culture Institute, as a clear response to the cultural implications of de-industrialization and the shift to the tertiary sector. The Plan articulated a six-pronged approach to the cultural as a knowledge society challenge: to make the city a significant content producer; to make culture a key element of social cohesion; to integrate the city in the flows of digital culture; to dynamize the city's historic heritage; to reconcile the needs of the component

(Continued)

(Continued)

cities in the larger city-region space; and to project it as a key player on the international cultural scene (London Development Agency, 2006). The framework has been debated, revised and updated since then, in particular a revision carried out in the wake of the 2004 Forum and presented in a report entitled New Accents 2006 (Barcelona Culture Institute, 2006). Significantly, quite unlike the Olympic Games, the Forum is perceived locally as a failed enterprise, not least because the vast architectural infrastructure created for it did not become a permanent asset afterwards. Content-wise, the Forum also proved ephemeral. Hence the turn towards a more citizen-oriented approach in the 2006 document, which contains a Preface by the political head, the Councillor for Culture, in which he underlines that several transformative phenomena associated with globalization and environmental issues

> are generating new needs and new challenges, while placing the cities as the territories where the opportunities and dangers ... reveal themselves in the raw ... a whole set of elements to which cultural policies act, or should act, as a counterweight, not always an easy role and one which needs to be played from a view of them [sic] as a city project, inevitably shared with all the people, institutions and sectors that act every day in the culture of Barcelona. (Barcelona Culture Institute, 2006)

New urban infrastructures and refashioned city spaces more than anything else have nevertheless been the main containers of that 'city project': the 1992 Olympic Games, the 2004 Forum and a host of other cultural developments since then. When, in 1999, the Royal Institute of British Architects awarded the city its Gold Medal, it lauded 'a pragmatic urban strategy [that] ... has transformed the city's public realm, immensely expanded its amenities and regenerated its economy, providing pride in its inhabitants and delight in its visitors' (cited in Paz Balibrea, 2004: 205). Faced with such a boilerplate encomium, however, one might pose some critical questions – that apply to the experience of many cities, not just this one. How much does the massive investment in flagship building and urbanism contribute to the actual cultural life of any city, apart from the display of symbolic capital that they and the events they contain may represent as vehicles of politico-symbolic signifying? Can the city escape the pitfalls of gentrification, the dislocation of neighbourhoods, the inevitable removal of their original inhabitants? How to counter the seemingly unavoidable urban speculation driven by large-scale real estate business interests through processes that deploy the aesthetic dimension in political ways and at the same time aestheticize the political (Paz Balibrea, 2004)? Such questions have indeed been posed within the local cultural elite itself and by the Executive Committee of the Culture Council, leading it to advocate in its recent annual reports a turn to other lines of action, such as making the city a more effective content producer, forging a larger local consumption base through arts education that can stimulate both talent and social demand for cultural goods and services, creating 'arts factories' – affordable public spaces for creative activities – fostering the international export of local cultural products, or providing connectivity tools for local cultural operators. There has also been an emphasis on a broader notion of culture that encompasses creativity in science and technology, notably in the domains of bio-technology and bio-medecine.[4]

Initially conceived in a welfare state rationale that saw major new urban projects as a public service, a first phase of urban renewal led by Oriol Bohigas in the early post-Franco years gave way to a different rationale of urban reconfiguration, one that hewed ever more closely to the global scripts of architectural monumentality and creativity. Driven by an alliance between private interests and local politicians, huge projects such as the Vila Olímpica, Poblenou, Diagonal Mar or Sant Andreu/Sagrera that transformed what had previously been industrial and/or working-class areas bore little resemblance to 'the small-scale, detailed, respectful urban project intended to bring direct benefit to the most depressed neighbourhoods and their inhabitants' (Paz Balibrea, 2004: 213). One can therefore wonder about the extent to which the monumental remaking of the cityscape and spectacular infrastructure-generated and generating world events have actually delivered cultural benefits to all the city's inhabitants. International branding aims have been realized to be sure, but what about shared and sustainable urban livability for all? A number of dissatisfied or dissenting voices have indeed been heard, as in the case of the ambitious urban regeneration project in the derelict central district Poblenou, entitled Districte d'Activitas 22@BCN, where there has been resistance and public protest by the incumbent community (Križnik, 2005).

On the other hand, and on a largely positive note, the 'buzz' created, the creation of delivery mechanisms for the creative industries and the fostering and incubation of innovation, and the encouragement of multi-stakeholder involvement (at least among culture and cultural industries players) have without doubt made for a 'creative city'. A distinct exemplarity also characterizes the City Council's response to the intercultural challenge: the fast-growing heterogeneity of the city's population (the number of foreign residents rose from 2 per cent in 1998 to 17 per cent in 2010), as it seeks to reconcile the imperatives of shared citizenship and cohesion with a cosmopolitan ethos appropriate to the migratory flows it is receiving, not just from the rest of Spain (as occurred in the mid-twentieth century) but from the entire world. Thus Barcelona has adopted an 'Interculturality Plan' for coexistence in diversity, carried out with the help of 200 entities and literally thousands of citizens. It has created a 'New Citizens Portal' based on principles such as 'equality between rights and duties, acknowledgement of cultural diversity, improvement of community relations and social cohesion'.[5] The Plan has put in place a set of Reception Guidelines aimed at promoting intercultural relations through the systematic and gradual development of common areas and initiatives that can enable positive interaction. Yet these institutional initiatives also have their limits; as top-down exercises how can they transform entrenched monocultural attitudes and mindsets? And the architectonic emphasis of Barcelona's cultural remaking poses its own problems. The Raval zone, for example, now resplendent with gleaming new institutions of European high culture, although itself not actually gentrified, is inhabited mainly by recent immigrants whose cultural capital gives them scant access to this kind of cultural offer. Yet, despite these shortcomings, in the judgement of many, no other European city is rising so systematically to the challenge of generating local-level community coexistence, *convivencia* and inclusion.

The creation of enabling legal and administrative frameworks, together with governance mechanisms to professionalize the public management of culture, has been a second *leitmotiv*. Such precepts are slowly beginning to be heeded, but the pace needs to be stepped up. The record is still patchy in this regard, as emerges from the policy successes and failures recorded in this volume. In some regions, particularly South Asia, national polities have not yet adapted to the realities of a new metropolitan age. The nation has not yet empowered municipalities to enact and implement policies for culture in any significant way. In fact, the disempowerment applies in other fields as well and, indeed, for sometime now many have urged that urban governance be reformed accordingly. In India, for example, either the central government in Delhi or the state government still dominate the limited degree of policy thinking that exists at the urban level. Thus the city of Jaipur's cultural positioning is determined not by the city authorities but by those of the Indian state of Rajasthan, of which it is the capital. In Mumbai, as Lambah tells us in her chapter (24), civil society elites have taken the initiative in preserving the city's architectural heritage, as indeed they have across the entire country, notably through the efforts of the various local chapters of the Indian National Trust for Art and Cultural Heritage (INTACH). In a different context, but in like fashion, Savchak and McAusland tell the story of L'viv, where a non-governmental entity, created by a handful of local citizens, has replaced the city authorities in order to put in place a framework for cultural policy development (Chapter 19); and Vasconcelos-Oliveira emphasizes the key role played by a private organization, Sesc, in the cultural life of São Paulo (Chapter 27).

Governments have long been urged to frame cultural issues as multifaceted, cross-sectoral ones. Lack of such joined-up governance is often the key problem, as Jiménez points out in respect to Mexico City (Chapter 23), where coherence among the different levels of government – or even within cultural institutions – is strikingly absent. Cultural choices often pose vexed questions of value and values in relation to employment, social policy, income and resource distribution, or redistribution, gender inequality and the environment (more on this below). For Janet Merkel, however, the experience of Berlin demonstrates that culture is often 'an almost unmanageable policy field'. Precisely because it cuts through so many other policy areas, responsibility for it can no longer be clearly allocated clearly to one department. For them, of the essence is a kind of 'mainstreaming', whereby culture is not seen as a separate policy field but as a dimension in all fields. Nailing down that cross-cutting dimension, however, is easier to advocate than to accomplish.

Implicit in all the chapters is a fourth key idea, namely that any cultural policy worth the name has to be formulated on the basis of a thorough audit of the cultural and other resources available. Allen Scott made the point in 2008, referring specifically to the cultural industry sector as an engine of local development, that the essential first task is 'to map out the collective order of the local economy along with the multiple sources of the increasing-returns effects that invariably crisscross through it. It is this collective order more than anything else that presents possibilities for meaningful and effective policy intervention' (2008: 318). Top-down planning may not achieve the desired effect; finely tuned bottom-up measures are, on the other hand, essential. In this volume, Klaic broadens the ambitions of such mapping and ordering by recognizing a potential new stakeholder: the university. The world's rapidly globalizing universities, he argues, can be drivers of knowledge economy development, or provide much needed skills locally, over and above their role in boosting city prestige. On an even broader canvas, Lobato draws attention to the fact that there is now a global map of informal cultural practices and interactions. Taken together, these expansions necessarily transform our view of local cultural assets and rights, as well as of our vision of cultural production and consumption. It is not possible for any urban cultural policy to formalize or discipline cultural production circuits that are not available through the conventional channels; a new kind of articulation between the policy-maker and the informal realm remains to be invented.

But beyond the mechanics of implementation, what lines of emphasis on the 'right', the 'good' or the 'harmonious' in terms of city cultural policy are brought to the fore in the volume? There are many of these and rather than attempt a rapid summary of them all, we might more usefully explore five in some degree of depth.

Questions of value and values

First, the need to be vigilant regarding perverse outcomes when cultural infrastructures and programmes serve branding and place marketing and are designed to position the city as a 'global' player. The most obvious of these is gentrification, already abundantly analyzed in the literature, the process whereby refurbished spaces become expensive spaces – pushing out the original inhabitants (Chapter 12). Globalized narratives, not the least of which is Florida's 'creative class' paradigm, all too easily divert policy from local access, engagement, inclusion and participation. The effects of these narratives on local identity and sense of place, on cultural engagement and pride as well as on the sustainability of the cultural infrastructures put in place can all be problematic. As Lily Kong pointed out in the third volume of this series, 'creative industries' discourses and policies external conceptions 'do not always translate unequivocally into an indigenous artistic development' (2010: 173). In the present volume, her analysis of culture-derived city branding processes argues that a standardized formula is being applied everywhere, generating homogeneity instead of distinctiveness. Because the attendant outcomes are not always beneficial to the city's own inhabitants, the practices of city branding need to be carefully assessed in the context of a broader 'agenda of ambition'. Likewise, 'spectacularization' processes homogenize cityscapes, contradicting each city's search for prestigious distinctiveness by using a limited pool of 'star architects' and 'global' global architectural firms (Ponzini Chapter 7). Moreover, paradoxical urban effects and disappointments occur when complex contextual requirements such as accessibility/availability of financial, social and cultural capital for complementary social activities are not met. Critical analysis needs to stress, as does Elsheshtawy, that physical infrastructure in and of itself may simply mask unpleasant socio-political realities unless there is a much broader social and cultural engagement. Yet, as Stuart Cunningham reminds us in Chapter 8, 'political leaders are partial to the siren song of the "edifice complex"'.

That siren song largely explains a second phenomenon – politicians' preferences for cultural democratization over cultural democracy. In a now familiar dichotomy, the former seeks to provide access to a predetermined set of cultural goods and services, while the latter seeks to give them tools of agency, voice and representation in terms of their own cultural expressions. The first assumes that a single cultural canon determined on high can be propagated to 'the masses'. Nor has it been successful, as the unequal distribution of cultural capital in society has made access to culture either problematic or unsolicited by the intended beneficiaries, while the scale of market-driven cultural industries has reduced the reach of subsidized cultural provision. Cultural democracy, on the other hand, which Pieterse and Gurney in Johannesburg or Vasconcelos-Oliveira in São Paulo advocate for, seeks to augment and diversify access to the means of cultural production and distribution, to involve people in fundamental debates about the value of cultural identity and expression, while also giving them agency as regards the means of cultural production, distribution and consumption.

A third set of issues relates to the global script of creativity (Anheier and Isar, 2010). What emerges here is the need for nuance. 'One-size-fits all' approaches simply cannot work. Some of the well-tried formulae of spatial clustering or concentration are being superseded: as in the suburbs of Brisbane and Melbourne analyzed by Flew and Gibson, the 'creative class' may not turn out to be where it is expected to be. 'Creative city' approaches frequently forget the local creative ecosystem and the fact that, as Cunningham also reminds us, the production and consumption of culture are blurring, and tomorrow's citizens/consumers will expect the two to be much more interdependent. Policies need to be shaped to suit both production and consumption, a point echoed by the Executive Committee of Barcelona's Culture Council (Box 32.1). This needs to go hand in hand with a policy blend of entrepreneurialism and social innovation of the kind practised in Vancouver (Chapter 30), which is based on stable participatory values, social progressivism and neighbourhood development. As Landry observes in Chapter 9:

Creativity is context driven. What is creative in one circumstance may not be in another. Whereas in the past we might have harnessed engineering prowess to solve urban infrastructure problems or public health issues, today needs are different. ... What is deemed to be creative in a small Albanian city like Korca or Lezhe will be different from what we expect from a Melbourne.

The arts activist cited in Chapter 8 found himself overburdened with the red tape created in the name of 'creative city' policy. In other words, direct public support has its limits; it cannot create quality – 'Picasso never got a grant', as Antoni Monegal has put it (personal communication) – and so creativity strategies should concern far more than direct support. Rather, they should seek to nurture enabling environments for cultural practice and beyond, for all spheres of local governance. The cultural sector is hoisted with its own petard here: it originated the 'creativity' discourse, but now the latter has taken on a life of its own, for the benefit of sectors other than the cultural. Indeed, the global script of 'creativity' has become a bit too hegemonic. As Pieterse and Gurney remind us, public life and cultural publics can be imagined differently and in terms other than the creative economy paradigm; economic infrastructures ought to be seen as secondary to ecological and social-cultural infrastructures. One example is in the Colombian city of Medellín (Arbeláez Tobón, Chapter 21), which has shown how systematic investments in education, leisure, social, public and low-key economic infrastructures in poor neighbourhoods, connected through a city-wide accessibility grid, can dramatically improve the quality of life for large numbers of people. Finally, as regards the promotion of informality, it is evident that in many ways market forces and commodification in the creativity paradigm conspire against it. Aksoy and Robins detect in Istanbul, for example, 'a calculated assault on the principle of informality, which has been a significant factor, a social and organizational resource we can say, in the practices of daily life in Istanbul' as well as the 'unmaking of the city's historic cultural and social diversity'.

A fourth set of issues concerns the ever increasing heterogeneity of urban societies, 'mixing bowls' for a new trans- or intercultural ethos. This 'interculturalism' should involve not only the cultures of minority ethnic groups, but also changed conditions for everyone, in which the relations between people belonging to different cultures must be nurtured through mutual translation and dialogic exchange that increase the mixing of cultures rather than merely 'manage' or celebrate a mosaic of different and separate cultures. We need to shift from speaking of 'different cultures' to a stress on 'cultures in difference', so that cultural practice on the ground can feed into the continuing production of difference (Bennett, n.d.). The paradox here is that, by its very nature, the intercultural project is rooted in person-to-person contacts, in creative and intellectual practice, not in official policy and action. It has to be a freely willed individual stance, although it cannot be reduced, as Touraine reminded us, to interpersonal relations; it leads to the 'construction of general forms of social and cultural life' (Touraine, 1997: 210). It cannot be brought into being by official pronouncements, declarations, or symbolic gestures, yet the ways in which cultural diversity is envisioned and acted upon by governments and by social custom – and often the politicians who govern us act or speak in relation to diversity because of what they think social custom wants or is – determine whether it leads to greater societal creativity and innovation or, on the contrary, to conflict, violence or exclusion (Dancygier, 2010).

The opposing ideal could be expressed in a word that doesn't exist in English but does in Spanish: *convivencia*. Attaining it requires a new spirit of local, city-based interculturalism. As Wood analyses it in Chapter 3, this in turn challenges the capacities of the local political culture and bureaucratic machinery to break out of its silos and work transversally and holistically – for example, in the organization of public space, as formerly public domains have been increasingly appropriated into privatized commercial and residential areas accompanied by increased security and exclusion. Or through cultural institutions such as museums, galleries, theatres and libraries that have almost invariably been created in very different times for very different audiences from the ones they now must serve. Today, they need to better promote a more inclusive and plural public culture that recognizes a multiplicity of cultural rights and empowers all those who have a stake in that public culture. A growing number of city museums, for example, have become proactive with regard to cultural diversity, as they strive to represent the knowledge, experience and practices of all those who constitute the urban population. The objective is to build

a polyphonic sense of self-esteem and identity. This requires an embrace of a much broader range of arts and creative activity, as integral components of a living cultural life in which the museum, although based most of the time on a historical legacy, is a fully-fledged actor. It would obviously include the classic tasks of conserving and managing cultural heritage, but also that of revealing and recording the contemporary, emerging voices, values and traditions of a culturally-diverse society.

And, last but not least, the job of relating ordinary people to the wider environment within which they too may contribute to the development of sustainable cultural systems. As Roy Ballantyne and David Uzzell put it in a recent article, museums also will have to demonstrate their added value in educating visitors about important general issues of the day. Thus 'they will need to design exhibits that address issues such as racism, migrations, homelessness … environmental issues, environmentally sustainable behaviour' and the like (2011: 7). And we do need to remember that this is not an issue for the global North alone, for as Lucina Jiménez reminds us, in other regions as well, city governments are out of step with citizen demand as regards the management of urban space for coexistence in diversity.

A fifth key area is the environment. 'Sustainability' has become a catchword, mostly used in ways that diverge considerably from the World Commission on Environment and Development's 1987 concept, which saw sustainable development as a process 'that meets the needs of the present without compromising the ability of future generations to meet their own needs'. In the welter of current usages of the term 'sustainable', the powerful central idea of intergenerational responsibility has been either lost or relegated to the background. Instead, the word is deployed indiscriminately as an almost ritual qualifier to an array of processes. Thus it can refer, *inter alia*, to the maintainability of a broad societal process such as socio-economic development; or to the medium- or long-term viability of a project or institution, in particular its financial soundness; or to the ways in which certain practices may be conducive to a better quality of life. Although they may not be semantically orthodox, however, all of these understandings of sustainability have their usefulness – provided we say something specific and definable when we use the term in each of these different ways.

In the case of the city, a number of understandings are possible. Hewing close to the original idea, and especially with respect to the spectre of climate change, the big question for cities is how they can organize urban functions in ways that reduce their 'carbon footprint' to the maximum. How can their plant and operations be modified so as to consume less non-renewable energy? How can their modes of operation be changed so as to contribute as little as possible to environmental pollution?

There can be more metaphorical understandings too. As Duxbury, Cullen and Pascual argue in Chapter 5, the 'culture and sustainable development paradigm can renew the commitment as well as bridge the divide between diverging policy approaches, by bringing cultural issues and actors closer to general societal debates'. But as they also observe, there is still a good deal of work to be done in order to go beyond the 'feel good' impacts of deploying a buzzword. Further conceptual development is required, as is a much closer linking of theory and practice that recognizes the specificities of places and cultures. Already this agenda is being advanced through many grassroots experiments of non-profit organizations and community activists, and an increasing number of urban planners and officials are devising new ways of thinking about and organizing collective life. As Morris reminded us in volume 4 of the series, climate change is not merely a global process acting on the environment,

it is also a global process acting on the societies that govern and maintain that environment. Both require a new and creative spirit of conservation and renewal. The environment requires permanent reassessment of the societal values, norms and expectations attached to it (Morris, 2011).

The way such reasoning broadens the frame of reference for 'culture' leads us to a final set of observations. These have to do with a divide and a disjuncture. The divide is the one the co-editors alluded to in their Introduction: between two types of cultural policy research, client-driven and instrumentalist on the one hand, and more critically-informed academic conceptualizations on the other. The disjuncture is the one that exists between the reality – which is that cultural policy is overwhelmingly arts or creative industry policy – and the rhetoric – which is that the true aim of cultural policy is culture as 'way of life' or 'identity'. Cities, however, have no choice but to bridge the divide and eliminate the disjuncture; they must combine theory and practice, the critical and the constructive. The 'visceral pain, pleasure and desire lines of the real city' (Pieterse and Gurney) interpellate not just the arts but also questions of community and belonging, of identity and difference, of collective remembering and forgetting and of inclusion and exclusion.

Box 32.2 An integrated urban revitalization process in Tel Aviv–Jaffa

Tel Aviv–Jaffa (TLV), founded in 1909, is growing rapidly in economic and cultural influence, and is ranked No. 50 on the Global Cities Index (www.atkearney.com/index.php/News-media/2010-global-cities-index). Recently, *Lonely Planet* (2010) named TLV the third 'hottest city', and praised its leisure, entertainment, and culture. Situated on the Mediterranean coast, it is a vibrant city with numerous cultural spots, restaurants, and bars open day and night. Often called 'a non-stop city' for that reason, it has become a magnet for a variety of tastes and populations, including international business and communication professionals and creative artists, as well as domestic and international tourists. TLV is characterized by a hedonistic spirit and informal atmosphere and is often seen as an antithesis to the historical capital city of Jerusalem. The 'White City of Tel-Aviv', so-called because of the outstanding Modern Movement urbanism of its construction, was inscribed on UNESCO's World Heritage List in 2003.

Between 2001 and 2004, a comprehensive planning process was initiated in an attempt to integrate the cultural and economic spheres. This followed three types of strategies implemented between 1983 and 2004 (Molin, 2010): real estate development for elite culture; development of community art projects; and development of culture and creative quarters. The new strategic lines were: (1) development of a

(Continued)

(Continued)

major economic and cultural center of metropolitan and national standing and culture capital with cultural facilities for all; (2) a city for all of its residents; (3) citizen-oriented governance; and (4) an attractive urban environment (City, 2006). The strategic plan thus emphasized culture as the main component of the city's identity, and as the driving force that influences the city's economic and social fabric. In this aspect, Tel Aviv has followed other cities in the world that have implemented culture-led urban development strategies to promote urban renewal and revitalization (Evans, 2005; Miles and Paddison, 2005).

Since its inception, TLV has been a center of cultural creativity. As home to the majority of Israeli artists and major cultural institutions, such as the Batsheva Dance Company and the Israel Philharmonic Orchestra, the city combines an interesting mix of culture and art forms. The vision presented in the plan and the strategic lines formulated strive to safeguard TLV's central cultural and economic position in the country as a metropolis. The strategies that have been formulated for the promotion of the cultural scene involve: the concentration of cultural activities in five defined cultural quarters, each of which should have a brand of its own, often centering around heritage or historical landmarks as a catalyst for renewal (e.g., the Old Jaffa port or the old train station); incentives for cultural institutions and artists by allocating municipal financial resources; incentives for cultural entrepreneurs; partnerships with the private sector; investment in building and renovation of major cultural institutions such as the Habima National Theater; art in the public domain; and attracting international cultural tourism. These strategies were proposed with the aim of encouraging original artistic work, innovation, and diversity, and in an attempt to attract a critical mass of cultural institutions, artists, and consumers (City, 2010). At the same time, many different courses of action have been designed to maintain TLV at the pinnacle of Israel's economy. In 2010, a series of indicators were put in place in order to assess the results (City, 2010). Among these indicators were the increase in audience participation. Between 2000 and 2008, the number of people who attended dance and theater performances in TLV increased by 57 per cent and 39 per cent, respectively. A similar trend has been found among visitors to museums. There has also been increased diversification of cultural offerings, especially in alternative music arts (City, 2010). On the economic and social plane, there has been an increase in the growth domestic product (GDP) per capita, as well as in the number of persons employed in the city, and in the number of apartments built. Concomitantly, the city's status has risen as an economic center of financial and business services and its income from local sources has increased (City, 2010). Other indicators monitored point to positive changes in the urban and social environment, including high resident satisfaction. Nonetheless, differences in social and economic indicators have been noted between the northern and central areas of the city in comparison to the southern part, which is inhabited by people of low socio-economic status.

Tel Aviv is thus in the midst of an ongoing urban revitalization process – a process that is evident in the changing cultural and economic scene as well as in Tel Aviv's physical appearance and attractiveness.

Shulamit Shulov Barkan

References

City (2006) *The strategic plan for Tel Aviv Yafo.* Tel Aviv: Municipality of Tel Aviv, Strategic Planning Unit.

City (2010) *Indicators for monitoring the city.* Tel Aviv: Municipality of Tel Aviv, Strategic Planning Unit.

Evans, G. (2005) 'Measure for measure: evaluating the evidence of culture's contribution to regeneration, *Urban Studies*, 42(5/6), 959–983.

Lonely Planet Publications (2010) *Lonely Planet's Best in Travel 2011.* London: Lonely Planet.

Miles, S. and Paddison, R. (2005) 'Culture-led urban regeneration', *Urban Studies*, 42(5/6), 833–839.

Molin, E. (2010) 'Development of culture strategies in cities and their implication for local population'. Unpublished doctoral thesis. Haifa: Technion, Israel Institute of Technology.

Notes

1 As mentioned in a previous volume (Anheier and Isar, 2008) much of this practical policy advice, particularly on 'the creative city', was elaborated by British consultants and think tanks in the 1990s – notably Charles Landry and colleagues at Comedia (Landry, 2000) – and consolidated by the impact and uptake of Richard Florida's work in the early 2000s.

2 These recommended stances figure among those that the present writer – informed notably by the work of Landry and others at Comedia – elaborated on behalf of UNESCO (1999) over a decade ago. It matters little that the advice was for national governments, for if there is one thing the chapters in this volume have shown for sure, it is that practically all the major generic cultural policy challenges are experienced more directly and intensely at the city level.

3 The continuity, it must be said, is based on 32 years of Socialist Party administration of the city. At time of writing, just after the Spanish local elections of May 2010, in which the long-incumbent party was defeated, it is too early to tell whether it will be maintained, changed or abandoned…

4 The author is very grateful to Professor Antoni Monegal, Chair of the Executive Committee (composed of independent experts) of Barcelona's Culture Council (*Consell de la Cultura*) for the insights he kindly shared on a previous draft of this note, as well as to Jordi Pascual at UCLG (see Chapter 5) for his comments. Neither of them is of course responsible for the author's judgements expressed here.

5 See www.bcn.cat/novaciutadania/index_en.html.

REFERENCES

Anheier, H. and Isar, Y.R. (eds) (2008) *The Cultural Economy. The Cultures and Globalization Series 2*. London: Sage.

Anheier, H. and Isar, Y.R. (eds) (2010) *Cultural Expression, Creativity and Innovation. The Cultures and Globalization Series 3*. London: Sage.

Ballantyne, R. and Uzzell, D. (2011) 'Looking Back and Looking Forward: The Rise of the Visitor-centered Museum', *Curator*, 54, 1: 1–8.

Barcelona Culture Institute (2006) *New Accents 2006. Barcelona Strategic Plan for Culture*. Barcelona: Institut de Cultura. Available at: www.bcn.es/plaestrategicdecultura/pdf/StrategicPlanBCN.pdf (accessed 19 May 2011).

Bennett, T. (n.d.) 'Culture and Difference: The Challenges of Multiculturalism'. ESRC Centre for Research on Sociocultural Change, The Open University, Milton Keynes. Unpublished typescript.

Dancygier, R.M. (2010) *Immigration and Conflict in Europe*. New York: Cambridge University Press.

Kong, L. (2010) 'Creative Economy, Global City: Globalizing Discourses and the Implications for Local Arts', in Helmut Anheier and Y.R. Isar (eds) *Cultural Expression, Creativity and Innovation. The Cultures and Globalization Series 3*. London: SAGE.

Križnik, B. (2005) 'Forms of Local Resistance: No al 22@'. Paper for the University of Ljubljana and the Institut d'Arquictura Avançada de Catalunya. Available at: www2.arnes.si/~uljfarh5/kriznik_noal22@.pdf

Landry, C. (2000) *The Creative City. A Toolkit for Urban Innovators*. London: Earthscan.

London Development Agency (2006) *Barcelona Case Study: Strategies for Creative Spaces*. London: London Development Agency.

Marshall, T. (ed.) (2004) *Transforming Barcelona*. London: Routledge.

Morris, B. (2011) 'Not Just a Place: Cultural Heritage and the Environment', in Helmut K. Anheier and Yudhishthir R. Isar (eds), *Heritage, Memory and Identity. The Cultures and Globalization Series 4*. London: SAGE, pp. 124–135.

Paz Balibrea, M. (2004) 'Urbanism, Culture and the Post-industrial City: Challenging the 'Barcelona Model', in T. Marshall (ed.), *Transforming Barcelona*. London: Routledge, pp. 205–224.

Scott, A. (2008) 'Cultural Economy: Retrospect and Prospect', in Helmut Anheier and Y.R. Isar (eds) *The Cultural Economy. The Cultures and Globalization Series 2*. London: Sage.

Touraine, A. (1997) *Pourrons-nous vivre ensemble? Egalité et différence*. Paris: Fayard.

UNESCO (1999) *The Value of Culture* (position paper for the forum *Development and Culture* co-organized by the Inter-American Development Bank and UNESCO, Paris, 11–12 March 1999). UNESCO document.

World Commission on Environment and Development (1987) *Our Common Fututre* (Brundtland Report). New York: Oxford University Press.

CHAPTER 33

ETHNOGRAPHIC SNAPSHOTS: VISIONS OF CITIES
Mieka Ritsema

This essay is built around snapshots of Hanoi, Cape Town and Detroit that demonstrate how large-scale development projects transform not only the built environment but also the cultural fabric of everyday life. Cultural policy discussions that relate only to art or artifacts neglect the major issues thrown up by globalization in cities around the world. This essay examines how urban policies that emphasize achievement of 'world-city status' are transforming the cultural life of cities. Often these transformations tangibly impact the art, artists, and physical urban artifacts that cultural policy seeks to protect.

Introduction

While urban settlements have historically served different purposes as religious, political, or commercial centers, cities in the twenty-first century have more in common than ever before. In a globalizing era, municipal policies appeal to global imaginaries, global capital, and global visitors, often packaging local culture and identity for international consumption. Centers of financial and political power, such as New York City, São Paulo, or Tokyo, securely represent integration in the global system, while smaller cities pursue 'world-city status' through a range of efforts, including policies that favor mega-projects like stadia, subdivisions or highways. Cape Town's appeal to world-city status, for example, is characterized by multi-million dollar investments to replace a centrally-located stadium and nearby urban infrastructure for the World Cup; concurrently, the city battles with poor residents over services, notably access to adequate housing. Such decisions to invest in large-scale development projects are transforming not only the built environment but also the cultural fabric of everyday life in cities around the world.

For this volume, which is dedicated to examining the relationship between cultural policy and governance in cities, I have chosen to articulate both prose and photography in order to consider how major urban policy decisions to support mega-projects are fundamentally reshaping the cultural life of cities. With its complex genealogy (Williams, 1988), the concept of culture continues to represent a range of meanings in contemporary public and intellectual life. While cultural policy typically stresses artistic creativity and cultural heritage, an anthropological view of culture emphasizes systems of meaning, value, and symbols. Cultural policy is often enlisted to protect important local artifacts, such as architecture or fine art, but often overlooks culture in terms of lived experience; however, it is everyday cultural life that provides the context for the production of heritage and art. Cultural policy discussions that relate only to art or artifact neglect the major policy decisions driving globalization in cities around the world. Relying on an anthropological definition of culture, this essay examines some implications of urban policies that, through an emphasis on achievement of 'world-city status', are transforming the cultural life of cities. In many cases, these transformations tangibly impact the art, artists, and physical urban artifacts that cultural policy seeks to protect.

The textual snapshots presented in this essay capture dramatic changes to the built environment and cultural life of each city that are the result of explicit policies supporting mega-projects and wooing global capital. Despite an extraordinary range of responses to globalization, contemporary city-making processes demonstrate remarkable similarity in increasing inequities and disparities within cities, resulting in socially and spatially divided cities (UN-HABITAT, 2008). My snapshots visualize the impacts of, and responses to, social and economic processes of globalization in Hanoi, Cape Town, and Detroit. Recent photographs from these diverse cities demonstrate instructive similarities in response to global pressures that are rapidly changing lives, livelihoods, and environments. That these cities differ significantly from one another in terms of cultural, historical, and political context makes the case even more instructive for considering how policy decisions regarding large-scale public investment impact everyday life in cities around the world.

In addition to focusing on global capital and mega-projects at the expense of local livelihoods, municipalities often do not value locally produced art until it generates a global audience. Top-down cultural policy at times fails to recognize the artistry in the everyday. I therefore conclude with examples of two artists who now famously represent their cities out of the cumulative waste of the cities themselves. For Tyree Guyton and Nek Chand, whose artistic contributions emerged from the destruction of Detroit and construction of Chandigarh respectively, cultural policy and municipal support took many years to catch up. Both artists represent grassroots responses to urban issues rather than to top-down results of cultural policy. The art installations represent urban culture in terms of both the systems of meaning that emerge from everyday life as well as cultural policy's emphasis on artistic creativity and heritage.

Hanoi, a 1000-year-old capital

Hanoi, the political capital of Vietnam, celebrated 1000 years in 2010. The city's rich cultural heritage is a result of centuries of global influence incorporating elements of Chinese and French occupations to Soviet and now Western-style living (Ngoc, 2008). After decades of war and communist governance, the state policy of *Doi Moi*, or economic renovation, which began in 1986, enabled the creation of a private sector and opened the door to foreign investment. Although reforms have resulted in national poverty reduction, inequalities are increasingly visible in urban Vietnam, largely in response to market-driven housing policy (Gough and Tran, 2009; Waibel, 2006).

The construction of so-called 'new urban areas', which are massive, gated, mixed-use development projects, characterizes Hanoi's investment in world-city status. Built on agricultural land, these mega-projects are displacing the villages and rural livelihoods that have surrounded this political center for centuries. The scale and pace of global investment in new urban areas is supported by municipal policy as well as a lucrative land market. One of Hanoi's first new urban areas, Ciputra Hanoi International City, a joint venture with an Indonesian developer, combines high-rise residential buildings and single-family homes on its nearly 405 hectares (Waibel, 2006). Villagers who once grew rice, flowers or vegetables for local consumption are selling their land use rights to large, residential development projects in which they are not likely to be able to afford to live, and in which they certainly could not maintain their traditional farming practices.

The new 'Master plan of Hanoi by 2030 and a vision of 2050', exhibited to the public in April 2010, highlights urban expansion through the development of satellite cities at the expense of agricultural land and livelihoods. In 2008, Vietnamese state policy extended Hanoi's administrative boundaries into neighboring provinces and districts which resulted in an immediate doubling of the capital's population to 6.2 million and more than tripling of the land area to 3,300 km² (Vietnews, 2010). As exemplified by Ciputra, The Manor, and many other new urban areas, Hanoi's agricultural lands are being replaced by high-end, private development at an unprecedented rate and scale, resulting in increasing social and spatial divisions and tensions. Meanwhile, efforts for cultural preservation in the historic city have stalled in the face of meager municipal and popular support (Logan, 2000; Waibel, 2004). Hanoi's Ancient Quarter – where street names signify different market guilds – remains a thriving commercial center in the city;

Photo 33.1 Keangnam Hanoi Landmark Tower, Vietnam
An office and residential complex, the Keangnam Hanoi Landmark Tower by South Korean-based Keangnam, will become the tallest building in Vietnam upon completion. Livelihoods and cultural practices sustained by agriculture are increasingly unviable in this city dominated by a market economy. (Photographer: Mieka Ritsema)

yet, there is little implementation of cultural policy to preserve this architectural heritage (Logan, 2000). Preservation is particularly difficult because the character of the market area lies not in individual buildings, but in the composite vibrancy created through the interplay of mixed-use development and lively street life (Tran, 2010). The rush for tourist dollars is rapidly changing the atmosphere of this centuries-old commercial center as residents, who are themselves keen to benefit, now prefer to replace traditional houses and trades with hotels and businesses directed at tourists.

Municipal policy decisions regarding land use and global capital support the shift from rural to urban life and from dense, mixed-use settlement to sprawling gated enclaves. Though Hanoi has yet to experience the growth of slums on a scale similar to the world's major capitalist urban settlements, the growth of gated, wealthy enclaves certainly mirrors cities elsewhere in the world. Vietnam's transition from a predominantly agrarian to an urban capitalist economy raises many questions about the concurrent cultural shift in livelihoods, values, and heritage in the quest to modernize. In response to Hanoi's transformation, Huu Ngoc, the celebrated Vietnamese ethnologist, wrote, 'At the dawn of the twenty-first century, in face of globalization, it is essential that Vietnamese culture develops a balance which ensures the harmonious development of both culture and the economy'

Photo 33.2   Quiet residential street in Ciputra Hanoi International City
In Ciputra Hanoi International City, this quiet residential street overseen by security guards provides a sharp contrast to the vibrant street life elsewhere in the city. Resembling fortified enclaves around the world, Hanoi's 'new urban areas' include privatized educational, security and recreational facilities. (Photographer: Mieka Ritsema)

(2008: 524). How Hanoi might attain that balance remains to be seen.

Cape Town, a tourist city

As South African cities struggle with the enduring legacy of apartheid, municipal decisions for public investment appear to harden rather than loosen the boundaries of racially segregated neighborhoods. In contrast to Hanoi's strict communist-era government, which mandated social equality, Cape Town's apartheid-era government legislated social and spatial hierarchies based on racial classification. The legacy of inequality continues to impact nearly every aspect of everyday life in South Africa today, from access to education to health care to housing.

Cape Town's tourist industry is no exception. Most international visitors remain in the city center, shopping at the V&A Waterfront or taking the ferry to Robben Island, riding the cable car up Table Mountain or visiting nearby beaches. While tourists may tour the townships, where the majority of black and colored residents live, few stay in lodging or eat in restaurants in the Cape Flats. Even during the 2010 World Cup, business did not significantly improve, as was anticipated. For example, at MaNeo's Bed & Breakfast in Langa, one of Cape Town's oldest townships, there was no increased demand for rooms, despite the establishment's affordability and proximity to the city center (MaNeo, 2010).

In the twenty-first century, Cape Town's investment in world-city status has been coupled to its tourist economy and the 2010 FIFA World Cup. In addition to replacing the stadium at Green Point, the municipality supported major upgrades to tourist infrastructure, including the airport, highways, and improvements to the city center, favoring the city's most well-developed areas. The mega-event proved to be a great success in terms of engendering significant national pride and improving the

Photo 33.3 Hanoi's streets
Hanoi's streets are typically lined with commercial buildings and small-scale entrepreneurs. The buildings are often mixed use, with the resulting commercial and residential interaction creating a vibrant streetscape. (Photographer: Mieka Ritsema)

Photo 33.4 The Atlantic side of Table Mountain, Cape Town
On the Atlantic side of Table Mountain, Cape Town's coast draws residents and visitors alike to the beaches near some of the country's most expensive real estate. (Photographer: Mieka Ritsema)

country's image (Pillay et al., 2009). The extent to which major sporting events like the World Cup has led to sustained economic development or poverty alleviation in cities, if at all, remains unclear (Burbank et al., 2002; Newton, 2009; Pillay and Bass, 2009).

In preparing to host the World Cup, Cape Town expended considerable effort to 'clean up' the city, not unlike other cities hosting major international events (Davis, 2006; Newton, 2009; UN-HABITAT, 2007). Efforts included formalizing elements of the informal economy and informal settlements prior to the event. Areas for informal vending, including the busy market at Cape Town Train Station, were organized and formalized by the city, reducing the total number of vendors and increasing the costs for small entrepreneurs (Keepile, 2010; Voice of the Cape, 2010). The government also attempted to develop formal housing in place of an informal settlement along the N2 highway leading from the airport to the city center, resulting in serious controversy (Legassik, 2008; Newton, 2009). Although the N2 Gateway project initially represented a solution to the extensive housing shortage in Cape Town, the effort suffered from broken promises, including forced relocations of residents to Delft, an area in the periphery of the city. Claiming their right of access to adequate housing and the illegality of forced evictions, residents protested, employing a range of methods, including demonstrations in the city center, blocking the N2 highway, and bringing their case to the South African Constitutional Court (COHRE, 2009; Legassik, 2008).

Despite talk of empowerment, cultural diversity, and development, Cape Town remains a highly segregated city, and government decisions have yet to produce equitable social transformation. Instead, building alternate housing for poor residents on the

Photo 33.5   Table Mountain, Cape Town
On the other side of Table Mountain, the views in the Cape Flats are dramatically different. As a result of efforts to 'beautify' the N2 highway leading from the Cape Town International Airport to the city center, the municipal government built housing in Temporary Relocation Areas in Delft, pictured here, in order to relocate people from an informal settlement constructed along the highway. (Photographer: Mieka Ritsema)

city's periphery, in areas like Delft, has reproduced patterns of apartheid-era segregation (Huchzermeyer, 2004; McDonald, 2008; Watson, 2002). As strategies to implement cultural policy, Hanoi's claim to value the preservation of its cultural heritage, on the one hand, and Cape Town's claim to value the transformation of its apartheid legacy, on the other, are both undermined by their respective policies which privilege development for high-income earners.

Detroit, a shrinking city

Although Miami and Los Angeles are better known for urban sprawl, Detroit's early twentieth-century expansion was characterized by low-density, single family homes. Consisting of an area of nearly 140 square miles, Detroit is larger than Boston, Manhattan, and San Francisco combined, and about 40 square miles are vacant (Pitera, 2010a). With a population of less than 1 million people,

Detroit continues to suffer the transition from its Fordist roots to a post-Fordist, global economy. The symbolic heart of early twentieth-century industrial ingenuity, Detroit now represents a history of urban disinvestment and abandonment that has been ongoing for more than 50 years.

Detroit's municipal investment in world-city status has focused on the core downtown area, where public and private developers invested heavily in the development of an entertainment district in the late 1990s. Anchored by the construction of two new stadia, Comerica Park and Ford Field, Detroit also hosts numerous performing arts organizations. The city claims Motown and Techno as well as an extensive art deco landscape. Detroit's downtown draws significant numbers of event tourists from neighboring suburbs to its sports games and arts performances. Though this temporal use of space swells the city's population during events, it fails to lure substantial numbers of new residents to populate its many vacant buildings. It also perpetuates

Photo 33.6   Brush Park neighborhood, Detroit
Single family homes, like this abandoned mansion in the Brush Park neighborhood, characterize Detroit's housing stock. Despite extensive marketing and visioning efforts, redevelopment and historic preservation have been slow to happen. (Photographer: Mieka Ritsema)

Photo 33.7   Downtown Detroit
Downtown Detroit's ubiquitous parking garages have alternative, temporary uses, including this rooftop after-party following the Jay-Z and Eminem 2010 concert in Comerica Park. While many neighboring high rises remain vacant, the automobile continues to generate income for the city, if only for event parking. (Photographer: Mieka Ritsema)

the dichotomy between city and suburb, where the former represents predominantly black, low-income residents and the latter predominantly white, middle- and high-income residents.

Detroit's investment in mega-projects has stimulated development in the core downtown area, but it has had little impact on most of Detroit's neighborhoods. The shrinking population and tax base have been accompanied by the withdrawal of city services, ranging from the closure of schools and police stations to lack of snow plowing and park maintenance (Vogel, 2005). Individual residents, community groups and non-profit organizations supported by foundations lead the way in envisioning new futures for Detroit (Lee Boggs, 2006; Parris, 2009; Pitera, 2010b). Urban residents have developed 'do it yourself' solutions to urban problems,

from caring for elderly neighbors to growing their own food and lighting their neighborhoods (Vogel, 2005). In the past five years, small-scale solutions have made national media headlines, but it remains to be seen how the city's reputation and the government's approach will change.

Creativity and everyday life in cities

Much has been written about artistic and cultural heritage from the perspective of major cultural institutions and cultural policies, and less attention has been paid to the artistic innovation that occurs in terms of the everyday cultural life of a city. A city's diverse residents participate in the continual process of creating urban culture(s) by engaging the values, symbols, meanings, and materials of everyday life. The development policies adopted in cities like Hanoi, Cape Town, or Detroit overlook small-scale, local processes of cultural production. Yet, it is in these contexts that innovative works of art and heritage take root. In this vein, it is instructive to explore two artistic examples that present a meaningful articulation of artistic creativity and city-making processes in the trajectories of two very different cities, Detroit and Chandigarh.

Tyree Guyton and Nek Chand are artists who have brought acclaim to their cities on opposite sides of the world. Guyton in Detroit and Chand in Chandigarh have created enduring artistic projects out of the rubble of the city itself. Both artists' projects have been targeted by their municipalities at some point in their careers, and both later received acclaim and recognition for their efforts. Detroit and Chandigarh represent alternative examples of urban decline and urban growth, yet it is important to reflect on the extraordinary artistry that

has emerged out of the ordinary and everyday in both cases.

While the government of India proclaimed its independence and modernity through the creation and construction of the city of Chandigarh, Nek Chand developed his artistic vision through materials salvaged from the city itself. A modernist city, Chandigarh was built after India's independence to become the new capital of Punjab following Partition in 1947. At the time, it was understood as a nation-making moment by Prime Minister Nehru, who stated in 1952, 'Let this be a new town, symbolic of the freedom of India, unfettered by the traditions of the past, an expression of the nation's faith in the future'. His words are enshrined on tourism signs that dot the city declaring Chandigarh's 'architectural marvels'. More famous than the capitol complex designed by legendary architect Le Corbusier, however, is the neighboring Rock Garden created by Nek Chand.

After finishing his day job as a road inspector for Chandigarh, Chand developed his passion night

Photo 33.8   Chandigarh, India
Since 1957, Nek Chand's vision has turned the debris of Chandigarh into an extraordinary Rock Garden. Chand has used rocks, housing fixtures, ceramics, and many other types of salvaged material in his work. The sculptures in this photo are made from broken bangles. (Photographer: Mieka Ritsema)

after night, surreptitiously (Nek Chand Foundation, 2002). With material salvaged from villages destroyed for the impending city and the waste produced during the city's construction, Chand created more than 25 acres of winding paths, sculpture, and waterfalls. Chandigarh's City Museum states that the city itself is one of the greatest urban experiments of the twentieth century, and it was perhaps this experimental creativity that inspired Chand. In an interview, he said, 'I thought, Why should I not build a kingdom too? A kingdom of gods and goddesses' (Gerrard, 1997). Unlike the expertise brought to build Chandigarh, the Rock Garden was the innovation of a man who was not trained as an artist but was inspired by the city being built around him. Although Chandigarh represents a different case than Hanoi, Cape Town, or Detroit, the point of including it here is to emphasize how an individual's everyday experience can lead to an artistic vision that produces international acclaim for a city.

While Chand developed his Rock Garden in secret for many years, Tyree Guyton began his artistic career by publicly challenging the city of Detroit. In the process, Guyton transformed Heidelberg Street in Detroit's East Side from a space of abandonment to an international tourist attraction. Like many city neighborhoods, the East Side suffered from a withdrawal of city services, crime, and neglect. Using the city itself as his canvas, Guyton transformed the streets from spaces of fear to spaces of safety, conviviality, and creativity (Guyton, 2010).

Made with materials salvaged from the city itself, the Heidelberg Project represents the work of one man with a different vision for Detroit. Guyton exemplifies the 'do-it-yourself' attitude characteristic of Detroiters, a critical aspect of local cultural practice

Photo 33.9 **Detroit's East Side streets**
Since 1986, Tyree Guyton's vision has turned Detroit's East Side streets into an artistic wonderland. Using the mundane materials of everyday life, the Heidelberg Project inspires a sense of place and community in Guyton's Detroit neighborhood.
(Photographer: Lily Baum Pollans)

that is generally ignored by municipal policy seeking large-scale solutions to the city's problems. For both Guyton and Chand, their municipalities threatened to destroy their work, and the city of Detroit did in fact demolish several of Guyton's installations which were viewed as contradictory to the city's image (Nasar and Moffat, 2004). Over decades, both artists have engaged the community, the city, and a global audience in imagining different futures for their respective cities.

Conclusion

In terms of resiliency and ingenuity when facing change, institutions often lag behind individuals. The recognition both Nek Chand and Tyree Guyton have received from local and global audiences encouraged their cities to embrace their work and ultimately have supported their cities' global aspirations. Both artists innovatively recycle mundane objects from everyday life in the city for their artwork, and in both cases, the artists' extensive installations emerged from years of dedication and hard work devoted to the city itself. Fashioning art and creating a sense of place from the materials at hand seems to be as compelling, if not more, than mega-projects like stadia and subdivisions for contributing to a city's image.

These examples demonstrate not only the artistry in the everyday, but how urban development policy has the potential to over-shadow the very elements of a city that contribute to the measure of its global significance. While there are extensive literatures critiquing development and neoliberalism in cities around the world, this chapter is intended to question the parameters of cultural policy by considering comparative urban context. While it is practical for cultural policy to emphasize artistry and heritage, expanding the realm of the cultural to include lived experience means that the realm of policy must also be extended to include major urban development decisions. Understanding these relationships in different cities thus becomes more difficult, but also more important as municipalities continue to design and implement contradictory policies.

The patterns of policy-making that significantly impact cultural practices and cultural life require further exploration, especially in conjunction with cultural policy. Responding to the city of Cape Town's urbanization policy, Spiegel et al. (2005: 32) state, 'Policy needs to be flexible, differentiated, and needs-driven if it is to accommodate the realities of social differentiation and stratification process that lie beneath the surface of gender and race divides.' Applying this perspective to cultural policy would seem to be a useful approach for cities seeking to understand and market the identities, experiences, and attractions that make them unique and desirable 'world cities' in the twenty-first century.

REFERENCES

Burbank, M. J., Andranovich, G., and Heying, C. H. (2002) 'Mega-events, urban development, and public policy', *The Review of Policy Research* 19(3): 179–202.

COHRE (2009) 'N2 Gateway project: Housing rights violations as "development" in South Africa', report by COHRE. Geneva: Centre on Housing Rights and Evictions.

Davis, M. (2006) *Planet of Slums*. London: Verso.

Gerrard, N. (1997) 'It's rubbish. But it is art', *The Observer Review*, June 8.

Gough, K. V. and Tran, H. A. (2009) 'Changing housing policy in Vietnam: Emerging inequalities in a residential area of Hanoi', *Cities* 26: 175–186.

Guyton, T. (2010) 'The Heidelberg Project', website video, www.heidelberg.org/.

Huchzermeyer, M. (2004) *Unlawful Occupation: Informal Settlements and Urban Policy in South Africa and Brazil.* Trenton, NJ, and Asmara: Africa World Press.

Keepile, K. (2010) 'Cape traders to be moved ahead of World Cup', *Mail & Guardian Online*, April 26, www.mg.co.za/article/2010-04-26-cape-traders-to-be-moved-ahead-of-world-cup.

Lee Boggs, G. (2006) 'Detroit: Space and place to begin anew', paper presented at the University of Michigan. Available at: www.boggscenter.org/u-of-m-10-06.shtml.

Legassick, M. (2008) 'Western Cape housing crisis: Writings on Joe Slovo and Delft', report. Cape Town: Western Cape Anti-Eviction Campaign and Socialist Alternative.

Logan, W. S. (2000) *Hanoi: Biography of a City*. Sydney: University of New South Wales Press.

MaNeo (2010) Personal communication made at MaNeo's Bed & Breakfast, Langa, Cape Town, South Africa.

McDonald, D. A. (2008) *World City Syndrome: Neoliberalism and Inequality in Cape Town*. New York: Routledge.

Nasar, J. and Moffat, D. (2004) 'The Heidelberg Project – Detroit, Michigan', *Design Observer*, www.designobserver.com/media/pdf/The_Heidelberg_659.pdf.

Nek Chand Foundation (2002) 'About Nek Chand', www.nekchand.com/nek.html.

Newton, C. (2009) 'The reverse side of the medal: About the 2010 FIFA World Cup and the beautification of the N2 in Cape Town', *Urban Forum* 20: 93–108.

Ngoc, H. (2008) *Wandering through Vietnamese Culture* (4th edn). Vietnam: The Gioi Publishers. (1st edn, 1995.)

Parris, Jr., T. (2009) 'Community groups fight the mortgage crisis on the home front', ModelD. Available at: www.modeldmedia.com/features/cdcs20009.aspx.

Pillay, U. and Bass, O. (2009) 'Mega-events as a response to poverty reduction: The 2010 World Cup and urban development', in U. Pillay, R. Tomlinson, and O. Bass (eds.), *Development and Dreams: The 2010 Legacy of the World Cup*. Cape Town: HSRC Press, pp. 76–95.

Pillay, U., Tomlinson, R., and Bass O. (eds.) (2009) *Development and Dreams: The 2010 Legacy of the World Cup*. Cape Town: HSRC Press.

Pitera, D. (2010a) 'Neighborhood retooling', presentation to the International Honors Program. Detroit, Michigan, August 30.

Pitera, D. (2010b) 'Productive residue: The casting of alternative public space', in G. Wilkins (ed.), *Distributed Urbanism*. New York: Routledge.

Spiegel, A., Watson, V., and Wilkinson, P. (2005) 'Women, difference, and urbanization patterns in Cape Town, South Africa', *Anthropology Southern Africa* 28(1&2): 31–38.

Tran, H. A. (2010) 'Ancient Quarter history', presentation to the International Honors Program. Hanoi, Vietnam, November 18.

UN-HABITAT (2007) *Enhancing Human Safety and Security: Global Report on Human Settlements 2007*. London: Earthscan.

UN-HABITAT (2008) *State of the World's Cities 2010/2011: Bridging the Urban Divide*. London: Earthscan.

Vietnews (2010) 'Hanoi plans green, modern capital', *Vietnews*, April 12, www.vietnewsonline.vn/News/Society/Environment/14320/Hanoi-plans-green-modern-capital.htm.

Vogel, S. (2005) 'DIY city services', in Philipp Oswalt (ed.), *Shrinking Cities: International Research,* (Vol. 1). Germany: Hatje Cantz, pp. 462–469.

Voice of the Cape (2010) 'Traders take to CTN streets', *Voice of the Cape*, February 24, www.vocfm.co.za/index.php?&section=news&category=&vocnews=&article=51541.

Waibel, M. (2004) 'The Ancient Quarter of Hanoi: A reflection of urban transition processes', *ASIEN* 92: 30–48.

Waibel, M. (2006) 'The production of urban space in Vietnam's metropolis in the course of transition: Internationalization, polarization, and newly emerging lifestyles in Vietnamese society', *Trialog* 89(2): 43–48.

Watson, V. (2002) *Change and Continuity in Spatial Planning: Metropolitan Planning in Cape Town under Political Transition*. London: Routledge.

Williams, R. (1988) *Keywords: A Vocabulary of Culture and Society*. London: Fontana.

PART 2   INDICATOR SUITES

Introduction

Overarching Suites

— **Trends in Urbanization**
— **City Networks and Rankings**
— **City Comparisons**

City Suites

— **Abu Dhabi**
— **Berlin**
— **Istanbul**
— **London**
— **L'viv**
— **Mexico City**
— **New York City**
— **São Paulo**
— **Shanghai**

Describing and Comparing Culture in Cities Globally:

Introducing the Indicator Suites — Michael Hœlscher

References

All about Shanghai and Environs. A Standard Guidebook (Edition 1934-35). Shanghai: The University Press. Online: http://www.virtualshanghai.net/Original_Text.php?ID=5.

Anheier, H. K. (2004) *Civil Society: Measurement, Evaluation, Policy*. London: Earthscan.

Anheier, H.K. (2007) Introducing 'cultural indicator' suites. In H.K. Anheier & R. Isar (eds.), *Conflicts and Tensions* (pp. 335-347). London: Sage.

Anheier, H. K. & Hoelscher, M. (2010) Creativity, Innovation, Globalization: What International Experts Think. In H.K. Anheier & R. Isar (eds.), *Cultural Expression, Creativity and Innovation* (pp. 421-433). London: Sage.

Beaverstock, J. V., Smith, R. G., Taylor, P. J., Walker, D. R. F. & Lorimer, H. (2000) 'Globalization and world cities: some measurement methodologies'. *Applied Geography*, 20, 43-63.

Berking, H (ed.)(2008) *Die Eigenlogik der Städte: neue Wege für die Stadtforschung*. Frankfurt: Campus.

Buckley, C. (1998) 'Rural/urban differentials in demographic processes: The Central Asian states'. *Population Research and Policy Review*, 17, 71-89.

Castells, M. (1989) *The informational city : information technology, economic restructuring, and the urban-regional process*. Oxford: Blackwell.

Dodman, D. (2009) 'Blaming cities for climate change? An analysis of urban greenhouse gas emissions inventories'. *Environment and Urbanization*, 21, 185-201.

Evans, G. (2009) 'Creative Cities, Creative Spaces and Urban Policy'. *Urban Studies*, 46, 1003-1040.

Fischer, C.S. (1975) 'Toward a Subcultural Theory of Urbanism'. *American Journal of Sociology*, 80, 1319-1341.

Fischer, C. S. (1995) 'The Subcultural Theory of Urbanism: A Twentieth-Year Assessment'. *American Journal of Sociology*, 101, 543-577.

'Our world is shrinking, while cities are expanding into each other, continuously reshaping our (and their) sense of place within a global horizon. As cities compete for relevance they are challenged to claim both situated difference and global connectedness.'

— (Göktürk et al. 2010: 1)

Introduction

Each volume of the 'Cultures & Globalization' series consists of two parts. The first part contains analyses and explorations of various aspects of the volume's theme. The second part complements these chapters with selected quantitative and qualitative data. These data are displayed in an easily accessible way in the form of what we call Indicator Suites, following insights from information graphics (Tufte 2001).

In the first four volumes of the series, the structure of the Indicator Suites followed a conceptual scheme. This can be represented as a matrix with three perspectives of globalization (economic, political and cultural globalization) and four aspects of culture (as a system of meaning and values, as an economic system, as a political aspects system and as a system of sites and movements). All these were analysed on four different levels (the transnational, the national, organizations and the regional level, and individuals). This conceptual scheme and its background are explained in more detail in Anheier (2007). However, the indicator suites of the current volume have a different starting point. The main reason is the book's focus on cities, which implies a specific level of analysis. One advantage of this approach is to enable a close link between the narrative chapters and the data section. Nevertheless, the aim is still to bring in other levels as well by putting city trends into a wider context of globalization. In this respect, the appendix to this Introduction offers an overview of the many city-related indicators found in previous volumes of the series.

Part 2 consists of twelve indicator suites. Nine deal with cities covered as city profiles in Part 1. Three suites take on comparative perspectives: one compares the nine cities, a second looks at urbanization, and a third examines city networks and rankings.

Why cities?

Since the early days of urban sociology the city has been understood as a kind of laboratory for modernization processes (Simmel 1903). Urban lifestyles, labelled as urbanism (Wirth 1938), have been especially prone to new forms of individual identity and community living. One reason for this is the sheer size of city populations, allowing subcultures to develop a critical mass and to cross-fertilize each other (Fischer 1975,1995).

Another reason is that cities throughout history have been the destination of migration. The resulting heterogeneity of urban areas in terms of different life-styles certainly contributes to their creativity (e.g. Baycan-Levent 2010). However, it also makes them contested places where different groups put forward claims of many kinds (see Harvey 2008; Lefebvre 2011). And while many of the emerging opportunities and urban problems are of an economic nature, cultural and social aspects definitely also play a crucial role as well. All this challenges city governance on how to manage this internal diversity.

Besides a more or less internal view of singular cities, a more relational perspective has evolved. Cities are increasingly networked and linked by commercial, people, goods, services and other flows. They are also competitors in a global market for corporations, the 'creative class' (Florida 2005), and for media attention. National governments conceive larger cities as 'growth machines' (Molotch 1976) or 'economic powerhouses' (Van Winden 2010: 101) for their national economies as a whole. Especially, the creative or cultural industries and the knowledge economy generally are often seen by policy makers as means of urban development (Flew 2010; Knight 1995; Van Winden und Van Den Berg 2004). As elaborated in the Introduction and in many chapters of this volume, this stance calls for strategic cultural policies and governance of cities (see Evans 2009; Lazzeretti und Cinti 2009). However, it is often difficult to combine the aims of internal integration and external attraction.

The selected cities deal with these demands and tensions quite differently. As such, not only single cities can be seen as laboratories of modernity, but one can also use the multitude of cities with their different approaches as a kind of real-life quasi-experiment in globalization. While each city has its own contexts and logics, it is nevertheless possible to draw some important overarching conclusions by comparing their policies and solutions (e.g. Hill 2004). Besides the qualitative analyses presented in the previous chapters, the following indicator suites present some more quantitative data as well.

Overarching Suites

Urbanization is one of the most important demographic trends of our world today. The United Nations reported that from 2008 on, more than half of the world's population lives in cities (Unfpa 2007). For Europe and the Americas the figure is over 80 per cent. Ever more urban agglomerations are turning into megacities, especially in Asia and in less developed countries generally. One important reason for this is rural exodus, fuelled by expectations of better opportunities in cities than in rural

Flew, T. (2010): 'Toward a Cultural Economic Geography of Creative Industries and Urban Development: Introduction to the Special Issue on Creative Industries and Urban Development'. *The Information Society: An International Journal*, 26, 85 - 91.

Florida, R. (2005) *The Flight of the Creative Class. The New Global Competition for Talent.* New York: HarperCollins.

GaWC (Globalization and World Cities Research Network) (2010) *The World According to GaWC 2010*. Online resource. Available from http://www.lboro.ac.uk/gawc/world2010.html.

Göktürk, D., Soysal, L. &Türeli, I. (eds.)(2010) *Orienting Istanbul. Cultural Capital of Europe?* Abingdon: Routledge.

Harvey, D. (2008) 'The Right to the City'. *New Left Review*, 53, 23-40.

Hill, R. C. (2004) 'Cities and nested hierarchies'. *International Social Science Journal*, 56, 373–384.

Knight, R.V. (1995) 'Knowledge-based Development: Policy and Planning Implications for Cities'. *Urban Studies*, 32, 225-260.

Lazzeretti, L. & Cinti, T. (2009) 'Governance-specific Factors and Cultural Clusters: The Case of the Museum Clusters in Florence'. *Creative Industries Journal*, 2, 19-35.

Lefebvre, H. (2011) *The production of space.* [reprint] Malden: Blackwell.

Molotch, H. (1976) 'The City as a Growth Machine: Toward a Political Economy of Place'. *American Journal of Sociology*, 82, 309-332.

Neuman, M. (2005) 'The Compact City Fallacy'. *Journal of Planning Education and Research*, 25, 11-26.

Rössel, J. (2012) Methodological Nationalism. In: H.K. Anheier & M. Juergensmeyer (eds.), *Encyclopedia of Global Studies*. London: Sage.

Sassen, S. (1991) *The Global City. New York, London, Tokyo.* Princeton (NJ): Princeton University Press.

Simmel, G. (1903) Die Großstädte und das Geistesleben. In Th. Petermann (ed.), *Die Großstadt. Vorträge und Aufsätze zur Städteausstellung* (pp. 185-206). Dresden: GeheStiftung.

Taylor, P. J. (2005) 'Leading World Cities: Empirical Evaluations of Urban Nodes in Multiple Networks'. *Urban Studies*, 42, 1593-1608.

Trust for London and New Policy Institute (2010) *Income inequality in London compared with other English regions*. Retrieved September 7, 2011, from London's poverty profile Web site: http://www.londonspovertyprofile.org.uk/indicators/topics/inequality/income-inequality-in-london-compared-with-other-english-regions/

Tufte, E. R. (2001) *The Visual Display of Quantitative Information*. Cheshire, CT: Graphics Press.

UN Habitat (2001) *Cities in a Globalizing World. Global Report on Human Settlements 2001*. London: Earthscan.

UN Habitat (2008) *State of the World's Cities 2010/2011. Bridging the Urban Divide*. London: Earthscan.

UN Habitat (2011) *Cities and Climate Change. Global Report on Human Settlements 2011*. London: Earthscan.

UNFPA (United Nations Population Fund) (2007) *State of World Population 2007. Unleashing the Potential of Urban Growth*. New York: UNFPA.

Urban Age (2006) *Urban Age Summit Berlin Newspaper*. Online resource. Available from http://www.urban-age.net/0_downloads/UA_Summit_Berlin_Newspaper.pdf.

Van Winden, W. (2010) 'Knowledge and the European City'. *Tijdschrift voor economische en sociale geografie*, 101, 100–106.

Van Winden, W. & Van Den Berg, L. (2004) *Cities in the Knowledge Economy: New Governance Challenges*. Rotterdam: Euricur - European Institute for Comparative Urban Research.

Wirth, L. (1938) 'Urbanism as a Way of Life'. *American Journal of Sociology*, 44, 1–24.

areas, which results in massive social, economic and ecological problems. However, while this trend has been seen as a major threat, recent research also suggests that we should be cautiously optimistic. It seems that cities themselves are often not the problem, but mainly high rates of population growth. Analyses show that city populations often exhibit lower birth rates (e.g. Buckley 1998), have on average a higher economic productivity, and often even show lower per capita pollution than people living in rural areas (Un Habitat 2008, 2011). However, larger cities also often have the highest levels of social inequality within their countries (e.g. Trust for London and New Policy Institute 2010). For this reason, the first suite tries to illustrate the phenomenon of urbanization from different angles.

The second overarching suite, *City networks and rankings*, draws attention to an important aspect of urbanization. Cities are not only located within their nations, but within a dense web of cities, establishing transnational networks, relationships, and hierarchies between them. Cities are an integral part of the 'space of flows' (Castells 1989), and Sassen has prominently shown how global cities' division of labour operates (Sassen 1991). An important indicator of world city status is the connections to other influential cities (e.g. Taylor 2005) [i]. These networks of cities, some of which have higher GDPs than mid-sized countries, are the true places of globalization, as they are at the same time locations for international companies' headquarters, for international non-governmental organizations and the destination for national and international migrants. One might argue whether cities are also the places where most innovations originate (as some analysts claim that most innovations come from the periphery), but the cities are definitely the places where new ideas can flourish and spread. And in the opinion of cultural experts the diversity that can be found within cities fosters cultural creativity (Anheier & Hoelscher 2010: 423).

Besides the nine indicator suites dealing with single cities in more detail, which are described in the next paragraph, a third suite compares them with regard to important dimensions related to culture and creativity. Such *city comparisons* allow us to put the cities in context. The idea of comparing cities on multiple dimensions in an easily accessible way, as is done in this suite, is also used by others. It parallels the idea of the civil society diamond (Anheier 2004), only here it is located at the city-level instead of the country-level. The Urban Age project also uses similar techniques to display their information on cities (Urban Age 2006). [ii]

The nine city suites

While the suites described so far deal with comparative issues, the following take account of each city's own logic (Berking 2008). The nine cities presented in more detail are Abu Dhabi, Berlin, Istanbul, London, L'viv, Mexico City, New York, São Paulo and Shanghai. [iii] All city suites follow a similar outline, with data on the development of its population, questions of migrants and ethnic diversity, overall and cultural budgets, the composition of the labour market, with a special focus on the creative economies, foreign tourists as an indicator of the city's overall attractiveness, and data on select cultural institutions or events.

London and *New York* are two classical 'global cities' with strong global linkages (Sassen 1991). They probably best represent the type of the Western Metropolis that combines economic and cultural vitality. While London, also being the capital of its country, is clearly by far the most important city in the country, New York, although having a large impact, is less crucial within the US, as there are other globally important American cities like Los Angeles or Chicago.

Berlin and L'viv complement London as European cities. Berlin was chosen because of its contested history. Over forty years, the city was divided into a Western part, belonging to West Germany, and an Eastern part, the capital of former East Germany. Since reunification in 1990, the city has developed a new dynamic. However, while some claim that it is one of the culturally most vibrant cities in Europe, its economic power is still lagging behind that of most comparable cities.

L'viv is included as a medium-sized city. Again, its history as a post-Soviet city makes it an example for the dynamics that emerged in Eastern Europe after 1989. The town is striving to combine the legacy of the twentieth century in a creative and forward looking way with its current situation as well as with its pre-communist history.

Abu Dhabi and Istanbul represent two very different examples of larger cities in the Middle East, and both are also cities where cultures intersect. *Istanbul*, an European Capital of Culture in 2010, sits on the edges of both the European and the Asian continents. And for many centuries now it has integrated traditions from both. Although growing very fast in recent years, it maintains a strong historical legacy. *Abu Dhabi*, on the other hand, has become a global cultural player only quite recently. However, with massive investments in cultural infrastructure, often in cooperation with prestigious Western partners such as the Louvre, the emirate is trying to establish itself as an important cultural hotspot.

i
See Beaverstock (2000) on some measurement issues for world city status.

ii
The "Urban Age" project is probably one of the most advanced initiatives of city comparisons (see http://www.urban-age.net/).

iii
The formerly included Johannesburg had to be dropped.

iv
Especially in the developing world a functioning urban planning that is able to deal with the sometimes explosive growth has to be designed in the first place. However, in these cases the softer approaches can already be built into the newly developing structures right from the start.

359

Shanghai, as the only Asian city in the sample, also exhibits such a centrally planned approach to improvements of the cultural infrastructure, though on a somewhat different level. With a first global appearance in the early twentieth century ('the most cosmopolitan city in the world' [All About Shanghai and Environs 1935]), and supported by China's claim to be one of the leading countries of the world, cultural developments today seem to be based on economic and political power as well as self-confidence.

Last, but not least, with *Mexico City* and *São Paulo* two Latin American cities are part of the indicator suites in this volume. Mexico City is one of the largest urban agglomerations worldwide. It is the economic, political, and cultural capital of Mexico and of Central America as a whole, and operates as a point of intersection for the whole region, connecting North- and South America. With regard to population size, São Paulo is the largest city in the southern hemisphere (Vasconcelos-Oliveira compares it with the second largest city in South America, Buenos Aires, in chapter 27). Its strong regional influence in both economic and cultural terms is complemeted by its globalization networks (GaWC 2010).

Concluding remarks

City life, as different as it may be from one location to another, is shaping the experiences of an ever increasing majority of the world's population. And cities, as modernity, have always at least two aspects: they offer opportunities as well as threats. Cultural clashes and economic inequalities characterizing them can do both: lead to increased creativity and cultural hybridity, resulting in new cultural forms and expression, as well as in increased economic activity; or lead to increased tensions and conflicts. Often they do both at the same time. The same appears with regard to ecological sustainability: while cities often experience severe problems with, for example, pollution, water supply and traffic congestion, their per capita use of natural resources is often lower than comparative figures for smaller villages and towns (see, for example, the discussion on the 'compact city', e.g. Dodman 2009; critically Neuman 2005).

To deal with heterogeneity, traditional top-down administrative urban planning is certainly still necessary, but needs to be supplemented by softer governance approaches, taking cultural issues into account (Un Habitat 2001: Part II). [iv] New governance approaches, generating synergy effects by bringing city administration, economic actors and civil society together, are sought after. Public-private partnerships are but one instrument discussed with regard to this. Part 1 of this volume introduces examples of these new approaches, and Part 2 tries to put them into context.

The indicator suites that follow can in no wise provide a full account of the richness and dynamic of the nine cities. Data limitations and space prohibit this. Nevertheless, the following pages should give readers an initial overview and provide them with references for further inquiries. With this, the book contributes to a wide range of initiatives trying to overcome methodological nationalism (Rössel 2012) in the social sciences by highlighting the importance of sub-national units for the analysis of globalization processes.

Overview of city-related data in previous volumes of the "Cultures & Globalization" series

Data labels of suite	Data Point	Page
Volume I		
Global Civil Society / Extensity + Intensity	Top 10: NGO Secretariats by cities	359
	WTO Ministerial Conference Attendance	360
Global Sites + Events/ Hong Kong + Mumbai	Hong Kong Population by Ethnicity (2001; % of total population)	476
	Hong Kong Visitor Arrivals (in millions)	476
	Hong Kong Inward + Outward Movements of Aircraft + Ocean Vessels (in millions)	476
	Hong Kong International Trade (Exports + Imports in $US Millions)	476
	Mumbai Population Growth (Change 1950 -200 + Forecast 2015)	477
	Mumbai % Share Religions (2001)	477
	Mumbai % of Migrants (% of all migrants, %of total population in Mumbai)	477
	Mumbai Population, Literacy + Work (by Gender)	477
	Mumbai Foreign Direct Investment (by top ten countires and % of all approved Proposals 2004)	477
	Mumbai Foreign Direct Investment (Total #of Proposals approved 2005)	477
Global Sites + Events/ New York City	NYC Demographics: Ethnic Breakdown of Population (By Borough 2001)	478
	NYC Top 20 Countries of Origin for focign-born Citizens (2000)	478
	NYC Demographics: Top 10 Languages Spoken at Home (Population <5yrs in 2000)	478
	Port of NY + NJ: Value of all cargo Imports + Exports (2003+2004 in $US thousands)	479
	NYC: Fortune 500 Companies with a yearly revenue over 20 bill. (2003)	479
Global Sites + Events/ Los Angeles	Los Angeles: Top US Ethnic Newspapers Published (estimated circulations 2001)	480
	Los Angeles Port: Exports + Imports (1988–200)	481
Global Sites + Events/ London	London Population by ethnic group (April 2001)	482
	London Religious Diversity	482
	London: Top City Based Global TNCs	482
	London: Most Diverse Boroughs (2001)	482
Global Performance Art	Art gallery area, Manhattan and Brooklyn, 1987-2007 International Philharmonic Tour Locations	293
	Estimated # Of Cultural Estabsilhments in NY (Manhattan) + Los Angeles Counties (2004)	495
Volume II		
Culture As A System Of Sites + Movements/ Global Sites + Events Global Sites + Events / Global Cultural Centers + Cities/ NY + LA	Estimated # Of Cultural Estabsilhments in NY (Manhattan) + Los Angeles Counties (2004)	509
	Estimated % Breakdown of Cultural Establishments in NY + LA (2004)	508
	Estimated # + % Breakdown of Cultural Employees in NY County (Manhattan) + LA County	510
	The Embeddedness of NYC`s Cultural Industries (estimated # of creative workers in NYC outside the Creative Industries)	511
	Top 15 Public Cultural Corporations Headquartered in New York City (2007)	512
Global Sites + Events / Global Cultural Centers + Cities/ Tokyo	Top 20 Cultural Industry Corporations Headquartered in Tokyo (2007)	514
	# of Cultural Facilities Tokyo (2005)	515
	Estimated # of Cultural Establishments in Tokyo Metro Area (2004)	515
Global Sites + Events / Global Cultural Centers + Cities/Singapore	Public Cultural Corporations Headquartered in Singapore (2007)	516
	# of Major Art Companies (1995, 2000, 2005)	517
	Estimated # of Creative Establishments + Employees in Singapore by Service Industry (2004)	517

Trends in Urban- ization

References

Hoornweg, D. (2010) *Cities and Climate Change. An Urgent Agenda*. Urban Development Series Knowledge Papers, Dec. 2010, Vol 10. Washington: World Bank. Retrieved August 1, 2011, from http://siteresources.worldbank.org/ INTUWM/Resources/340232-1205330656272/ CitiesandClimateChange.pdf

Megacity (2011) Retrieved August 3, 2011, from Wikipedia: http://en.wikipedia.org/wiki/Megacity

Satterthwaite, D. (2002) *The ten and a half myths that may distort the urban policies of governments and international agencies*. Working Paper. Department for International Development. Retrieved August 3, 2011, from http://www.ucl.ac.uk/dpu-projects/21st_ Century/myths/myths.htm.

Data Sources

1
UN Habitat (2008) State of the World's Cities 2010/2011. Bridging the Urban Divide. London: Earthscan. Page 12. Retrieved July 29, 2011, from http://www.unhabitat.org/pmss/ listItemDetails.aspx?publicationID=2917

2
United Nations, Department of Economic and Social Affairs, Population Division (2010) World Urbanization Prospects : The 2009 Revision. CD-ROM Edition - Data in digital form (POP/ DB/WUP/Rev.2009). Retrieved July 27, 2011, from http://esa.un.org/unpd/ wup/index.htm.

3
Urbanization by country. Retrieved July 29, 2011, from http://en.wikipedia.org/wiki/Urbanization_ by_country (data originally from CIA World Factbook)

4
City Mayor Statistics: Fastest Growing Cities. Retrieved July 29, 2011, from http://www. citymayors.com/statistics/urban_growth1.html

5
Morris, I. (2010) Social Development. Manuscript. Stanford University. Retrieved July 29, 2011, from http://www.ianmorris.org/ docs/social-development.pdf.

The twenty-first century is increasingly seen as the *urban age*. The United Nations has estimated that by the end of 2008 over 50 per cent of the world's population lived in cities. Twenty-six agglomerations have populations of more than 10 million people (*Megacity*, 2011). An urbanization level of 70 per cent is forecasted for 2050 (Data Point 1).

What Do We Know?

• Although around half of the world's population lives in urban areas, this figure differs by world regions (Data Point 1). Northern Europe and North and South America have the highest rates, with more than 80 per cent of the population living in urban areas, and Eastern Africa and South Central Asia with fewer than 40 per cent.

• Tokyo has been the largest city for more than 50 years (Data Point 2). At the beginning of the new century, however, New York lost second place to the fast-growing Indian megacities of Delhi and Mumbai and the somewhat slower-growing São Paulo and Mexico City. London, Paris, and Moscow dropped off the list of the largest 15 cities before 2000.

• Singapore and Hong Kong, as city-states, have the highest level of urbanization. The United Kingdom and Venezuela also have urbanization levels higher than 90 per cent. However, in some African, Asian, and Caribbean states fewer than one in five citizens live in a city (Data Point 3).

• Beihai, China, is predicted to be the fastest growing city of the world between 2006 and 2020, with an annual growth rate of more than 10 per cent. Cities in industrially developed countries have obviously had smaller growth rates, as all the cities included (with the exception of Toluca) are in countries with medium to low development (Data Point 4).

• Although megacities are a relatively new phenomenon, urbanization as a trend has a long history. Two thousand years ago, Rome had around 1 million inhabitants (Data Point 5).

• Cities differ not only according to their size, but also, with massive consequences for their inhabitants, according to their density. Mumbai, for example, has more than 10 times the number of people per square meter as New York (Data Point 6). Additionally, distribution within the cities is not equal either. Urban Age Project researchers and Hoornweg (2010) have given examples of how to display densities within cities.

• Similarly unequal is the distribution of large urban agglomerations (more than 5 million inhabitants) across regions as it is predicted for the coming years. Eastern and South Central Asia will have by far the largest number of such agglomerations, followed by North and South America (Data Point 7).

• Data Point 8 supports the claim that cities are more productive than rural areas. All but one city produced a larger share of the national gross domestic product (GDP) than its population share would suggest. The interesting exception is Sydney.

• The importance of cities is underlined by the fact that some cities have larger economies than many countries (Data point 9). Tokyo and New York, for example, have larger GDPs than Korea, Canada, or Australia.

• Sustainability is an urgent issue for cities. Data Point 10 displays the relationship between GDP and the emission of greenhouse-gas equivalents for larger cities across the world. New York and Tokyo are outliers with regard to GDP, but Moscow and Shanghai, although producing much less wealth, have equally high emissions. So, productivity is but one factor influencing a city's ecological footprint, and other factors also play a crucial role.

What Are The Issues?

The trend toward people's life experiences increasingly being shaped by urbanization buttresses the claim made throughout this volume that cities are increasingly central actors of cultural policy and governance. However, some questions remain. First, an international definition of *city* has still not been agreed on, and varying definitions by some larger countries could increase or decrease the world's level of urbanization by some percentage points (Satterthwaite, 2002). Second, urbanization can take quite different forms. Although many European cities have long histories and a relatively settled urban fabric, some newly emerging megacities are characterized by chaotic conditions and large slum areas. *Urbanization* can, therefore, mean quite different things, from increased inequality (cities exhibit larger differences in income) to improved cultural and even ecological living conditions. After long years of pessimism regarding the status of future cities, a new discussion is emerging that stresses the positive side, such as increased productivity and even better sustainability under certain circumstances. However, intelligent governance on different levels—international, national, and regional—and even within certain city districts is desperately needed to overcome problems of integration and social inequality.

6
City Mayor Statistics: The largest cities in the world by land area, population and density. Retrieved July 27, 2011, from http://www.citymayors.com/statistics/largest-cities-density-125.html.

7
UN Habitat (2011) Cities and Climate Change. Global Report on Human Settlements 2011. London: Earthscan. Retrieved July 29, 2011, from http://www.unhabitat.org/downloads/docs/GRHS2011_Full.pdf

8
UN Habitat (2008) State of the World's Cities 2010/2011. Bridging the Urban Divide. London: Earthscan. Page 19. Retrieved July 29, 2011, from http://www.unhabitat.org/pmss/listItemDetails.aspx?publicationID=2917

9
Hoornweg, D. (2010) Cities and Climate Change. An Urgent Agenda. Urban Development Series Knowledge Papers, December 2010, Vol 10. Washington: World Bank. Retrieved August 1, 2011, from http://siteresources.worldbank.org/INTUWM/Resources/340232-1205330656272/CitiesandClimateChange.pdf.

10
Hoornweg, D. (2010) Cities and Climate Change. An Urgent Agenda. Urban Development Series Knowledge Papers, December 2010, Vol 10. Washington: World Bank. Page 17. Retrieved August 1, 2011, from http://siteresources.worldbank.org/INTUWM/Resources/340232-1205330656272/CitiesandClimateChange.pdf.

1 **Urbanization Level Per Region and Tipping Point** (Urban vs Rural Population)

Region	Tipping point before 2010 (year)	2010 urban (%)	Tipping point after 2010 after (years)	2050 urban (%)
World	–	50.6	–	70
More developed regions	Before 1950	75	–	86
Europe	Before 1950	72.6	–	83.8
Eastern Europe	1963	68.8	–	80
Northern Europe	Before 1950	84.4	–	90.7
Southern Europe	1960	67.5	–	81.2
Western Europe	Before 1950	77	–	86.5
Less Developed Regions	–	45.3	–	67
Africa	–	40	2020	61.8
Sub-Saharan Africa	–	37.3	2030	60.5
Eastern Africa	2005	23.7	2032	47.6
North Africa	1993	52	–	72
Southern Africa	–	58.8	–	77.6
Western Africa	–	44.6	–	68
Asia	–	42.5	–	66.2
Eastern Asia	–	48.5	2020	74.1
South-central Asia	–	32.2	2023	57.2
South-eastern Asia	1980	48.2	2013	73.3
Western Asia	1962	66.3	2040	79.3
Latin America and the Caribbean		79.4	2013	88.7
Central America	1965	71.7	–	83.3
South America	1960	83.7	–	91.4
Rest of the World				
North America	Before 1950	82.1	–	90.2
Oceania	Before 1950	70.6	–	76.4

	1950	1955	1960	1965	1970	1975	1980	1985	1990	1995	2000	2005	2010
Tokyo	2	1	1	1	1	1	1	1	1	1	1	1	1
Delhi									11	6	6	2	2
Sao Paulo			15	13	8	5	4	4	4	4	4	5	3
Mumbai		15	14	15	15	14	10	6	5	5	5	6	4
Mexico		12	12	8	4	3	3	3	3	3	2	3	5
New York	1	2	2	2	2	2	2	2	2	2	3	4	6
Shanghai	9	5	5	11	14					13	7	7	7
Kolkata	8	11	11	12	12	9	8	9	7	7	8	8	8
Buenos Aires	6	6	6	7	7	7	7	8	10	9	9	10	11
Los Angeles	11	9	7	6	5	6	6	7	8	8	10	11	12
Rio de Janeiro	14	13	13	14	13	11	11	11	12	12	12	14	14
Osaka	10	10	8	5	3	4	5	5	6	10	11	15	
Seoul						15	12	10	9	11			
Cairo							15	14	14	14	14		
Paris	4	4	4	3	6	8	9	12	13	15			
Moscow	5	7	10	10	10	10	13	13	15				
London	3	3	3	4	9	12	14	15					
Chicago	7	8	9	9	11	13							

3 Eleven Countries (> 1 million inhabitants) with Highest and Lowest Levels of Urbanization (2008)

Singapore	100
Hong Kong	100
Puerto Rico	98
Kuwait	98
Belgium	97
Qatar	96
Venezuela	93
Uruguay	92
Israel	92
Argentina	92
United Kingdom	90
Burkina Faso	20
Malawi	19
Rwanda	18
Nepal	17
Ethiopia	17
Niger	16
Sri Lanka	15
Uganda	13
Trinidad and Tobago	13
Papua New Guinea	12
Burundi	10

0 10 20 30 40 50 60 70 80 90 100

4 The World's Fastest Growing Cities

(estimated growth rate 2006-2020 above 4%)

Beihai (China)	10.58
Ghaziabad (India)	5.2
Sana'a (Yemen)	5
Surat (India)	4.99
Kabul (Afghanistan)	4.74
Bamako (Mali)	4.45
Lagos (Nigeria)	4.44
Faridabad (India)	4.44
Dar es Salaam (Tanzania)	4.39
Chittagong (Bangladesh)	4.29
Toluca (Mexico)	4.25
Lubumbashi (Congo)	4.1
Kampala (Uganda)	4.03

0 2 4 6 8 10 12

5 Largest Cities in Historical Perspective

Key: City / Size

"Western"

Beidha, Basta, Çatalhöyük 1,000	Tell Brak 4,000	Uruk 45,000
Mureybet 500	Çatalhöyük 3,000	Uruk, Tell Brak 5,000

Thebes 50,000 — Rome 1,000,000 — Cordoba 200,000 — London 900,000

Memphis, Ur 60,000 — Babylon 150,000 — Constantinople 450,000 — Cairo 400,000 — London 6,600,000

8000 BCE 7000 BCE 6000 BCE 5000 BCE 4000 BCE 3000 BCE 2000 BCE 1000 BCE 500 BCE 1 BCE / CE 500 CE 1000 CE 1500 CE 1800 CE 1900 CE

"Eastern"

Jiangzhai, Jiahu 300 — Luoyi, Feng 35,000 — Chang'an 500,000 — Kaifeng 1,000,000 — Beijing 1,100,000

Dadiwan 5,000 — Linzi 80,000 — Luoyang 200,000 — Beijing 678,000 — Tokyo 1,750,000

Fengcheng-Nanshui 11,000

6 Cities and their Population Density

(2007; people per sqKm; Top 10 and selected cities)

Mumbai (1)	29,650
Kolkata (2)	23,900
Karachi (3)	18,900
Lagos (4)	18,150
Shenzhen (5)	17,150
Seoul/Incheon (6)	16,700
Taipei (7)	15,200
Chennai (8)	14,350
Bogota (9)	13,500
Shanghai (10)	13,400
Sao Paulo (25)	9,000
Mexico City (27)	8,400
Istanbul (32)	7,700
London (43)	5,100
Buenos Aires (46)	4,950
Barcelona (48)	4,850
Tokyo/Yokohama (50)	4,750
Manchester (58)	4,000
Berlin (65)	3,750
Paris (69)	3,550
Los Angeles (90)	2,750
Torino (94)	2,700
Johannesburg/East Rand (100)	2,500
New York (114)	2,050
Vancouver (123)	1,650
Melbourne (127)	1,500
Marseille (154)	1,199
Brisbane (167)	950
Abu Dhabi (201)	700

7 Number of Large Urban Agglomerations

by Geographic Aggregates: • 2000   • 2010   • 2020

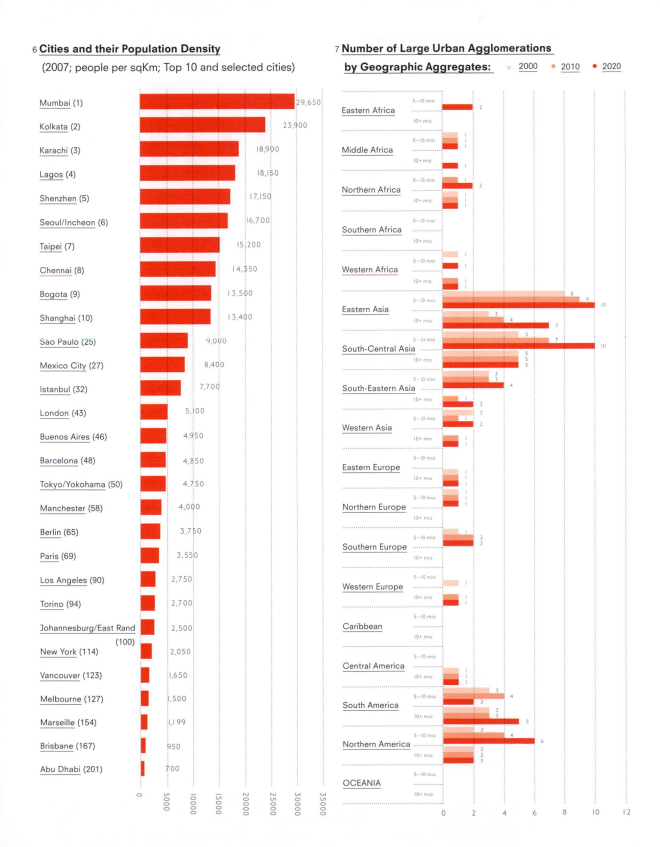

369

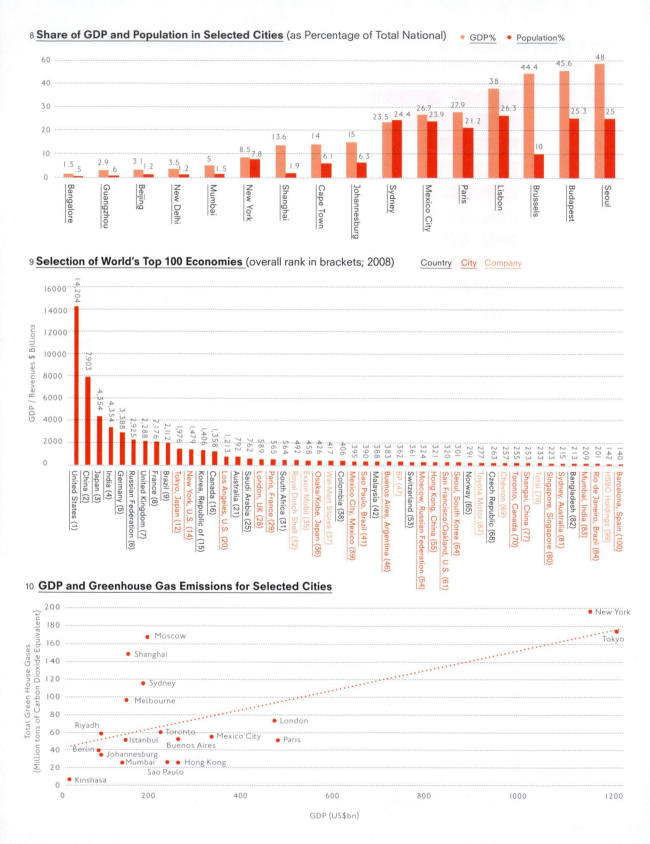

8 Share of GDP and Population in Selected Cities (as Percentage of Total National) ● GDP% ● Population%

Bangalore 1.5 / .5
Guangzhou 2.9 / .6
Beijing 3.1 / 1.2
New Delhi 3.5 / 1.2
Mumbai 5 / 1.5
New York 8.5 / 7.8
Shanghai 13.6 / 1.9
Cape Town 14 / 6.1
Johannesburg 15 / 6.3
Sydney 23.5 / 24.4
Mexico City 26.7 / 23.9
Paris 27.9 / 21.2
Lisbon 3.8 / 26.3
Brussels 44.4 / 10
Budapest 45.6 / 25.3
Seoul 48 / 25

9 Selection of World's Top 100 Economies (overall rank in brackets; 2008)   Country   City   Company

GDP / Revenues $ Billions

United States (1) 14,204
China (2) 7,903
Japan (3) 4,354
India (4) 4,354
Germany (5) 3,388
Russian Federation (6) 2,925
United Kingdom (7) 2,288
France (8) 2,176
Brazil (9) 1,976
Tokyo, Japan (12) 1,479
New York, U.S. (14) 1,406
Korea, Republic of (15) 1,358
Canada (16) 1,213
Australia (21) 792
Saudi Arabia (25) 762
London, UK (28) 589
Paris, France (29) 565
South Africa (31) 564
Royal Dutch Shell (32) 492
Exxon Mobil (35) 458
Osaka/Kobe, Japan (36) 426
Wal-Mart Stores (37) 417
Colombia (38) 406
Mexico City, Mexico (39) 395
Sao Paulo, Brazil (41) 390
Malaysia (42) 388
Buenos Aires, Argentina (46) 383
BP (47) 362
Switzerland (53) 361
Moscow, Russian Federation (54) 324
Hong Kong, China (55) 321
San Francisco/Oakland, U.S. (61) 320
Seoul, South Korea (64) 301
Norway (65) 291
Toyota Motor (67) 277
Czech Republic (68) 263
Chevron (69) 257
Toronto, Canada (70) 255
Shangri, China (77) 253
Total (79) 233
Singapore, Singapore (80) 223
Sydney, Australia (81) 215
Bangladesh (82) 213
Mumbai, India (83) 209
Rio de Janeiro, Brazil (84) 201
HSBC Holdings (99) 142
Barcelona, Spain (100) 140

10 GDP and Greenhouse Gas Emissions for Selected Cities

Total Green House Gases (Million tons of Carbon Dioxide Equivalent)

New York
Tokyo
Moscow
Shanghai
Sydney
Melbourne
London
Riyadh
Toronto
Istanbul
Mexico City
Buenos Aires
Paris
Berlin
Johannesburg
Mumbai
Hong Kong
Sao Paulo
Kinshasa

GDP (US$bn)

City Networks and Rankings

References

Castells, M. (1989) *The informational city: Information technology, economic restructuring, and the urban-regional process.* Oxford: Blackwell.

Hoelscher, M. (2010) Measuring creativity and innovation. In H. K. Anheier & R. Isar (Eds.), *Cultural expression, creativity and innovation* (pp. 317–328). London: Sage.

Potts, J., & MacDonald, T. (2011) *Why the bloody hell live there? First estimates of a cultural consumption price index by Australian region.* Unpublished paper, ARC Centre of Excellence for Creative Industries and Innovation, Brisbane, Queensland, Australia.

Sassen, S. (1991) *The global city: New York, London, Tokyo.* Princeton, NJ: Princeton University Press.

Staiger, U., Steiner, H., & Webber, A. (eds.) (2009) *Memory culture and the contemporary city: Building sites.* Houndsmills, Basingstoke, England: Palgrave Macmillan.

Taylor, P. J. (2005) 'Leading world cities: Empirical evaluations of urban nodes in multiple networks'. *Urban Studies*, 42, 1593–1608.

Therborn, G. (2002). 'Monumental Europe: The national years. On the iconography of European capital cities'. *Housing, Theory & Society*, 19, 26–47.

Data Sources

1
http://www.lboro.ac.uk/gawc/globalbuzz.html, retrieved June 3, 2011

2
http://en.wikipedia.org/wiki/Abu_Dhabi#Twin_towns_-_sister_cities

http://www.berlin.de/rbmskzl/staedteverbindungen/staedtepartnerschaft_ueberblick.de.html

http://www.greatistanbul.com/sister_cities.htm
http://en.wikipedia.org/wiki/List_of_twin_towns_and_sister_cities_in_the_United_Kingdom#London

http://en.wikipedia.org/wiki/Lviv#Twin_towns_.E2.80.94_sister_cities

http://en.wikipedia.org/wiki/List_of_twin_towns_and_sister_cities_in_Mexico

Single cities are important. Equally important, however, important are the networks, relationships, comparisons, and so forth in which cities are embedded. As Saskia Sassen (1991) has shown, even at the level of top global cities there is a kind of division of labor. Therefore, this suite complements the city suites by shedding light on some obvious and more subtle inter-linkages between different cities, establishing hierarchies and spaces of flows between them (Castells, 1989). Although this suite focuses on the city sample of this volume and some important cases, for many data points additional city data are available.

What Do We Know?

• 'Global Buzz' measured by the Globalization and World Cities Research Network pertains to the economic, political, social, and cultural connectedness of cities over time (September 2009 – August 2010). New York and London mainly kept their top positions over this year, but longer term reports will show whether new competitors arise (such as Shanghai, with an increase from 1.66 per cent to 3.39 per cent; Data Point 1).

• City twinning is a means for exchange across borders, but also for positioning one's city in the international hierarchy. Although the intensity of relations between twin or 'sister' cities might vary, a pattern is nevertheless visible. Again, London and New York have the most prestigious sister cities, with nearly all being capitals. London, Berlin, and New York also have on average the largest sister cities (Data Point 2).

• A large range of different city rankings exist. Although some of them are just a means to increase the circulation of certain media or attention toward certain companies, some are academically based and aimed at increasing knowledge (e.g. Hoelscher, 2010, for a discussion of quality aspects of rankings). Data Points 3 to 5 present different approaches. The Foreign Policy Global Cities Index compares major world cities on five dimensions: business activity, human capital, information exchange, cultural experience, and political engagement. The usual suspects take the lead. PriceWaterhouseCooper's Cities of Opportunity looks at similar dimensions, although with different names: intellectual capital and innovation, sustainability, demographics, livability, and lifestyle assets. Again, New York, London, and Paris are at the top, joined by Sydney.

• The Intercultural City Index takes quite a different approach. The joint action of the Council of Europe and the European Union is more of a policy-driven self-assessment tool and network than a mere ranking. Its aim is to support the further improvement of the cultural, social, and political integration of minorities within the partaking cities. Although most cities are satisfied with regard to their cultural and civil life, there seems to be room for improved governance processes (Data point 5).

• The following graphs focus even more on the network aspect. Networks of companies, as well as the location of international governmental and nongovernmental organizations such as the United Nations or the International Olympic Committee, are often used as indicators for World City status (e.g., Taylor, 2005). Data Point 6 shows where international nongovernmental organizations were founded and where they have their current headquarters. The analysis is based on data collected by Tom Davies. Only those cities that have been mentioned at least twice are displayed. Geneva, London, and Paris stand out as the most important places in this respect. The strong European dominance might, however, be the result of a data bias.

• One important means of city branding is architecture (see chapters by Kong and Ponzini, this volume). Public buildings, such as monuments (Staiger, Steiner, & Webber, 2009), museums, or government buildings (Therborn, 2002), are often used to highlight a city's status as a global city. Globally popular architects play a significant role here. Data Point 7 includes public projects built between 2000 and 2011 designed by the nine most prominent architects of the Baunetz ranking. Although the Southern Hemisphere is virtually not present, the East and West show strong relationships.

• The last three data points refer not to the city as a whole, but to urban dwellers and their individual use and perception of the city they live in. The first shows data from an interesting Australian research project, which aims to compare the price of cultural consumption for different places (Potts & MacDonald, 2011). Living in remote towns increases the price of cultural consumption significantly, hampering equal access to culture for the respective population groups (Data Point 8).

• Besides such objective measures, how citizens perceive their city is also important. Data Points 9 and 10 report results from the European Urban Audit. Overall, a clear majority of people are satisfied with the cultural facilities in their home towns. Most also see foreigners as good for their city. Luxembourg and Stockholm have the highest values, both benefiting from large shares of foreigners because of international organizations.

What Are The Issues?

Most city rankings come to similar conclusions: London, New York, Tokyo, and some other Western cities regularly occupy the pole positions, joined by some 'rising stars' in the East. However, the benefits of such rankings are sometimes unclear, as they are of different scientific value,

Attention: Mexico Cities Wikipedia site (http://en.wikipedia.org/wiki/Mexico_City#Twin_towns_.E2.80.94_Sister_cities) lists some additional cities (e.g. Tokyo) http://en.wikipedia.org/wiki/List_of_sister_cities_in_New_York

http://www.prefeitura.sp.gov.br/cidade/secretarias/relacoes_internacionais/cidadesirmas/index.php?p=1066

http://www.shfao.gov.cn/wsb/english/Sister_Cities/index1.html

In general, ambigious cases have been dropped from the list. Only cities that could be confirmed as sister cities by different sources were taken into account.

http://www.geobytes.com/CityDistanceTool.htm?loadpage

Distance between cities: http://www.mapcrow.info/

Population of Sister Cities: Wikipedia-Sites of these cities, retrieved April 29, 2011

3
http://www.foreignpolicy.com/articles/2010/08/11/the_global_cities_index_2010, retrieved October 25, 2010

Foreign Policy (2008) The 2008 Global Cities Index. *Foreign Policy* Nov/Dec 2008, 68-76. Available from http://www.foreignpolicy.com/articles/2008/10/15/the_2008_global_cities_index

Data for 2008 also available from http://www.atkearney.com/images/global/pdf/The-2008-Global-Cities-Index.pdf (accessed June 3, 2011)

4
PriceWaterhouseCooper (2011) *Cities of Opportunities*. (Pages 12 f.). Retrieved July 7, 2011, from http://www.pwc.com/us/en/cities-of-opportunity/2011/pdfdownload.jhtml

5
http://www.coe.int/t/dg4/cultureheritage/culture/cities/Index/, retrieved June 3, 2011

Intercultural cities is a joint action of the Council of Europe and the European Union and BAK Basel have provided expert support for the development of the INDEX

6
http://www.staff.city.ac.uk/tom.davies/Organizations.html, retrieved June 3, 2011

Additional information was retrieved from the websites of the specific organisations / associations

7

Selection of architects based on the "Baunetz" ranking with regard to their appearance in internationally wellknown architectural journals (http://www.baunetz.de/ranking/?area=ranking&type=int&lang=en;

Architects with a score above 100 in both rankings June/July 2010 and Nov/Dec 2010 were selected (though might exhibit a bias towards European architects).

Then their respective information in the English Wikipedia was used to select projects (only official / public / infrastructure buildings; only built projects; only since the year 2000) (all websites accessed January 20, 2011).

http://en.wikipedia.org/wiki/Herzog_%26_de_Meuron

http://en.wikipedia.org/wiki/Dominique_Perrault

http://en.wikipedia.org/wiki/David_Chipperfield

http://en.wikipedia.org/wiki/Kerry_Hill
Kerry Hill is mentioned in Wikipedia, but without projects. Additional information was therefore retrieved from: http://archnet.org/library/parties/one-party.jsp?party_id=1076

http://en.wikipedia.org/wiki/SANAA
http://en.wikipedia.org/wiki/Baumschlager-Eberle
http://en.wikipedia.org/wiki/Jean_Nouvel
http://en.wikipedia.org/wiki/Bjarke_Ingels_Group
http://en.wikipedia.org/wiki/Steven_Holl

8

Jason Potts and Trent MacDonald (2011) *Why the bloody hell live there? – First estimates of a Cultural Consumption Price Index by Australian region.* Working Paper. ARC Centre of Excellence for Creative Industries and Innovation (CCI): Queensland University.

9

European Commission (2009) Perception Survey on quality of life in European Cities. *Flash Eurobarometer Series #277.* Gallup Organisation. Pages 98 f. Retrieved July 26, 2011 from http://ec.europa.eu/public_opinion/flash/fl_277_en.pdf

10

European Commission (2009) Perception Survey on quality of life in European Cities. *Flash Eurobarometer Series #277.* Gallup Organisation. Pages 110 f. Retrieved July 26, 2011 from http://ec.europa.eu/public_opinion/flash/fl_277_en.pdf

and many draw only on a limited set of indicators (see Hoelscher, 2010). However, alternative approaches looking at new and interesting data, such as the Intercultural City Index or Sustainability Indices, are emerging. Different research networks (e.g. Urban Age, GaWC) try to find new ways of in-depth analysis of not only the numbers, but also the content and meaning of linkages, allowing a more detailed analysis of the very important city hierarchies, networks, and relations. These new techniques, together with the inclusion of additional cities, will help to paint an ever more appropriate picture of the important role cities are playing in economic, political, social and cultural globalization processes.

1 Global Buzz - Extent of Cities' Global Connectedness (Sep 2009 - Aug 2010)

	Sep-09	Oct-09	Nov-09	Dec-09	Jan-10	Feb-10	Mar-10	Apr-10	May-10	Jun-10	Jul-10	Aug-10
•••• New York	8.37%	9.04%	9.14%	5.96%	5.80%	4.74%	5.53%	5.85%	5.24%	4.28%	5.46%	5.47%
•••• London	4.33%	4.74%	5.08%	5.02%	4.40%	3.75%	4.71%	5.01%	4.83%	3.76%	5.12%	4.37%
— Paris	2.49%	2.94%	2.35%	2.11%	2.93%	4.00%	3.31%	2.96%	3.04%	2.23%	2.54%	2.44%
— Sao Paulo	0.36%	0.44%	0.55%	0.43%	0.40%	0.29%	0.41%	0.52%	0.40%	0.41%	0.35%	0.40%
•••• Shanghai	1.66%	2.02%	2.44%	1.70%	2.26%	1.98%	1.97%	2.45%	2.66%	3.56%	3.68%	3.39%
— Tokyo	4.55%	4.62%	2.53%	1.91%	2.42%	2.06%	2.33%	3.07%	2.47%	1.73%	3.10%	2.68%
— Berlin	1.15%	1.28%	1.15%	1.15%	1.10%	1.74%	1.90%	1.62%	1.52%	1.29%	1.50%	1.49%
— Johannesburg	0.36%	0.39%	0.37%	0.52%	0.19%	0.14%	0.34%	0.63%	0.65%	0.56%	0.71%	0.24%
•••• Mexico City	0.40%	0.50%	0.35%	0.59%	0.44%	0.18%	0.39%	0.69%	0.55%	0.56%	0.45%	0.70%
•••• Melbourne	0.77%	0.84%	1.10%	0.88%	1.06%	0.90%	0.93%	1.23%	1.34%	0.77%	1.64%	0.96%
— Mumbai	2.29%	1.80%	1.39%	1.10%	1.65%	1.18%	1.13%	1.40%	1.49%	7.52%	2.04%	1.23%
•••• Abu Dhabi	0.58%	0.72%	1.21%	1.13%	0.78%	1.52%	1.30%	0.70%	0.58%	0.47%	0.41%	0.26%
•••• Istanbul	0.55%	0.57%	0.44%	0.37%	0.44%	0.20%	0.54%	0.61%	0.62%	0.39%	0.58%	0.64%

2 Sister City Relations (Selected dimensions and cities)

Region	# of Sister Cities (SC)	# of Capitals in SC	# of Cities on other Continents	Average Distance to SC (in Km)	Mean Size of Population of SC
Abu Dhabi	8	5	6	6,972	2,812,554

List of Sister Cities

Bethlehem, Palestinian Authority; Brisbane, Australia; Delhi, India; Houston, US; Iquique, Chile; Madrid, Spain; Minsk, Belarus; Nicosia, Cyprus

Berlin	17	15	8	4,693	6,004,373

Beijing, China; Brussel, Belgium; Budapest, Hungary; Buenos Aires, Argentinia; Istanbul, Turkey; Jakarta, Indonesia; London, UK; Los Angeles, US; Madrid, Spain; Mexico-City, Mexico; Moscow, Russia; Paris, France; Prague, Czech Republic; Tashkent, Uzbekistan; Tokyo, Japan; Warsaw, Poland; Windhoek, Namibia

Istanbul	50	20	31	3,830	2,732,502

Almaty, Kazakhstan; Amman, Jordan; Athens, Greece; Barcelona, Spain; Beirut, Lebanon; Berlin, Germany; Budapest, Hungary; Busan, South Korea; Buenos Aires, Argentina; Cairo, Egypt; Cologne, Germany; Constanta, Romania; Constantine, Algeria; Damascus, Syria; Dubai, United Arab Emirates; Durres, Albania; Filipe, Bulgaria; Florence, Italy; Habana, Cuba; Ho Chi Minh, Vietnam; Houston, USA; Isfahan, Iran; Jakarta, Indonesia; Jeddah, Saudi Arabia; Johor Bahru, Malaysia; Kabul, Afghanistan; Kazan, Russia; Khartoum, Sudan; Lahor, Pakistan; Mary, Turkmenistan; Mexico City, Mexico; Odessa, Ukraine; Osh, Kyrgyzstan; Paris, France; Plovdiv, Bulgaria; Prague, Czech Republic; Rabat, Morocco; Rio de Janeiro, Brazil; Rotterdam, Holland; Samarkant, Uzbekistan; Sarajevo, Bosnia and Herzegovina; Shanghai, China; Shimonoseki, Japan; Saint Petersburg, Russia; Skopje, FYRO Macedonia; Stokholm, Sweden; Strasbourg, France; Toronto, Canada; Venice, Italy; Warsaw, Poland; Xi'an, China

London	10	9	6	5,188	7,545,927

Beijing, China; Berlin, Germany; Bogotá, Colombia; Moscow, Russia; New York City, US; Kuala Lumpur, Malaysia; Paris, France; Rome, Italy; Tehran, Iran; Tokyo, Japan

L'viv	16	1	4	1,051	722,884

Banja Luka, Bosnia and Herzegovina; Budapest, Hungary; Freiburg im Breisgau, Germany; Grozny, Russia; Kraków, Poland; Kutaisi, Georgia; Łód , Poland; Lublin, Poland; Novi Sad, Serbia; Przemy l, Poland; Rishon LeZion, Israel; Rochdale, UK; Rzeszów, Poland; Saint Petersburg, Russia; Samarkand, Uzbekistan; Wrocław, Poland

Mexico City	18	9	8/15	5,640	4,086,334

Arequipa, Peru; Beijing, China; Beirut, Lebanon; Bogotá, Colombia; Chicago, US; Cuzco, Peru; Guatemala City, Guatemala; Kaliningrad, Russia; Lima, Peru; Los Angeles, US; Madrid, Spain; Nagoya, Japan; Panama City, Panama; Rio de Janeiro, Brazil; San Salvador, El Salvador; Santiago, Chile; São Paulo, Brazil; Toronto, Canada

New York	10	9	9	8,056	5,989,565

Beijing, China; Budapest, Hungary; Cairo, Egypt; Jerusalem, Israel; Johannesburg, South Africa; London, UK; Madrid, Spain; Rome, Italy; Santo Domingo, Dominican Republic; Tokyo, Japan

Shanghai	45	11	32	8,420	2,527,291

Aden, Yemen; Alexandria, Egypt; Algiers, Algeria; Antwerp, Belgium; Barcelona, Spain; Basel, Switzerland; Busan, South Korea; Casablanca, Morocco; Chicago, US; Colombo, Sri Lanka; Cork, Ireland; Dubai, United Arab Emirates; Dunedin, New Zealand; Espoo, Finland; Gothenburg, Sweden; Guayaquil, Ecuador; Haifa, Israel; Hamburg, Germany; Hamhung, North Korea; Ho Chi Minh City, Vietnam; Istanbul, Turkey; Karachi, Pakistan; Liverpool, UK; London, UK; Manila, Philippines; Maputo, Mozambique; Marseille, France; Milan, Italy; Montreal, Canada; Osaka, Japan; Oslo, Norway; Piraeus, Greece; Port Vila, Vanuatu; Porto, Portugal; Rosario, Argentina; Rotterdam, Netherlands; Saint Petersburg, Russia; San Francisco, US; São Paulo, Brazil; Sarajevo, Bosnia and Herzegovina; Tashkent, Uzbekistan; Valparaiso, Chile; Windhoek, Namibia; Yokohama, Japan; Zagreb, Croatia

São Paulo	32	14	22	9,238	2,396,360

Amman, Jordan; Asuncion, Paraguay; Beijing, China; Bucharest, Romania; Buenos Aires, Argentina; Chicago, US; Cluj-Napoca, Romania; Coimbra, Portugal; Cordoba, Spain; Damascus, Syria; Funchal, Portugal; Góis, Portugal; Hamburg, Germany; Havana, Cuba; La Paz, Bolivia; Leiria, Portugal; Lima, Peru; Lisbon, Portugal; Luanda, Angola; Macau, China; Mendoza, Argentina; Milan, Italy; Montevideo, Uruguay; Naha, Japan; Ningbo, China; Osaka, Japan; Santiago de Compostela, Spain; Santiago, Chile; Seoul, South Korea; Tel Aviv, Israel; Toronto, Canada; Yerevan, Armenia

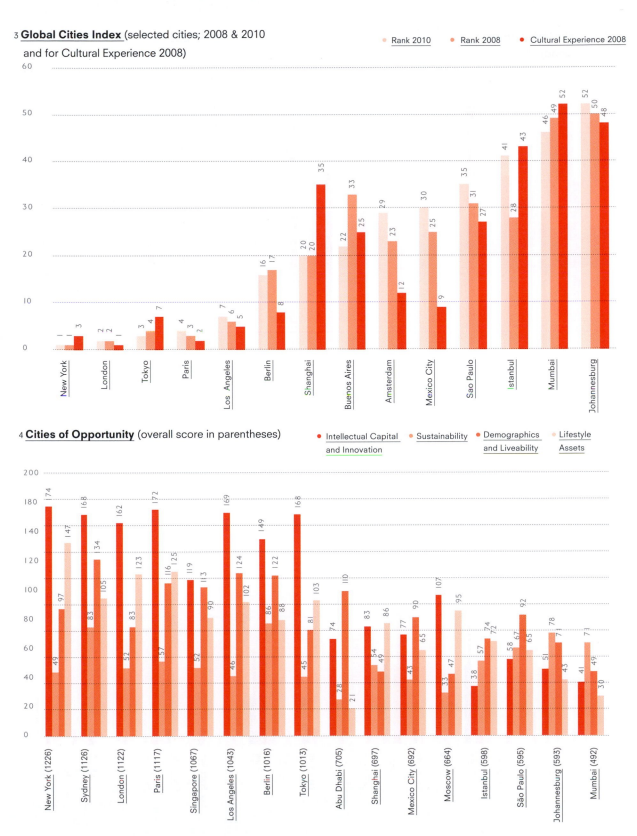

3 **Global Cities Index** (selected cities; 2008 & 2010 and for Cultural Experience 2008)

● Rank 2010   ● Rank 2008   ● Cultural Experience 2008

4 **Cities of Opportunity** (overall score in parentheses)

● Intellectual Capital and Innovation   ● Sustainability   ● Demographics and Liveability   ● Lifestyle Assets

5 Intercultural City Index

(100 = good) (2010)

- Intercultural City Index
- Subdimension: Cultural and Civil life
- Subdimension: Governance

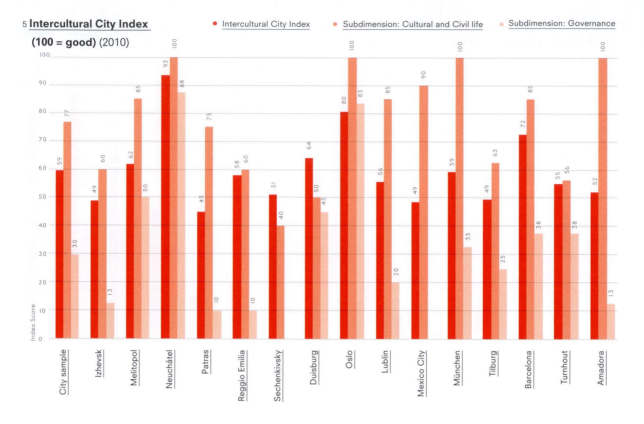

6 Location of Selected INGOs: Foundation and Current Headquarter (years refer to the year of foundation of INGOs)

Location of Foundation Before 1945 1945-1989 Since 1990   Location of Headquarter Before 1945 1945-1989 Since 1990

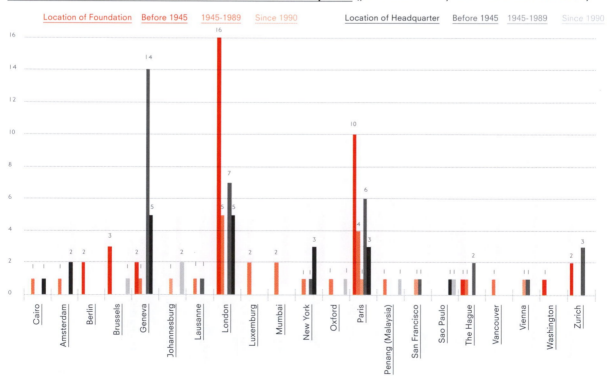

Public Projects Designed by the "Top 9" Architects of the Baunetz ranking (2000 –2011)

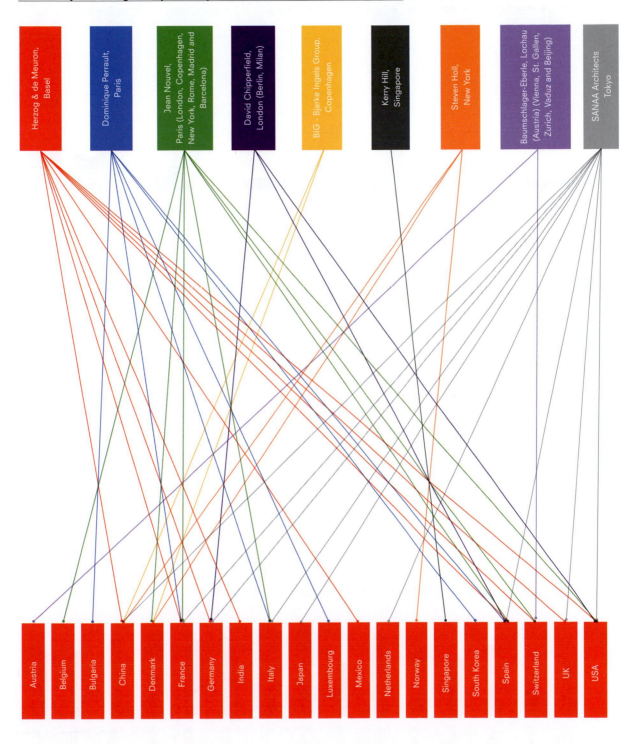

8 Cultural consumption price index estimates (Australian Cities, 2011)

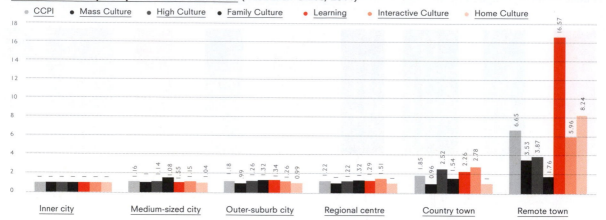

Legend: CCPI · Mass Culture · High Culture · Family Culture · Learning · Interactive Culture · Home Culture

	Inner city	Medium-sized city	Outer-suburb city	Regional centre	Country town	Remote town
CCPI		1.16	1.18	1.22	1.85	6.65
Mass Culture		.99	.99	1	0.96	3.53
High Culture		1.14	1.26	1.22	2.52	3.87
Family Culture		1.08	1.32	1.32	1.54	1.76
Learning		1.55	1.34	1.29	2.26	16.57
Interactive Culture		1.15	1.26	1.51	2.78	5.96
Home Culture		1.04	0.99	1	1	8.24

9 Satisfaction with cultural facilities such as concert halls, theatres, museums and libraries in European cities (2009)

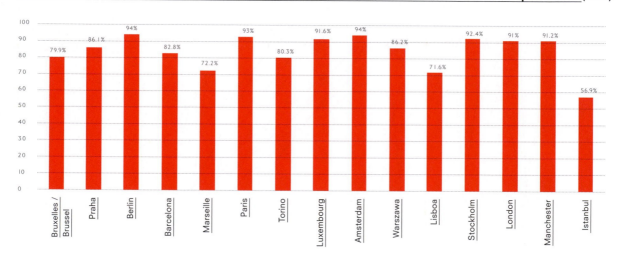

City	%
Bruxelles / Brussel	79.9%
Praha	86.1%
Berlin	94%
Barcelona	82.8%
Marseille	72.2%
Paris	93%
Torino	80.3%
Luxembourg	91.6%
Amsterdam	94%
Warszawa	86.2%
Lisboa	71.6%
Stockholm	92.4%
London	91%
Manchester	91.2%
Istanbul	56.9%

10 The Presence of Foreigners is Good for this City (percentage agreed) (2009)

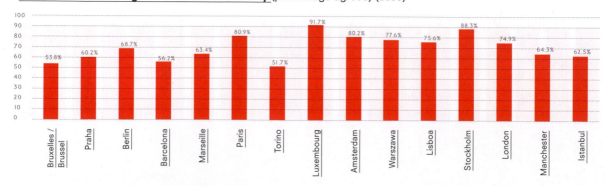

City	%
Bruxelles / Brussel	53.8%
Praha	60.2%
Berlin	68.7%
Barcelona	56.2%
Marseille	63.4%
Paris	80.9%
Torino	51.7%
Luxembourg	91.7%
Amsterdam	80.2%
Warszawa	77.6%
Lisboa	75.6%
Stockholm	88.3%
London	74.9%
Manchester	64.3%
Istanbul	62.5%

City Comparisons

References

Florida, R. (2002) *The rise of the creative class and how it's transforming work, leisure, community and everyday life.* New York: Basic Books.

Florida, R. (2005) *Cities and the creative class.* New York: Routledge.

Hendricks, J. (1999) Creativity over the life course—A call for a relational perspective. *International Journal of Aging and Human Development*, 48, 85–111.

Huntington, S. P. (1996) *The clash of civilizations and the remaking of world order.* New York: Simon & Schuster.

While the following nine suites present cities in more detail, this suite offers a comparative overview of all of them. Data were collected for six dimensions, each related to a city's heterogeneity. The basic hypothesis is that greater heterogeneity across these dimensions contributes to a city's capacity for what could be called 'positive creative developments'.

The six dimensions are:

• *Foreign-born residents and migrants:* A larger share of foreign-born residents or migrants increases the amount of new and foreign cultural capital and networks brought into the city. This in turn spurs the creation of new and hybrid cultural trends and ways of living. The share of foreign-born residents and migrants can also be interpreted as an indicator of a city's attractiveness to migrants from other countries and cultures.

• *Size of the 25–39 age group:* Although all inhabitants of a city contribute to its cultural life, people in their 20s and 30s are seen as especially creative and open to new developments, as well as being in the most productive phase of their working life (this is only a very rough estimate, because differences certainly exist depending on country and city context as well as individual life trajectories; e.g. Hendricks, 1999).

• *Religious inhomogeneity and share of largest religious denomination:* Religion is often seen as one of the most important cultural influences, and the two are sometimes even equated (as is mainly the case in Huntington's 1996 *The Clash of Civilizations and the Remaking of World Order*). Here, it is used as another indicator of cultural heterogeneity within a city. High values show low heterogeneity. Therefore, inverse figures (100 minus the percentage of the largest denomination) are shown.

• *Employment Rate:* This dimension contributes mostly indirectly to a city's cultural capacity. However, a sound economic basis and a less pressured public budget for basic needs allows a city to invest in culture in the first place. High levels of unemployment, however, are an indicator for underlying social and economic problems. Therefore, inverse figures are again shown.

• *Percentage of citizens with higher education:* People with a higher level of education can more easily gain benefits from their creativity. Many creative jobs have some kind of higher education as basic prerequisite. Richard Florida (2002, 2005), especially, has emphasized the positive impact of people with higher education on cities (see Cunningham, this volume, for a discussion of this theory).

• *Employees in the service industry:* The cultural or creative economy belongs mainly to the service industry. Because reliable and comparable data on the extent of the creative economy at the city level are hard to find, the share of employees in the service industry as a whole is taken as a proxy for this figure.

Cities are compared along these six dimensions. However, the results should be interpreted with caution, because the data stem from different data sources or from different years. For one data point, religious homogeneity, no data were available for Shanghai; for Istanbul, only country-level data could be found.

Year of data collection

Region	Foreign-born migrants	25–39 age group	Religious Inhomogeneity	Employment Rate	Citizens with higher education	Third-sector Employees
Abu Dhabi	2009	2009	No year	2008	2009	2008
Berlin	2009	2009	2009	2009	2008	2009
Istanbul	2010	2010	2010	2009	2009	2009
London	2001	2001	2009	2010	2008	2010
L'viv	2001	2010	2001	2010	2010	2009
Mexico City	No year	2000	2000	2010	2010	2010
New York	2009	2000	2000	2010	2000	2009
São Paulo	2000	2010	2000	2009	2004	2009
Shanghai	2000	2000	No data	2007	2000	2008

With regard to employees in the service industry, clear differences are detectable between the cities in more developed countries (with values well above 80 per cent) and those in less-developed countries (e.g., Shanghai, with just over 50 per cent, and Istanbul, with 58 per cent).

Huge differences can also be observed with regard to foreign-born citizens and religious uniformity, with only the last relating to the level of development in at least some way. Abu Dhabi has by far the most foreign-born residents, and the South and Latin American cities have the least. Religious heterogeneity is highest in New York, followed by London and Berlin (in which the largest religious group is actually made up of atheists, at more than 60 per cent). It is lowest in Istanbul (mainly Muslim) and Mexico City (mainly Catholic).

The percentage of people with higher education shows differences as well. In London, nearly one in three citizens holds some kind of higher education certificate. In L'viv, this figure is only around 5 per cent; in Mexico City, just above 2 per cent. However, these figures have to be interpreted carefully because reliable data on education are often difficult to obtain.

The share of people between ages 25 and 39 lies between 22 per cent and 29 per cent (Berlin and L'viv at the lower end, Mexico City and Istanbul at the upper end), with the outstanding exception of Abu Dhabi, with more than 40 per cent in this age group (probably because of the number of migrant workers).

Abu Dhabi

1, 2 , 4 , 5 , 5b

SCAD - Statistics Centre Abu Dhabi (2010) *Statistical Yearbook 2010 Abu Dhabi*. Retrieved June 6, 2011, from http://www.abudhabi. ae/egovPoolPortal_WAR/ShowPropertySe rvlet?nodePath=%2FAdsic+Repository%2 FSites%2FPortal%2FContent%2FADSIC %2FEN%2FStandardDocuments%2FDow nloads%2Fstatistical-yearbook-abu-dhabi-2010%2Fpdf%2F%2Fcm%3Adata

3

@llo' Expat Abu Dhabi (2011) *People, Language and Religion*. Retrieved June 23, 2011, from http://www. abudhabi.alloexpat.com/abudhabi_information/ people_language_religion_abudhabi.php

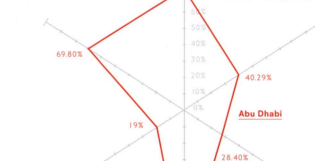

Berlin

1

Amt für Statistik Berlin-Brandenburg (2010) *Statistischer Bericht A1-6 hj2/09 - Melderechtlich registrierte Ausländer im Land Berlin am 31. Dezember 2009*. Retrieved June 23, 2011, from http://www.statistik-berlin-brandenburg.de/ publikationen/Stat_Berichte/2010/SB_A1-6_hj2-09_BE.pdf

2

Amt für Statistik Berlin-Brandenburg (2010) *Statistischer Bericht A1-10 A6-2 j01-09 - Ergebnisse des Mikrozensus im Land Berlin 2009*. Retrieved June 23, 2011, from http://www.statistik-berlin-brandenburg.de/ Publikationen/Stat_Berichte/2011/SB_A1-10_ A6-2_j01-09_BE.pdf

3 , 4

Amt für Statistik Berlin-Brandenburg (2010) *Die kleine Berlin-Statistik 2010*. Retrieved June 23, 2011, from http://www.statistik-berlin-brandenburg.de/Produkte/kleinestatistik/ kBEst_2010.pdf

5

Amt für Statistik Berlin-Brandenburg (2010) *Statistisches Jahrbuch 2009 Berlin*. Retrieved June 23, 2011, from http://www.statistik-berlin-brandenburg.de/PRODUKTE/jahrbuch/jb2009/ BE_Jahrbuch_2009.pdf

5b

Amt für Statistik Berlin-Brandenburg (2010) *Statistisches Jahrbuch 2010 Berlin*. Retrieved May 22, 2011, from http://www.statistik-berlin-brandenburg.de/Produkte/jahrbuch/jb2010/ BE_Jahrbuch_2010.pdf

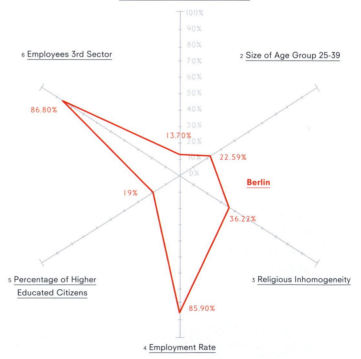

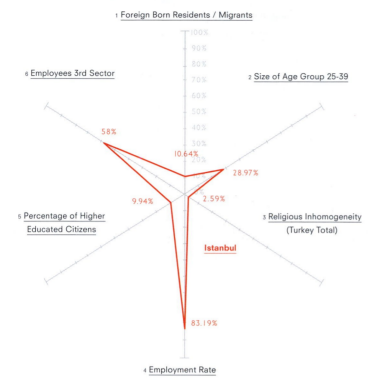

Istanbul

1
ESA UN, International Migrant Stock, 2008 revision. Retrieved June 10, 2011, from http://esa.un.org/migration/p2k0data.asp
2
Turkish Statistical Institute (n.d.) *Address Based Population Registration System* (ABPRS). Retrieved July 5, 2011, from http://report.tuik.gov.tr/reports/rwservlet?adnksdb2=&ENVID=adnksdb2Env&report=turkiye_il_yasgr.RDF&p_il1=34&p_kod=2&p_yil=2010&p_dil=2&desformat=pdf
3
Association of Religion Data Archives (n.d.) *National Profiles Turkey*. Retrieved July 5, 2011, from http://www.thearda.com/internationalData/countries/country_226_1.asp
4
Turkish Statistical Institute (n.d.) *Bölgesel Göstergeler, TR10 Istanbul 2009*. (Retrieved July 5, 2011, from http://www.tuik.gov.tr/Kitap.do?metod=KitapDetay&KT_ID=0&KITAP_ID=196)
5
Turkish Statistical Institute (n.d.) *Address Based Population Registration System* (ABPRS). Retrieved July 5, 2011, from http://report.tuik.gov.tr/reports/rwservlet?adnksdb2=&ENVID=adnksdb2Env&report=wa_il_cinsiyet_yas_egitim_koyseh.RDF&p_kod=2&p_il1=34&p_xkod=egitim_kod&p_yas=6&p_sehkoy=1&p_yil=2010&p_dil=2&desformat=pdf
5b
Urban Age (n.d.) *Urban Age City Data, Istanbul, Urban Workforce*. Retrieved Jly 5, 2011, from http://urbanage.net/cities/istanbul/data/2009/

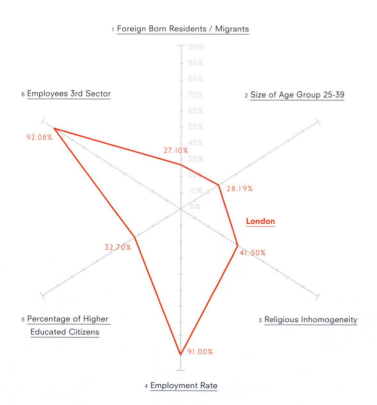

London

1
MPI Data Hub (n.d.) *Londondatasheet*. Retrieved June 23, 2011, from http://www.migrationinformation.org/datahub/gcmm/Londondatasheet.pdf
2
Office for National Statistics (n.d.) Census 2001. Retrieved June 23, 2011, from http://www.statistics.gov.uk/census2001/pop2001/LONDON.asp
3
Greater London Authority (2010) *Annual Population Survey - Population by religion*. Retrieved June 23, 2011, from http://data.london.gov.uk/datafiles/demographics/population-by-religion-london.xls
4
Office for National Statistics (2011) *Regional Profile - London Economy*. Retrieved June 23, 2011, from http://www.statistics.gov.uk/cci/nugget.asp?id=2286
5
NOMIS (n.d.) *Annual Population Survey - Employment and Skills*. Retrieved June 23, 2011, from http://data.london.gov.uk/datafiles/employment-skills/qualifications-of-working-age-population-GCSE.xls
5b
Office for National Statistics (2010) *Labour Market Statistics* -December 2010: London. Retrieved June 23, 2011, from http://www.statistics.gov.uk/downloads/theme_labour/Monthly-LMS/lmsmonthly1210.zip

385

L'viv

1 , 3
Wikipedia (2011) *Lviv*. Retrieved June 23, 2011, from http://en.wikipedia.org/wiki/Lviv
2
Lviv Investment Portal (2010) *Age and Family Status*. Retrieved February 22, 2011, via e-mail.
4
Lviv Investment Portal (2010) *Unemployed Citizens*. Retrieved January 26, 2011, via e-mail.
5
Lviv Investment Portal (2010) *Percentage of Higher Educated Citizens*. Retrieved January 26, 2011, via e-mail.
5b
Lviv Investment Portal (2010) *Number of employees by types of economic activity in Lviv for 2009 (thousands persons)*. Retrieved June 8, 2011 from http://www.investinlviv.com/what-do-we-offer/human-resources-and-education/labour-market/

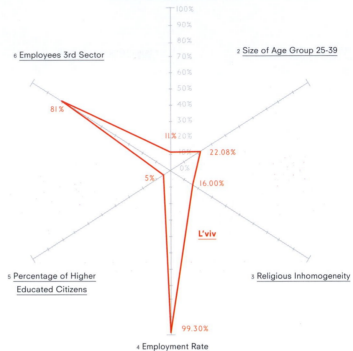

Mexico City

1
Urban Age (2006) Towards and Urban Age. *Urban Age Summit Berlin, November 2006*. Retrieved on August 26, 2011, from http://www.urban-age.net/0_downloads/UA_Summit_Berlin_Newspaper.pdf (page 12, with no data source given there).
2 , 3
INEGI (n.d.) *XII Censo General de Población y Vivienda 2000 - Población de 5 Anos y Más por Delegación, Sexo y Religión, y su Distribución Según Grupos Quinquenales de Edad*. Retrieved June 23, 2011, from http://www.inegi.org.mx/sistemas/TabuladosBasicos/LeerArchivo.aspx?ct=3475&c=16852&s=est&f=1
4 , 5
INEGI (2010) *Censo de Poblacion y Vivienda 2010 - Mexico en Cifra, Distrito Federal*. Retrieved June 23, 2011, from http://www.inegi.org.mx/sistemas/mexicocifras/
5b
INEGI (n.d.) Encuesta Nacional de Ocupación y Empleo (ENOE). *Distrito Federal*. Retrieved May 22, from http://www.inegi.org.mx/sistemas/tabuladosbasicos2/indesttrim.aspx?c=26232&s=est

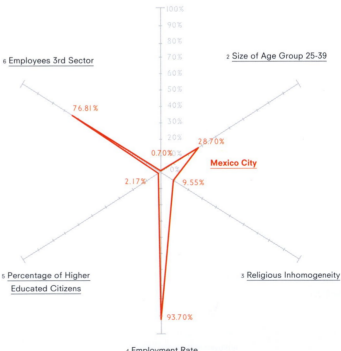

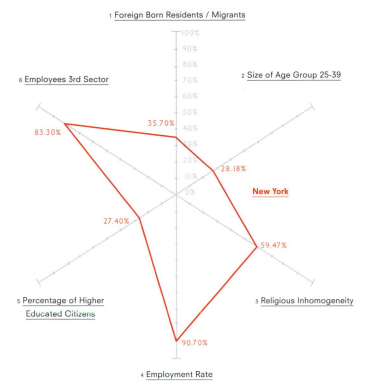

1 Foreign Born Residents / Migrants

6 Employees 3rd Sector

2 Size of Age Group 25-39

83.30%

35.70%

28.18%

New York

27.40%

59.47%

5 Percentage of Higher Educated Citizens

3 Religious Inhomogeneity

90.70%

4 Employment Rate

New York

1, 4
NYCEDC (n.d.) *Demographics.* Retrieved June 23, 2011, from http://www.nycedc.com/NewsPublications/NYCEconomics/DataResources/Documents/Demographics%201a.pdf

2
U.S. Census Bureau (n.d.) *Census 2000 Summary File 1.* Retrieved May 20, 2011, from http://factfinder.census.gov/servlet/QTTable?_bm=y&geo_id=16000US3651000&-qr_name=DEC_2000_SF1_U_DP1&-ds_name=DEC_2000_SF1_U&-lang=en&-_sse=on

3
Social Explorer (n.d.) *Major Religions.* Retrieved June 23, 2011, from http://www.socialexplorer.com/pub/reportdata/HtmlResults.aspx?reportid=R10016163&ItemsPerPage=6

5
U.S. Census Bureau (n.d.) *State & County QuickFacts - New York (city), New York.* Retrieved June 23, 2011, from http://quickfacts.census.gov/qfd/states/36/3651000.html

5b
Bureau of Labor Statistics (2009) *May 2009 OES Estimates.* Retrieved June 23, 2011, from ftp://ftp.bls.gov/pub/special.requests/oes/oesm09ma.zip

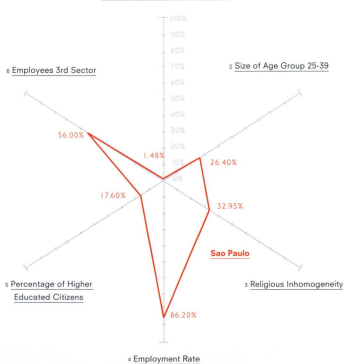

1 Foreign Born Residents / Migrants

6 Employees 3rd Sector

2 Size of Age Group 25-39

56.00%

1.48%

26.40%

17.60%

32.95%

Sao Paulo

5 Percentage of Higher Educated Citizens

3 Religious Inhomogeneity

86.20%

4 Employment Rate

Sao Paulo

1
Secretaria Municipal de Desenvolvimento Urbano (n.d.) *Nacionalidade da População Município de São Paulo 1920 a 2000.* Retrieved May 22, 2011, from http://smdu.prefeitura.sp.gov.br/historico_demografico/tabelas/pop_nac.php

2
Instituto Brasileiro de Geografi a e Estatística (n.d.) *População residente, por grupos de idade, segundo os municípios e o sexo.* Retrieved June 23, 2011, from http://www.censo2010.ibge.gov.br/sinopse/index.php?dados=26&uf=35#topo_piramide

3
Sistema IBGE de Recuperacao Automática (n.d.) *População residente por cor ou raça e religião - Brasil, Região, UF e Região Metropolitana.* Retrieved June 23, 2011, from http://www.sidra.ibge.gov.br/bda/tabela/protabl.asp?c=2094&z=cd&o=7&i=P

4
Fundação Seade (n.d.) *Taxa de Desemprego, por Tipo de Desemprego e Experiência Anterior de Trabalho - Município de São Paulo - 1985-2009.* Retrieved June 23, 2011, from http://www.seade.gov.br/produtos/ped/framostrassunto.php?assunto=0

5
Fundação Seade (n.d.) *Distribuição dos Ocupados, por Nível de Instrução - Município de São Paulo - 1985-2004.* Retrieved June23, 2011, from http://www.seade.gov.br/produtos/msp/emp/emp6_031.xls

5b
Investe São Paulo (n.d.) *Mercado de Trabalho.* Retrieved May 22, 2011, from http://www.investimentos.sp.gov.br/porque/mercado%20de%20trabalho?lang=en

Shanghai

1
Urban Age (n.d.) *Demographic Profile - Etnicity*.
Retrieved June 23, 2011, from http://urban-age.
net/0_downloads/profiles/Shanghai_General.xls
2
Urban Age (n.d.) *Demographic Profile - Age
Pyramid*. Retrieved June 23, 2011, from http://
urban-age.net/0_downloads/profiles/Shanghai_
General.xls
4
Shanghai Municipal Government (2008) *As
unemployment rate falls, migrants find abundant
jobs (09/05/2008)*. Retrieved June 23, 2011
from http://www.shanghai.gov.cn/shanghai/
node17256/node18151/userobject22ai30095.html
5
Urban Age (n.d.) *Education - Qualification levels*.
Retrieved June 23, 2011, from http://urban-age.
net/0_downloads/profiles/Shanghai_General.xls
5b
Shanghai Statistics (2011) *Shanghai Statistical
Yearbook 2009*. Retrieved March, 2011, from: ???

1 Foreign Born Residents / Migrants

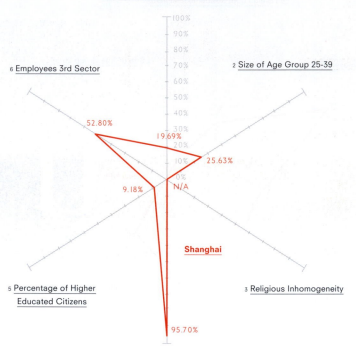

6 Employees 3rd Sector

2 Size of Age Group 25-39

52.80%

19.69%

25.63%

N/A

9.18%

Shanghai

5 Percentage of Higher
Educated Citizens

3 Religious Inhomogeneity

95.70%

4 Employment Rate

Abu

Dhabi

References

Kapiszewski, A. (2006) *Arab versus Asian Migrant Workers in the GCC Countries.* United Nations Expert Group Meeting on International Migration and Development in the Arab Region. UN/POP/EGM/2006/02. Retrieved from http://www.un.org/esa/population/meetings/EGM_Ittmig_Arab/P02_Kapiszewski.pdf

National Media Council (2010) *United Arab Emirates Yearbook 2010.* London: Trident Press. Retrieved from http://www.uaeinteract.com/uaeint_misc/pdf_2010/Yearbook2010_EN/#160

Data Sources

1
Tedad - The UAE 2005 Census (n.d.). Population in Main Cities. Retrieved June 6, 2011, from http://www.tedad.ae/english/statistic/main_cities.html

2
SCAD - Statistics Centre Abu Dhabi (2010). Statistical Yearbook 2010 Abu Dhabi. Retrieved June 6, 2011, from http://www.abudhabi.ae/egovPoolPortal_WAR/ShowPropertyServlet?nodePath=%2FAdsic+Repository%2FSites%2FPortal%2FContent%2FADSIC%2FEN%2FStandardDocuments%2FDownloads%2Fstatistical-yearbook-abu-dhabi-2010%2Fpdf%2F%2Fcm%3Adata

3
SCAD - Statistics Centre Abu Dhabi (2010). Statistical Yearbook 2010 Abu Dhabi. Retrieved June 6, 2011, from http://www.abudhabi.ae/egovPoolPortal_WAR/ShowPropertyServlet?nodePath=%2FAdsic+Repository%2FSites%2FPortal%2FContent%2FADSIC%2FEN%2FStandardDocuments%2FDownloads%2Fstatistical-yearbook-abu-dhabi-2010%2Fpdf%2F%2Fcm%3Adata

4
5
SCAD - Statistics Centre Abu Dhabi (2010). Statistical Yearbook 2010 Abu Dhabi. Retrieved June 6, 2011, from http://www.abudhabi.

The Arab world has gained much from the persistently high and seemingly unsatisfiable demand for oil. Abu Dhabi, with one of the world's biggest oil reservoirs, has taken advantage of this situation over the last three decades. After setting up a basic infrastructure for the needs of international companies, Abu Dhabi began, like Dubai, to search for future economic prospects but has chosen a slightly different means of development. It engages much more in developing infrastructure for leisure and culture than in trying to establish itself as a hub for finance, trade, business and transport.

Some facts about Abu Dhabi

• The population of Abu Dhabi's capital region has multiplied by a factor of five in the past 25 years. An acceleration in population growth occurred from the mid-1990s until around 2008. Since then, growth has slowed down (Data Point 1). The national and foreign populations of Abu Dhabi have grown in similar ways: although the acceleration in growth of the national population was slightly lower than that of the foreign population, its acceleration did not slow during the past few years. Abu Dhabi's large share of foreigners, who make up around 75 per cent of its population, is remarkable (Data Point 2).

• In 2009, Abu Dhabi spent about 11 per cent of its budget on governmental development projects (Data Point 3), whereas almost 60 per cent was spent on covering recurrent administrative expenditures of the city's and the federal government.

• Abu Dhabi's administration is heavily engaged in developing the city's infrastructure. The two main enterprises founded for that purpose are closely tied to the government and have exclusive rights to overview and subcontract all projects that are contributing to a new infrastructural urban fabric. Much attention seems to be paid to cultural development, such as education, heritage and cultural memory, and perhaps most important, an orientation toward cultural assets that are 'Western' in nature (see chapters by Elsheshtawy and Ponzini, this volume). The development of the new city district on Saadiyat Island, dedicated to culture and high-class leisure and living, incurred an expenditure of US$27 billion and is intended to be fully implemented by 2020 (Data Point 4), with cultural core institutions already being built now. Most of these cultural institutions are joint ventures between Abu Dhabi's development enterprises and well-established Western museums (e.g., the Louvre) and educational facilities (e.g., the Sorbonne).

• Abu Dhabi's current cultural infrastructure seems to be underdeveloped in relation to that of other global cities. For more than a million inhabitants, the city has just 10 cinemas (Data Point 5). However, a relatively high number of media publishing businesses are located in Abu Dhabi. Current investments in culture therefore may change Abu Dhabi's cultural infrastructure over the next decade in a fundamental way. First, one can observe an overall expansion, with a strong focus on Western high culture. Second, there are some voices calling for stronger references to the emirates own culture.

• The structure of employment in Abu Dhabi's jobs is different from that of most other cities in the indicator suites. While the share of about 90 per cent of jobs in the service industry, featuring service occupations and highly skilled labor, is not that differently, Abu Dhabi exhibits a very large share of elementary and crafts and related trades occupations within this sector. There is virtually no industrial sector (Data Point 6).

• Most of Abu Dhabi's workers and employees are foreigners (82 per cent or nearly 3.9 million workers in 2008). They are especially concentrated in blue-collar jobs and service sectors (Data Point 6b). Although exact figures are difficult to find, major expatriate communities in the United Arab Emirates are from India (1.2 million), Pakistan (450 thousand), Sri Lanka (160 thousand), Egypt (140 thousand) and the Filipines (120 thousand; data for 2002, Kapiszewski, 2006: 10).

• Abu Dhabi is working to establish Western style high culture and high-class leisure facilities to attract tourists. Most visitors are from the other United Arab Emirates states, followed by Europe and Asia (Data Point 7).

What Are The Issues?

Compared with the other cities in the indicator suites, Abu Dhabi stands out in various ways. Politically, it is ruled by a monarchy and its extended family. Economically, its oil reserves guarantee a high income for the state and its citizens, but only for a foreseeable future.

In reaction to this, Abu Dhabi is trying to establish itself as a regional cultural capital. This effort is not just underscored by interest in Western cultural assets such as museums and leisure facilities, but also by the promotion of educational infrastructure dedicated to its people and the region's needs. Concern on the latter score is linked to the issue of emiratization ('policy of expanding participation of the country's citizens in the workforce', National Media Council, 2010, p. 159), pointing to the lack of nationals employed.

In conclusion, Abu Dhabi will have to struggle with tensions emerging from its claim to be a globalized and modern city and its call for 'emiratization'. It is also still an open question what the specific contributions of this city to a global culture will look like, because its cultural highlights are not locally produced, but are imports from established foreign institutions.

ae/egovPoolPortal_WAR/ShowPropertySe rvlet?nodePath=%2FAdsic+Repository%2 FSites%2FPortal%2FContent%2FADSIC %2FEN%2FStandardDocuments%2FDow nloads%2Fstatistical-yearbook-abu-dhabi-2010%2Fpdf%2F%2Fcm%3Adata

6
SCAD - Statistics Centre Abu Dhabi (2010). Statistical Yearbook 2010 Abu Dhabi. Retrieved June 6, 2011, from http://www.abudhabi. ae/egovPoolPortal_WAR/ShowPropertySe rvlet?nodePath=%2FAdsic+Repository%2 FSites%2FPortal%2FContent%2FADSIC %2FEN%2FStandardDocuments%2FDow nloads%2Fstatistical-yearbook-abu-dhabi-2010%2Fpdf%2F%2Fcm%3Adata

6B
SCAD - Statistics Centre Abu Dhabi (2010). Statistical Yearbook 2010 Abu Dhabi. Retrieved June 6, 2011, from http://www.abudhabi. ae/egovPoolPortal_WAR/ShowPropertySe rvlet?nodePath=%2FAdsic+Repository%2 FSites%2FPortal%2FContent%2FADSIC %2FEN%2FStandardDocuments%2FDow nloads%2Fstatistical-yearbook-abu-dhabi-2010%2Fpdf%2F%2Fcm%3Adata

7
SCAD - Statistics Centre Abu Dhabi (2010). Statistical Yearbook 2010 Abu Dhabi. Retrieved June 6, 2011, from http://www.abudhabi. ae/egovPoolPortal_WAR/ShowPropertySe rvlet?nodePath=%2FAdsic+Repository%2 FSites%2FPortal%2FContent%2FADSIC %2FEN%2FStandardDocuments%2FDow nloads%2Fstatistical-yearbook-abu-dhabi-2010%2Fpdf%2F%2Fcm%3Adata

SCAD - Statistical Centre Abu Dhabi (2009). Statistical Yearbook 2009 Abu Dhabi. Retrieved June 6, 2011, from: http://www.abudhabi. ae/egovPoolPortal_WAR/ShowPropertySe rvlet?nodePath=%2FAdsic+Repository%2 FSites%2FPortal%2FContent%2FADSIC %2FEN%2FStandardDocuments%2FDow nloads%2Fstatistical-yearbook-abu-dhabi-2009%2Fpdf%2F%2Fcm%3Adata

1 **Population Over Time (Abu Dhabi Region)** (1975–2009)

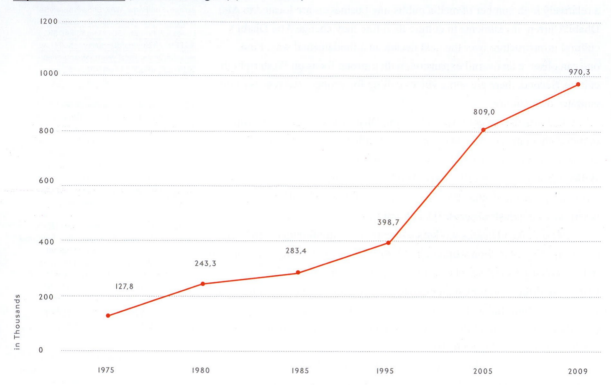

2 **Population by Nationality (Abu Dhabi / Emirate)** (1975–2009)

● Nationals ● Non-Nationals

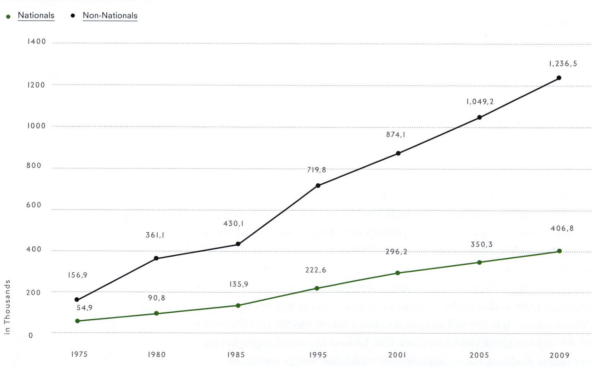

3 **Distribution of Public Expenditures by Type** (2009; %; Emirate)

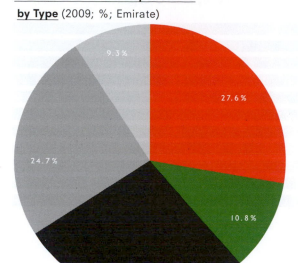

- ● Recurrent Department Expenditure
- ● Development Expenditure
- ● Contribution to the Federal Government
- ● Aid and Loans
- ● Capital Payments

4 **Cultural Investment**

- ● Museums ● Universities ● Leisure

Name of Institution	Building Costs	Extended Investments
Guggenheim	400 mill USD	3 billion USD
Louvre	110 mill USD	562 mill USD
Zayeed National Museum	—	—
Maritime Museum	—	—
NYU	—	—
Sorbonne	—	435.7 mill USD
Zayed University	—	1.116 billion USD
Ferrari Theme Parc	AED 10.9 billion	2.97 billion USD

5 **Number of Printing Press Shops, Book Stores, Publishers,...** (2009; Region)

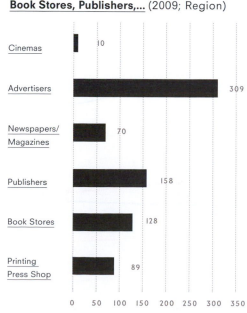

6 **Estimated Employed Population**
(2008; Emirate; 15 years and over by main occupation)

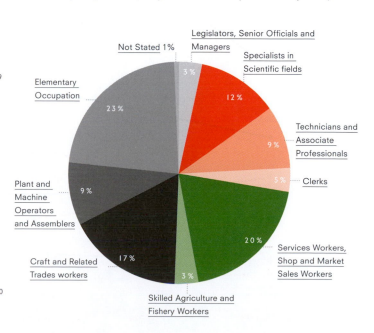

6B Non National Share of Estimated Employed Population (15 years and over by Main Occupation) (Mid - 2008)

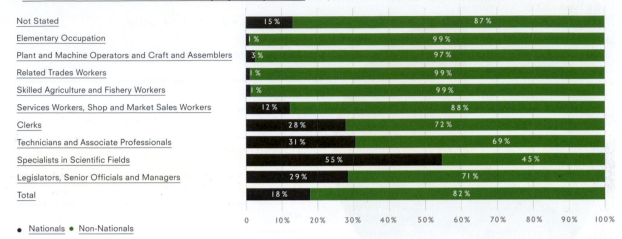

Occupation	Nationals	Non-Nationals
Not Stated	15%	87%
Elementary Occupation	1%	99%
Plant and Machine Operators and Craft and Assemblers	3%	97%
Related Trades Workers	1%	99%
Skilled Agriculture and Fishery Workers	1%	99%
Services Workers, Shop and Market Sales Workers	12%	88%
Clerks	28%	72%
Technicians and Associate Professionals	31%	69%
Specialists in Scientific Fields	55%	45%
Legislators, Senior Officials and Managers	29%	71%
Total	18%	82%

● Nationals ● Non-Nationals

7 Guests of Hotel Establishments by Nationality (Abu Dhabi Emirate) (2008)

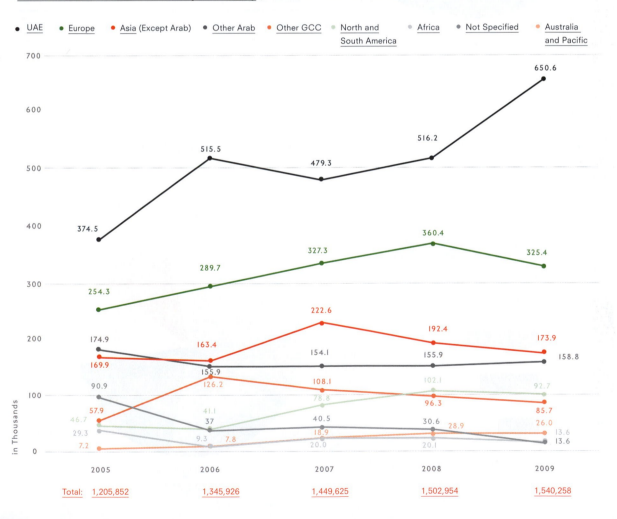

● UAE ● Europe ● Asia (Except Arab) ● Other Arab ● Other GCC ● North and South America ● Africa ● Not Specified ● Australia and Pacific

	2005	2006	2007	2008	2009
Total:	1,205,852	1,345,926	1,449,625	1,502,954	1,540,258

Berlin

References

Amt für Statistik Berlin-Brandenburg (2009) *Statistisches Jahrbuch 2009*. Berlin: Kulturbuch-Verlag. Retrieved July 15, 2010, from http://www.statistik-berlin-brandenburg.de/produkte/jahrbuch/jb2009/BE_Jahrbuch_2009.pdf

Amt für Statistik Berlin-Brandenburg (2009) *Statistisches Jahrbuch 2009* [Statistical Yearbook]. Berlin: Kulturbuch-Verlag. Retrieved from http://www.statistik-berlin-brandenburg.de/produkte/jahrbuch/jb2009/BE_Jahrbuch_2009.pdf

Mundelius, M. (2009) Einkommen in der Berliner Kreativbranche: Angestellte Künstler verdienen am besten [Employed Artists Earn Most] *Wochenbericht des DIW Berlin* (No. 9/2009). Berlin: Deutsches Institut für Wirtschaftsforschung. Retrieved from http://www.diw-berlin.de/documents/publikationen/73/diw_01.c.95339.de/09-9-1.pdf

Senatsverwaltung für Stadtentwicklung (2006) *Berlin: Orte der Internationalität*. Berlin: Technische Universität Berlin, Institut für Stadt- und Regionalplanung. Retrieved from http://opus.kobv.de/zlb/volltexte/2008/6343/

Senatsverwaltung für Wirtschaft, Technologie und Frauen (2011) *Konjunkturdaten Arbeitslosigkeit: Arbeitslosenquote Berlins im Vergleich mit Deutschland* [Data on Unemployment: Unemployment rates Berlin in comparison with Germany]. Retrieved from http://www.berlin.de/imperia/md/content/sen-wirtschaft/konjunkturdaten/c_04.pdf?start&ts=1302079728&file=c_04.pdf

Teipelke, R. (2011) *Impression of skyrocketing rents in Berlin now officially confirmed by rent index report*. Retrieved from http://placemanagementandbranding.wordpress.com/2011/06/03/impression-of-skyrocketing-rents-in-berlin-now-officially-confirmed-by-rent-index-report/

Data Sources

1
Einwohnerentwicklung von Berlin (n.d.). Retrieved May 22, 2011, from http://de.wikipedia.org/wiki/Einwohnerentwicklung_von_Berlin

Unlike other major European cities such as Rome, Paris, or London, Berlin was contested and politically instrumentalized for more than 40 years. In the aftermath of World War II, Berlin lost more than one million inhabitants (Amt für Statistik, 2009). The West was part of the Federal Republic of Germany, and the East was part of the German Democratic Republic, which surrounded the whole city. This situation retarded the city's development in some aspects; yet, it also led to some sort of inter-German competition and doubling with regard to some prestigious cultural institutions.

However, since German reunification in 1990, the city has prospered, at least in cultural and tourism-related terms, while at the same time, many parts of Berlin, especially in the east, experienced a loss of industrial infrastructure and the manufacturing base. The current transformation of the city has opened up space for creative processes and (relatively) cheap rents alike. One, qualitative, indicator for its growing popularity is the fact that more and more international artists choose Berlin as a place to live and work and that more firms in the creative economy are opening up offices in the city.

Some facts about Berlin

• Although many other large cities have grown over the past decades, the population of Berlin remains the same size as in the mid-twentieth century, at around 3.4 million (Data Point 1). The share of migrants is slightly higher than 13 per cent. The overwhelming majority of immigrants come from Europe. Turkish (24 per cent of all immigrants) and Eastern European people make up the largest groups. However, the number of Asian migrants is also considerable (Data Point 2).

• Although a vibrant city, Berlin is not rich by German standards, because it does not have a broad industrial base and its unemployment rate is around double that of the country as a whole (14 per cent compared with eight per cent; Senatsverwaltung, 2011). As a result, social security is the largest part of Berlin's financial budget, and financial services is the third largest (Data Point 3). The second biggest share is education, science, and research, paying, *inter alia*, for three large universities. Overall, Berlin spent €22.6 billion in 2011. In its cultural budget, the two most important spending items are the 'Staatstheater' (comprising inter alia the *Stiftung Oper*, *Deutsches Theater*, and *Volksbühne*) (45 per cent) and heritage, memorials, and museums (21 per cent). The latter pays for different UNESCO World Heritage Sites. The film industry, an important aspect of Berlin's creative economy, gets €16 million (figures for 2009; Data Point 4).

• Looking at central cultural venues in Berlin, the city exhibits one of the richest publicly funded cultural infrastructures globally. However, due to financial problems, more than half of the smaller public libraries in different quarters of the city were closed down between 2000 and 2008 (Data Point 5).

• Like most larger cities in developed countries, Berlin's labor market is characterized by a large share of jobs in the service sector (86 per cent; Data Point 6). Twenty thousand artists and 80,000 other workers in the creative industries produced a relatively large share of Berlin's gross domestic product, 10 per cent overall (Mundelius, 2009). Building and construction (5 per cent) is an important branch because the city is still in the process of restructuring after its reunification 20 years ago and is also trying to conserve older treasures (seven housing complexes built in 1913–1931 were inscribed on the UNESCO World Heritage List in 2008). As a result, rents and housing prices have been rising substantially in some areas of Berlin but are in most cases still far below those of many comparable cities (Teipelke, 2011).

• Berlin has become increasingly attractive as a holiday destination, as considerably larger numbers of foreign tourists indicate (Data Point 7). Its share of all tourists has risen from 26 per cent in 1994 to more than 36 per cent in 2010. Tourists come mainly from the United Kingdom (330,000), Italy (280,000), and the United States (260,000), accounting for around 30 per cent of all foreign tourists.

• The international film festival *Berlinale* is one of the big cultural events in the city, and it is closely connected to its film industry in Babelsberg (e.g., movies such as Lang's 'Metropolis,' Tarantino's 'Inglorious Basterds') and other places. With guests from over 120 countries and journalists from more than 80, the film festival is also acknowledged internationally (Data Point 8).

What Are The Issues?

Berlin has a complex, often tragic history, with destruction in World War II and division in the years afterward. During the past 20 years, it has become one of the cultural hotspots of Europe. Additionally, being the (new) capital of the world's fifth largest economy, it also plays an important political role (146 foreign embassies; Senatsverwaltung, 2006). However, its size and economic power are much lower than those of other important European capitals such as London or Paris, which results in enormous structural challenges because resources for maintaining and improving its position are sometimes lacking. The future will show whether Berlin will be able to incorporate these trends in a meaningful and sustainable way, bringing it closer to the status of a true world city, or whether the city will find it difficult to adapt. One of the key issues for Berlin, constantly debated, is the cultural and economic integration of migrants (an official policy exists only since 2005).

2
Amt für Statistik Berlin-Brandenburg (2009). Die kleine Berlin-Statistik 2009. Retrieved May 22, 2011, from http://www.statistik-berlin-brandenburg.de/produkte/KleineStatistik/kBEst_2009.pdf

Amt für Statistik Berlin-Brandenburg (2010). Pressrelease from 03/31/2010 - No. 97. Retrieved May 22, 2011, from http://www.statistik-berlin-brandenburg.de/pms/2010/10-03-31a.pdf

3
Senatsverwaltung für Finanzen (2010). Haushaltsplan von Berlin für die Haushaltsjahre 2010/2011. Retrieved May 22, 2011, from http://www.berlin.de/imperia/md/content/senatsverwaltungen/finanzen/haushalt/2010_2011_band_01_hg_uebersichten.pdf?start&ts=1289891980&file=2010_2011_band_01_hg_uebersichten.pdf

http://www.berlin.de/imperia/md/content/senatsverwaltungen/finanzen/haushalt/2010_2011_band_01_hg_uebersichten.pdf?start&ts=1289891980&file=2010_2011_band_01_hg_uebersichten.pdf

4
Senatskanzlei Kulturelle Angelegenheiten (2009). Kulturausgaben der Hauptverwaltung des Landes Berlin (ohne Bezirke). Retrieved May 22, 2011, from http://www.berlin.de/imperia/md/content/sen-kultur/bescheinigungen/eckdaten_kulturhaushalt_2004_bis_2009.pdf?start&ts=1271331265&file=eckdaten_kulturhaushalt_2004_bis_2009.pdf

5
Amt für Statistik Berlin-Brandenburg (2009). Die kleine Berlin-Statistik 2009. Retrieved May 22, 2011, from http://www.statistik-berlin-brandenburg.de/produkte/KleineStatistik/kBEst_2009.pdf

6
Amt für Statistik Berlin-Brandenburg (2010). Statistisches Jahrbuch 2010 Berlin. Retrieved May 22, 2011, from http://www.statistik-berlin-brandenburg.de/Produkte/jahrbuch/jb2010/BE_Jahrbuch_2010.pdf

7
Senatsverwaltung für Wirtschaft, Technologie und Frauen (n.d.). Tourismus in Berlin. Retrieved May 22, 2011, from http://www.berlin.de/sen/wirtschaft/abisz/tourismus.html#ex

8
Berlinale (n.d.) Berlinale 2005 Facts & Figures. Retrieved May 22, 2011, from http://www.berlinale.de/en/archiv/jahresarchive/2005/01_jahresblatt_2005/Pop-up_Berlinale_2005_in_Zahlen.html

1 **Population Over Time** (1950–2009)

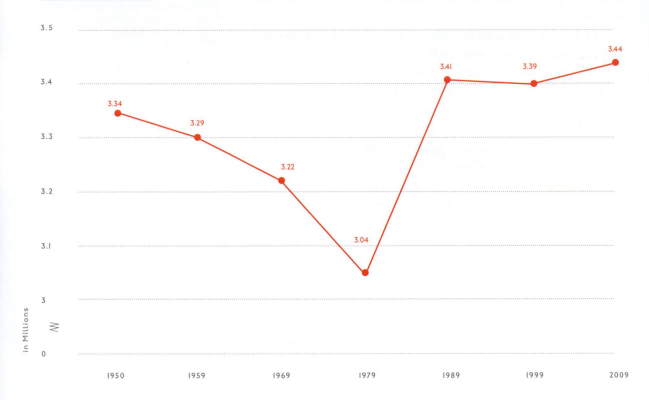

2 **Origins and Total Share of Migrants in Berlin** (2000–2009)

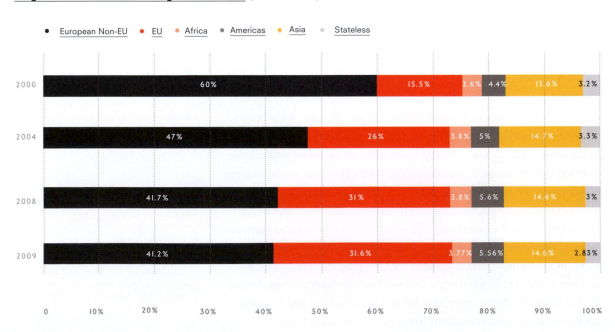

3 **Budget Shares by Sectors** (2011)

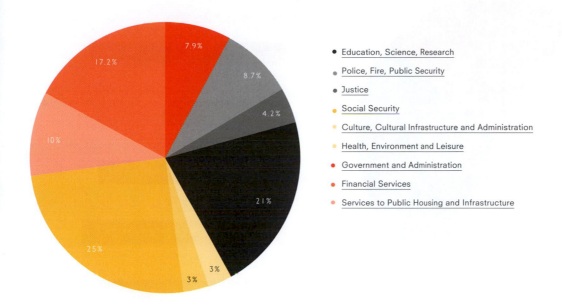

- ● Education, Science, Research
- ● Police, Fire, Public Security
- ● Justice
- ● Social Security
- ● Culture, Cultural Infrastructure and Administration
- ● Health, Environment and Leisure
- ● Government and Administration
- ● Financial Services
- ● Services to Public Housing and Infrastructure

4 **Cultural Budget Breakdown**
(2004, 2009 estimated; in Millions €)

5 **Cultural Venues / Institutions**
Number of Institutions (2000–2008)

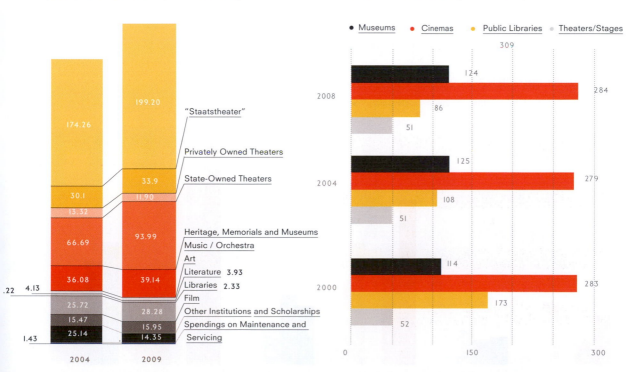

6 Sectors of Employment (2009)

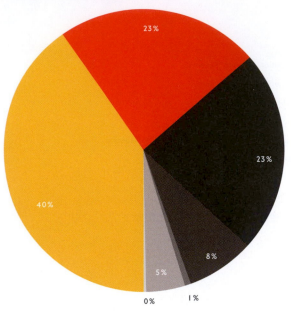

- 23%
- 23%
- 40%
- 5%
- 0%
- 1%
- 8%

- Public And Private Services
- Finance, Real Estate, Business Services
- Trade, Transportation And Hospitality
- Manufacturing
- Goods-Producing
- Building And Construction
- Agriculture And Fishing   Total employed (in thousands): **1665.6**

8 Berlinale (International Film Festival): Countries of Origins of Press and Accredited Guests

- Accredited Guests   - Journalists

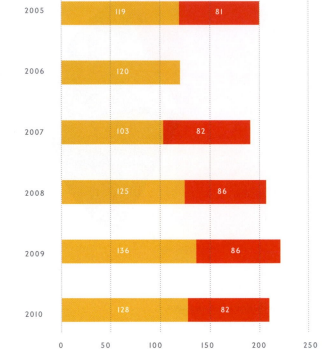

Year	Accredited Guests	Journalists
2005	119	81
2006	120	
2007	103	82
2008	125	86
2009	136	86
2010	128	82

7 Foreign Tourists - Top -Ten (1994, 2005, 2010)

- UK   - Italy   - Netherlands   - USA   - Spain   - Denmark   - France   - Switzwerland   - Sweden   - Austria

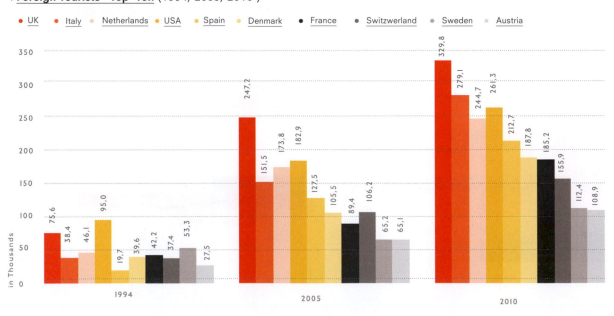

in Thousands

1994: 75,6 · 38,4 · 46,1 · 95,0 · 19,7 · 39,6 · 42,2 · 37,4 · 53,3 · 27,5

2005: 247,2 · 151,5 · 173,8 · 182,9 · 127,5 · 105,5 · 89,4 · 106,2 · 65,2 · 65,1

2010: 329,8 · 279,1 · 244,7 · 261,3 · 212,7 · 187,8 · 185,2 · 155,9 · 112,4 · 108,9

Istan–bul

References

Aksoy, A., & Enlil, Z. (2011) *Cultural Economy Compendium*: Istanbul 2010. Istanbul: Istanbul Bilgi University Publications.

Aksoy, A., & Robins, K. (2011) 'Heritage, memory, debris: Sulukule, don't forget.' In H. K. Anheier & Y.R. Isar (eds), *Heritage, memory & identity* (pp. 222–230). London: SAGE.

Göktürk, D., Soysal, L., & Türeli, I. (eds) (2010) *Orienting Istanbul: Cultural capital of Europe?* Abingdon, UK: Routledge.

Koch, G. (2009) 'Innovation in urban Räumen.' In U. Matthiesen & G. Mahnken (eds), Das *Wissen der Städte. Neue stadtregionale Entwicklungsdynamiken im Kontext von Wissen, Milieus und Governance* (pp. 83–94). Wiesbaden, Germany: VS Verlag.

Navaro-Yashin, Y. (2011) 'Knowing the city: Migrants negotiating materialities in Istanbul.' In H. K. Anheier & Y. R. Isar (eds), *Heritage, memory & identity* (pp. 231–238). London: Sage.

Said, E. W. (2003) *Orientalism*. London: Penguin Books.

Short, J. R. (2006) *Global metropolitan: Globalizing cities in a capitalist world.* New York: Oxon.

Data Sources

1

TURKSTAT, General Population Census Figures (1965-2000). Retrieved June 10,2011, from http://tuikapp.tuik.gov.tr/nufusmenuapp/menu.zul

TURKSTAT, Population Figures based on Residency Registration Records (2007- 2010). Retrieved June 10.2011, from http://www.tuik.gov.tr/VeriBilgi.do?tb_id=39&ust_id=11

2

ESA UN, International Migrant Stock, 2008 revision. Retrieved June 10, 2011, from http://esa.un.org/migration/p2k0data.asp

3

http://www.ibb.gov.tr/en-US/Organization/Birimler/ButceveDenetimMd/Documents/2004_2005_ana_yatirim_kalemleri.pdf, accessed June 14, 2011

"Our world is shrinking, while cities are expanding into each other, continuously reshaping our (and their) sense of place within a global horizon. As cities compete for relevance they are challenged to claim both situated difference and global connectedness."

— (Göktürk et al. 2010: 1)

When cities are framed by the concepts of local situation and global links, questions arise concerning image construction, cultural policy making, forms of communication, and exchange on a global scale and in correspondence with existing national policies. Emerging definitions of global cities as 'arena(s) for a constellation of distinct social interests that are negotiating the global-local connection' (Short, 2006: 7) or as scenes of transcultural knowledge formation (Koch, 2009: 93) direct the focus of sociological research toward analyses of balancing and combining global and local elements in cultural, social, and political domains within urban spaces.

As a representative case study, the city of Istanbul offers a distinctive basis for such analyses: its historical background, which almost no publication about the city fails to begin with; its connected cultural, religious, and historic ethnic diversity and transculturality; its geographical position, to which both of the first points are connected; and the recent, globally oriented cultural policy plans in and for Istanbul form the thematic frame. Needless to say, all of these factors were part of the case the city authorities made for its selection as a 'European Capital of Culture' in 2010.

The following data points are brief, exemplary indicators for urban processes unfolding in Istanbul under the influence of globalization. An underlying question is whether Istanbul can define itself as a transcultural, global city of trade and culture.

Some facts about Istanbul

• There is steady population growth, albeit with decreasing gains and birth rates (Data Point 1). In comparison with Turkey's other large cities, Istanbul has the highest population growth rate, raising its rank in the U.N. World City Ranking from 29 in 1980 to 20 in 2010. This increase could suggest a further growth in Istanbul's social significance, and thus also its political significance, on a national basis.

• Although no reliable data on foreign-born people in Istanbul are available, the small numbers for Turkey overall suggest that their number in Istanbul is also quite small (Data Point 2). However, closer analyses of the population's composition in terms of internationality are needed.

• Because the city continues to grow rapidly, and because many districts are in the process of urban redevelopment, large investments into the urban infrastructure, including traffic and parks, are needed, as can be seen from the city's budget (Data Point 3). These processes accompany replacements and expropriation, with sometimes severe consequences for inhabitants and their local identities (see Aksoy & Robins, 2011; Navaro-Yashin, 2011). Detailed information on Istanbul's cultural budget was not available.

• In line with the city's strategy of establishing itself as a global cultural hotspot, the number of cultural events supported by the municipality has increased significantly over the past few years (Data Point 4). The strikingly high number of theater performances has decreased slightly, leading to a more even distribution across different cultural activities.

• Istanbul's numerous cultural institutions have attracted many visitors, and increasingly so (Data Point 5). The lower figures for library use are probably because each user is counted (registered) only once, regardless of number of visits, whereas for other activities each visit is counted.

• Overall, a huge increase in jobs can be observed for Turkey as a whole between 2003 and 2008 (Data Point 6). The percentage increase (155 per cent) is largest for construction and for real estate, indicating the already-mentioned growth in urban redevelopment. In the same time, the number of people working in the cultural economy doubled from 133 751 to 268 477.

• Although the figures for local and foreign artists at the Istanbul Biennial, an international arts exhibition, do not show a clear trend (one reason is probably that it has a large international share from the start), the Istanbul Biennial's impact has certainly risen. It started in 1987 with around 10,000 visitors and no international press accreditation. In 2009, it had more than 100,000 visitors (6,000 international) and 600 accredited international journalists (personal communication (January 11, 2011), Ö. Ece, Istanbul Foundation for Culture and Arts).

What Are The Issues?

Istanbul is a city of intersections. It mixes old traditions with the newest developments in art and culture, not the least in architecture. Sitting on the edge of two continents, it combines oriental and occidental (see Said, 2003, for a critical discussion of these terms) ways of living and thinking. Economically, it still has large industrial and new postindustrial industries and service sectors. At the same time, Istanbul's share of the Turkish cultural economy is 46 per cent (Aksoy & Enlil, 2011). The question is whether the city will be able to integrate all this heterogeneity creatively, or if these tensions will tear the city apart, giving rise to social, political, and cultural distortions. Cultural policy and governance will have a crucial role to play in fruitfully combining local identities with global demands.

4
IBB Annual Reports. Retrieved June 10, 2011, from http://www.ibb.gov.tr/tr-TR/BilgiHizmetleri/Yayinlar/FaaliyetRaporlari/Documents/2010/giris.html

5A
Aksoy, A and Enlil Z (2011). Cultural Economy Compendium: stanbul 2010. Istanbul: Istanbul Bilgi University Publications, p.199

5b
http://www.tuik.gov.tr

6
TURKSTAT, Some basic indicators and employment by economic activity, NACE Rev 1.1. Retrieved June 14, 2011, from http://www.tuik.gov.tr/VeriBilgi.do?tb_id=30&ust_id=9

7
Aksoy, A and Enlil Z (2011). Cultural Economy Compendium: stanbul 2010. Istanbul: Istanbul Bilgi University Publications, p.199

1 Population Over Time in Different Turkish Cities

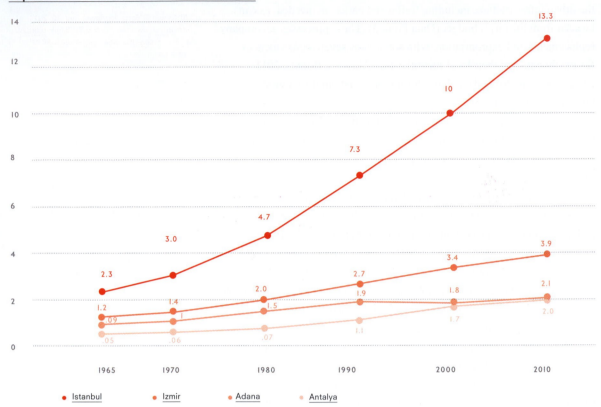

- Istanbul
- Izmir
- Adana
- Antalya

2 International Migrants in Turkey (1990–2010)

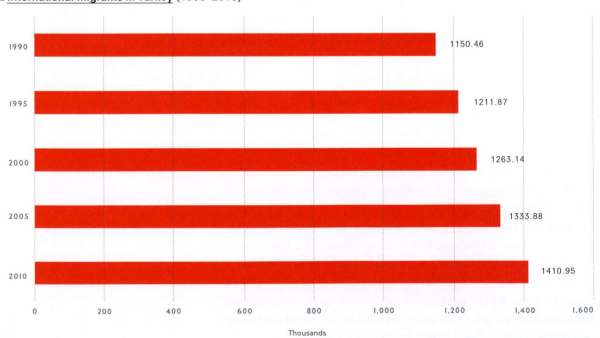

Year	Thousands
1990	1150.46
1995	1211.87
2000	1263.14
2005	1333.88
2010	1410.95

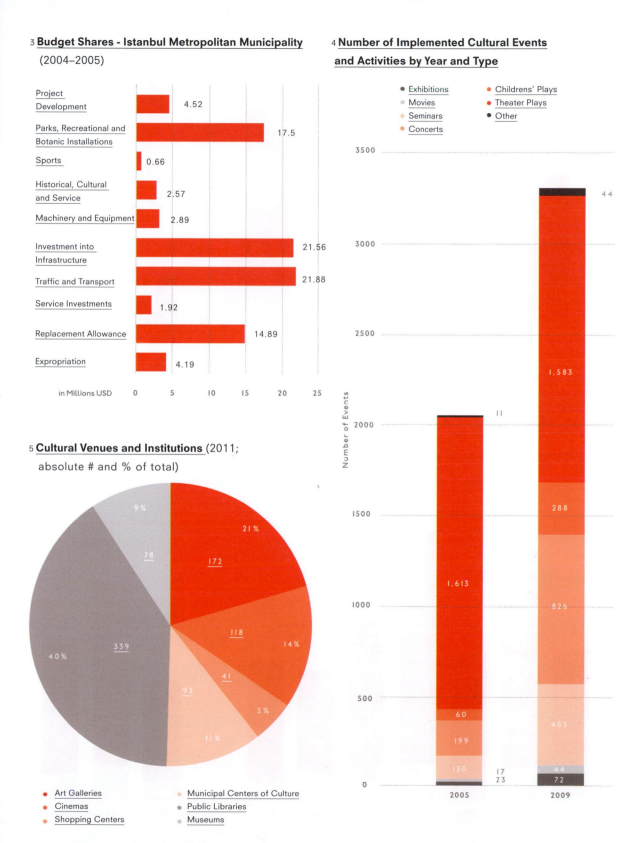

3 Budget Shares - Istanbul Metropolitan Municipality
(2004–2005)

Project Development	4.52
Parks, Recreational and Botanic Installations	17.5
Sports	0.66
Historical, Cultural and Service	2.57
Machinery and Equipment	2.89
Investment into Infrastructure	21.56
Traffic and Transport	21.88
Service Investments	1.92
Replacement Allowance	14.89
Expropriation	4.19

in Millions USD   0   5   10   15   20   25

4 Number of Implemented Cultural Events and Activities by Year and Type

- ● Exhibitions
- ● Movies
- ● Seminars
- ● Concerts
- ● Childrens' Plays
- ● Theater Plays
- ● Other

Number of Events

3500
3000
2500
2000
1500
1000
500
0

2005
- 44 (2009 top)
- 11
- 1,613
- 60
- 199
- 130
- 17
- 23

2009
- 44
- 1,583
- 288
- 526
- 453
- 44
- 72

5 Cultural Venues and Institutions (2011; absolute # and % of total)

- 9% — 78
- 21% — 172
- 14% — 118
- 5% — 41
- 11% — 92
- 40% — 339

- ● Art Galleries
- ● Cinemas
- ● Shopping Centers
- ● Municipal Centers of Culture
- ● Public Libraries
- ● Museums

405

6 Sectoral Distribution of Employment in Turkey (2003–2008)

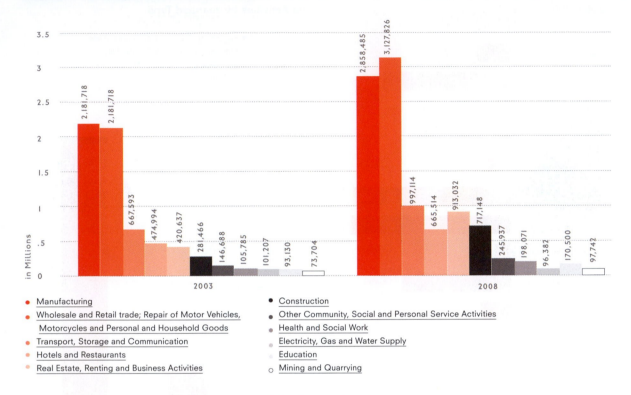

in Millions

- Manufacturing
- Wholesale and Retail trade; Repair of Motor Vehicles, Motorcycles and Personal and Household Goods
- Transport, Storage and Communication
- Hotels and Restaurants
- Real Estate, Renting and Business Activities
- Construction
- Other Community, Social and Personal Service Activities
- Health and Social Work
- Electricity, Gas and Water Supply
- Education
- Mining and Quarrying

7 Istanbul Biennial: Foreign and Local Artists or Artist Groups Over Time
- Local   - Foreigner

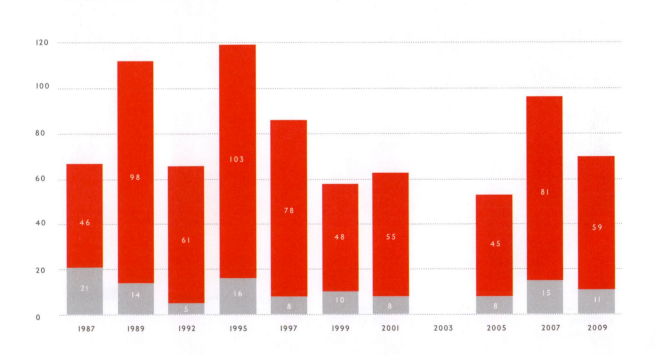

London

References

Trust for London and New Policy Institute (2010)
*Income inequality in London compared with
other English regions*. Retrieved September
7, 2011, from London's poverty profile Web
site: http://www.londonspovertyprofile.org.uk/
indicators/topics/inequality/income-inequality-in-
london-compared-with-other-english-regions/

Data Sources

1
Demographia.com (2001). Greater London, Inner
London & Outer London Population & Density
History. Retrieved May 27, 2011, from http://
www.demographia.com/dm-lon31.htm

Greater London Authority (2011). GLA
Population Projections 2010 Round, SHLAA,
Borough SYA. Retrieved May 25, 2011, from
http://data.london.gov.uk/datastore/package/
popproj-2010rnd-shlaa-borough-sya

2
Greater London Authority (2008). ONS Ethnic
Group Population Estimates: Mid-2006.
Retrieved May 30, 2011, from http://www.
london.gov.uk/archive/gla/publications/
factsandfigures/dmag-update-15-2008.pdf

3
Greater London Authority (2010). The Greater
London Authority's Consolidated Budget and
Component Budgets for 2010-11. Retrieved May
30, 2011, from http://static.london.gov.uk/gla/
budget/docs/1011budget.pdf

4
Department for Culture and Sports (2010).
Resource Accounts 2009-10. Retrieved July 6,
2011, from http://www.culture.gov.uk/images/
publications/2010_DCMS_Resource_Accounts.
pdf
4B
Arts & Business(n.d.). Private Investment in
Culture 09/10 - Benchmarking Tool. Retrieved
May 30, 2011, from http://benchmarking-tool.
artsandbusiness.org.uk/region/london/sector/
all/size/large

London's size and constant growth has led to its central position in contemporary discussions around globalization. The largest Western city in 1800, London was the largest city in the world in 1900 and only dropped out of the top 15 largest cities in 1990 (see Trends in Urbanization suite). Nevertheless, it still ranks at the top of virtually every world city ranking (see City Networks and Rankings suite).

Some facts about London

• London's population growth accelerated in the mid-nineteenth century. A population decrease began in the 1960s and continued until the 1980s. The 1990s brought a turning point; since then, the population has been on the increase (Data Point 1).

• A large share (31 per cent) of its total population is foreign-born (Data Point 2). The United Kingdom is the 'mother country' of the Commonwealth, an outcome of the decolonization process, which commenced with India's independence in 1947 and continued in the 1960s. For some years, citizens of Commonwealth countries enjoyed special advantages with respect to migration and work permits in the United Kingdom. Additionally, since 1990 the UK has proved to be more open towards Eastern Europeans than many other countries of the European Union.

• London's city budget reveals a highly diversified funding system, with income from many different sources and cross-financing between different organizations. The London Development Agency and Transport for London, for example, are almost entirely financed through their own earned income. About 84 per cent of London's budget expenditure goes to the Metropolitan Police Authority. When the costs for the Fire and Emergency Planning Department are added in, this percentage rises to 97 (Data Point 3).

• London's cultural sector receives funding from two main sources, the national Department for Culture, Music, and Sports and private funding (data on funding through the local authorities was not traceable). London draws about 19 per cent of the department's total national budget for recreation, culture, and religion, thereby receiving a much larger share of the budget than its share of the U.K. population. Only expenditures for the subcategories religious and other community services (6 percent), broadcasting and publishing services (0.2 percent), and recreational and sporting services (13.5 percent) do not privilege London (Data Point 4).

• Private funding differs in its distribution to different areas of the United Kingdom. London draws 68.2 per cent of the UK's total private investment in culture (and 83 percent of individual donations). Private investments include individual donors as well as business investment and trusts and foundations. Donations tend to be made to more prestigious, major organizations, whereas smaller organizations are more or less neglected by the private sector (Data Point 4b).

• The higher-than-average investments by the government as well as private financiers result in a rich cultural infrastructure: 215 theaters and concert halls, 184 museums, and 395 libraries (Data Point 5). This very good infrastructure, together with the city's cultural heterogeneity (see next section) probably contributes to London's ranking first in the Cultural Experience category in the Global Cities Index (see City Networks and Rankings suite).

• Service jobs make up 96 per cent of London's employment. Although consumer services is the largest single category (21 per cent), London also accommodates a highly diversified and elaborate business and financial service sector structure. As a result, 24 per cent of its total employment are located in high-value businesses and business-supporting services (Data Point 6).

What Are The Issues?

London is one of the most important financial services centers in the world. Moreover, it is the cultural and creative hub of the United Kingdom. Highly-paid jobs as well as moderately to low-paid jobs are found in London, which attracts both highly educated and skilled personnel and migrants looking for a better future. This mix creates a highly diversified population and serious social tension resulting from income inequality and problems of access and participation (Trust for London and New Policy Institute, 2010). This tension undoubtedly contributed to the outbreak of riots in London in 2011.

Overall, the financial crisis and more generally a decrease in British influence in the world puts pressure on London. Concerns have been raised regarding whether investments made in the preparation for the 2012 Olympic Games and similar mega-events have been well spent or whether the money would have been better used to improve London's overall infrastructure and support social issues (see chapter by Oakley, this volume).

5
London Development Agency (n.d.). London - A cultural Audit. Retrieved May 30, 2011, from http://static.london.gov.uk/mayor/culture/docs/cultural-audit.pdf

6
"Greater London Authority (2007). Working Paper 25 - An expenditure-based approach to employment sectors in London. Retrieved May 30, 2011, from http://legacy.london.gov.uk/mayor/economic_unit/docs/wp_25.pdf"

7
London Development Agency (n.d.). London Visitor Survey Annual Report 2008. Retrieved May 30, 2011, from http://www.lda.gov.uk/Documents/London_Visitor_Survey_Annual_Report_2008_8202.pdf

1 **Population Over Time** (1801-2006)

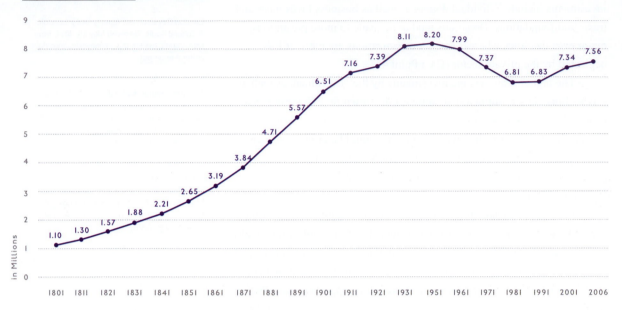

in Millions

1.10 · 1.30 · 1.57 · 1.88 · 2.21 · 2.65 · 3.19 · 3.84 · 4.71 · 5.57 · 6.51 · 7.16 · 7.39 · 8.11 · 8.20 · 7.99 · 7.37 · 6.81 · 6.83 · 7.34 · 7.56

1801 1811 1821 1831 1841 1851 1861 1871 1881 1891 1901 1911 1921 1931 1951 1961 1971 1981 1991 2001 2006

2 **Ethnicities in Greater London** (2006)

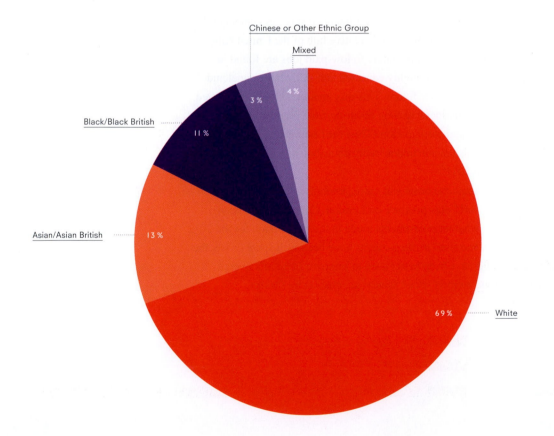

Chinese or Other Ethnic Group

Mixed

Black/Black British — 11 %

3 %

4 %

Asian/Asian British .... 13 %

69 % ——— White

410

3 **The Greater London Authority's Budget** (2009/10)

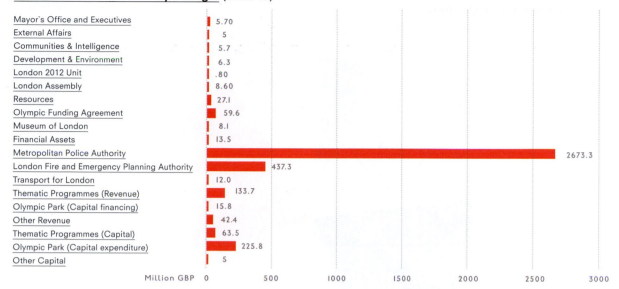

	Million GBP
Mayor's Office and Executives	5.70
External Affairs	5
Communities & Intelligence	5.7
Development & Environment	6.3
London 2012 Unit	.80
London Assembly	8.60
Resources	27.1
Olympic Funding Agreement	59.6
Museum of London	8.1
Financial Assets	13.5
Metropolitan Police Authority	2673.3
London Fire and Emergency Planning Authority	437.3
Transport for London	12.0
Thematic Programmes (Revenue)	133.7
Olympic Park (Capital financing)	15.8
Other Revenue	42.4
Thematic Programmes (Capital)	63.5
Olympic Park (Capital expenditure)	225.8
Other Capital	5

4 **Spending on Recreation, Culture and Religion by DCMS** (2008/2009) ● London ● UK

4B **Private Investment in Culture** (2009/2010) ● Business Investments ● Individual Giving ● Trust & Foundations

Spending on Recreation, Culture and Religion (Million GBP):

	London	UK
Recreational and Sporting Services	53.5	396.6
Cultural Services	344.3	1563.2
Broadcasting and Publishing Services	0.2	102.7
Religious and Other Community Services	1	16.3
R&D, Recreation, Culture and Religion	0.7	3.3
Recreation, Culture and Religion Not Elsewhere Classified	13.1	60.2

Private Investment in Culture (Million GBP):

	Business Investments	Individual Giving	Trust & Foundations
All Organizations Sizes (1124)	73.16	299.11	75.79
Small Organizations (242)	.84	.34	.78
Medium Organisations (603)	6.9	6.3	10.12
Large Organisations (181)	12.13	14.42	15.08
Major Organisations (98)	53.22	278.02	49.78

5 **Cultural Venues/Institutions** (2007)

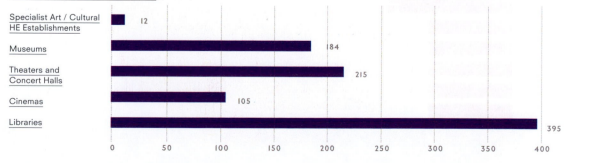

Specialist Art / Cultural HE Establishments	12
Museums	184
Theaters and Concert Halls	215
Cinemas	105
Libraries	395

6 Total Employment in London by Category (2005)

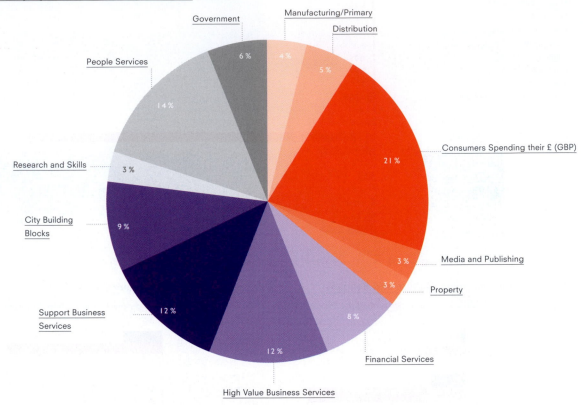

- Government 6 %
- Manufacturing/Primary 4 %
- Distribution 5 %
- Consumers Spending their £ (GBP) 21 %
- People Services 14 %
- Media and Publishing 3 %
- Property 3 %
- Research and Skills 3 %
- Financial Services 8 %
- City Building Blocks 9 %
- Support Business Services 12 %
- High Value Business Services 12 %

7 London Tourists' Main Home Countries (2008)

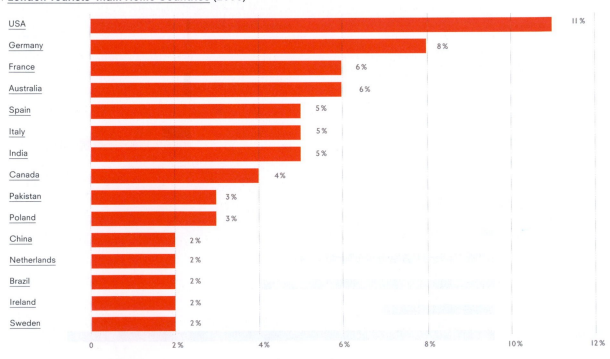

- USA 11 %
- Germany 8 %
- France 6 %
- Australia 6 %
- Spain 5 %
- Italy 5 %
- India 5 %
- Canada 4 %
- Pakistan 3 %
- Poland 3 %
- China 2 %
- Netherlands 2 %
- Brazil 2 %
- Ireland 2 %
- Sweden 2 %

L'viv

Data Sources

1

Wikipedia (2011). Lviv. Retrieved June 7, 2011, from http://en.wikipedia.org/wiki/Lviv

Wikipedia (2011). The population of the city. Retrieved June 7, 2011, from http://uk.wikipedia.org/wiki/%D0%9D%D0%B0%D1%81%D0%B5%D0%BB%D0%B5%D0%BD%D0%BD%D1%8F_%D0%9B%D1%8C%D0%B2%D0%BE%D0%B2%D0%B0

2

Wikipedia (2011). The population of the city. Retrieved June 7, 2011, from http://uk.wikipedia.org/wiki/%D0%9D%D0%B0%D1%81%D0%B5%D0%BB%D0%B5%D0%BD%D0%BD%D1%8F_%D0%9B%D1%8C%D0%B2%D0%BE%D0%B2%D0%B0

3

Lviv City Administration (2009). Information on Expenditures of the municipal budget of Lviv, 2009. Retrieved June 7, 2011, from: http://www.city-adm.lviv.ua/lmrdownloads/finansy2009/vydatky2009.xls

4

Lviv City Administration (2009). Information on Expenditures of the municipal budget of Lviv, 2009. Retrieved June 7, 2011, from: http://www.city-adm.lviv.ua/lmrdownloads/finansy2009/vydatky2009.xls

Located in the western part of Ukraine, L'viv's long tradition as a city goes back to the thirteenth century and the city's culture has flourished under different political leaders, nations, and political systems (see Savchak & Knudsen McAusland, this volume). Today, the city can claim to be culturally diverse, thanks to its history of changing regimes and circumstances, as well as by its geographical vicinity to Hungary, Slovenia, Poland, Romania and Belarus. L'viv presents itself as a cultural focal point in the region, seeking to feature its post-Soviet development without denying its history. The city has maintained a vast number of historical buildings and institutions that makes its cityscape distinct. It joined the Organization of World Heritage Cities in 1998.

What Do We Know?

• In the decade between the break up of the Soviet Union in 1991 and 2001, L'viv lost more than 10 per cent of its population. Since then, it has recovered slightly but has not yet regained its former population size (Data Point 1).

• Political events have repeatedly caused some ethnic group or the other to be expelled from the urban community. During World War II, most of L'viv's Jewish community was extinguished by the Nazis; the fall of the Soviet regime caused the departure of many of the city's Russian population after 1989 (Data Point 2).

• Education is the main sector of the city's public expenditure (26 per cent). Social security and welfare rank second at 19 per cent, and the share of healthsector is 17 per cent. Investment in construction accounted for almost 16 per cent of the budget in 2009. Cultural concerns rank last in expenditures at only 2.6 per cent (Data Point 3).

• Breaking down the expenditures for cultural purposes reveals that the main share is dedicated to arts education for children, coming in at nearly half of the sector's budget (Data Point 4). Generally, the largest amount goes to institutional cultural infrastructure such as theaters (14 per cent), libraries (15 per cent), museums (10 per cent), and orchestras (9 per cent). Only a small share, 5 per cent, is spent on independent institutions, cultural clubs and other types of venues outside the public sector.

• Even though only a small amount of the city's budget is invested in independent clubs and venues, about 140 cultural clubs enrich the social life of city residents. In contrast to only 11 cinemas, the city has 29 theaters, 59 museums and a relatively large number of libraries (Data Point 5).

• L'viv's history is manifest in its vast richness of architectural jewels, with 285 sites claiming cultural heritage status.

What Are The Issues?

L'viv strives to develop its image as a mix of cultural, economic, and educational advantages. The city's established traditional cultural scene, however, sometimes is not open enough to allow new cultural structures to prosper (see the recommendations by Savchak and Knudsen McAusland, this volume). While the overall unemployment rate is quite low (see City Comparisons suite), it faces a challenge in moving the service sector of employment toward highly skilled labor so as to retain graduates in the city and attract young and culturally oriented people from all over Ukraine and the broader surrounding region.

[5]
Savchak, Ihor (2010). Cultural Policy and Governance in a New Metropolitan Age - Case of Lviv (Ukraine). Chapter draft

[6]
Lviv Investment Portal (2010). Number of employees by types of economic activity in Lviv for 2009 (thousands persons). Retrieved June 8, 2011 from http://www.investinlviv.com/what-do-we-offer/human-resources-and-education/labour-market/

[7]
Lviv City Administration (2010). Competitiveness Strategy of Lviv Review survey entry of tourists. Retrieved June 8, 2011 from http://www.city-adm.lviv.ua/lmrdownloads/turystu/2010_11_18_Inbound_Tourism_Survey_Repor__UKR.pdf

Population of L'viv by birth and by religious adherence

Place of birth	Percent
L'viv	56%
L'viv oblast (province in Western Ukraine surrounding L'viv)	19%
Ukraine, but in the East	11%
Former Republics of the USSR (Russia)	7 (4)%
Poland	4%
Western Ukraine, but not L'viv oblast	3%

Religious adherence	
Ukrainian Greek Catholic Church	45%
Ukrainian Orthodox Church – Kiev Patriarchate	31%
Ukrainian Autocephalous Orthodox Church	5%
Ukrainian Orthodox Church (Moscow Patriarchate)	3%
Other faiths	3%

Source: State Statistics Committee of Ukraine (without year). All-Ukranian population census 2001. Retrieved from http://2001.ukrcensus.gov.ua/eng/.

1 **City Population** (1989, 2001, 2007, 2010)

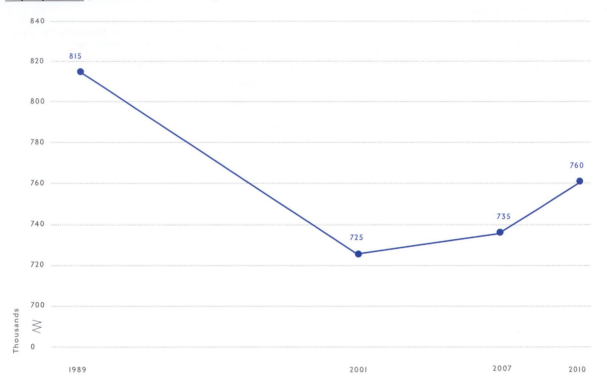

2 **Ethnic Composition L'viv** (1900–2001) ● Ukrainian ● Poles ● Jews ● Others

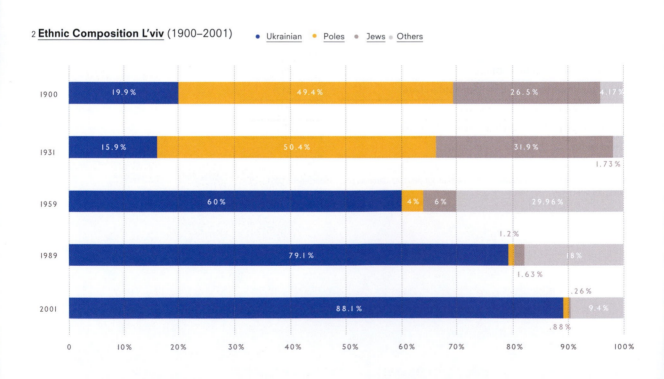

3 **Budget Expenditure by Sectors** (2009)

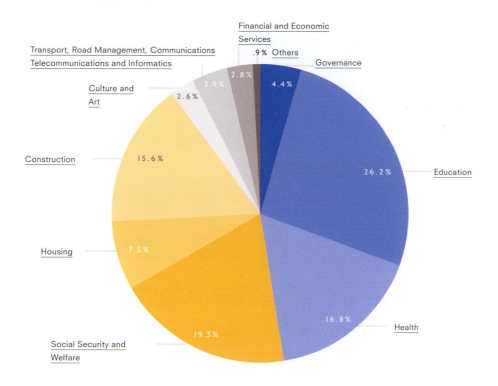

Financial and Economic Services .9 %

Transport, Road Management, Communications Telecommunications and Informatics 3.9 %

Culture and Art 2.6 %

Construction 15.6 %

Housing 7.5 %

Social Security and Welfare 19.3 %

Others 2.8 %

Governance 4.4 %

Education 26.2 %

Health 16.8 %

4 **Culture and Art Budget Breakdown** (2009)

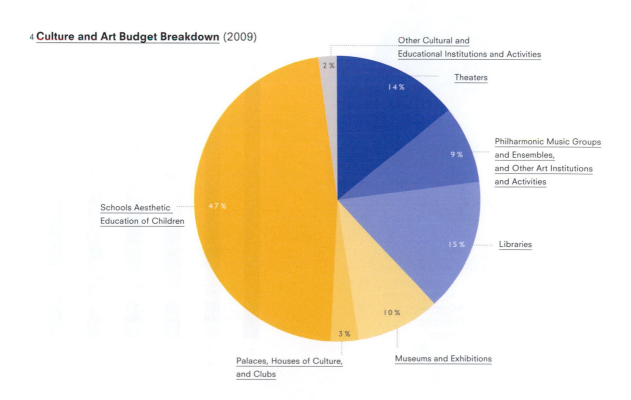

Other Cultural and Educational Institutions and Activities 2 %

Theaters 14 %

Philharmonic Music Groups and Ensembles, and Other Art Institutions and Activities 9 %

Libraries 15 %

Schools Aesthetic Education of Children 47 %

Museums and Exhibitions 10 %

Palaces, Houses of Culture, and Clubs 3 %

5 **Cultural Assets** (2010)

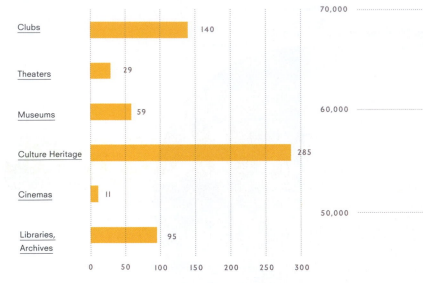

Clubs	140
Theaters	29
Museums	59
Culture Heritage	285
Cinemas	11
Libraries, Archives	95

0   50   100   150   200   250   300

7 **Number of Foreign Tourists** (2002–2007)

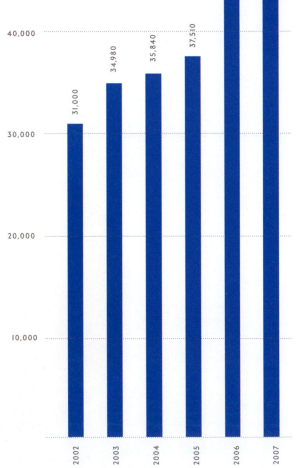

2002	31,000
2003	34,980
2004	35,840
2005	37,510
2006	47,360
2007	58,280

6 **Employees by Types of Economic Activity** (2010)

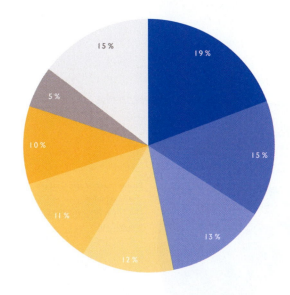

- 19 %
- 15 %
- 13 %
- 12 %
- 11 %
- 10 %
- 5 %
- 15 %

- ● Industry
- ● Health Care and Social Assistance
- ● Trade, Repairing of Cars, Household Products and Personal Consumption
- ● Activity of Transport and Communications; Financial Activitiy
- ● Utilities and Individual Services; Activity in Culture and Sport Spheres
- ● Government
- ● Education
- ● Others

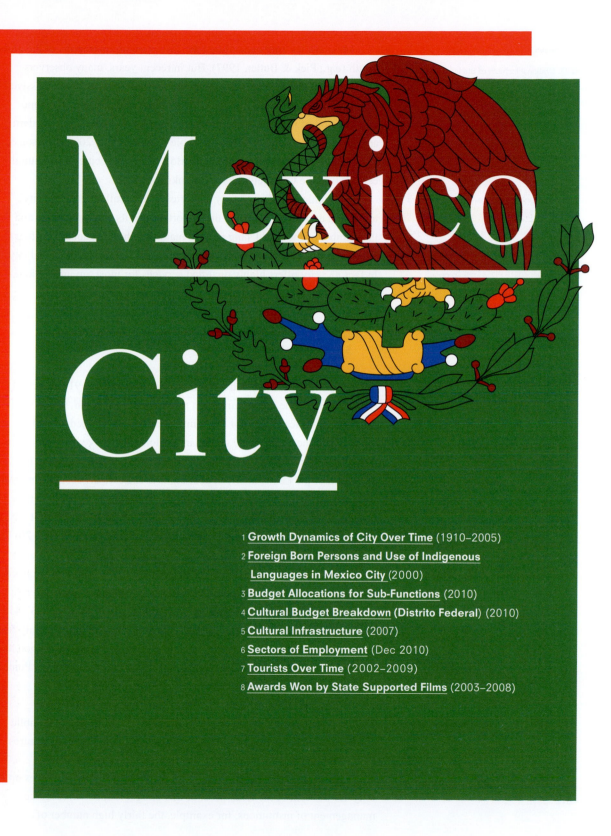

Mexico City

References

INEGI (National Institute of Statistics and Geography) (2011) *Population Census for 2010.* Retrieved from http://www.censo2010.org.mx/

Mexico City (2011) Retrieved from http://en.wikipedia.org/wiki/Mexico_City

Negrete, M. P. (2009) 'Santa Fe: A "global enclave" in Mexico City.' *Journal of Place Management and Development,* 2(1), 33–40.

Newson, L. A., & King, J. (2009) *Mexico City through history and culture.* New York: Oxford University Press.

Organisation for Economic Co-operation and Development (2004) *OECD territorial reviews Mexico City.* Paris: OECD. Retrieved from http://www.oecdbookshop.org/oecd/get-it.asp?REF=0404051E.PDF&TYPE=browse

Pick, J. B, & Butler, E. W. (1997) *Mexico megacity.* Boulder, CO: Westview Press.

Data Sources

1

INEGI (n.d.). Censo de Población y Vivienda 1930. Retrieved May 22, 2011, from http://www.inegi.org.mx/sistemas/TabuladosBasicos/LeerArchivo.aspx?ct=764&c=16767&s=est&f=1

INEGI (n.d.). Séptimo Censo General de Población 1950. Retrieved May 22, 2011, from http://www.inegi.org.mx/sistemas/TabuladosBasicos/LeerArchivo.aspx?ct=845&c=16765&s=est&f=1

INEGI (n.d.). Censo General de Población 1970. http://www.inegi.org.mx/sistemas/TabuladosBasicos/LeerArchivo.aspx?ct=960&c=16763&s=est&f=1

INEGI (n.d.). XI Censo General de Población y Vivienda 1990. Retrieved May 22, 2011, from http://www.inegi.org.mx/lib/Olap/consulta/general_ver4/MDXQueryDatos.asp?proy=cpv90_pt

INEGI (n.d.). Conteo de Población y Vivienda 1995. Retrieved May 22, 2011, from http://www.inegi.org.mx/lib/Olap/consulta/general_ver4/MDXQueryDatos.asp?proy=cpv95_pt

INEGI (n.d.). XII Censo General de Población y Vivienda 2000. Retrieved May 22, 2011, from http://www.inegi.org.mx/lib/Olap/consulta/general_ver4/MDXQueryDatos.asp?proy=cpv00_pt

INEGI (n.d.). II Conteo de Población y Vivienda 2005. Retrieved May 22, 2011, from http://www3.inegi.org.mx/sistemas/iter/consultar_info.aspx

INEGI (n.d.). Censo de Población y Vivienda 2010. Retrieved May 22, 2011, from http://www.inegi.org.mx/sistemas/mexicocifras/default.aspx?src=487&ent=09

Mexico City long exemplified the fast-growing metropolis of the global South (e.g., Pick & Butler, 1997). But in recent years, many observers have stressed that the city has grown past its limits and is facing massive structural problems.Still, Mexico City, with the idiosyncratic, dynamic combination of its ancient historical past (see Table 1) and more modern approaches to arts and culture as a whole (e.g., Negrete, 2009; Newson & King, 2009), can compete with the world's other great cities and cultural centers (see the City Networks and Rankings suite).

Economically, Mexico City classifies as a so-called 'gateway city' to Central and South America: the importance of its stock exchange and the number of the world's big players making it their headquarters (four companies in the Fortune 500) do not qualify it as a top-notch global city. In fact, the city offers highly qualified services for most top international companies and many specific networking functions are carried out.

Some facts about Mexico City

Its population increased more than tenfold between 1910 and 1990 (Data Point 1). The rate of migration to the *Distrito Federal*, which is the proper Mexican name for the administrative unit, peaked around the 1940s. With the boom of the secondary sector, unemployed workers from more rural destinations across Mexico were drawn to the capital. In the aftermath of the Latin American debt crisis in the early 1980s, this migration flow ceased rapidly. However, the still-growing larger metropolitan area population is estimated to be more than 20 million people, making it the 'largest metropolitan area in the Western hemisphere' (*Mexico City*, 2011).

• Indigenous culture in Mexico City—when compared with Oaxaca and Chiapas—is rather marginalized and appears to have further declined. In 2011, the indigenous population in Mexico City was estimated to be 141,710, however, no real census exists (INEGI, 2011). More than 37,450 citizens are estimated to speak Nahuatl. Overall immigration is mainly from other Mexican states, followed by the United States. This phenomenon has resulted in a comparatively low number of foreign-born people (Data Point 2). Mexico City certainly cannot be labeled an immigration city.

• The largest shares of the city budget are spent to provide very basic services and infrastructure. Urbanization, public safety, and public administration as well as potable water make up the largest expenditures (Data Point 3).

• As a result, the budget for culture, recreation, and sports makes up only 1.4 per cent of the total. Most of this budget is spent on resource management of institutions, for example, the fairly high number of museums in Mexico City (e.g., *Museo de Arte Moderno, Museo Nacional de Antropología, Museo Nacional de Arte, Museo Frida Kahlo*; Data Point 4).

• The Distrito Federal has less than 10 per cent of the inhabitants of the country as a whole, but as the capital of the nation, it has a huge overrepresentation of cultural infrastructure (Data Point 5). Parts of this infrastructure are not managed by the city government, but by the federal government.

• Compared with many Western global cities, Mexico City's share of the manufacturing sector is still considerable (Data Point 6). However, Mexico City experienced a huge increase in service employment (from 62 per cent to 73 per cent between 1990 and 2000; OECD, 2004). Professional, financial, and corporate services already make up more than 10 per cent of employment.

• Hotels in Mexico City were booked significantly more often by national tourists (Data Point 7). However, international tourists spent almost as much money. The city's Benito Juárez International Airport has been listed among the top 30 airports since 2008, considering total air traffic movement.

• The (federal) government's increasing investment in film production seems to pay off (Data Point 8). The state-controlled (since 1958) Churubusco studios have attracted international interest for more than 60 years: from the golden years of Mexican cinema until the contemporary *Nuevo Cine Mexicano*.

What Are The Issues?

For years, the city's core has struggled with infrastructure problems: these include vital sectors such as supply of fresh water; traffic overload, resulting in severe air pollution; and the poor state of construction in the most densely populated, less developed housing areas.

In addition, Mexico City is in the midst of a cultural–political war: since the election of Ebrard Casaubon, the left-of-center, liberal mayor (more precisely, the head of government of the Distrito Federal), the government has passed some legislation that touch upon traditional concern's of the city's Catholic majority. These issues include, for example, same-sex marriage, granting women the right to abort 12 weeks into pregnancy, and the simplification of divorce.

Sound cultural policies and governance in Mexico City are necessary to be able to contribute to a reduction of the ecological, social and cultural tensions that are evident. However, until now the city lacks a coherent and participative approach (see Jiménez Lopez, this volume).

Table 1: United Nations Educational, Scientific, and Cultural Organization World Heritage Sites in Mexico City

Site	Date of Inscription
Historic center of Mexico City and Xochimilco	1987
Luis Barragán House and Studio	2004
Central University City Campus of the Universidad Nacional Autónoma de México	2007

Retrieved from http://whc.unesco.org/en/list

2
INEGI (n.d.). II Conteo de Población y Vivienda 2005. Retrieved August 4, 2011, from http://www.inegi.org.mx/est/contenidos/proyectos/ccpv/cpv2005/default.aspx

3
Secretaría de Finanzas (n.d.). Federal District Legislative Assembly: Expenditure Budget Act Federal District Financial Year 2010, Allocation of Budget Expenditures of the Federal District [Translated from English into English]. Retrieved April 9, 2011, from http://www.finanzas.df.gob.mx/egresos/
4
Secretaría de Finanzas (n.d.). Programa Operativo Anual 2010. (Pages 71 ff.) Retrieved April 9, 2011, from http://www.finanzas.df.gob.mx/documentos/POA_2010.pdf
5
Sistema de Información Cultural (n.d.). Espacios Culturales. Retrieved May 22, 2011, from http://sic.conaculta.gob.mx/consulta2/

Sistema de Información Cultural (n.d.). Cine. Retrieved May 22, 2011 from http://sic.conaculta.gob.mx/index.
6
INEGI (n.d.). Encuesta Nacional de Ocupación y Empleo (ENOE). Distrito Federal. Retrieved May 22, from http://www.inegi.org.mx/sistemas/tabuladosbasicos2/indesttrim.aspx?c=26232&s=est
7
Dirección General de Planeación y Desarrollo Turístico (2009). Secretaría de Turismo, Indicadores estadísticos del sector, 2002 - 2010. Retrieved May 22, 2011 from http://www.mexicocity.gob.mx/general/descargar.php?id=Indicadores_a_Dic_09.pdf

8
IMCINE (2009): Indicadores de la industria cinematográfica en méxico. Retrieved May 26, 2011, from http://www.imaginationfilmsonline.com/13_indicadores.pdf

1 **Growth Dynamics of City Over Time** (1910–2005)

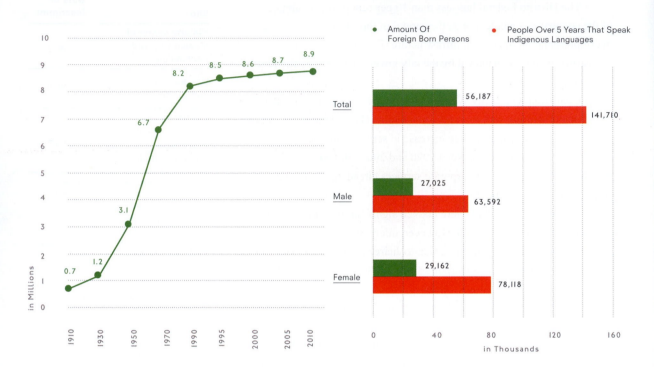

2 **Foreign Born Persons and Use of Indigenous Languages in Mexico City** (2000)

● Amount Of Foreign Born Persons

● People Over 5 Years That Speak Indigenous Languages

Total	56,187 / 141,710
Male	27,025 / 63,592
Female	29,162 / 78,118

in Thousands

3 **Budget Allocations for Sub-Functions (Distrito Federal)** (2010)

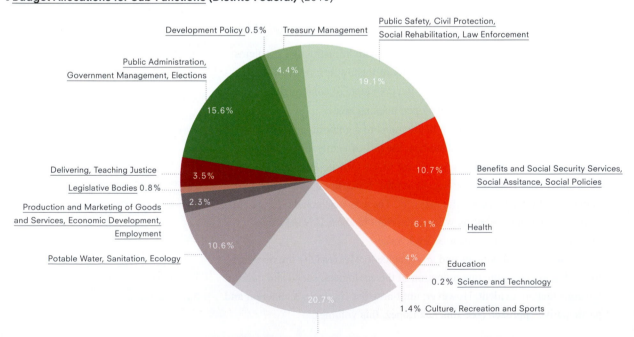

Development Policy 0.5%
Treasury Management 4.4%
Public Safety, Civil Protection, Social Rehabilitation, Law Enforcement 19.1%
Public Administration, Government Management, Elections 15.6%
Benefits and Social Security Services, Social Assitance, Social Policies 10.7%
Health 6.1%
Delivering, Teaching Justice 3.5%
Legislative Bodies 0.8%
Production and Marketing of Goods and Services, Economic Development, Employment 2.3%
Education 4%
Science and Technology 0.2%
Potable Water, Sanitation, Ecology 10.6%
Culture, Recreation and Sports 1.4%
Urbanization, Housing, Transportation 20.7%

422

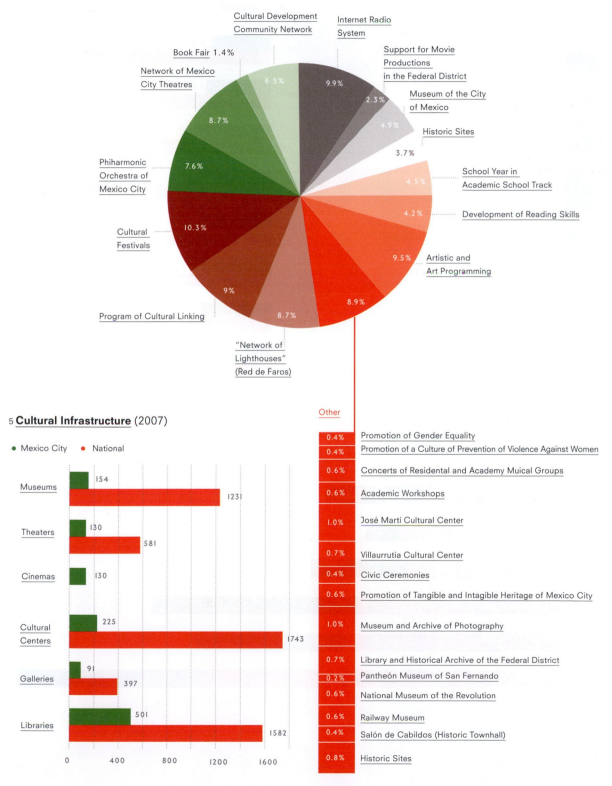

4 <u>**Cultural Budget Breakdown (Distrito Federal)**</u> (2010)

Cultural Development Community Network

Internet Radio System

Book Fair 1.4%

Network of Mexico City Theatres

Support for Movie Productions in the Federal District

Museum of the City of Mexico

Historic Sites

Phiharmonic Orchestra of Mexico City

School Year in Academic School Track

Development of Reading Skills

Cultural Festivals

Artistic and Art Programming

Program of Cultural Linking

"Network of Lighthouses" (Red de Faros)

6.5%
9.9%
2.3%
4.9%
3.7%
8.7%
7.6%
4.5%
4.2%
10.3%
9.5%
9%
8.7%
8.9%

5 <u>**Cultural Infrastructure**</u> (2007)

● Mexico City   ● National

	Mexico City	National
Museums	154	1231
Theaters	130	581
Cinemas	130	
Cultural Centers	225	1743
Galleries	91	397
Libraries	501	1582

0   400   800   1200   1600

Other

0.4%	Promotion of Gender Equality
0.4%	Promotion of a Culture of Prevention of Violence Against Women
0.6%	Concerts of Residental and Academy Muical Groups
0.6%	Academic Workshops
1.0%	José Martí Cultural Center
0.7%	Villaurrutia Cultural Center
0.4%	Civic Ceremonies
0.6%	Promotion of Tangible and Intagible Heritage of Mexico City
1.0%	Museum and Archive of Photography
0.7%	Library and Historical Archive of the Federal District
0.2%	Pantheón Museum of San Fernando
0.6%	National Museum of the Revolution
0.6%	Railway Museum
0.4%	Salón de Cabildos (Historic Townhall)
0.8%	Historic Sites

6 **Sectors of Employment (Mexico City)** (Dec 2010)

0.4%	Unspecified
0.4%	Agriculture, Forestry, Hunting And Fishing
0.4%	Mining And Quarrying And Electricity
15.6%	Manufacturing
6.8%	Construction
22.2%	Trade
7.3%	Restaurants and Accommodation Services
7.6%	Transport, Communications, Mail and Storage
10.5%	Professional, Financial And Corporate
9.8%	Social Services
12.3%	Miscellaneous Services
6.8%	Government And International Agencies

7 **Tourists Over Time** (2002–2009)

● International ● National

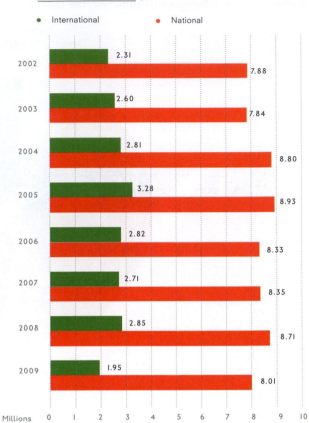

Year	International	National
2002	2.31	7.88
2003	2.60	7.84
2004	2.81	8.80
2005	3.28	8.93
2006	2.82	8.33
2007	2.71	8.35
2008	2.85	8.71
2009	1.95	8.01

Millions 0 1 2 3 4 5 6 7 8 9 10

8 **Awards Won by State Supported Films** (2003–2008)

● International ● National

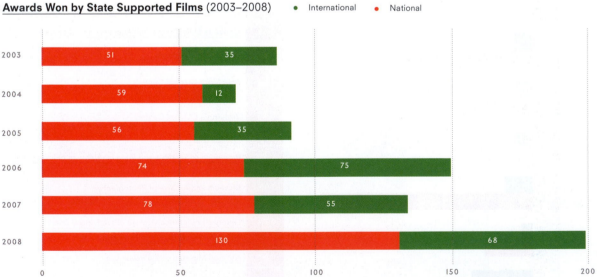

Year	National	International
2003	51	35
2004	59	12
2005	56	35
2006	74	75
2007	78	55
2008	130	68

0 50 100 150 200

New York City

References

Berg, B. F. (2007) *New York City politics: governing Gotham.* New Brunswick: Rutgers Univ. Press.

Currid, E. (2007) *The Warhol economy: How fashion, art, and music drive New York City.* Princeton, NJ: Princeton University Press.

Foner, N. (Ed.) (2005) *Wounded city. The social impact of 9/11.* New York, NY: Russell Sage Foundation.

Data Sources

1

Demographics of New York City (n.d.) Retrieved May 20, 2011, from http://en.wikipedia.org/wiki/Demographics_of_New_York_City

2

U.S. Census Bureau (n.d.) *New York - Race and Hispanic Origin for Selected Large Cities and Other Places: Earliest Census to 1990.* Retrieved May 20, 2011, from http://www.census.gov/population/www/documentation/twps0076/NYtab.pdf

U.S. Census Bureau (n.d.) *Census 2000 Summary File 1.* Retrieved May 20, 2011, from http://factfinder.census.gov/servlet/QTTable?_bm=y&-geo_id=16000US3651000&-qr_name=DEC_2000_SF1_U_DP1&-ds_name=DEC_2000_SF1_U&-_lang=en&-_sse=on

U.S. Census Bureau (n.d.) *2007 American Community Survey 1-Year Estimates.* Retrieved May 20, 2011, from http://factfinder.census.gov/servlet/ADPTable?_bm=y&-qr_name=ACS_2007_1YR_G00_DP5&-geo_id=16000US3651000&-ds_name=ACS_2007_1YR_G00_&-_lang=en&-redoLog=false

New York City Department of City Planning (2011) *NYC Total and Foreign-born Population 1790 - 2000.* Retrieved May 20, 2011, from http://www.nyc.gov/html/dcp/html/census/1790_2000_hist_data.shtml

3

New York City Council (2009) *FY2010 Expense and Contract Budget Resolutions. Schedules A and B.* Retrieved May 21, 2011, from http://www.nyc.gov/html/omb/downloads/pdf/adopt09_expreso.pdf

New York City, sometimes called the global capital of the world, has been a city of migration since its beginnings. Indeed it is the place of origin of the term *melting pot*, coined more than a century ago. The largest city in the United States and one of the largest cities in the world (see Trends in Urbanization suite), its five boroughs are associated with a cosmopolitan lifestyle and luxury but also with crime and urban decay. Throughout its history, New York City has repeatedly faced serious challenges, ranging from deindustrialization and crime to the 9/11 terrorist attacks in 2001, as before. The city reduced its high crime rate by creating and enforcing strong policies and reestablishing abandoned neighborhoods, and revitalized its economy by focusing on financial industries. New York City is not just a very real place but also a symbol of the dreams of the ambitious and the adventurous. More than any other city, it reflects the spirit of the urban in the twentieth century.

Some Facts about New York City

• By the end of the 1960s, New York City's population was around 7.8 million people. Suburbanization in the 1970s resulted in massive population loss until the beginning of the 1980s. Population growth reappeared in the 1990s (Data Point 1).

• Since the 1980s, the number of Asian migrants has risen, and the 1990s saw growth in the number of foreign-born people classified as other or mixed (Data Point 2). New York City's immigrant population is striking not just in number but in its extreme heterogeneity. In 1644, when the city was still called *Nieuw Amsterdam*, more than 20 languages were spoken. In 2005, nearly 36 per cent of the population was foreign born, and more than 170 languages (some linguists count up to 800) were spoken. Immigrant children, who grow up in a world in which ethnic diversity is a fact of life, bring in their different backgrounds and create cultural hybrids with a distinct New York flavor.

• The social and educational sectors receive the highest share of public expenditures, more than 60 per cent of the $60 billion city budget. The police and fire departments share 12 per cent, and the Department for Cultural Affairs (DCA) receives 0.3 per cent (Data Point 3).

• The administration's role in New York City's cultural economy seems limited, but the city has in fact established the largest cultural funding agency in the United States, the Department of Cultural Affairs (DCA). The DCA supports the city's cultural life and 33 large city-owned cultural institutions, with a total annual budget of approximately $160 million. A closer look at DCA's budget (Data Point 4) shows that 65 per cent goes to large and well-established institutions. About a third of the department's expenditures are distributed among several small and lesser known institutions and to cultural programs benefiting city residents.

• The city is also home to a vast and diverse nonprofit cultural community, which encourages creativity (Currid, 2007, pp. 181–185). Nonprofit and private organizations play a crucial role in the funding of cultural activities.

• In addition to DCA-financed and non-profit institutions, there are a number of privately financed and commercially oriented organizations. Connected to the city's world-famous Broadway, but also expanding beyond this iconic area, are 86 museums and 163 stages and theaters (Data Point 5) (for a detailed analysis of all these cultural institutions see Halle and Mirrer, this volume).

• New York City's employment structure is heavily service oriented. About 97 per cent of the jobs in New York City are located in the tertiary sector (Data Point 6).

• The 9/11 terrorist attacks resulted in a massive decrease in the number of international tourists visiting New York City. Four years later, the city had recovered, and the number of international tourists grew by more than 30 per cent over the next 5 years (Data Point 7).

What Are The Issues?

A modern metropolis with aging infrastructure, New York City faces problems of limited capacities: availability of affordable space for living and for creating new enterprises. Although the city continues to benefit from its 'command and control' functions in the global economy, which help to reinforce the local finance, insurance, and real estate industries, the shock waves from successive recent financial crises are still being felt. Emerging industries such as the cultural sector and tourism, while important, seem too small to propel New York City's economy. Also, infrastructural problems such as waste and sanitation management, or in general all issues concerning environmental tasks, are serious challenges. The city is additionally burdened with the reconstruction of the World Trade Center site. The 9/11 attacks perceptibly changed the local political environment. The fading acceptance of newer immigrant communities and further migration might harm the city's long-term development (Foner, 2005). Such hindrances will make it all the more difficult to resolve structural problems such as labor market tensions and social and infrastructural chasms, calling for new forms of governance (Berg, 2007).

4
New York City Council (2009) *FY2010 Expense and Contract Budget Resolutions. Schedules A and B.* Retrieved May 21, 2011, from http://www.nyc.gov/html/omb/downloads/pdf/adopt09_expreso.pdf

5
NY.com (2011) *Museums in New York.* Retrieved May 21, 2011, from http://www.ny.com/museums/all.museums.html

NY.com (2011) *Broadway Theaters.* Retrieved May 21, 2011, from http://www.ny.com/theater/on-broadway/theaters.html

NY.com (2011) *Off-Broadway Theaters.* Retrieved May 21, 2011, from http://www.ny.com/theater/off-broadway/theaters.html

NY.com (2011) *NYC Dance Venues.* Retrieved May 21, 2011, from http://www.ny.com/dance/venues.html

NYC.com (2011) *Movies.* Retrieved May 21, 2011, from http://www.nyc.com/movies/

New York Public Library (n.d.) *Locations and Hours.* Retrieved May 21, 2011, from http://www.nypl.org/locations

6
U.S Bureau of Labour Statistics (n.d.) *QCEW State and County Map.* New York. Retrieved May 21, 2011, from http://beta.bls.gov/maps/cew/US?start_over=true

7
nycgo.com (n.d.) *nyc statistics.* Retrieved May 22, 2011, from http://www.nycgo.com/articles/nyc-statistics-page

8
Alliance for the Arts (n.d.) *Top 100 Cultural Institutions in New York.* Retrieved June 9, 2011, from http://www.allianceforarts.org/get_the_facts/071910%20Crains%20top%20100.xls

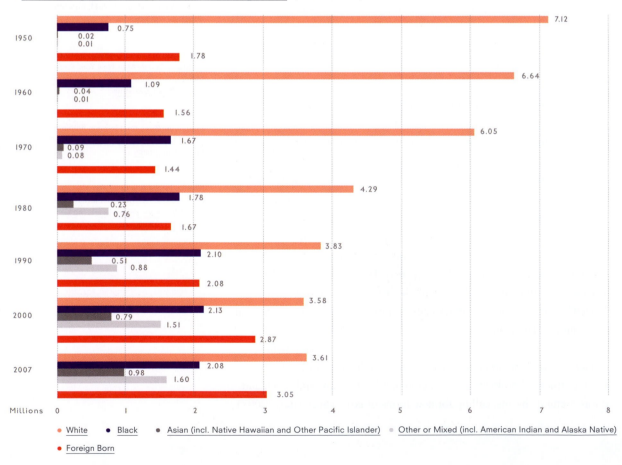

● White   ● Black   ● Asian (incl. Native Hawaiian and Other Pacific Islander)   ● Other or Mixed (incl. American Indian and Alaska Native)

● Foreign Born

3 **Citybudget New York - Fiscal Year** (2010)

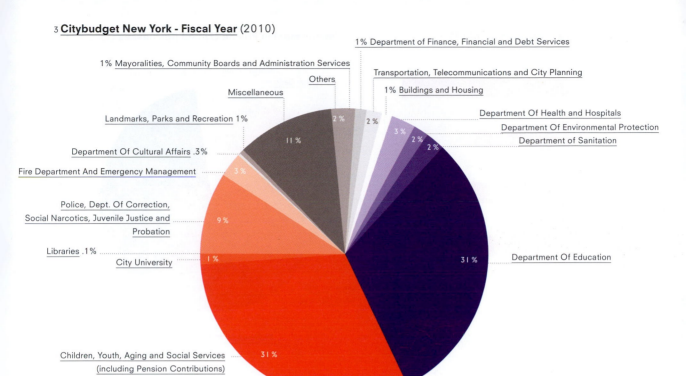

1% Department of Finance, Financial and Debt Services

1% Mayoralities, Community Boards and Administration Services

Transportation, Telecommunications and City Planning
1% Buildings and Housing

Others

Miscellaneous

Department Of Health and Hospitals
Department Of Environmental Protection
Department of Sanitation

Landmarks, Parks and Recreation 1%

Department Of Cultural Affairs .3%

Fire Department And Emergency Management

2%

2%

3%

2%

2%

11%

3%

Police, Dept. Of Correction,
Social Narcotics, Juvenile Justice and
Probation

9%

Libraries .1%

City University

1%

31% Department Of Education

Children, Youth, Aging and Social Services
(including Pension Contributions)

31%

4 **Budget Breakdown Department Of Cultural Affairs - Fiscal Year** (2010)

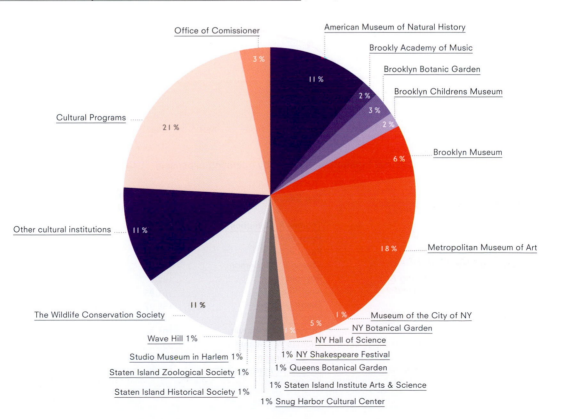

Office of Comissioner

American Museum of Natural History

Brookly Academy of Music

Brooklyn Botanic Garden

Brooklyn Childrens Museum

Cultural Programs

3%

11%

2%

3%

2%

21%

Brooklyn Museum

6%

18% Metropolitan Museum of Art

Other cultural institutions

11%

11%

The Wildlife Conservation Society

Wave Hill 1%

Studio Museum in Harlem 1%

Staten Island Zoological Society 1%

Staten Island Historical Society 1%

1%

5%

1%

Museum of the City of NY
NY Botanical Garden
NY Hall of Science
1% NY Shakespeare Festival
1% Queens Botanical Garden
1% Staten Island Institute Arts & Science
1% Snug Harbor Cultural Center

429

5 Cultural Venues / Institutions (2011)

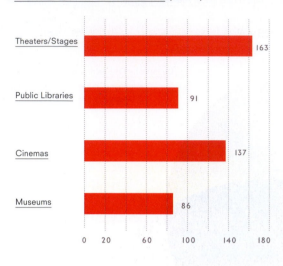

- Theaters/Stages — 163
- Public Libraries — 91
- Cinemas — 137
- Museums — 86

0 20 60 100 140 180

6 Employment in Private Owned Businesses (June 2010)

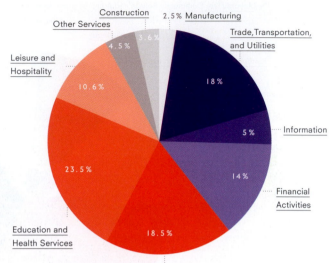

- Construction — 3.6%
- Other Services — 4.5%
- Manufacturing — 2.5%
- Leisure and Hospitality — 10.6%
- Trade, Transportation, and Utilities — 18%
- Information — 5%
- Financial Activities — 14%
- Education and Health Services — 23.5%
- Professional and Business Services — 18.5%

7 Foreign Tourists to New York (2000–2010)

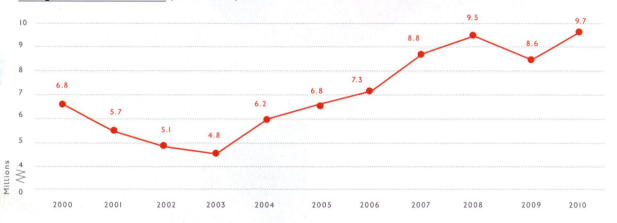

Millions

2000	2001	2002	2003	2004	2005	2006	2007	2008	2009	2010
6.8	5.7	5.1	4.8	6.2	6.8	7.3	8.8	9.5	8.6	9.7

8 New York City's 12 Largest Cultural Institutions (Ranked by operating expenses)   **City Owned**   Privately Owned

Organization	Top Executive(s)	2008 Operating Expenses (in Millions)	2009 Attendance
Metropolitan Museum of Art	Thomas P. Campbell	309.30	4,768,115
Metropolitan Opera Association	Peter Gelb	265.74	–
New York Public Library	Paul LeClerc	264.85	17,976,307
Wildlife Conservation Society	Steven E. Sanderson	182.35	–
Lincoln Center for the Performing Arts	Reynold Levy	162.67	302,515
Thirteen (WNET New York and WLIW 21)	Neal Shapiro	161.95	–
Museum of Modern Art	Glenn D. Lowry	158.47	2,839,197
American Museum of Natural History	Ellen V. Futter	144.74	4,800,000
Brooklyn Public Library	Dionne Mack-Harvin	101.54	–
Queens Borough Public Library	Thomas W. Galante	99.91	15,000,000
Carnegie Hall	Clive Gillinson	83.31	750,000
Solomon R. Guggenheim Foundation and Museum	Richard Armstrong	64.77	1,300,000

São Paulo*

References

Hoornweg, D. (2010) *Cities and climate change: An urgent agenda (Urban Development Series Knowledge Papers*, Vol. 10). Washington, DC: World Bank. Retrieved from http://siteresources.worldbank.org/INTUWM/Resources/340232-1205330656272/CitiesandClimateChange.pdf

Data Sources

1

Secretaria Municipal de Desenvolvimento Urbano (n.d.). População nos Anos de Levantamento Censitário Município e Região Metropolitana de São Paulo, Estado de São Paulo e Brasil 1872 a 2010. Retrieved May 22, 2011, from http://smdu.prefeitura.sp.gov.br/historico_demografico/tabelas/pop_brasil.php

2

Secretaria Municipal de Desenvolvimento Urbano (n.d.). Nacionalidade da População Município de São Paulo 1920 a 2000. Retrieved May 22, 2011, from http://smdu.prefeitura.sp.gov.br/historico_demografico/tabelas/pop_nac.php

3

Secretaria de Finanças e Desenvolvimento Econômico do Município de São Paulo; Fundação Seade (2003). Despesa Realizada, segundo Funções e Subfunções de Governo Município de São Paulo 2002-2003. Retrieved May 22, 2011, from http://www.seade.gov.br/produtos/msp/index.php?tip=met4&opt=s&tema=FPU&subtema=1

4

Instituto Brasileiro de Geografi a e Estatística - IBGE, Diretoria de Pesquisas (2007). Sistema de Informações e Indicadores Culturais 2003-2005. Estudos e Pesquisas - Informação Demográfi ca e Socioeconômica Número 22. Retrieved May 22, 2011, from http://www.cultura.gov.br/site/wp-content/uploads/2008/04/indic_culturais2005.pdf

5

Fundação Seade (n.d.). Equipamentos Culturais, por Tipo, segundo Subprefeituras e Distritos Município de São Paulo 2002. Retrieved May 22, 2011, from http://www.seade.gov.br/produtos/msp/cul/cul1_002.xls

São Paulo is the largest city in Brazil and in South America overall. Its universities and diversified cultural infrastructure contrast with its dense and rapidly created urban infrastructure. The poorer outskirts and slums (*favelas*) contrast with the city center, which is home to business, trade, and established cultural institutions. Nonetheless, the city seeks to create a network of cultural centers across the city to encourage cultural participation across its many neighbourhoods.

Some Facts about São Paulo

• São Paulo grew quickly between the 1950s and the 1980s, with its population nearly quadrupling. Since then, the growth rate has dropped to below 2 per cent. Today, the city is home to more than 11 million inhabitants (Data Point 1).

• Until the early twentieth century the city was a popular destination for emigrants from Europe and other parts of the world. This resulted in a share of foreigners of more than 30 per cent in the 1920s. However, São Paulo lost this status, and the figure of foreign-born residents shrank to 2 per cent or lower in the 2000s accordingly (Data Point 2).

• Most of São Paulo's financial budget is spent on education, health, social services, and security. Expenditures on culture account for only around US$60 million (R$140 million), or 1.2 per cent of the city's budget in 2005 (Data Point 3). These expenditures are financed by three sources, the national government, the federal state of São Paulo and the city's municipal government. The federal state subsidies increased considerably since 2003, reaching around US$450 million (R$796 million) in 2009, while expenditures by the municipal government pretty much stayed the same, at least until 2005 (Data Point 4).

• Services and commerce in São Paulo together total less than 60 per cent (Data Point 6), which is low compared with the other global cities in the indicator suites. The city's dependence on industrial production is made precarious by increased international competition. The cultural sector accounts for around 6 per cent of employment, though with a larger share between younger age groups (see table below).

• Between 2004 and 2010 the number of international tourists coming to São Paulo has grown by more than 30 per cent (Data Point 7).

• São Paulo's efforts in cultural activities are reflected in the rising number of international events happening in the city every year: an increase from 21 in 2004 to 79 in 2009. In relative terms, this increase is much larger than for Brazil as a whole (from 113 to 293). Foreign visitors to cultural events in São Paulo come from many nationalities. Argentines and people from the United States are the two largest groups, with around 11 per cent each (Data Point 8).

What Are The Issues?

São Paulo's accelerated growth in the second half of the 20th century led to a densely populated urban space and the extensive urbanization of the region close to São Paulo City. Still, the impact of population growth is traceable in diverse social inequalities and infrastructure struggles. Although São Paulo's cultural efforts are well demonstrated by the data presented in this suite, the city has a problem with equal access for all social groups and inhabitants of different parts of the city (see Vasconcelos-Oliveira, this volume).

São Paulo will probably have to struggle with reforming the employment sector in the near future. Services and commerce together total less than 60 percent (Data Point 6), which is low compared with the other global cities in the indicator suites. Production of industrial commodities faces trade and environmental challenges. When talking about the city's dependence on industrial production, one must bear in mind the international competition. The issue of environmental pollution also plays into the relationship between the city and its industrial sector. São Paulo is an urban agglomerate and the dense center of the city's broader metropolitan area. Managing the sources of pollution and lowering emissions without constraining production will probably be a matter for the future for the federal state government and São Paulo City (e.g., Hoornweg, 2010).

6
Investe São Paulo (n.d.). Mercado de Trabalho. Retrieved May 22, 2011, from http://www. investimentos.sp.gov.br/porque/mercado%20 de%20trabalho?lang=en

7
Ministério do Turismo (n.d.). Estudo da Demanda Turística Internacional - 2004-2009. Retrieved May 22, 2011, from http://www.dadosefatos. turismo.gov.br/export/sites/default/dadosefatos/ demanda_turistica/internacional/download_ internacional/Estudo_da_Demanda_Turxstica_ Internacional_-_2004-2009.pdf

8
Fundação Getulio Vargas (2009). Pesquisa do Impacto Econômico dos Eventos Internacionais Realizados no Brasil - 2007/2008. Retrieved May 22, from http://www.dadosefatos.turismo.gov. br/export/sites/default/dadosefatos/demanda_ turistica/Eventos/Download_eventos/Relatxrio_ Final_-_Estudo_do_Impacto_Econxmico_de_ Eventos_Internacionais_realizados_no_Brasil.pdf

Employees in the cultural sector by age groups (2003)

	Total Employees (in thousands)	Cultural Sector Employees (in thousands)	Cultural Sector Share of total employment (%)	Share of Age Groups in Cultural Sector (%)
All Ages	19768	1225	6,2	100
10 to 24	4029	342	8,5	27,9
25 to 49	12124	702	5,8	57,3
50+	3616	181	5	14,8

Source: http://www.seade.gov.br/produtos/anuario/index.php?anos=2003&tip=ment&opt=temas&cap=2&tema=dem#1

Urban Population Over Time (1950–2010)   ● Population   ● Average Annual Change

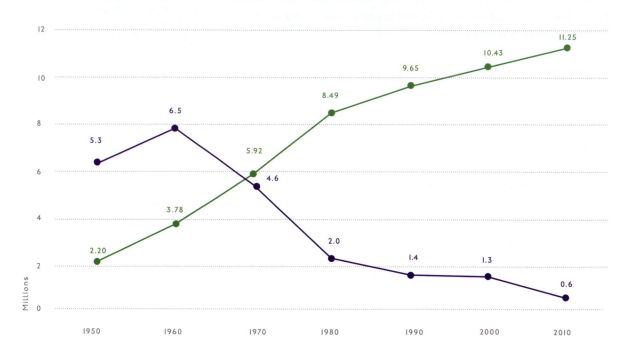

Share of Nationalities (1920–2000)

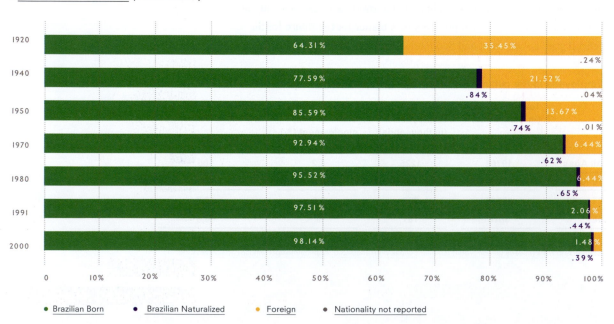

● Brazilian Born   ● Brazilian Naturalized   ● Foreign   ● Nationality not reported

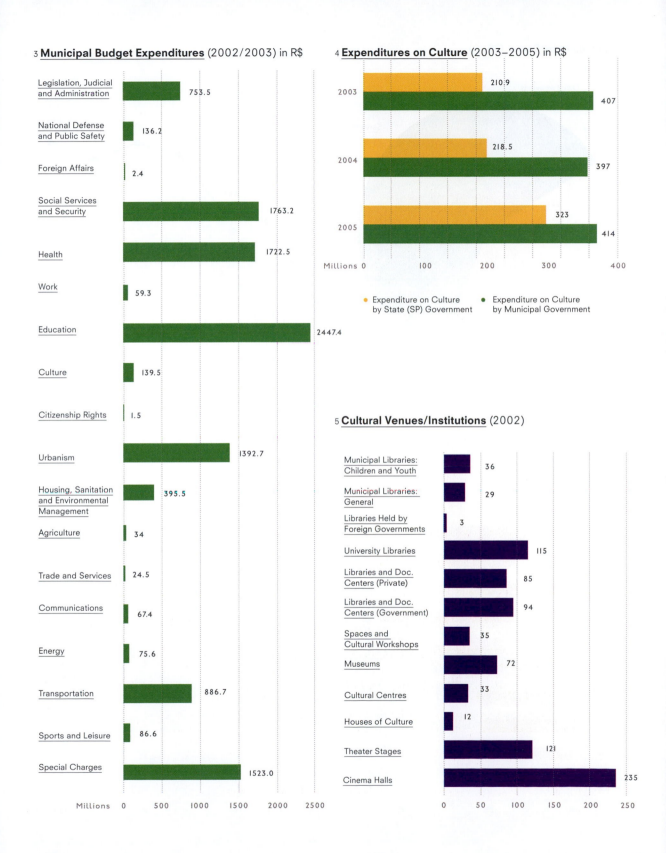

3 **Municipal Budget Expenditures** (2002/2003) in R$

Legislation, Judicial and Administration	753.5
National Defense and Public Safety	136.2
Foreign Affairs	2.4
Social Services and Security	1763.2
Health	1722.5
Work	59.3
Education	2447.4
Culture	139.5
Citizenship Rights	1.5
Urbanism	1392.7
Housing, Sanitation and Environmental Management	395.5
Agriculture	34
Trade and Services	24.5
Communications	67.4
Energy	75.6
Transportation	886.7
Sports and Leisure	86.6
Special Charges	1523.0

Millions 0   500   1000   1500   2000   2500

4 **Expenditures on Culture** (2003–2005) in R$

Year	Expenditure on Culture by State (SP) Government	Expenditure on Culture by Municipal Government
2003	210.9	407
2004	218.5	397
2005	323	414

Millions 0   100   200   300   400

● Expenditure on Culture by State (SP) Government
● Expenditure on Culture by Municipal Government

5 **Cultural Venues/Institutions** (2002)

Municipal Libraries: Children and Youth	36
Municipal Libraries: General	29
Libraries Held by Foreign Governments	3
University Libraries	115
Libraries and Doc. Centers (Private)	85
Libraries and Doc. Centers (Government)	94
Spaces and Cultural Workshops	35
Museums	72
Cultural Centres	33
Houses of Culture	12
Theater Stages	121
Cinema Halls	235

0   50   100   150   200   250

6 **Employment by Sector** (2009)

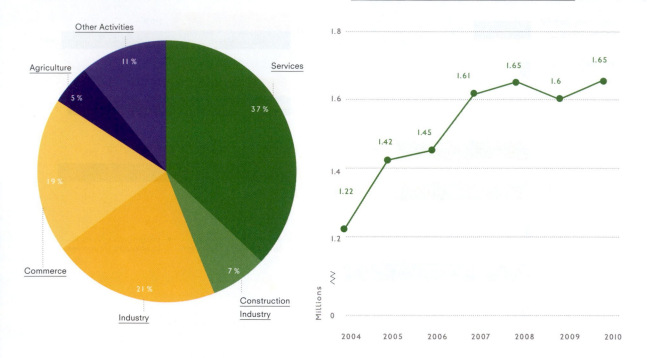

Other Activities — 11 %
Agriculture — 5 %
Services — 37 %
Commerce — 19 %
Industry — 21 %
Construction Industry — 7 %

7 **Number of International Tourists Over Time** (2004–2010)

1.22 · 1.42 · 1.45 · 1.61 · 1.65 · 1.6 · 1.65

Millions

2004 2005 2006 2007 2008 2009 2010

8 **"Top12" Home Countries of Foreign Visitors at Events in São Paulo** (2007/2008)

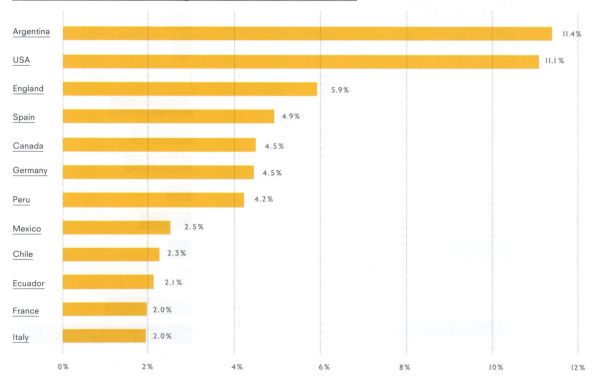

Country	Percent
Argentina	11.4%
USA	11.1%
England	5.9%
Spain	4.9%
Canada	4.5%
Germany	4.5%
Peru	4.2%
Mexico	2.5%
Chile	2.3%
Ecuador	2.1%
France	2.0%
Italy	2.0%

0% 2% 4% 6% 8% 10% 12%

Shanghai

References

All About Shanghai and Environs.
A Standard Guidebook. (Edition 1934-35).
Shanghai: The University Press. Retrieved May
17, 2011, from http://www.virtualshanghai.net/
Original_Text.php?ID=5.

Chen, X. (ed.)(2009) *Shanghai Rising: State Power
and Local Transformations in a Global Megacity.*
Minneapolis: University of Minnesota Press.

Murr, B. (2008) *Shanghai, Wirtschafts- und
Stadtentwicklung.* Report WKO Außenwirtschaft
Österreich. Retrieved May 17, 2011, from http://
portal.wko.at/wk/pub_detail_file.wk?AngID=1&D
ocID=839316&ConID=314369&rct=j&q=Shangh
ai:_Wirtschafts_und_Stadtentwicklung_Murr&ei=
HnfSTfDrG8rysgb80byiCQ&usg=AFQjCNHGxb
3WqRfgM7B5KsUSKIJJsLnLsQ&cad=rja.

Shanghai Statistics (2004) *Statistical Yearbook
2004 of Shanghai.* Retrieved May 10, 2011,
from http://www.stats-sh.gov.cn/2004shtj/tjnj/
tjnj2004.htm.

Shanghai Statistics (2010) *Statistical Yearbook
2010 of Shanghai.* Retrieved May 10, 2011,
from http://www.stats-sh.gov.cn/2004shtj/tjnj/
tjnj2010e.htm.

The 12th Five-Year Plan of Shanghai. Retrieved
May 17, 2011, from http://www.e-gov.org.cn/
ziliaoku/zhengfuguihua/201101/115485.html.

Wu, W. (2004) Cultural Strategies in Shanghai:
Regenerating Cosmopolitanism in an Era of
Globalization. *Progress in Planning 61* (3), 159-180.

Data Sources

1
http://www.stats-sh.gov.cn/2003shtj/tjnj/nje09.
htm?d1=2009tjnje/E0304.htm,http://www.stats-
sh.gov.cn/2003shtj/tjnj/nj10.htm?d1=2010tjnj/
C0202.htm, accessed May 10, 2011

2
http://www.stats-sh.gov.cn/2003shtj/tjnj/nje06.
htm?d1=2006tjnje/E0305.htm, accessed
May 10, 2011

3
http://www.stats-sh.gov.cn/2004shtj/tjnj/
tjnj2006E.htm#, accessed May 10, 2011

3a
http://www.stats-sh.gov.cn/2003shtj/tjnj/nje10.
htm?d1=2010tjnje/E0404.htm, accessed
May 10, 2011

Shanghai, sitting at the mouth of the Yangtze River, became a world city during the nineteenth and early twentieth centuries because of its favorable port location and its opening up to foreign trade in 1842. Although Shanghai possesses little of the ancient Chinese empire's cultural legacy compared with Beijing, it occupies its significant place in the modern culture of China by acting as a space of encounter between Chinese tradition and Western modernity. This has generated new kinds of hybrid modernities in which not only 'East meet West', but – acknowledging the crucial importance of Japanese influence – 'East meets East'.

The most populous city in China, with a registered population reaching 14 million and a transient population of about 5 million, Shanghai covers an area of 6,340.5 square kilometers. Equally as large is its economy, with a gross domestic product of $250 billion in 2009. Shanghai remained China's economic powerhouse after 1949, benefiting enormously from the opportunities afforded by the opening up of global trade. Its import and export volume reached $515.4 billion in 2009. In 2007, three quarters of its total trade consisted of the import and export volume of around 10,000 foreign companies, which employed a quarter of all employees and gained a growth in profits of 37.9 per cent in that year (Murr, 2008).

Shanghai presents itself to the world as a cosmopolis. One would expect culture to play a major role in that representation. How is this taking place and what impact does globalization have on Shanghai's culture?

Some Facts about Shanghai

• *International attraction*: Besides its financial attraction for foreign investors, Shanghai is also attractive to the growing number of foreigners living there. Within 9 years, the number of foreign residents in Shanghai tripled, reaching 152,000 in 2009 (Data Point 2). The majority are employees of foreign companies; however, international students are becoming a larger percentage, increasing from 5.7 to 10 per cent (Shanghai Statistics 2004, 2010). In 2009, more than 4 million foreign tourists visited Shanghai (Data Point 7).

• *Transnational exchange:* Shanghai is or was twinned with almost 70 cities from all six continents. It also has a platform for international exchange. The number of international exhibitions in Shanghai, let alone the Shanghai Expo, is increasing, together with exhibition space, which may indicate an increase in scale (Data Point 8).

• *Shanghai culture unbound?* After the opening up of China to the outside world, Shanghai's culture regained the vitality it had at its peak during the 1930s. Between 1990 and 1995, around $121 million was spent annually on building locations and organizing big events. This figure doubled in the years from 1996 through 2000 (Yin, 2000, as cited in Wu, 2004, p. 168), contributing to a well-developed physical cultural infrastructure (Data Point 5), though with much less money spent on programming. Moreover, Shanghai is beginning to have a voice in the international art field. Launched in 2007, the SH Contemporary, an exhibition of Asian contemporary art, has attracted the participation of almost 100 cities every year (Data Point 9).

• *Municipal cultural strategy:* Despite its strong economy, Shanghai's industry is still primarily manufacturing, though this has increasingly moved to the periphery of the city and become more hi-tech oriented (Data Point 6). The city authorities have also promoted scientific, technological, and knowledge-based industries, as part of an attempt to diversify and move up the value chain. The adoption of the term 'creative industries' in 2005 was part of this; the city has yet to fully work out the relationship between these agenda and that of 'culture'. Nevertheless, the aim of constructing Shanghai as a cultural cosmopolis is formulated in the current 5-year plan (2011–2015), which focuses on more large scale infrastructural investment (*The 12th Five Year Plan*, 2011). In 2009, around US$5 billion (¥35 billion) were spent on education (Shanghai Statistics, 2010). The trend toward increasing expenditures in culturally relevant sectors is clear (Data Point 3, Data Point 4; see Chen, 2009, on the importance of Shanghai's city government).

What Are The Issues?

Although Shanghai has made a lot of infrastructural investments in culture and the cultural industry is booming, the question remains as to which central values form the basis of the city's development and cultural identity. The current rapid development claims to build on and integrate at least parts of the legacy – of buildings, global image etc. – of this metropolis, distinguishing it from other Chinese, but also Western cities (Wu, 2004; O'Connor and Gu, this volume). There exists even a special term for this Shanghaian mix: hai pai culture. But is it a superficial 'reconstruction' using clichéd images or will it provide the resources for a new modern vision of the city?

In recent years, some of Shanghai's indicators have shown increases slowing, sometimes even declining. Whether this is a short-term impact of the financial crisis, or whether the described current phase of rapid development in Shanghai is coming to an end, has to be shown by the future.

4
http://www.stats-sh.gov.cn/2003shtj/tjnj/nje06.htm?d1=2006tjnje/E0506.htm, accessed May 10, 2011

5
http://www.stats-sh.gov.cn/2003shtj/tjnj/nje09.htm?d1=2009tjnje/E2201.htm,http://www.stats-sh.gov.cn/2003shtj/tjnj/nj10.htm?d1=2010tjnj/C2102.htm, accessed May 10, 2011

6
http://www.stats-sh.gov.cn/2003shtj/tjnj/nj10.htm?d1=2010tjnj/C0215.htm, accessed May 10, 2011

7
http://www.stats-sh.gov.cn/2003shtj/tjnj/nje09.htm?d1=2009tjnje/E0721.htm

http://www.stats-sh.gov.cn/2003shtj/tjnj/nj10.htm?d1=2010tjnj/C0620.htm

http://www.stats-sh.gov.cn/2003shtj/tjnj/nj06.htm?d1=2006tjnj/C0823.htm

http://www.stats-sh.gov.cn/2003shtj/tjnj/nj.htm?d1=2004tjnj/C0822.htm

http://www.stats-sh.gov.cn/2003shtj/tjnj/nj07.htm?d1=2007tjnj/C0723.htm

8
http://www.stats-sh.gov.cn/2003shtj/tjnj/nje09.htm?d1=2009tjnje/E0716.htm, accessed May 10, 2011

http://www.stats-sh.gov.cn/2003shtj/tjnj/nj10.htm?d1=2010tjnj/C0615.htm, accessed May 10, 2011

9
http://www.stats-sh.gov.cn/2003shtj/tjnj/nj10.htm?d1=2010tjnj/C0615.htm, accessed May 10, 2011

The Cultures and Communication Series 3, p. 362

10
Eileen Chang: "Love", April 1944 in Shanghai Translated by P.Y. Toh in October 2007, originally published in the Magazine, Volume 13, No.1,1944

1 __Population Over Time__ (1978–2009)

2 __Resident Foreigners in Shanghai__ (2000–2009)

- Japan
- Republic of Korea
- Singapore
- Germany
- United Kingdom
- Canada
- United States
- Australia
- France
- Malaysia
- Other

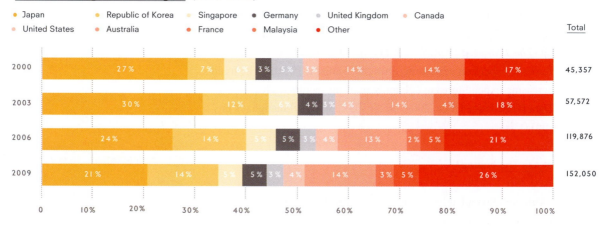

Year	Total
2000	45,357
2003	57,572
2006	119,876
2009	152,050

3 __City Budget: Local Fiscal Expenditure__ (1980–2005)

- Capital Constructions
- Technical Updates and Transformation of Enterprises
- Science and Technology Promotion
- City Maintenance
- Science, Education, Culture and Health Care
- Administration
- Other

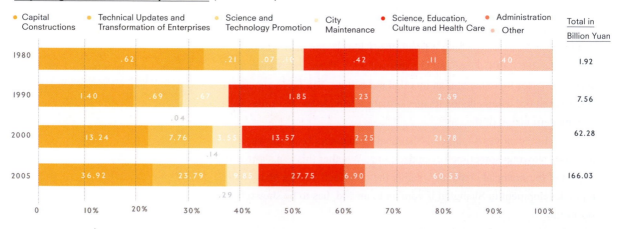

Year	Total in Billion Yuan
1980	1.92
1990	7.56
2000	62.28
2005	166.03

4 **Budget Break Down "Science,Education, Culture and Health Care"** (in million Yuan and share) (1980–2005)

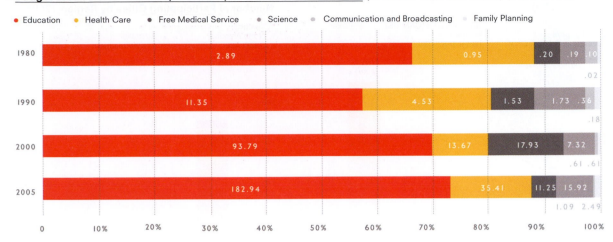

5 **Number of Cultural Venues/Institutions** (1995–2009)

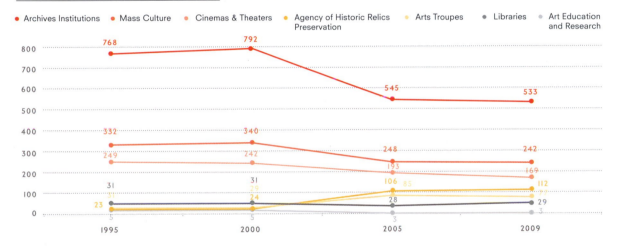

6 **Distribution of Labour Force** (2009)

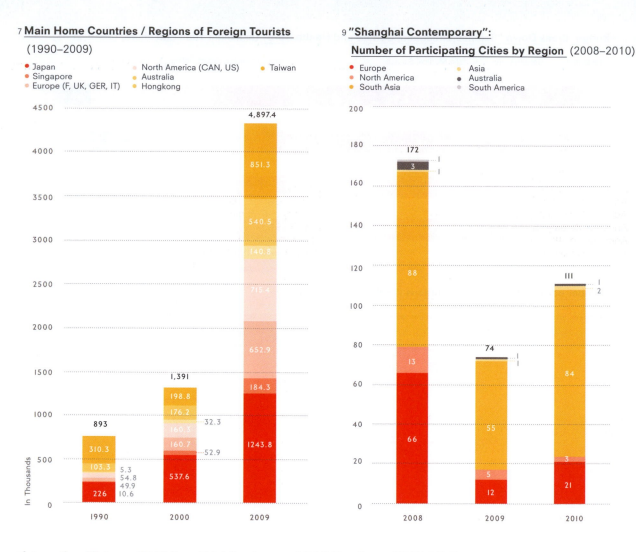

7 <u>**Main Home Countries / Regions of Foreign Tourists**</u>

(1990–2009)

- Japan
- Singapore
- Europe (F, UK, GER, IT)
- North America (CAN, US)
- Australia
- Hongkong
- Taiwan

4,897.4
851.3
540.5
140.8
71.4
652.9
184.3
1243.8

1,391
198.8
176.2
160.3
160.7
32.3
52.9
537.6

893
310.3
103.3
5.3
54.8
49.9
10.6
226

In Thousands

1990   2000   2009

9 **"Shanghai Contemporary":**

<u>**Number of Participating Cities by Region**</u> (2008–2010)

- Europe
- North America
- South Asia
- Asia
- Australia
- South America

172
3
88
13
66
1
1

74
1
1
55
5
12

111
1
2
84
3
21

2008   2009   2010

8 <u>**International Fairs and Exhibitons Total Numbers and Exhibition Space**</u> (2003–2009)

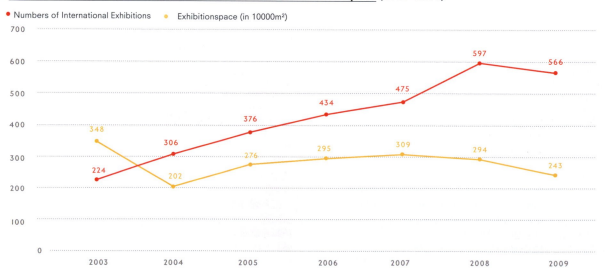

- Numbers of International Exhibitions
- Exhibitionspace (in 10000m²)

700
600   597   566
500   475
434
400   376
306
300   348   276   295   309   294   243
224   202
200

2003   2004   2005   2006   2007   2008   2009

INDEX